Wells Fargo

An Illustrated History

by Noel M. Loomis

with over 300 illustrations

In 1852, an express company was formed in San Francisco by Henry G. Wells and William G. Fargo. This company was to serve the gold fields both as a mail service and as a bank, and in so doing to become the most famous trade name of the West: Wells Fargo.

This is the story of Wells Fargo and of the people who created it and developed it into the four-billion-dollar institution that it is today.

From the early days, Wells Fargo was a symbol of faith. One could hire the company to do any chore—from escorting wives to California, to delivering a battalion of soldiers for an Indian war, to buying a bottle of eye medicine. Wells Fargo carried hundreds of millions of dollars worth of gold dust and gold coin, and no shipper ever lost a penny. Speed and safety were the guiding principles, and every man in the West believed and relied on this. A town wasn't a town in Gold Rush days without a Wells Fargo office, and when the express arrived in a mining town, everybody would gather.

A detailed and incisive history with over 300 illustrations, this book captures the flavor of the West and the excitement of one of the great institutions of past and present America.

WELLS
FARGO

Noel M. Loomis

WELLS FARGO

Clarkson N. Potter, Inc./Publisher
NEW YORK
DISTRIBUTED BY CROWN PUBLISHERS, INC.

Library of Congress Catalog Card Number: 68–17309
Printed in the United States of America
First Edition
Published simultaneously in Canada by
General Publishing Company Limited
Designed by Shari de Miskey

This book is especially dedicated to

LITTLE MARY
(Jacqueline Mary Liljenberg)

who at the age of ten months was demonstrating the
feasibility of being an individualist
without being a rebel

Acknowledgments

Through the several years of gathering material for this book from a body of information that has never been replete with facts, the author has been most grateful for the more-than-willing cooperation, the substantial enthusiasm, and the tactful suggestions of Miss Irene Simpson, director of the History Room at the Wells Fargo Bank in San Francisco; Miss Simpson also furnished much material, and she read the manuscript and pointed out many errors of detail.

There has been excellent help from John O. Theobald, Phoenix, Arizona; Mrs. N. B. Lacy, New Hampshire Historical Society; Mary K. Dempsey, Montana Historical Society; William E. Ellis, editor of *Motorland;* O. O. Winther, Indiana University; Helen Giffen, Society of California Pioneers; W. Neil Franklin, National Archives; Jane F. Smith, National Archives; Allan R. Ottley, California State Library; W. N. Davis., Jr., State Archives; F. Waddell Smith, who read the portion relating to the Pony Express; Vernon F. Perrigo, M. D.; Helen Harding Bretnor, Bancroft Library; Charles Hans, Vice-president of Wells Fargo & Company; the several officers of the Wells Fargo Bank who supplied information and material; and the many others who are named throughout the manuscript.

The general plan of the book, the arrangement of materials, and the conclusions drawn therefrom, as well as the final responsibility for accuracy, are the province of the author.

—Noel M. Loomis

San Diego State College,

Contents

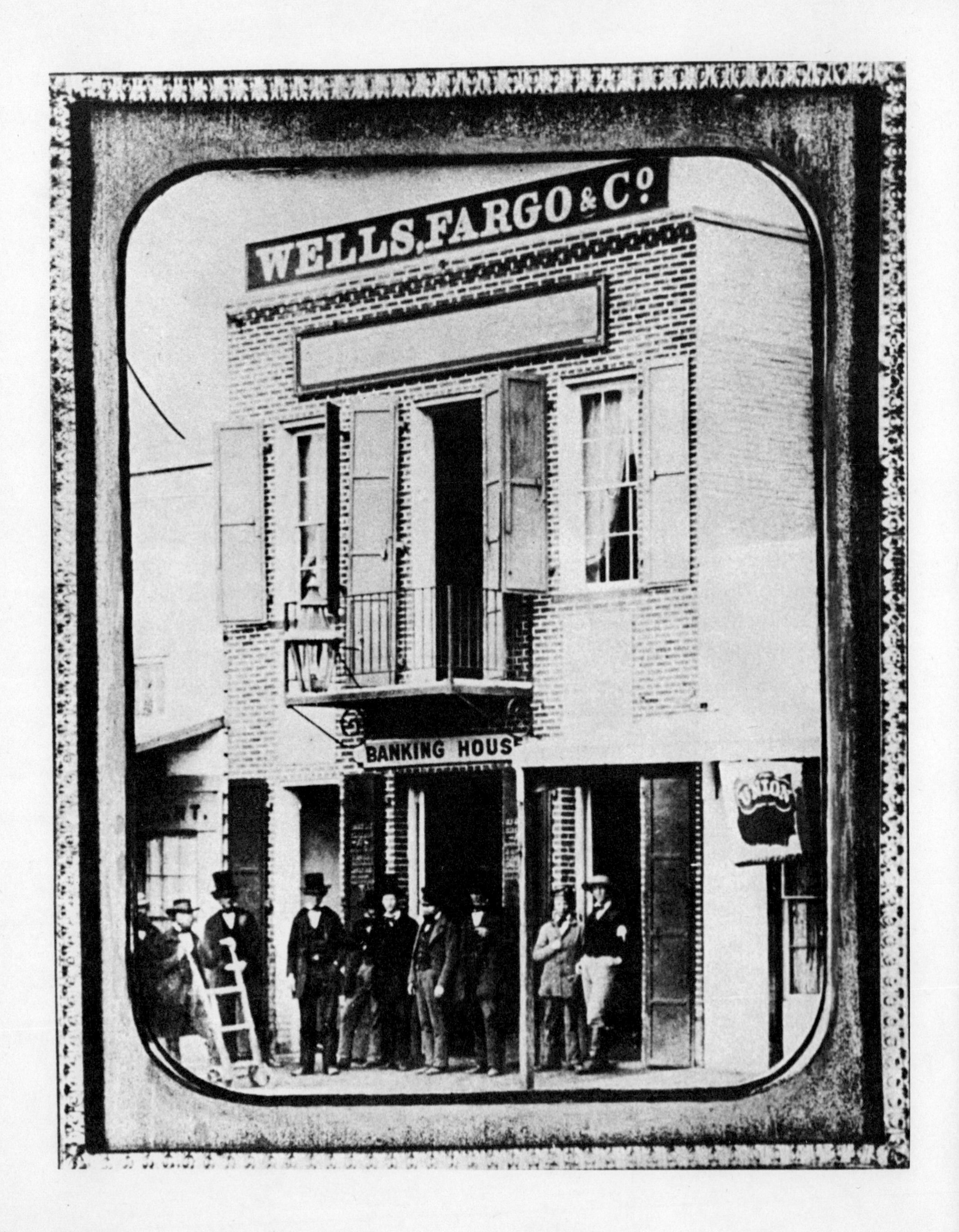
WELLS, FARGO & Co
BANKING HOUS

1852
The Beginning

THE HISTORY OF WELLS, FARGO & Company is the story of an express and banking company made up of individualists who battled for business every inch of the way, who usually—but not always—thought clearly and logically, who took risks, who beat down and bought out their competitors, who never declined a chance to be of service. The company made extraordinary profits and paid astonishing dividends, and yet it seems not to have gambled with its depositors' welfare. It went through crisis after crisis. In one year it paid 122 percent dividends, in another year 315 percent. It was such a plump melon that it was raided again and again by speculators and financiers, and yet somehow its massive reputation carried on, and even the raiders bowed to the magic name of Wells Fargo.

When Edward H. Harriman completed his conquest of the company in 1905, he was appalled to find that the Wells Fargo bank had more capital stock than it had deposits, and proposed to put an end to the banking activities—but was persuaded not to. The bank could not make any money that way, but the name Wells Fargo was far too valuable to drop, so he moved the express business east but sold the bank to Isaias W. Hellman. Five years later his executors cut up $30,000,000 in cash in the vaults of the express company, which had always had a peculiar surplus account called "reserve."

That reserve account is a revealing factor in the philosophy behind the Wells Fargo management. For if there is one thing about Wells Fargo that every employee, from janitor to president, has believed in solidly for more than a hundred years, it is that Wells Fargo is good. To a Wells Fargo employee—even to the president—that massive reserve belonged there because it meant that Wells Fargo could weather any calamity. Wells Fargo was good.

The history of Wells, Fargo & Company is not that of a great banking company involved in failures or scandals and it is not that of a great express company that came to dominate the West; it is the history of a company that has always been good.

This is not a very spectacular or dramatic thing, seen against the turmoil of the failures of the Adams Express Company of California; Page, Bacon & Company; Palmer, Cook & Company; or the Bank of California; but somehow doing what is right seems to have a virtue of its own if continued long enough, and there *is* drama in the activities of this company that time and again kept its doors open

Wells, Fargo & Company's first home in the West, the red-brick banking house built by Samuel Brannan (and probably the bricks were made by Brannan's Mormons, since they were brickmakers). At this early date (presumably 1852), the company had the words "Banking House" over the door.

while other and bigger bankers closed theirs. It is, however, a drama that must be seen broadly. It must be understood as a part of the times, a part of the place, a part of the events, a part of the people. In this light, perhaps Wells, Fargo & Company is notable for what it did *not* do, for the people came to expect Wells Fargo to do only what was right.

The history of Wells Fargo is also the history of San Francisco and the California Gold Rush, for Wells Fargo was created because of the Gold Rush and it operated through the wild early years when most companies were broken by the Gold Rush and by the speculative fevers it brought into being. It is also the story of men who went into a strange new country, adjusted to conditions there, found ways to be of service, and made a profit as they went along.

One of the important services rendered by Wells Fargo was the carrying of mail. In 1852, the United States Post Office Department found it utterly impossible to keep up with all the new mining camps in a country where fifty thousand men swarmed over the rugged mountains or toiled knee-deep in icy water. In fact, a letter addressed to Aloysius Q. Jones at Jackass Flat or Squabbletown or Growlersburg or Pinch-Em-Tight or Git up and Git or Puckersville, might well confound the postmaster as he wondered where such a mining camp could possibly be in a wild, mountainous area some 100 by 180 miles. It didn't really make any difference, anyway, because the nearest post office to the mining camps was at New Auburn, and by the time the letter got to New Auburn, Aloysius Q. Jones had moved on to some new diggings at Lousy Level or New Jerusalem or Bogus Thunder.

On the other hand, one could address a letter to "John Smith in the California Mines, from his mother in Utica, New York," turn it over with a dollar to a Wells Fargo man, and feel that it had a chance to be delivered. And, by golly, it did. And was.

In the days of the California Gold Rush, letter-carrying was an important part of every express company's business. The Post Office was slow getting started in California, and the miners—most of them away from their families—seemed more impatient over the lack of mail than over anything else. Even before the discovery of gold (in 1847), one Charles L. Cady established the first express in California by carrying letters from San Francisco to Sutter's Fort or Fort Sacramento at twenty-five cents apiece, but in 1849 Alexander H. Todd, California's first great expressman, carried letters to Sacramento and various mining camps for one ounce of dust, worth sixteen dollars—which, however, included forty cents government postage and twenty-five cents rake-off to the postmaster for letting Todd take the letters out of the office. Todd had two thousand names on his list of miners who did not object to paying that much money for a letter—and sometimes that was more gold than a miner found in a week!

Through the fifties, the delivery of mail was a substantial part of the business of most express companies in California, but by no means the only part of their business, since express includes parcels, bullion, coin, food, heavy machinery, wives and children, and literally anything that can be transported.

The word "express" means "rapid conveyance." In the time of Wells Fargo, the word was taken literally, and the men who carried the mail and the packages were so thoroughly honest and sincere—and capable—that eventually the name Wells Fargo became synonymous with rapid conveyance.

But there is an equally important factor in the transportation and delivery of goods, mail, gold, or human beings: reliability—a quality on the part of the expressman that gives the shipper faith that the expressman can be trusted implicitly. Perhaps an equally good word is "integrity." Wells Fargo excelled in reliability as much as in rapidity. For over sixty years a man could turn over to a Wells Fargo employee a letter to his sweetheart, a bundle of stock certificates, a box of gold, or his wife (bringing wives to California by express was quite a business in the 1850's), and *know* that it would be delivered in good shape to the addressee. Wells Fargo never spared any expense or effort in making that assurance as nearly positive as human skill and determination could make it. Wells Fargo had the concept, and its employees had the pride, the steadfastness, and the resources to uphold it.

There is not much to distinguish between express carrying objects of intrinsic value and express carrying communications. In the 1300's, the One Inca had live fish brought up from the sea to Cuzco by runners bearing them in baskets of water; that was an express—a word that always carries a strong connotation of organization or system to maintain the desired speed. In 1805, the word "express" was used when Governor Alencaster of New Mexico sent an obscure Indian interpreter named Pedro Vial to stop the Lewis and Clark Expedition on the Missouri River. He reported to the commandant-general at Chihuahua: "If the news is usual, I will send it by the regular express; if unusual, I will send it by an extraordinary express."

In the United States in the 1830's, there was no organized express for the use of the public; there was no parcel post; there was no way to send a package to somebody in a distant town except by the kindness (for appropriate fees) of any number of stagecoach drivers, canal-boat captains, and teamsters, but the United States was beginning to move in many directions, and the need for an express service was becoming apparent.

Then Martin Van Buren was elected President in 1836, and during his time in office the power reaper came into use; the electric telegraph and the revolver were invented; and the railroads started their great boom that was to revolutionize the nation. All was not on the good side, however, for it was in the early 1830's that cholera began to scourge the country. That period was also a time of overextension of credit and wildcat banking, with resultant overspeculation in western lands and overstimulation of industrial production.

But still a way had not been found to express things from one place to another.

It is a little hard to imagine (or is it?), but Congress had passed an act to distribute a surplus from the federal treasury to the states, and the government withdrew its deposits from the land banks and thus precipitated the panic of 1837. Once the panic had run its course, business again burgeoned with all the energy of a new and vigorous country. In a nation where electric power was unheard of but where steam power was used to run boats and turn machinery; where coal-gas streetlights were very modern and friction matches were coming into common use; where America's principal characteristic was still its go-ahead-iveness—in such surroundings was the modern express-business born. Business was expanding and its needs were growing, and the need to move things from one place to another was pressing.

The system used to transfer packages—whether of merchandise, promissory notes, stocks and bonds, bullion, or specie—was haphazard at its very best. If you wanted to send a package to a friend in New Hampshire, it was pretty involved and catch-as-catch-can. If a man wanted a package of tea or a coffee grinder or a horse collar from Boston, he tried to find a friend who was making the trip and who would have time to handle the purchase. If a banker wanted to send a package of stock certificates to a bank in Boston or a bundle of bank notes (there was no national currency), he too would look for a friend. However, friends did not go to Boston with regularity, while banking went on every day, so it got to be common practice for a banker or broker to rush down to the railroad depot or the steamship dock just before departure time and try to find a friend who was making the trip. Perhaps he did not see a friend, but the depot master or the ship captain would suggest "So-and-So, the man with the sandy beard," and it often happened that a banker would entrust a package of valuable papers or coin to a stranger, and hope for the best. Apparently this was reasonably successful and the losses not great, but the service was erratic.

Then, too, the mission often was not as simple as a mere delivery; it might involve a collection and the return of that collection to New York City. Therefore, although life was not as crowded then as it would be a hundred years later, many missions required time and effort, and occasionally they imposed responsibility.

Thus, with the increase of business resulting from the great expansion of the railroads, and particularly from the boom in cotton following the success of the cotton gin, the stage was set for a professional errand boy—an expressman of competence and responsibility.

According to Alvin F. Harlow, in *Old Waybills,* probably the very first expressmen in the United States advertised in the Boston *Sentinel* in 1789, at which time they said:

> The proprietors of the mail stages beg leave to inform the publick that they have employed two faithful trufty perfons, who go in the Stages from this town to New York and back, and who will execute any commifsions they fhall pleafe to intruft them with, on reafonable terms. Newfpapers from either place, carefully delivered at 2s 3d per annum. Inquire at Stage Houfe, near the Mall. January 31, 1789.

Since the *Sentinel* bears no further reference to that early offer of service, it probably did not last long. It is interesting, however, to realize that almost fifty years elapsed after that, before the express business really got a foothold. In the meantime, of course, stage drivers continued to pick up a few shillings by carrying mail and small parcels.

There is a tradition that the drivers usually transported such items in their big top-hats, and certainly one such driver—Benjamin P. Cheney, who afterward became a prominent expressman and who in 1854 was named a director of Wells Fargo—said that carrying packages in his hat had made him bald. In those days, too, the stagecoach driver delivered verbal messages, collected notes and bills, bought goods on order, and carried money. He often carried mail because postage rates were very high, and he also carried newspapers. Newspaper publishers were involved in such rivalry that they themselves hired special expresses to obtain the text of President Jackson's December, 1830, message to Congress.

It may be that the first systematic expressman was one Silas Tyler, who attached a car (in those days about the size of a one-horse wagon) to the end of the Boston & Lowell Railroad in 1835, and carried packages but apparently nothing for the banks. The railroad seems to have been in partnership with him, but in 1836 he sold his interest to W. C. Gray, who carried parcels and acted as a bank messenger. In those days, it seems likely that the railroad was a partner in the express business, for Gray had a pass good for six months.

There were others who experimented with the express idea: David T. Brigham, S. S. Leonard, Dean and Davenport, Dow's Express, James W. Hale, and B. D. and L. B. Earle (who started on the Boston & Providence in 1834), so it is difficult to say who thought up the idea, or even that any one person thought it up. But what can be said is that a man named William F. Harnden turned it into a successful business. Apparently Harnden also was the first to call himself an "expressman." (It is worth noting that many men later to become important figures in American Express, Adams Express, and Wells Fargo started out with Harnden.)

Harnden, a small, slight man afflicted with tuberculosis or incipient tuberculosis, was a ticket agent for the Boston & Worcester, worn down by the six-

James W. Hale, an early expressman, apparently one who, like Benjamin P. Cheney, carried the express in his hat. From "Harper's Monthly Magazine," August 1875.

Two stagecoach advertisements from a Boston newspaper from September, 1843; the first one offers express services: "All packages, messages, &c., entrusted to the driver in the morning, will be faithfully attended to, and an answer returned the same day, if requested." Passengers would be called for in any part of Boston.

'TIME IS MONEY.'
COACHES & RAIL ROAD
From Medway to Boston.

A LINE of Stages, in connection with the Dedham Branch Rail Road, will run daily, Sundays excepted, on and after August 21st, leaving the Temperance House, West Medway, at 7 o'clock A. M., passing through Medway Village, Rockville, East Medway, Medfield, West Dedham, and arriving in Dedham Village in season to take the 10 o'clock A. M. train for Boston.

Passengers, by taking this route, can arrive in Boston at half past ten A. M., and, on their return will take the 3 o'clock P. M. train from Boston, leaving them nearly five hours to transact business, and arrive at Medway at half past six.

Fare, from Medway to Boston, $1 00
do do Medfield do 75
do do W. Dedham do 37½

All packages, messages, &c., entrusted to the driver in the morning, will be faithfully attended to, and an answer returned the same day, if requested.

☞ Books kept at the Washington Coffee House, Boston, and passengers, by leaving their names, will be called for in any part of the city.

S. D. BUTLER, Agent

September, 7, 1843.

FARE REDUCED
On the Old Line of Mail Stages between Boston and Woonsocket Falls!

A Mail Stage leaves Doolittle's City Tavern, Brattle Street, Boston, daily, Sundays excepted, at 11 A. M.; passes through Dedham, West Dedham, Medfield, East Medway, Rockville, Franklin Centre, and South Bellingham, to Woonsocket Falls, every Monday, Wednesday, and Friday, returning the alternate days by the same route.

Every Tuesday, Thursday, and Saturday, passes through Dedham, Medfield, East Medway, Medway Village, West Medway, North and South Bellingham, to Woonsocket Falls, returning the alternate days by the same route.

Fare, from Boston to W. Falls, $1 00
do do Franklin, 75
do do Medway, 75
do do Medfield, 62
do do West Dedham, 50
do Dedham to Medfield, 25
do do Medway, 50

The proprietors of this daily line of stages feel grateful for past favors, and assure the public that they can travel by this line as cheap as by any other whatever.

JOSEPH MILLER,
BLAKE PARKER.

August 31, 1843.

teen-hour days. On a trip to New York to visit a friend who was an agent for a steamboat, Harnden asked what he could do for a living that would not be as onerous as his job, and his friend suggested that he make a business of delivering the many parcels that his friend, as agent, was frequently asked to send by "somebody."

There are other stories about the beginning that are more dramatic, but this one seems reasonable. Harnden made arrangements with a railroad and a steamboat company, and on February 23, 1839, announced that he would "run a car through from Boston to New York and vice versa four times a week," to collect drafts and forward merchandise. (The word "car" was advertising exaggeration, for all his business was carried in a carpetbag for some time.) The newspapers then referred to his "package express," and it is worth noting that he apparently delivered newspapers free to other newspapers for the favorable items they might print about him. This free carriage of newspapers continued as a standard form of good-will advertising (now known as "creating a public image") for many years.

In the Philadelphia *Courier* for August 29, 1840, Harnden advertised "Harnden's New York and Boston Package Express, daily via Stonington." His offices then were at Third and Market streets, Philadelphia; 2 Wall Street, New York; and 8 Court Street, Boston. It rather seems that the express business arose almost simultaneously with the railroad business, for most early express advertisements indicate the use of railroad transportation, and Harnden's is not an exception. His card says, "Close cars will be run through from New York to Boston, daily, for the transportation of specie, bank notes, and packages and parcels of goods of all kinds." ("Close cars" probably means "closed cars," which indicates that safety was already an important consideration.)

Harnden's offer of services described a true express: that is, the rapid conveyance of items. A second statement, however, pertains to something other than express:

William F. Harnden, who is often considered the "father of the express business," with his carpetbag. From "Harper's Monthly Magazine," August, 1875.

Alvin Adams, founder of the great Adams Express. From "Ballou's Pictorial Drawing-Room Companion," Vol VIII (1855), p. 108.

Advertisement of Adams & Co.'s Express in the Wooster (Massachusetts) "Palladium," December 3, 1845. Signed by Alvin Adams and W. B. Dinsmore, and offering, even at that early date, express service to Philadelphia, Washington, Pittsburgh, and St. Louis, and forwarding service to Europe.

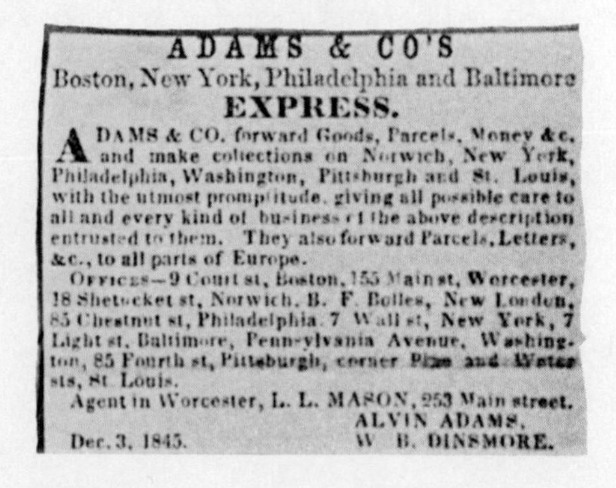

ADAMS & CO'S
Boston, New York, Philadelphia and Baltimore
EXPRESS.

ADAMS & CO. forward Goods, Parcels, Money &c. and make collections on Norwich, New York, Philadelphia, Washington, Pittsburgh and St. Louis, with the utmost promptitude, giving all possible care to all and every kind of business of the above description entrusted to them. They also forward Parcels, Letters, &c., to all parts of Europe.

OFFICES—9 Court st, Boston, 155 Main st, Worcester, 18 Shetucket st, Norwich. B. F. Bolles, New London, 85 Chestnut st, Philadelphia. 7 Wall st, New York, 7 Light st, Baltimore, Pennsylvania Avenue, Washington, 85 Fourth st, Pittsburgh, corner Pine and Water sts, St. Louis.

Agent in Worcester, L. L. MASON, 253 Main street.

ALVIN ADAMS,
Dec. 3, 1845. W. B. DINSMORE.

Particular attention will be paid by W. H. to purchasing goods, paying and collecting drafts, notes and bills. He will promptly transact any and all business which may be entrusted to his charge.

He was already going into banking.

The primary function of a bank is to lend or borrow money, to issue it, or to care for it, and also to receive various valuable papers and bullion as a purchase or for discount. Therefore, it seems inevitable that, under the conditions, the expressman would carry out many of the functions of a banker; this is indicated by Harnden's "paying and collecting drafts, notes and bills." It is certain that this sort of activity is far beyond the mere transportation or conveyance of papers or articles. And since there was no telephone or telegraph, and the expressman was the sole direct contact between a bank in New York and a bank in Boston, he would sometimes have to exercise some judgment.

For instance, a merchant in New York might send to a wholesaler in Boston a package of bank notes that included notes from a bank in Alexandria, Virginia; and, since nearly all bank notes were discounted at various rates,[1] the wholesaler might not want to accept them at the remitter's figure, and it might well be that the expressman of that day would suggest a compromise figure in the interest of expediting business. Or he might be handed a bundle of notes with instructions to get the best deal possible for them. In such simple ways, and in many others not as simple, the expressman found himself unable to avoid entirely the functions of a banker.

Alexander Todd gives a good explanation of the natural evolution of expressmen into banking in California:

It was not long before the miners came to us to get us to take care of their money for them. It was a very common thing for me to start out from Stockton with two horses loaded down with gold dust. The miners had no opportunity for taking care of their dust, and we were obliged to have safes at our different offices, and our express business soon merged into a banking business. We charged them for taking care of their dust ½ percent per month, and they gave us the privilege of using it also. That was termed a general deposit. A special deposit was when a miner would bring in his dust, and put his name on it, and put a seal on it, and for keeping such deposits in our safe, we charged him

J. P. DAVIS,
SUCCESSOR TO A. LOW'S SALEM AND *BOSTON EXPRESS.*

THE subscriber having purchased of Mr A. Low his
EXPRESS BUSINESS,
BETWEEN SALEM AND BOSTON,
would respectfully inform his friends, and the late customers of this line, and the public generally, that he will continue to call at the usual places,
FOR THE CONVEYANCE OF
Parcels, Packages, Bundles, Merchandize, &c., &c.,
TO AND FROM BOSTON.
Present arrangements will be as follows, viz: A Light Wagon (over the Turnpike) will leave Salem EVERY DAY, at 9¼ o'clock, A. M., and returning, will leave Boston at 3 o'clock, P. M.

THE PARCEL EXPRESS,
via E. R. Road, will leave SALEM at 10¼ o'cl'k, AM. Leave BOSTON at 4 o'cl'k PM.
All orders attended to promptly, and faithfully executed.
Wagons for HEAVY GOODS will run daily, as usual.
Particular attention paid to the transportation of Seamen's baggage.

—OFFICES:—
In Salem, as usual; in Boston, at the Rail Road Exchange, Court Square.
Salem, Apr 5, 1849. J. P. DAVIS.

NOTICE. The subscriber, having disposed of his Express Business between Salem and Boston, to Mr. J. P. DAVIS, would confidently recommend him to his late customers and the public generally.
ADRIAN LOW.
Salem, April 5, 1849. 3m

HARNDEN'S NEW YORK AND BOSTON PACKAGE EXPRESS, daily via Stonington.
Office south east corner of Third and Market streets, Philadelphia—No 2 Wall street, New York—No 8 Court street, Boston.
Close cars will be run through from New York to Boston, daily, for the transportation of specie, bank notes, and packages and parcels of goods of all kinds.
Goods sent by this line will be forwarded as directed to any part of the State of Massachusetts, New Hampshire, Vermont, Maine and Connecticut, immediately on their arrival at Boston.
Particular attention will be paid by W. H. to purchasing goods, paying and collecting drafts, notes and bills. He will promptly transact any and all business which may be entrusted to his charge.
N. B. All goods must be marked "Harnden's Express," and sent to office as above before 12 o'clock, M.
Merchants in Philadelphia and Baltimore, who have goods brought over from England; in "Cunard's Mail Line of Steamers" to Boston, can have Mr. H. pass them through the Custom House, and forward them immediately as directed.

REFERENCES.
Philadelphia { Messrs. Carey & Hart, " E. W. Clark & Co.
New York { " Goodhue & Co. " John T. Smith & Co.
Boston { " Bryant Sturgis & Co. " Weeks, Jordan & Co.

ROBT. MONTGOMERY, Agent, S. E. corner Third and Market streets, Philad.
D. BRIGHAM, Jr. Agent, No. 2 Wall street, N. York.
WM. F. HARNDEN, Proprietor, No. 8 Court street, Boston. je 20 1y

N. Y. & E. R. R. Express,
For the transportation of Boxes, Bales, Parcels, Packages, &c. &c.,
Wells, Butterfield & Co., Proprietors.
CLOSES for the West at 4 P. M.
" " East, at 5 "
Arrives from the West, 3 25, A. M.
From the East, 4 30, P. M.
Office at the Hat Store, 4 doors above the Bridge, Owego. F. RAYNSFORD, Agent.

BURGESS AND JOHNSON'S EXPRESS,

(Left) *Advertisement of J. P. Davis in the Salem "Register," September 9, 1850.*

(Right) *Advertisement of New York and Erie Rail Road, owned by Wells, Butterfield & Co., in the Owego (N. Y.) "Gazette" for July 29, 1852.*

FAST LINE.
OPPOSITION TO SISK & CO.'s SLOW LINE!!

FARMERS & DROVERS' N. Y. & ERIE R. ROAD, Fowarding and Market Line. From Owego to New York, DAILY (Sundays excepted,) per *Freight or Express Trains,* (as owners of property prefer,) for all kinds of Produce, Live Stock, &c., &c.
Liberal advances made in Cash on consignment.—Office at F. Raynsford's Hat, Cap & Clothing Store, Ithaca st., Owego, where the proceeds of all property received will be paid punctually in Bankable money.
N. B. Being no longer connected with Sisk & Co.'s *slow line,* but shipping as above, by the fastest line that runs the road, the subscriber takes this opportunity of saying to the farmers of this and adjoining counties, that he is now enabled to offer them better facilities for disposing of their produce, than ever; and respectfully solicits a continuation of their consignments, assuring them that the business will be attended to with promptness and dispatch, and would also remark that a large stock of fashionable Hats, Caps & Clothing can always be found on hand, and for sale at a little less prices than else where in Owego.
Owego, April 18, 1850. F. RAYNSFORD.

Advertisement of F. Raynsford in the Owego (N. Y.) "Gazette," dated April 18, 1850. Note the emphasis on "Sisk & Co.'s slow line."

1% a month. All the security the miner had was our receipt, stating that we had so much of his property on hand.

It had been so in the 1840's, and it was so in the 1850's, when Henry Wells and William Fargo went into partnership to carry on an express business in the Gold Country of California. It was to continue so for more than half a century, until Edward H. Harriman, displeased because the bank had more assets than deposits, caused the two functions—express and banking—to be definitely separated. In the beginning, however, the two functions were hardly recognized as separate.

Most of the men who were to become prominent in the express business, started in the 1830's or the 1840's. L. B. and B. D. Earle, who sometimes are said to have started the express business, had run an express between New York and Boston in 1835 and had accepted whatever came their way. The Earles, however, do not seem to have weathered the panic of 1837 too well. Henry E. Wells, a Vermont Yankee, was moving freight and passengers over the Erie Canal, and William Harnden made his first trip on March 4, 1839, as an "express-package carrier" between New York and Boston.

Alvin Adams went into business as a partner in Burke & Company's Express, running between Boston and Worcester, in 1840. Burke, discouraged, soon sold out to Adams for $100 (payable $10 a month), and in 1841, Adams established service between Boston and New York and then from New York to Albany. (Henry Wells was Harnden's agent for a while in Albany.) Then Adams went into partnership with Ephraim Farnsworth and later with William B. Farnsworth.

By 1850, Adams was advertising service among Boston, New York, Philadelphia, and Baltimore. He would "forward Goods, Parcels, Money &c. and make collections on Norwich, New York, Philadelphia, Washington, Pittsburgh and St. Louis, . . . They also forward Parcels, Letters, &c., to all parts of Europe." This advertisement, from the Wooster (Massachusetts) *Palladium* of October 20, 1850, is dated December 3, 1845, and signed by Alvin Adams and W. B. Dinsmore. The company first was known as Adams & Company, but in 1854, Adams would absorb Harnden & Company and become

Adams Express Company, one of the great express companies of America, and the first of the big companies to go into California with success.

Advertisements of the smaller companies also throw light on express operations of early days. For instance, J. P. Davis bought Adrian Low's line, and advertised in the Salem *Register* on September 9, 1850:

J. P. DAVIS, SUCCESSOR TO A. LOW'S SALEM AND *BOSTON EXPRESS.* The subscriber having purchased of Mr. A. Low his EXPRESS BUSINESS, BETWEEN SALEM AND BOSTON, would respectfully inform his friends, and the late customers of this line, and the public generally, that he will continue to call at the usual places, FOR THE CONVEYANCE OF *Parcels, Packages, Bundles, Merchandize, &c., &c.,* TO AND FROM BOSTON. Present arrangements will be as follows, viz: A Light Wagon (over the Turnpike) will leave Salem EVERY DAY, at 9¼ o'clock, A. M., and returning, will leave Boston at 3 o'clock, P. M. THE PARCEL EXPRESS, via E. R. Road, will leave Salem at 10½ o'cl'k, AM. Leave Boston at 4 o'cl'k PM. All orders attended to promptly, and faithfully executed. Wagons for HEAVY GOODS will run daily, as usual. Particular attention paid to the transportation of Seamen's baggage.

A note by the former owner is appended:

NOTICE. The subscriber, having disposed of his Express Business between Salem and Boston, to Mr. J. P. Davis, would confidently recommend him to his late customers and the public generally. ADRIAN LOW.

At about the same time, one F. Raynsford obviously parted with an established line and started one of his own. Apparently the parting was not amicable, for the advertisement in the Owego (N. Y.) *Gazette* for October 17, 1850, says:

FAST LINE. OPPOSITION TO SISK & CO.'S SLOW LINE!! FARMERS & DROVERS' N. Y. & ERIE R. ROAD, Fowarding and Market Line. From Owego to New York, DAILY (Sundays excepted,) per *Freight or Express Trains,* (as owners of property prefer,) for all kinds of Produce, Live Stock, &c., &c.

Liberal advances made in Cash on consignment,— Office at F. Raynsford's Hat, Cap & Clothing Store, Ithaca st., Owego, where the proceeds of all property received will be paid punctually in Bankable money.

N. B. Being no longer connected with Sisk & Co.'s *slow line,* but shipping as above, by the fastest line that runs the road, the subscriber takes this opportunity of saying to the farmers of this and adjoining counties, that he is now enabled to offer them better facilities for disposing of their produce, than ever; and respectfully solicits a continuation of their consignments, assuring them that the business will be attended to with promptness and dispatch, and would also remark that a large stock of fashionable Hats, Caps & Clothing can always be found on hand, and for sale at a little less prices than else where in Owego. F. RAYNSFORD.

That's telling 'em! And how do you like the plug for the hat, cap, and clothing business!

In 1841, Wells, Fargo & Company was not yet organized, but Henry Wells (acting as agent for Harnden at Albany), left Harnden's company to become a messenger for (and partner in) Pomeroy & Company, between Albany and Buffalo, New York. This company, operating west of Albany (where Adams had not wanted to operate—probably because there was no railroad to Buffalo at that time), had as partners Wells, George E. Pomeroy, and Crawford Livingston, and was successful. Wells even figured out a way to ship oysters by stagecoach at $3 a hundred to the people of Buffalo.[2]

During 1842 and 1843, there was a depression, the result of federal legislation to provide very broad bankruptcy laws—so broad that the ensuing economic setback was called the "debt repudiation depression." The express companies, however, seemed to prosper in spite of the depression.

In 1842, William G. Fargo, the second member of the American West's most famous partnership (who had been a conductor or agent—or both—for the Auburn & Syracuse Railroad), became a messenger for Pomeroy & Company, and in 1843 became Pomeroy's agent at Buffalo. Pomeroy's business was expanding, and it was running into New York City by steamboats on the Hudson River.

In 1845, Wells, Fargo, and Dan Dunning organized Wells & Company's Western Express (as of April 1) to operate from Buffalo to Cincinnati, St. Louis, and Chicago via steamships, stagecoaches, and wagon trains (for there were no railroads to those far western places). From Albany to Buffalo alone a messenger still had to travel by four different railroads, a stagecoach, and by private conveyance, and the trip required four nights and three days.

Wells was then forty years old, Roman-nosed, and believed in the government staying out of affairs that were none of its business. He had already backed down the government in its attempt to start a rival express line,[3] and, in 1845, Wells saw another need and set out to respond to it. The charge for carrying a letter at that time was twenty-five cents from New York to Buffalo, and there was no law that absolutely precluded competition, so Wells set a price of six cents for transportation of letters between those two points, had some orange-colored stamps printed, and was in business. Soon Wells was carrying a great many letters while the United States' carrier had only a few. This situation irked the government, and it obtained indictments against that reprehensible practice. But Wells's men kept carrying mail, and were arrested—only to be bailed out by friends. The express company promoted public meetings and circulated petitions to ask that the express companies not be interfered with in their attempts to do an honest business. Then Wells tried to make an agreement with the Post Office Department to carry the government mail at five cents a letter for the entire country!

The government did not accept Wells's offer because such an arrangement would have thrown 16,000 postmasters out of business, but it changed the letter rate to five cents (not over three hundred miles) and ten cents. The fight with the government lasted three years, and certainly Wells's was the kind of spirit that was to rule Wells Fargo for several generations. Strange to say, in 1851, the government made the letter rate three cents for distances not over three thousand miles, and it rather seems that Henry Wells had a great deal to do with low postage rates.

In those early years, little was thought about banking as a separate business. Rather, it was an adjunct of the express business—but any kind of business was important to men like Wells and Fargo.

In 1844, George Pomeroy withdrew from the company, but Thaddeus Pomeroy became a junior partner, and it seems that Crawford Livingston remained, and that William G. Fargo came into the firm, which became Livingston, Wells & Company.

William Harnden died in 1845, and the business of his firm, already suffering because Harnden had put too much of his attention on immigration from Europe, continued to fall off—perhaps under the pressure of Wells and Fargo and the thriving Adams company.

The Mexican War came in 1846, and by 1847, the country was in a postwar boom. Alvin Adams bought the Harnden routes to the south and east, and began to operate into St. Louis through Baltimore, Washington, Pittsburgh, Cincinnati, and Louisville. The express business was spreading out.

There were many, many name changes in the early years. In 1846, Wells and Fargo separated for a time when Wells sold his interest in Western Express to William Livingston. Western Express became Livingston & Fargo, and Wells went to New York to work for Livingston, Wells & Company. In 1847, Crawford Livingston, whose association with Wells had started in Pomeroy & Company, died, and Johnston Livingston came into the firm, which changed its name to Wells & Company. (However, it will appear later that Livingston, Wells & Company continued to operate in Europe.)

A new and fairly important firm appeared in 1848 or 1849, when John Butterfield (who ten years later would establish the Butterfield Overland Mail, the most famous of all early mail lines) and James D. Wasson began carrying express between New York and Albany. At first, both the Butterfield line and the Wells line paid the New York Central $100 a day for using their cars, but by 1849 Butterfield & Wasson had a contract on all the New York Central lines, and Wells was shut out.

An advertisement from the Owego (N. Y.) *Gazette* for July 29, 1852, by F. Raynsford shows that Wells and Butterfield had gotten together:

> N. Y. & E. R. R. Express. For the transportation of Boxes, Bales, Parcels, Packages, &c. &c., Wells, Butterfield & Co., Proprietors. Closes for the West at 4 P. M. Closes for the East, at 5 P.M.... Office at the Hat Store, 4 doors above the Bridge, Owego. F. RAYNSFORD, Agent. BURGESS AND JOHNSON'S EXPRESS, Closes for the North at 5 P. M. Arrives from the North at 8 P. M.

Apparently Raynsford sold out to Wells, Butterfield & Company,[4] which was running east and west (perhaps between New York and Cleveland, Ohio, while Burgess and Johnson probably ran between Owego and Buffalo). Sisk's *slow line* probably had expired.

INCORPORATED by the LEGISLATURE of the STATE of NEW YORK.

No. 113 — 100 Shares

New Granada Canal and Steam NAVIGATION COMPANY.

CAPITAL $2,000,000

SHARES $25 EACH.

This is to certify, that Henry Wells is entitled to One Hundred Shares of the Capital Stock of the NEW GRANADA CANAL AND STEAM NAVIGATION COMPANY not transferable under two Years from June 1st 1855 and then only at the Company's Office, personally or by Attorney, and upon surrender of this Certificate.

In Witness Whereof we have hereunto affixed our hands and the seal of the Company.

New York, September 7th 1855.

M Starbuck SECRETARY Henry Wells PRESIDENT.

A stock certificate signed by Henry Wells, president of the New Granada Canal and Steam Navigation Company, in 1855. There is no record of this company in the governmental archives of New York, where this certificate was issued, but it is Number 113, and indicates that possibly in 1855 Henry Wells interested himself in building a canal across the Isthmus of Panama. The original is in the History Room, Wells Fargo Bank. (The picture bears no resemblance to New Granada, but such pictures were made from stock cuts and often meant little.)

In the meantime (in 1848), gold had been discovered in California (short of war, possibly the single most important event in United States history —with deference to the Louisiana Purchase and the Treaty of Guadalupe-Hidalgo), and events were in the making to change the whole world, and especially to give Henry Wells and William G. Fargo a chance to prove themselves under the most trying conditions —for Wells, Fargo & Company was first, last, and always a California company.

At that time, there was no organized mail service of any kind between the Atlantic and the Pacific coasts, since California had been a part of the United States for about a year and was not even a state, and so the gold discovery, made in January, 1848, was not immediately known in the East. The first hint of it in the East, a rather casual reference in a booster edition of the California *Star,*[5] was supposedly taken across the Rocky Mountains and the endless prairies of the Great Plains by pack mule, and reached the East probably in July or August but was treated with skepticism.

Colonel Richard B. Mason, the military governor of California (now that California no longer belonged to Mexico), made a trip to the mines and confirmed the news. Then he sent a messenger, Lieutenant Lucien Loeser, through Panama with an official letter and 230 ounces, 15 pennyweight, and 5 grains of gold as evidence of the finds. The gold was displayed by the War Department and duly assayed by the Treasury, and on December 5, 1848, President Polk, in a message to Congress, verified the startling news that gold of great purity (894 fine) had been found in California, in unknown but probably extensive quantity. The electrifying news was flashed from Washington to New York by electric telegraph, and soon was traveling all over the world. A few days later the first guidebook to

California designed for gold miners (or at least designed to get the gold from the pockets of would-be miners)[6] was offered for sale, and the great rush was on—the most astounding migration ever known to man.

Pawnbrokers did a tremendous business, loaning money to excited men who in turn bought patent pocket filters, California rubber boots, collapsible California beds, patent gold-washing machines, and firearms,[7] and used the rest of the money to buy flour and bacon and passage on a ship—or a share in an emigrant company to go overland through Utah or along the Gila Trail or through Mexico. Many would never reach California because of starvation, lack of water, accidents, violent tempers, Indian massacres, and the deadly cholera, but those who did reach the Land of Promise would need services (express, banking, and mail), and these rough men in a rough country were not inclined to quibble over costs (or to exercise much patience).

It seems there had been an overland-mail trip in 1846 from Oregon City to Weston, Missouri, but probably not more than one such trip. In 1847, ship captains were offering to accept mail for Panama, to be transshipped there to the East. The first California express got under way when Charles L. Cady, in 1847, carried mail (at twenty-five cents a letter) from San Francisco to Sutter's Fort, or Fort Sacramento, twice a week. And in the following year (1848), Sam Brannan's paper, the California *Star,* made a substantial gesture toward an overland express by announcing on January 15 that the California Star Express would leave San Francisco April 1 for Salt Lake and Independence, Missouri (which it expected to reach in sixty days), and would carry letters for fifty cents.

The *Star*'s bitterly disliked rival, the *Californian* (California's very first newspaper), said on March 1 that it also had completed arrangements for a mail, and would carry letters at the same price, newspapers at twelve and a half cents, "to be paid in advance." The *Californian* expected to go via Salt Lake City and the South Pass in Wyoming in thirty days or less. Heavy snows in the mountains, however, caused postponement of its departure until April 15. The rivalry between the two papers is evident, because the *Star* said later: "Our Overland Mail left on April 2." It turned out later that the mail expected to wait two weeks at Sutter's, so one may assume

BANKERS.

WELLS, FARGO & CO.

NEW YORK AND CALIFORNIA EXPRESS

....AND....

Exchange Company

CAPITAL.......................................$[illegible]

D. N. BARNEY..................President.
T. M. JANES....................Treasurer.

DRAW BILLS OF EXCHANGE,

.... IN SUMS TO SUIT ....

ON ALL THE CITIES OF THE UNITED States and Canada; Union Bank of London, London; and Royal Bank of Ireland, Dublin.—Advance on Gold Dust consigned for Assay, and receive Deposits, General and Special.

EXPRESS

Forwarders and Commission Agents.

SHIP TREASURE at the Lowest Rates, and insure under our own open policies, held with the best English Companies, viz.:—Indemnity Mutual Marine; Marine Insurance; Royal Exchange Insurance, and London Assurance.

FORWARD FREIGHT AND PARCELS to all parts of the United States and Canadas, and through the "AMERICAN AND EUROPEAN EXPRESS AND EXCHANGE COMPANY," to all parts of Europe;—Execute Commissons, make Collections and Purchases, and attend promptly to all matters pertaining to the Express business.

FORWARD DAILY EXPRESSES, in charge of experienced and faithful Messengers, to all the Towns and Mining Camps in California; Semi-Monthly to Oregon and intermediate points on the Northern Coast; Port Townsend and Olympia; to San Diego and intermediate points on the Southern Coast; and by every vessel to the Sandwich Islands.

☞ For the better security of ourselves and the public, Agents in California, Oregon and Washington Territories, are furnished with "Appointments", or Commissions, specifying their powers as our Agents. Such "Appointments" they are required to keep exposed to the public view in their places of business.

OFFICE—Corner California and Montgomery sts.

LOUIS McLANE,
General Agent for California.

G. W. BELL,
SAM'L KNIGHT,
Superintendents.

ja31-6m

Fessenden's Patent Pocket Filter,

An article adapted to the wants of the traveller, especially to those of the California Emigrants and Miners. Manufactured and for sale, Wholesale and Retail,

Corner of Beach and South Streets, Boston.

A Wells Fargo advertisement in the San Francisco "Herald," August 1, 1858, and a small advertisement in a Boston newspaper in 1850 for a "patent pocket filter."

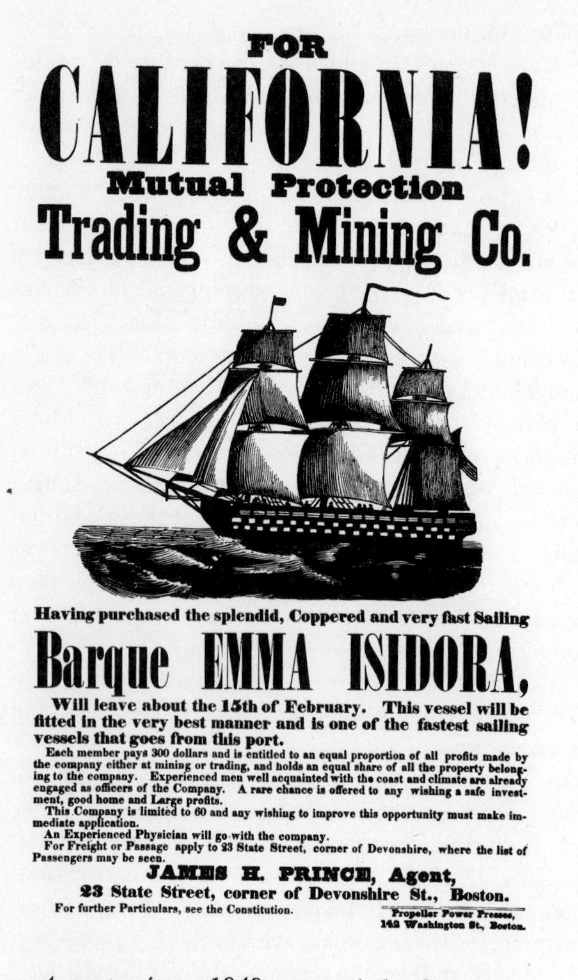

FOR
CALIFORNIA!
Mutual Protection
Trading & Mining Co.
Having purchased the splendid, Coppered and very fast Sailing
Barque EMMA ISIDORA,
Will leave about the 15th of February. This vessel will be fitted in the very best manner and is one of the fastest sailing vessels that goes from this port.
Each member pays 300 dollars and is entitled to an equal proportion of all profits made by the company either at mining or trading, and holds an equal share of all the property belonging to the company. Experienced men well acquainted with the coast and climate are already engaged as officers of the Company. A rare chance is offered to any wishing a safe investment, good home and Large profits.
This Company is limited to 60 and any wishing to improve this opportunity must make immediate application.
An Experienced Physician will go with the company.
For Freight or Passage apply to 23 State Street, corner of Devonshire, where the list of Passengers may be seen.
JAMES H. PRINCE, Agent,
23 State Street, corner of Devonshire St., Boston.
For further Particulars, see the Constitution.
Propeller Power Presses,
142 Washington St., Boston.

A poster from 1849—one of the first, since the departure was scheduled for February 15. As usual, it sounded very conservative: experienced men in charge, a physician engaged, company limited to sixty. They all started that way. Each passenger was to pay $300, and it was to be a mutual enterprise, with each member entitled to an equal share of the proceeds. Few of the "one for all—all for one" deals worked out so as to satisfy anybody. In fact, few of them were still in effect by the time the men (or some of them) got to California. The men in the companies quarreled; often the "experienced" men had had no experience west of the Hudson River. Printed by permission of the American Antiquarian Society.

the April 2 departure was largely propaganda. The *Californian* stayed by its guns, and said its (second?) mail would positively leave May 22—but, three days later, the *Star* said: "Another EXPRESS will leave our office on the 20th of June for Independence. Letters 50¢, papers 12½¢." So the *Star* would carry newspapers too—but it is safe to assume that no copies of the *Californian* would be in the pack. Then, on May 17, the *Star* said: "Dr. Jones' Eastern Mail will leave town this morning for Independence, via Salt Lake."

It is said that a "Mr. Gray of Virginia"[8] did carry the *Star*'s first express, and reached St. Joseph by early August, 1848. (Strangely enough, however, his stories of the discovery of gold—which he can hardly have failed to tell—were not printed in Missouri newspapers.[9])

It seems doubtful that the *Star's* second express (referred to as "Dr. Jones' Eastern Mail," probably a reference to E. P. Jones, Sam Brannan's green-spectacled first editor), got any farther than the mines, for by June 20, the announced time of departure, the *Star*'s proprietor and its editor at that time, Edward C. Kemble, had folded the *Star* completely and gone to the gold fields. Likewise, it is doubtful that the *Californian* ever sent out its May 22 express, because the *Californian* had folded before the *Star,* and its editor also had gone to the Gold Country.

Apparently it was a year before San Francisco began to settle down and assume its role as headquarters for the Gold Country, for it was not until April 12, 1849, that the first bankers advertised in the *Alta California,* the firm of Roach & Woodworth, which addressed itself to the miners:

> To Gold Diggers, and others!! Remittances to the United States and Europe, can be made in sums from $10 to $10,000, in Bills of Exchange, Drafts, Letters of Credit, Gold Dust, or Coin, at the same rates as cost of transportation only, apply to Roach & Woodworth, Parker House. Highest price paid for Gold Dust, in Gold or silver coin. Apr. 12, 1849. 14tf

On June 21—over two months later—three more firms got into the banking business: Simmons, Hutchinson & Co., exchange brokers and commission merchants; Burgoyne & Co., bankers and commission merchants; and Moffat & Co., assayer.

In that same issue of the *Alta California* (June 21), Whitney & Ely's Atlantic & Pacific Express advertised for the first time, offering services

> via Panama and the Isthmus of Darien [the Isthmus of Panama], to connect with Adams & Company's Express to the United States. Gold in small parcels. Articles of any description not exceeding 100 pounds in weight. The safes of this Express will cross the Isthmus with the United States Mail, and under the same protection. Elisha Ely, San Francisco. Charles A. Whitney, Panama.

On June 18, Whitney & Ely had forwarded a shipment of letters and packages from San Francisco via Panama, New Orleans, and Havana, and presumably it turned over its goods to Adams in New York. However, that attempt did not get very far, and the company was superseded in October by Adams & Company.

There are various modern references to the fact that either the American Express Company or Livingston, Wells & Company was the first eastern express company in California, but it is hard to substantiate either of these thoughts. There was a "Robert Wells & Company, Merchants," that advertised in the *Alta* in early 1849, and one "Thomas G. Wells, Exchange and Banking Office," advertised in the *Pacific News,* September 15, 1849—but neither indicates any connection with Henry Wells or with any express company.[10]

On September 1, 8, and 15, 1849, the *Pacific News* carried an advertisement for Haven & Livingston, San Francisco, California. That firm offered:

> Foreign and Inland Exchange in connection with Livingston, Wells & Co., New York, having agencies in all the principal Atlantic cities, Great Britain and France, [and] offer their services in the various branches of their business. Bullion, gold dust, packages, etc., etc., received and forwarded to any of the above places. Orders filled and the articles returned with the utmost dispatch. Drafts on New York, Philadelphia, and other large cities. Articles of value received for safe keeping. Office in New York, 10 Wall Street, in Philadelphia, 48 South Third Street. Haven & Livingston, Clay Street.

There had been at least three Livingston brothers; William A. was in business with Fargo; Johnston

A placard or flyer for Warren & Co., merchants at Mormon Island in the Gold Country, who promised to run an express and mail service to the river steamers. From the Bancroft Library, Berkeley, University of California.

Livingston was in Wells & Company; and Crawford had died in 1847. It is not inconceivable that either William or Johnston was in partnership with Haven, but this is not the American Express Company and it is not Livingston, Wells & Company.

An item of considerable interest, in view of the importance of mail-carrying to the early express companies, is the advertisement in the *Pacific News* of September 15, 1849, for the "Strangers' & Miners' Registry Office, Parker House." This announcement graphically illustrates the difficulties of finding a given person in the mines or of being found. "References—J. W. Gray, First Alcalde, San Francisco," it says, or "Ward & Co." The announcement is signed by Winants & Co., and describes the services offered:

Subscribers to this Registry can obtain through it, information of their friends in the mines or elsewhere, in California; send and receive letters to and from the Post Office and friends, and have other business transacted with security and dispatch.

No price is given for this service, but various reports indicate that others offered the registry service for one dollar per registration.

Palmer, Cook & Company started an express business in its early days, but abandoned it in 1851. Ira B. Cross says that American Express had an office in San Francisco in 1850, but Cross is not too reliable on such details. Inasmuch as John Butterfield vetoed extension of American Express' activities to California in 1852, it does not appear that American ever had an office in San Francisco.

A lot of men were trying, but few had the sagacity and tenacity to put the effort across. It is strange, too, since the need and the demand for transportation of articles from one place to another was so great. Todd and Gregory and many others got into the field in 1849, but the first eastern company to become firmly established was Adams, which, on October 31, 1849, sent Daniel Hale Haskell to California. The Adams announcement in the *Alta California* for November 8, 1849, offered express service to the East, and said:

Gold dust bought, also forwarded to any of the above places, and bills of exchange given in any amounts. Letter-bags made up and forwarded by a special messenger in each of the steamers.

Adams had started as an express company but was already in the banking business by buying gold; it was in the mail-carrying business. But apparently it did not yet consider itself a banker, or the other bankers in town did not consider it so, because an announcement of banking hours (9 to 4) on October 20, 1850, is signed by Argenti & Company; Page, Bacon & Company; Wells & Company (not Henry Wells); Burgoyne & Company; James King of William; B. Davidson; and Tallant & Company. Adams' name is absent.

It does not appear that Adams & Company was dragging its feet, however, for by early 1851 it was the leading express company on the Pacific Coast. It may be observed, too, that Adams offered a special messenger with its letter-bags; this implies that it would send messengers with its express shipments by sea—which is exactly what it did. Not until Wells Fargo should come on the scene would there be another express service that would regularly send a messenger with its shipments.

"Messenger service" meant that a man would travel with the shipment at all times, personally seeing to its transfer, whether from ship to shore, stagecoach to railroad, muleback to man. The messenger was not only to see to the proper transfer of the express, but he was also to protect it in every way possible from holdup men, from flood, from sinking, from fire. In short, his job was to see that the goods were delivered.

In 1851, Augustus Elliott went all the way through from San Francisco to New York and back, accompanying his own shipments and making a round trip every two months, but in January, 1852, he advertised that he would ship through Nicaragua (Vanderbilt's new route had just opened), and it appears that the messenger service was not continued —probably because Elliott was sending a shipment every two weeks when the steamers sailed, and could neither be in four places at once nor hire men to do the job. (However, there is some evidence that he did continue the messenger service, and, if so, he was ahead of Wells Fargo in this respect.[11])

Thomas Gihon was a special messenger who demonstrated the kind of integrity that made the big express companies famous for reliability, when the *Tennessee* went on the rocks just north of the Golden Gate on February 6, 1853, with sixteen hundred passengers aboard. Gihon, an Adams messenger, had twelve or fourteen trunks of money and packages, and a number of women (wives of pioneers and woman schoolteachers), so, when the vessel struck, he first ran to notify the women in his care; then he launched a boat and began taking women ashore. A few men tried to rush the boat, but he kept them back with a pistol. He worked like a Trojan all that morning, and then, as the ship began to break up, Gihon asked if he might be allowed to take his express off the ship ahead of the passengers' baggage. He had worked so diligently that that was permitted, and the passengers helped. (Most of the baggage was saved also.) Then the passengers held a dinner and passed resolutions to the effect that Thomas Gihon was a great hero. Wells Fargo had no small competition in early California.

Wreck of the Tennessee. From Frank Soulé, et al., "Annals of San Francisco."

Thomas O. Goold was another. He was in the steamer *Atlantic* that was wrecked on Fisher's Island off the East Coast, November 25, 1846, a few miles out of New London, Connecticut. The *Atlantic* was battling a furious gale and became unmanageable and began to drift. She struck on the rocks and went to pieces in a few hours. Most of the seamen and experienced passengers escaped by jumping from the leeward as each wave ran out, but others, "in their fright and ignorance," jumped overboard from the windward side into deep water, and were immediately drowned. Goold saved the money and valuables of Adams & Company, and saved twenty persons from drowning, for which gallantry he received a gold watch and chain from Adams, and a medal from the Boston Humane Society.[12]

Wells Fargo did not get into California until 1852, and it has been suggested that Henry Wells and William G. Fargo were deliberately holding back to see how long the gold boom would last, but that does not seem entirely characteristic of them. It may be assumed, as a matter of fact, that both men wanted to get into California earlier, but had not been able to do so, since in 1850 they had become partners in a new company, the American Express, and were held back by some of the partners. Three aggressive companies—Livingston, Fargo & Company; Wells & Company; and Butterfield & Wasson[13]—had united in 1850, and the new company was doing well.[14] In its third year, however, Henry Wells and William G. Fargo pointed out that in 1851 some $60,000,000 in gold had come to the East from California, and that there was a profit in carrying so much gold.[15] At that time, Adams was carrying most of it,[16] and Wells and Fargo proposed to send American Express into California to challenge Adams; they believed there was plenty of business for both companies.[17] Contrariwise, however, John Butterfield and two others on that board opposed the extension, probably on the theory that the Gold Rush could hardly last.[18]

Perhaps both Wells and Fargo were satisfied to try it outside the corporate structure of American. At any rate, by May 20, 1852, according to their

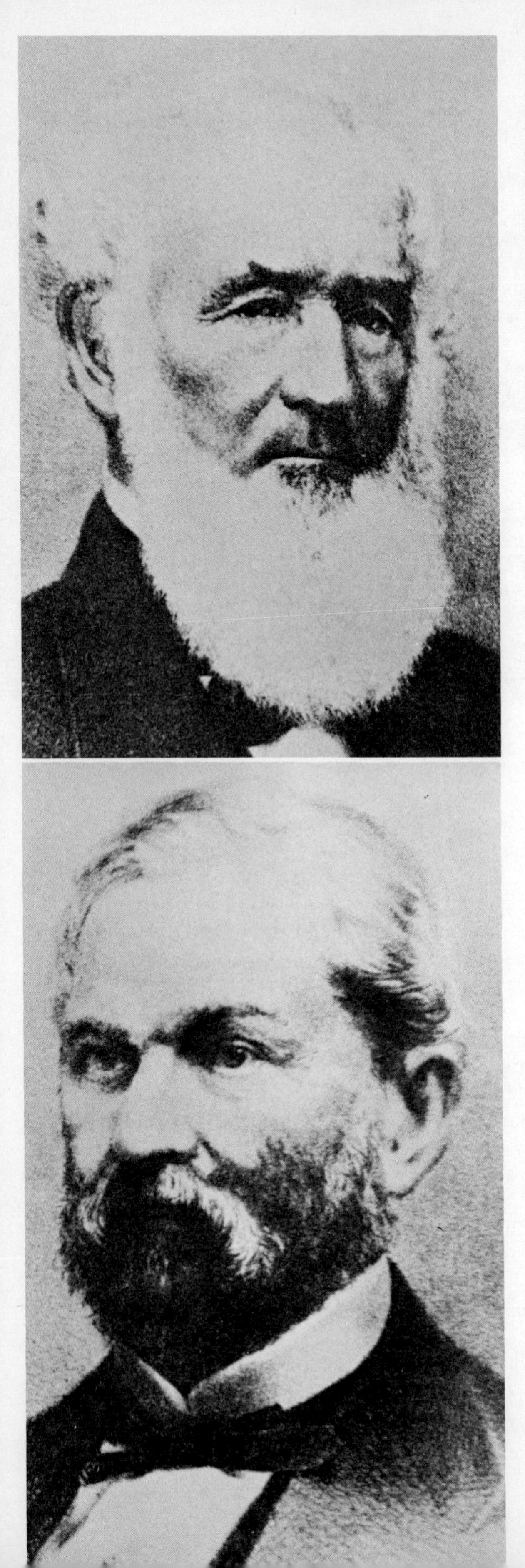

Henry Wells and William G. Fargo, founders of Wells, Fargo & Company. Wells was born in Thetford, Vermont, December 12, 1805, was in a number of early express companies, was president of American Express Company on its founding in 1850, and with Fargo organized Wells, Fargo & Company in 1852. He was president of American Express until 1868; founded Wells College for women in Aurora, New York, and died in Glasgow, Scotland, in 1878. William George Fargo was born in New York in 1818, and got into the express business in 1842. He and Wells in 1844 organized the first express company to run west from Buffalo. He was secretary of the American Express Company at its founding, and became president in 1868. He was president of Wells, Fargo & Company 1870–1872, and died in Buffalo, New York, in 1881.

announcement in *The New York Times,* they had formed a new company called Wells, Fargo & Company, with the following men on the board: Henry Wells, William G. Fargo, Johnston Livingston, Elijah P. Williams, Edwin B. Morgan, James McKay, Alpheus Reynolds, Alex M. C. Smith, and Henry D. Rice.[19] Wells Fargo was on the way, and it may be worth noting that Edwin B. Morgan, a banker and financier of Auburn, New York, was elected president of the new company.

Wells, Fargo & Company was capitalized at $300,000. There were to be 3,000 shares at $100; $5 per share was to be paid immediately, and the stock would be issued, fully paid, for $25, which seems to provide a capital of $75,000 for the commencement of their operations. Full payment, incidentally, was called on April 23.[20]

The company sent two agents to California. The first one, Samuel P. Carter, to run the express business, arrived in California June 27 on the *Oregon,* and the company's announcement appeared in the *Alta California* on July 3, 1852, headed, "Wells, Fargo & Company's Atlantic and Pacific Express—a joint-stock company." It would:

> undertake a General Express Forwarding Agency and Commission Business; the purchase and sale of Gold Dust, Bullion, and Bills of Exchange; the payment and collection of Notes, Bills and Accounts; the Forwarding of Gold Dust, Bullion and Specie, also Packages, Parcels and Freight of all descriptions in and between the city of New York and the city of San Francisco, and the principal cities and towns in California; connecting at New York with the lines of the American Express Company; the Harnden Express; Pullen, Virgil & Co.'s Northern and Canada Express; and Livingston, Wells &

Co.'s European Express. They have established Offices and faithful Agents in all the principal cities and towns throughout the Eastern, Middle and Western States; energetic and faithful messengers, furnished with iron chests for the security of treasure and other valuable packages, accompanying each Express upon all their lines, as well in California as in the Atlantic States. They will immediately establish offices at all the principal towns in California, and run messengers on their own account for the purpose of doing a general Express business.

Several facts are noticeable in this announcement. First, Wells Fargo was to be a joint-stock company. This is the kind of association in which each partner cannot stand on his corporate identity but is responsible as an individual; each shareholder has more to say about the affairs of the company, but he is at the same time assuming much more risk. Therefore, it appears that the assumption of this type of company is an indication of the men who made it up: They were individualists, not afraid to assume more risk if they could have more to say about the business. Second, there is no emphasis on banking service. Third, Wells Fargo assured customers that messengers would travel with all shipments, as was customary in the East. Fourth, offices would be established in all principal towns of California, and "as soon as such arrangements are completed, notice will be given."[21]

It may be noted too that at that early time—their first announcement of services in California—Wells Fargo mentioned "iron chests"; obviously, then, the iron chest had been in use in the East, and Carter must have come to California supplied with a number of them.

Wells, Fargo & Company's offices were in "S. Brannan's new fire-proof block, Montgomery st., between California and Sacramento."[22] Wells, Fargo & Company,[23] preparing to go into business in San Francisco, apparently arranged with Sam Brannan to erect a building for them diagonally across the street from the Parrott Building, the first stone building in San Francisco.[24]

On June 1, 1852, shortly before Wells Fargo's Mr. Carter arrived in California, there were four aggressive advertisers for express, as shown in the *Alta California*.

One was Gregory's Atlantic and Pacific Express; it advertised the "only express by the Nicaragua route, and the best possible facilities by Panama"; it also had a messenger on two steamers daily for Sacramento and the Gold Country, "with a safe and stateroom for the utmost security." It issued drafts payable at sight for the remittance of funds to other persons, and it bought "clean gold dust."

The second express company in the *Alta*'s column was Hunter & Company's Express, which obviously had a strong tie-up with Adams; Hunter said it was the only express company in El Dorado, Placer, and Calaveras counties authorized to draw bills of exchange on Adams; it sold checks, bills of exchange, and drafts[25] payable by Adams; it collected accounts; it forwarded gold dust but did not offer to buy it; its office was with the Adams office in both San Francisco and Sacramento. It, of course, ran a daily express to mining towns in the counties named, and connected with Adams Express for the southern mines.[26]

Rhodes & Lusk's Express ran weekly from San Francisco to Yreka. It forwarded letters, packages, and treasure, it made collections, it sold drafts, and it forwarded gold dust to the mints at Philadelphia and New Orleans but did not offer to buy gold dust.

The fourth was a company that ranked with Gregory in importance: Todd's Express, which ran daily throughout the southern mines (to which Stockton was the point of entry); Todd made collections, and forwarded treasure and packages; he was a successor to Reynolds, Todd & Company, and his office was with Gregory.

There was, of course, Adams & Company, which was pretty well in control of the express and banking business in California.

This was the situation when Wells Fargo went into San Francisco and into the building already built for them by Sam Brannan. Hunter was well established in the Middle Mines, Todd in the Southern Mines, and Gregory all over, while Adams, saying nothing at that particular time, was everywhere also. Nevertheless, it was a booming country, and there was no reason for Wells Fargo to fear competition. In fact, it rather seems that, on the whole, Wells Fargo thrived on competition.

Carter, Wells Fargo's agent, did not immediately begin receiving gold for transport in any volume, because, when the *Oregon* sailed from San Francisco on July 31, she carried $600,000 for Adams, $682,014 for Page, Bacon, and $21,710 in gold for

Samuel Brannan. From Frank Soulé, et al., "Annals of San Francisco."

Wells Fargo. (Since Page, Bacon was not in the express business, it may be assumed that its amount represented purchases.)

Wells Fargo's man who would handle the banking business in California (Reuben W. Washburn, a banker) arrived in San Francisco, July 10, on the *Tennessee,* along with eleven deaths from cholera. He carried files of Eastern and Panama newspapers and 65 packages for Wells Fargo, while Adams had 310 packages on the same ship.

Washburn issued Wells Fargo's first exchange on July 13, 1852, and Wells Fargo, by that act, was definitely in the banking business, although there were not, as yet, more than minimal facilities for holding money. No change was made in the Wells Fargo card in the *Alta California*. The company was doing a great deal of advertising in other ways, however.

One of the best descriptions of Wells Fargo's early services appears in a poster printed to advertise its establishment in Placer County; the poster is dated August 25, 1852, six weeks after Washburn reached San Francisco:

> Placer County Branch of Wells, Fargo & Co.'s Express! A joint stock company—capital, $300,000. Composed from, and connecting with, the American Express Company; Livingston, Wells & Co.; Wells, Butterfield & Co.; Livingston, Fargo & Co.; the Harnden Express; and Pullen, Virgil & Co., in the United States and the Canadas, and Livingston, Wells & Co., throughout all parts of Europe.

They seem to have added three new companies (but no unfamiliar names) in their connections.

> Furnished with the most ample means—with the best possible facilities for transportation—with energetic and faithful Messengers for the conveyance of Treasure and Valuable Packages on all their lines—and, most of all, with a business reputation of several years' standing

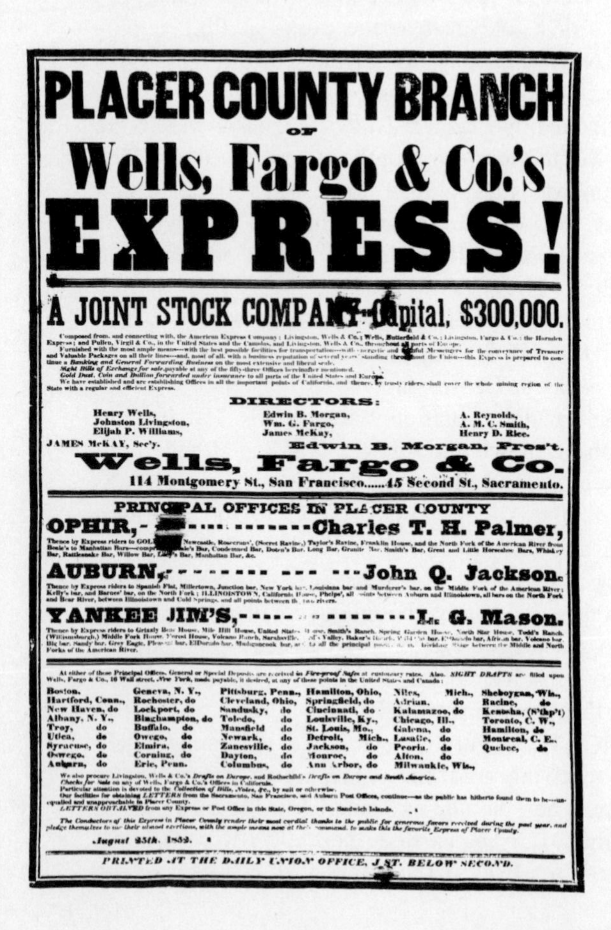

The Placer County poster of 1852. The original is in the History Room, Wells Fargo Bank.

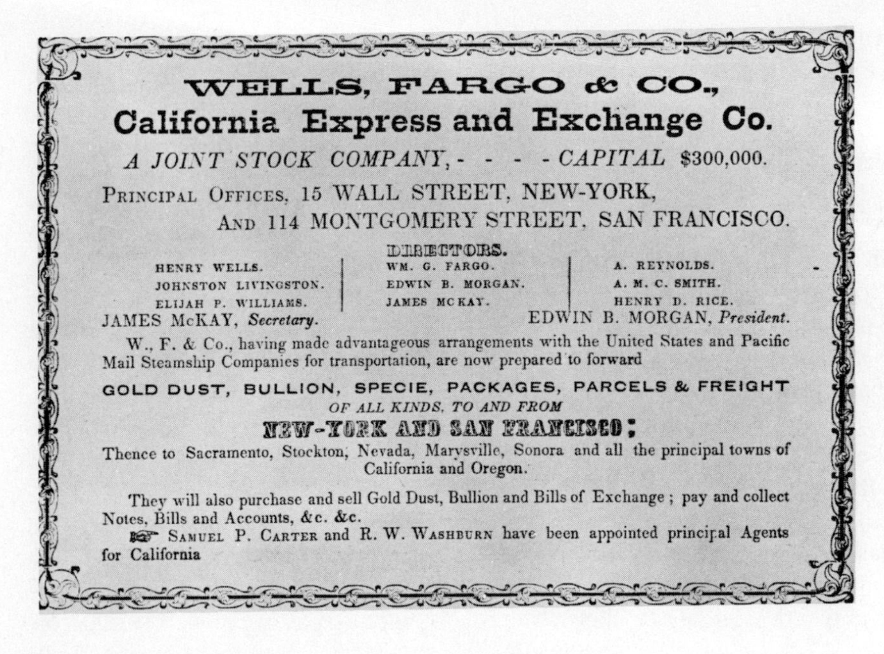

WELLS, FARGO & CO.,
California Express and Exchange Co.

A JOINT STOCK COMPANY, - - - - CAPITAL $300,000.

PRINCIPAL OFFICES, 15 WALL STREET, NEW-YORK,
AND 114 MONTGOMERY STREET, SAN FRANCISCO.

DIRECTORS.

HENRY WELLS.	WM. G. FARGO.	A. REYNOLDS.
JOHNSTON LIVINGSTON.	EDWIN B. MORGAN.	A. M. C. SMITH.
ELIJAH P. WILLIAMS.	JAMES MCKAY.	HENRY D. RICE.

JAMES McKAY, *Secretary.* EDWIN B. MORGAN, *President.*

W., F. & Co., having made advantageous arrangements with the United States and Pacific Mail Steamship Companies for transportation, are now prepared to forward

GOLD DUST, BULLION, SPECIE, PACKAGES, PARCELS & FREIGHT
OF ALL KINDS, TO AND FROM
NEW-YORK AND SAN FRANCISCO;

Thence to Sacramento, Stockton, Nevada, Marysville, Sonora and all the principal towns of California and Oregon.

They will also purchase and sell Gold Dust, Bullion and Bills of Exchange; pay and collect Notes, Bills and Accounts, &c. &c.

☞ SAMUEL P. CARTER and R. W. WASHBURN have been appointed principal Agents for California

A card (probably circulated from house to house) from about 1852, to advertise the company's services. The original is owned by B. C. Pearce, a vice-president of the Wells Fargo Bank.

throughout the Union—this Express is prepared to continue a *Banking and General Forwarding Business* on the most extensive and liberal scale. *Sight Bills of Exchange for sale,* payable at any of the fifty-three Offices hereinafter mentioned. *Gold Dust, Coin and Bullion forwarded under insurance* to all parts of the United States and Europe. We have established and are establishing Offices in all the important points of California, and thence, by trusty riders, shall cover the whole mining region of the State with a regular and efficient Express.

Here, for the first time as far as can be determined, Wells Fargo announced its banking services: sight bills of exchange, checks, drafts, and collections —not the same as transporting packages. Then it published its "Principal Offices in Placer County" and the agents in charge of them:

Ophir—Charles T. H. Palmer. Thence by Express riders to Gold Hill, Newcastle, Rosecrans' (Secret Ravine), Taylor's Ravine, Franklin House, and the North Fork of the American River from Beale's to Manhattan Bars—comprising Beale's Bar, Condemned Bar, Doten's Bar, Long Bar, Granite Bar, Smith's Bar, Great and Little Horseshoe Bars, Whiskey Bar, Rattlesnake Bar, Willow Bar, Lacy's Bar, Manhattan Bar, &c.

Auburn—John Q. Jackson. Thence by Express riders to Spanish Flat, Millertown, Junction bar, New York bar, Louisiana bar and Murderer's bar, on the Middle Fork of the American River; Kelly's bar, and Barnes' bar, on the North Fork; Illinoistown, California House, Phelps', all points between Auburn and Illinoistown, all bars on the North Fork and Bear River, between Illinoistown and Cold Springs, and all points between the two rivers.

The word "bar" does not refer to a cocktail emporium, even though, strangely enough, the miners were not unaccustomed to mixed drinks.[27] The word "bar" refers to a gold-bearing bar of gravel.

Yankee Jim's—L. G. Mason. Thence by Express riders to Grizzly Bear House, Mile Hill House, United States House, Smith's Ranch, Spring Garden House, North Star House, Todd's Ranch (Williamsburgh,) Middle Fork House, Forest House, Volcano Ranch, Sarahsville, Bird's Valley, Baker's Ranch, Wild Cat bar, ElDorado Bar, African bar, Volcano bar, Big bar, Sandy bar, Grey Eagle, Pleasant bar, ElDorado bar [there may have been two], Madigancook bar, and to all the principal points on the Dividing Ridge between the Middle and North Forks of the American River.

Whatever else Carter and Washburn were doing, they were not sitting on their hands.

So much for the express routes in Placer County. The poster then describes other services:

At either of these Principal Offices, General or Special Deposits are received in *Fire-proof Safes* at customary rates.

This apparently means that Wells Fargo was receiving deposits as a bank.[28]

"Also," the poster says, "*Sight Drafts* are filled upon Wells, Fargo & Co., 16 Wall street, *New York,* made payable, if desired, at any of these points in the United States and Canada"; fifty-two places in the East are named, substantially the same as those named before, with a number of new towns in Ohio, Michigan, and Wisconsin.

"We also procure Livingston, Wells & Co.'s *Drafts on Europe,* and Rothschild's *Drafts on Europe and South America. Checks for Sale* on any of Wells, Fargo & Co.'s Offices in California." Selling checks was a good business because frequently the checks were not presented for payment until considerably later.

Particular attention is devoted to the *Collection of Bills, Notes, &c.,* by suit or otherwise. Our facilities for obtaining *Letters* from the Sacramento, San Francisco, and Auburn Post Offices, continue—as the public has heretofore found them to be—unequalled and unapproachable in Placer County. *Letters Obtained* from any Express or Post Office in this State, Oregon, or the Sandwich Islands [Hawaii].

And a final sendoff ends this comprehensive offer of services:

The Conductors of this Express in Placer County render their most cordial thanks to the public for generous favors received during the past year [?], and pledge themselves to use their utmost exertions, with the ample means now at their command, to make this the favorite Express of Placer County.

There is no question that Wells, Fargo & Company was after the banking business with fervor. Perhaps Washburn, the banking manager of Wells Fargo, knew what he was doing. In the *San Francisco Directory* for 1852-53, Wells Fargo had a page advertisement saying:

Wells, Fargo & Co., Bankers and Exchange Dealers. W. F. & Co., in connection with their *Express Business,* will also transact a general Banking, Exchange and Collection Business. General and Special Deposits received. Collections and Remittances made in all parts of California, Oregon, the Atlantic States and Europe, with promptness and dispatch. Gold Dust, Gold and Silver Coin, and Bullion, bought and sold. Money advanced on Gold Dust deposited for transmission or coinage. Sight Exchange on New York and Boston, for sale at current rates. Drafts also drawn payable at the following places, viz:

And it names fifty-one towns, having added "Pittsburg," several towns in Ohio and Michigan, Louisville, St. Louis, and some in Wisconsin.[29] By the time of this publication (probably late in 1852), Wells Fargo was thoroughly committed to an all-out effort toward the banking business of San Francisco.

The next advertisement in the *Alta California* appeared on October 10, 1852, at which time the company advertised as Wells, Fargo & Co.'s Express, and said:

Our next regular semi-monthly Express for New York and all parts of the Atlantic States, Canada and Europe, will be dispatched in charge of our regular through messenger, Mr. John J. Kelly, by the Pacific Mail Steamship Co.'s steamship *Oregon,* Captain A. V. H. Leroy, on Saturday, October 16th, at 7 o'clock, A. M. Treasure received for shipment until Friday, October 15th, at 5 P. M., and fully insured. Small packages and parcels received until 12 o'clock, midnight. Bills of exchange drawn on New York, payable in our principal office, No. 16 Wall street, and at our agencies in Boston, Hartford, New Haven, Albany, Troy, Utica, Syracuse, Oswego, Auburn, Rochester, Buffalo, Cleveland, Sandusky, Columbus, Louisville, Ft. [!] Louis, Toledo, Cincinnati, Detroit, Chicago, Milwaukee, Peoria, Galena, Toronto, C. W., Hamilton, C. W., Montreal, C. E., Quebec, C. E. [Signed] Wells, Fargo & Co., 114 Montgomery street.

This ad started on October 10 and ran seven times.

At the same time, under the head of "Banking," cards were run by Duncan, Sherman & Co., New York; the Savings Bank of California; F. Argenti & Company;[30] James King of William; Palmer, Cook & Company; and Adams & Co., but not by Wells Fargo.

James King of William was a man who tried his hand at various things; he would soon start the San Francisco *Bulletin* and attack anybody who might get in his way.[31]

Palmer, Cook & Company was only a banking house, and for a few years would be rather important in California, but eventually would go under from attacks by James King of William.[32] Adams & Company was pushing for banking business. F. Argenti & Company offered little or nothing more than did Wells Fargo; it could draw on banks in New York, London, Liverpool, and Paris; it would buy "good, clean gold dust" at the highest prices, or would forward it to New York or England, covered by insurance.

Wells Fargo apparently did not advertise again in the *Alta California* until December 27, when it announced express to New York "and New Orleans" by the *Northerner*. As before, it would accept gold and packages, and said it would draw bills of exchange payable at sight in the places previously listed (except Hartford and New Haven, which apparently had been dropped) and a number of new ones: Erie, Pottsville, Stonington, Reading, Providence, and Philadelphia. It appears that American Express had been busy in the East.[33]

It is noteworthy that Wells Fargo had added service to New Orleans, "Direct from Aspinwall by U. S. Mail steamers." It may or may not be significant that Wells Fargo was staying away from Vanderbilt's Nicaragua line. And well it might, since trouble was brewing in Nicaragua.[34]

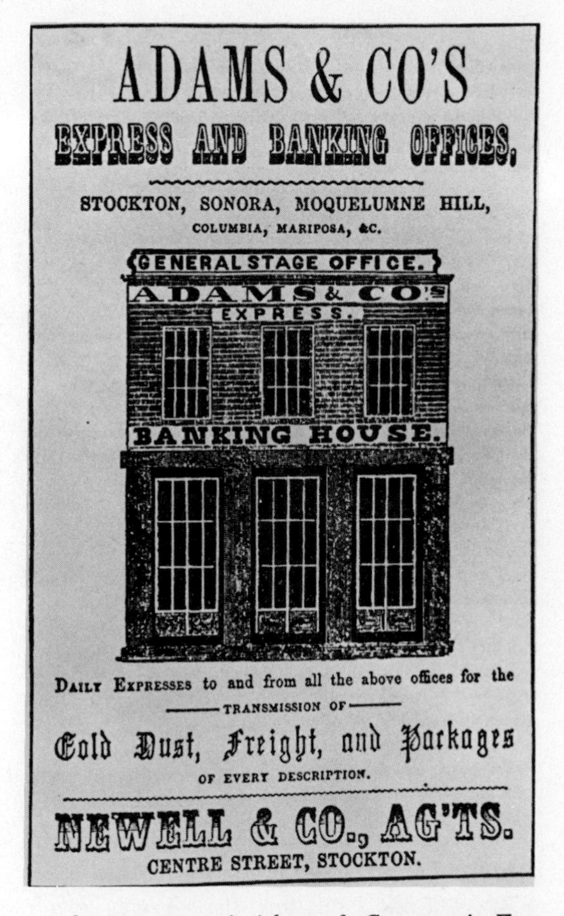

Advertisement of Adams & Company's Express and Banking Offices, from Colville's "City Directory of Sacramento for the Year 1854–5"; print from the Bancroft Library, Berkeley, University of California.

Another wild and tempestuous aspect of life that involved more than one banker in both San Francisco and New York, and did its part in leading to the failure of some big houses, was that of the filibuster. In keeping with the wild and freewheeling spirit of adventure and the consciousness of manifest destiny (that is, that it was America's manifest destiny to rule the continent from sea to sea), there were other factors that made opportunity for the filibusterer, or, perhaps, forced opportunity on him: The fact that Frenchmen in the Gold Country were ill suited to mining, and not too well disposed to work in harmony with other nationalities; the general feeling that Mexico and the Central American countries were badly ruled, unable to defend themselves, and so oppressed that the people would welcome any relief; the inordinate ambition of small men who had, generally speaking, failed at everything else; and the wildness of the first years of gold and lawlessness, which led men to the feeling that might made right.[35] All these, and perhaps others, led men like Gaston, Count de Raousset-Boulbon, and "the gray-eyed man of destiny," William Walker, to try their fortunes in other countries.

There were two common excuses offered by the filibusterers: First, that Mexicans (in particular) were badly treated by their government, and needed help and direction to develop their natural resources —especially their mines; second, that they were harassed by the Apaches (which was true), and that a few good men with rifles would be looked on as saviors.

In the spring of 1851, Joseph C. Morehead, quartermaster-general of California, led some men

The mission of Cocóspera, near which the early filibustering party of Pindray stayed for a short while. From J. Ross Browne, "A Tour Through Arizona," in "Harper's Monthly Magazine," January, 1865.

(variously reported at from forty-five to several hundred) toward Baja California and Sonora, but the expedition broke up and Morehead returned to California to try again.

At about the same time, the Mexican government, aware of its own helplessness, began to tamper with the idea of inviting foreign colonists, hoping to solve some of the problems on Mexico's frontier, and especially in Sonora. Therefore, in November, 1851, Charles de Pindray took eighty-eight Frenchmen to land in Cocóspera Valley in northern Sonora; objective: to develop agriculture and to search for minerals. However, the Apaches respected Pindray's men no more than they did Mexicans, and presently Pindray became truculent toward the Mexican authorities, and finally wound up with a bullet in his forehead—either a suicide, a victim of a quarrel, or a removal by the Mexican government.

Lepine de Segondis in March, 1852, took some eighty men to exploit the mines in the Gila Valley.[36] They went to the Santa Cruz Valley but did not stay long, because little gold was found there.

The Mexican government by that time was becoming as distrustful of the French as it was of the aggressive Anglo-Americans, and so it was cautious of Raousset-Boulbon when he came into Sonora in June, 1852, with some two hundred men. It was true also that United States authorities were beginning to feel uncomfortable over the anti-filibustering section of the treaty between Mexico and the United States, and there was some talk that Boulbon's arms would be seized in San Francisco, but it was not done.

Patrice Dillon, the French consul in San Francisco, was one of the chief encouragers of Boulbon (as he had been of Pindray and others), but it seems likely that the chief backers were bankers, since the openly avowed objective of Boulbon was the famous Planchas de Plata (Silver Plate Mines) on the present northern border of Sonora, between the old town of Guevavi and the mission of El Saric—reputed to be very rich but abandoned in the 1740's. The middleman between Boulbon and the Mexican government was the great French-Mexican banking house of Jecker, Torre & Company, and opposed to Boulbon (because Jecker, Torre had invaded an area that was not its own) was the financial giant of the Pacific Coast of Mexico, Barron, Forbes & Company, which had headquarters down the coast at Tepic.

At this point, it is obvious that Boulbon was involved in the intricacies of Mexican politics, at which anybody but a Mexican is an amateur, but Boulbon, probably unaware, went ahead, more intent on being somebody than on making his project successful. Trouble brewed between Boulbon and, first, his men and, second, the Mexican officials. It may be that Barron, Forbes had bought Sonoran officials to make things difficult for Boulbon. Nevertheless, Boulbon eventually captured Hermosillo, but failed to follow through. He surrendered to General Blanco in Guaymas in late 1852, and left his men to shift for themselves while he went back to San Francisco to organize another expedition.

The filibustering was really an overflow from the general feeling that had brought men to California to pick up gold nuggets from the ground, and it involved many prominent men and some bankers, so it is important to observe that this is one of the things that Wells Fargo apparently did not go into.

In California, in the last two months of 1852, there were three significant events that gave Wells Fargo a chance to prove its mettle.

First was the national election, in which the Democrat, Franklin Pierce, beat the Whig, Winfield Scott, by a small majority. At the election, Wells Fargo took it upon itself to obtain and deliver to San Francisco "carefully prepared special returns" from the gold fields. The national outcome would not be known for a month (having to come by steamer), but California results were known quickly, and Wells Fargo made many friends by this service. Wells Fargo had, from the beginning, carried newspapers from one town to another, and there are many notations of this on editorial pages: "Our respects to Wells Fargo for a bundle of newspapers from San Francisco, bringing our intelligence to the 5th," or, from the New York *Tribune* for September 26, 1854: "We tender our thanks to R. Lord, Esq., Purser of the *Prometheus* and to Wells Fargo & Co.'s Express, for the prompt delivery of California papers."[37]

The second important event was a great fire in Sacramento in early November (the day of election, in fact), in which some twenty-six blocks were burned and some $5,000,000 damage done (including destruction of the Wells Fargo office). Wells Fargo worked like a hundred Trojans in that disaster, collecting money, subscribing money, and carrying (free of charge) bundles of clothing and boxes of food contributed by San Francisco, Marys-

Franklin Pierce, Democratic President of the United States, 1853–1857. From "The White House Gallery of Official Portraits of the Presidents."

J Street in Sacramento City during the flood. From the "Illustrated News," March 19, 1853.

ville, and other towns for relief of the needy in Sacramento.

The Alta California brought the news of the fire to the people of the state:

> *Awful Conflagration!* SACRAMENTO IN ASHES! Six Lives Known to Be Lost! Twenty-five Hundred Buildings Burned!! *Dreadful Destitution Among the Sufferers!* . . . We have the following full report of this disastrous event, prepared for us by Mr. Reed, the Express Messenger of Adams & Co. At 11½ o'clock on Tuesday evening a fire broke out in the millinery shop of Madame Lanos, . . . Gregory's Express Messenger furnishes us with the following additional particulars . . . One thing is certain: Sacramento will be rebuilt within a month, far better than ever before.

Wells Fargo does not appear to have gotten in on the spreading of the news, or the publicity for aid rendered (as far as the *Alta* is concerned), but Wells Fargo was doing its good deed nevertheless.

Soon after the holocaust in Sacramento, heavy floods from the Sacramento River hit the Gold Country, and again Wells Fargo did herculean service in supplying isolated miners with mail and food over impassable trails, so that the San Francisco *Herald* was moved to say, on December 17, that "Wells Fargo, a firm which has gained rapidly in public favor and is now fully and successfully established, made extraordinary exertions to supply the press here with the first news—they succeeded. They are very prompt and often in advance in furnishing us with news from the most remote towns of the interior."

It seems Wells Fargo messengers were favoring the *Herald,* perhaps because the Wells Fargo office was closer to that of the *Herald* than it was to that of the *Alta California.*

Although it was said later that Washburn was not

an aggressive man, obviously the Wells Fargo agency in San Francisco was not dragging its feet those first six months of 1852, for by the end of the year the Wells Fargo sign and the Wells Fargo green iron shutters were on Wells Fargo buildings in twelve towns in California.[38] Wells Fargo had established an agency at Sacramento, a little north and east of San Francisco—which was roughly a supply point for the Middle Mines; from Sacramento it went north to Marysville, which was a trading point for the Northern Mines. In July it had made arrangements with Hunter & Company at Placerville to handle Wells Fargo business in El Dorado County. Then Gregory's Express abandoned its route in Placer County, and Wells Fargo took over its routes and agencies in August. On September 1, Wells Fargo had arranged connections at Marysville and Sacramento with Rhodes & Lusk's Shasta Express for northern California and southern Oregon. And on September 1, arrangements were made with Todd's Express for business in the Southern Mines.

By September 1, a new brick building housed Wells Fargo in Sacramento. In October, semimonthly service was arranged to Portland via Pacific Mail, and a Portland agency set up. In December, as noted, semimonthly service was established to New Orleans.

It rather seems that Wells, Fargo & Company's first six months were busy and successful, and certainly they were typical of the years to come.

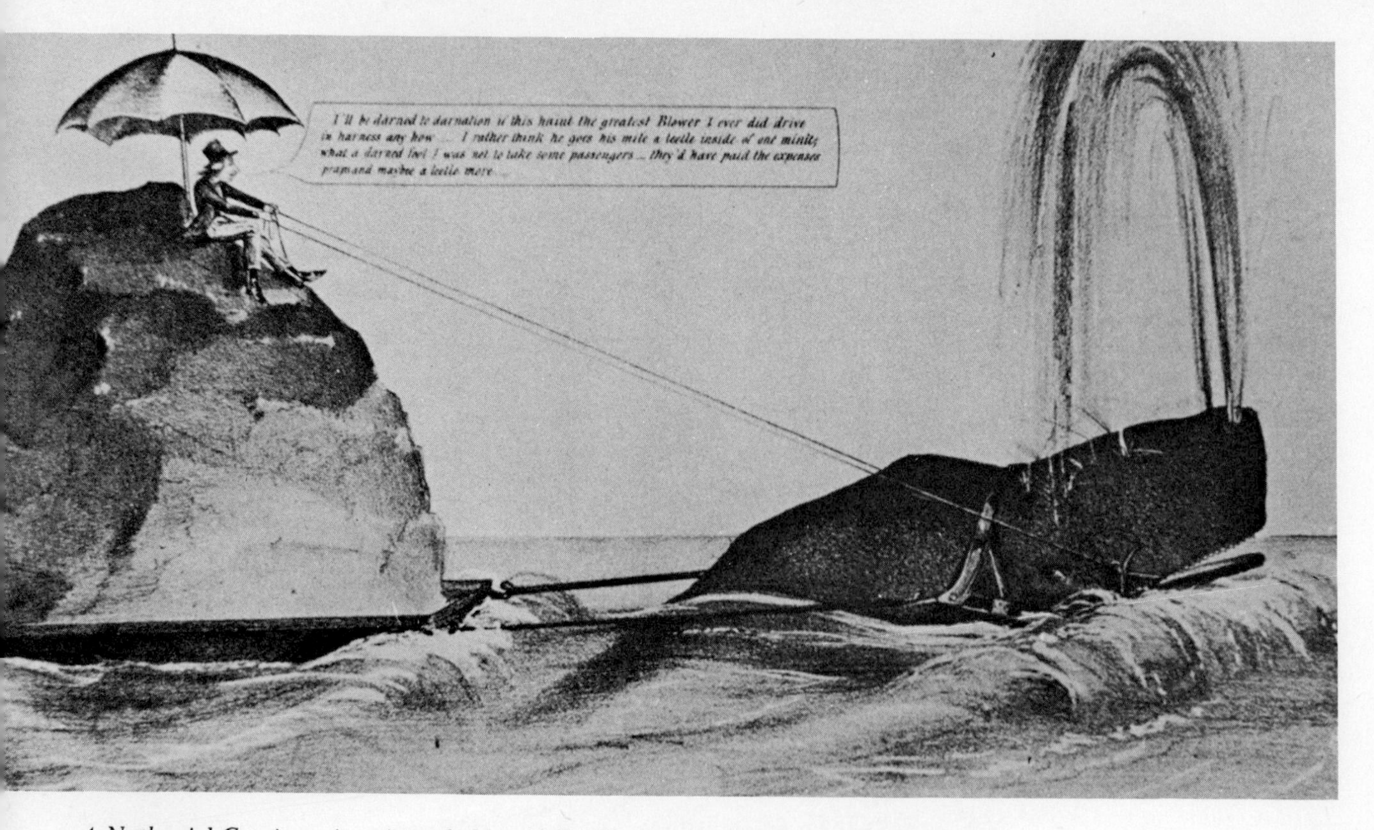

A Nathaniel Currier print of (probably) 1849. The caption reads: "California Gold. An accurate drawing of the famous hill of gold, which has been put into a scow by the owner, and attached to a Sperm Whale who is now engaged in towing it around the Horn, for New York." The balloon reads: "I'll be darned to darnation if this haint the greatest Blower I ever did drive in harness any how—I rather think he gets his mile a leetle inside of one minit; what a darned fool I was not to take some passengers—they'd have paid the expenses praps and maybe a leetle more—" The East was inclined to consider the Gold Rush a joke. The original print is owned by the California Historical Society.

A scene to represent the early rush of miners from Yerba Buena. From Frank Soulé, et al., "Annals of San Francisco."

Gold—The "Ruin" of California

WELLS FARGO WAS ORGANIZED TO DO business in California, and lost no time adjusting itself to the strange conditions there—for the Mother Lode Country was (and still is) like nothing else anywhere. That condition started in the hectic days of 1848, when San Francisco, the fountainhead of all the Gold Country's eccentricities, gradually became aware of the discovery of gold, but it also had some roots in California's Spanish and Mexican background.

California had been a long way from Madrid and a long way from Mexico City, and had been settled by priests who had acquired great tracts of land for their missions, and by regal favorites who had acquired huge estates to raise cattle and sheep. Inasmuch as supply ships did not come up the coast very often, living was inclined to be primitive even for the wealthy landowners, but it certainly was quiet. There was some change, however, when Mexico revolted successfully against Spain in 1821, and again in the early 1830's when the property of the missions was taken out of ecclesiastical hands. In the meantime, a few "Boston men" (captains of Yankee ships) had come to California, had liked it, and had stayed, but they had generally married Spanish girls and had adapted themselves to the Spanish way of life.

In 1846, however, the United States and Mexico went to war, and changes came fast. After a few hectic weeks, General Kearny became military governor of California, and things began to hum as discharged soldiers settled in the state and a few curious Anglo-Americans moved in to impose their culture upon the land.

The Spaniards, so long isolated from their native countries, tended to accept the new regime rather gracefully, and, with the exception of the stirring-up of things by men like Captain John Charles Frémont, affairs rocked along rather smoothly for almost exactly a year. Then the restless Americans found gold in the tail race of Sutter's mill near what is now Coloma. The Spaniards had lived in California for eighty years, but they had stayed largely in the valleys and plains and so had not come in contact with the gold of the Mother Lode (east, northeast, and southeast of San Francisco). However, word came down from the mountains to San Francisco in February that gold had been discovered—and San Francisco, generally speaking, yawned.

The two newspapers, the *Californian* and the California *Star,* seemed reluctant to give credence to the reports, possibly because they disliked each other so much. The *Californian* (which Sam Brannan's *Star* had said, most ungallantly, was published by "a lying sycophant and an overgrown lickspittle"—to which the *Californian* had responded by observing that "if you lie down with dogs, you must rise up with fleas. . . . The present editor is wearing breeches made for a *boy*") published the first rumor of gold, and it was therefore promptly denied by the *Star,* which headed its item: "The Mineral Mania—All not coal [*sic*] that glitters";[1] the following week, however, the *Star* conceded that there was something to it.

The *Star*'s editor then went to look for himself. The *Californian* printed another report, and on May 3 said that "seven men with picks and spades could gather $1,600 worth of gold in fifteen days." Three days later (May 6) the *Star* said: "We have returned and resumed our labors. . . . Full flowing streams, mighty timber, large crops, luxuriant clover, fragrant flowers, gold and silver. Great country, this." It almost seems that they didn't want to believe it, though it has been hinted that Sam Brannan suppressed the news to give himself time to get entrenched in the Gold Country.

But the village of San Francisco[2] ceased to yawn. Everybody headed for the mountains, and within a few days San Francisco was deserted. Storekeepers were without goods and without customers, so they locked the doors and went to the mines themselves. Only the very old and the physically incapable stayed at home, and suddenly both newspapers found themselves without advertisers and without subscribers.

Then the *Star* gave some hint that perhaps Brannan was indeed indulging in a minor bit of hanky-panky (no novelty to Sam) when it said on May 20:

> El Dorado Anew.—A terrible visitant we have had of late—a *fever* which has well nigh depopulated a town. . . . And this is the *gold fever*. . . . Was there ever any thing so superlatively silly? . . . We are inclined to believe the reputed wealth . . . all sham—a supurb take in, as was ever got up to "guzzle the gullible."

The *Star*'s tortuous syntax might be more cogent if it were not so vociferous. But then the *Star* added a completely contradictory note: "Beyond a question . . . no richer mines of gold have ever been discovered upon the face of the continent." It does seem possible that Brannan, the owner, was establishing stores in Sacramento and perhaps other places in the Gold Country, and that the editor was under orders to ignore the discovery—but slipped.

A letter to the editor of the *Californian* doubts if "ever the sun shone upon such a face as is now being enacted in California, though I fear it may prove a tragedy before the curtain drops." It admonished the editor: "I consider it your duty, as a conservator of the public morals and welfare, to raise your voice against the thing. It is to be hoped that General Mason will dispatch the volunteers to the scene of the action, and send these unfortunate people to their homes, and prevent others from going thither."

It would have been a good trick if anybody could have done it, for the editor of the *Star* had already sent his booster edition to the East to give the gold discovery away, and within six months the whole world would be converging on the Gold Country.

On May 24, the *Californian* denied the deploring of its contributor. "Neither can we believe that the consequences of this 'mania' will be so *very* ruinous to the future prospects of California," it added, and it revealed its own feeling by suggesting that its subscribers who had left or who were about to leave for the Gold Country, could have their papers forwarded to New Helvetia (Sutter's place) if they would leave their address at the office.

Then the *Californian* in its next issue gave up: "The whole country, from San Francisco to Los Angeles, and from the seashore to the base of Sierra Nevada, resounds with the sordid cry of gold! Gold!! GOLD!!! while the field is left unplanted, the house half builded, and everything neglected but the manufacturers of shovels and picks"; and the *Star* on May 27 conceded disaster: "Never within the last three years has the town presented a less lifelike, more barren appearance than at the present time, never so inactive, so void of stir. . . . Every thing wears a desolate and sombre look, every where, all is dull, monotonous, dead." In another item it said: "Latest accounts from the Gold Country are highly flattering," and it admonished: "Pay up before you GO (every body knows WHERE). Papers can be forwarded to Sutter's Fort with all regularity."

That week, on May 29, the *Californian* issued a slip announcing its suspension of publication. Its last columns had bulged with news of gold and advice on how to weigh it, and its mournful farewell was not entirely consistent but hardly to be unexpected in the feverish excitement of the times.

The *Star* announced the *Californian*'s apparent demise: "Gone to ———. The *Californian* ceased issue with the annunciatory slip of Tuesday last. Verdict of inquest—fever."

Benjamin R. Buckelew, editor of the *Californian*,

had gone to the mines. But in the following week, the *Star* itself gave up: "In fewer words than are usually employed in the announcement of similar events, we appear before the remnant of a reading community with the material or immaterial information that we have stopped the paper—that its publication ceased with the last regular issue. We have done. Let our word of parting be, Hasta luego." Both Sam Brannan and his editor had gone to the mines, having, like the *Californian,* issued a slip to announce that the *Star* would be published no more.

It was June, and the second big exodus started from San Francisco. Those few, like the editors, who had held the fort, now gave it up and went to the mountains to look for gold. There was no skilled or unskilled labor available in the town; shops were closed, newspapers suspended, facilities nonexistent; soldiers and sailors deserted, and ships were stranded in the harbor because the captains could not hire anybody to load coal or wood for them—their own crews having deserted, and in some cases their officers.

The *Californian* was published several times during the summer and early fall, and on September 2 (its third issue since its suspension), it noted that it was the only newspaper published in the territory "since the advent of the 'golden era,' when the *Star* ceased to twinkle." Buckelew was considerably more gentle than Kemble or Brannan.

San Francisco had felt the golden touch, and would not be sane again for many years—some say forever.[3]

The real problem was about to develop, for in December President Polk's verification of the gold find set off a world-wide fever that caused streams of immigrants to pour into San Francisco: Peruvians, Mexicans, Chileans, Prussians, Irishmen, Englishmen, and Welshmen; Malayans in native dress; South Sea Islanders; Chinese by the thousands; Hindus in their turbans. Frenchmen organized a national lottery and sent thousands of men to the mines. Overnight, San Francisco became the world's most cosmopolitan city.

All these came through San Francisco into the Gold Country, and they were added to by thousands arriving from the Atlantic states on ships that went around the Horn. The stream of emigrants going overland to Oregon to get free land, turned south in Utah and went for gold; hundreds of men formed emigrating companies in New England and sailed on ships for Panama or Nicaragua; many more traveled a hundred trails through Texas and northern Mexico,[4] crossed at Fort Yuma, and struggled across the great Anza Desert, or they wound their precarious way through Mexico and finally dragged their weary bodies into one of the Mexican ports on the Pacific coast. Mexicans wound across the desert from Sonora in long trains of mules and burros;[5] Russians came down from Alaska; Australians poured in as fast as sailing ships would carry them. The whole world funneled its gold-hungry men through San Francisco to the mines.[6]

An advertisement from the Paris newspaper "Debats" for the California lottery. You bought tickets for 100 francs and perhaps won a trip to California. The company says it has already sent 406 persons to California on the Jacques-Lafitte, *the* Grétry, *the* Uncas, *and the* Louisiana. *The whole world was converging on California, but the idea was especially appealing in France because that country was suffering a severe depression. The company promised to furnish food, houses, equipment, and all necessaries for the miners; the company claimed it had deposited 560,000 francs for the first four expeditions. From microfilm owned by Abraham P. Nasatir.*

San Francisco in 1849, showing the ships cluttering the bay. A Currier & Ives print.

A poster advertising the sailing of the Ospray *for San Juan, Nicaragua, and Chagres, Panama, in 1852.*

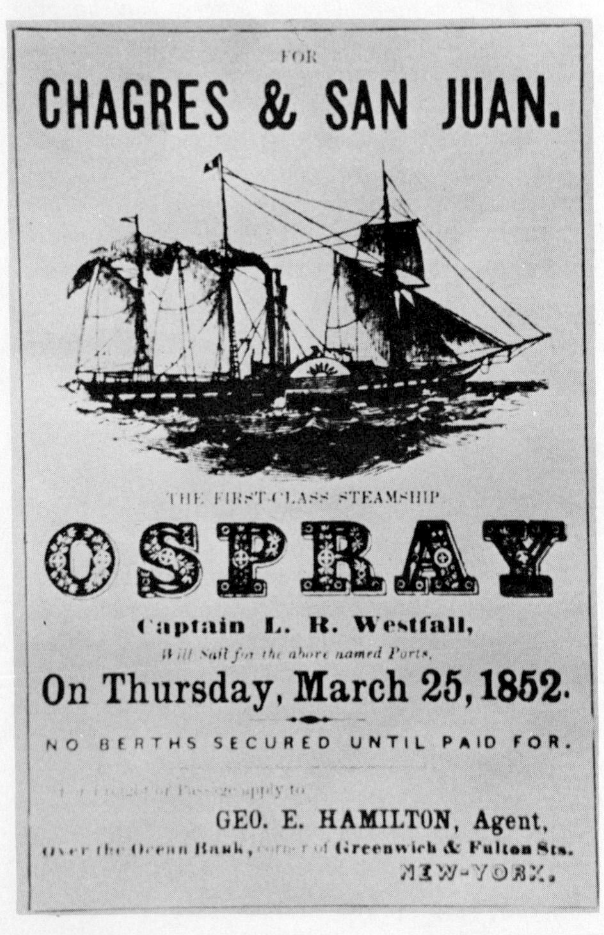

Opposite:
A French map of California in 1849 by C. Arnaud. The "Auriferes Region" is very plain. Printed by permission of Carl I. Wheat.

A poster from the Archives of the Paris Police, announcing tickets for 10 francs in a lottery in which ten men might win trips to California. From microfilm owned by Abraham P. Nasatir.

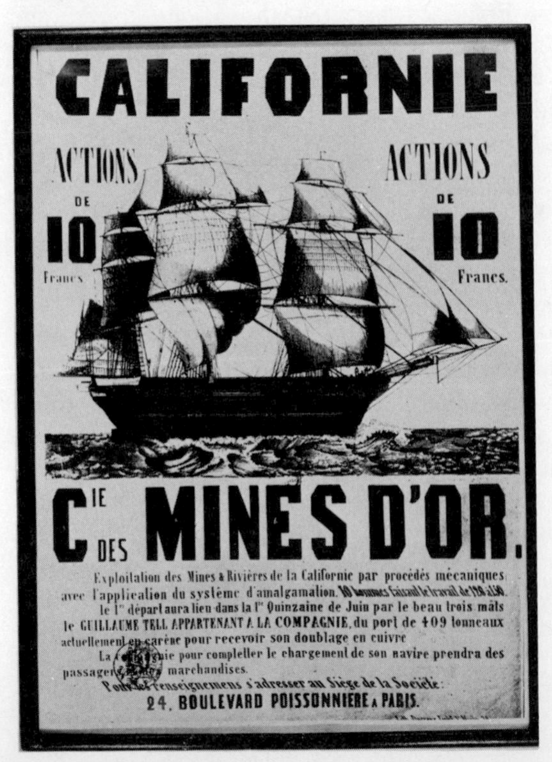

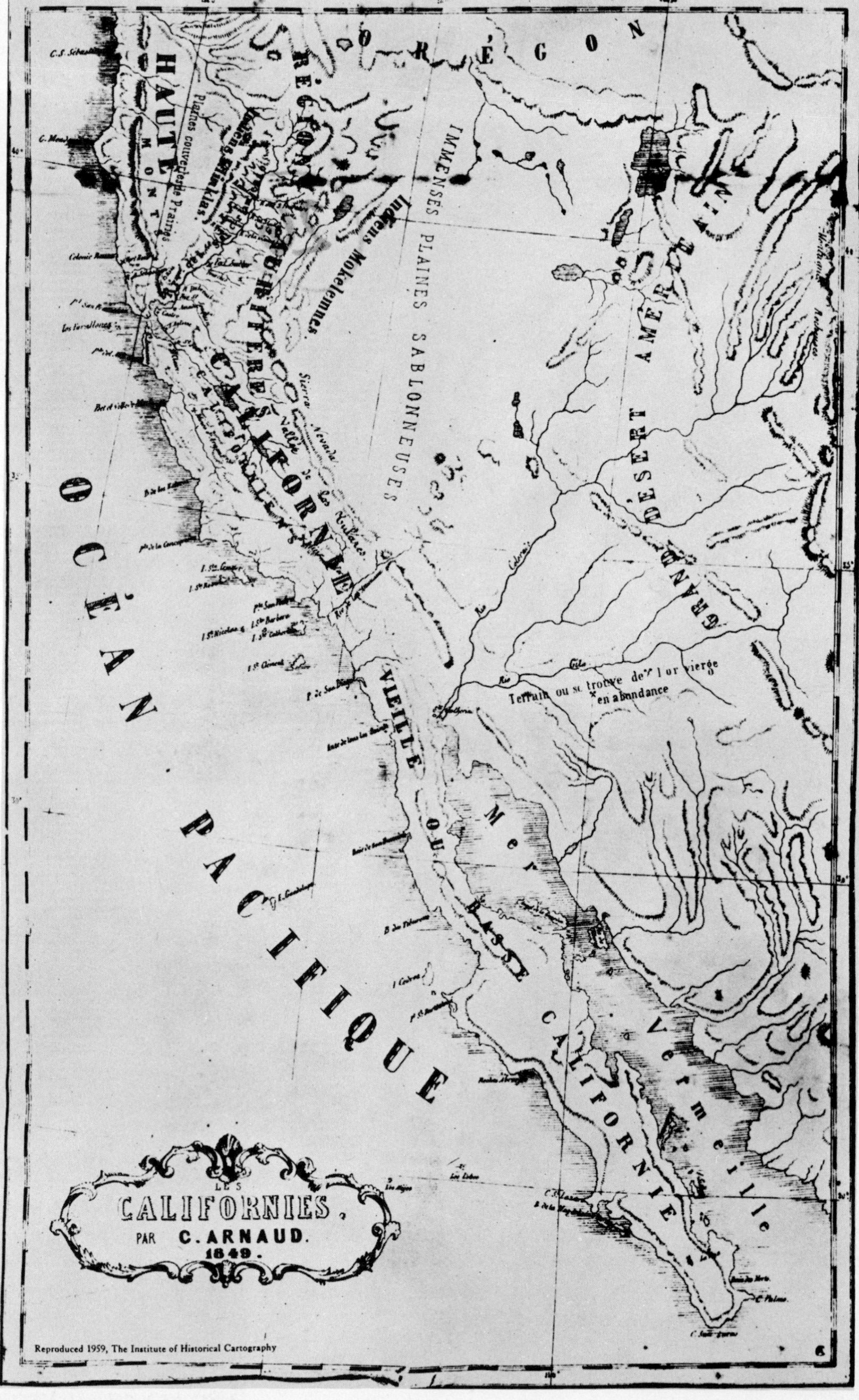
ORÉGON
HAUTE
CALIFORNIE
IMMENSES PLAINES SABLONNEUSES
Indiens Mokelemnes
Plaines couvertes de Prairies
Sierra Nevada
OCÉAN PACIFIQUE
GRAND DÉSERT AMÉR
Terrain ou se trouve de l'or vierge en abondance
VIEILLE OU BASSE CALIFORNIE
Mer Vermeille
LES CALIFORNIES, PAR C. ARNAUD. 1849.
Reproduced 1959, The Institute of Historical Cartography

A party of obvious Mexicans (referred to as Spaniards in California, except that Mexican women in those days rode sidesaddle on the right) headed for the Gold Country. From Thomas Armstrong, "Scenes of Wonder and Curiosity in California," published by Hutchings and Rosenfield.

Through 1849 there was order in the Gold Country, but by the winter of 1849–1850 there was trouble. The many nationalities did not always get along. Americans having no luck hated the Mexicans and the Chileans and the Chinese, and claimed the gold was theirs because the land was theirs. The French were ill-suited to work in the mines, and did not fraternize.

There was no organized law in such an explosive country, and in 1851, both in San Francisco and throughout the Gold Country, men began to take the law in their hands—sometimes through a Committee of Vigilance, sometimes through a group of miners impatient with thievery and murder. A very common item in the early Gold Country newspapers says: "A jury of miners yesterday found John Jones guilty of murdering George Smith, and hanged him to an oak-tree west of town."

Prices of course went out of sight. A pick or a shovel might sell for $10 (as against a normal price of fifty cents); flour was $100 a barrel; bread was $1 a loaf and none to be had; it cost $1 apiece to get a shirt washed (if you were lucky enough to have an extra one), and some miners sent their shirts to China to be laundered.

The average miner did not make much; unless a man was industrious or lucky, he would not make enough to pay for his meals. But a few were both industrious and lucky, and one man panning out $1,000 worth of gold in two hours would offset one hundred lonely, hungry, ill-equipped, and discouraged men who wished they could somehow get passage back home.

Naturally, many had come for adventure, for excitement, but many had left wives and children at home and had come for a quick stake. Some made it; some did not. Some went back home; some didn't bother; some died alone and unknown. Wives were still looking for husbands two generations later, and sometimes a mother never heard from her son until after he met a sad and unhappy end. James P. Casey, just before he was hanged by the Committee of Vigilance in 1856, made an anguished plea: "I have an aged mother in the Atlantic States, and I hope she will never hear how I died. . . . Oh, my mother! my mother! I hope she will never hear of this. Oh, God! have mercy on my mother; comfort her in her affliction."

Casey was only one.

The miner worked from dawn to dark at back-breaking labors. He dug gravel, carried water, built sluiceways, and constructed dams. He formed companies for the bigger projects such as dam-building, and at least one heroic band labored mightily in the icy water to build a dam to divert water so they would all make more money, only to have a flood wash it out almost immediately; they built it again, and then found that the gravel was poor and they made about $1.50 per day.

From the New York *Tribune* of July 25, 1854, there is a good description of the work in water control:

El Dorado Mines.—A correspondent of *The Mountain Democrat,* from the Middle Fork of the American River, says:—The extensive dry diggings and ravines in the vicinity of Pilot Hill, and at Hogg's Diggings, have been worked since '49, and pay well yet. Water is now scarce, but as the Pilot Creek Canal Company intend running a branch of their ditch by Spanish Bar, through Greenwood Valley, to the above places, we shall soon have plenty. At the present time the most prominent feature in this section of the county, is the extensive preparations being made for river mining. At Poverty, Green Mountain and Maine bars, the miners have already let out their contract for fluming. At Murderer's Bar the foundations for their large flume are already laid. At the latter place, the miners have one of the largest and best dams in the country, which was built last year. The high water last winter had no effect upon it, and the structure is now in good condition. This will be a great saving to those interested; and probably the miners will be at work in the bed of the river sooner than any other company on the American River. It would be useless to say anything in relation to the richness of the deep crevices running across the river at Murdock's Bar. The water, "pay dirt" and rocks, all have to be raised by steam and water-power. To facilitate their operations, several of the claim-holders have joined their claims, obtained a charter, and will work their claims as a joint-stock company. In the cañon below the bar, the fluming timbers are all on the ground. A company has been organized for the purpose of tunneling around the falls through a high bluff of rocks just above the town. When that is completed, several bars, within two miles up the river, that the miners have never been able to work on account of [lack of] water, can then be worked to good advantage. The "jam" at the falls now flows the water back a long distance.

It was difficult building those dams and flumes, and the workers or miners at night spent what money they had carousing, or they stayed in their tents and by candlelight wrote long and touching letters to their loved ones; they organized dances in which men with white rags on their sleeves or on the seats of

Gold diggers on the Sacramento, according to an early lithograph from the Peters Collection in the Smithsonian Institution. It is quite a collection of characters: Indians, a Negro, a beaver hat, felt hats, shirtsleeves, and coat-tails. A bunch of men is fighting in the middle distance at the right, and we strongly suspect that the tiny log counter in the foreground, with a slanting roof, marks the site of a saloon.

their pants were "women"; they gambled at monte; they held church on Sunday.

They were busy—but perhaps part of the reason for their busyness was the lack of mail, and their trying to forget. They were unbelievably homesick, and they wanted to hear from their families more than they wanted anything else in the world.

Into this emotion-charged situation came the express companies. The miners were in a wild, primitive country and had no supplies except those brought up from San Francisco by an occasional express; they had letters brought haphazardly by other miners until the express companies began to make a business of carrying letters. Even after the expresses began to bring mail, it was not all clear sailing, because for some men, $1 a letter was too much to pay. But they managed. One man who had had no luck was one day confronted with eight letters, and had only $7 to his name—but he had $1 coming for a day's labor, and got his letters.

However, at first even the expresses were not very well organized, and there was dissatisfaction among the miners until the bigger express companies put the service on a more systematic basis.

Wells Fargo, of course, was one of those who did so.

Into the hectic Gold Country world of rough men and great human hunger, Wells Fargo made its entry in June, 1852, and its progress was so rapid that Henry Wells made a trip of inspection to California, arriving in San Francisco, February 5, 1853, on the *Oregon*. He looked over the San Francisco office and then wrote a letter to Colonel Morgan, the banker-president of Wells Fargo who was a long-time friend of Wells, commenting on the progress of the company in California and incidentally offering some information on the Harnden Express:

Our Internal Express here is one of the most profitable that I ever knew for its age. . . . I will go up to all our offices. If Pardee or someone else comes he will go along with Carter and me. . . . I am perfectly satisfied with all Carter's Arrangements. They have been Judicious and well timed, liberal but not extravagant & such as have given him the confidence of the best men of the Town.

You may recollect Brigham of the Harnden Express[7] was spoken of & he has kindly offered to take charge of our interests here in connection with the Vanderbilt line of steamers [through Nicaragua] at the moderate salary of Ten Thousand a Year. Carter is worth two of him. In fact he is the man for the position . . . but he will [wants to] come back & remain here [in the East] . . .

This is a great Country & a greater people. Our Express is just in from Sacramento & the mines & our Waybill for New York will amount to nearly $3000.[8] The amt. going forward by this Steamer as you will see is the largest ever shipped from this Port. Had the express got in from the Southern mines we should have had some Two Hundred Ounces more to add to our amount.

At any rate, Henry Wells was pleased with what he found in San Francisco—and well he should have been, for in the six months of 1852, Carter and Washburn had made astonishing progress; they had offices and agents in at least a dozen towns, and had connections all over the Gold Country. They were beginning to do the kind of business that would pour profits into the coffers of Wells, Fargo & Company.

The attitude of the management is well represented by Henry Wells, but so far the lower levels have been neglected—the little man, the clerk or agent in the office in the Gold Country. Fortunately, there is a good picture of such a man in the letters of John Q. Jackson. Jackson was agent for Gregory at Auburn in Placer County, but, as seen in the August 25, 1852, poster, he changed over to Wells Fargo; he explained the reason in a letter to his brother on October 23, 1852:

Mother says rolling stones gather no moss—but whether they do or not I am always going to roll when the "ship is about to sink" and rolling will save me. Gregory had a large amount of drafts protested [that is, other banks refused to honor them] which has nearly ruined him and his business—he is now engaged in a suit with his New York Agts in regard to their protesting his drafts when they had funds of his in their hands sent to meet them when presented—how it will terminate I don't know but I do know that by the change I have made it is a great advantage to me, . . .

It appears that Gregory probably lacked capital, and it is not impossible that one or more of the big companies in the East had something to do with it.

Jackson was only twenty-one years old and may be forgiven for the vanity he shows in describing his new position:

A miners' ball without women but with plenty of stomping enthusiasm. From the "Century Magazine," Vol. XLII (1891).

Edwin B. Morgan, first president of Wells, Fargo & Company (and until D. N. Barney became president in 1853). From the History Room, Wells Fargo Bank.

This is a responsible position and one, by which, in my good management of business and conduct, I have gained the utmost confidence of the "Heads" of the Concern in San Francisco and Sacramento. [Auburn is about twenty miles northeast of Sacramento.] What I have to do is quite confining—staying in my office all day till 10 at night buying dust, forwarding & receiving packages of every kind, from and to everywhere—filling out drafts for the Eastern mails in all sorts of sums, from $50 to $1000 and drawing checks on the offices below, when men wish to take money to the cities, as it is a great convenience to them to have a check instead—and it saves us the trouble of shipping coin up from below for purchasing dust—I have just come from the Post Office, from which I have got 100 letters to be forwarded to the different parts of the country to which they are ordered by Express, on these I make $25 as my charge on each is 25¢—this comes around twice a month and I generally get out about a dozen 3 times a week besides—letters from within the state—this alone pays quite a sum—nothing like my expenses however, as they are necessarily heavy, but not so heavy but that they leave me a handsome sum each month on all my income . . . all my letters on business are to be written always five or six each night and the same number during the day. The Gold dust bought during the last two days is to be cleaned, weighed, sealed and packed ready to be forwarded in the morning—My books balanced—letters to be sorted for the different offices to which they are to be forwarded—a list made of those received from Sacramento to day—and bundled for the river messenger who leaves at Daylight.

Jackson also told his father about a different part of his duties:

My position throws me in contact with the heaviest business men of the state—Bankers, Lawyers, Judges, Merchants & all do business through us. I received a few days since from San Francisco a contract between two parties, for settlement, one of the parties is here having left New York under obligations to give one third of his net profits in this country while he remained here, not less than eighteen months—he has made five or six thousand dollars but being a very slippery fellow has all his funds in money and cannot be brought to any thing like reasonable terms, the party owning the third has given me instructions to let him off at $1000 if he will pay no more. He is very willing to pay this but I am

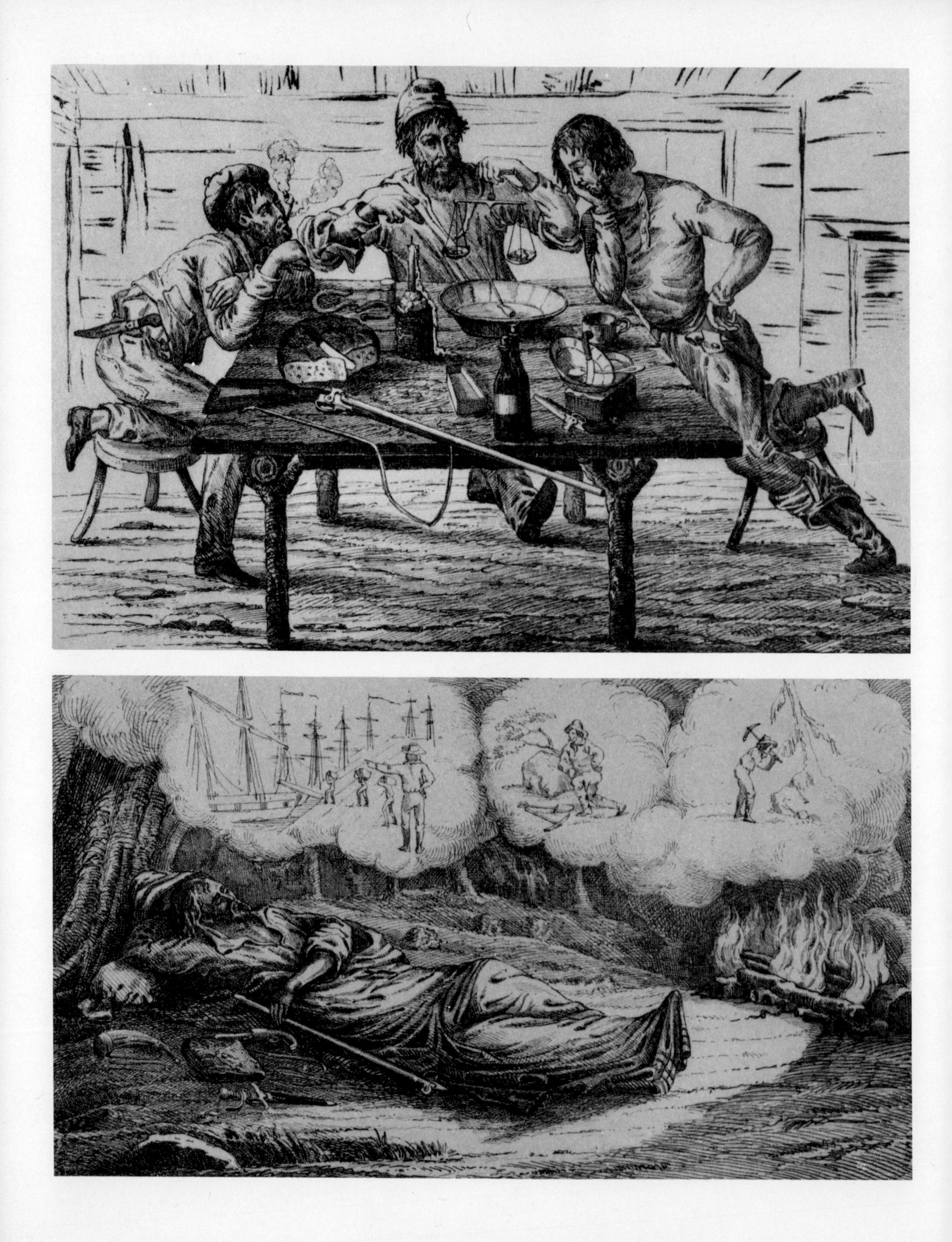

holding off as I think that more can be got out of him after a while. I am going to be well paid for my services as the case is left wholly to my judgment to make such terms as I think advisable—even less than $1000. In a few days I will close the matter and will no doubt give all concerned satisfaction. This kind of business I have a good deal of to do and have now on hand over $3000 in notes for collection to be forwarded through express to all parts of the country.[9]

This letter shows one way of financing one's passage to the mines—later called grubstaking. It also shows Jackson exercising a great deal of initiative for a twenty-one-year-old (he had gone to the mines at eighteen). But most of all, this letter shows that the individual agent was carrying out exactly the service that Wells, Fargo & Company offered in its advertising: "Collection of Bills, Notes, &c., by suit or otherwise."

By April, 1853, a young Yale graduate, Charles T. Blake, became an agent for Wells, Fargo & Company at Michigan City, and went to work "buying dust, writing drafts, shaving notes, and in fact doing a general banking and express business." Blake's letters describing his work are not detailed until 1860, when he went to work for Charles T. H. Palmer, the Wells Fargo agent at Folsom. Some changes had taken place since 1852, but not such as seriously to affect his work. Adams Express Company and Page, Bacon had failed in 1855, and Palmer, Cook & Company in 1856; the San Francisco mint had opened in 1854, giving miners an additional outlet for their gold, and giving express companies the business of transporting coin (mostly $20 gold pieces) to the interior. The Sacramento Valley Railroad had been put through to Folsom in 1856, and the stage lines had moved their headquarters to Folsom.

However, it does not appear that there was any essential difference in the kind of business that Wells Fargo carried on, and in the way of handling it in an office. For transportation in the nonrailroad country, the company had a heavy wrought-iron safe, as in 1852, but it was built into the back seat of the coach and could be sat on.[10] It had a padlocked door on top, and Blake's description of his duties sounds fairly typical of all Wells Fargo offices in the Gold Country:

Every day when the stages come in, these doors and padlocks are taken off and carried to the office and kept over night. The cars [railway train] come in to connect with the up country stages every morning at quarter before eight, and by that time we had to be through breakfast and down at the office. Two of us used to go over and carry over the iron doors and padlocks and distribute them among the coaches. A messenger came up on the cars who had everything arranged so that as soon as the cars reached the platform he handed out the treasure, put up in bags marked with the names of the different offices. These I distributed among the different stages and locked all the safes, while the other man and the messenger occupied themselves in getting the various parcels and packages of heavy freight put aboard. The passengers crowd from the cars on to the stages so that before you get half through your rounds you have to empty the stage of its passengers in order to get at the safe.

(Blake disliked the Chinese intensely, and called them "selfish, piggish, depraved, and impudent"; he thought they ought to be driven out of the state, apparently not knowing that they were fond of Wells Fargo.)

By the time Blake and his co-workers got the gold dust on the train, they would have to work out the packages and mail that had been brought by the train. This "occupied the time pretty fully for about an hour every morning. As soon as I got leisure, I would come back to the office, clear out my furnaces, get the fires ready to start, do what little putting to rights was required and was ready for my assay customers."[11]

The company might buy the gold; it might send it to the mint; it might ship it to the East. In any event, the practice was much as it always had been: The miner would bring in, say, $1,000 worth of dust to be assayed. The miner then could draw against that dust in Wells Fargo checks and send them out in payment. The bank would honor the checks and

Two lithographs in San Francisco. The two men watching the other weigh his gold seem pretty nonchalant about it. It may be worth noting that the man dreaming has at hand no visible digging tools, but, instead, a knife, a pistol, a powder horn, and a rifle. From the Peters Collection in the Smithsonian Institution.

charge the miner 1/15 percent a day for the use of the money. (Interest rates were usually about 2 percent a month.) The check procedure enabled a man to do business on a small capital.

It was Blake's job to make the assays, and it was his business to get the gold into circulation as fast as possible, since gold lying in a safe made no money for anybody.

"Some of our customers that lived nearest came in early in the morning," says Blake, "and we used to get their dust into bars by half past ten o'clock, at which time the up country stages began to come in bringing the bulk of our gold either in the hands of passengers or by Express. From that time till 12 o'clock, when the San Francisco train went down, we were driven very close. All the large bars that did not need to be combined, we chipped [for assay] and sent down in the noon train, thereby saving a day on them. It was a close shave sometimes. I have had the melted gold in the fire when the five-minute bell rang, poured it, dressed the bar, chipped it, weighed, sealed and waybilled[12] it, and had it on the cars in time. The melting was usually finished by half past one, when if there was not a press of work, I went to dinner with the rest. As a general thing, two days in a week however, I lost my dinner and would not get up to the house until nine o'clock in the evening. . . . One day when we had a big rush I did not finish my work until four o'clock next morning. . . ."

Whereas in the early 1850's it was not an uncommon duty of an express company to undertake the safe delivery of women and children from the East to their husbands or relatives in California, by 1860 a bigger burden was sometimes undertaken. The company was handling a great deal of heavy freight —as it always had—on one occasion sending one hundred tons of freight to Washoe by wagon trains. Also, on one occasion, Blake delivered in Washoe three companies of United States soldiers and twenty thousand pounds of baggage (Wells Fargo furnished the meals; apparently they agreed to deliver the soldiers in good shape, and accepted all necessary responsibilities in that connection).

In 1863, Blake went to San Francisco, and "Mr. [Louis] McLane . . . told me that I should have the agency in any place I might choose to locate. Now the reputation of this firm is very high on this coast, so that to be an agent of theirs in any place gives one position at once, and the profits of an agency in any important place amount often to $250 a month and seldom fall lower than one hundred."

So Blake chose to go to Boise, in Idaho Territory, and his next letter is from Walla Walla, in Washington Territory:

I start from here in the lighest possible trim as to Express apparatus. A small forwarding receipt book, a check book, a lot of waybills, and an agency appointment, with a few franks [stamps], are all my stock in trade. . . . I am to start tomorrow morning with a mule passenger train which is going through with about a dozen passengers. The distance is three hundred miles and we expect to make it in about ten days. I had to buy in Portland a complete outfit, blankets, pistols, knife, packing bags, etc., reminding me very strongly of old '49 times. . . . Save the Pictorial newspapers for me as I may want to have you send them up. Freight from Portland to me will be $1.50 per pound, but newspapers bring $1.00 apiece. . . .[13]

He comments on the gold and the men hunting it, and the entire circumstances must have been almost identical with those in California a few years earlier:

Every one of these creeks [that run into the Boise River] and the gulches leading into them and the whole hillsides between them seem to be rich in gold. Men working with cradles on little points in the hills take out $100.00 a day to the man. . . . The dust here is poor, a rough quartzy looking gold like that from Millers Defeat [in California], fineness ranging from 750 to 850. It is almost the only currency here and is paid out full of sand as it was in old California times, at $16.00 per oz. . . .

Very soon we came on miners at work, men whipsawing and making shingles, etc., and very soon came out on a little flat ridge, and . . . came into a little square . . . and were in the town of Placerville. . . . One of the crowd said to our guide "Can you tell us anything about Wells Fargo & Co.? We understood that they were going to establish an agency here." "Yes," says the guide, "they are, and that man in spectacles is the agent." The next instant I heard a shout taken up and repeated through the whole town "Wells Fargo have come." In less than three minutes I was surrounded by an excited crowd of two or three hundred men, who hardly allowed me time to get my saddle off from my mule before they almost dragged me into a large unfinished building on the Plaza, as they called the square. The carpenters were at work, but were stopped at once, the

A saloon in the mines, and five miners working a long tom. Lithographed in San Francisco by Britton & Rey. From the Peters Collection at the Smithsonian Institution.

shavings were cleaned out, one man ran for a whiskey keg to make me a stool and another brought in a pair of scales and a yeast powder box to put gold dust in and installed himself to weigh for me. I had brought in with me about 400 letters, and now proceeded to call them over. As the news of my arrival spread, the crowd increased and for eight mortal hours my tongue had to wag without cessation. I disposed of a great many letters at a dollar apiece and about eight o'clock at night broke up business in spite of the crowd, being very hungry and tired and started out to get something to eat. This was my introduction to Placerville.

It was Placerville, Idaho Territory, but it may as well have been Placerville, California, in 1850:

I found my hands full as long as I staid. I was busy from morning till night and very soon began to see that there was a great deal of money in the country. . . . Everything reminded me of '49 times in California. Money was easily made and recklessly spent. Nearly every finished house in the town was a gambling saloon and all were crowded every night. Fighting, shooting, etc., were every day occurrences. During the day there would probably be half a dozen fights and two or three shooting scrapes, and as all the gambling houses kept a band of music in each in full blast, the uproar and confusion would be perfectly deafening. . . . A man came riding through the Plaza very fast, and as he passed this party [of drunken men] one of them jerked out his revolver and fired a couple of shots after him. "There's no harm done [the shooter said], I didn't hit him."

Placerville is a small town about half the size of Michigan Bluff. . . . I have rented one of the best houses fronting on the plaza at $150.00 a month. It is yet a mere shell, but I have a board fixed up in one corner for a counter and take in letters and packages. I have no office furniture, no blanks or anything. . . . My stock in trade consists of about 50 envelopes, two or three quires of paper, a forwarding receipt book, some pens, ink, a stock of sealing wax, and some way bills. Envelopes for this coast we sell at 50 cts. apiece [including delivery]. States do. [ditto] 75 cts. We get letters from Oregon P. Offices for 50 cts. apiece. I should judge from appearances that the letter business alone would reach $1,000.00 a month. We charge 5 per cent on treasure to Portland, and merchants think it quite reasonable.

Alas for Blake's hopes! He got a shipment of gold coins from Portland and paid it all out for dust. He made a trip to Portland, and the steamboats on the river gave him free passage and meals because he represented Wells Fargo, but somebody in the Wells Fargo office thought the Boise route was too long and too dangerous, and had already decided to withdraw the Boise agency.[14]

Blake found Portland people hostile toward Wells Fargo for discontinuing the agency, and he himself was disappointed, for he felt that the office would clear $500 a month for him and $5,000 for Wells Fargo.[15]

Whatever Wells Fargo's mistakes may have been, they were more than offset by the good judgments and the friendly actions of everybody from Henry Wells down to the clerks who melted the gold and carried the trunks. It does not seem that Charles Blake's feeling toward the Chinese was commonly held by Wells Fargo people. It seems rather that Wells Fargo operated on the theory that one man's money was as good as anybody else's—and that, in its essence, adds up to democracy. But Wells Fargo people went considerably beyond that in helping out after the fire in Sacramento and during the great floods along the Sacramento River. Perhaps that adds up to sympathy. All in all, it was the right company in the right place at the right time.

1853
A Year of Races and Records

THE ENTIRE PERIOD OF THE 1850's was to a very considerable degree one of uncertainty in San Francisco. The fall of 1850 brought the first depression to the Gold Country, particularly because eastern merchants had unloaded great quantities of merchandise there. This depression continued through 1851 and 1852, and the winter of 1852, when California was overcrowded with emigrants of all kinds, was one of widespread destitution. That fall there had been a promise of improvement; during the winter there was much rain and snow (and that meant the mines would be working in the spring), but work three or four months in the future was no help to people who had nothing. The *Alta California* said on February 12, 1853:

> We have had among us a large class of unfortunates during the winter. The streets of San Francisco have supplied a living to hundreds, either by acts of charity, the giving of alms at the street door, or by the tolerance of a class whose wants have driven them into every conceivable method of wringing a dime from the passer-by.... There has never been so deplorable an exhibition of mendicancy in our streets as may be witnessed daily at this time,... hundreds of destitute men and scores of women and children besieging the pockets of society in public and private, indoors and out. Troops of girls perambulate the streets day and night with hand organs, tambourines and essays at vocal music.... Little girls... are to be found in front of the city saloons at all hours of the day, going through their graceless performances.

But gold was still coming out of the mines, and on February 16 the biggest shipment of gold up to that time left San Francisco on three ships—the *California,* the *Panama,* and the *Brother Jonathan.* The total was almost $4,000,000, and of this total, Page, Bacon & Company shipped $1,000,000; Adams shipped $500,000; and Wells Fargo shipped $73,448. To pinpoint Wells Fargo's place in gold shipping, it should be noted that B. Davidson at the same time shipped $332,800; Burgoyne & Co. shipped $310,000; Drexel, Ratner & Church shipped $90,000; and F. Argenti shipped $30,000. There were eleven others named (all with smaller sums than that of Wells Fargo), and "miscellaneous shippers" accounted for $214,364. Although Henry Wells was pleased by the company's progress, obviously he did not gauge it entirely by the amount of gold shipped, even though he commented favorably on that too.

On July 7, Carter went home, to be replaced by Colonel William Pardee, who continued to go forward.

Henry Wells arrived in San Francisco in February, 1853, for his inspection, and apparently his visit suggested more capital for the company, because the board called for 5 percent payments on February 19, February 21, and March 11, 1853. It is not entirely clear as to whether this was an assessment additional to the original $25, or in fulfillment of the $25 per share. The minutes say:

An eight-mule team and three six-ox teams on the long trip to the Gold Country. From William M. Thayer, "Marvels of the New West."

All subscriptions having been paid in full, as per Association agreements, stocks and notes deposited by original subscribers were ordered surrendered to makers or representatives on May 3, 1853.[1]

The company needed capital about May 1, and borrowed $50,000 on Wells Fargo stock. On May 3, the capital stock of the company was increased from $300,000 to $500,000.

In the busy month of September, 1853, Wells Fargo bought out Alexander Todd's express company, and continued another policy that it had followed from the beginning: buying out the opposition. Adams had done it with great success, and Wells Fargo would continue.

On November 26, Colonel Morgan resigned as president, and the directors elected to succeed him Danford N. Barney, who was making a name in the East as a young and able financier. Johnston Livingston resigned as treasurer on the same day, and Thomas M. Janes was appointed in his place.

When William Tecumseh Sherman arrived in San Francisco in April, 1853, he found the following banking companies: Page, Bacon & Company and Adams & Company in Parrott's new granite building;[2] Wells, Fargo & Company; Drexel, Sather & Church; Burgoyne & Company; James King of William; Sanders & Brenham; Davidson & Company; Palmer, Cook & Company; and others. Lucas, Turner & Company would soon be another.

It did not take long, however, for Wells Fargo to encounter other opposition than that of competing companies. The first holdup of a gold-carrying expressman had been committed in 1851, but the business had not progressed very rapidly. However, in April, 1853, the agent of Adams Express Company at Mormon Island (a man named Nichols) was held up by seven men who got $7,000. Adams promptly offered $2,000 reward plus one fourth of the recovered treasure. From that time on, the express companies were considered fair game by ambitious holdup men, and many rewards were offered and paid by all companies active in the express business.

However, the express companies could not afford to neglect the important factor of getting there first. In the aggressively tempestuous area that fanned out east, northeast, and southeast from San Francisco—and to quite an extent in other parts of California and in Nevada as well—tempers were short and patience was at a premium. In a word, the general attitude was primitive (in many respects, not at all an uncomplimentary word), and so the men in the mines and others elsewhere tended to have great respect for the strongest or the fastest. Indeed, what else was there, in such a new and fast-changing

New York expressmen putting on a parade at Christmas, 1852. The American Express Company seems to dominate the N. Y. & E. R. R., the Thompson River R. R., and Wells, Butterfield & Company. The building in the background appears to be the American Express Company Building at 10 Wall Street. From "Gleason's Pictorial Drawing-Room Companion," Vol. IV (1853).

Danford N. Barney, president of Wells, Fargo & Company, 1853–1866; from a portrait owned by his great-grandson, Austin D. Barney, Hartford, Connecticut. Some writers make it "Danforth," but in 1869 his brother, A. H. Barney, spelled it "Danford," and in 1871 D. N. Barney signed the articles of association of the New York Elevated Rail Road Company "Danford N. Barney." His grandson was named Danford Newton Barney, and died in the 1950's.

country, to base an opinion on? So it was that great emphasis was laid on the speed of an express, and for many years the phrase was used (especially by those express companies that carried mail through Nicaragua and thereby beat the mail steamers, which sent the mail across Panama): "through ahead of the mails." That meant that an express company, picking up government-stamped mail in New York two days after the regular mail steamer left, could go through Nicaragua and deliver mail in San Francisco a day or two ahead of the regular mail via Aspinwall and Panama City. Cornelius Vanderbilt used that phrase, "through ahead of the mails," constantly in securing his hold on freight, express, and passenger business.[3]

The blessed days of setting records and even of running out-and-out races were at their peak, perhaps, in the early steamboat days on the Mississippi River, but they certainly were revived in the competition for passenger business to the Gold Country. As fast as Pacific Mail got a big new ship and advertised it (usually about three hundred tons heavier than it was), Vanderbilt or some lesser competitor would put on a ship announced as still heavier, and passenger business would follow the tonnage. Ships were constantly announcing new and better times as engines were built bigger and more powerful, and a new record set by a ship would result in a crowded passenger list on the next Steamer Day.[4]

This respect for the first one to get there was reflected from the beginning in the express companies, in whose feats, from the very first, public interest was often as high as it had been in the speed trials on the Mississippi River a few years earlier.

Alexander Todd (according to *Old Waybills*) claimed to have beaten the Adams man to Stockton in April, 1851, when both were carrying President Fillmore's message. Both had been determined to get the message to the mines first. But, back in San Francisco, Todd had figured the Adams people would watch him, so he went into a theatre while his partner packed the express in an India-rubber sack. The steamer for Stockton had already gone, and the Adams messenger started by rowboat. As soon as the Adams man was out of sight, Todd took a boat to Oakland, and went to Stockton on horseback. He got there about 2 o'clock in the morning and "delivered the message to the printers there," then went on to Mariposa, still "supplying the message" (undoubtedly he had many copies of the New York *Herald*). His route from Stockton to Mariposa and back took three days.

In the meantime, the Adams rowboat messenger got lost in the bayous and was picked up by a steamboat captain. Todd's regular messenger was on that boat (the *Jenny Lind*), and so the Adams man bribed the captain to put him off before they reached Stockton, so he could get ahead of the regular Todd messenger. The Adams man pulled into Stockton triumphantly on Tuesday, and was somewhat chagrined to discover that Todd, who had left San Francisco Saturday, had delivered his message on Sunday.

Adams got even in March, 1852, when the regular mail steamer *Tennessee* unloaded her cargo in San Francisco. The Adams messenger started on the steamboat *Bragdon* for Stockton, but presently left the steamboat with two other men. He went on to Stockton in a rowboat, and twenty-four hours later pulled into Stockton and "placed the intelligence half a day in advance of the regular conveyance," according to the Stockton *Journal*.

A little later (in 1855), the Wells Fargo messenger from New York had detailed instructions to enable him to make an impression on the newspapers. On his way north in the Pacific, he was to prepare a careful alphabetical list of all letters that he carried for San Francisco; he was to get the ship's purser's report (list of passengers) and put it, with his letter list, in the letter bag. When the ship should approach San Francisco, Wells Fargo's news boat would come by, and the Wells Fargo man was to throw the bag of letters and the bag of newspapers (or several bags) into the boat. The messenger was warned to have all the bags of newspapers on deck, and to "be ready for him, so as not to miss fire."

The newspapers also contributed their ingenuity to being first. The *Alta California,* following the election of 1856 (when James Buchanan was elected), sent a printer to Acapulco with type cases and a chase. The steamers stopped there, and the printer caught the Pacific Mail steamer *Golden Age* and sailed back to San Francisco. Of course, he saw the eastern papers, and all he had to do was set the results in type for the *Alta* and make up the form and lock it up, then pack it and pad it. (He had ample time for all this.) Then he delivered the locked-up form to a man in a boat (probably the

A lithograph (1853) for the American Express Company that mentions also Thompson & Company's Express in Canada, and Wells, Fargo & Company's California Express. From the Honeyman Collection at the Bancroft Library, Berkeley, University of California.

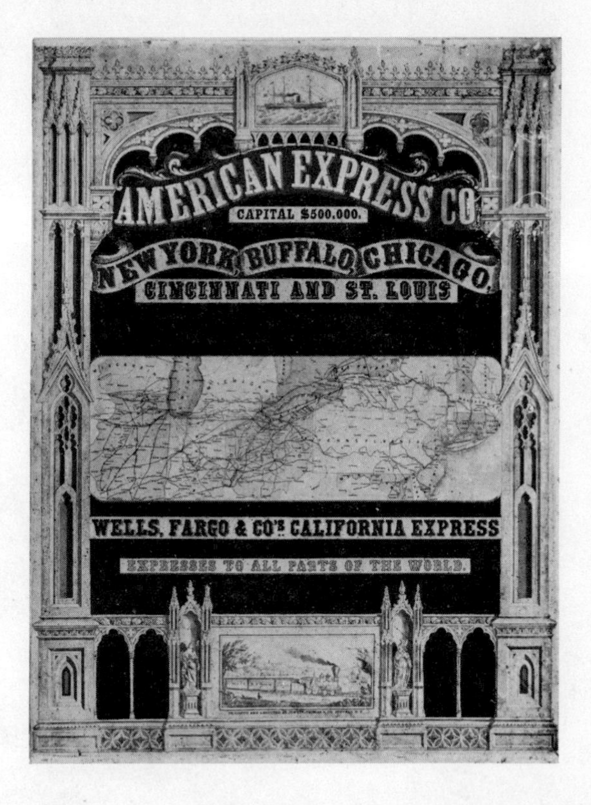

Wells Fargo news boat), and enabled the *Alta* to scoop every other paper in San Francisco—particularly the *Bulletin,* now edited by Tom King, brother of the dead James King of William. Tom screamed, "Fake", long and righteously—and he had a well-taken point—for the ship had docked at 8:30 P.M. and the extra had come out at 9 P.M. He knew that handspiking of type just wasn't that fast. But Tom King was something of a novice at the newspaper game. He probably was a better editor than James, but this time had to eat crow.[5]

The spirit of competition was keen and it was vigorous, and in those days it was not considered reprehensible to win.

With all Wells Fargo's competitive spirit, it apparently stayed away from Vanderbilt and his Nicaraguan line—the "Opposition Route," as it was advertised—for the first year or so. While other and smaller companies seemed to embrace the chance to make the trip "ahead of the mails," Wells Fargo and Adams seem to have gone along with the Pacific Mail Company. While Vanderbilt had cut the transit time from New York to San Francisco to twenty-six or twenty-four days (and cheerfully predicted twenty-one days, and advertised "ahead of every other line"), two promoters in 1853 got a government contract to carry mail from New Orleans to Vera Cruz and then across Mexico to Acapulco. They hired express riders and bought stagecoaches, and made the four hundred miles over the Sierra Madres in five and a half days. Some mail was carried over this route, which was scheduled to go from New Orleans to San Francisco in sixteen days, but the promoters had overlooked a small item: They depended on Pacific Mail steamers to pick up the mail at Acapulco, apparently without any sort of contract. Since Pacific Mail had the government's mail contract in the Pacific Ocean, it is understandable that their steamers ceased to call at Acapulco, and so the Veracruz line did not last very long. Charles P. Kimball's Noisy Carriers, as usual, used the Veracruz line while it lasted, and stamped their mail, "by independent line, ahead of everything."

However, Wells Fargo seems not to have been swayed by such upstarts. It continued to stay with the Pacific Mail Company. On the whole, big companies stayed by big companies,[6] and perhaps it is a good thing that Wells Fargo stayed away from the Vanderbilt line, for that line's ships developed a habit of going to the bottom.

It is true that the Pacific Mail's *Tennessee* was wrecked in February, 1853, but no baggage or passengers were lost, and presumably Wells Fargo benefited from Thomas Gihon's (the Adams man) heroic efforts on that occasion.[7] But in August, 1852, the Vanderbilt ship *Pioneer* went down with losses; in February, 1853, the Vanderbilt ship *Independence* was lost in one of the worst wrecks on the Pacific coast (three hundred passengers drowned); and in April, the Vanderbilt ship *S. S. Lewis* was lost. Probably Wells Fargo officials were duly grateful that they had not had any miners' wives and children on those ships.

On April 10, 1853, an advertisement in the *Alta California* carried the information that the Accessory Transit Company had bought out Vanderbilt in Nicaragua. This line was also called the Nicaragua Steamship Company, and Cornelius K. Garrison was

Wreck of the ill-fated steamer Independence *off Santa Margarita Island, February 16, 1853.*

Vanderbilt's Independence *went down off Santa Margarita Island, Baja California, on February 16, 1853, and some 300 lives were lost—apparently from sheer carelessness or incompetence. From the "Illustrated News," 1853.*

A poster (probably from 1849). Apparently Clarke's General Agency Office was acting as a broker for passage to California. Every ship that could be floated in those days was called "first class," but the word "ventillated" indicates that there had already been some repercussions from overcrowded and unventilated ships on which people had been jammed into holds designed only for merchandise or bulk goods. Printed by permission of the American Antiquarian Society.

A portrait of Commodore Vanderbilt, engraved by A. H. Ritchie. Vanderbilt sold out to Garrison and then promptly went to Panama and started another transit company.

the transit company's agent in San Francisco. The Accessory Transit Company had been a small company that operated mule-drawn stagecoaches over twelve miles of road from San Juan del Sud, on the west shore of Nicaragua, to Lake Managua; and a small lake steamer and some river steamers to San Juan del Norte on the eastern side. There was considerable mystery as to why the great Vanderbilt would sell out to a pocket-size company. Some thought it was due to the fact that he received forty thousand shares of stock that could be traded on the market, as well as a mortgage for $150,000. Others said later that the Accessory Transit Company had to pay Vanderbilt $40,000 a month. At any rate, Garrison[8] had become an important man in San Francisco, and it would not be long before Wells Fargo would be using his Nicaraguan line.

Vanderbilt had operated the Opposition Line through Nicaragua a little over two years, but, as soon as he sold out to Garrison and the Accessory Transit Company, he went to Panama to organize his Independent Opposition Line to battle everybody: George Law on the east side, Pacific Mail and the Nicaragua Steamship Company (or Accessory Transit Company) on the west. The Panama Railroad Company, an important factor, was not controlled by any of his competitors and so could be used by him; and the port of Aspinwall was owned by the Panama Railroad Company. On September 20, 1853, therefore, the commodore began operations with a new ship of two thousand tons, the *Uncle Sam*. With two other ships, Vanderbilt began to make the other three lines uneasy, for no one ever knew what Vanderbilt would do next.

In December, 1853, the first direct and open contest occurred between Wells Fargo and Adams. Daniel Haskell, who managed Adams in California, operated on a lavish scale, and employed as manager I. C. Woods, who seemed also helpful in the spending of money, and so Adams had acquired a

A portrait of Cornelius K. Garrison, who bought the Nicaragua transit company from Vanderbilt.

An early woodcut of Californians crossing the Isthmus of Panama on mules. From "Gleason's Pictorial Drawing-Room Companion," Vol. II (1852).

very decided predominance in express and banking matters. However, the men who were at the head of Wells Fargo (several of them officials of American Express[9]) were not entirely novices at the express business, and one of their first moves in California was to cut the freight rate from New York; it had been sixty cents, and they reduced it to forty cents. By the end of 1853, they had built a fine office in Sacramento (to replace the one burned out in the fire of 1852), and a substantial two-story red brick building in Columbia, with great iron doors that had cost $125 apiece for freight to be shipped around the Horn.

Adams was boasting of their messengers' crossing the Isthmus of Panama in twenty-four hours, and assuring customers that they were never behind with their express to New York, and *always in advance* with dust at the Philadelphia mint. Exactly how they could manage that when the smaller opposition was shipping through Nicaragua, they do not say. However, the two big express companies, Adams and Wells Fargo, had grown up and survived under cutthroat competition, and it is safe to say that no small company would be ahead of either one very long, as it is also reasonably safe to guess that neither one was ahead of the other one very long. However, Adams outraced Wells Fargo to deliver President Franklin Pierce's message to Congress, December 5, 1853.

It developed into a race without a formal challenge. The two companies had previously competed with each other between Sacramento and Portland. In this case, the message was expected to arrive in late December, and both companies went through the country hiring horses ahead of time, and Adams got the best horses, so apparently at that time Adams men knew more about horses than did Wells Fargo men.

Shipping.

NICARAGUA STEAMSHIP COMPANY.

FOR NEW YORK AND NEW ORLEANS, via SAN JUAN.

The Shortest, Healthiest, and Quickest Route.

ONLY 12 MILES LAND CARRIAGE—MACADAMIZED ROAD.

THE ONLY THROUGH LINE GIVING TICKETS WHICH INCLUDE THE ISTHMUS TRANSIT.

THROUGH AHEAD OF THE MAILS.

THE FAVORITE STEAMER SIERRA NEVADA, J. H. BLETHAN, Commander, Will sail from Jackson Street Wharf, for SAN JUAN DEL SUD, on Monday, Jan. 16th, at 12 o'clock, noon.

Treasure for Shipment will be received up to 6 o'clock A. M., Jan. 16th.

The Mail Bag will close Fifteen Minutes before the sailing of the Steamer.

C. K. GARRISON, Agent, Corner Sacramento and Leidesdorff streets.

ja11

C. K. Garrison was advertising his Nicaragua Steamship Company in San Francisco in January, 1854, and was still saying (as he perhaps was entitled to say), "Through ahead of the mails."

The telegraph was not in use in California then, but the companies thought the message might arrive as early as December 28. In the meantime, horses had been kept saddled, and as soon as the message

WELLS, FARGO & CO.

BANKERS

AND

EXCHANGE DEALERS.

W. F. & CO.,

In connection with their EXPRESS BUSINESS, will also transact a general

BANKING, EXCHANGE AND COLLECTION BUSINESS.

GENERAL AND SPECIAL DEPOSITS RECEIVED.

COLLECTIONS AND REMITTANCES

Made in all parts of California, Oregon, the Atlantic States and Europe, with promptness and dispatch.

GOLD DUST, GOLD AND SILVER COIN, AND BULLION,

BOUGHT AND SOLD.

Money advanced on GOLD DUST deposited for transmission or coinage.

SIGHT EXCHANGE

ON NEW YORK AND BOSTON, FOR SALE AT CURRENT RATES.

DRAFTS

ALSO DRAWN PAYABLE AT THE FOLLOWING PLACES, VIZ:

ALBANY, NEW YORK,
TROY, " "
UTICA, " "
SYRACUSE, " "
OSWEGO, " "
AUBURN, " "
GENEVA, " "
ROCHESTER, "
LOCKPORT, " "
BUFFALO, " "
BINGHATON, "
OWEGO, " "
ELMIRA, " "
CORNING, " "
ERIE, PENNSYLVANIA,
PITTSBURG, "
HARTFORD, CONNECTICUT,
NEW HAVEN, "
CLEVELAND, OHIO,
SANDUSKY, "
TOLEDO, "
MANSFIELD, "
NEWARK, "
ZANESVILLE, "
COLUMBUS, "
DAYTON, "
HAMILTON, OHIO.
SPRINGFIELD, "
CINCINNATI, "
LOUISVILLE, KENTUCKY,
DETROIT, MICHIGAN,
JACKSON, "
ANN ARBOR, "
KALAMAZOO, "
NILES, "
ADRIAN, "
MONROE. "
CHICAGO, ILLINOIS,
GALENA, "
LASALLE, "
PEORIA, "
ALTON. "
ST. LOUIS, MISSOURI.
MILWAUKEE, WISCONSIN,
SHEBOYGAN, "
RACINE, "
KENOSHA, "
MONTREAL, CANADA EAST,
QUEBEC, " "
HAMILTON, " WEST,
TORONTO, " "

WELLS, FARGO & CO.

NO. 114 MONTGOMERY STREET,

SAN FRANCISCO.

An advertisement from the San Francisco Directory for 1852–53. From the History Room, Wells Fargo Bank.

In the middle of the nineteenth century, one of the most popular sports of newspapers was to bemoan the awful toll of life and the dreadful suffering and slaughter caused by wrecked ships and trains. In this picture, a locomotive blows up near the top, while a ship is on fire. In the right background, a building seems to be exploding, while the Grim Reaper rides atop a locomotive, scythe at the ready, and another skeleton looks out the engine cab; people are strewn all over, about to be killed by the iron horse, and one is actually under the wheels of the monster; steam from the cylinders scalds all who are hapless enough to lie there, and in the distance a string of cars falls off a high bridge (presumably the rear end of the same train). From "Harper's Weekly," September 23, 1865.

was received, the riders for the two companies set out. According to William S. Lowden, who rode for Adams, the race was close from San Francisco to Tehama, and Wells Fargo was in the lead at Marysville. They were changing horses every four or five miles. The Adams rider reached Tehama a little ahead, and there the race really commenced. The bags of mail weighed fifty-four pounds, and the rider from Tehama to Shasta changed horses nineteen times. He did not touch the ground but once, and that was at Prairie House, where the man in charge of the Adams horse was engaged in a fist fight with the man in charge of the Wells Fargo horse. At all other changes, the rider leaped from one galloping horse to another, and reached Shasta (sixty miles) in two hours and thirty-seven minutes. From Shasta to Weaverville the run was after dark in a light snow—but Wells Fargo was beaten by the time its rider reached Shasta, for the Adams rider then was halfway to Yreka. The race cost Adams & Company about two thousand dollars, but undoubtedly the company considered the victory worth the price.

Apparently the message itself was not very exciting (as indeed it does not seem so today), because the *Alta California* did not print it until January 13. But, like the scientist who glories in pure research, those two companies raced for the pure joy of flexing their muscles.

At that time, railroads were multiplying so fast (mostly short lines) in the East, that they were impossible to keep track of, but it is interesting to observe that there were so many accidents that some doubted that the railroad would ever replace the horse. Newspapers in general reported every accident in detail, with gory reports by victims and much use of the words *awful, dreadful, ghastly, terrible,* and *unspeakable* (for instance: "Passengers Burned Alive by Steam in Horrible Railroad Accident"); there were countless editorials on the unendurable situation, and the *Illustrated News,* June 18, 1853 (in what actually was a very mild tone), said:

> *Manifest Destiny—Clear the Track.*—A lightning line is now running from Chicago to New York, and passengers are put through in a flash, and not unfrequently, as the public is aware, in a crash, going with Mr. Doolittle and his "First Locomotive," "slam bang to eternal smash." Truly, we are "a bustin people." We must be blowing something up. The steamboat folks blow up their passengers, and the editors blow up the steamboats. We all come down, and if alive, progress or propel again. The tanks "bust," the bilers "bust," and we "bust" with indignation. We consider ourselves entitled to the track, and if old fogy folks fail to clear it, we put it through, and put them through. "Keep off the crossing." Manifest destiny is just ahead of us, but we are bound to head it. Even the lightning must soon be greased, or be abandoned as an old highway to slow going thunderbolts. So we go, and so keep going. A man who cannot keep up with this age had better get out of it. If he can't get out, we help him. "Life and limb at the passenger's risk, and no accountability for freight or baggage." Buy your ticket and make your will—take your seat and go to praying.

Obviously the men of Wells Fargo, American, and Adams did not pay much attention to newspapers while there was work to do.

On September 2, Pardee's appointment as resident director in California was made. By that time, Carter was already home, and it may be that some of the board's subsequent actions stemmed from Carter's reports on conditions in California.

At the time of Pardee's appointment, Wells Fargo also bought Livingston, Wells & Company for $15,000, payable in Wells Fargo "scrip." It was contemplated that the company would use the name of Livingston, Wells & Company in Europe, and an agent was appointed for Paris.

Also in 1853, the Wells Fargo New York offices were moved to 82 Broadway. Perhaps the most significant item, however, appears on September 2, when the board heard that the operations of Wells Fargo had already earned $30,000 profit. In a period of a little over a year, starting from scratch, the company had shown a 40 percent profit, and it was no longer a question of possibility, but rather a problem of exercising good management, showing aggressiveness, using good sense—all aspects in which the men of Wells Fargo obviously excelled. The company had already taken the first big step in what today is called "building a public image." It had established in the minds of the people of California a reputation for helpfulness, for service, and most of all for integrity, and this reputation today constitutes almost an aura around the name of Wells Fargo.

1854
The Last Great Year of Gold

THE YEAR 1854 WAS THE LAST GREAT year of gold prosperity. There would be much more gold taken from the fabulous Mother Lode, but 1854 was the last big year, and after that year, people began to think of other things than mining. Emigrants continued to come to California, but more tradesmen stopped in San Francisco and began to spread out through the country, and even to get as far south as Los Angeles and San Diego.

Business in the year 1853 had started with a rush because of the water available to wash gravel in the streams, but again there had come a surplus of goods, and that had precipitated another depression in the latter half of 1853. At the same time, San Francisco had greatly overbuilt, and the New York *Tribune* said February 15, 1854:

> Since our last review of the market, business has assumed a more unsettled and depressed aspect, owing to the large imports of every description of goods. The arrivals during the past fortnight have been twelve from the Atlantic borders and fifteen from European and Pacific foreign ports. The scarcity of money and the necessity of meeting freight bills, with instructions from consignors to realize as soon as possible, caused a vast amount of every description of goods to be forced on the market. A large amount of goods have been sold, but at low rates. Our market is glutted, with no outlet, or any prospects for months to come. The sacrifice of goods has just begun. . . .
>
> It was supposed by all that rain was the only requisite to cause a revival in trade, [but] the rains have come and gone, the miners are hard at work, and in many instances are doing well; but trade has not revived.

It seems that forty or fifty vessels were reported on the high seas en route to San Francisco with still more goods, and so the prospects were doubly gloomy. This report was printed March 14. The general trend in business, it seems, might have been overcome but for some other factors not immediately evident: the forgeries of Honest Harry Meiggs, the political-economic manipulations of Palmer, Cook & Company, and the extravagances of Adams & Company. All in all, it was the making of a first-class depression.

Interest rates, which had always been high in San Francisco (from 1 to 2 percent a month), went up to 7 and 10 percent a month. Joseph Palmer was supporting both Frémont and David Broderick in politics, though Frémont and Broderick were bitter political enemies; Palmer failed to pay interest on state bonds held in the East, although Palmer, Cook & Company had received the money from the state, and Duncan, Sherman & Company in New York (later to be abused by San Franciscans), without being asked, advanced $60,000 to pay the interest and save the credit of California.

Money rates were high, but banking at its best was not easy in early California because of the impermanency and instability of people who wanted

A native bongo on the Chagres River, with California emigrants and their baggage aboard. From F. N. Otis, "History of the Panama Railroad."

This was said to be one way of crossing the Isthmus. The traveler, somehow covered with a cloak made of vegetation, is sitting on a board seat, with his feet tied up to keep them out of the way. He must have been ill, to travel in this uncomfortable fashion. From "Gleason's Pictorial Drawing-Room Companion."

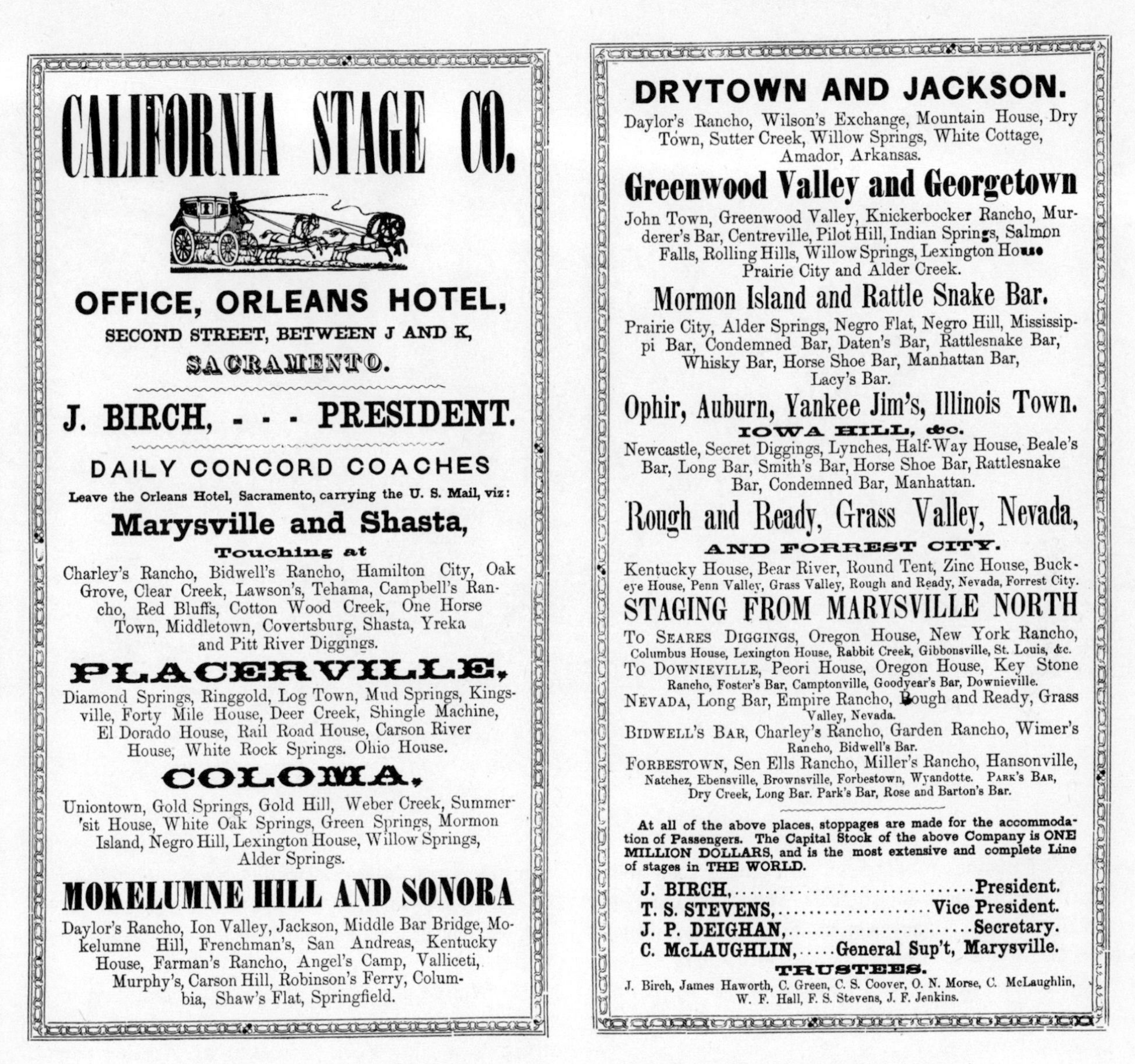
CALIFORNIA STAGE CO.

OFFICE, ORLEANS HOTEL,
SECOND STREET, BETWEEN J AND K,
SACRAMENTO.

J. BIRCH, - - - PRESIDENT.

DAILY CONCORD COACHES
Leave the Orleans Hotel, Sacramento, carrying the U. S. Mail, viz:

Marysville and Shasta,
Touching at
Charley's Rancho, Bidwell's Rancho, Hamilton City, Oak Grove, Clear Creek, Lawson's, Tehama, Campbell's Rancho, Red Bluffs, Cotton Wood Creek, One Horse Town, Middletown, Covertsburg, Shasta, Yreka and Pitt River Diggings.

PLACERVILLE,
Diamond Springs, Ringgold, Log Town, Mud Springs, Kingsville, Forty Mile House, Deer Creek, Shingle Machine, El Dorado House, Rail Road House, Carson River House, White Rock Springs. Ohio House.

COLOMA,
Uniontown, Gold Springs, Gold Hill, Weber Creek, Summer'sit House, White Oak Springs, Green Springs, Mormon Island, Negro Hill, Lexington House, Willow Springs, Alder Springs.

MOKELUMNE HILL AND SONORA
Daylor's Rancho, Ion Valley, Jackson, Middle Bar Bridge, Mokelumne Hill, Frenchman's, San Andreas, Kentucky House, Farman's Rancho, Angel's Camp, Valliceti, Murphy's, Carson Hill, Robinson's Ferry, Columbia, Shaw's Flat, Springfield.

DRYTOWN AND JACKSON.
Daylor's Rancho, Wilson's Exchange, Mountain House, Dry Town, Sutter Creek, Willow Springs, White Cottage, Amador, Arkansas.

Greenwood Valley and Georgetown
John Town, Greenwood Valley, Knickerbocker Rancho, Murderer's Bar, Centreville, Pilot Hill, Indian Springs, Salmon Falls, Rolling Hills, Willow Springs, Lexington House Prairie City and Alder Creek.

Mormon Island and Rattle Snake Bar.
Prairie City, Alder Springs, Negro Flat, Negro Hill, Mississippi Bar, Condemned Bar, Daten's Bar, Rattlesnake Bar, Whisky Bar, Horse Shoe Bar, Manhattan Bar, Lacy's Bar.

Ophir, Auburn, Yankee Jim's, Illinois Town.
IOWA HILL, &c.
Newcastle, Secret Diggings, Lynches, Half-Way House, Beale's Bar, Long Bar, Smith's Bar, Horse Shoe Bar, Rattlesnake Bar, Condemned Bar, Manhattan.

Rough and Ready, Grass Valley, Nevada,
AND FORREST CITY.
Kentucky House, Bear River, Round Tent, Zinc House, Buckeye House, Penn Valley, Grass Valley, Rough and Ready, Nevada, Forrest City.

STAGING FROM MARYSVILLE NORTH
To SEARES DIGGINGS, Oregon House, New York Rancho, Columbus House, Lexington House, Rabbit Creek, Gibbonsville, St. Louis, &c.
To DOWNIEVILLE, Peori House, Oregon House, Key Stone Rancho, Foster's Bar, Camptonville, Goodyear's Bar, Downieville.
NEVADA, Long Bar, Empire Rancho, Rough and Ready, Grass Valley, Nevada.
BIDWELL'S BAR, Charley's Rancho, Garden Rancho, Wimer's Rancho, Bidwell's Bar.
FORBESTOWN, Sen Ells Rancho, Miller's Rancho, Hansonville, Natchez, Ebensville, Brownsville, Forbestown, Wyandotte. PARK'S BAR, Dry Creek, Long Bar. Park's Bar, Rose and Barton's Bar.

At all of the above places, stoppages are made for the accommodation of Passengers. The Capital Stock of the above Company is ONE MILLION DOLLARS, and is the most extensive and complete Line of stages in THE WORLD.

J. BIRCH, ... President.
T. S. STEVENS, ... Vice President.
J. P. DEIGHAN, ... Secretary.
C. McLAUGHLIN, ... General Sup't, Marysville.

TRUSTEES.
J. Birch, James Haworth, C. Green, C. S. Coover, O. N. Morse, C. McLaughlin, W. F. Hall, F. S. Stevens, J. F. Jenkins.

James Birch's California Stage Company (the world's biggest stage-line company), showing nine lines daily leaving Sacramento in Concord coaches, carrying the mail, and five lines leaving Marysville. From Colville's "City Directory of Sacramento for the Year 1854–5." From the Bancroft Library, Berkeley, University of California.

Three wagons, each one labeled "California," cross the endless prairie, drawn by cattle, following a trail marked by skeletons of other cattle. From Alonzo Delano, "Life on the Plains."

to borrow. Businesses were run on a lavish scale and living was done on a lavish scale, and often the two got mixed. Much money was made in a hurry sometimes, and likewise it could be lost in a hurry.

How much banking Wells Fargo was doing is not at all evident, but the express department was doing a growing business.

Early in 1854, James E. Birch, a young man,[1] made a move that must have been welcome to Wells Fargo, for he consolidated some three fourths of the stage lines in California into one company, the California Stage Company. Where twelve or fifteen stage lines had run out of Sacramento, now only one would operate. That would seem to eliminate the haphazard catch-as-catch-can competition between Wells Fargo and Adams for stage connections. It would tend to reduce the fierce rivalry, but it would also tend, one suspects, to make the work monotonous. For a while there would be other ways in which the two big companies could compete, but, as an afterthought, one may wonder if perhaps the stage-line consolidation signaled the end of the first big era of freewheeling competition, and the beginning of an era when hardheaded business would prevail.

But Wells Fargo showed no signs of pulling in its horns in 1854, for on January. 17, the board of directors in New York increased its working capital to $150,000, and on March 1 declared a dividend of 10 percent.

In April, the United States mint was opened in San Francisco, causing changes in the sale or handling of gold, for now dust could be made into coins (principally $20 "gooses") without the long delay and the uncertainty of shipment to Philadelphia or to Europe. The mint also put more coins into circulation. For too long business had been done in bags of dust or by the thimbleful (uncertain measurements at best). Likewise, there was the feeling that an assay from the mint was absolutely reliable, and it must have had the effect of putting pressure on careless assayers.

Assaying had long been an occupation of some suspicion. There is no hint that the big banking companies—Adams, Wells Fargo, or Page, Bacon—were ever anything but reliable, but individuals in the assaying business engaged in many crooked practices: chipping the bars, adeptly abstracting a couple of ounces of dust from a lot (even under the eyes of the miner), or undervaluing the fineness of a bar so as to buy it cheap.

A typical item in the San Francisco *Herald* for June 29, 1854, gives an idea of the problem:

Caught at last.—Complaints have several times been made at the police office, of a broker named McCann, who keeps an exchange office on Pacific street, emblazoned with the most inviting cards of high prices for gold dust, etc., by miners who have gone to the establishment, but found that their bag, after being placed in his scales, lost much of its weight, but how or by what manner the dust had been abstracted has up to the present time remained a puzzle. McCann was arrested several times, and on each occasion the dupe stated that he had weighed his dust at the mines—never opened it—came down here—attracted by the high prices offered to be paid at this establishment, went in, but when the bag was weighed it was found that it was some ounces short, though his eyes were fixed on the scales all the time, and he failed to detect any foul play. This is the complaint which has been made on several occasions. Yesterday, Officer Morton disguised himself as a miner, and having procured a bag of gold dust, went to Adams & Co.'s Express Office, and had it weighed. It was found to contain 28 oz. He then proceeded to McCann's establishment and offered it for sale. The dust was placed on the scales, when lo! 8 ounces mysteriously disappeared. McCann was immediately arrested and brought to the station house; but the most wonderful thing of the whole is, that the scales and weights were examined, and nothing wrong could be discovered. The whole matter was investigated before the Recorder, but no light was thrown on the mysterious transaction.

The weights and the scales were all taken away, but there was nothing found which would be evidence against the defendant; and we are left to presume that there is some sleight-of-hand—some manipulation of which we know nothing—some art that this man has studied, practiced and brought to perfection, so as to defy even those who are standing by to detect him. The Recorder then said, whether he would commit him for trial or not he could not at present say, but he would take the case under advisement, and would give a decision on Monday next.

Knowing the temper of those early miners, one can say with assurance that he would not care to be in McCann's boots whether he was held or not. (There is no explanation as to how it actually was done.)

An advertisement in the San Diego *Herald* on May 29, 1851 (the first issue of that newspaper), advises miners that the "United States Assay Office" was established by Congress "with a view to afford them the actual value of their Gold Dust. When free from sand or quartz, it will yield you from seventeen to eighteen dollars per ounce! We are authorized by the government, under the supervision of an Assayer, appointed by the President and Senate of the United States, and have given heavy bonds for the faithful discharge of our duties. You may now realize the full value of your labors." That certainly implies that there had been problems in the assay business. This advertisement is signed by Moffat & Company. But it is easy to understand that Moffat & Company did not carry as much weight as did the United States mint.

In July, 1854, Wells Fargo bought another active competitor, Hunter & Company, and this consolidation left Wells Fargo and Adams pretty well in command of the express business in California. Page, Bacon & Company seemed to have more banking business than did anybody else, but that company did not handle express. Adams probably led Wells Fargo in express and was just under Page, Bacon in banking. Wells Fargo was after the banking business, but its shipments of gold dust do not indicate much more than half the volume done by either of the other two companies.

Up to that time, San Francisco had had six disastrous fires almost entirely without insurance, but had promptly (if flimsily) rebuilt each time. The streets were still quagmires during rainy periods, and the delivery of mail was still unbelievably inefficient except when it was carried by an express company. When a mail steamer came in, long lines of men gathered before the post office, to wait sometimes two days for the mail. Men or boys often got in line only to be able to sell their places later to impatient miners for perhaps five dollars. The rowdy and boisterous tried to push in the post-office door before the mail was up, and intimidated a clerk who went for a bucket of water. The clerks worked as long as they were able, and then lay down on the wooden floor to rest.[2]

In the early days, long lines of miners gathered at the post office, hoping for mail, and waited many hours. Some men stood in line as an investment, and later sold their places for $5. Mail clerks worked twenty-four hours at a stretch after a ship came in with mail. From Frank Soulé, et al., "Annals of San Francisco."

It was a transitional era. Previous to 1854 there had been failures here and there, but by 1854 some of the companies were pretty big and involved, and in early San Francisco it was easy for a careless and free-spending manager to find his company insolvent. To quite an extent, this type of situation was due, as it often is, to the fast-growing and rapidly shifting population—typically frontier and typically careless.

The total population of California in 1850, according to the census, had been 117,000, not counting Indians, and by 1852 it was 264,000, of which only 22,000 were women. Obviously, with a ratio of less than one woman for ten men, frontier conditions still prevailed. With rare exceptions, the only women in mining camps were prostitutes, and even those were so scarce that they often were accorded the respect usually reserved for good women. Prostitutes, of course, were imported from France, Latin America, and China in large numbers—large, that is, compared to the total female population.

A respectable woman, on the other hand—especially a woman of obvious class—was respected, adored, and revered. The hunger of men for women is often interpreted as a sex hunger, but it is far more than that: a hunger bone-deep but at the same time indefinably spiritual, so that the first reaction of most men, on beholding a woman after a long period of male-only society, is to be in awe of the wonders of creation. As Bancroft puts it:

> The influence of woman is strikingly exhibited in California during the . . . camp era. A hush then fell upon the revelling miners at the appearance of a woman in their secluded haunts, so a chivalrous respect surrounds her still wherever she moves. She may travel alone throughout the land, assured of respect and protection; many entertainments are made free to her in order to attract more male patronage.[3]

The streets of early San Francisco were in dreadful shape, and here a gentleman, unlucky enough to step into the water, fights off rats with his cane while a rat climbs the dress of the woman on the left, and another runs up the leg of the woman on the right. From Frank Soulé, et al., "Annals of San Francisco."

This latter was true even in San Francisco, where in 1854 and later, a theatre owner would announce the first row of seats reserved for ladies, in the hope —always fulfilled—that men would come for the sake of seeing a woman. Bancroft also says: "The divine halo shields even the fallen class." It is needless to say that when respectable women came into the Gold Country, prostitutes began to lose their position of honor, because good women would not stand for it.

That transition was not sudden, however; witness the eminence of Julie (or Julia C.) Boulette in Virginia City, Nevada, who was given a grand public funeral in January, 1867, after dying of strangulation by a person or persons unknown.[4]

The funeral was held from the engine house on B Street, the members of whose company were "her best friends." Julie always had great interest in any matter connected with the fire department, and any Virginia Citian would rise up in anger if anyone should suggest that she recognized a well-packaged market for her services. The day of her funeral was stormy and disagreeable, but the procession was led by the Metropolitan Brass Band, followed by sixty members of Virginia Engine Company No. 1 in uniform, wearing their badges in mourning. Julie was buried in the firemen's plot in the Flower Hill Cemetery, where she still lies, surrounded by a white picket fence. As an indication of the mixture of emotions felt toward a woman in a pioneer country, it is worth noting that, although the respectable women of Virginia City pulled down their window curtains as the procession passed, the band, on its return to town, mournfully played, "The Girl I Left Behind Me."

There was still a great conglomeration of nationalities in San Francisco, and this was made worse by the fact that an unusually high proportion of the population was of criminal character from Australia, from Chile, from France, and from other countries.[5]

The streets of San Francisco were laid out straight (as they had been in 1849), and were generally surfaced with clay. Houses were invariably flimsy, made of rough boards, unpainted, with calico or any cheap cotton goods nailed on the studdings and joists of the walls and ceilings. Some of the best hotels had most of their rooms separated from others only by canvas partitions, and the sounds and smells were literally indescribable in polite language. Unhappily, too, such accommodations were not for men alone; they were accorded feminine arrivals from the East without discrimination, and many a woman must have spent her first California night in disgust and terror.

Barrooms, gambling houses, and "dance halls" were crowded with drunken revelers,[6] and brass bands blared day and night in the tawdry places of amusement. The prices of food varied a great deal according to the news from the mines, but it was not unusual to pay three dollars for a breakfast of ham, two eggs, and coffee. Gambling "prevailed to an extent heretofore unheard of and unknown." Monte and roulette tables were "encircled continually day and night" by booted, whiskered men, and covered with bags of gold dust and "heaps of doubloons" and Mexican dollars, which were incessantly changing hands in enormous amounts. "Pistols and revolvers, fired in recklessness or fun, made the air musical with loud reports or whistling messengers, while, at other hours, intoxicated men, mounted on fleet horses, were rushing to and fro."

Since there had not been many small coins in San Francisco and since many foreign coins were legal tender all over the United States, foreign coins were well accepted in San Francisco. Mexican currency had been first, and then milreis from Brazil, doubloons from Spain, Peru, and Ecuador, francs and five-franc pieces from France, pesetas from Spain, zwanzigers from Austria, crowns from England, florins and guilders from Holland, and rupees from India were circulated freely, and at first nobody minded. But many of those coins were not worth as much as they passed for. The franc, for instance, worth about twenty-five cents, commonly passed for a quarter or two bits; the rupee, worth forty-one cents, passed for fifty cents, or four bits. Money was so easily come by in those days that any small silver coin passed as a bit and was valued at one real—the Mexican one eighth of a dollar. In 1856, the *Bulletin* complained that the Danish pistareen, worth seventeen cents, was passing for twenty-five cents. Even an American dime passed for a bit (twelve and a half cents).

Colonel R. B. Mason, the military governor of California, had tried to make gold legal tender in California but had not been successful, and so currency, like most other things in early California, was freewheeling. However, by 1854 business was beginning to settle down, and miners realized that a merchant who paid them $18 an ounce for dust, but paid it in French francs valued at twenty-five cents, was actually getting the dust at $14.40 and could take it down the street and sell it to Wells Fargo and make $3.60 an ounce. It was then (in 1854) that sentiment began to arise against foreign coins (coincident, of course, with the establishment of the mint in San Francisco). Foreign coins would continue to circulate rather freely through the 1850's, but ordinary people began to watch the silver content and the value in dollars.

Another practice going out of style was the pinch of gold dust. Small purchases were made for so many pinches of dust—a pinch being whatever amount the merchant could raise between his forefinger and thumb. Sometimes, when a man asked for a job (especially as a bartender), the prospective employer would ask, "How much can you raise in a pinch?" Obviously a man with a big finger and thumb could raise more dust, and his services would be more desirable. Many a bartender, it is said, would wet his finger and thumb, drop the dry dust into the proprietor's till, and rub off the wet dust in his own vest pocket. But by 1854 the pinch was going out of favor, along with foreign coins.[7] Business was settling down.

There was always a great number of newspapers published, and newsboys yelling their papers in many languages added to the confusion, while fire engines drawn by draft horses clanged and rumbled their way to and fro to officiate at the many fires in town. Hacks and buses careened through the muddy streets, while private carriages proceeded more sedately. Elegance was no protection for anybody, for an illiterate miner with a bag of dust felt that he was just as good as anybody else.

Nevertheless, there was progress, as a reporter recorded in the New York *Tribune,* September 26, 1854:

> The city is improving at a wonderful rate. The streets in the business portion of the City are being rapidly filled up three, four, five and six feet, to the new grade; and the old houses are raising and new ones building on all sides. It looks singular to see the houses standing on stilts one day, high above the streets, and the next day the street is filled in and planked, and in a week it looks like a new neighborhood. Many of the streets are altogether impassable with piles of brick and lumber, and the excavations for sewers, and the heaps of earth hauled to fill in the new grade. I think I may safely say that within a few years San Francisco will be a beautiful city.

Wells Fargo was at one end of Montgomery Street, and Telegraph Hill with its famous semaphore to announce the ships was at the other end. When the arms of the semaphore went up, their position indicated the kind of ship,[8] and bells and whistles created a din. A fire company would rush to the dock, and a band would spring up from somewhere—for a ship meant mail, newspapers, and packages, and sometimes loved ones. After the ship docked and began to unload, long lines formed at the post office and at the express offices.

There were, of course, other and quieter men in San Francisco—fruit growers, fishermen, vintners, ranchers, coal miners, loggers—but by and large it was and still is a city of freewheeling and fast dealing. It is spectacular and colorful, and one is still expected to keep his own eyes open. It is perhaps the last stronghold of urban individuality.

The bay (on the east and north of the town) was still crowded with ships (often described as a "forest of masts"), many of which, deserted as early as 1849 or as late as yesterday, had been turned into hotels. Some were anchored where they floated; others were pulled up on shore; still others were broken up and their lumber used for building.

In 1854, Honest Harry Meiggs came into the banking picture with considerable impact. Meiggs had come to San Francisco early, and by 1850 was a prominent lumber dealer and mill owner. He

FIGURE 2.—RIDING DRESS.

the head. These terminate in drooping sprays, falling upon the neck.—The Dress is of *moire antique,* low upon the shoulders, and *demi-basquée* before and behind. It is covered almost entirely with white blonde, three rows of which ornament the corsage, and being continued, drape the sleeves. The skirt also is covered with three blonde flounces overlapping each other. The first two are looped up at the side by clusters of orange flowers with branching sprays. Smaller bouquets also ornament the corsage and the sleeves.

FIGURE 2.—The Hat, from which our sketch is taken, is of fine Leghorn. Other fabrics of straw, made in similar style, are worn. The rim is looped up at the sides—more closely upon that side where the feather is worn—by two wide bands of white watered satin ribbon. A twisted band of this ribbon, together with rosettes and strings, also ornaments the hat, which is completed by a gracefully floating plume.—The Habit is composed of Cashmere or Saxon cloth. Light green is a favorite color, though this is not imperative, since the color should always be such as to harmonize with the complexion of the wearer. It is enriched by elaborate needlework of trailing vines and flowers, with an arabasque border. The sleeves, which are embroidered in like manner, are slashed upon the under-sleeve and cross-laced by cords which terminate in tassels. The sleeves are made flowing, and do not have the *mousquetaire* cuff.—The *Gilet* is of white *poult de soie,* likewise embroidered upon the collar. It is cut away rounding at the bottom, where it is fashioned like the old Continental waistcoat. Above this the breast of the coat may be confined by loops, which do not, however, slip over the button directly opposite, but over the one next below. The cords from the opposite sides thus form a cross-lacing with lozenge-shaped openings.—The Chemisette is of lace, fulled at the top, with an edging of Valenciennes lace. The size of our page does not admit of the insertion of the skirt in the illustration. This is made quite full, and may be ornamented with needle-work to match that of the boddice.

Of MANTILLAS there are several elegant novelties. Among the most noteworthy of Mr. BRODIE'S recent importations are some elegant scarfs and mantillas of Chantilly and Guipure lace. The delicate tracery of the one of these materials, and the transparency and picturesque effect of the other, peculiarly adapt them for the summer months. There are also novel styles of open-worked Canton crape scarfs and mantles, the beauty of whose designs and the elaborateness of whose manufacture fully equal any thing that has been produced in the Flowery Land.

In BONNETS we notice no very special novelties. They still continue to be made small, very small, with round crowns, and of the most transparent tissues. They are worn a trifle closer to the cheeks than heretofore. The trimming is chiefly bestowed upon the inside and around the front, the back being comparatively unornamented.

By 1854, our equestrienne is wearing a fine Leghorn hat (which has a plume, of course). The habit or jacket is of cashmere or saxon cloth, light green, with elaborate needlework; the chemisette is of lace. The saddle seems to have an extra horn on the right, which must be a slip on the part of the artist. From "Harper's Monthly Magazine," July, 1854.

Honest Harry Meiggs, who got away with half a million dollars or so and precipitated a banking panic in San Francisco, and wound up building a railroad from Lima to Cerro de Pasco in the Peruvian Andes. From "Scribner's Monthly," August, 1877.

bought land and expended a great deal of city money on improvements, as he was alderman for three terms. Then the price of land dropped, and Meiggs found himself in trouble, and turned to forgery.

He found the opportunity in city warrants. In 1853, the city had been extending the streets, building sewers, and using a great deal of lumber. To pay for the material and the labor bills of contractors, the city used scrip[9] in sums of $100, $500, $1,000, and $5,000, which were readily accepted by the city's bankers at 50 or 60 percent for loans. Meiggs, especially, was a favorite with the banks, for he borrowed much and paid the interest (sometimes as much as $30,000 a month) promptly on loans taken against the scrip as collateral, and, in fact, offered more collateral than the amount usually required. Meiggs had a large home, and sawmills around Mendocino, and in general lived like a rich man. One day, however, William Tecumseh Sherman, the director of the Lucas, Turner & Company banking branch in San Francisco, discovered that Meiggs owed them, as principal or endorser, about $80,000—all secured by scrip or city warrants; at the same time, Meiggs had accounts in other banks, and borrowed freely from them all.[10]

On the next steamer day, Meiggs came to the bank to get a draft on Philadelphia for $20,000, for which he offered his note and the usual collateral. Sherman told him that their draft was the same as cash, and since Meiggs already owed them heavily, the bank could not sell him a draft except for cash; in fact, Sherman said, he wanted Meiggs to reduce his account to $25,000. Meiggs took him to a mercantile house to show him that his (Meiggs's) business could not fail, but Sherman refused to issue the draft except for cash. The mercantile firm then agreed to take Meiggs's debts at the bank except for $25,000, and secure their part by mortgages on real estate and city warrants; they gave Sherman three acceptances[11] for the amount.

The three acceptances matured and were paid; then one morning Meiggs and his family and brother were missing (the brother had been elected city controller), and it was discovered that he had sailed for South America on a lavishly fitted yacht.

As soon as Meiggs's flight was known, San Francisco exploded with excitement and wild rumors; everybody ran to and fro to secure his money, and the mercantile house that had reduced his account with Lucas, Turner & Company failed. The total of Meiggs's liabilities ran up to about $1,000,000, and then it was discovered that much of Meiggs's scrip was a forgery, for it had been issued fraudulently. He had gotten hold of a book of warrants and used them as he desired. Meiggs's flight, says Sherman, set off a series of failures in San Francisco that extended into 1856. Many business firms and small bankers were affected by it—and perhaps some large ones—but, through it all, Lucas, Turner & Company was not affected, and Wells, Fargo & Company remained as steady as a rock.[12]

As a matter of fact, in January of 1854 Wells Fargo moved into what probably was a bigger building. It was called the Express Building, and it also was built by Sam Brannan, a few doors from Wells Fargo's first building and right across the street from the Parrott Building and Adams & Company.[13]

There has long been a tale about the Parrott Building that may or may not be apocryphal. If true, it might explain one factor in the success of Wells Fargo. It seems that John Parrott, the banker who had made a fortune in Mazatlán, to save money had imported the building stones from China—but they were keyed in Chinese symbols. That should not have been a problem, for there were Chinese masons in San Francisco, but they refused to work on the building. Finally Parrott sent to China for the man who had bossed the stone cutting, and he looked over the stones and the site and said: "These stones are all cut and marked for the opposite corner, where no evil influences will be encountered. This building is on the wrong location."

Parrott had already bought the land on the northwest corner, of course, but the Chinese man shook his head; the gods would not allow such a building to prosper. But Parrott was stubborn, and went ahead to erect the building. The Chinese people were shocked but not unfriendly; they offered to exorcise the building (which would involve mostly burning some papers and throwing rice and tea), and the contractor agreed to go along with it. However, after the building was completed, the contractors decided they had had enough monkey business, and would not allow the rites to be held.

The Chinese then took cognizance of the hex on the Parrott Building, and refused to enter it, but went diagonally across the street to Sam Brannan's "new red brick building," the first home of Wells Fargo, and burned incense and offered prayers for the success of the new company (Wells Fargo).[14]

In January, 1854, Wells Fargo moved into its second building, and was then on the very corner that the Chinese had said was good when the Parrott Building was going up, and for many days there was a solemn procession of Chinese through the bank day after day, ostensibly paying tribute to Taoi Pah Shing Kwun, appropriately the god of wealth. (It would have been heresy to suggest that one reason for the procession was that a Chinese man had set up a stand down the street and was charging his

Three envelopes, all bearing Wells Fargo insignes, to Gui Fah at Orleans Bar, Chinaman Ah Shing At (care of Sun Gee Lee & Co.) at Crescent City, and John Brown, Chinese, at Sawyers Bar. From the History Room, Wells Fargo Bank.

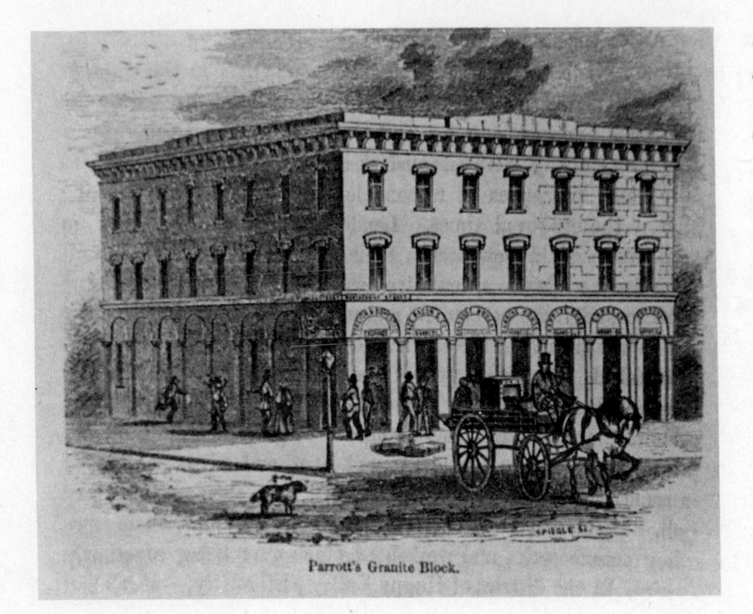

Parrott's granite block, built of stone imported from China but built on the wrong corner of the intersection. So said a Chinese stonemason brought from China to straighten things out. (They built it there anyway, because Parrott already owned the lot.) The dray is bearing a safe. The legends over the doors say: "Page, Bacon & Co. Foreign & Domestic Exchange. Page, Bacon & Co., Bankers. Gold Dust Bought. Banking House. Express. Express," and some too faint to be read. From Frank Soulé, et al., "Annals of San Francisco."

The second Wells, Fargo & Company building, the "Express Building." Pollard & Company seems to have one door, and perhaps uses that end of all three floors, while Wells Fargo has separate doors for banking and express. This building was across the street from the Parrott Building, and in this picture is considerably more elegant, even to the handsome rigs and stylish horses. A newsboy is selling papers. From the History Room, Wells Fargo Bank.

Montgomery and California streets, looking north in June, 1854. On the left is the Parrott Building, where the United California Bank is today, and on the right is the Express Building, with Wells, Fargo & Company signs very prominent. Down the block is the home of the "Alta California." The street does not look much like this today, especially at five o'clock in the afternoon. From Frank Soulé, et al., "Annals of San Francisco."

countrymen a small fee for the right to walk through the Wells Fargo Building and render proper tribute to Taoi Pah Shing Kwun.)[15]

The new building of 1854, says Soulé, was on a lot valued at $100,000, on the northeast corner of the intersection of California and Montgomery (Adams, in the Parrott Building, was on the northwest corner[16]); the Wells Fargo building was 75 feet high, with four stories and a basement, had a Montgomery Street front of 68 feet and a California Street front of 62½ feet, and was valued at $180,000. Wells Fargo & Company, "bankers and express agents," occupied the lower floor with Pollard & Company, real estate and money brokers. It was about that time that San Francisco had one of its worst cold spells—when ice froze up to an inch thick—but that did not stop the Chinese tribute to Taoi Pah Shing Kwun.

In a San Francisco newspaper of February 1, 1854, appears an item to the effect that Wells Fargo was about to establish an express and banking business throughout Oregon and Washington territories; J. M. Vansycle, "for the past year general superintendent of Wells Fargo in California, leaves to take up residence in Oregon." Vansycle was one of the oldest Wells Fargo agents in California, the item says, having started in 1853 when Wells Fargo was less than two years old!; he had been the Wells Fargo agent at Stockton.

By that time, Wells Fargo was shipping through Nicaragua as well as Panama, for an item in the *Alta California* for February 17, 1854, offers the information that Wells Fargo had just shipped $30,000 in treasure by the Pacific Mail Steamship Company's steamer *California,* via Panama, and $6,000 by the Nicaragua Steamship Company's steamer, *Brother Jonathan,* via San Juan.

On March 2, the *Alta California* said that Wells Fargo had shipped (on March 1) $60,800 by the *John L. Stephens,* a Pacific Mail steamer, and also $63,100 by the *Sierra Nevada,* a Nicaragua Steamship Company ship destined for San Juan del Sur (often called San Juan del Sud). On March 17, the *Alta California* said that Wells Fargo had shipped $80,200 by the *Golden Gate,* a Pacific Mail steamer, and $69,550 by the *Cortes,* a Nicaragua Steamship Company vessel. On March 27, the newspaper reported the arrival of the Nicaragua company's *Brother Jonathan* from San Juan, and the passengers included "Wells, Fargo & Company's messengers," one of whom reported on the accident at Virgin Bay on Lake Nicaragua March 2, in which nineteen gold-laden persons were drowned.

On April 27, Wells Fargo advertised in the *Alta California,* saying, "Our regular express for the Atlantic States and Europe will be dispatched on Monday, May 1st, at noon, by the steamers" *Panama* (a Pacific Mail ship to Panama), *Cortes* (a Nicaragua Steamship Company ship to San Juan del Sur), and *Uncle Sam* (an Independent Line steamer to San Juan). This ad said that a "special messenger on each steamer" would accompany the shipments, and the ad ran for several days. A new ad of the same wording announced shipments May 16 by the *Golden Gate* (Pacific Mail) and the *Brother Jonathan* (Nicaragua Steamship Company). Adams Express Company ran similar ads, so it rather seems that the two big companies (and some smaller ones) were using both routes freely by that time.

Again, the New York *Tribune* reported on July 25 that Wells Fargo had shipped $138,000 on the *Pacific,* a Nicaragua Steamship Company vessel, for San Juan.

Gold-mining was still going on, and some important finds were made, as told in the *Tribune* for July 25 (quoting from the *Nevada Journal*):

> We learn from Mr. Birdseye, who has just returned from Iowa City, that the mines in these rich diggings still continue to yield prospects, which, even in the extravagant history of California, have few equals. . . . Not a single company . . . but has succeeded in finding rich dirt. . . . Excitement up to the highest pitch. Last week the Jamison Company took out for their week's work $15,000. . . . At Independence Hill, one mile above Iowa City, . . . good leads. Some four miles above Iowa Hill, the same lead has been opened by several persons. . . . Those who have visited there say that the scene presented reminds them very forcibly of Nevada [Nevada City] in 1850 when all around was hurry, confusion and anticipation. Everything is unsettled; newcomers constantly crowding in, all in hope of getting a sight at "the elephants." . . . The same may be said of Forest City, Minnesota, Smith's Diggings, Camptonville, New-Orleans Flat, etc. . . . Dry Creek is now being flumed again. . . .
>
> C. G. Lake, Esq., Agent for Wells, Fargo & Co., at Angel's Camp, writes us that on the 10th and 11th instant, he purchased there gold dust to the amount of 325 ounces. This speaks well for that vicinity, and

shows a large population engaged in mining operations.

[The Grass Valley *Telegraph* says:] In Grass Valley miners have been more than ordinarily successful—as an evidence: Messrs. Wells, Fargo & Co. bought on Saturday evening $14,000 worth of dust, in small parcels. A new hotel has been opened in the flourishing mining town of Forest City, which cost $10,000. A new town called Mobile has been laid out, about one mile and a half south-west of Iowa Hill, and a saw mill, stores and dwellings are to be immediately erected. The Drakeville Company took out over $1,800 the past week. . . . The Independent Company at Forest Hill is succeeding well with their tunnel. They washed out on Saturday last, in eight hours, eighty ounces. From two pans of earth was recently taken forty-two ounces of gold, and a single person washed out in one day $1,000.

Shades of Bet-a-Million Gates! Man's oldest dream—the dream of getting rich quick—must have been fanned to white heat by these reports.

On the same day, the *Tribune* reported that Wells Fargo had shipped $117,600 in treasure by the *John L. Stephens* for Panama (Wells Fargo was fifth in quantity shipped; Page, Bacon shipped $362,000). On the *Pacific* for San Juan, Wells Fargo shipped $138,000, against Page, Bacon's $404,000. The three big companies—Page, Bacon; Wells, Fargo; and Adams—were shipping heavily through Nicaragua. On September 25, 1854, the *Prometheus* arrived in New York with $110,500 from Wells Fargo; $224,236 from Adams; $417,000 from Duncan, Sherman & Co.; and nothing from Page, Bacon. Duncan, Sherman had nothing on the other two ships.

A receipt dated at Rattlesnake Bar October 9, 1854, is evidence of Wells Fargo's banking activities, for it says: "$400.00. Received from Jacob Hoffner on General Deposit in our office Four Hundred Dollars in coin which we hold payable to his order on presentation of this certificate properly endorsed. Palmer & Baldwin. No. 52." It is endorsed by Jacob Hoffner and stamped, "Paid."[17]

The Wells Fargo agent at Auburn, John Q. Jackson, gives a pretty good idea of the political situation in California in the fall of 1854, in a letter dated September 15 and addressed to his father:

I received a letter from Jimmy last mail containing a good deal of general news which I was glad to receive.

We have just got through with our election of congressmen and county officers. As you doubtless have

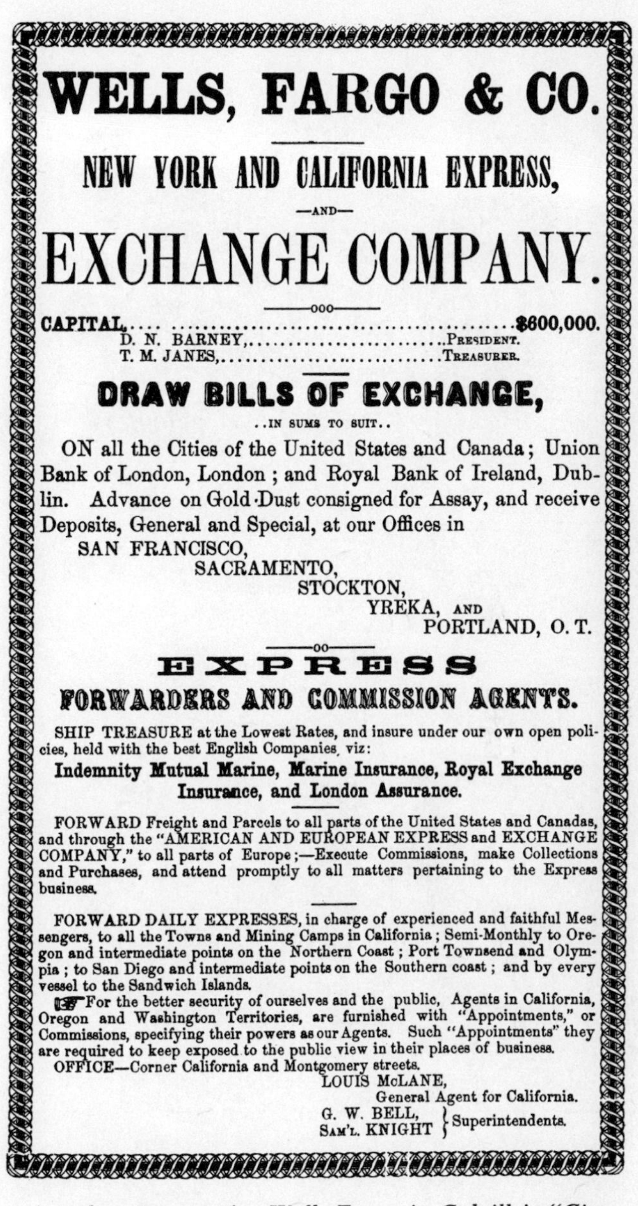

An advertisement for Wells Fargo in Colville's "City Directory of Sacramento for the Year 1854–5, from the Bancroft Library, Berkeley, University of California.

Night in the Log Cabin.
Camping out.
Going to work.
Hole gives out
New diggings Struck
Next day.
Lith. & Pub. by Britton & Rey. Cor. Montg. & Comm.l Sts S.F.

A Britton & Rey lithograph entitled "Scenes in a Miner's Life." Obviously nobody lingered when new diggings were located. From the Peters Collection at the Smithsonian Institution.

A Chinese man working a pan and another operating a rocker, while another digs and two more carry. From R. Guy McClellan, "The Golden State."

seen a great deal in the newspapers regarding California politics, tis unnecessary for me to say much in way of preface to post you up. The democratic party unfortunately had Mr. Broderick as an aspirant for the U. S. Senate and solely on his account the party was a good deal divided—in this county particularly so—excitement running very high and bets innumerable made on the strength of the two democratic tickets; this led to the election of the whole whig ticket from constables to State Senator.

To give you some idea of betting I might mention one instance—that of the present sheriff of this county who had occupied the office for four years and heretofore had a strong political influence—he being a strong Broderick man and anxious to have one of his deputies receive the nomination in the convention used every exertion for that purpose. The anti-Brodericks in convention were the stronger party and the cry was soon raised by the Brodericks that *they* did not receive fair play and bolted the convention; the result was the formation of two and the nomination of two county tickets (Democratic). Both parties were incensed against each other and willingly allowed the whigs to run into office sooner than give way for a compromise. Astin (Sheriff) spent in canvassing the county some $500 or $1,000 and bet some $4,000 besides on his party ticket all of which he lost—the anti-Broderick ticket polling more votes by 500 than his. The betting was not confined to him but was indulged in pretty generally by most of those who felt interested in the matter. I hardly know who are the most disappointed the winners or losers. There is a great deal of talk and commotion still and it will be some time yet before the ordinary quiet is restored. As for the people generally both whigs and democrats they are glad of the change and hope for a better administration of county affairs for the next two years.

He also gives some information about Wells Fargo:

The business of our company is constantly increasing and we have for a long time past done a large share of it in this county. Auburn as it is situated is the place of the most business of the county having four roads from different sections coming into it on all of these are arriving and departing at all times of the day and on

It looks like "Whittington's Express," and it is being pulled over the Sierra Nevadas by two dogs—neither one of which seems to be a Husky. This was printed in "Hutchings' California Magazine," 1856, and is entitled "The California Dog Express." In 1887, William M. Thayer used the same picture (but without the words "Whittington's Express"), and said it was the first express of Fargo and Wells over the Rocky Mountains (in his book, "Marvels of the New West").

Entitled "The Overland Route," this drawing seems to depict emigrants in many different stages of travel. From Alonzo Delano, "Life on the Plains."

$400 00/100 Rattlesnake Bar. Oct 9. 1854
Recieved from Jacob Hoffner
on General Deposit in our Office Four Hun=
dred Dollars in coin which we hold payable to his order on presentation of this cer=
tificate properly Endorsed
No 52. Palmer & Baldwin

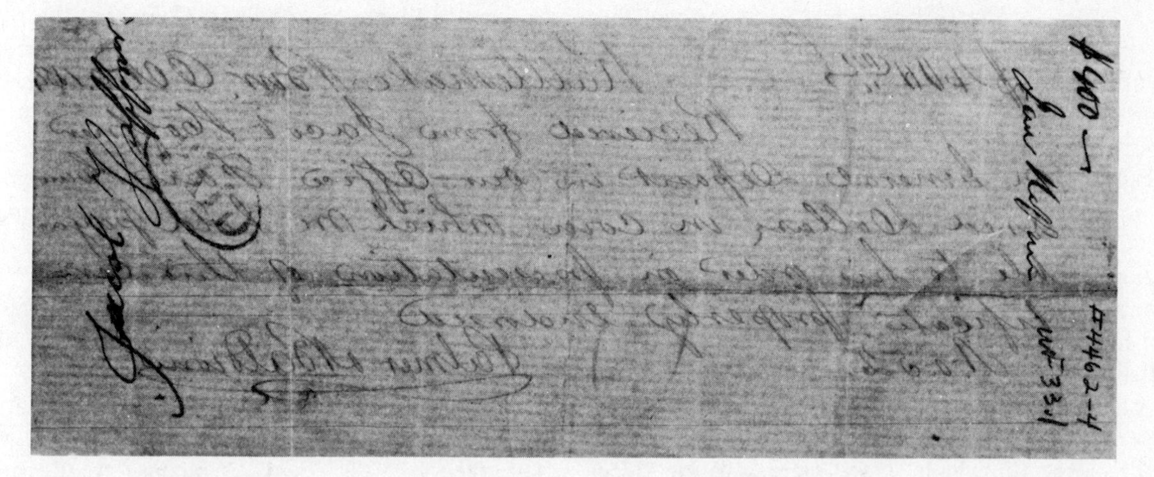

A receipt given by Palmer & Baldwin at Rattlesnake Bar. Endorsed on the back by the depositor, Jacob Hoffman, and stamped on the front, "Wells Fargo & Cos. Express. Rattlesnake. Paid." From the History Room, Wells Fargo Bank.

which are carried our expresses of treasure of which has to pass through the office here. The amount of gold dust bought at the offices of Yankee Jims, Iowa Hill and Michigan Bluff, in the aggregate, is from $8,000 to $10,000 for the month, at this office from $30,000 to $50,000 and at Rattlesnake Bar office from $30,000 to $40,000. Shipments are made of these amounts once or twice a week centering here from whence they are sent to the Sacramento office from there to the S. F. Mint. When we make a shipment tis frequently 100 to 150 pounds about as much as one likes to shoulder to and from the stages.

From these figures, it is seen that the five offices named were shipping some $160,000 a month or close to $2,000,000 a year. His shipments averaged about $35,000—which means that he was shipping about once a week or oftener. He makes some general remarks about the business, about a bulldog, and about mining:

The Express and Banking business is a pleasant one with the exception of some few of its functions—taking away the great haste in dispatching matter which we are forced to do for want of more time. I have no trouble except simply owing to the care of the treasure which is placed in this office. Were it not for this feeling of responsibility and trust I would be as light hearted and happy as a bird.

As a friend, counsellor and safeguard we have one of

the largest bull dogs I ever saw in any country. He weighs 128 pounds and is a very intelligent and noble fellow—is devoted to his business and takes as much interest in the office, seemingly, as any one connected with that establishment. The first artist that come along I will have his daguerreotype taken and forwarded that you may have a look at him.

The mining in the rivers now is in full blast and some claims paying remarkably well. I go to a place called Murderers Bar, six miles distant, once a week to purchase the dust dug there. I hear a great deal of complaint among the miners—many are doing nothing. While one man is making 10 or $20 for day there are a dozen who are scarcely making board. The claims at this place are very deep.[18]

In five years San Francisco had been through the terrors of lawlessness and the subsequent Vigilance Committee of 1851; it had been invaded by Tammany politicians from the East and Chivalry fire eaters from the South; the Broderick faction had already (in 1854) built up a powerful organization of ward heelers and controlled judges (such as Ned McGowan), and was getting in shape for another Vigilance Committee; in 1854, it had already given rise to several filibustering expeditions to Mexico, and there would be more in the next few years. Here was the spirit that later led a mob to sack the office of Etienne Derbec's highly successful French newspaper, *L'Echo du Pacifique,* upon the assassination of President Lincoln in 1865. Here was the spirit that would send a monster petition (75,000 signatures) to Washington to ask for an overland mail service.[19] So it was an explosive situation when Wells Fargo faced its first big test: the banking crisis of 1855.

San Francisco had grown up wild, woolly, and full of fleas, and was about to start paying for it. Conditions were about to change. Adams had already closed its doors for a short time, but in 1855 it would close them for a longer time.

The crisis of 1855 came directly from the attitude of the people. Specifically, it arose from banking—not from express—but the two functions were still so closely intertwined that the fall of one would mean the fall of the other.

Wells Fargo's business was growing, and it was making money. In September, 1854, it paid a 5 percent dividend. And that made 15 percent for the year.

It seems also that officers and directors during the spring and summer of 1854 became convinced that Wells Fargo's purchase of Livingston, Wells & Company had been brought about by some unspecified misrepresentation on the part of Henry Wells, Johnston Livingston, William N. Babbitt, and S. DeWitt Bloodgood, and the directors requested these men to refund the stock issued to them in payment or to reimburse Wells Fargo appropriately, and to accept return of the Livingston, Wells & Company business; the board also requested Wells and Livingston to refund $35,000 because of fraud and misrepresentation.

Since all these men were involved in Wells Fargo, and many of them in American Express, and several of them in Livingston, Wells & Company, the issues involved are by no means clear. However, no radical changes appear in the makeup of the board. In fact, there would be few changes in the board's personnel until 1866.

A report of gold shipments on November 17 shows that Page, Bacon & Company handled $417,000 worth of gold to Panama on that date, Adams $350,000, and Wells Fargo $177,000. Wells Fargo's total was still considerably less than that of either of the others, but it had gained greatly since its February 16, 1853, shipment of $73,448.

The directors in 1854 were Danford N. Barney, president; James McKay, secretary; Edwin B. Morgan, Henry Wells, E. P. Williams, A. Reynolds, Johnston Livingston, William G. Fargo, and William I. Pardee. Thomas N. Janes was treasurer. Reynolds resigned in September and Benjamin P. Cheney, the great expressman, was elected in his place.

On March 1, 1854, a dividend of 10 percent was paid, and on September 2, a dividend of 5 percent was paid.

In 1854, Count Raousset-Boulbon made his second filibuster into Sonora, and this time he was financed by San Francisco capitalists, according to implications by Bancroft,[20]—though it appears that the backing was not forthcoming as liberally as promised when rumors circulated that the United States government was about to crack down. It was also said that wealthy and influential citizens of Sonora had promised financial assistance, also probably true, although such promises are dubious in the extreme. At any rate, Boulbon, backed this time by Felix Argenti, an Italian banker of San Francisco, sailed for Sonora again in May (1854), accompanied by Augustus G. M. Bowen, cashier of Argenti's banking house (Argenti bought the ship and paid for the supplies taken aboard it). The ship capsized, but Boulbon reached Guaymas with his cargo (and the ship). Boulbon distributed arms and ammunition among the Frenchmen who had preceded him (some four hundred), and the Mexican General Yañez closed battle with Boulbon's forces in Guaymas. The Frenchmen lost 48 dead and 78 wounded; 313 were taken prisoner. The Frenchmen were well treated except for Boulbon, who was tried by a court-martial, convicted, and sentenced to death. That was in August, 1854. Felix Argenti had lost his investment.

In late 1853 and early 1854, William Walker got into the filibustering ring by landing at La Paz, in Baja California, with forty-five men. His destination was Guaymas, but the country arose against him while he was awaiting recruits, and he campaigned northward up the long peninsula to the border near San Diego, nine hundred miles from La Paz, where he surrendered with what was left of his force, now tattered, worn, weary, hungry, and tired. It is not known who financed Walker's 1854 sashay into Mexico, but it is obvious that considerable money was required for transportation, food, clothing, and arms, and since Walker was later financed to an incredible extent by bankers in San Francisco, New Orleans, and New York, it seems very likely that he had some financial backing from San Francisco for his Baja California venture.

Count Gaston de Raousset-Boulbon, the Wolf Cub, who ended his life before a firing squad in Guaymas, Sonora. From Frank Triplett, "Conquering the Wilderness."

COUNT RAOUSSET-BOULBON.

1855
The Great Banking Panic

THE FALL AND WINTER OF 1854–1855 was a time of depression in the East, and was not helped in California because there was no rain in the mines, which meant that the placer miners, who depended on running water, could not work the gravel. There had been some changes in the mining process, too. Whereas in the first days, nearly all mining was done by placer (that is, by swirling the water around a pan or by directing it through a wooden trough), the richness of the mines had lessened since that time, and hydraulic mining had been started in 1852 (in which a powerful stream of water was directed against a hillside, often from a boat, to wash down gravel in large quantity).

The net effect of these developments, and the rise in quartz-mining (which required heavier machinery) tended to make mining an occupation of big companies. The individual miner was out of work, and he drifted to the cities and towns. In 1854, also, it was becoming openly known that corruption in government in California was widespread, and people were losing confidence. There had been over-speculation in stocks and goods, both in San Francisco and in the East, and it would seem that the break should have come in San Francisco, since everybody speculated in everything there, from gold-mining stocks to wormy flour. However, the break came from the East, and reached San Francisco later.

In January, the directors of Wells Fargo gave some attention to the matter of insurance on the shipment of express. They noted that there had been considerable risk in the early years, and that therefore all shipments had been customarily insured, but the directors felt the risk had lessened, and they authorized the Executive Committee (first time mentioned) to assume the risk on shipments valued at not over $20,000—an account to be kept of all risks assumed. McKay, Barney, and Johnston Livingston were appointed an insurance committee.

At that time, January 15, the business in California was not giving satisfaction, and on January 15, Pardee, the express manager in California, was authorized to employ an assistant. A month later, the directors authorized the employment of a man to go to California with full power to act for the board (but no information appears as to the identity of the man employed—if there was one).

There was an ominous portent when the *Golden Age* arrived in San Francisco on January 30, 1854, with news of the failure of mercantile houses in the East, in St. Louis, and in New Orleans. Christmas holidays in the East had been gloomy; many men were out of work, and city administrations and public committees of citizens were raising relief money. The *Placer Times* took note of this depressing news, and compounded it in these words:

"Trade [in California] is utterly prostrate, and the pecuniary embarrassments of the mercantile classes have never been equalled since the settlement of the country by the Anglo-Americans. The principal cause producing this state of things has frequently before been alluded to by us—the absence of sufficient rain to enable the miners to prosecute their labors." All this, compounded with reckless credit and equally reckless buying, had been observed before, but, as to be expected, without serious effect.

On February 15, the directors of Wells Fargo voted a dividend of 5 percent, so it does not appear that their business in California was in trouble; perhaps it merely was not growing fast enough.

However, disaster soon struck California from the East when the Pacific mail steamer *Oregon* arrived February 17 with the news that Page & Bacon of St. Louis had failed. That was the parent bank of Page, Bacon & Company in San Francisco; it had speculated heavily in stocks and bonds of the Ohio and Mississippi Railroad, then in construction between St. Louis and Cincinnati; the railroad company got in trouble, and Page & Bacon found its drafts dishonored in New York, and was forced to close.

William Tecumseh Sherman was brevetted captain for service in the Mexican War, but resigned his commission in 1853 and went to San Francisco to manage the branch bank of Lucas, Turner & Company. In 1861, he was commissioned colonel in the Union army, and this picture, printed in "Harper's Weekly" for January 24, 1863, shows him as a major general.

The *Alta California* gives quite a different turn to the story. It says that Page & Bacon owned an immense amount of real estate and that its credit was good, although it had "extended many favors" to businessmen in the tight money market. The *Alta* says that $60,000 worth of drafts were protested[1] in New York by Duncan, Sherman & Company. That, of course, would precipitate a closing-in by other banks and a panic among depositors, then a run on the bank.

The *Alta* says that Bacon was in New York and had a cargo of iron worth $1,400,000 that he could have liquidated within an hour, but that he had no chance. He went to the office of Duncan, Sherman & Company with William H. Aspinwall, wealthy owner of the Pacific Mail Steam Ship Company, and arranged for drafts to be honored to the amount of $100,000, and assumed the matter was closed. But, says the *Alta,* he was notified twenty minutes before closing time that the drafts would be protested unless he could deposit $60,000 in cash before closing time.

This, the *Alta* says, was an act not only of bad faith but also of premeditated malice, a trick and a fraud without excuse or apology. The *Alta* says that even at that moment $40,000 was on the way from New Orleans, and that the steamer from California arrived a day or two later with enough gold to pay off the drafts and leave $120,000 in the hands of Page & Bacon. The *Alta* further assures its readers that, although the senior partner of St. Louis was also the senior partner of San Francisco, the San Francisco house was distinct from the St. Louis house, and that the failure in St. Louis would have no effect in San Francisco. It seems, however, that Page & Bacon had just drawn a million dollars from Page, Bacon & Company, so perhaps the tie was closer than the *Alta* believed.

William Tecumseh Sherman throws a different light on the affairs of Page, Bacon & Company when he says that during the winter of 1854–1855 he received frequent intimations in letters from Lucas, Turner & Company in St. Louis to Lucas, Turner &

Company in San Francisco to the effect that Page & Bacon was in trouble, having committed itself much too heavily in the Ohio & Mississippi Railroad and having to borrow money to pay for materials and to make large advances to contractors. Page, says Sherman, was a wealthy man, but not a banker. Also, says Sherman, the "headman" in California was Henry Haight, who was "too fond of lager-beer" to be trusted with such a large business.

Public meetings were held and resolutions of confidence in Page, Bacon & Company were passed. The company itself published a communication saying, among other things, that it was not so closely tied to the St. Louis bank as to be affected by its failure; that it was quite solvent and would continue to do business as usual. Thirty prominent businessmen said, in an advertisement in the *Alta California,* they would take Page, Bacon certificates of deposit for merchandise. Perhaps they all ignored a letter in the same issue of the *Alta California,* from New York, saying that actually Page & Bacon had had $250,000 protested in drafts, that they were in worse shape than they claimed, and were bound to close in a few days, no matter if Duncan, Sherman & Company had not protested their drafts.

Depositors began to withdraw their money from the Page, Bacon bank, and rumors began to circulate through the city. The withdrawal commenced slowly on February 18, but increased steadily through the twenty-first. The bank paid its demands and tried to quiet the rumors, but the run was on. On the twenty-second, after paying out a total of $600,000, the officers closed the doors because their deposits were below $100,000.

When the run started, Haight called on Sherman for help; Sherman went to see him, and found that Haight had been drinking; Haight's manner was extremely offensive, but Sherman was willing to buy, with cash, a fair portion of his bullion, notes, and bills, provided that Page, Bacon would not fail.

Other financial leaders of San Francisco were there, and Haight wrote out a paper saying: "We, the undersigned property-holders of San Francisco, having personally examined the books, papers, etc., of Page, Bacon & Co., do thereby certify that the house is solvent and able to pay all its debts," and asked them to sign it. Haight proposed to publish that statement in the morning papers, but Sherman asked Captain J. L. Folsom, a former classmate of his at West Point, if he had personally examined the accounts. Folsom said he had not, whereupon Haight asked rudely, "Do you think the affairs of such a house as ours can be critically examined in an hour?" Sherman pointed out that their signatures on such a paper would be endorsements and would render them liable; he said also that his partner B. R. Nisbet had learned the banking business in the house of Page, Bacon and that Lucas, Turner & Company kept exactly the same books, so that the accounts could be examined by morning. Folsom and Parrott demanded a count of the money in the vault, but Haight "angrily refused," and they all declined to sign the paper.

While the run was developing on Page, Bacon, smaller runs were developing on Adams, Wells Fargo, A. S. Wright, and Robinson and Company's Savings Bank, and when Page, Bacon closed, these secondary runs went into full swing. On the twenty-third, these four banks all closed their doors, and San Francisco was in a panic. Courts adjourned. Business, wholesale and retail, stopped completely. Montgomery Street, the street of banks, was jammed with people, mostly workingmen and miners, and a few women (mostly Mexicans). Women sobbed, men muttered threats, and occasionally a man gave way to hysteria. The greatest press was around the Adams office, which was in the Parrott Building where Page, Bacon & Company had its offices. More than one man had planned to withdraw the thousands he had worked for and saved since the beginning of the Gold Rush, and return home to his wife and family in the East, only to find that suddenly, in a matter of hours, his savings were gone and he was without even steamer fare.

On the twenty-third, Sherman's bank was besieged by men and women wanting their money. All who wanted it were paid promptly. Some exchanged their certificates of deposit for gold bars. Others accepted Sherman's word of honor that their money was safe. It was pouring rain that day, but the crowds milled in the streets, with "all the excitement and confusion of a battle, for the fortunes and honor of many were at stake." But in spite of the predictions that all banks would be forced to close that day, Lucas, Turner & Company remained open until closing time—practically the only bank in San Francisco that did so. Sherman's caution had paid off.[2]

Adams & Company was not in as bad shape as

was Page, Bacon. It had spent a large amount of cash for gold dust to be shipped on the *Uncle Sam,* but it said it was solvent and circulated cards to that effect. However, it soon paid out over $200,000, and then closed its doors with considerable money left (the amount was never determined, but it was thought to be from $400,000 to $600,000).

Now began some tightrope-walking at that company. Alvin Adams had made a trip to California to inspect the properties there, and had been wined and dined by Daniel Haskell and I. C. Woods, lauded by the newspapers, and praised by public meetings, but the fact was that Daniel Haskell had become rich and no longer was as capable or as careful as he had been; with Woods in charge, apparently far less scrupulous, there were some unhealthy things going on, but Alvin Adams was not supposed to see them, and apparently did not. Another report says that Haskell had retired and was living in the East when the crash came.

James King of William was also in the Adams picture. He had opened a small bank in San Francisco in 1849, but in 1854 had closed it, paid off some depositors, and made arrangements with Adams & Company to pay the rest. Somehow or other, in the process he became cashier of Adams & Company at $1,000 a month—part of which was applied to the money he owed Adams. Those who liked King always said that he had no knowledge of the careless ways of Adams & Company, but those who did not like him were quick to point out that James King of William managed to be on the scene in such matters more often than could be accounted for by chance.[3]

Nevertheless, the Adams company withdrew all the cash it could from the branches with which it had telegraphic communication, and that withdrawal caused the Sacramento office to close early on Friday. Wells Fargo, too, posted a notice at noon Friday, saying that it had paid out all its coin and bullion, but the express office remained open.

At Grass Valley, the Adams office closed, and crowds of miners surged into town and threatened to sack the office—but did not. Wells Fargo stayed open there until most of its deposits were paid out.

At Placerville, Adams closed at 9 o'clock in the morning, while Wells Fargo paid out as long as its funds lasted.

At Nevada City, the news came in at 10 o'clock; a few deposits were given to special customers, and then it was announced that the branch was out of money. Wells Fargo paid out until 2 o'clock and was forced to suspend.

At Columbia, the manager had already moved his cash to the vault of the Tuolumne Water Company, and declined to pay the crowd of depositors. At Sonora a mob burst into the Adams office and got the cash ($49,000), but later it appeared that most of the rioters were not even depositors, but burst open the iron door for the excitement of it. A large part of the money paid out found its way into the hands of lawyers, who, for percentages, withdrew the attachments they already held against Adams & Company.

At Jamestown, the Page, Bacon & Company vault was broken open by angry depositors, but found empty. (However, the *Alta* for February 25 carried a story that Page, Bacon denied they had had a vault broken open at "Jackson," and said they had no agency or vault at that town.)

In Marysville, the manager of Mark Brumagim & Company, bankers, remained open one hour after the regular closing time to accommodate depositors who might want to withdraw their money.

Adams & Company went into a tempestuous receivership, and I. C. Woods on February 24 issued a card avowing he had surrendered his private property to the receiver, and said: "My entire private property I have surrendered to the creditors of Adams & Co., subject to judgements in favor of clerks of the concern, whose labor and fidelity have built it up, and whose earnings remain unpaid." (Woods had been manager of the bank.)

Although Page, Bacon's failure was a disastrous one, the people did not greatly blame it, feeling that it had gone broke trying to help Adams, and also considering that its staying open until it had paid out all funds available was a way of playing fair. But the public feeling toward Adams was one of antagonism and bitterness because it had closed its doors with a great deal of money and dust still in its vaults, and also because of many strange circumstances, the mysterious transfers of assets, and the ultimate disappearance of several hundred thousand dollars worth of assets.

At 10 o'clock on Saturday evening (February 24), the officers of Wells, Fargo & Company completed an investigation of their own books, and

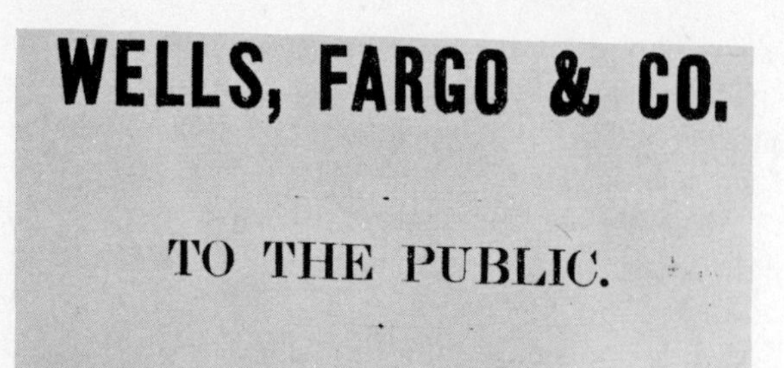

WELLS, FARGO & CO.

TO THE PUBLIC.

As there seems to be some misapprehension and misrepresentation as to the tenor of the Bill of Complaint filed against Mr. PARDEE, of the above house, on which an injunction issued and a Receiver was appointed, it is due to you that it should be at once removed. The suspension of this House, to my mind, was the result of a mere panic, and nothing more; but after it had occurred, it was due to the Public that its assets should be at once placed in such a shape, that all the Creditors would in any possible contingency receive their entire debts, share and share alike. Under our statutes and decisions, no other course was left than to apply to the Court for an injunction and a Receiver, and it was necessary to state, as a ground, in the Bill, that the House was for the moment *unable to meet its debts in coin*; that is, that there was a TEMPORARY INSOLVENCY. But for these, court attachments and useless litigation might have exhausted, in unnecessary costs, much of those means that belong to the Creditors. As counsel for the House, who drafted the bill and obtained the injunction and Receiver, I can assure the people of California, that this suspension is merely a temporary one—that no man need lose a dollar by it, and that the resumption of the House and a continuation of its hitherto prosperous business may be considered as morally certain.

GEO. C. BATES,
Attorney, &c.
Firm of BATES, LOVE & LAWRENCE.

Sunday, February 25, 1855.

Wells, Fargo & Company was not "insolvent" very long. This copy of its notice to the public is from the California Historical Society, San Francisco.

published the following card in the *Alta* on Sunday morning:

> Wells, Fargo & Co. have completed a balance of their accounts this day, and find to the credit of their house, above every liability, $389,105.23; and only ask of their friends a few days to convert some of their assets, to resume payment.

On the next day (Sunday), Wells Fargo published a card or placard to advise the public as to the reasons for certain steps it had taken:

> WELLS, FARGO & CO.
> TO THE PUBLIC.
>
> As there seems to be some misapprehension and misrepresentation as to the tenor of the Bill of Complaint filed against Mr. Pardee, of the above house, on which an injunction issued and a Receiver appointed, it is due to you that it should be at once removed. The suspension of this House, to my mind, was the result of a mere panic, and nothing more; but after it had occurred, it was due to the Public that its assets should be at once placed in such a shape, that all the Creditors would in any possible contingency receive their entire debts, share and share alike. Under our statutes and decisions, no other course was left than to apply to the Court for an injunction and a Receiver, and it was necessary to state, as a ground, in the Bill, that the House was for the moment *unable to meet its debts in coin;* that is, that there was a TEMPORARY INSOLVENCY. But for these, court attachments and useless litigation might have exhausted, in unnecessary costs, much of those means that belong to the Creditors. As counsel for the House, who drafted the bill and obtained the injunction and Receiver, I can assure the people of California, that this suspension is merely a temporary one—that no man need lose a dollar by it, and that the resumption of the House and a continuation of its hitherto prosperous business may be considered as morally certain.
>
> Geo. C. Bates, Attorney, &c.
> Firm of Bates, Love & Lawrence.
>
> Sunday, February 25, 1855.[4]

It is interesting to observe that the Chinese demonstrated their complacent faith in Wells Fargo (and in the benevolence of Taoi Pah Shing Kwun) by declining to withdraw their money from Wells Fargo and by continuing, even during the panic, to ship their gold dust from all over the mining country to Wells Fargo in San Francisco.[5]

Wells, Fargo & Company obviously was in better shape than either Page, Bacon or Adams, and, while its officials in San Francisco anxiously watched the outpouring of cash, its agents in the Gold Country had their own problems. At Marysville, the agent was C. H. Hedges, and he had a great deal of gold dust that he had accepted from merchants in Marysville. He got an order from San Francisco to close the bank; it was twenty minutes before three, and he sat with his watch in hand until closing time, then had the doors closed and told the clerks to return after getting something to eat. He had a thousand accounts from men who trusted Wells Fargo, and he had no intention of letting them down. He bought all the buckskin bags he could find, and told the clerks that, no matter what the condition of other Wells

Fargo banks, the one in Marysville was sound, and he was determined to protect his depositors. He therefore instructed the clerks to take the money and dust on general deposit and pack it in the buckskin bags (each of which held from $1,000 to $5,000 in dust) and mark it "special deposit"—and the books must be made to correspond with the bags. They worked until 2 o'clock the next morning, and Hedges felt it was a night's work well done. He had protected his depositors. The next morning, to his great relief, he received a telegram from San Francisco, saying that he was to open the bank as usual.

At Auburn, the Adams office closed early Friday morning, but armed men compelled the manager to open the vault, and by 10 o'clock the branch was cleaned out. Wells Fargo there apparently was not hurt, but the experience was harassing for John Q. Jackson, the manager there:

> Yesterday & today have been days long to be remembered by me. On the night of the 22nd I was present at a ball given in the place where I remained till 4 a.m. at that hour I retired to bed to snatch a few hours sleep before beginning the days work. At 8 o'clock I was awoke up by a messenger handing me a telegraphic dispatch from our firm below, to the effect that *Adams & Co.* had failed and to prepare for a run. Here was a pleasant message and I instantly got up & at the moment I reached the door crowds were running towards the office, I knew that our funds would not meet all our outstanding drafts certificates etc. and would not commence paying. Very soon Adams & Co. here had paid out all their funds and still were short some $20,000.00. The crowd were now furious and banking hours drawing nigh—What was worse still was my being alone in the office—My assistant a short time since being transferred to the Iowa Hill Office. I saw no other plan but to open and let it go as far as it would—Paying out commercial and the work got pretty warm when two or three of my personal friends came forward and offered their assistance to the extent of their means. One of them being very popular and a *substantial* man his presence seemed to allay all excitement and to instill confidence, as to our means, to the crowd. As they dispersed and the matter became a little quieted I went outside and made arrangements for funds nearly to the amount of all the demands against us—The time ran smoothly till about 4 p.m. when it was telegraphed that *Wells Fargo & Co. had suspended in San Francisco*. This fell like a death knell to me but as far as this office was concerned I would weather it—When the news was spread around the crowd commenced assembling and pretty soon the paying out was lively—but as there seemed to be no lack of funds & my giving personal assurance of their safety all was quieted for the day—This morning I received a dispatch from San Francisco Office that their house would open on Monday next and through the day have received several of the same purport. We have had but little trouble so far today [Saturday], & I am in hopes we will go through the storm safely. This is certainly the proudest time of my life and I only wish that my *masters' other agents* together with themselves may be so successful in the end as I have been. The bankers have been put to a frightful test and many having abundant means forced to suspend—As I understand it W. F. & Co. in San Francisco had plenty of dust & assayed bars, but ran short of coin. Monday I feel assured will bring us a better day and one that will establish the credit of the firm to a greater degree than it has ever enjoyed heretofore. Of course their standing effects me in every way & their fall would be equal to the same thing with me. The steamer Uncle Sam on account of all the suspensions which have taken place is detained till Monday when she sails.[6] I send you two daily papers which will give you some idea of the excitement throughout the country. In haste, Your affectionate son, Jno. Q. Jackson.[7]

Most of the smaller banks in San Francisco survived. Some of them endured short runs, but in the end they had more money than they started with, for those who had withdrawn their money from the big companies needed a place of safety.

Wright's Miners' Exchange Bank and Robinson & Company's Savings Bank finally went under.

It was during this great panic that Louis Remme, a French-Canadian cattleman, made his famous ride to Portland. Remme had driven down the valley on February 23, had sold his cattle for $12,500 in gold, and had deposited the money at the Adams bank. The next morning as he ate breakfast in Bremond's restaurant in Sacramento, he opened the Sacramento *Union* and read that Adams had suspended. He left his breakfast and ran to the Adams office, which was surrounded by a mob. He reached a clerk with his deposit certificate in his hand, but was sent to the end of the line.

His first thought, as he saw the long line of men waiting to get their money, was to go to another town, but he knew all towns in the state would be the same. Then he would have to go to another state:

Oregon. He would go to Portland. That meant he would have to hurry to San Francisco to take the next ship, the *Columbia.* There was no telegraph to Portland, and the office there would not know. But, on the other hand, everybody on the ship would know, and it would never work. He had to reach Portland *before* the ship.

Remme had no intention of giving up his $12,500 without a fight, but he knew that there was only one way to get to Portland first: He would have to ride horseback.

It was a seven-hundred-mile ride, but Remme decided fast. He went to the wharf and caught a stern-wheeler leaving for Knight's Landing, forty-two miles upriver. He got a horse from Knight and rode straight north. He rode all day and all that night, buying fresh horses as he had to have them. Seventy hours from Knight's Landing he reached Yreka near the Oregon border. He snatched an hour's sleep at rare intervals, and rode through Hungry Creek, Bear Creek, and Jacksonville, wondering if he could beat the steamer. At the moment, the steamer seemed to have all the odds in her favor, but Remme kept going. On the fifth day, he reached Eugene, and at sunrise of the sixth day he was at French Prairie. He reached Oregon City at 10:30, and crossed the Willamette into Portland at noon.

He went to the Adams office, and the agent examined his certificate of deposit, saw that it was valid, and paid Remme in gold.[8]

If he paid in dust or in coin, Remme must have had about fifty pounds of gold. At that time, a cannon boomed, and the *Columbia* was coming up the river. He had beaten the ship by about an hour. He had also made a great ride: seven hundred miles in six days.

I. C. Woods, the manager of Adams & Company, had been taking care of himself. He had built the port town of Ravenswood and a farm called Woodside Dairy in present Menlo Park, and had taken a large sum of gold and had hidden it in a frame-and-mud house. However, Maurice Dooley, owner of a line of stages and heavy depositor with Adams, took a gun and forced Woods to pay him $80,000, the amount of his deposit. Woods fled to Sydney, Australia, disguised as a woman; later he was seen in Honolulu. The Adams books disappeared and later were found floating in the bay, some important pages missing—which added up to the fact that $269,000 of assets had disappeared, perhaps to Australia.[9]

It seems an undeniable fact that Woods sent "coin, dust, and bullion" out before the close of the bank, and that property ended up with Palmer, Cook & Company. There was severe criticism because Adams closed so soon.

Woods's assets were sold at auction by the sheriff, and the proceeds presumably were applied to the liquidation of the firm.

Now James King of William, who should have been well satisfied to be quiet, got back into the limelight by borrowing $500 from friends to establish the San Francisco *Bulletin,* in which he made furious attacks on all bankers and expressmen involved in the failures, and accused Palmer, Cook & Company of being politicians rather than bankers.

But James King was always vitriolic and reckless, and it seems dubious that his charges against that firm had any foundation. It is doubly sad, then, that his charges had much to do with the failure of Palmer, Cook & Company two years later, after King was dead from a bullet following his caustic attack on James P. Casey, publisher of the Sunday *Times.*

Edward Bosqui, who worked for Palmer, Cook & Company, says that King's attitude toward the firm was caused by an insolent turndown when King applied to Edward Jones, junior partner of Palmer, Cook & Company, for a loan just after he started publishing the *Bulletin.* King said Jones would live to regret his action, and a few days later published a violent attack on the firm, and that was followed day after day by malicious and untrue charges, and people began quietly but steadily to withdraw their deposits. One may examine some of James King's words in the issue of October 11, 1855, in which he editorializes on the reasons for the postmaster's charging as much as $137 a year box rent; he says it is because Palmer, Cook & Company charge exorbitant rent ($18,000 a year for the post office), and he calls them the Uriah Heaps of San Francisco bankers; "those delectable gentlemen"; "these sneaking, surety-giving moneylenders"; he says:

> these political wire-pullers and un-bank-like gentlemen have laid their ubiquitous fingers on part of the money thus wrung from the people of this city. They are unlike other bankers, because forevermore they are at some scheme to elect, not good men to office, but their own, or such as can be so fashioned; and then becoming

This service of plate apparently consisted of a coffee- or teapot (properly inscribed), a sugar bowl, a creamer, and a fourth container (a condiment dish?). Usually they were of silver plate, but sometimes they were of sterling and very valuable. This picture, printed in "Gleason's Pictorial Drawing-Room Companion" for 1852 (Vol. II), is of a service presented to John B. Adams, "popular conductor on the Western Railroad between Springfield and Albany."

bondsmen for them, get hold of public money with which to bribe and corrupt other public officers, both State and Federal. . . . Oh, Uriah Heap, Uriah Heap, Uriah Heap, *'umble* Uriah Heap, *where* are your laurels now? They are all faded, and *clean gone* forever![11]

Yes, King should have known when he was well off, because in the California *Chronicle* on November 5, 1855, a letter was printed from William L. Newell that said aloud what a lot of persons were thinking:

To James King of William: . . . I charge you with having, by cunning deception and fraud, in the early days of the gold fever of '50 and '51, secured the confidence of the community, with the *premeditated* intention of using said confidence for the purpose of swindling those who put trust in your *assumed* honesty; . . . that you were cognizant of and a participator in the whole of the rascality of I. C. Woods and others. . . . I charge you . . . with assisting in the process of having the gold dust and treasure of that concern [Adams & Co.] carted away from their banking house during the night; and of being in council with Woods and Cohen in the back office of Palmer, Cook & Co. after these transactions. . . . You took and gnawed the bone given you by I. C. Woods, and the moment he was powerless, you turned like a cur and bit the hand which had saved you from ruin . . . you never would have the honesty to say one word to the public could you have had the privilege of *stealing* and carrying away the amount which you desired.[12]

It sounds like the barking of an angry dog except that it is remarkably consistent with James King's operations.

However, James King was not the only one to exercise invective against Palmer, Cook & Company, because the Sacramento *Daily Union* said on July 31, 1856:

Like a vampire, this Banking House clings to the body politic, sucking its substance through all political changes, and yet execrated by the masses of the people, upon whose substance it feeds; and finally, to replete itself, it blasts the credit of the body upon which it has so long been preying. It is not our intention to indulge in speculations, but we have heard it suggested now, as it was when Duncan, Sherman & Company so nobly stepped forward to save the State before, that these men, whose business it is to deal in State securities, may have a design in prostrating our credit, in order to buy up the State indebtedness, at a low rate, and then by an equally skillful movement, put those evidences up again.

In an article in the New York semiweekly *Tribune* bylined "Our Own Correspondent," resentment against all the companies is stated in strong fashion:

During the past six months three of the most prominent banking-houses in this city have failed—Page, Bacon & Co., Adams & Co., and Burgoyne & Co. . . . Page, Bacon & Co. have been popular bankers and largely accommodated their customers. . . . These bankers have been nothing more nor less than speculators. . . . This is plainly seen in the case of Adams & Co., who have thousands of dollars of assets that are not now and never were worth a farthing.

Now these Bankers have "caved," what do the shrewd people of the East think of the costly service of plate in Broadway to be presented to Mr. H. [Haight] of the firm of P. B. & Co.? Who pays $15,000 for this plate? It is said the merchants of San Francisco, as a testimonial of respect, &c. But is any person so shallow as to suppose that the merchants of this city would give $15,000 to a banker because he had loaned them money at three per cent per month? Nonsense. These men are pets of P. B. & Co., who have had large accommodations and expect more. They will pay for the plate whenever P. B. & Co. will give them the money to do it. And P. B. & Co. will pay poor depositors when these plate-men pay their notes, which will not be the case with all of them, I venture to say, in the year 1855. Of a similar character are all "plate" operations.

It might be interesting to observe that, in the same dispatch, Wells Fargo appears as the largest shipper of "specie," with $115,646; Drexel & Company is second with $100,000; and William Seligman & Company is third with $26,600. It did not take Wells Fargo long to top the list.

Less than three months later (in the issue of August 28, 1855), the *Tribune* says:

Adams & Co.'s affairs are getting more and more complicated. There is a report of the referee pending before the District Court, which awards Merick G. Reed et al $180,000 of the assets. A controversy has arisen between the creditors as to who of the attaching credits shall have precedence. In the meantime, James King of Wm., late manager of the banking department of the business, has threatened an expose and published three communications, which detail the manner in which he became connected with the house. On the 17th, Alfred A. Cohen [the receiver] assaulted him in the street, received a Roland for an Oliver, and came off second best. Cohen's brother was fined $300 for assaulting T. W. Park, one of Alvin Adams's attorneys. All this was caused by the failure of Woods and Adams & Co.

Street fights and cowhiding scrapes have attracted public attention for two weeks past. Montgomery street nearly every day has offered one of these interesting occurrences—none, however, resulting in anything serious. Two fights, of the more dignified and regular order, are announced. The parties are Yankee Sullivan and Joe Winrow, and J. Reiner and Ed. McKugen—the first for $2,000 and last $500 a side.

Well!

Cohen had not wanted to be the receiver anyway—but no matter, James King was after everybody.

A more prosaic paragraph—but a significant paragraph—in the same story says:

Overland immigration will scarcely amount to one quarter of the same last year. The Indians are troublesome on the plains, which probably deters many who would otherwise come. The price of cattle is advancing accordingly (since oxen will not be arriving in quantity).

It was claimed that Alvin Adams had sold his interest in Adams & Company of California before the crash, but proof is lacking. Nevertheless, Adams felt the opprobrium deeply, and finally resigned the presidency of Adams & Company late that year (1855), because he felt his presidency was detrimental to the company's interests.

Some of the Adams employees in California got together and formed the Pacific Express, which went into the Alta Express in 1857, which was bought up by Wells Fargo in 1858.

William J. Pardee, manager of the express department, had been appointed receiver[13] for Wells Fargo, and found it had some $400,000 over and above all liabilities. One report in the *Alta* says that Wells

Fargo opened on Tuesday morning, and paid out coin all day. Business was very light, and freight to the interior was much smaller than usual. It rained all day Tuesday, and that may have held some persons back from rushing to get their money at Wells Fargo, although the reporter said: "Public attention is altogether too much taken up with the affairs of the Bankers to permit a calm to supervene just yet; and the excitement, although it has greatly died away, still seems to be merely slumbering. The crowds which occupy Montgomery Street each hour of the day sufficiently demonstrate the fact that there is still a possibility of danger, although we sincerely hope that it is now all over." By "danger," he meant, of course, a riot, sacking of the banks, and possibly a lynching.

Wells, Fargo & Company got over the panic in good shape. It had banked prudently and carefully, and was in excellent condition, and its express operations continued. The San Francisco bank of Wells Fargo had closed on Friday, February 23, but reopened on Monday, according to another report.

It was a little primitive, but it was a lot better than crossing Panama by bongo and muleback. From F. N. Otis, "History of the Panama Railroad."

This picture of Alvin Adams was printed in "Harper's Monthly Magazine" for August, 1875.

It was not long before it became apparent that Adams & Company was not nearly as solvent as Woods had said—that it had assets to the extent of only about half its liabilities.

The company's debacle was complete, and nine years later it still owed half a million dollars, with assets for about 5 percent of the total. Liquidation of the Adams affairs took about ten years, and, in the end, the lawyers got most of it, the depositors almost nothing.

On March 3, the *Alta California* announced important news received by the steamer *Sonora:* The bill providing a transcontinental telegraph had passed both houses of Congress, and, as soon as the President should affix his signature, California could be assured of no longer being cut off from the world. Also, passengers on the *Sonora* had been held up an hour at the Isthmus summit to celebrate the completion of the Panama Railroad, another important item in connecting California with the East. The *Sonora* carried a large amount of express freight for both Adams and Wells Fargo.

Also, it was said that $650,000 in gold from Page, Bacon & Company had been received in New York, and that $300,000 of that sum was available to Page & Bacon to pay its obligations. It must have been small comfort to the depositors in San Francisco who had lost their money.

The *Alta California* suspended its Sunday edition on March 4, but the *Herald* continued to publish, and its Sunday edition for that date shows an advertisement for Wells, Fargo & Co.'s Southern Coast Express to Monterey, Los Angeles, San Diego, and the Kern River Mines. The Pacific Express was already advertising as a joint-stock company formed by the late employees of the Adams company, to do business in about the same fashion as had Adams, but the advertisement said, "The business will be strictly and solely a Forwarding one, having NO CONNECTION WITH BANKS OR BANKERS." It was signed by R. G. Noyes, president.[14] Joseph Palmer was on the board of trustees.

Banking houses advertising in the *Herald* at the same time are Lucas, Turner & Company; Drexel, Sather & Church; Forbes & Hancock; F. A. Seilliers; Abel Guy; and Pioche, Bayerque & Company; interestingly, Page, Bacon & Company's card was still running also.

There was announced in the same issue a meeting of the depositors of Adams & Company at the National Hall "for the purpose of appointing a committee to investigate the relationship existing between Alvin Adams and the firm of Adams & Company in California. Also to investigate the position of I. C. Woods and James King of Wm. with said firm, and for the further purpose of ascertaining the true value of the assets." It was signed by "A Depositor."

There were extensive disastrous effects of the panic on San Francisco businesses. During 1855, there were 197 business failures in the town, with total liabilities over $8,300,000 but assets of only $1,500,000. But 1855 did not see the end, because in 1856 there were 140 more failures, including the final dissolution of Palmer, Cook & Company, with total liabilities of $3,500,000.

As for Wells Fargo, it emerged as the shining light of express companies and bankers. It had been tried and not found wanting. In the summer, Wells Fargo, probably needing more room, moved into the Parrott Building, got the Chinese people to exorcise it, and called it the Wells Fargo Building. From those dark and hectic days of February, 1855, Wells Fargo emerged as the dominant express and banking company of the West.

Survival of the banking panic did not mean that Wells Fargo had no other problems in 1855; as a matter of fact, a major problem that year occurred in connection with the carrying of mail.

One of the very great handicaps under which the post office operated in California was the act of Congress that provided mail service. As a result, among the instructions issued to the first postal agent, William Van Voorhies, was one to the effect that he should install post offices in San Diego, San Pedro, Santa Barbara, Monterey, and San Luis Obispo (none of which was in the Gold Country), and other offices in the interior provided "the expense thereof [could be] defrayed out of the net proceeds of such office." Since not many mining camps stayed established long enough to even think of paying for the upkeep of a post office, it was an ironic provision.

Nor did the postal service get much better. In fact, the express companies performed a real service in the carriage and delivery of mail. And still the expense, inconvenience, uncertainty, and delay involved in getting mail through official channels was annoying to those looking for letters from home. In

1851, the ship service had been increased to twice monthly from its original once-a-month schedule, but that did not help the lonely miner in Jackass Gulch or Mad Mule or Sublimity. It rather seems that by 1855, when the population was well over 300,000, the people were nearing the end of their patience—so much so that the *Alta California* printed one of the most bitter attacks on the inefficiency and corruption of the postal service.

> The Postmaster intimates that the Post Office now affords facilities equal to those of any Express Company.... The opinion of the Postmaster is sadly at variance with most men of the community, for it is generally believed that the Expresses are much more expeditious than the mails, as is evidenced by the fact that so many letters are sent by the Expresses, notwithstanding the fact that, besides paying postage, the Express charge must also be paid. The letter of Mr. Weller... proves conclusively that the present post office system is the most outrageous tyranny ever imposed upon a free people. It forbids us sending letters by such means of conveyance as we may prefer, without paying an odious and onerous tax to the government.
>
> The whole system, as now conducted, is utterly useless. It is so clearly and undeniably a nuisance, that we had hoped the press generally would have taken up the subject, for then it would in time be abolished.... The Post Office system, so far as California is concerned, is a humbug and a nuisance.... The Expresses willingly carry letters for a bit[15] each, to the Atlantic States,... and yet surely and safely.

Wells Fargo caught the mail steamers without fail, whereas the post office, it seems, very often did not get its mail to the ships in time.

"Our business men generally prefer to pay the double postage," the *Alta* said.

> He who depends on the mail for his newspaper, finds his neighbor who relies on the Express, will have it read through, and can lend it to him, while he is waiting for the Post Office to open....
>
> People have got an idea that the Post Office is a great blessing; and so it once was. But the people have got ahead of it.... Congress at the last session, while everywhere else it materially reduced the rates of postage, increased it for us. They not only increased it, but they required us to pay an increased postage whether we make use of the mails or not.... There is a regular system of espionage set over us to bleed us if we break into the Government monopoly. To sum all up, it is a tyrannical and useless institution and ought to be abolished. Let this matter be borne in mind by the people... and Congress will not long force it upon us.

Strong language! And yet not entirely without justification. The government, of course, had many problems—if that helps. For instance, the salary of a postmaster was fixed at $2,400 a year, and he was required to give bond, but a sailor or a teamster could make $300 a month and almost as much more from moonlighting, and have no problems with a bond and no financial accountability.

Naturally, too, the post office officials were displeased at the express companies' taking over their function, and such a deeply intrenched and wideflung arm of the government was not likely to give up without a fight. Alexander Todd had understood that and had had himself sworn in as a postal clerk when he started carrying mail. (His business of buying worn copies of the New York papers for $1 and selling them in the Gold Country for $8 had no direct connection with his postal activities.) However, the postmaster at San Francisco cut in on Todd's profits by charging him twenty-five cents for each letter Todd carried. (More likely, it was to allay his annoyance at having Todd hold up the line of men waiting for mail while Todd went down his list of some two thousand names and forced the clerk to look for each one.[16]) Before long, the postmasters at Stockton and Sacramento did the same thing—and thus letters from the East, at first, cost sixty-five cents per half ounce in postage. (In the very beginning a letter had cost the miner $16 in his hands.)

The express companies generally did not go through the formality of putting their agents under the Post Office, but set their rates for what the traffic would bear, and continued to deliver mail to the Gold Country and to pick it up. Wells Fargo had a letter-collection service in San Francisco, and by 1862 its green boxes on various corners of San Francisco competed with the red boxes of the Post Office Department. (It is said, too, that Wells Fargo boxes got the most business.)

Much later (after 1870), Wells Fargo had its famous band of letter ponies—some thirty-five ponies that were kept saddled and waiting—and for twenty-five cents a Wells Fargo rider would deliver a letter anywhere in the city.[17]

However, in 1854, the Post Office Department

had a fight to keep the letter business in its own hands, and one of its first moves was to require that all letters carried by anybody whatsoever must bear a United States postage stamp, and it threatened that any express found with letters without such stamps would be fined $50; therefore, both Wells Fargo and Adams announced in the *Alta California* in January, 1854, that all letters carried by them must bear a post-office stamp or be carried in a post-office envelope.

In March, the usual mail did not stop at San Diego, and the San Diego *Herald* screamed about it on April 8:

The steamer *John L. Stephens* was distinctly seen by one of our Pilots, on Friday last, the 31st ult., close off Point Lobo, but she did not heave to. This is really too bad, as the mail she brought from the Atlantic States will not now reach us, till the 17th; that is to say, if the steamer *Goliah* continues *her late* regularity.[18]

We ask with all humiliation, if we are ever going to have any relief from this tardiness? *Seventeen* days difference in our receipts of perhaps important dispatches. Are not our relations with Mexico of such a nature that we should know something of what is going on? Is our military post, now being augmented, to be cut off from *direct* communication with the heads of the different departments at Washington? Are we to continue to send all our correspondence destined for the Eastern States, to San Francisco first? We sincerely hope not, and *crave* some amelioration of our present condition. . . .

Acknowledgments are due, and we hereby tender them to Purser Flemming, of the *Goliah,* to Purser Dean of the *Fremont,* to Adams & Co., to Wells & Co., and last, though not least, to J. W. Sullivan, for innumerable favors received from all during the present week. Without you, gentlemen, we should have no intelligence of passing events, either on the Atlantic or Pacific coast, seeing that the *regular* mail steamers no longer call here.

Mail was much more than a means of satisfying curiosity. Inasmuch as many men in California had left behind their wives and families, there was a very deep and genuine concern over the welfare of those at home. Such a case was that of one Joseph Glines, who, in 1851, left his wife and four daughters in Wisconsin while he went to the mines to make his fortune. Glines was a sober family man, and went for nothing except the stake that every man dreams about but so few obtain. Some time after he got to Rough and Ready, a fifth daughter was born, but before Glines even found out her name, the mother got cholera and died, and the new daughter got cholera and died. Then Joseph Glines was in a far-away land, unable to return to his four motherless daughters, unable even to send them money. He had to gather himself as best he could and write a letter of reassurance to his oldest daughter, and encourage her to hold the little family together until he could get back to Wisconsin.

Will you not, my dear Lucinda, write me a letter? . . . . I long for the time to come when I shall return. I have often thought what a comfort it would be, if you could be with me. . . . Imagine yourself by the side of your Pa, on a pleasant Sabbath evening. We will pluck some beautiful wild pinks which fall in our path . . . and a thousand other wild flowers. . . . We look over a dense, heavy forest of pine, a range of mountains still covered with snow. Toward the setting sun we see high mountains. Further to the south, . . . the broad and beautiful valley of the Sacramento . . . thousands of cattle, horses and mules grazing.

He was having a hard time getting to the subject that weighed so heavily on his mind, but he finally did it in verse:

'Tis now one year since I left home, and all to me on earth so dear. It pleased an all-wise providence to call from earth, unto the skies, one held in fond remembrance whose soul is now in Paradise. On you and Mary, now devolves the care of little sisters dear, be gentle, mild and kind to all. Teach Caroline and Libby well, that they may fear the sinner's road, to shun the path of vice and hell, and walk in that which leads to God. Go visit oft, the sacred spot where you have laid your Mother dead, and do not let it be forgot that you or I may lie there near.

But I must close my letter for it is now late at night, and the boys are snoring away while I am sitting in the corner writing off my knee. O! how often do I think of you, my dear children. Indeed, it is seldom that you are absent from my thoughts. Give my love to your grandmama, and best respects to any inquiring friends. I send you all my love, and a thousand kisses to little Libby.[19]

A helpless father with an overburdened heart was not likely to be patient with poor mail service.

A good description of mail service in the early days may be taken from a "Pocket Letter Book" of

Gregory's Express—a small (less than three by five inches folded) stapled notebook of forty blank pages covered with paper black-coated on the outside and printed in gold:

to facilitate correspondence between . . . [illegible] of towns, and the mining district of California, and . . . tants of the United States. Gregory's United States and California Express. [The inside cover says:] This Line, . . . being invariably ahead of the mails, the best medium is presented to the care of mercantile houses, or well-known residents, in San Francisco or other parts of California, by which means their earlier delivery may be insured. Letters directed simply to "California," or "at the mines," will not be forwarded, as little probability exists of their reaching the persons so vaguely addressed. After addressing the letter, enclose it in an envelope, and direct to J. W. GREGORY, post-paid to New-York.

The writer of this letter, William Miller, also gives a picture of the miner's feeling about mail:

December the 7 1851 i received your leter yester day dated sep the 6, 1851 i was glad to hear from you for I have looked for letters until i got tiard of asking the post masters for letters. this is the 15th letter that I have rote to you since i left home and received 4 letter from you and the friends . . .

He comments on California. Though some did not like it, he is one of the many who did:

i am sorry to here that thare has been so many deaths around you this is a very healthy country as i would like to se [?] and the best climate it isent to cold or to hot it haint so chaingeable as the states is wre I had [?] this last summer and fill 6 months of dry weather i dont recollect of its raining enough to wet mans shirt sleaves this is the country that i would like to live in if there was some sosiety as there is in the states but as there is none i escpect to return to the states some time in fifty-two if i live and keep my health and make enough money i maynt come home ontil nexct fall . . .

His next sentences give a picture of economic conditions, social conditions, and some other things:

i am working for $100 a month that would be big wages in the states i am well ia present and i hope these few lines may find you the same the boys is all well at present Johy is 75 miles southe a working for four dollars a day and grub i sent my best respets to you all and the serronding friends this sunday night and i must quit and go to bed and be ready for mornings grnd [grind?] and then i must towhal [does he mean *trabajo*?] all day hard for quottro paso [*cuatro pesos*—four dollars] res [?].

The suffering immigrants here seem to be in various postures of supplication—some of them to God, some to dead or dying relatives. Since the moon is up, they are not suffering from heat, but they may be dying of thirst and starvation, and possibly cholera. From Frank Soulé, et al., "Annals of San Francisco."

As you have rote all about the ups and downs in your parts so i will rite to you something about the habits in this contry in this part the watch word is playing cards and gambling of all sorts. thare has bin a many a boy spoild by comeing to this contry he would get to playing cards and drinking and beting money and sometimes they would win and then they would think they kowed [knowed] it all and the first time they knew they los it all and then they would say i will try and get my money back again and then i will quit it and geting it back they loose as much more and so it goes as for my part they have the first dollar to get out of me yet if i do say it myself about 4 miles from this place whare i have worked this season the gamblers has killed several men they would get to betting and loose than raise fuss and the gambler would pull out a pistole an as like as not shoot him down as i dont like that way doing i dont go a near them i thint it is a poor place for a man to go to pass the time of anyhow but there is hundreds of people go ther on saturday night and sonday and rip and tare drink gmble and spend thare money . . .

i will tell you about the mines as near as i can they rivers is worked out they say so as to not make more than 3 to 5 dollars a day in the most [illegible] places there is some ravines that woul pay tollerable good wages if there was watter but it has the appearance of a dry winter and i think it is better to work for the wages that i am getting than run about to hunt beter digings and run they resk of finding worse they quartz rock is they principal mining about here now there is any amount of mills about here now they bigest part of them is a doing well i thin one or to men without a mahine cant do much rock that will pay forty dollars to 50 those mills can make money fast if they can get they rock up easy say one or two men go to getting up quarts on there one hook and it will cost them from 8 to 10 16 dollars a ton and then pay 1 to 2 dollars acording to the distance then 25 dollars a ton for crushing it yoursel it wont pay of they laber and suppose it only pays thirty or 40 dollars a ton and then a man would come out at they little end of the horn thats nothing more than common . . .

Then he tells of some of the high jinks of financing among the miners:

some times there will on[e] or two come to me and say to me i hav been a stakeing of a very rich lead dont you want a shear [share] in it i say to them do you think it is rich and they will say i dont think any thing about it i know it is i say to them you had better keep it and work it they sa nothing they have got more than they can work says one to me you are a fine son [?] looking fellow i will give you a chance to make your fortune if you will give me some say 100 hundred dollars some say 500 some say 1000 thousand il say to them do you think it is so much as that and the other one will sep [step] up and say y [?] pardner you are a fool for offering it so cheap as that and the other one would say i know it is cheap [but] being as i said i would let him have it i wont back out then he will say will you give to make the keen [?] i will tell him i will studdy on it an our or so directly here they come again and say are you agoing to take it i will tell them in a pigs eye i am and then they are mad enough they would think by the way i talked i was going to take it and them laughing to think how they was a going to cheat me.

William Miller.[20]

Undoubtedly it was the post office's insistence on its own prerogatives that led the *Alta* to print its caustic editorial of July 13, 1855—not entirely without justification. The post office carried the mail, it is true, but *efficiency* is hardly a word compatible with its service. Wells Fargo went far into the interior, into the Gold Country, and facilitated business by carrying mail and delivering it.

In 1855, the Post Office Department in Washington instructed the postmaster of San Francisco to seize all mail carried by express companies. But, as before and as afterward, the East reckoned without the wild spirit of the West. The businessmen of San Francisco dared the postmaster to seize their mail; the postmaster, wiser perhaps than his masters in Washington, did not try to enforce the order.

It rather seems that letter mail was an important part of Wells Fargo's business from two standpoints: It built up the people's faith in Wells Fargo's integrity, and it certainly made a profit for the company (or the company would not have gone to such lengths to carry it). It also brought Wells Fargo to thousands of miners as a company that could be depended on. And more: When a miner, three thousand miles from home and six months without a letter from his wife, espied the Wells Fargo man on his mule, and when that same man delivered into his hands the long-awaited letter from home—well, just how much more pleasant an image can any company create?

In the East, the officers must have watched with some concern over the events of that wild February of the banking panic, but they had not been idle. In January, they had discontinued the Paris office because the operation of the business of Livingston, Wells & Company was unprofitable, and the president was instructed to call upon that company for a settlement of the amount still due to Wells, Fargo & Company.

On May 14, the capital stock was increased to $600,000; the additional $100,000 was to be sold to stockholders at $80 per share, according to their present holdings, and any unsubscribed stock was to be sold on the open market.

On September 12, the directors voted another 5 percent dividend, making 10 percent for the year of 1855. The only change in the board of directors was in the addition of William I. Pardee, the general manager for California.

United States mail service in the Sierra Nevada Mountains, as illustrated in R. Guy McClellan, "The Golden State."

During the crisis or as a result of it, Thomas Janes, the treasurer of Wells Fargo, had been sent from New York to take charge of the company's operations, and in October he appointed Louis McLane general manager—soon after the headquarters was moved to the Parrott Building. (McLane is said to have been a navy lieutenant on the frigate *Savannah,* and was in Monterey in July, 1846, when Captain John D. Sloat [he was not made commodore until 1862], commander of the Pacific squadron of the United States Navy, ran up the Stars and Stripes over Monterey.[21])

The Bakersfield area, at the south end of California's great inland valley, got into the news again when the New York *Tribune* printed an item on August 28, 1855:

Kern River Again.—The Stockton Argus learns from a reliable gentleman just from the Kern River country that the miners on White River, Kern River, Greenhorn and Rich Gulch, and all through that vicinity, are now opening rich quartz veins. When he left Greenhorn there were nine *arrasters*[22] running, and nine or ten veins opened. The miners were all busy making *arrasters,* and men were wanted at $60 to $70 and board per month, but could not be hired. All hands were hunting and opening quartz veins; the veins were from four to ten inches wide, running through decayed granite and slate; they now pay $10 per day to the hand. The country is full of quartz veins, and the gold is very fine and generally diffused through the mass; there are not many rich spots or pockets in the veins, like other veins in other parts of the country, but all the veins are impregnated with fine flour gold, and paying fair wages, say 4 to 30 per cent to the pound [?]. He showed some very pretty specimens of quartz. . . . There are about one hundred miners in the Kern River region.

While the miners were busy making *arrastras,* other ambitious men were moving in other directions; in May, 1855, William Walker reentered the filibuster stage by sailing for Nicaragua with fifty odd men; he had a contract to take three hundred colonists, and on the strength of this contract he secured the necessary money to charter and fit out

The remains of an arrastra *built in the back country of San Diego County probably about 1900. The iron in the center revolved, suspending boulders or heavy iron weights to break up the ore. There is an old dam on Pine Creek about a quarter of a mile above this* arrastra, *and probably water was piped to the* arrastra *and run through it during the crushing, since the door on the south side would provide an outlet. Photograph by the author.*

Louis McLane in his younger days. From Ira Cross, "Financing an Empire."

a vessel with the backing of F. Argenti, the Italian banker.

Walker's brig, the *Vesta,* was still under attachments to the tune of $350, and in fact was host to a deputy sheriff trying to collect a meat bill, but Walker got under sail just the same; all his men had had military experience, and all were armed. Fit colonists all! And as soon as Walker got his men into Nicaragua, he attacked a garrison of one thousand soldiers in Rivas, one of Nicaragua's principal towns; one hundred natives were killed. It now appears that Walker was playing politics and trying to put himself in position to acquire considerably more than the original 170 acres per man. Walker fought a number of battles, and was reinforced by more men from San Francisco. Walker had taken sides in a civil war and was hoping to pull off a coup and become the virtual owner of Nicaragua. It is easy to see that in such a bold enterprise there were vast fortunes to be made overnight if Walker should be successful; a whole country was at stake, and Walker fought Nicaraguans, Guatemalans, Costa Ricans, and Salvadorians before it was over. In 1857, he canceled the contract of the Accessory Transit Company, and brought down the wrath of Vanderbilt, who organized an expedition from Costa Rica[23] that captured the lake and river transportation and hampered Walker considerably.

Meanwhile, the U. S. sloop-of-war *Cyane* had shelled the Nicaraguan town of San Juan del Norte and aroused the indignation of the American press.

William Walker, the gray-eyed man of destiny who failed at everything he tried. Educated in law and medicine, experienced as a politician and as a newspaper editor, he even failed to fall in love with a desirable girl in New Orleans who wanted him (fortunately for her). Like many filibusterers, he died before a firing squad, after fighting, at one time, Great Britain, Cornelius Vanderbilt, and several Central American republics.

Parker H. French, of notoriety in many fields, arrived on the scene and initiated an abortive attack on Fort San Carlos but was defeated. French went to Washington as minister from Nicaragua, but was not recognized. He was also involved in fund-raising, and as a matter of fact a great deal of money was poured into Nicaragua by American bankers during those bloody times, but most sources (perhaps all sources) are noticeably reticent in naming the men who financed Walker's filibuster in Nicaragua.[24]

Edward Bosqui says that Palmer, Cook & Company was not involved in the Walker affair, but Wiltsee's *Gold Rush Steamers* says that the *Uncle Sam* arrived in Nicaragua in October with a box of bullion containing $20,000 in gold bars consigned by Palmer, Cook & Company to J. Cook, Jr., New York.[25]

C. J. Macdonald had just arrived in San Juan del Sur as a special agent of Palmer, Cook & Company to see to the safe conduct of passengers and treasure across the isthmus of Nicaragua for the Accessory Transit Company, and he authorized the agent of the Accessory Transit Company to deliver the $20,000 worth of gold bars to Colonel C. C. Hornsby[26] of Walker's army. The delivery was fully receipted. Then the agent of the transit company went to the American minister and protested the delivery. Walker said the facts were true enough, but he, as head of the government in Nicaragua, authorized it. Some high-level hanky-panky was going on, and the only one who protested was the agent—not Palmer, Cook & Company. Joseph N. Scott, the agent who protested, said, on the other hand, that Walker placed a strong guard on the steamer *San Carlos* under Scott's charge, and demanded the box "supposed to contain twenty thousand dollars."[27]

It was a real fight between Garrison and Vanderbilt, and Walker was in on the ground floor. He blocked the crossing of Vanderbilt's passengers, and Vanderbilt retaliated by organizing an army of three thousand Costa Ricans.[28]

It seems that C. K. Garrison sold the transit company to William Garrison, and Vanderbilt sued C. K. Garrison for $500,000. In fact, suits of all kinds popped up in various courts, and during this time it was learned that Vanderbilt had received $40,000 a month from the transit company.

Verily, there were many opportunities for a banker with a slight flair for speculation to go wrong in those times in Nicaragua, and a large amount of money will always be sourceless as far as the records are concerned.

The filibustering activities are important in San Francisco's banking history because of the known bankers who put up money for them, the others who are unknown, and the possible effect of their losses on other banks in San Francisco, as well as the ultimate effects if they had been successful in their backing.

While some were gambling during those years, it appears that Wells, Fargo & Company stayed out of all such questionable complications. However, during 1855, Wells Fargo started a rate war that led to a general agreement with competing companies within six months. It may be assumed that Pacific Express was the company aimed at.

In September, 1855, a fire in Grass Valley gave Alonzo Delano, the Wells Fargo agent there, a chance to advertise Wells Fargo.

> A fire broke out in the United States Hotel and rapidly spread to the adjoining buildings. The vault of Wells Fargo & Company withstood the hottest of the fire and preserved its valuable contents. The loss was especially great because the merchants had just laid in large stocks of goods for the fall trade . . . the most notable example of energy of action (of the people of Grass Valley) was that of A. Delano, agent for Wells, Fargo & Company. About an hour after the astonished sun had gazed upon the scene of desolation, a frame shanty was seen moving down the hill from the west end of the town. Slowly but surely it advanced and was backed up against Wells, Fargo & Company's brick vault, which was still standing among the ruins. In a few moments "Old Block" appeared with a sign on which was painted, "Wells, Fargo & Co.'s Express Office." In less than eight hours after the cry of fire had alarmed the midnight air, "Old Block" stood smiling behind his counter, amid the smouldering ruins and with the ground still warm beneath his feet, ready, as he said, "to attend to business."[29]

With men like that, how could Wells Fargo lose?

On December 31, 1855, Wells, Fargo & Company had agencies in fifty-five towns in California, Idaho Territory, Arizona Territory, and Oregon; the towns were Angels Camp, Auburn, Benicia; Boston (Idaho Territory); Camp Seco, Camptonville, Carrollton, Cherokee, Coloma, Columbia, Crescent City, Diamond Springs, Downieville, El Dorado, Fiddletown, Forest City, French Bar, Georgetown, Goodyear Bar, Grass Valley, Hornitos, Iowa Hill, Jackson, Jamestown, Los Angeles, Mariposa, Marysville, Michigan Bar, Michigan City, Mok Hill, Mormon Island, Napa City, Nevada (City), New York; Oroville, Arizona Territory;[30] Petaluma, Philadelphia, Placerville; Portland, Oregon; Prairie City, Rattlesnake, Red Bluff, Rough and Ready, Sacramento, San Andreas, San Francisco, San Jose, Shasta, Sonora, Stockton, Timbuctoo, Vallecito,[31] Volcano, and Yankee Jim's.

A list dated only six weeks earlier had appeared in the *Bulletin,* giving the address of the new location in New York (82 Broadway), and listing the agents at "principal offices." This list shows three offices at places not mentioned in the list from L. O. Head's "Minutes": Colusa, Doton's Bar, and Ione Valley. It is also informative in the names of agents:

Angels Camp: C. G. Lake, agent.
Auburn: J. Q. Jackson, agent.
Benecia: Shirley & Co., agents.
Coloma: Wm. McConnell & Co., agents.
Columbia: Wm. Deagener, agent.
Colusa: John W. Wood, agent.
Crescent City: D. W. McComb, agent.
Diamond Springs: O. McKnight, agent.
Doton's Bar: Palmer & Baldwin, agents.
El Dorado: T. J. Orgon, agent.
Georgetown: Conness & Reed, agents.
Grass Valley: A. Delano, agent.
Honolulu: R. Coady, agent.
Hornitas: Barton & Barkley, agents.
Ione Valley: Milo H. Turner, agent.
Iowa Hill: T. B. Hotchkiss, agent.
Jackson, E. E. Barney, agent.
Jamestown: B. Randall, agent.
Los Angeles: H. R. Myles, agent.
Mariposa: J. B. Condon, agent.
Marysville: C. H. Hedges, agent.
Michigan Bar: Kingsbury & Kingsley, agents.
Michigan City: C. T. Blake, agent.
Mokelumne Hill: J. P. Gilley, agent.
Monterey: A. Smith, agent.
Mormon Island: Luman Smith, agent.
Nevada: Wm. Hewett, agent.
Oregon City: John M. Bancher, agent.
Panama: Hurtado & Bros., agents.
Petaluma: S. C. Hayden, agent.

A receipt given by Baldwin & Co., Wells Fargo agents at Rattlesnake, in 1855 for a check for $100 that they forwarded to San Francisco for collection. The original is in the History Room, Wells Fargo Bank.

WELLS, FARGO & CO'S
EXPRESS & EXCHANGE COMPANY,
CAPITAL, $500,000,
PRINCIPAL OFFICES, { 16 WALL-STREET, NEW-YORK, 114 MONTGOMERY-ST., SAN FRANCISCO.

Wells, Fargo & Co's Express.

Value, $ Rattlesnake Mch 2d 1855

Received from John Peller

Check from Forest City Office #281. "One Hundred"

Addressed Wells Fargo & Co

which we agree to forward to San Francisco for collection

and deliver proceeds to order of John Peller

W. F. & Co.. will not be responsible for the contents of any valuable package unless that value is expressed in the receipt. nor will they be responsible for any loss or damage from Fire, or the dangers and accidents of Navigation and Transportation. from goods being improperly packed, or from any cause whatever. unless the same be proved to have occurred from the fraud or gross negligence of ourselves. our agents or servants.

For the Proprietors,

Baldwin & Co
agts.

Placerville: Alex Hunter, agent.
Portland: Jas. O'Neil, agent.
Rattlesnake Bar: Baldwin & Co., agents.[32]
Red Bluff: E. W. Goodrich, agent.
Sacramento: W. B. Rochester, agent; A. B. McNeil, cashier.
San Andreas: Kolberg & Co., agents.
San Diego: E. B. Pendleton, agent.
Santa Barbara: F. J. McGuire, agent.
Santa Clara: Straney & Bros., agents.
San Jose: Elliott Reed, agent.
Shasta: Samuel Knight, agent.
Sonora: W. H. Simmons, agent.
Stockton: J. M. Vansyckle, agent; T. R. Anthony, cashier.
Vallecito: L. Dinkelspiel & Co., agents.
Volcano: Hanford & Downs, agents.
Yankee Jims: W. Winchester, Jr., agent.

Directors and officers for 1855 were the same as those at the end of 1854. On February 15, 1855, a dividend of 5 percent was paid, and on September 12, a like dividend was paid.

All in all, San Francisco and, indeed, all of California endured a severe blow in 1855, but the boundless go-ahead-ism was still there. The new gold discoveries at the Kern River mines in the Bakersfield area were in the process of development, but the most important factor was a change in the way of doing business.

1856
Year of the Vigilantes

THE HECTIC FINANCIAL EVENTS OF 1855 marked a change in the conduct of business in California, or even, perhaps, brought it about. More nonminers were coming to California all the time, and they were looking for some stability. Perhaps the old free-and-easy method of doing business—trust and hope because there may be a big strike tomorrow—would never entirely disappear, but it was about to undergo some serious changes. Wells, Fargo & Company was firm in the saddle as the leading express company and the leading banking company in California; the Sacramento Valley Railroad was finished on February 22, 1856, to Folsom (and stopped for lack of money; its owners had wanted to go on to Placerville).

An unpleasant situation had developed in the express business in the latter part of 1855, perhaps as a result of Wells Fargo's rate war: The express business had earned for Wells Fargo in September, 1855, exactly $21.69, but in October it had lost $1,634.49, in November $1,940.92, and in December $3,712.80—a total operating loss for the last four months of 1855 of $7,127.27. It was this fact that prompted the board of directors on February 20, 1856, to appoint Louis McLane, general agent for California; Garrett W. Bell, superintendent of the exchange department; and Charles F. Higgins, superintendent of the express department, an executive committee for California; and, a few days later (on March 5) T. M. Janes a special agent for California, "with full powers."[1]

Early in January, 1856, Wells Fargo published in the *Alta California* a new list of offices corrected as of January 1, and this list is different enough from the one in the *Herald* in 1855 to warrant reproduction. The list now is divided into two sections, of which the first is "express and banking agencies": Sacramento, Stockton, Marysville, and Shasta (with the same agents as in 1855); and Portland, with Jas. O'Neill as agent.

The second section is of "express agencies"; there are many different names among the agents, and there are twenty-four new agencies. A great many changes had been made in the preceding two months:

Angel's Camp: C. G. Lake, agent.
Auburn: J. Q. Jackson, agent.
Benicia: Shirley & Co., agent.
Campo Seco: Root Bros., agent.
Camptonville: Stephen Dorsey, agent.
Carrollton: Palmer & Baldwin, agent.
Cherokee: George W. Turney, agent.
Coloma: W. McConnell & Co., agent.
Columbia: Wm. Daegener, agent.
Colusi [Colusa]: John H. Wood, agent.
Crescent City: D. W. McComb, agent.
Diamond Springs: E. N. Strout, agent.
Downieville: B. M. Fetter, agent.
El Dorado: T. J. Orgon, agent.
Fiddletown: J. W. Kendall, agent.
Forest City: H. W. Theall, agent.
French Bar: Peck & Co., agent.
Georgetown: Conness & Reed, agent.

UNITED STATES MAIL STEAMSHIP COMPANY, 309

Connecting with the Pacific Mail Steamship Company,

Carrying the Great United States Mail for California and Oregon, via Aspinwall and Panama.

CHEAPEST AND BEST ROUTE.

Leaving New York at 2 P. M., on the 5th and 20th of each month, FROM WARREN STREET PIER, NORTH RIVER.

The public are informed that the P. M. S. S. Co. always have ONE OR MORE EXTRA STEAMERS laying at Panama, to provide against accidents; and as these facilities are not possessed by any other line on this or any other route to California, this is the only line that can guarantee through passages without detention, and at the lowest rates.

The U. S. M. S. Co. have 10 first class steamers on the Atlantic, and the Pacific Mail S. Co. 16 first class steamers plying between Panama and San Francisco, commanded by government officers, each steamer having a surgeon at the service of the passengers.

Passengers will be landed at the Railroad Wharf at Aspinwall, free. Transit of the Isthmus at the passenger's expense. The railroad is in operation to Gorgona, doing away with the river navigation. The expense of the transit varies from $12 to $30, according to amount of baggage. For Freight or passage apply to

CHARLES A. WHITNEY,

At the Office of the Companies, 177 West Street, cor. Warren, New York.

A card to advertise the United States Mail Steamship Company in the Atlantic Ocean, and the Pacific Mail Steamship Company in the Pacific Ocean, carrying the Great United States Mail for California and Oregon. From the collection of Edgar B. Jessup.

The Wells Fargo express office in the Parrott Building. On the left are the mail-boxes, and at the left rear is the door to the bank. There is "Interior Express" (probably West Coast) and "New York Express" (which probably included most express sent by steamer). Original sketch by Durin Van Vleck, later an associate of William Keith. From the History Room, Wells Fargo Bank.

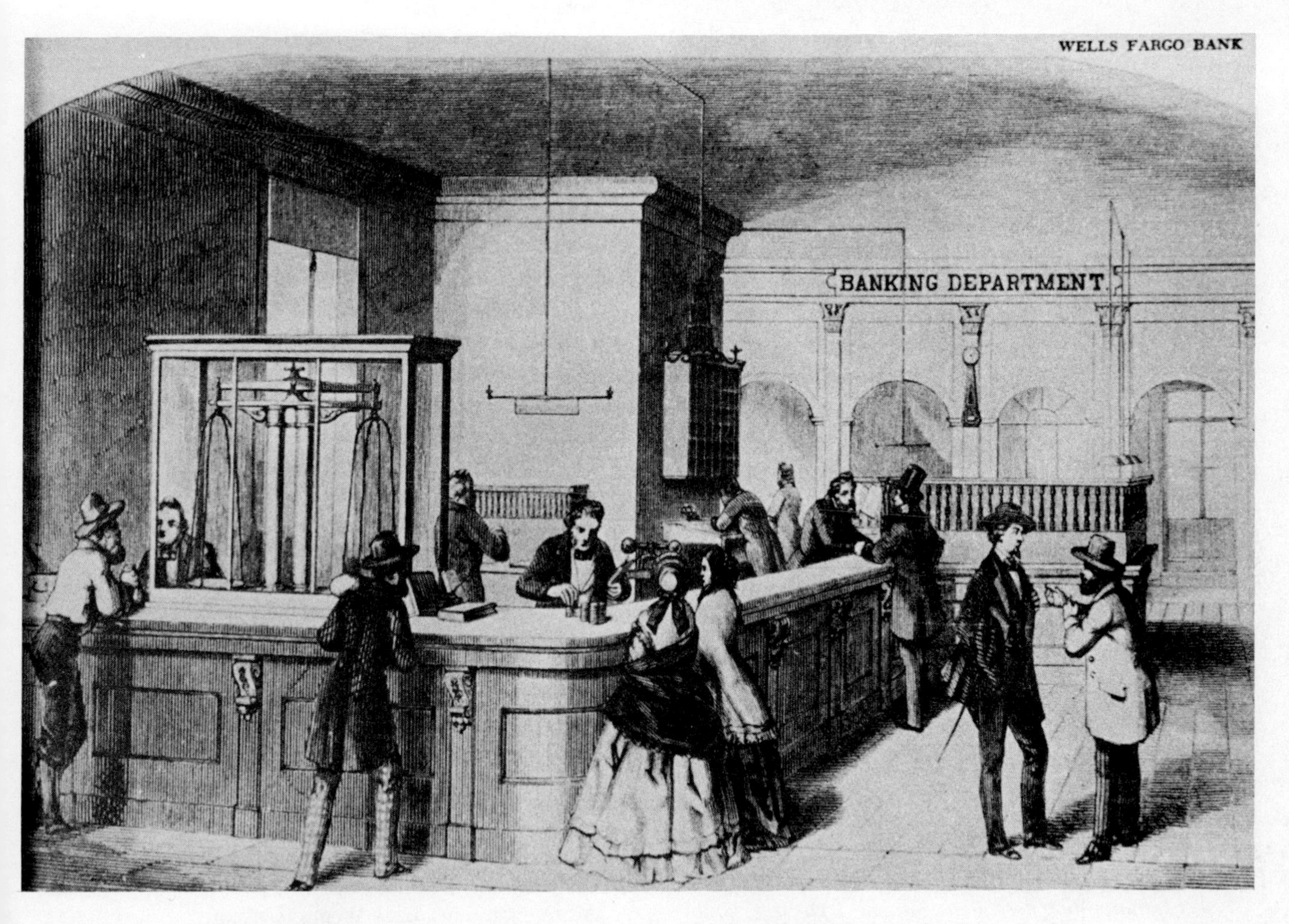

The Wells Fargo banking department in the Parrott Building. At the left are the famous gold scales, in the center a teller is counting out gold coin ($20 pieces, obviously), and in the background a single bookkeeper works at his accounts. Banking then was a department of Wells, Fargo & Company (and technically would remain so—although an important one—for over fifty years). From the History Room, Wells Fargo Bank.

Goodyear's Bar: Beauchamp & Wood, agent.
Grass Valley: C. B. Haskell, agent.
Greenwood: E. C. Ferguson, agent.
Honolulu: R. Coady & Co., agent.
Hornitas: Burton & Barker, agent.
Ione Valley: J. W. Gish, agent.
Iowa Hill: T. B. Hotchkiss, agent.
Jackson: S. P. Dorsey, agent.
Jamestown: B. Randall, agent.
Knight's Ferry: G. W. Dent, agent.
Los Angeles: H. Alexander, agent.
Mariposa: J. B. Condon, agent.
Michigan Bar: Kingsbury & Pollard, agent.
Michigan City: C. T. Blake, agent.
Mokelumne Hill: J. P. Gilly, agent.
Monterey: M. & L. Little, agent.
Mormon Island: ——— Rohrer, agent.
Napa City: E. R. Weaver, agent.

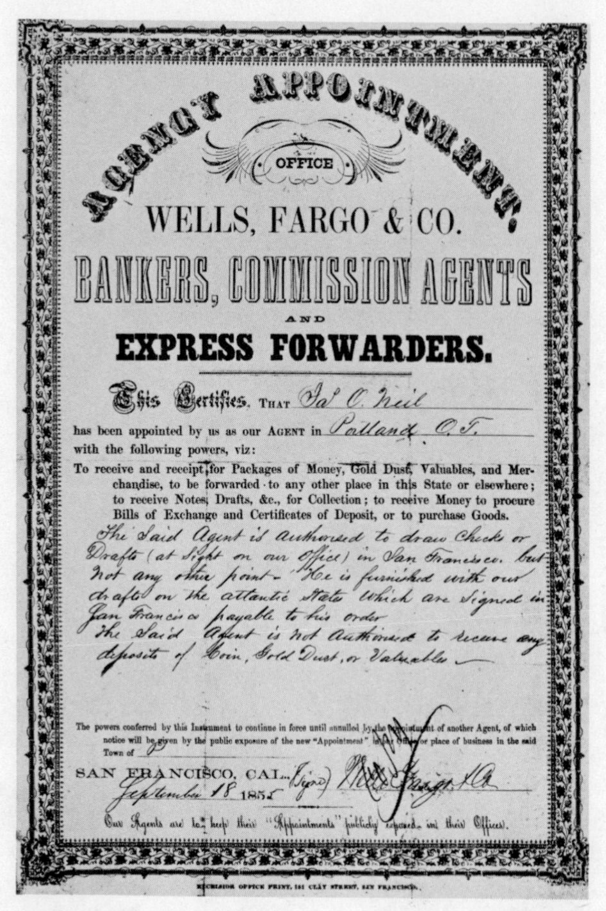
AGENCY APPOINTMENTS.

OFFICE

WELLS, FARGO & CO.

BANKERS, COMMISSION AGENTS

AND

EXPRESS FORWARDERS.

This Certifies, THAT Jas O. Neil

has been appointed by us as our AGENT in Portland O. T.

with the following powers, viz:

To receive and receipt for Packages of Money, Gold Dust, Valuables, and Merchandise, to be forwarded to any other place in this State or elsewhere; to receive Notes, Drafts, &c., for Collection; to receive Money to procure Bills of Exchange and Certificates of Deposit, or to purchase Goods.

The Said Agent is authorised to draw Checks or Drafts (at Sight on our Office) in San Francisco. but not any other point - He is furnished with our drafts on the atlantic States which are Signed in San Francisco payable to his order

The Said Agent is not authorised to receive any deposits of Coin, Gold Dust, or Valuables —

The powers conferred by this Instrument to continue in force until annulled by the appointment of another Agent, of which notice will be given by the public exposure of the new "Appointment" in our Office or place of business in the said Town of

SAN FRANCISCO, CAL. September 18 1855 (Signed) Wells Fargo & Co

Our Agents are to keep their "Appointments" publicly exposed in their Offices.

EXCELSIOR OFFICE PRINT, 151 CLAY STREET, SAN FRANCISCO.

An agency appointment for Jas. O. Neil at Portland, Oregon Teritory, dated September 18, 1855. It is signed merely, "Wells, Fargo & Co." Only one or two men had the right to sign that way, according to Frederick L. Lipman—the president and the treasurer, and possibly the vice-president.

Nevada: C. H. Mead, agent.
Oregon City: J. N. Bancker, agent.
Orleans Flat: Jas. R. Spencer, agent.
Oroville: Jas. McWilliams, agent.
Panama: Hurtado & Bros., agent.
Petaluma: S. C. Hayden, agent.
Placerville: W. H. Mansfield, agent.
Prairie City: H. F. Kellum, agent.
Rattlesnake Bar: Baldwin & Co., agent.
Red Bluff: E. W. Goodrich, agent.
Rough and Ready: E. B. Comstock, agent.
San Andreas: Wood K. Knight, agent.
San Diego: E. B. Pendleton, agent.
San Jose: Elliott Reed, agent.
Santa Barbara: F. J. McGuire, agent.
Santa Clara: Strasser & Bro., agent.
Sebastopol: J. W. Dudley, agent.
Sonoma: E. B. Weaver, agent.
Sonora: E. S. Osgood, agent.
Timbuctoo: A. Stewart, agent.
Vallecito: L. Dinkelspiel & Co., agent.
Volcano: Hanford & Downs, agent.
Yankee Jim's: W. Winchester, Jr., agent.
Doton's Bar has been dropped.

Two facts are obvious: The number of agencies has almost doubled, and Wells Fargo has gone down the coast to San Diego. Likewise, there have been many changes in personnel. It seems that much of the deficit in profit must have come from the expense of establishing new offices; it also appears that the established agencies were considerably shaken up in late 1855.

Also, it may be significant that Louis McLane was using the *Alta California* more than it had been used formerly; he was running a fairly long advertisement for Wells Fargo's banking services, and a quite long advertisement of express services.

This advertisement ran through January, 1856; through February (corrected as of February 1); and well into March (corrected as of March 1). The March list shows changes of agents, moves of agents from one place to another, and several new agencies:

Drytown: Burt & Co., agent.
Folsom: Luman Smith, agent.
Indian Diggings: Alex McGregor, agent.
Jackson: W. S. Butler, agent.
Mormon Island: Ezra Woolson, agent.
Murphy's: J. Palache, agent (new agency).
Napa City: J. W. Dudley, agent (moved from Sebastopol).
Nevada: C. H. Mead, agent.
Oregon City: J. N. Banker, agent.
San Andreas: Wood K. Knight (name corrected).
San Juan: Clark & Seely, agent.
Sebastopol: R. Corwin, agent.
Shasta: A. B. Brown (in addition to the "banking and express" agency).
Sonoma: Fred Rohrer, agent (probably moved from Mormon Island).
Sonora: W. H. Simmons, agent.
Sutter Creek: Handford & Wildman, agent (new).
Uniontown (H. B. [Humboldt County?]): B. F. Wyman, agent (new).
Vallejo: G. R. Jaques, agent (new).

Yankee Jim's: S. P. Dorsey, agent (moved from Jackson).

Wells Fargo in its advertising warns that agents must keep their appointments on display;[2] therefore, it is appropriate to consider the form and wording of an "appointment." The printed appointment of James O. Neil [sic] at Portland, Oregon, reads as follows:

Agency Appointment. Office Wells, Fargo & Co. Bankers, Commission Agents and Express Forwarders. This certifies, that Jas. O. Neil has been appointed by us as our Agent in Portland, O. T. [Oregon Territory] with the following powers, viz:

To receive and receipt for Packages of Money, Gold Dust, Valuables, and Merchandise, to be forwarded to any other place in this State or elsewhere; to receive Notes, Drafts, &c., for Collection; to receive Money to procure Bills of Exchange and Certificates of Deposit, or to purchase Goods.

[This paragraph hand-written] The Said Agent is authorized to draw Checks or Drafts (at Sight on our office) in San Francisco, but not any other point. He is furnished with our drafts on the Atlantic States which are signed in San Francisco payable to his order. The Said Agent is not authorized to receive any deposits of Coin, Gold Dust, or Valuables.

[Printed] The powers conferred by this Instrument to continue in force until annulled by the appointment of another Agent, of which notice will be given by the public exposure of the new "Appointment" in our Office or place of business in the said Town of P.

San Francisco, Cal., September 18, 1855.

(Signed) Wells Fargo & Co.

Our Agents are to keep their "Appointments" publicly exposed in their Offices.[3]

The Portland agent's banking powers were definitely separated from his activities as express agent, for he could receive money, gold dust, or valuables for forwarding but not for deposit.

In January, 1856, there were many banking advertisements in the *Alta California* by: Drexel, Sather & Church; Parrott & Co. (Parrott was the owner of the Adams Express building into which Wells Fargo had moved after the big panic of 1855); Lucas, Turner & Co.; Alsop & Co. (for Duncan, Sherman & Co., which had been vigorously blamed by the *Alta* for the downfall of Page, Bacon & Co.); F. Argenti, Cavallier & Co.; a direct advertisement for Duncan, Sherman & Co. and another for Alsop; C. K. Garrison & Co. (he had started in Panama); Lubeck & Co. (exchange on Australia); Daniel Gibb & Co.; Cross & Co.; Belloc Frères & Lescau [?]; and J. B. Moller & Co.

Nowhere is there an advertisement for Palmer, Cook & Company, which was about to get into great trouble over its handling of state funds.

Later in the year, one of the important banking firms of California was organized: Garrison, Morgan, Fretz & Ralston. Cornelius K. Garrison had been mayor of San Francisco; William C. Ralston would be president of the Bank of California and would go down in the crash of 1875.

A great many less significant but nevertheless important things were going on, as told in the New York *Tribune* for January 1, 1856:

A curious article of *real soap* has also been discovered [in Table Mountain], which closely resembles castile soap, and moreover answers an excellent purpose for washing. Specimens have been exhibited all over the State; and it is a fixed fact that a *mountain of soap* exists in California. By what process the ingredients were thrown together it is impossible to say.[4]

Sebastopol celebrations have been held in various towns of the interior.[5]

The levee in Sacramento has been strongly repaired and large additions made to it [to prevent another flood].

Sacramento is now lighted with gas.

Two horse thieves were hung at Union City, Almeda County, on the 28th ult.

The *Alta California* reports San Francisco's celebration of the fall of Sebastopol on November 26 at South Park.

An immense pavilion was erected for this purpose . . . under which was stretched ten tables, each 230 feet long, and preparations were made for seating 4,000 guests. A dinner was provided for the multitude, unexampled in variety and profusion, and all the preliminaries were made to render it the grandest affair of the kind ever known in California. Toasts and speeches were duly prepared, mammoth bands and orchestras got together, and at the appointed hour the immense pavilion was densely crowded, while thousands of spectators surrounded it on the outside. All went well until the period arrived for toasts and speeches, when the crowd, rendered merry from a free use of wine, concluded to spend the evening in a grand "jollification," rather than in listening to speeches in French and English. [And why not?] The closing portion of the celebration was therefore very ludicrous, very good natured, and to be compared to nothing perhaps but the "confusion of tongues" at Babel. The cost of this demonstration was not less than $20,000. [It does not tell who paid the bill.]

In that same issue of January 1, 1856, the New York *Tribune* reported the arrival of the *George Law* in New York, bringing treasure that had reached Panama on the *Golden Age*. Wells Fargo leads the list of remitters with $278,250.

And finally, there is the usual (or not unusual) flock of optimistic reports from the mines:

> *Table Mountain.—The Union Democrat* says that Messrs. Bowman, Bond, McCartle & Co., washed out about one third of the dirt they took from their shaft during the day—realizing five pounds of gold in the same number of hours [at $500 a pound]. On Tuesday we were present when the same parties washed half a pan, which produced about $50 worth of beautiful coarse dust.
>
> *The Columbia Clipper* said on the Tuolumne River, some Frenchmen in the bed of the river on Wednesday last took out $3,500 from about 200 pans of dirt. On the following day the riffle was so completely filled with gold that the men ceased working.
>
> *The Calaveras Chronicle* says that the Lone Star Quartz Company "cleaned up" last week, and from eighty days grinding obtained $1,740.
>
> At Angel's Camp, C. G. Lake, Esq. [the Wells Fargo agent], last Sunday purchased upward of fifteen pounds of dust from quartz mills.
>
> We know one party not a quarter of a mile from town, who have for many weeks past washed out from *sixteen* to *twenty pounds* of gold for the week.
>
> *The Mountain Democrat* contains the following:
>
> *Rich.*—A prospect of *one hundred and ten dollars* to the pan was taken out of the Nashville Tunnel, on Cedar Hill, last week by McCamee & Co.

The *Tribune* seems to have been bullish on California in general, for it said that "agricultural affairs are improving, and it is believed that the largest wheat crop ever sown will be put in the coming year." And there was still more glorious news from the Gold Country:

> The mines are at this time [about November 15, 1855] yielding immensely. . . . Table Mountain still continues a marvel for richness, and vast sums of the precious metal are daily extracted from it. The whole mountain is being pierced with tunnels. . . . To purchase a claim to one hundred feet of this mountain would require a fortune. Thousands of miners who have recently recorded claims here by the right of discovery and possession, now feel sure of making the "pile" for which they came to California.

Whatever else might happen, the news at that moment was enough to start a new wave of migration.

Freight via Panama that year was generally twenty-five cents a pound; Pacific Express tried to cut it to twenty cents a pound, but it was soon back to twenty-five. During that year, Wells Fargo brought to San Francisco, among other things, barrels of cocoa, a "complete set of type," and 51 boxes of ink. The ink may have been carbon black and linseed oil to make printers' ink, or it may have been nutgall or some other coloring matter to make writing fluid.

It was in 1856 that Wells Fargo and other express companies got into a fight with the Sacramento *Union* but decided that wisdom was the better part of valor. The *Union,* perhaps inspired by statistics that showed the state legislature had paid several times as much to express companies as to the post office for carrying mail,[6] scourged the "monopolists" [?] and said that legislative material ought to be carried by the post office. (A strange monopoly, indeed!) The *Union*'s editorials annoyed the express companies so much that they organized a boycott against the *Union,* and so notified it in these words:

> Inasmuch as you have, after all the facilities extended to you by the different Expresses for increasing your circulation throughout California, published statements injurious to our business and derogatory to the character of all engaged in the Express business, we the undersigned Agents for the different Express companies in this place, have signed an agreement as follows: That we will not carry to you any files of papers, and that we will not carry any papers from your office, either for exchanges, to subscribers or agents. That we will give you a fair chance to test the facilities the mail offers over the Expresses, and to show you that we repudiate the idea of giving to boys or *newspaper writers,* watches or any other trinkets for the purpose of bribing them to "blow" for us.

The notice was signed by Wells Fargo, Pacific Express (the reorganization of Adams Express), G. H. Wines, and Langton & Company. Bold words—but the express companies had reckoned without the power of the press. The *Union* published their notice and said also that the express companies were common carriers and had no right to decline the *Union*'s business. Other newspapers promptly took up the cudgel, as newspapers were wont to do in those days, and the Placerville *American* said:

> We can hardly conceive how one or more Express Companies can hope to browbeat or bully the Press of California. Else why . . . unless their faith was strong that theirs was the power and theirs the determination to use it. . . . If it has come to this, that we may not express our views and the views of the masses, in relation to the manner in which our public servants disburse the money of their constituents—if we may not urge upon the Legislature the exercise of a commendable economy without being denounced by a conspiracy of Express Companies and a league entered into for the evident purpose of preventing an expose of the very frauds they themselves would perpetrate, from reaching the ears of the great mass of California readers—if it has come to this, the sooner that open hostility between the two interests is declared, the better.[7]

The express companies probably were guilty of using all the influence they could on the legislature, but under any circumstances their position was indefensible. Perhaps they would not have bridled over the *Union*'s idea, which was essentially correct, if the *Union* had been more circumspect in its language. Be that as it may, the express companies found themselves engaged in the classic sport of sticking their necks out. That game did not last long, however, for within a few days, the Wells Fargo agent at Sacramento backed water, followed by the other three, so the Placer *Press* could say on February 2: "Wells, Fargo & Co. on Thursday brought us our regular *Union,* for which we thank them." Hostilities had ceased before they had gotten out of hand.

In 1856, Wells Fargo finally conceded the mail-carrying right to the post office. In June, 1855, a former employee of the Adams Company, Henry Reed, had organized a Penny Express to carry letters to several towns at five cents a letter. In the *Alta* on June 25 he announced the rate, with the provision that collect-on-delivery letters would be ten cents. Stimson's Express was carrying letters for twelve and a half cents, and Pacific Express carried them in California and Oregon for ten cents, which included a three-cent government envelope.

Probably it was the cutthroat competition. Whatever it was, in September, 1856, Wells Fargo gave up the long fight with the Post Office Department by announcing that Wells Fargo would thenceforth carry letters only in its own prepaid envelopes—an idea of Louis McLane. It went much further, however, for Wells Fargo bought government envelopes and franked them with its own name, and sold them for $10 to $12 a hundred. This automatically satisfied the post office, for it was getting its postage, and it eliminated the losses that arose from collect-on-delivery letters—a step the government also had recently taken. All express companies followed suit; some small companies sold the three-cent envelopes as low as $7 a hundred, which meant the express company would get four cents for carrying a letter.

The extent of the importance of mail to Wells Fargo is suggested by the fact that it was soon selling $15,000 worth of envelopes a month.[8]

All in all, 1856 did rather well, for that was the year the people of San Francisco—and, indeed, of all the mining country—got thoroughly fed up with corruption in government and organized the Second Committee of Vigilance.

As a result of the events of April and May, 1856, James King was murdered; James P. Casey was hanged by the Vigilantes; Charles Cora was hanged for the murder of "General" William H. Richardson, an officer of the law; the San Francisco *Herald* would lose heavily for being too slow to back up the Vigilantes; Ned McGowan, a judge, would leave the country; and a state supreme court justice would be held for attempted murder of the hangman of Casey and Cora. Through all these events, Wells Fargo seems to have held its composure and not gotten involved.

A man named David C. Broderick had come out early from New York and had brought with him the Tammany Hall politics of that period. Broderick was virile and aggressive and not much troubled by scruples, so it was not long before he was in control of San Francisco politics, and, indeed, powerful in California politics. As a Democrat, he was elected to the state senate in 1850, and served as lieutenant-

David C. Broderick, who was a first-rate Tammany ballot-box stuffer on a small scale, but unsuccessful when he got into the United States Senate. He was killed in a duel by Judge David C. Terry in 1859. From the California Historical Society.

James King of William, banker with Adams & Company when it failed, then editor of the "Bulletin," which he started and used to attack everybody he did not like and some that he might have liked. James P. Casey, who murdered him, was no better than he should have been, but King asked for it if any man ever did. It was unfortunate for Casey that he ran headlong into William T. Coleman's Vigilantes. From Ira Cross, "Financing an Empire."

governor. However, he had his eye on a senatorial seat in the national Congress, and maneuvered by all means, fair and foul, to win it. He controlled ballot boxes and judgeships, one of his most notorious kept judges being Ned McGowan, whom Broderick himself called a "ballot stuffer." In this year of 1856, patronage, favoritism, and corruption were so utterly rampant in San Francisco that Broderick ran headlong into the Second Committee of Vigilance, which was organized primarily to reestablish some semblance of honest government.[9]

The tempestuous events of the Committee of Vigilance started—or, rather, broke out—over James King of William, who was about to tread roughshod for the last time. In 1855, while he castigated everybody in connection with the Adams failure, and particularly lambasted Palmer, Cook & Company because they would not release the funds deposited in their keeping, he had found time to create new enemies. In November of that year, a gambler named Charles Cora shot and killed William H. Richardson, a United States marshal, without apparent justification.[10] Cora was arrested and put in jail, and a tremendous crowd gathered and shouted, "Hang him! Hang him!" Speakers addressed the crowd and took votes on the matter.

A contemporary artist's reconstruction of James P. Casey's murder of James King of William. King had said he carried a gun, but he apparently did not use it. A Pacific Express wagon is in the background (P. E. was organized from the wreckage of Adams).

The bells of the firehouses began to ring—the traditional signal for a hanging. Sam Brannan, the builder of Wells Fargo's first and second homes, addressed the crowd and urged immediate execution; then he was arrested for inciting a riot, but released at once.

James King singled out William Mulligan, the jailkeeper, for his major invective in the *Bulletin*: "Hang Billy Mulligan!" he demanded. "That's the word! If Mulligan lets Cora escape, hang Billy Mulligan, and if necessary to get rid of the sheriff, hang him—hang the sheriff!"

James King was anything but temperate.

Cora was tried. His mistress, whose name was not then Cora, and the publisher of the Sunday *Times,* James P. Casey, spent a great deal of money on lawyers, and the jury failed to agree.

Casey's *Times* went after King's *Bulletin,* saying, among other things, that King's brother Thomas had tried to get the dead Richardson's job. Thomas denied it, and asked the name of the man who had given him that information. Casey refused to give it. Then James King revealed that Casey had been in Sing Sing. Casey went to the *Bulletin* office and remonstrated, and King ordered him to get out.[11]

Casey waited for King and shot him in front of the Pacific Express Company office with a navy revolver (usually about .54-caliber). At fifteen paces, the ball struck King in the left breast. King cried, "Oh God! I am shot!" and staggered into the express office, while Casey went to the police to give himself up.

Inflammatory San Francisco exploded in wrath. The Vigilance Committee held meetings. The streets were crowded with angry people, and the army and navy were called on to avoid a riot. King had made many persons angry at him, but his shooting united all factions that were opposed to the corrupt elements. The Vigilance Committee reorganized under the presidency of William T. Coleman,[12] and soon had six thousand members, then eight thousand. The mayor asked the governor for militia to put down the Vigilantes, but Coleman told the governor it would only cause trouble, and that the people were tired of inefficiency and corruption. It appears that perhaps Governor Johnson told Coleman to go ahead and clean things up but be quick about it.

William Tecumseh Sherman, who had mistrusted Honest Harry Meiggs and who was later to be prominent in the Civil War, expressed himself vigorously against the "rioters," who immediately pointed to some of Sherman's own swervings from the straight and narrow path. Sherman prudently remained quiet.[13]

The three forms of power—civil, under Broderick's faction; military, under Sherman; and social, under Coleman—seemed unalterably opposed.

Coleman was realistic, and knew that in such a fluid situation, possession was all important, so he dispersed 3,000 Vigilantes under arms throughout the city, and planned a march against the jail. It was Sunday, and a New Hampshire man said: "When you see these damned psalm-singing Yankees turn out of their churches, shoulder their guns, and march away like that, you may know that hell is going to crack shortly!" And indeed it was.

The Vigilantes marched through the streets and

Fort Vigilance, also called Fort Gunnybags, where the Vigilantes held James P. Casey and Charles Cora, tried them, and hanged them from the windows. (Probably the street numbers were put on later.) Some contemporary pictures of the hangings in a huge square do not seem realistic.

EXECUTION OF JAMES P. CASEY & CHARLES CORA,

.... BY THE ....

Vigilance Committee of San Francisco, on Thursday, May 22nd, 1856, from the windows of their Rooms, in SACRAMENTO STREET, BETWEEN FRONT AND DAVIS.

JAMES P. CASEY AND CHARLES CORA,

WERE hung by the Vigilance Committee at precisely twenty minutes after one o'clock—the former for the murder of JAMES KING OF WM., and the latter for the murder of Gen. WILLIAM H. RICHARDSON. Both persons had been tried before the Committee, and found guilty. A promise had been made to Casey that he should have a fair trial, and be permitted to speak ten minutes. These conditions had doubtlessly been observed. Casey was informed on Wednesday afternoon, that he had been condemed to be hung. While under the charge of the Vigilance Committee his spirit appeared to be unbroken. When awaken, after a sleep, he would frequently strike the floor with his hand cuffs, and swear fiercely at his fate. During the evening previous to his execution, the Right Rev. Bishop Allemany attended Casey, who had been educated in the Roman Catholic religion. During the night he was restless, and passed a portion of the time in pacing his room.

Cora attracted less attention, and conducted himself more quietly.

At eight o'clock, on Thursday morning, the General Committee was notified that Casey and Cora would be executed at half-past one, and ordered to appear under arms. During the morning preparations were made for the execution. Beams were run out over two of the windows of the Committee Room, and platforms about three feet square extending out under each beam. These platforms were supported next the house by hinges, and outside by ropes, extending up to the beams. Along the streets, for a considerable distance on each side of the place of execution, were ranged the Committee—more than three thousand in number—some on foot with muskets, and others on horseback with sabres. No outsiders were permitted to approach within a hundred yards. Beneath the place of execution wese several cannon and caissons ready for use if necessary. The houses in the vicinity were covered with spectators; and in the streets were collected, probably, not less than eight or ten thousand persons.

At a quarter past one o'clock Casey and Cora were brought out upon the platforms. The former was attended by the Rev. Father Gallagher. The arms of both were pinioned at the elbows. The noose was placed around Cora's neck, when he stepped upon the platform and stood firm as a statue, a white handkerchief being wrapped around his head. The noose was placed around Casey's neck, but at his request removed, while he had some three or four minutes conversation with his priest. He then came forward and addressed the people as follows:

"GENTLEMEN, FELLOW CITIZENS:—I am not guilty of any crime. When I am dead, when I am laid in my grave, let no one dare traduce my character or asperse my memory. Let no man exult over me, or point to my grave as that of an assassin. I am guilty of no crime. I only acted as I was taught—according to my early education—to avenge an insult. Let not the Alta, the Chronicle, and the Globe, persecute my memory; let them no more proclaim me a murderer to the world. Let them not insult me after death. I have an aged mother in the Atlantic States, and I hope that she will never hear how I died. I trust she will never know I am executed on a charge of murder. I am not guilty of any such crime."

About this time Father Gallagher touched Casey, and said: "Pray to God to pardon you for your crime; pray God to save your soul."

Casey, after a moment's hesitation, spoke again:

"Oh, God, pardon and forgive me. Oh, my mother! my mother! I hope she will never hear of this. Oh, God! have mercy on my mother; comfort her in her affliction. Oh, God! have mercy on my soul! Oh, my God! my God! I am not guilty of murder—I did not intend to commit murder."

After he had concluded, the noose was again adjusted, his eyes bandaged, and, as he was about to step forward, he faltered, and was about to sink, when the arms of two men were extended and supported him to the fatal spot.

Both prisoners being prepared, the signal was given, and, at the same moment, the souls of James P. Casey and Charles Cora were launched into eternity; and their bodies became an inanimate mass of corruption. Neither of them struggled much, Casey showing the most physical suffering.

From the time the prisoners appeared at the window until the drop fell, the immense mass of people stood uncovered, and the utmost silence was maintained, not a shout being heard, or a loud word spoken. The bodies continued to hang for nearly an hour as they were executed. Although a great many persons were in sight at the time, awaiting the climax of the tragedy, there were many others scattered about town, who had supposed the affair would be postponed. The news spread rapidly through the city, and in ten minutes after the death of Casey, great numbers of men were to be seen rushing down Clay, and Washington, and Commercial streets, as though it were a matter of life and death to get a sight of the spectacle. The bodies were then taken down and handed over to the Coroner.

For sale at M. Ullmann's corner of Washington and Sansome street. [TOWN TALK, PRINT.]

May 22nd 1856

Loaned by W. H. Myrick, Mayfield.

This flyer shows the two men hanging. They had walked out onto small platforms from the windows, and the platforms were dropped to effect the execution. The streets were crowded, and some three thousand Vigilantes were under arms. From the original in the History Room, Wells Fargo Bank.

drew up in front of the jail with a six-pound cannon trained on the door. The twenty lawmen inside, not wanting to resist 3,000 determined men, gave up Casey and then Cora.

King had been shot on Wednesday, and was still alive. Every doctor in town who wanted his name in the papers had gathered to consult over his case, and a surgeon had been called from Los Angeles. Somebody had put a sponge in King's wound, and it was still there. Dr. Beverly Cole said it ought to come out, and offered to take it out, but the other gentlemen of medicine voted him down.

It was a tender situation for Casey; if King should die, Casey would be tried for murder. Meantime, feelings in San Francisco did not cool off; if anything, they became more inflamed. A placard said:

> . . . The law here is a mockery; the weak, the poor, the stranger, may pay his misdeeds by the forfeiture of his liberty or his life; but the rich villain, the powerful gambler, stalks through our streets with bowie-knife or revolver to work out his wicked will. . . . There is a point beyond which patience degenerates into cowardice . . . when the law is effete, or its protection becomes tyrannical, resistance becomes the duty of every freeman. . . . Law and its courts are a farce; murder stalks amongst us and must be checked. Then up, friends, and let the majority of the people try the presumed murderer, and then, if he be guilty, executed.

It was signed, in the manner of the times, "Brutus."

King began to improve, but there was no lessening of public indignation over his shooting. In Sacramento and in other towns in the Gold Country, public meetings were held; opinion was expressed in favor of the Vigilance Committee, and local Vigilance Committees were formed; it was proposed to organize a state-wide Committee. Contributions poured in to Coleman, and eventually reached the enormous sum of $350,000. A woman said: "What is to be done with Casey? If the men don't hang him, the women will!"

Casey had been antagonized, and he had done no more than many others—but he had done it at the wrong time. The public was fed up with Broderick and his gang, and the excitement, once loosed, would not subside without vengeance. Perhaps those who say that the law should not be concerned with vengeance are right—but this was not the law, but public opinion, which had been outraged long enough.[14]

The end came on Tuesday, when James King of William died, ending a stormy career. The streets were soon crowded with people. Bells tolled all over town, and great crowds gathered around the Vigilantes' headquarters, where Casey and Cora were held. All places of business closed; flags were at half-mast; buildings were draped with black cloth.

The Committee of Vigilance proceeded at once to try both Casey and Cora; they organized a court with judge and jury; they called witnesses; they appointed counsel for both sides, and their deliberations were swift but fair. Cora was found guilty by a bare majority;[15] Casey was convicted unanimously. Both were sentenced to be hanged at the time of King's funeral: the next day (May 22, 1856) at noon.

On that day, Vigilante companies of both infantry and cavalry patrolled the streets. At 12:45, two small platforms were thrust from two windows of the Committee's building, and two beams were pushed out from the roof—each with a noose hanging from it. The platforms were held up by ropes from the rooms. A man named Sterling A. Hopkins agreed to act as hangman.

The ceremony was brief. Cora appeared, arms and legs bound, a white handkerchief over his face; the noose was placed around his neck. Casey was pale, his eyes bloodshot, his speech incoherent. He denied being a murderer. He was twenty-nine years old, and spoke for seven minutes, uttering the impassioned plea: "Oh, God! my poor mother! Oh, God!"

The signal was given, and both platforms dropped together and the men died with very little struggle.[16]

There were many, many repercussions from that tempestuous summer. Arguments, fistfights, and duels over the rightness of the Committee's actions raged for years; those against the Committee (or those who had been adversely affected by its actions) called its hangings mob violence, and even the President of the United States at one point, at least, was asked to send troops to preserve order (which he declined to do).[17]

Those who favored the Committee pointed out the obvious fact that, under Broderick's machine, the forces of law and justice had broken down, and that (contrary to the soft attitude of many reformers today) a few hangings had an exemplary effect. Indeed they had, and William T. Coleman quietly emerges as one of the strong men in California history. But all the events of that wild spring and summer had not yet transpired when James King of William was laid in his grave, forever stopped from his fuming, ranting, and raving (or was he?). In fact, the subsequent events make it seem somewhat incredible that Coleman's "government within a government" was able to maintain its equilibrium for so long.[18]

The most dangerous crisis for the Committee of Vigilance came over the impetuous and ill-advised actions of the fire-eating southerner, Justice David S. Terry. Terry had his own ax to grind, and there is no evidence that he was, as one writer suggests, an extremist for law and order; rather, one suspects, he wanted his side to win, and, in spite of his own insistence that he was a "gentleman," he seems not to have cared how that winning was accomplished. Terry exerted a great deal of influence over John N. Johnson, the Know-Nothing[19] governor elected in the upset of 1854. The term "Know-Nothing" seems to have applied to Johnson in more ways than one, since Bancroft characterizes him as inept, unintelligent, and subject to all the demands of expediency in his self-interest; in fact, says Bancroft, he was no better than President Pierce—and that was very bad indeed in the eyes of Hubert Howe Bancroft.

David S. Terry, the fire-eating southerner who fought the Vigilantes and who later, among many other ruffian acts, killed Broderick in a duel. Terry professed to be proud of his status as a "gentleman," but his actions were totally inconsistent.

It is Johnson who told Coleman to get it over with and be quick about it, presumably, and it is Johnson of whom the irresponsible editor Parker H. French said, in the back-handed way of the times, "Johnson never drinks."

French, a man of questionable character—to put it charitably—had started overland through northern Mexico leading a train of Gold Rush emigrants in 1849, had formed a group and split off the main party, and later attacked the main party; part of his right arm was amputated in Chihuahua, and another piece was amputated later. His item in the California Daily *Register,* May 20, 1857, says:

The rumor afloat that Governor Johnson baptized himself alongside the *John L. Stephens,* under the influence of an *ardent spirit* to see *Well-her* [John L. Weller] on board—that it was he [Johnson] making the boat reel, and not the boat making him! is entirely untrue. These are tight times, and he was in a tight place; but to say that he was "tight," would expose the sayer to indictment for libel, and imprisonment with the editor of the *Sacramento Age,* and we will not be engaged in such an outrage as even permitting such a rumor to go uncontradicted. For Johnson never drinks —no, never! never!! never!!! By *gin-go,* never! Do you, Governor?

Quite a display of insinuation.

In March, 1855, on a steamboat, French was shot in the leg, and the Sacramento State *Journal* said it was gratified to say that French was recovering slowly.[20]

Terry influenced Johnson to get help from General Wool, the United States military commander in California, and to put Sherman in charge of the

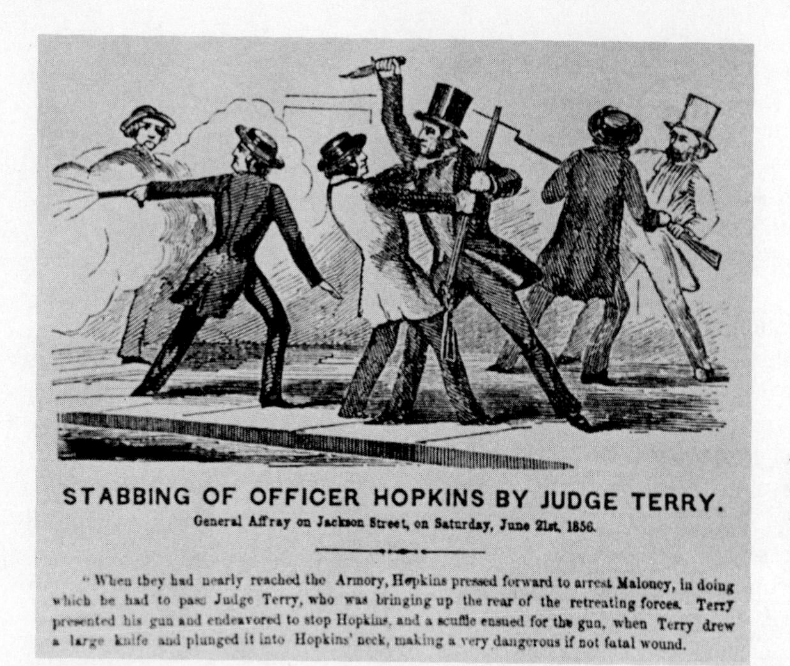
STABBING OF OFFICER HOPKINS BY JUDGE TERRY.
General Affray on Jackson Street, on Saturday, June 21st, 1856.
"When they had nearly reached the Armory, Hopkins pressed forward to arrest Maloney, in doing which he had to pass Judge Terry, who was bringing up the rear of the retreating forces. Terry presented his gun and endeavored to stop Hopkins, and a scuffle ensued for the gun, when Terry drew a large knife and plunged it into Hopkins' neck, making a very dangerous if not fatal wound.

A contemporary woodcut of the stabbing of Sterling A. Hopkins, the hangman of Casey and Cora. Terry emerges as a full-scale Tammany demagog.

military forces in San Francisco. Sherman wanted arms and ammunition and a 32-pound cannon, but Wool backed out of it.

Terry issued a writ of habeas corpus for a man who was held by the Committee (which had arrested many lesser violators of the peace), but the Committee told the deputy sheriff writ server to go jump in the bay. Terry was enraged, and Sherman issued a draft call, naming the disturbance a civil war, and asking all good citizens to cease resistance to the courts. The Vigilantes pointed out that they were not opposed to the operation of the courts—provided they should operate. The governor declared the county in a state of insurrection, and asked Wool for three thousand rifles and a few cannon.

All this time, David S. Terry was busily promoting his own insurrection against the Vigilantes, and feeling was so high in the city that the Committee of Vigilance turned its headquarters at 41 Sacramento Street into a fort with six brass cannon, swivel guns loaded with grape, and one hundred riflemen behind a breastworks of tow sacks filled with sand (the sand being hauled and the bags being filled by two hundred teamsters). The streets were cleared for two blocks in all directions, and armed men walked the streets and gathered in low-voiced groups.

Broderick promptly organized a Law and Order party and held mass meetings, unmolested by the Vigilantes. Terry deserted his supreme court bench and brought the business of the court to a halt, but Terry seems not to have been concerned about that.

The Committee was compiling a black list of notorious law breakers, arresting them and trying them. Some already had been put on board ship and warned never again to let the sun set on them in San Francisco. By June 9, the Vigilantes had a battery of artillery, a battalion of cavalry, a French legion, and three regiments of infantry. The Committee's headquarters was christened "Fort Gunnybags."

The Committee continued with its business (Casey and Cora having been hanged) by arresting, trying, and sentencing lesser criminals. Sherman wisely resigned as commander of the state's forces in San Francisco.

The Vigilantes arrested two notorious scoundrels, Rube Maloney and John G. Phillips, but released them. Then the two were unwise enough to go around town making threats, so the Committee sent Sterling A. Hopkins, the man who had hanged Casey and Cora, to arrest them. He found them in an office with Terry and others; Terry drew a pistol on Hopkins, and Hopkins retired, but presently returned with four assistants to find the two scoundrels guarded by Terry and four others, all armed with double-barrel shotguns. Terry and Hopkins got into a hassle, and Terry, who had a pistol in his hand to start with, drew a bowie knife and thrust it six inches into Hopkins' neck.

Terry and his cohorts retired to an armory without loss of time. Hopkins was taken to a firehouse and a doctor was called. The Vigilantes issued orders for Terry's arrest, and within a few minutes the streets were filled with hurrying men wearing white badges in their left lapels, all converging at Vigilante headquarters. Merchants left customers standing, mechanics dropped their tools, and "draymen sprang from their seats, stripped their horses of the harness, all save the bridle, and, mounting, rode briskly away to the scene of action, leaving their loaded trucks standing in the street."

Colonel Olney, of the Vigilantes' war committee, who was laid up with a bad ankle, commandeered a kerosene delivery wagon and drove over the cobblestones furiously, says Bancroft, scattering empty kerosene cans—and a few full ones—over the street. (He promised to pay for the kerosene.)[21]

The Vigilantes demanded the surrender of the Terry force. The commander of the armory tried to deal, but the Vigilantes told him to open up or they would blow up the building. However, the Vigilantes agreed to protect Terry and Maloney from violence by persons not of the Vigilance Committee, and took them away. There were wild rumors that 500 Texans were going to attack Vigilante headquarters, but the Vigilantes surprised all armories in the city and crippled the law and order forces, taking several hundred prisoners and several thousand rifles and muskets.

Now the Vigilantes had a problem: If Hopkins should die, they would be bound to hang a justice of the supreme court. Hopkins, it now seems, *walked* into the firehouse, and went into shock. His wife and mother were there, and apparently his wife's morals were notorious if not bad, and the two women were more interested in the purse that might be made up for them than they were in Hopkins' recovery.[22] Bancroft indicates that Hopkins was not of the stuff of good martyrs, and in fact knew of his wife's derelictions and probably profited from them. The Vigilantes had a poor hero and an active and aggressive enemy, for Terry, Johnson, Sherman, and many others put all the pressure possible on the Vigilantes to get Terry out of the hoosegow. Mrs. Terry visited him daily and put on some touching scenes until the Vigilantes stopped it. Some Vigilantes lived at headquarters; others carried cocked pistols in their hands as they went home at night. The rumor was that Texans were going to carry gunpowder into the sewers and blow up the headquarters. Captain Boutwell, commander of the U.S. warship *John Adams,* demanded that Terry be placed on his ship as a prisoner of war; the implied threat was that he would open fire on the headquarters. The Vigilantes countered by stationing two hundred picked riflemen on tugs near the *John Adams*—but about that time, Boutwell had a chat with Admiral Farragut, and decided that the interests of the service required him to put to sea. Insolently enough, he said he had been stirred by the appeals of Terry's distressed wife and by the dictates of humanity. Old Navy men will wonder what kind of regulations they had in 1855. Farragut did not care for Boutwell's impetuosity, and told him to stay put and simmer down.

Terry was placed on trial by the Vigilantes on June 27, charged with resisting arrest by violence, committing an assault with a deadly weapon, and several breaches of the peace: an attack on "Mr. Evans" of Stockton; on "Mr. King" in Stockton; and on J. H. Purdy in San Francisco—rather an astonishing list for such a self-admitted gentleman as Terry.

Terry claimed self-defense and was permitted to bring in witness after witness. The heat continued against the Vigilantes, but they stood firm. Hopkins' condition was critical, and mass meetings demanded Terry's conviction, the governor's resignation, the mayor's resignation, the sheriff's resignation, the district attorney's resignation, the county clerk's resignation, the assessor's resignation, the surveyors' resignation, a judge's resignation, the coroner's resignation, the school superintendent's resignation, and three justices' of the peace resignations. Most of the Vigilantes had business or jobs that needed tending, but they kept on with Terry's trial, while Terry's friends in high places continued to try to overpower the Vigilantes by sheer pressure.

The trial was held seven days a week and lasted twenty-five days. In the meantime, Hopkins fortunately recovered; Terry was then found guilty on all counts except that concerning Purdy, and secretly ordered to be discharged. It seems that a part of the Committee released him because he was a gentleman and used to finer things—although exactly what application that has, if true, is still not clear. As a matter of fact, Terry had not borne up too well under the strain, especially since two other men had been tried during his trial, found guilty, and hanged.

The people were not happy over Terry's release, for there were a great many who thought that a man of gentle birth had no more right to kill than did a hoodlum, but Terry was released, and that was the end of the Committee's most rigorous test. The Committee's purpose was to get some of the most notorious criminals out of San Francisco, and to restore the sanctity of the ballot box. And in its many judgments during those tempestuous times, it made substantial moves in that direction, not disbanding finally until 1859.

How the men of Wells Fargo managed to stay neutral during those hectic events is not apparent, but, at a time when one's sympathies alone could cause him to prosper or go broke, Wells Fargo seems to have stayed neutral successfully.[23]

Louis McLane, general agent of Wells Fargo, must indeed have been a prudent man, to walk the tightrope of public opinion without wavering to either side—but apparently he did so.

In 1856, Palmer, Cook & Company got into trouble for its various machinations between politics and banking.[24] The state treasurer, Henry Bates, bought state warrants, controller's warrants, and state scrip with the coin and bullion of the state—against state law. He made, says Bancroft, $15,000 that way in 1856. Also, the law requiring public money to be kept in the fireproof vault in the capital, and forbidding deposit with any firm, was violated, and Palmer, Cook & Company found itself holding, without having put up security, $88,520 due in New York as interest on state bonds, which money, says Bancroft, the company's officers used for the company or for themselves. Agents and bankers absconded, and the treasurer gathered up all the money in the treasury (about $15,000 short of the amount needed) and delivered it to Wells, Fargo & Company to be expressed to New York. Then Bates borrowed $20,000 from Wells Fargo and put it in the state's vaults, partly in United States money and partly in California $10 pieces (worth twenty-five cents less than United States coins). Bancroft complains because this loan was entirely repaid in United States coins.[25]

Partly in connection with these events, the year 1856 also brought about the failure of Palmer, Cook & Company and 139 other firms with liabilities of over $3,000,000. Edward Bosqui gives James King credit for this crash, but it must be observed that King, vicious as he unquestionably was, received material assistance from ambition, carelessness, and violation of law on the part of Palmer, Cook & Company. In June, the firm failed for the second time to pay the interest on state bonds in New York, and soon thereafter failed to meet its own drafts there. At that time also it had underwritten bonds for state officials to the amount of $583,000. It had also supported the filibusterer William Walker in Nicaragua, and had played a leading part in the presidential campaign of John Charles Frémont.[26] Joseph Palmer also had bought large blocks of real estate on credit, and altogether it does not seem that Joseph Palmer, the senior partner of the firm, adhered to banking principles. The immediate cause of the failure, of course, was the firm's refusal to pay its drafts ("refusal" meaning "failure"). The firm suspended July 29, 1856, and was legally dissolved January 21, 1857.

Five large firms went down with Palmer, Cook & Company, owing a total of $987,000.

The presidential campaign of 1856 was one that caused trouble to many people with money, for many firms, banking and others, poured money into the purses of their favorite parties. In 1856, the country had been flooded with immigrants from Europe, and many of them were Catholics; the labor unions had begun to fight the immigrants, and so arose the Know-Nothing party, a nativist movement aimed at Catholicism and the foreign-born; in some cities like New York the two interests clashed in bloody riots. In 1856, too, the issue of slavery was a very violent point of conflict. Frémont represented the new Republican party, which stood for woman suffrage, abolition of slavery, and quite a number of isms; it was generally said that Frémont was for the North. Millard Fillmore, who had filled out Harrison's term as President, was nominated by the Know-Nothings and also by the dying Whig party; he favored the status quo. James Buchanan, the Democratic candidate, was said to favor the South.

The campaign was vicious. Each side attacked every other side, and went to great lengths of "logic" and "facts" to prove the other side was all wrong.

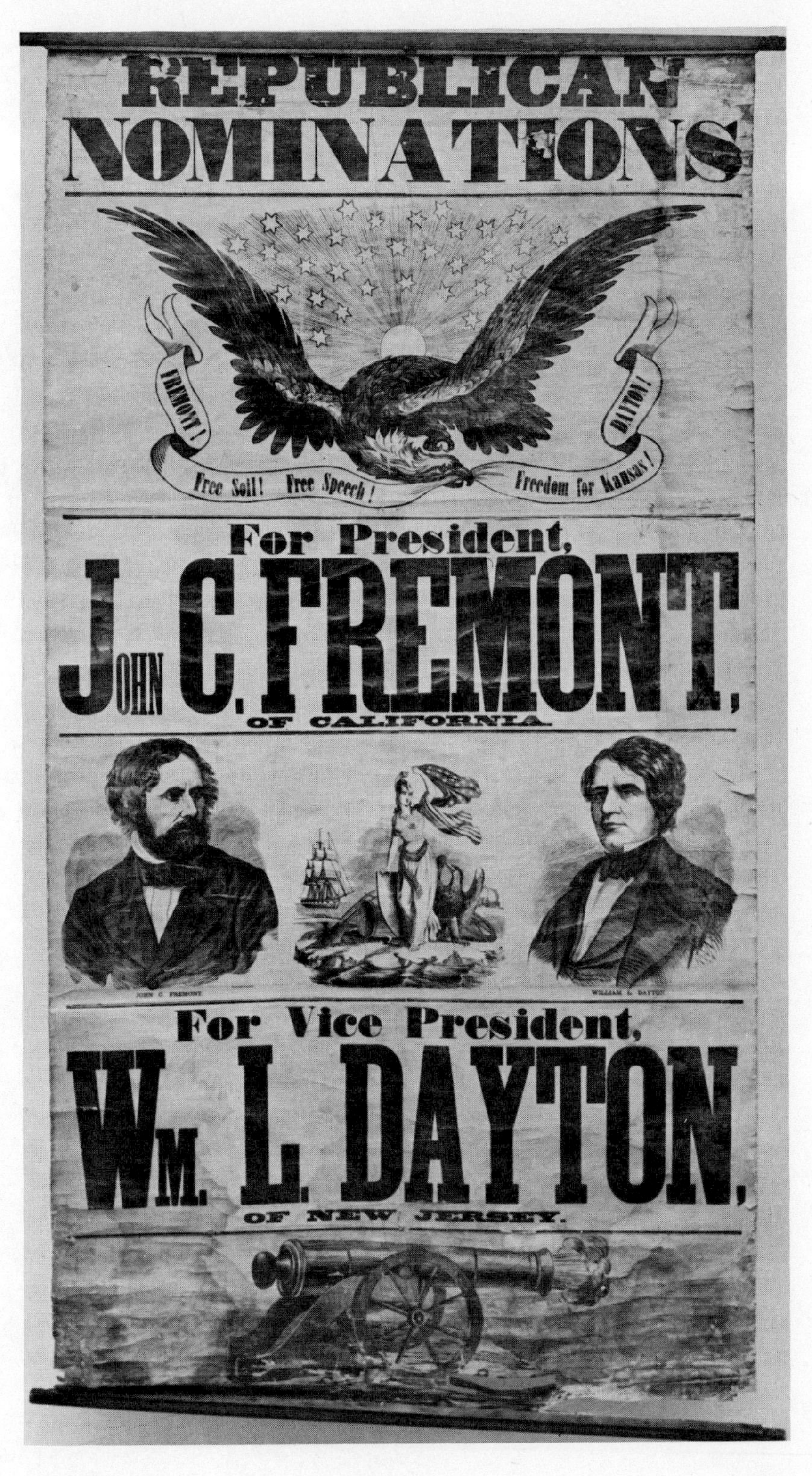

A political campaign banner of 1856 from the Ralph E. Becker Collection at the Smithsonian Institution. "Free Soil! Free Speech! Fremont!" Also, "Freedom for Kansas!"

In this cartoon from the Library of Congress collections, Pierce is carrying Buchanan on his shoulders, Frémont is on a cart being pulled through the "Abolition [of slavery] Cess Pool" and aided by Horace Greeley and Henry Ward Beecher with a "Beecher's Bible" (a rifle) in his hands, while Fillmore rides in a carriage labeled "American Express" and gives it a plug just to make sure.

James Buchanan, Democrat, who believed in letting things alone, was elected over Frémont and Fillmore in 1856. From "The White House Gallery of Official Portraits of the Presidents."

A campaign cartoon showing James Buchanan being crushed under the weight of the Cincinnati platform of the Democratic party, while the Republican slogan has been enlarged to: "Free Soil, Free Speech, Free Press, Free Men & Fremont." From the collections of the Library of Congress.

Henry A. Wise, a prominent Virginia politician, attacked Know-Nothingism with all his eloquence:

> Having swept the North, the question was: How can this ism be wedged in the South? and the devil was at the elbow of these preachers of "Christian politics" to tell them precisely how. [Catcalls, derisive cheers, and other manifestations from the Know-Nothing element of the meeting.]
>
> . . . There is a religious element—the Protestant bigotry and fanaticism—for Protestants, gentlemen, have their religious zeal without knowledge, as well as the Catholics. [A voice: "True enough, sir."] Well, how were they to reach them? Why, just by raising a hell of a funk about the Pope!
>
> . . . How can the conservative Whigs of Alexandria join hands with Democrats and go over to them in Know-Nothing Lodges? [Cheers.] A Whig of the North and a Whig of Alexandria cannot shake hands with each other in our presence, but . . . let the Whig of the North become a Know-Nothing, and then behind the curtain these gentlemen can shake hands and honeyfuggle with each other. [Much laughter.] I will deceive no man; I will honeyfuggle no voter. [Laughter] I will condescend to nothing unbecoming a gentleman.[27]

Feeling over the country was remarkably similar to that of 1965: Public meetings were held, riots were not infrequent, and inflammatory speeches and equally inflammatory pamphlets were common. It was only five years before the Civil War. And with everybody taking sides, it is a little strange that Wells Fargo did not get into the race, for certainly its parent, the American Express Company, did so, while Horace Greeley and Henry Ward Beecher got on the Frémont band wagon, and Buchanan seemed to rock along on the strength of Franklin Pierce's administration, fairly unnoticed and hardly considered to be a winner. (In a political cartoon in the Library of Congress, the three candidates are shown racing toward the Capitol—Buchanan on the shoulders of Pierce, Frémont bogged down in the "abolition cesspool," and Fillmore riding in a stylish carriage labeled "American Express." Apparently that advertisement did not satisfy the American Express contribution, so Fillmore is saying, in a balloon: "Founded by Washington, the only sure Line to Washington is the American Express." The cartoon is pro-Fillmore, but how that unusual speech ever got into it can be best answered by facts that probably are no longer available.)

In that tempestuous year, Wells Fargo apparently managed to keep its skirts clean—no small accomplishment in a town of such vivid likes and dislikes.

On January 3—if it had not done so before—Wells Fargo said in the *Alta California*: "Our next regular express will be dispatched via Panama per Pacific Mail Steam Ship Company's steamship *Golden Gate,* and via Nicaragua per Nicaragua Steamship Company's steamer *Uncle Sam* in charge of special messengers." So, Wells Fargo had begun shipping regularly through Nicaragua as well as Panama. Whether this had any connection with William Walker's presence in Nicaragua, is hard to know, but Walker was in his heyday in Nicaragua in 1856, and Freeman & Company and the Pacific Express Company both advertised shipments through Nicaragua in charge of special messengers.

On June 4, a board of control was created for Wells Fargo, to be composed of McLane, Bell, and Higgins. McLane or his successor was to have full authority in California.

On October 24, the board of directors of Wells Fargo approved the first contract between Wells Fargo and Messrs. Brigham, Rowe, McNeil, Skidmore, and Baker (according to the Head manuscript) to provide for establishment of express rates and a division of earnings. This is the first time a division of earnings is mentioned in Wells Fargo minutes, and this may be the first time the company agreed to such a contract.[28]

The office of Livingston, Wells & Company was closed in Paris in October, and apparently Henry Wells turned over to Wells Fargo forty-eight shares of stock of the United States Express Company at $90 per share to settle the company's claim against him in the Livingston, Wells & Company matter. It is interesting to note that the board returned this stock to Wells, together with the dividend payable December 1.

The directors in 1856 were the same as those for 1855 except that William I. Pardee resigned from the board and was replaced by Thomas M. Janes.

The *Alta California* on November 22 showed that Wells Fargo shipped $426,531 in treasure; that Drexel, Sather & Church was next with $325,000. The total for November was $4,569,308.

It does not appear that any dividend was declared in 1856. On the contrary, the minutes show that the

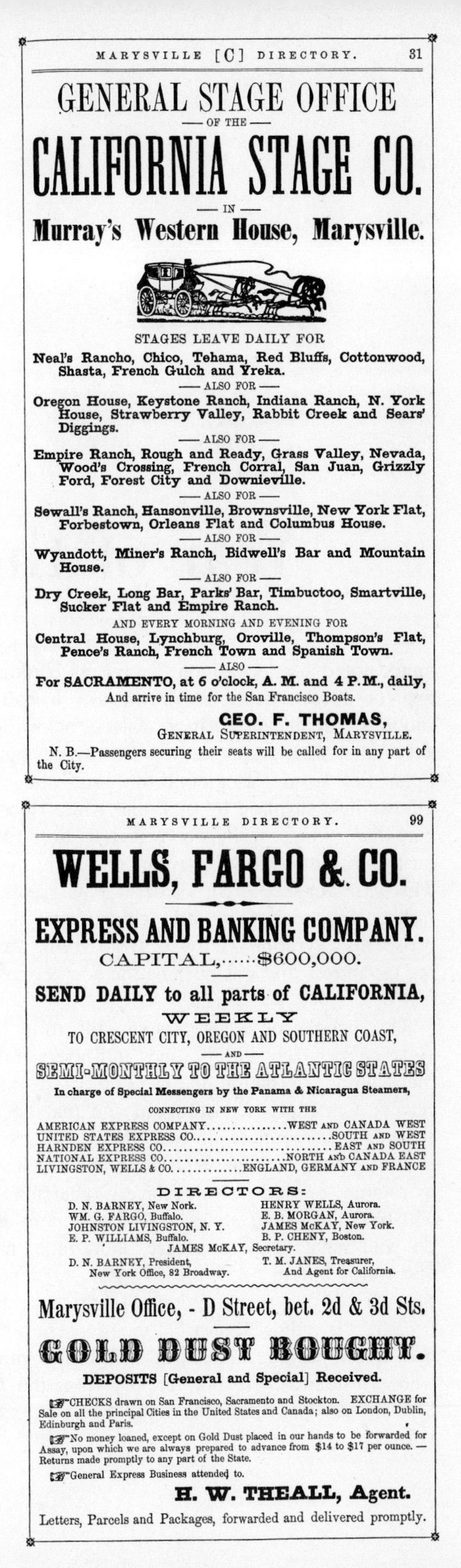

Advertisement of the California Stage Company, James Birch's mammoth organization, in Amy's "Marysville Directory for the Year Commencing November 1, 1856. From the Bancroft Library, Berkeley, University of California.

"funds of the company had been loaned, bills discounted, and credit given in California indiscriminately, occasioning disastrous losses," and on November 17, the board of directors "ordered the practice discontinued"[29] except on special authority of the board.

Obviously, however, Wells Fargo was not embarrassed, for it stood solidly through the fall of Palmer, Cook & Company, and it was on hand when needed. Though "disastrous losses" were experienced, it must be assumed that in other respects the company was a going concern.

Notes in the Minutes show twelve new offices opened in 1856, not previously accounted for: Chinese Camp (in Tuolumne County), Drytown (in Amador County), Folsom, Greenwood (in Eldorado County), Indian Diggins (in Eldorado County), LaGrange (in Stanislaus County), Martinez (in Contra Costa County), Monterey, Napa Springs (in Napa County), Ophir (in Placer County), San Juan (in San Benito County), Santa Rosa, and Trinidad. Wells Fargo was still growing, opening a new office at the rate of one every three weeks.

Another interesting year was ahead: 1857, a year of grasshoppers and panic all over the nation. It would also be the year when the first organized and maintained transcontinental (or overland) mail and express route would become a reality, and would launch Wells, Fargo & Company into another phase of its far-flung activities.

It was also a year in which Wells Fargo would carry almost $60,000,000 in gold.

Advertisement for Wells, Fargo & Company, showing the capital up to $600,000, and connections with American, United States, Harnden, National, and Livingston, Wells. Near the bottom it says: "No money loaned . . ." From Amy's "Marysville Directory for the Year Commencing November 1, 1856." From the Bancroft Library, Berkeley, University of California.

1857
Year of the Jackass Mail

THE YEAR 1857 MIGHT HAVE BEEN AS much noted for its fashions as for its banking and express developments. A drawing of a ball dress shows a magnificent creation of lace, billowing pink silk, tulle, and grape leaves—the whole built tier upon tier from the ground up, and the various billows held in place by pink and white ribbons! A gorgeous thing, really, constructed over a huge bustle, with the skirt fully five or six feet in diameter. This extravagance of dress perhaps is typical of a fast-moving society, a little giddy from the gold prosperity, gyrating wildly to avoid seeing or hearing the unrest that was pushing the country into civil war.

The people of Kansas were still torn by the violence between slavery and antislavery factions; the Kansas legislature in 1857 adopted the proslavery Lecompton constitution, and that became a source of contention all over the United States—including the California legislature. Kansas had been a raiding ground for proslavery guerrillas from Missouri and other states, who swept into Kansas on wild night raids to pillage, loot, rape, murder, and burn, but in 1857 the free-state men got into the spirit of the thing, and the Territory of Kansas became "Bleeding Kansas" for sure. These affairs had a tempestuous effect in California, many of whose residents were but recently from the United States, many of them from the states directly involved.

This is the year of the Dred Scott decision, which held, by implication, that the Missouri Compromise of 1820 had always been unconstitutional because it had discriminated against slavery; and which contained the United States Supreme Court decision that a Negro, free or slave, could not be a citizen and therefore could not bring a suit in the courts. The California Daily *Register,* edited by Parker H. French, waxed eloquent from indignation at the decision:

> The great fountain of human equities, the august tribunal, armed with a mighty nation's power, and once possessing a nation's confidence, is now defiled, and flows in slimy, muddy drops, from the agitation of a Southern oligarchy.[1]

It is also the year during which the Mormons of Utah broke out in rebellion against the government because Congress had refused the admission of Utah as a state (on the ostensible ground that polygamy was against the law); the United States sent troops into Utah. Connected with this was the Mountain Meadows Massacre, in which 120 emigrants of a wagon train were murdered by Indians allegedly incited and led by Mormons. Altogether, it was a year of turmoil and violence. It is also the year during which Borden's Eagle Brand Condensed Milk first came on the market.

Henry A. Crabb, another man who wanted to be something he was not and who played politics with Mexicans for the possession of Sonora. He died in 1857 before a firing squad, even though his wife was a Mexican girl from an important family. From the Arizona Pioneers' Historical Society.

An advertisement in "Hutchings' California Magazine" for Sam Brannan's Bank in 1857.

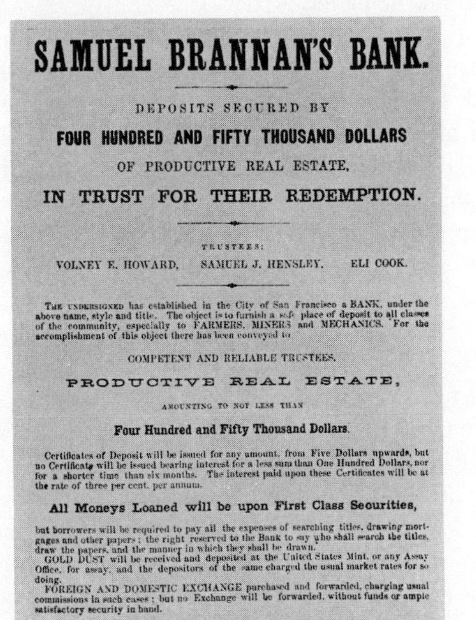

SAMUEL BRANNAN'S BANK.

DEPOSITS SECURED BY

FOUR HUNDRED AND FIFTY THOUSAND DOLLARS

OF PRODUCTIVE REAL ESTATE,

IN TRUST FOR THEIR REDEMPTION.

TRUSTEES:

VOLNEY E. HOWARD, SAMUEL J. HENSLEY, ELI COOK.

THE UNDERSIGNED has established in the City of San Francisco a BANK, under the above name, style and title. The object is to furnish a safe place of deposit to all classes of the community, especially to FARMERS, MINERS and MECHANICS. For the accomplishment of this object there has been conveyed to

COMPETENT AND RELIABLE TRUSTEES,

PRODUCTIVE REAL ESTATE,

AMOUNTING TO NOT LESS THAN

Four Hundred and Fifty Thousand Dollars.

Certificates of Deposit will be issued for any amount, from Five Dollars upwards, but no Certificate will be issued bearing interest for a less sum than One Hundred Dollars, nor for a shorter time than six months. The interest paid upon these Certificates will be at the rate of three per cent. per annum.

All Moneys Loaned will be upon First Class Securities,

but borrowers will be required to pay all the expenses of searching titles, drawing mortgages and other papers; the right reserved to the Bank to say who shall search the titles, draw the papers, and the manner in which they shall be drawn.

GOLD DUST will be received and deposited at the United States Mint, or any Assay Office, for assay, and the depositors of the same charged the usual market rates for so doing.

FOREIGN AND DOMESTIC EXCHANGE purchased and forwarded, charging usual commissions in such cases; but no Exchange will be forwarded, without funds or ample satisfactory security in hand.

THE BANK IS SITUATED IN THE

CITY OF SAN FRANCISCO,

On the Northeast Corner of MONTGOMERY and CALIFORNIA STREETS,

And will be open daily, (Sundays and Holidays excepted,) from 9 A. M. until 4 P. M.; on every Saturday evening from 7 to 9 o'clock, and on the night previous to the sailing of the steamers from 7 o'clock until 11 P. M.

SAMUEL BRANNAN.

SAN FRANCISCO, October 31st, 1857.

A ball dress as shown in "Harper's Monthly Magazine" for December, 1857

Parker H. French came back on May 21 in a lighter vein when he commented on femininity:

> But a year or two since, the advent of females in the mining regions was hailed as a novelty. [But] female influence has built up cities, made bleak hills and desert wastes a blooming garden. Refinement has shaken off the shackles of King Alcohol and the demon gambling. Cheered by woman's smile, the sturdy miner delves deep for gold.

French commented on the wind in San Francisco (May 20):

> These sea breezes are the salvation of the city during the summer months. They carry off all the odors of decomposed vegetation and filth, accumulating in by-places, on the outskirts. . . . This city is fast becoming famous for its varied occupations, and the up-town streets resound with the cries of bawling itinerants vending fruit, vegetables, fish and various other wares. They go about with carts or baskets, from morning to night, sending up a sound familiar to all who have lived in any of the larger Eastern cities. Lately we have seen the old-fashioned handcart, with jingling bells, going through the streets to pick up rags, and the valiant Frenchman with his two cows peddling fresh milk, has become one of the features of the place.

Probably the factor of most concern to bankers, however, was the panic of 1857. Railroads were being built everywhere, and the companies were overcapitalized and the lines overbuilt. The great flow of gold from California, and the gold discovery in Australia, caused prices to rise, and encouraged a mania for speculation, while at the same time the United States' reserve of specie dwindled. Generally speaking, across the United States, rainfall was scanty and crops were very poor; some regions suffered from infestations of grasshoppers. On top of everything else, gold production dropped for 1857, and the entire country on both coasts was practically bankrupt.

The last of the Sonoran filibusters occurred in this year when Henry A. Crabb led some eighty-seven Californians to a tragic rendezvous at Caborca. Crabb had come across northern Mexico, apparently with Parker H. French in 1850, had been successful in business in the Gold Country, had married a Mexican girl from a wealthy Sonoran family, and had become a state senator. But it seems that he wanted to be a governor or a United States Senator, and so embraced the Know-Nothing cause, but he lost when the election was held in the state senate. Crabb, unlike most of the filibusterers in Sonora, was an American (a Virginian)—not a Frenchman. Unlike them, too, he was already successful, but it appears that he was ambitious and impatient; he was in his thirties when he went to Sonora.

He formed an intrigue against the governor of Sonora, undoubtedly aided by his wife's family, but he failed to realize that the Mexicans were hard to beat at that sort of thing. He should have gauged the Mexicans better, because thousands of Sonorans had migrated to the Gold Country, and many wealthy Sonorans had settled in San Francisco and gone into business there.

But Crabb, perhaps piqued because he had lost a United States senatorial election in the legislature, gathered some ninety malcontented miners, disgruntled ex-politicians, and other worthless men (and a few substantial ones), and set out on foot for Sonora via the Yuma crossing, pretending that he had a contract to furnish men to work the mines of Sonora and fight the Apaches.

Typical of so many of his kind, Crabb promptly turned over the hard work to somebody else: He delegated his partner, John Cosby, to raise one thousand men and come by sea; then he set out for Sonora. There, he found that the government had changed hands, and the new governor considered Crabb's presence undesirable, and, in fact, called him a filibusterer and threatened death. Crabb encountered armed resistance, but in the bland assumption that the Mexicans would be on his side as soon as he should get under way, advanced to the small town of Caborca in northern Sonora, only to find himself involved in streetfighting. After six days of fighting, Crabb surrendered, trusting to the promises of Hilario Gabilondo that his men would be given safe conduct home. Some of Crabb's men were opposed to the surrender, pointing out that surrender to a Mexican officer generally meant death, but Crabb insisted that surrender was the best way out.

Crabb and eighty-seven men were shot in the back in the plaza, and their bodies left unburied. Crabb's head was severed, and eventually found its way to

San Francisco, where it was exhibited in a jar of alcohol, or whiskey, or mescal, or perhaps even formaldehyde. It was destroyed or lost in the fire of 1906.

Such was the feeling of Americans in California at that time that Parker H. French said in the San Francisco *Register* that he had just established:

> Twist it and turn it as you will, their death was naught but cold-blooded, inhuman butchery, under the foulest, false pretences— . . . Whatever may now be said of their intentions, whatever of obloquy may be cast on their ultimate aims, no one will refuse them a tear-drop of compassion—no one refuse to respect their memory, while hundreds will boil over with indignation in thinking of the means by which the party was routed. [!]
>
> We cannot forebear a few personal allusions. Mr. Crabb was a gentleman in every sense of that word. He may have erred in judgment once; but a more truly noble, brave, chivalric, whole-souled man, "take him for all in all," never trod the soil of California.

And one might add: "and seldom a more naive one."

However, the most important (and perhaps only) bit of information in French's tribute is the revelation that Crabb had been in trouble before—probably back in Virginia. Such a record was almost universal among filibusterers.

At two or three points, it seems that Crabb could have gone on to take Sonora if he had really wanted to, but, like most or all filibusterers, he declined to take the step. (Is it possible that such men are doomed to failure because they have the will to fail?)

Undoubtedly Crabb had received money from many different sources in California, but again it does not appear that Wells Fargo became entangled in this activity of such patent illegality.[2]

In many ways, the most important event of 1857, as far as Wells Fargo was concerned, is the establishment of the San Antonio & San Diego Mail Line (later called the Jackass Mail), the first transcontinental mail line in the United States—for this establishment of a cross-country mail route might be expected eventually to supersede the routes through both Panama and Nicaragua, for express as well as for mail. It seems doubtful that the San Antonio & San Diego ever carried a large volume of mail,[3] but it blazed the way and focused on the enterprise the attention of men like John Butterfield and his associates, who had the ability and the resources to make it successful.[4]

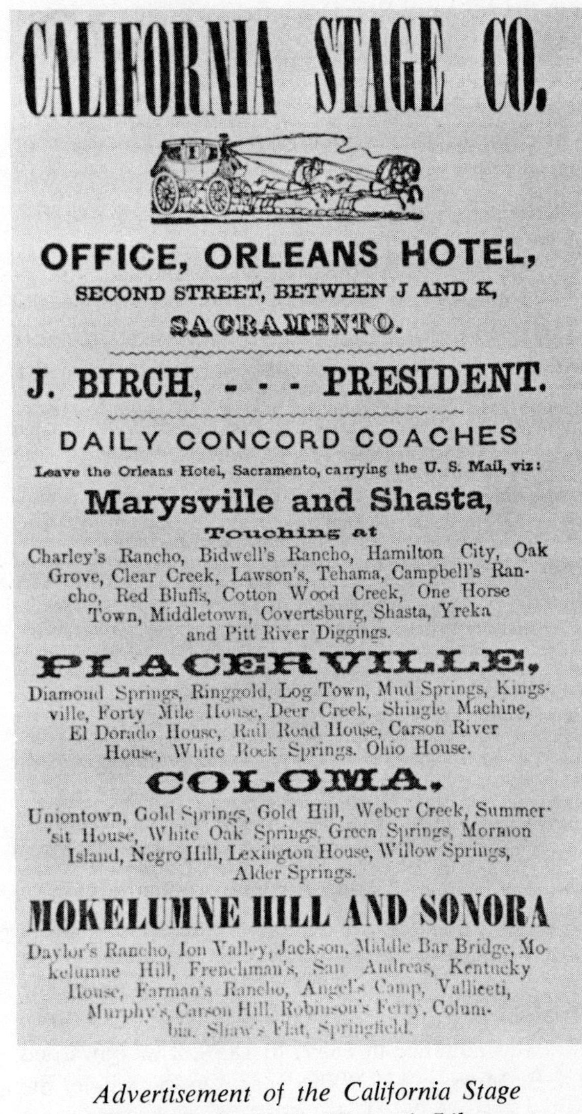

Advertisement of the California Stage Company. From the Bancroft Library, Berkeley, University of California.

There had been, of course, a number of attempts to establish mail service from East and West—most of them through Utah by what soon became known as the central route. Near the end of 1849, the Great Salt Lake Carrying Company was established to run from the Missouri River to Sutter's Fort in California (Sacramento), and carry passengers at $300 each or freight at $250 a ton. It was not a spectacular success.

In early 1850, the government moved to open an eighteen-foot post road from Fort Smith to San Diego. This effort, although in Congress, was not carried through, but it is important as the predecessor of the San Antonio & San Diego and the Butterfield Overland.

On the central route, a contract was let in 1850 to Samuel H. Woodson for monthly service from the Missouri River to Salt Lake City for $19,500 a year. Woodson in 1851 sublet the run from Fort Laramie, in eastern Wyoming, to Salt Lake City, to Feramorz Little and his Indian partner, Ephraim Hanks—who had a very difficult time. The route followed the Oregon Trail, had no stations, and went all the way with one set of animals; its schedule was thirty days, but it seldom went through on schedule. It was irregular and slow, and missed many trips altogether during the winter.[5]

In 1854, the contract for the east portion was awarded to W. M. F. Magraw (Independence to Salt Lake City), and ran until August 18, 1856.

On October 9, 1856, Hiram Kimball, a Mormon, acting for the B. Y. (Brigham Young?) Express Company, got a contract for service on the eastern leg, and, while he was making extensive preparations, Little and Hanks made one trip, but service was stopped by the Utah Indian War and the Mormon War, and the contract (for $23,000 a year) was annulled in 1857. In 1858, it was awarded to S. B. Miles at $32,000 a year. On the whole, the service east of Salt Lake City was poor—slow, irregular, uncertain, and often interrupted by violent trouble with Indians and by severe winter storms.

West of Salt Lake City the story was somewhat the same but the contractors were different. In 1851, a contract was awarded to Absalom Woodward and George Chorpenning[6] for monthly service between California and Salt Lake City. They started on May 1 but were harassed by Indians all summer and took over sixty days to reach Salt Lake City. Woodward was killed by Indians in November, and the carriers suffered frightfully from the deep snows and intense cold over the Sierras that winter. It was then that Snowshoe Thompson and others were called into service to carry the mail over the mountains. Snowshoe traveled between Placerville and Carson City and carried on his back as much as a hundred pounds.

The California Daily *Register* for May 21, 1857, spoke about Snowshoe Thompson: "The Sacramento *Union* states that Mr. Thompson, the Carson Valley Expressman, arrived in that city Tuesday afternoon . . . via Johnson's Cut-off, on horseback. . . . He encountered snow on the summit in spots from two or three feet deep." It seems that fifteen or twenty wagons from Salt Lake City were coming to Stockton to get goods from San Francisco, and Thompson had met other travelers:

> This side of Slippery Ford, Mr. Thompson met a party of seven men on their way to the States with thirty Spanish horses. They had gone by the wagon road, and had just reached Peavine Hill, on which they reported ten feet of snow, which they found to be rather troublesome. . . . He also met a party of emigrants in three wagons, twelve miles from Placerville, on their return to the States. They expected to cross the summit about the latter part of this week. They were from this city.

There are not many records of emigrants who returned to the United States in wagons.

In 1853, the compensation to Woodward and Chorpenning was increased to $30,000. In 1854, because of the severity of the mountain winters, the Chorpenning line was forced south by way of Los Angeles and the Mormon Trail (a route through San Bernardino and generally northeast through Las Vegas); it was changed to San Diego and then, in November, back to San Pedro; it used pack mules or pack horses, and ran by the southern route (usually called the Mormon Trail) until the summer of 1858.

French pointed out the need for a good wagon road in his *Register* May 21:

> The arrival of the Carson Valley expressman yesterday places us, this morning, in possession of news twenty-four days later from Great Salt Lake City than that received a short time since by the way of Los Angeles. [Twenty-four *days?*] The fact is brought home to us that the Calaveras route is preferred for wagons, and will be at once adopted. . . . The Salt Lake traders

propose to bring their wagons to Stockton and make their purchases in San Francisco. The position of Sacramento is quite as eligible, and this fact should serve as an admonition to our citizens to be up and stirring in the matter of the wagon road. Now is the time for action.

Both Adams Express and Wells Fargo sent express on the Chorpenning line from at least 1854 through 1858. Sometimes the mail and express were shipped to and from San Francisco from and to the southern terminus, and apparently this southern route was used until 1858.

James E. Birch was the moving force behind the San Antonio & San Diego; he is the man who in 1853 had consolidated all the stage lines from Sacramento to the Northern Mines into the giant California Stage Company, employing 150 persons and spending $75,000 a month in Sacramento alone. His stages ran south along the coast to Los Angeles, and his line was so successful that by fall the California Stage Company had declared at least five dividends of from 4 to 6 percent each. But Birch was more ambitious. It may have been partly a result of the fact that his young wife would not go to California with him. In 1855 he retired from active management to go east, and in 1857, after some two years of cultivating politicians, Birch won the contract to establish an overland mail, to run semimonthly, for $149,800 a year. In the face of great sectional rivalry (for naturally the North wanted a northern route), the contract was made to use the route along the thirty-second parallel through New Mexico and Arizona, following Cooke's route of 1846 (the Mormon Battalion) part of the way, and connecting East with West.

The line itself did not get off to a very strong start (although prompt enough). The San Antonio & San Diego contract was generally regarded as a preliminary to the real plum—the St. Louis to San Francisco run, with more frequent service—but in July, that run was awarded to a company headed by

The original John A. (Snowshoe) Thompson (spelled Thomson on his headstone at Genoa), who carried the mail over the high Sierras on Norwegian snowshoes (now called skis). From George Wharton James, "Heroes of California."

James E. Birch, founder of the San Antonio & San Diego Mail Company (the Jackass Mail). From the Historical Collection, Title Insurance and Trust Company, San Diego, California.

MISCELLANEOUS ADVERTISEMENTS.

OVERLAND TO THE PACIFIC.

The San Antonio and San Diego Mail-Line.

THIS Line, which has been in successful operation since July, 1857, is ticketing PASSENGERS through to San Diego and San Francisco, and also to all intermediate stations. Passengers and Express matter forwarded in NEW COACHES, drawn by six mules, over the entire length of our Line, excepting the Colorado Desert of one hundred miles, which we cross on mule-back. Passengers GUARANTEED in their tickets to ride in Coaches, excepting the one hundred miles above stated.

Passengers ticketed through, from NEW-ORLEANS, to the following points, via SAN ANTONIO:

To Fort Clark,............	Fare,	$52.	To Fort Bliss,..........	Fare,	$100.
" Hudson,.........	"	60.	" La Mesilla,.........	"	105.
" Port Lancaster,	"	70.	" Fort Fillmore,.....	"	105.
" Davis,............	"	90.	" Tucson,.............	"	135.
" Quitman,.......	"	100.	" Fort Yuma,.........	"	162.
" Birchville,......	"	100.	" San Diego,..........	"	190.
" San Elizario,...	"	100.	" Los Angelos,.......	"	190.
" El Paso,.........	"	100.	" San Francisco,.....	"	200.

The Coaches of our Line leave semi-monthly from each end, on the 9th and 24th of each month, at 6 o'clock A.M.

An armed escort travels through the Indian country with each mail train, for the protection of the mails and passengers.

Passengers are provided with provisions during the trip, except where the Coach stops at Public Houses along the Line, at which each Passenger will pay for his own meal.

Each Passenger is allowed thirty pounds of personal baggage, exclusive of blankets and arms.

Passengers coming to San Antonio can take the line of mail-steamers from New-Orleans five times a week to Indianola. From the latter place there is a daily line of four-horse mail-coaches direct to this place.

On the Pacific side, the California Steam Navigation Company are running a first-class steamer, semi-monthly, to and from San Francisco and San Diego.

Extra Baggage, *when carried*, 40 cents per pound to El Paso, and $1 per pound to San Diego.

Passengers can obtain all necessary outfits in San Antonio.

For further information, and for the purchase of tickets, apply at the office of C. G. WAYNE, 61 Camp Street, New-Orleans, or at the Company's Office, in San Antonio.

G. H. GIDDINGS, } Proprietors.
R. E. DOYLE, }

An early advertisement for the Jackass Mail, copied from "Touring Topics" by the Bancroft Library, Berkeley, University of California. The two-column format would have been unusual for a newspaper of 1858, and therefore it seems doubtful that this is a copy of an original.

John Butterfield, a director of the American Express Company. However, the Butterfield Overland was not to start service until September, 1858, and so Birch had a chance at least to make a mark.

Ships from New York or New Orleans would leave mail at Indianola, Texas, and a stagecoach would take it on to San Antonio. Birch's job was to take it from San Antonio across six hundred miles of wilderness (what Hafen correctly calls "one long battleground" with Indians—Comanches and Lipan Apaches) to El Paso, then through the deserts of New Mexico and Arizona to Yuma, across the Colorado Desert and the Laguna Mountains to San Diego, then either by ship to San Francisco, or by stage coach to Los Angeles and San Francisco.

Birch went to California probably in June, to buy animals and vehicles, to hire men, to establish stations, and to arrange for food and supplies to be delivered to those stations. The logistics were impressive, but Birch was a man of energy and resources.

The trip across the Colorado Desert would be by mules, which stood up better on the desert than did horses. Birch appointed Isaiah Churchill Woods, an expressman of some experience, general manager of the line, and thereby incurred the wrath of San Franciscans, who remembered him from the failure of Adams Express in 1855, and who were not too happy that San Diego had been designated the terminus of the stage line. It seems likely that the appointment of Woods may have had the most influence on the subsequent designation of the San Antonio & San Diego as the Jackass Mail.[7]

Beginning fare was $200 from San Antonio to San Diego, and passengers were allowed thirty pounds of baggage exclusive of blankets and firearms. The stages did not travel at night, and so the trip generally took from twenty-four to thirty or more days. A supply party out of San Antonio lost most of its animals to Comanches, but finally got through to San Diego in thirty-nine days. It was hailed with a salute of one hundred anvils,[8] and the San Diego *Herald* said its arrival was "the most important event which has ever occurred in the annals of San Diego," and said it "undoubtedly constitutes an epoch in the history of the Pacific coast of the Union, which will be recorded and remembered with great pride." (Actually, thirty-nine days was the time of the second mail; the first mail arrived with the second, and its time was fifty-four days.)

Some of the difficulties of the first cross-country mail line are indicated in a report made by Woods to the Postmaster General:

July 7 [1857].—We were due in Indianola this morning at daylight, but unfortunately grounded in a fog on a sand bar at the entrance of the bay, which lost us the connexion with the coach for San Antonio. . . .

July 19.—Today I despatch an extra train with stores for the road, and under instructions to go as far as Fort Lancaster, three hundred miles from here, and then to return. By this train I sent relays [mules] to be used by the up mail of the 24th. . . .

July 24.—I this morning despatched the mail coach from the Plaza [with] six men, well armed with rifles, and a Colt's pistol to each. Four saddles and accoutrements. Ropes, hopples [hobbles], shoeing tools, shoes and nails. Cooking utensils, and numerous minor articles. Provisions for thirty days, calculated to last to the Pimos [Pima] villages [on the Gila] and back to El Paso. Thirty-six mules.[9] Also $600 in cash to purchase supplies on the route.

August 1.— . . . The conductor of our train was compelled to remain all night in Castroville . . . in consequence of the herder having got intoxicated, and permitted six of our mules to stray. . . .

August 2.— . . . About 8 a. m. I met Captain Wallace, whom I had despatched on the 19th with relays . . . All that now remained of a fine outfit was the conductor and one man on borrowed mules. . . . One of them had his arm in a sling from a wound received in the fight. . . .

. . . On its way to Fort Lancaster, the Indians appeared suddenly on all sides of them from the chaparral, and commenced firing at the mules in the coach, the loose animals being a few hundred yards ahead. The frightened animals ran into a mezguer [a mesquite thicket?], turned short around, and broke the pole. . . . The conductor jumped from the box. A young man by the name of Clifford was either surrounded by Indians, or wounded so that he was unable to get away from the coach, and died fighting hand to hand with the Indians. The conductor got the mulada [mule herd] turned off from the road for the purpose of making a detour to escape, but the chase was so hot, and one saddle-mule having to be doubly mounted, they were compelled to betake themselves to running and leave the mules and property to their fate.

We lost coach and harness, 21 mules, provisions and equipment, $100 in money, and one box of personal property valued at some hundreds of dollars, . . .

The Indians were supposed to be Camanches. . . .

A party of infantry was kindly sent out by Lieutenant Fink, commander at Fort Hudson, to bury young Clifford and bring in the broken coach, if worth preservation. . . .

In carrying the mail we do not drive all the time from our morning start to the night camp. We stop four times during the day: twice for our two meals for breakfast and dinner; breakfast after the morning drive, dinner about 4 o'clock. We also stop once for a nooning, and once about sunset to graze the mules, at which hours they seem to feed best.

We stopped half an hour today at Camp Hudson, situated at the second crossing of the San Pedro, or the Devil's River; here I found the remnant of our coach, with the pole and ten spokes broken, the bars gone, the top all stripped, a bullet-hole through the body from a gun, carbine, or some piece carrying a heavy ball, and fired by the Indians. Made 42 miles today.[10]

Birch stayed in California only about two months and then went back East, but was drowned off Cape Hatteras in the sinking of the *Central America,* along with some three or four hundred others, including many prominent Californians. Giddings became general manager of the San Antonio & San Diego, and the business continued. By October, the time to San Diego had been cut to sometimes as low as twenty-two days; the line employed sixty-five men, and owned fifty coaches and four hundred mules. Its

The Central America *in pretty bad shape. "About eight o'clock," said the reports, "the ship began to settle rapidly, when she momentarily righted and went down stern foremost." Right here she seems to be sinking. From "Frank Leslie's Illustrated Newspaper," October 3, 1857.*

coaches made forty miles a day—not much compared to John Butterfield's day and night travel in 1858. The San Antonio & San Diego would run until 1861, but John Butterfield's contract overshadowed it, and it was doomed to a relatively small place in the affairs of Western transportation.

There seems to be, at the moment, no direct evidence that Wells Fargo used the San Antonio & San Diego, but since Wells Fargo maintained a station at Oroville in Arizona Territory, it does not seem reasonable to question it.

Advertisement of the Pacific Mail Steam Ship Company for the Golden Gate *in 1857.*

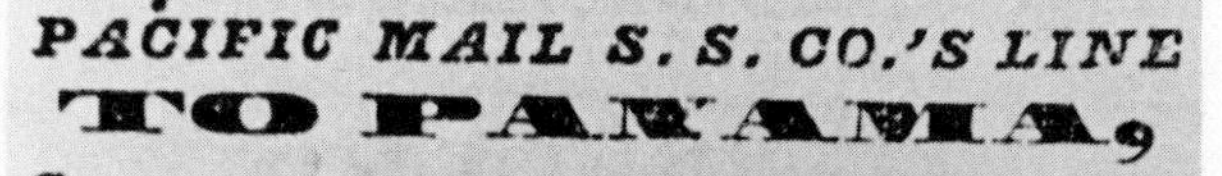

PACIFIC MAIL S. S. CO.'S LINE
TO PANAMA,
Connecting, via Panama Railroad, with the Steamers of the U. S. Mail Steamship Company at
ASPINWALL.
FOR NEW YORK AND NEW ORLEANS, DIRECT.
The Only Reliable and Safe Route.
Departure from Vallejo street Wharf.
The Favorite Steamship
GOLDEN GATE,
Will leave Vallejo street Wharf with the United States Mails, Passengers and Treasure, for PANAMA,
SATURDAY, July 20th, 1857,
At 12 o'clock, A. M, punctually.
Passengers by the P. M. S. S. Co.'s line are landed, on their arrival at Panama, upon the wharf at the Rail road terminus, by the Company's steam ferry boat, and proceed immediately by
RAILROAD ACROSS THE ISTHMUS,

In 1857, E. A. Rowe, the president of Pacific Express, was found guilty of speculating with state money and losing $124,000 (supposedly supplied to him by Henry Bates, the state treasurer to whom Wells Fargo had loaned $20,000 the year before), and was sent to prison.

Parker H. French got into the act in his *Register* on May 20:

> We have watched the progress of public outcry against these gentlemen with more than ordinary interest. They have been made the scape-goats of political rascals and public plunderers far more infamous than themselves. . . . Admitting that Dr. Bates is guilty as charged, he cannot be a hardened or bad man, for we are reliably informed that the blow thus given to his fair name, and the whirlwind of scorn that has overtaken him, has withered his life like the blast of the eastern sirocco. . . . We truly sympathise with that gentle being, who with bleeding heart and agonising brain, watches by the couch of him she has sworn to love and to honor. [Boo, hoo!]
>
> As to Col. Rowe, it was perfectly legitimate to contract with the State Treasurer for the payment of our July interest. . . . Mr. Rowe refused to make an expose of his private business, and for this he is incarcerated. Now, he may not be able to pay the interest, even though he should be disposed to do so, . . . because the legislature imprisoned him for a contempt offered their body.

A further note in the *Register* for May 21 gives this information: "The Sacramento *Union* says: Yesterday Henry Bates was again up before the Supreme Court on *habeas corpus,* for a reduction of bail. The Court denied the application. A writ of *habeas corpus* in the case of E. A. Rowe was also issued yesterday." He had refused to answer questions before a grand jury. "Rowe was taken before the Supreme Court yesterday. This accounts for his appearance on the streets. He was in charge of an officer."

Lucas, Turner & Company closed on May 1, 1857, without loss to the depositors.

The *Central America* went down in September off Cape Hatteras in a heavy sea; the engineer was accused of leaving his post and failing to feed coal to the fires, so the ship foundered and sank. Wells Fargo was the largest loser in coin and treasure; it had shipped $260,000 down on the Pacific Mail steamer *Sonora* on August 20, and that had been picked up at Aspinwall by the *Central America.* Wells Fargo was insured, however, under a running policy of $1,100,000 with four companies in London, and it may be presumed that the loss was paid. The total loss was $1,595,497.13 in treasure, and probably most of that was insured, but there were many losses in gold and in coin and drafts carried by passengers—possibly as much as half a million dollars' worth or more—and altogether the very heavy losses were difficult for California to bear. The general panic of 1857 might not have affected California very much if it had not been for this extraordinary loss. Drexel, Sather & Church lost heavily on the *Central America,* and it rather appears that that firm did not have insurance, for it suspended; it later paid off and resumed business in April, 1858.

The national panic started on October 23, 1857, by the closing of a large firm in New York, and quickly spread to Boston, Philadelphia, Baltimore, Washington, St. Louis, Cincinnati, Wheeling, Toronto, and all places in between with astonishing rapidity. Banking and mercantile firms of all kinds closed one after another, and by November 3 the country was paralyzed. On November 17, the San Francisco *Bulletin* printed a list of failures in the East—two long columns of six-point type that seem endless. However, it seems that San Francisco firms had already gotten themselves into good shape following the debacle of Palmer, Cook & Company, and there was no widespread failure in that city.

Wells Fargo seemed to go its unruffled way. Its directors did not change in 1857, and early in the year the notes from the Minutes say: "Conditions in California having improved somewhat, limited and well secured accommodations to certain parties were authorized on February 17, 1857." The parties are not named, nor is the extent of the accommodations defined, but this obviously means that they were starting again to make loans. It should be borne in mind that Wells, Fargo & Company was still basically an express company, and that this official recognition of the banking function was one more step toward development of that aspect of the business.

The Sisters of Mercy of San Francisco had a long appeal for funds for the ignorant, the sick, unemployed females, orphans, and fallen women in the *Register* for May 20, endorsed and paid for by nineteen men and firms including Lucas, Turner; Garrison, Morgan, Fretz & Ralston; Drexel, Sather & Church; and a number of other bankers; and Wells Fargo.

On May 20, the steamer *Sonora* took nearly $2,300,000 worth of treasure; Drexel, Sather & Church topped the list with $344,000, while Wells, Fargo & Company was second with $336,212.74.

On May 21, the California *Register* published a "Disaster Calendar" and noted that Captain Thomas, a resident of Sonora for six years, had been murdered by his barkeeper, an Italian; Thomas Walker was accidentally shot at Wisconsin Bar and died on the 14th; and a miner named Rice was stabbed at Quincy by William Harper, the result of a drunken quarrel. The *Register* also showed a characteristic shortness of temper when it said: "The Sonora *Herald* says that McCauley and Davis, convicted of murder, will certainly be hung by the people, if not by the law." It was almost enough to make a murderer crave justice.

Directors and officers for 1857 were the same as those for 1856. During the year, Charles F. Latham was appointed agent at Philadelphia, and also, two cash dividends were authorized: 5 percent on January 15 and 5 percent on July 30.

One list of "new offices opened during 1857" shows Gold Hill, Nevada (a forerunner of the great Comstock activity), Santa Cruz, Shaws Flat in Tuolumne County, Suisun in Solano County, Todds Valley in Placer County, Watsonville in Santa Cruz County, and Yreka. Another list of "agencies operated" shows a number of other changes, and deserves being given in full:

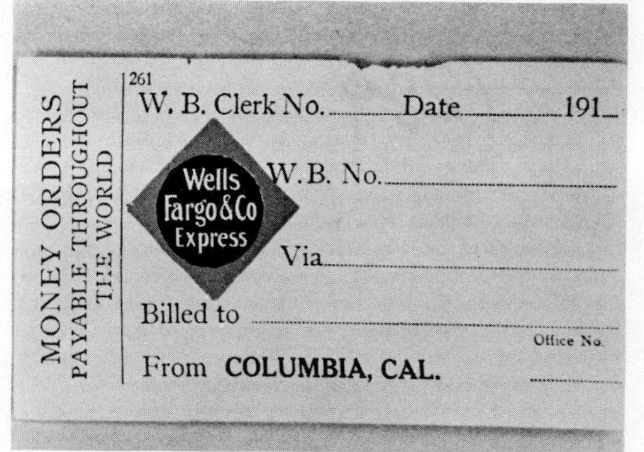

A Wells Fargo label from the office in Columbia, California, sometime after 1910. The pad of original labels is in the History Room, Wells Fargo Bank.

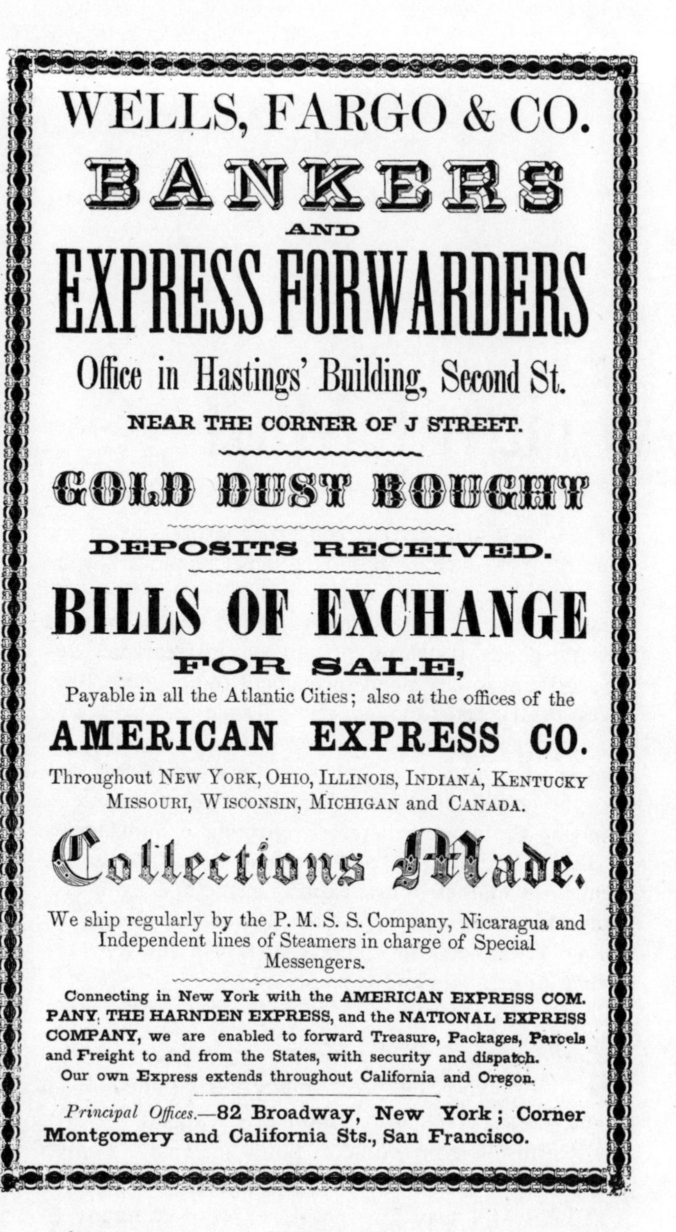

Advertisement for Wells, Fargo & Company in Amy's "Marysville Directory for the Year Commencing June, 1858." From the Bancroft Library, Berkeley, University of California.

Angels Camp, Auburn, Benecia, Boston, Camp Seco, Camptonville, Carrollton, Cherokee, Chinese Camp, Coloma, Columbia, Colusa, Crescent City, Diamond Springs, Downieville, Drytown, El Dorado, Fiddletown, Folsom, Forest City, French Bar, Georgetown, Gold Hill, Goodyear Bar, Grass Valley, Greenwood, Honolulu, Hornitos, Indian Diggins, Ione Valley, Iowa Hill, Jackson, Jamestown, Knights Ferry, La Grange, Los Angeles, Mariposa, Martinez, Marysville, Michigan Bar, Michigan City, Mok Hill, Monterey, Mormon Island, Murphy's Camp, Napa City, Napa Springs, Nevada, New York, Ophir, Oroville, Petaluma, Philadelphia, Placerville, Portland, Prairie City, Rattlesnake, Red Bluff, Rough & Ready, Sacramento, San Andreas, San Diego, San Francisco, San Jose, San Juan, Santa Barbara, Santa Clara, Santa Cruz, Santa Rosa, Sebastopol, Shasta, Shaws Flat, Sonoma, Sonora, Stockton, Suisun, Sutter Creek, Timbuctoo, Todds Valley, Trinidad, Uniontown, Vallecito, Vallejo, Volcano, Watsonville, Yankee Jim's, and Yreka.

The big year of 1858 was coming up. The Great Overland Mail of John Butterfield would get under way, running from St. Louis to San Francisco in twenty-five days. Wells Fargo would ship mail and express by the Butterfield route, and would control it within three years.

1858
The Great Overland Mail

In July, 1858, *Frank Leslie's Illustrated Newspaper* published a page on the American Express Company—which shows the great interest the public had in the thriving express industry at that time. A large woodcut shows the new five-story building of American Express at the intersection of Hudson and Jay streets in New York City; the building was of Westchester marble, and had two tracks laid in from the Hudson River Railroad. Its office department appears to have been quite ornate, and undoubtedly was the last word in 1858. Indeed, the item says it is "not surpassed by any private business structure in the country." The company's operations extended west to Iowa and Minnesota, and in 1857, the New York office alone had handled nearly 17,000,000 pounds of freight. The "money department" was separate from the freight department (banking department separate from express department), and before the panic of 1857, it had handled $2,000,000 in "treasure" (presumably coin, specie, gold dust, and gold bars). The value of money, goods, "and treasure" in the hands of the various agencies at certain times of the day amounted to over $5,000,000. The company had about a thousand employees, and its expenses were over $6,000 a day "whether the company do any business or not."

"The business ten years ago was a novelty," says *Leslie's*, but it is now one of the recognized institutions of the country. Yet, even at this day, some people ask what the express companies do! It would be easier to tell what they don't do in the way of business. Money, jewelry, goods, packages, presents, daguerreotypes, &c., &c., are sent to any point throughout the country. Bills, notes, drafts, and accounts are collected and paid. If a merchant sells goods to a Western customer that he does not know, or does not trust, the express company take the goods and deliver them at the customer's door, receiving the money therefor, returning it immediately to the seller. Butter, poultry, game, and fruits are brought to market by the express men. In short, everything almost that any person could do for himself by taking a journey, the express men will do for him, saving him trouble and expense.

Leslie's speaks of American's beginning, and says that "The whole express matter, contained in a single carpet bag, was frequently carried by Mr. Wells himself from point to point . . . Truly, a great result from a diminutive commencement!"

Adams still was the biggest express company in the East, while Wells, Fargo & Company was the biggest in the West, and there were many smaller ones, so it seems obvious that the country in general approved the two guiding principles of the express companies: promptness and safety. Express was faster than freight, and it was the only safe way to transfer valuables. American had instituted the col-

The American Express Company putting on a parade with eight black horses and plenty of silk hats. From an 1858 lithograph.

lect-on-delivery system by that time, but that innovation in business received only passing mention in *Leslie's*.

The proprietors of the biggest privately owned building in New York threw a big parade, with bands playing and with the directors riding in a huge express wagon drawn by ten magnificent horses. The directors, naturally, were in beaver hats and their best Prince Albert coats, and a thirty-one-star American flag floated in the breeze. The thirty-first star was for California, which had become a state in 1850.

American Express that year (1858) attempted to get into the travel business; it established a New York agency for the Atlantic Royal Mail Steam Navigation Company, and four months later reported a net profit of $603, but John Butterfield, perhaps too busy with the Great Overland Mail, led a move to get American out of the travel business. Harnden had done well at it, but Butterfield felt that it was too small to bother with.

The San Antonio & San Diego was still running, but probably not with much spirit, since its place had been superseded (by the announcement of the Butterfield contract) before it dispatched its first mail from San Antonio.[1] Northern California did not like it because it stopped at San Diego and because I. C. Woods was running it. They said the line "started in the middle and didn't go anywhere"; a passenger had to allow fifty or sixty days to make the trip from New Orleans to San Francisco. The company had only three substantial buildings on the route—at San Antonio, El Paso, and San Diego. Each of the other eighty-four stations had, at best, a mud shack and a brush corral, while most of them were no more than camping places. That would be changed under John Butterfield.

In those days there was a considerable division of opinion as to whether the post office should be self-supporting. One faction held that it was the duty of the post office to pioneer, to open roads to encourage emigration, while the other side felt that it ought to be a business and ought to be run as a business. Californians, however, were not misled by either argument. They wanted mail service and they said loudly that it was the government's duty to provide it even though the cost seemed exorbitant. Also, there was a considerable body of opinion in the West against the "steamship monopoly," and many Californians felt that there could be no answer to the mail problem until an overland service should be established.[2]

The bill that led to the establishment of the Great Overland (the Butterfield) route had become law on March 3, 1857, under the urging of Senator Gwin of California, Senator Rusk of Texas, and Representative Phelps of Missouri. Birch made a bid on the Great Overland contract and rather expected to get it, but the San Antonio & San Diego contract was signed the day before the Great Overland bids were opened.

The act of Congress left great latitude in the hands of Postmaster General Brown, who was from Tennessee. His personal reasons may have been important in choosing the route, but it does seem that the southern route is the only one open all winter long. Of course, it was well understood that emigration would follow any established route, and perhaps Brown wanted to encourage settlement of the southwest area in the hope of widening the slave territory.

Inasmuch as the contract was not to be let on the low bid, but rather on the Postmaster General's opinion of the bidder's ability to perform under the contract, and since John Butterfield was a friend of President Buchanan, it rather seems that James E. Birch did not have a chance at this contract. It may be that Birch too had friends in Washington, and that he was given the San Antonio to San Diego contract to satisfy them. Whatever did happen, it seems obvious that influence played a decisive part in the Overland Mail contract, and now indeed we wonder what faction of the American Express Company directorate had been backing Fillmore. It seems evident that, among the directors, they had backed both Fillmore and Buchanan, and one is left with the inevitable question: Who backed whom? And still a further question arises: Since they protected themselves with both Democrats and Know-Nothings, they must have protected themselves with Frémont too, for Frémont, the son-in-law of Thomas Hart Benton, always a man of great influence in Washington, believed in taking care of his friends always.[3]

At any rate, the storm broke when Brown announced the route. Even John Butterfield apparently did not like the southern route, but Brown insisted, and Butterfield went through with it. This route was from St. Louis by train to Tipton, Missouri; by stage to Springfield; Fort Smith, Arkansas; Preston on the Red River in Texas; Fort Belknap; across the Pecos River to El Paso; through present Lordsburg, New Mexico, and into Arizona at the north end of the Chiricahua Mountains; west to Tucson; north and west to Maricopa Wells; down the Gila River to Yuma; across the Colorado Desert, circling through Mexico to avoid the soft-sand dunes west of Yuma; through Vallecito and Warner Springs, northwest to Los Angeles, and up the coast to San Francisco.

The original officers of Butterfield's company, officially designated the Overland Mail Company, were John Butterfield, president;[4] William B. Dinsmore, vice-president; Johnston Livingston, secretary; Alexander Holland, treasurer. The directors were William G. Fargo, Hamilton Spencer, James V. P. Gardner, D. N. Barney, E. P. Williams, Marcus L. Kinyon, Hugh Crocker, Giles Hawley, and David Moulton.[5]

The route and terms of the contract were agreed to in September, 1857, and the service was to start in September, 1858. Surveying crews were sent out; roads were repaired and new ones were built; stations were located and built, wells dug, tanks built; eighteen hundred horses and mules were bought. Test runs were made, and schedules were worked out for supply trains and watermen as well as for the coaches. Two hundred and fifty coaches were ordered (most of them were celerity wagons—not Concords), and other vehicles were ordered. Harness was ordered. Conductors, drivers, station keepers, blacksmiths, mechanics, helpers, herders, and others were hired. A half interest in the California coast route was bought, and a steamboat bought for the Arkansas River. About $1,000,000 was spent before the coaches got under way. The total mileage was about 2,800. The coaches would run day and night, and the route had to be traversed in twenty-five days or less. They were to run semiweekly, and the government would pay the company $600,000 a year.[6]

John Butterfield's first and last rule was: "Remember, boys, nothing on God's earth must stop the United States mail!" and his 2,000 employees seemed to believe it. The drivers would use four, five, or six animals, depending on the terrain and the load; mules were used in Indian country (from Fort Belknap to Fort Yuma), and it was expected that the team would be changed at every station (every twelve or fifteen miles). On occasion, however, the stations were much farther apart, and a band of mules was driven with the coach to provide the changes.

The Concord coach had a capacity of some 4,000 pounds, and would seat nine passengers inside. The coaches were $1,400 each, and were lettered "Overland Mail Company" across the top on each side. The celerity wagon, invented by Butterfield, had the undercarriage of the Concord, but the top was a frame covered with canvas. Therefore, it had a lower center of gravity and was not as likely to turn over on rough roads. There was no provision for passengers to ride on top, but the inside seats could be made into a bed. The celerity wagon, or mud wagon, ran from Fort Smith to Los Angeles.

J. Waterman Ormsby, the New York *Herald-Tribune*'s reporter who was the first through passenger from east to west, said: "When the stage is full, passengers must take turns sleeping. Perhaps the jolting will be found disagreeable at first, but a few nights without sleeping will soon obviate that difficulty. . . . A bounce of the wagon which makes one's head strike the top, bottom or sides will be disregarded, and 'Nature's sweet restorer' found as welcome on the hard bottom of the wagons as in the downy beds of the St. Nicholas [Hotel]," but he did say that the "wagons and coaches can hardly be expected to equal the Fourth Avenue horse cars for comfortable riding." He said of the meals supplied:

John Butterfield, about 1858 or a little later. Butterfield had a hand in many early transportation projects, and is said to have had a very early company across the Isthmus of Panama.

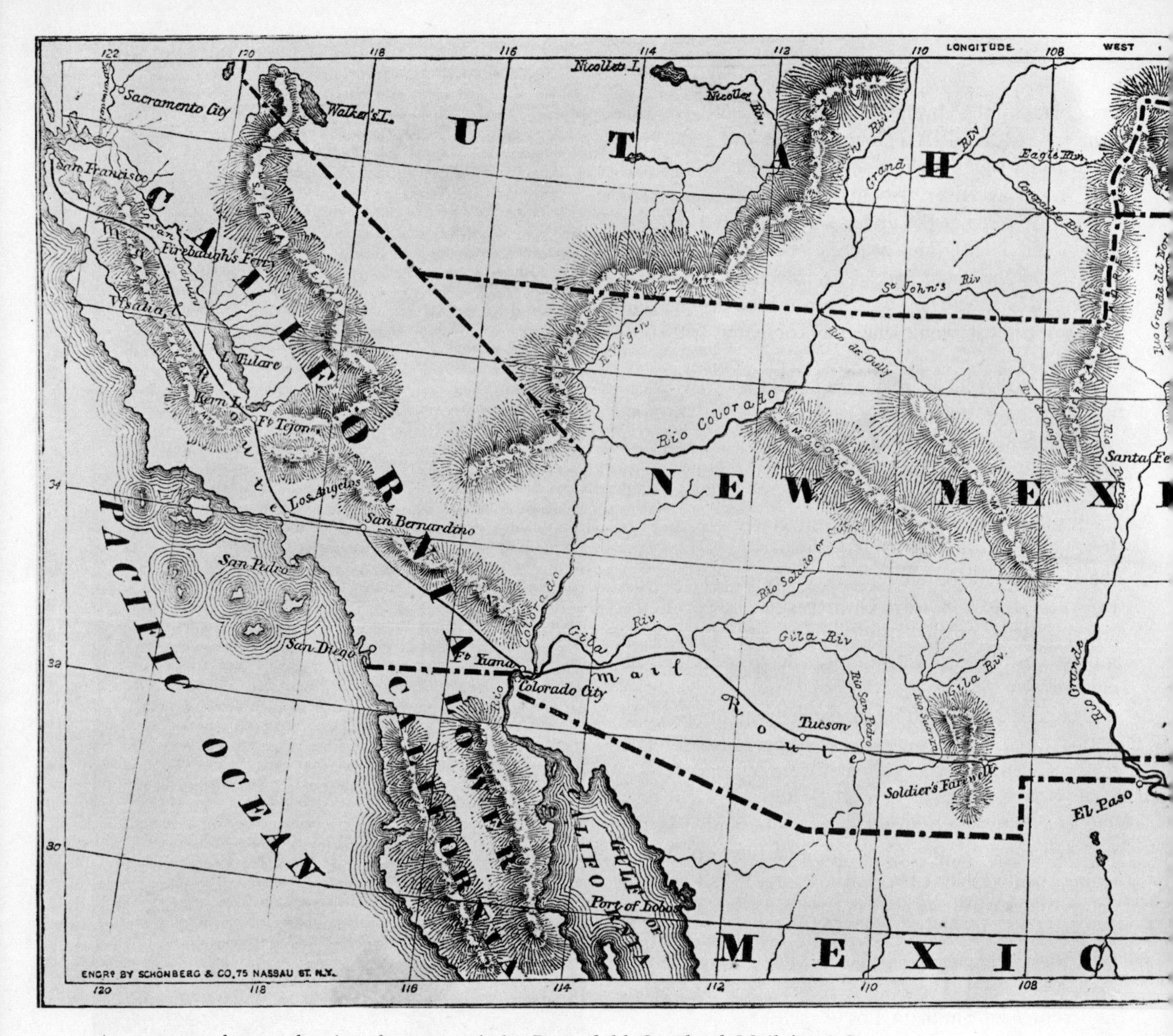

A pretty good map showing the route of the Butterfield Overland Mail from St. Louis and Memphis to San Francisco. From "Frank Leslie's Illustrated Newspaper," November 27, 1858.

"The fare could hardly be compared to that of the Astor House . . . consists of bread, tea, and fried steaks of bacon, venison, antelope, or mule flesh—the latter tough enough. Milk, butter, and vegetables can only be met with towards the two ends of the route." Other passengers spoke of jerked beef, mesquite beans, corn cake, black coffee, and "slumgullion" (which seemed most unsavory in reputation; perhaps, after a hard day's ride, it tasted better than it looked).

The problems of supply alone were enormous; each station, for instance, had to have up to 100 tons of hay a year—and hay cost $43 a ton in California, and had to be hauled long distances. Corn cost up to $5 a bushel at the station. Water had to be hauled; food had to be provided.[7]

The first mail left Tipton, Missouri, September 16, 1858, and reached San Francisco on Sunday morning, October 10. Ormsby says:

> It was just after sunrise that the city of San Francisco hove in sight over the hills, and never did the night traveler approach a distant light, or the lonely mariner descry a sail, with more joy than did I the city of San Francisco. . . . Finally we drew up at the stage office in

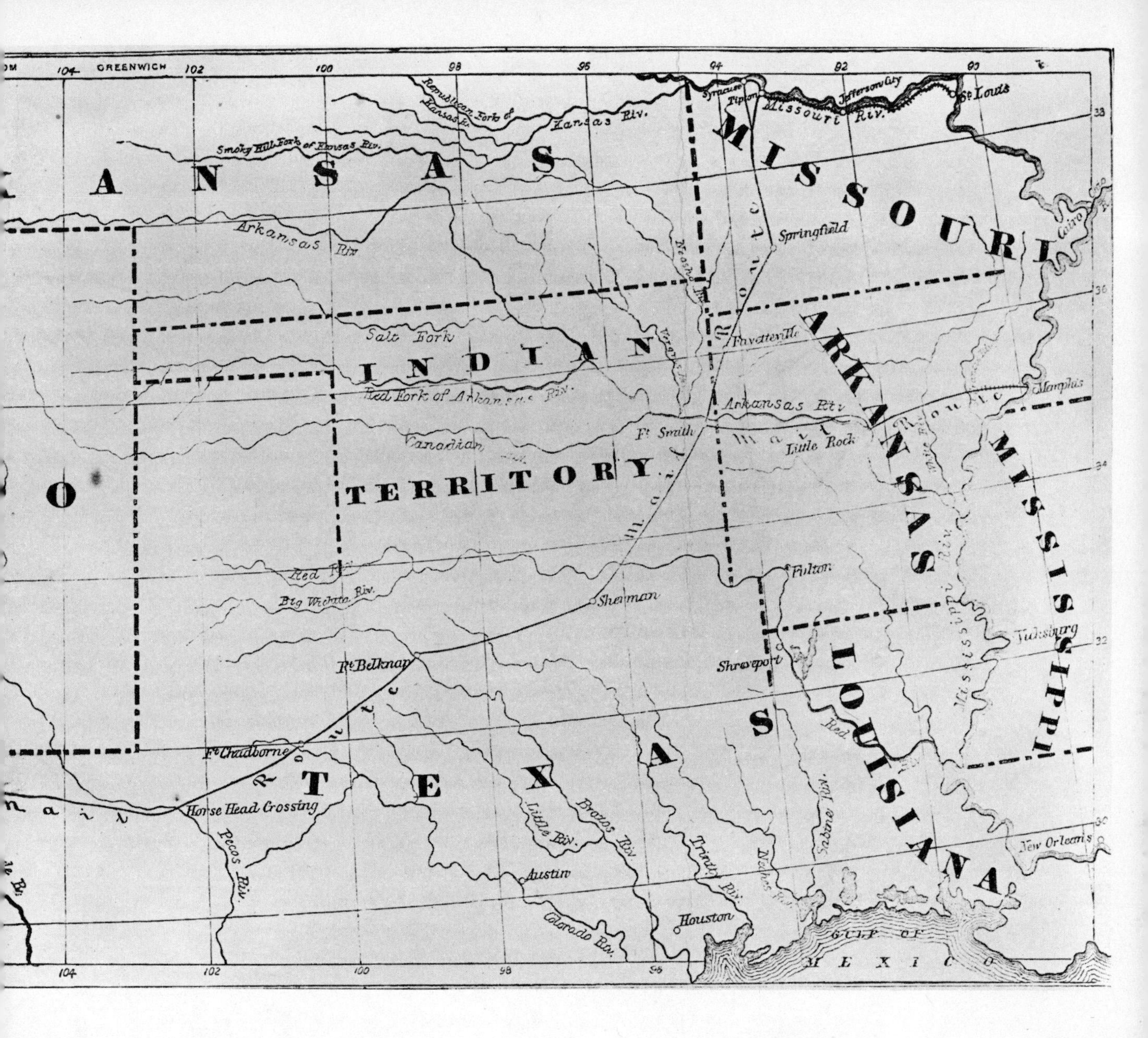

front of the Plaza, our driver giving a shrill blast of his horn and a flourish of triumph for the arrival of the first mail-bags. . . . It was 23 days, 23½ hours from St. Louis.

The *Alta California* issued an extra that day, and announced that the Overland had beaten the steamer mail by ten days. A mass meeting was held at Musical Hall on Monday night to celebrate the happy event, and probably it was a convivial meeting, for it elected a president, seventeen vice-presidents, and four secretaries. The president made an address and was followed by Ormsby, who evoked "terrific applause" (which he received "coolly"). Another speaker demanded that the time be shortened to eighteen days, and then resolutions were offered in praise of the Postmaster General—one of the few times in recorded history.

It is significant that Butterfield's first coach to the West carried some express packages for Wells Fargo.[8] Probably the express company had long before made arrangements with the Overland Mail Company.

The coaches traveled about 120 miles a day

REAR VIEW OF TUCSON.

In the early days, Tucson wasn't much. Even in 1858, it drew J. Ross Browne's ridicule as he designated this picture (in his series, "A Tour Through Arizona," in "Harper's Monthly Magazine") a "rear view of Tucson."

The Overland Mail coach starting from Tipton, Missouri, after picking up the mail from the railroad. John Butterfield, Jr., was driving this coach. From "Frank Leslie's Illustrated Newspaper," October 23, 1858.

The Overland Mail coach crossing a stream at night, preceded by a man on horseback holding a lighted lantern. From "Frank Leslie's Illustrated Newspaper," October 23, 1858.

John Butterfield, Jr., with what seems to be an oversized bow tie, who drove the first mail coach out of Tipton, Missouri. From "Frank Leslie's Illustrated Newspaper," October 23, 1858.

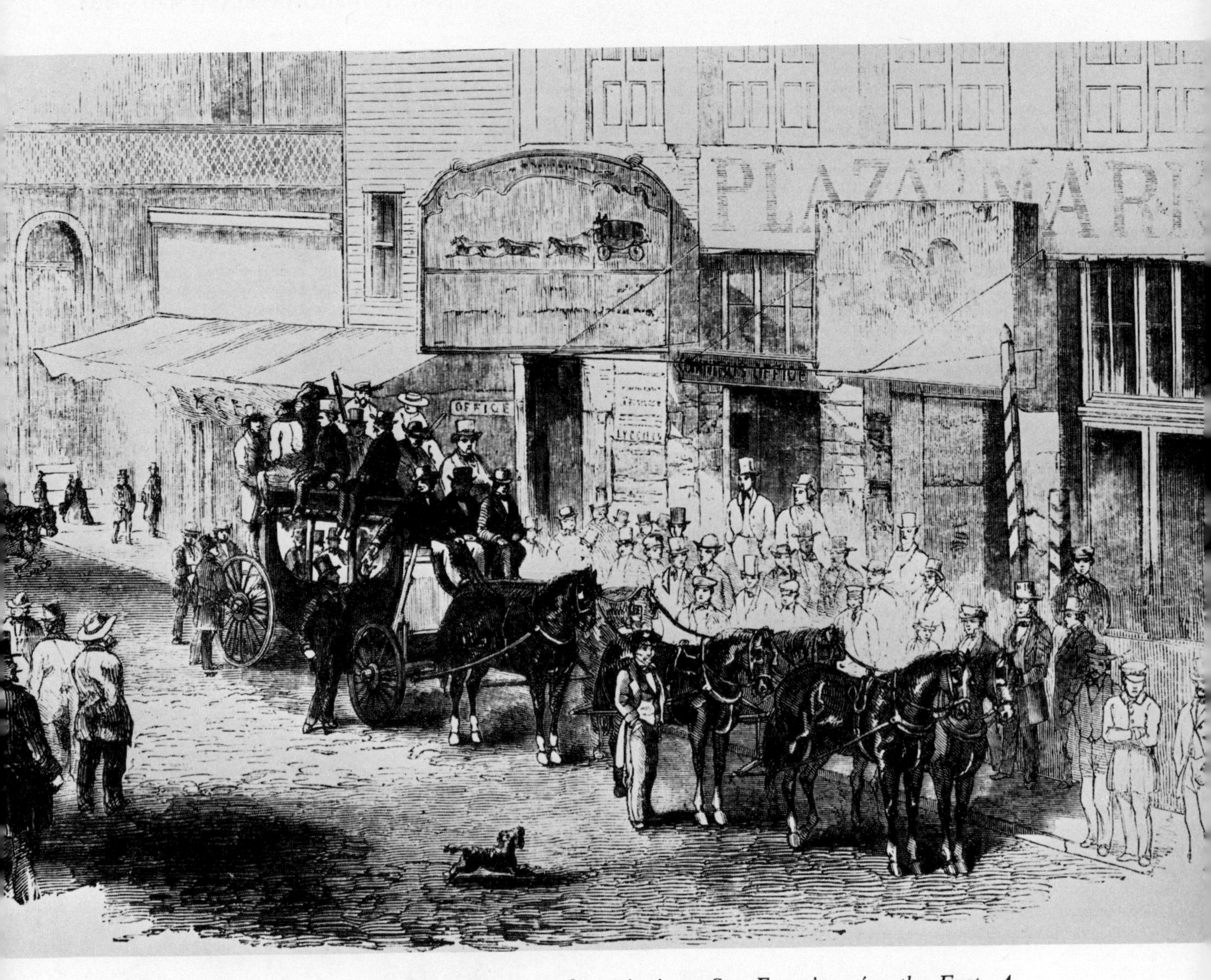

The Overland Mail starting on its first trip from San Francisco for the East. A woodcut made from a photograph for "Harper's Weekly," December 11, 1858.

(twenty-four hours)—an average of five miles an hour. On prairie lands they made as much as twelve miles an hour, but in the mountains the speed dropped to three miles an hour, and often the passengers had to walk.

The fare was generally set at $150 each way, or ten cents a mile for short trips. Passenger traffic was usually said to be good, as was express traffic, but mail income did not approach the cost to the Post Office Department. It was possible for a passenger to stay over at a station to get a rest from the day and night ordeal, but there was no assurance that he would get an early seat in another coach, and it was said that a passenger had stayed at a station as much as thirty days waiting for a chance to continue his journey.

However, perhaps even passenger business was not overwhelming, because statistics gathered from the San Francisco *Herald* and the St. Louis *Republican* show that in forty-seven stages reported (out of 104 possible during that time), there were eighty-five through passengers, west to east, and about the same number east to west. Seldom were there more than two, and sometimes none. One-way passengers probably were about 150 for the first year in each direction.[9] These figures would not indicate enough passenger traffic to be a very big factor.

It is said to be John Butterfield who introduced the conductor's horn, on which a long blast warned the station keeper to get ready to change teams and feed passengers.[10] All mail was accompanied by a conductor, who was the official horn blower.

There was great potential trouble from Indians, but it was usually limited to attacks on stations and especially to stealing stock. Only one open attack on a Butterfield coach was made successfully: in Apache Pass, just west of the New Mexico-Arizona state line, in 1861, when no mail was lost and nobody was killed.[11]

What did San Diego, bypassed by the Overland, think of the great event? Well, John Judson Ames, the editor of the San Diego *Herald*, was in San Francisco when the Overland arrived, but the *Herald* ignored it until November 13, when Ames said:

> Seats are engaged weeks in advance, and indeed the trip overland can only be indulged in by a few amateurs who are fortunate enough, in the lottery, to draw a prize . . . It is simply preposterous to expect the immense travel between California and the Atlantic states ever to be performed in stages. . . . Suppose the number of persons to be a thousand per month, each coach would have to carry 60 persons, and that would require 15 coaches with four passengers running every other day—an arrangement utterly beyond the power of any company. . . . Let it once be enacted that a national railroad will terminate at the Colorado.

Perhaps he had reason to be sour—but the big coaches continued to rumble across the continent, bearing people, mail, express, and gold, and only the Civil War would stop them. The San Antonio & San Diego would continue to run too, but it would use Butterfield coaches between El Paso and Vallecito; eventually the line between Yuma and San Diego would lose its mail contract. (The San Antonio & San Diego continued to operate, however, and was given a contract in 1861, after Butterfield's departure, to go the whole distance again, but was not able to fulfill it.)

Wells Fargo lost no time taking advantage of the new facilities, and sold envelopes stamped "Overland Mail, via Los Angeles." The *Alta California* of November 8 says:

John Judson Ames, legendary six-foot-six founder and editor of the San Diego "Herald," who steadfastly ignored the Butterfield Overland as long as he could, then scorned it. From the Historical Collection, Title Insurance and Trust Company, San Diego, California.

"Arrival of the Overland Mail. . . . Through the kindness of Messrs. Wells, Fargo & Co., we are in receipt of the St. Louis *Republican* and *Democrat* of October 14th, . . ." and continues exultantly: "The Isthmus routes, whether by Panama, San Juan, or Tehuantepec, will have to be regularly beaten by the mules of Mr. Butterfield."

It added: "The Overland edition of the *Alta California* attracted very general attention in St. Louis and other cities," and adds still another bit of information that does not wholly support the speculations of the San Diego *Herald* as to the lack of capacity of the stages to handle the traffic: "The stage brings no through nor way passengers."

About that time, there occurred another act that, to say the least, has not been habitual in America: The post office advertised for business. This particular item was in the San Francisco *Herald*:

> *Overland Mail via Los Angeles:* This mail is made up at this office at 10 p. m. every Sunday and Thursday. Letters for this route should be endorsed "Overland, via Los Angeles." Postage Three Cents per half-ounce, under 3,000 miles, and Ten Cents over that distance. C. L. Weller, P. M.

The advertisement is keyed: "oc6 law3mSat," which means it was to run once a week, Saturday only, for three months starting October 6.

On the whole, the Butterfield Overland Mail, like all the other mails to California, did not pay its way, although it may have made money from its express and passenger revenues. It did, however, provide a means of communication that, curiously enough, was to lead to its own undoing, for the distrust and hate over slavery had gone too far, and now communication, instead of bringing a modicum of understanding, added emphasis to the differences—fanned the fire that was leading to civil war.

It is not possible at this moment to know the exact time at which Wells, Fargo & Company began to obtain control of the Overland Mail Company, but it seems likely that the enormous cost of putting the line into operation (said to be over $1,000,000) charged against the paid-in capital ($2,000,000, but, says one report, only 5 percent paid in, which means $100,000) was so great that Wells and Fargo, seeing an opportunity to improve their express service and to tap a rich new field, came to the rescue with loans from Wells Fargo funds.[12] At any rate, the vast organization of John Butterfield continued to function well. The stages usually made the trip well under the contract time of twenty-five days, and never required more than twenty-six and a half days. By 1860, it was carrying more mail than was going by ocean, and by that time it had put wagons on the route exclusively for express. It was the longest stage line on earth, and one of the most successful.

Another curious aspect is apparent. Since John Butterfield had several times negated attempts of the American Express Company to extend its business, but since he himself had made a king-size gamble, one begins to wonder if there was not friction between him and other members of the board. Both he and Henry Wells were too hard headed to suffer in silence, and it may be that John Butterfield, in an attempt to make a place for himself in the sun, overstepped himself and merely put himself in the power of Wells Fargo.

On the central route, in May, 1858, John M. Hockaday became the contractor for two years on the eastern leg (Salt Lake City to Independence), and operated four-mule vehicles once a week for $190,000 a year. This line, then, combined with that of Chorpenning, meant a thirty-eight day schedule between Independence and Placerville in July, 1858, and this combination was the great competitor of John Butterfield on the southern route. Butterfield had the advantage, for his service was on a twenty-five-day schedule from St. Louis to San Francisco.

In 1858, Chorpenning returned to the original route of 1851, and in October the service was increased to weekly, and the equipment became six-mule coaches rather than pack animals; the trip from Placerville to Salt Lake City and return was on a sixteen-day schedule, and the pay was $130,000 a year.

Chorpenning and Hockaday maintained fair regularity, even in the winter. They employed men on snowshoes when they could not get through otherwise (especially on the west side), and upheld the central route, though somewhat feebly compared to the massive organization of Butterfield.

Actually, the government, which was the butt of much abuse (and sometimes rightly so), tried other ways to establish mail service to the West. On October 1, 1858, Jacob Hall received a contract for monthly service from Kansas City to Stockton, California, via Santa Fé; he was to use six-mule wagons and make the trip in sixty days, roughly along the 34th parallel, or the northern route through Arizona. The first eastbound mail left Stockton on November 1, 1858, but did not get through because of the Mohave Indians. It seems that only two westbound mails ever reached Stockton (the last one on May 22, 1859), and only four eastbound mails reached Kansas City, so it may be assumed that this attempt was not a roaring success, even though the people of Stockton were wildly enthusiastic for a while.

Another route, now little known, deserves to be recorded, because it was, for a while, a very strong competitor of all the overland routes, and mail shipped over it would reach San Francisco much sooner than by even the Butterfield Overland. This was the route across the Isthmus of Tehuantepec in southern Mexico.

The first mail over the Tehuantepec route reached San Francisco in November, 1858, from New Orleans in eighteen days, and all that winter and spring the time was regularly from fifteen to eighteen days. The mail went by steamer to Minatitlan on the Atlantic coast, from there up the Coatzacoalcos River by riverboat to a town called Suchil, then across the isthmus by Concord stagecoach to Tehuantepec or Ventosa, and from there up the Pacific coast by steamship. It appears that the Tehuantepec route was faster than any of the others, and it had much backing,[13] but it was not in the United States and therefore (perhaps especially because many Mexicans were hostile to it), although it carried much mail during its year or so of existence, it never was a serious threat to the overland lines.

In the latter part of 1858, then, strange as it may seem, the Hockaday-Chorpenning combination was a fairly strong competitor of Butterfield's route—perhaps because of intense sectional feelings and perhaps because the central route had a better territory to draw from.

A map from "Frank Leslie's Illustrated Newspaper" (December 18, 1858), showing the route through Panama and that through Nicaragua, the shortcut across the Isthmus of Tehuantepec, and one through Honduras that seems never to have been developed.

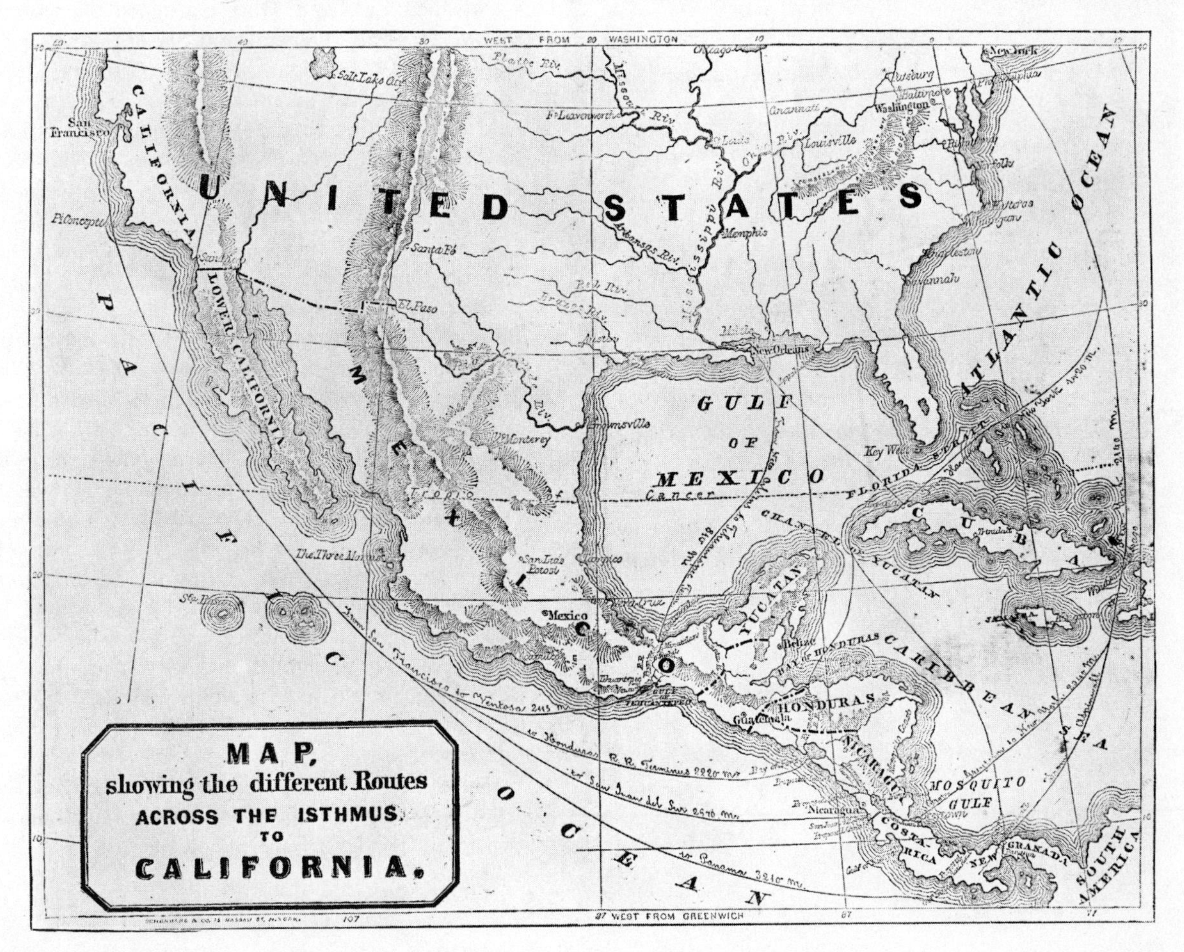

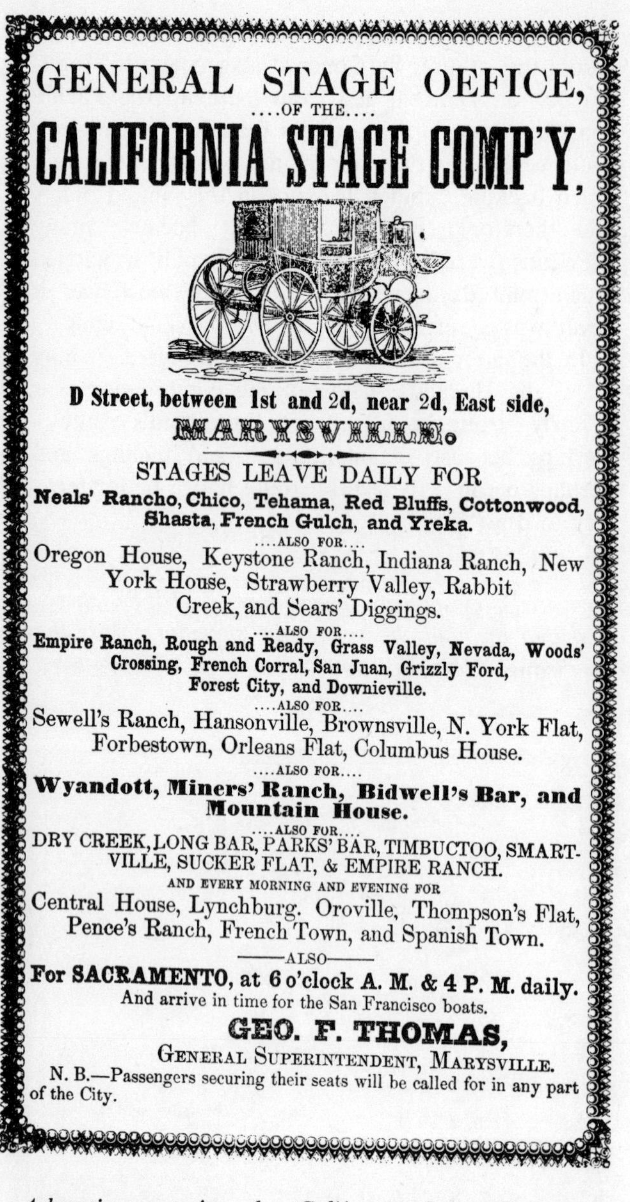

GENERAL STAGE OEFICE,
....OF THE....
CALIFORNIA STAGE COMP'Y,
D Street, between 1st and 2d, near 2d, East side,
MARYSVILLE.
STAGES LEAVE DAILY FOR
Neals' Rancho, Chico, Tehama, Red Bluffs, Cottonwood, Shasta, French Gulch, and Yreka.
....ALSO FOR....
Oregon House, Keystone Ranch, Indiana Ranch, New York House, Strawberry Valley, Rabbit Creek, and Sears' Diggings.
....ALSO FOR....
Empire Ranch, Rough and Ready, Grass Valley, Nevada, Woods' Crossing, French Corral, San Juan, Grizzly Ford, Forest City, and Downieville.
....ALSO FOR....
Sewell's Ranch, Hansonville, Brownsville, N. York Flat, Forbestown, Orleans Flat, Columbus House.
....ALSO FOR....
Wyandott, Miners' Ranch, Bidwell's Bar, and Mountain House.
....ALSO FOR....
DRY CREEK, LONG BAR, PARKS' BAR, TIMBUCTOO, SMARTVILLE, SUCKER FLAT, & EMPIRE RANCH.
AND EVERY MORNING AND EVENING FOR
Central House, Lynchburg. Oroville, Thompson's Flat, Pence's Ranch, French Town, and Spanish Town.
——ALSO——
For SACRAMENTO, at 6 o'clock A. M. & 4 P. M. daily.
And arrive in time for the San Francisco boats.
GEO. F. THOMAS,
General Superintendent, Marysville.
N. B.—Passengers securing their seats will be called for in any part of the City.

Advertisement for the California Stage Company for eight lines leaving Marysville, from Amy's "Marysville Directory for the Year Commencing June, 1858." From the Bancroft Library, Berkeley, University of California.

In 1858, Wells Fargo had practically a monopoly on the transportation of gold, and in that year it handled over $58,000,000 worth of gold bullion in California. Then Wells Fargo had a monopoly on the express business in Sacramento and in the Southern Mines; it traveled with the late James Birch's California Stage Company over 1,900 miles of lines.

In 1858, a new gold rush developed and for a time threatened to depopulate California: the gold rush to the Fraser River district in British Columbia, which turned out to be completely phony.

In 1858, Wells Fargo seems to have taken a definite step as a banking concern, because on that date it advertised in the San Francisco *Herald* as "Wells, Fargo & Co. New York and California Express and Exchange Company. Capital, $600,000." They would

draw bills of exchange, in sums to suit, on all the cities of the United States and Canada; Union Bank of London, London; and Royal Bank of Ireland, Dublin. —Advance on Gold Dust consigned for Assay, and receive Deposits, General and Special. EXPRESS Forwarders and Commission Agents. Ship Treasure at the Lowest Rates, and insure under our own open policies, held with the best English Companies, viz.:—Indemnity Mutual Marine; Marine Insurance; Royal Exchange Insurance, and London Assurance.—Forward Freight and Parcels to all parts of the United States and Canada, and through the "American and European Express and Exchange Company," to all parts of Europe.—Execute Commissions, make Collections and Purchases, and attend promptly to all matters pertaining to the Express business.—Forward Daily Expresses, in charge of experienced and faithful Messengers, to all the Towns and Mining Camps in California; Semi-Monthly to Oregon and intermediate points on the Northern Coast; Port Townsend and Olympia; to San Diego and intermediate points on the Southern Coast; and by every vessel to the Sandwich Islands. [It also carries the usual warning:] For the better security of ourselves and the public, Agents in California, Oregon and Washington Territories are furnished with "Appointments" or Commissions, specifying their powers as our Agents. Such "Appointments" they are required to keep exposed to the public view in their places of business.

Office—Corner California and Montgomery Sts.

Louis McLane, General Agent for California. G. W. Bell, Sam'l Knight, Superintendents.

Bill for a fireproof safe, No. 4½, weighing 1,460 pounds. It cost Wells Fargo $150—and another $50.25 to get it delivered. The original is owned by the California Historical Society.

Advertisement for Everts, Wilson & Company's Express at Marysville. It seems that even at that date, Everts, Wilson covered a nice territory including Rabbit Creek, Poorman's Creek, Onion Valley, Harrison's Diggings, Spanish Flat, City of '76, Barnard's Diggings, and Poverty Hill. From Amy's "Marysville Directory for the Year Commencing June, 1858," by courtesy of the Bancroft Library, Berkeley, University of California.

All this was run under the heading "Bankers," and it is interesting to observe that, under such a heading, the express business still gets the most space.

The treasurer, whose name generally appears as T. M. Ianes in the Head Minutes, appears here as T. M. Janes; this advertisement had been running since January 31.

The Head Minutes speak of the proposed purchase of a competitor when they say: "During the fall of 1857 and spring of 1858, conversations were had with the Adams Express Company in regard to Freeman & Company, California Express, but nothing definitely developed during the year in regard thereto." Perhaps Freeman wanted to sell but wanted too much money for its business.

Morgan resigned as director of Wells Fargo on July 20, and N. H. Stockwell was elected. Thomas M. Janes resigned in November, and Morgan was reelected. James McKay resigned as secretary in November, and Stockwell was elected secretary. Charles F. Latham, not a director, was elected treasurer in place of Janes.

Again the company paid 10 percent cash divi-

It's not exactly like the topless girls in a North Beach bar in San Francisco, but never think that the miners and cattlemen watching this performance were not aroused. You may note that, on both sides of the house, men in the boxes have feminine companionship, and these women do not look or act like wives. It is reminiscent of the Birdcage Theatre in Tombstone, Arizona, but this variety-show entertainment, complete with orchestra, was in Cheyenne, Wyoming, according to "Frank Leslie's Illustrated Newspaper" for October 13, 1877.

dends during the year—5 percent on February 1 and 5 percent on August 2.

The list of agencies "opened" during 1858 shows Forest Hill in Placer County, Olympia in Santa Cruz County, Oregon City in Oregon, Port Oxford in Oregon, Port Townsend in Washington, Poverty Bar in Sierra County (California), San Bernardino, Umpqua in Oregon, Victoria in San Bernardino County, Visalia in Tulare County, and Whatcom in Washington.

In reference to the latter part of 1858, Carl I. Wheat says:

> Wells, Fargo & Co.'s Express was at this period the most important agency for both express and mail service throughout California and particularly in the mining regions. It commenced its business in the state in 1852, and by a prodigious effort weathered the financial storm of 1855. By 1858, Wells Fargo went everywhere, did almost anything for anybody, and was the nearest thing to a universal service company ever invented. Next to the whisky counter and the gambling table, Wells Fargo's office was the first thing established in every new camp or diggin's.[14]

Three important developments were ahead for 1859: the discovery of gold in Colorado, the discovery of silver in the Comstock, and the beginning of the development of the network of stage lines on the eastern half of the central route (Utah to the Missouri River) that was eventually to attract Ben Holladay and then Wells Fargo.

It was also a memorable year because of the death of Rattlesnake Dick, a highwayman who had been pestering stagecoaches and getting away with the treasure for a number of years.

1859
The Fabulous Comstock

As early as 1850, Gold Rush emigrants had discovered gold north and west of Carson City, around Gold Hill and in Six-Mile Canyon, but the finds had never been rich, and the area remained a poor man's bonanza until 1859, when it was discovered, belatedly enough, that the ore was fabulously rich with silver, and the great rush started to Virginia City, then called Virginia Town.

The machinery needed for mining and refining, the tools, the supplies, and the men all were at hand in the California mines, just across the state line, to rush the great Comstock mines. And rush them they did. Men poured into the Gold Hill-Virginia City area by the thousands—booted, red-shirted, bearded—brawling, drinking, and always ready to fight. It had taken a year for the California rush to get under full steam, but the Comstock came into existence full blown. The dusty roads and passes across the Sierras were choked with men on foot, men on horseback, wagons pulled by horses, mules, and oxen. It was rugged country—but they were rugged men. It was said that ox teams of sixteen, twenty, and twenty-four animals were so thick on the road that if a driver had to pull out for any reason, he might have to wait all day to get back in line.

Aside from these personal aspects of the Comstock discovery, there were many of significance. That tremendous mountain of silver re-created the early days of 1849 and revived Sacramento and San Francisco with its flood of precious metal. A mint would be established at Carson City, Nevada, near Virginia City; huge fortunes would be made from the Comstock Lode, and those fortunes would lead into the Southern Pacific, the Central Pacific, the Bank of California, and the Nevada National Bank, and eventually into Wells Fargo itself.

The enormous sums of money to be made from the Comstock would play a major part in financing the Union during the Civil War, and, in fact, in holding the Union together; they would be responsible for Nevada's becoming a state in 1864; they would produce national senators and play a part in presidential campaigns; they would affect the economy of the entire world. And through it all, Wells Fargo had almost a monopoly on the express business. It was there, too, that Wells Fargo first became the actual owner of a stage line: the Pioneer Stage Line from Placerville to Virginia City.

Wells Fargo established a bank in Gold Hill in 1859, but it is not clear just when the company went into Virginia City. It rather appears that it had an express office there in 1860, for in that year it "quit buying gold" for a short time. At any rate, in 1861, the company built a new banking building in Virginia City on the east side of the main street.[1]

The building was of typical Wells Fargo construction: red brick with bright green shutters. And since the ground sloped away sharply from its front, it was built on a rock foundation that formed a

THIS!
THE WATER HERE IS POISON AND WE LOST SIX OF OUR CATTLE, DO NOT LET YOUR CATTLE DRINK ON THIS BOTTOM
As the trains headed across numerous mountain streams toward the Deer Creek ferry across the North Platte, many a hopeful family had the experience shown *below*.
Alonzo Delano, *Old Block's Sketch-Book, or, Tales of California Life*. 1856

A well organized die-off of all four horses hitched to a covered wagon by an emigrant. The implication is that the horses had drunk from gyppy or otherwise poisoned water—but seldom did four animals die so neatly. From Alonzo Delano's "Old Block's Sketch-Book."

basement. On the street a little farther south, in Gold Hill, another redbrick building without the shutters would be the Bank of California a few years later.

It was this year that Rattlesnake Dick reached the end of his rope. Stage robbery had started in April, 1852, when a gang under Reelfoot Williams held up the Nevada City coach and took $7,500 from the express company's box. A sheriff's posse took after the robbers and killed three of them, while Rattlesnake Dick escaped. His true name was Richard H. Barter, and supposedly he was the son of a British army officer, but he had prospected at Rattlesnake Bar in Placer County, and had served time for horse-stealing. He was said to have been killed in 1854, but it may have been another Rattlesnake Dick, for the stage robber seemed to keep right on. He got information about gold shipments from a prostitute in Shasta, and robbed a Wells Fargo mule train of $80,000 in 1855, a Rhodes & Lusk Express of $26,000 in 1856. He was captured but escaped and hid out in San Francisco, but soon found himself on the run because of the Vigilance Committee, and went back to his real love: stagerobbing. The year 1856 was a high point (or low point) in holdups; somebody was a holdup victim nearly every day that summer and autumn; there were many shoot-outs. Rattlesnake Dick was arrested more than once, but escaped from most of the jails in the Sierras.

Tom Bell's gang also was in its heyday in those months, and when there was too much heat on Rattlesnake Dick's gang, his outlaws merely shifted to Tom Bell. Bell operated on a grand scale but wound up with four hours to write letters before he swung from a tree. But Rattlesnake Dick kept going until August, 1858.

Gold coin, gold dust, and gold bullion were likely to be on every hand in those days, as happened one day in May when a banker's agent carrying $20,000 in dust in his carpetbag fooled some robbers who stopped the stage by telling them that a stage immediately behind them had plenty of treasure. The highwaymen did not find the dust in his carpetbag, but waited for the second coach. The second coach had a small safe for the Alta Express Company, which the robbers got—but they demanded the Wells Fargo box (which held $21,000 in gold). They broke open the box and helped themselves. Then two dust buyers galloped up to catch the stage, with

$16,000 in dust with them. The dust buyers were lucky, because the robbers fled.

In the year 1858, Wells Fargo lost many shipments. Robbery was so common that one miner kept three live rattlesnakes in the trunk where he cached his dust.

It was in July that Rattlesnake Dick got his just deserts. He was recognized by a man in Auburn, who got two deputies and went after him. In a gunfight, the man who had recognized him was killed, while Rattlesnake Dick, wearing fine black trousers and a cream-colored vest, got a bullet from breast to back that wounded vital organs, and another from side to side that also wounded vital organs. He got away—but not far. They found him a mile from the scene of the fight, with a bullet through his brain.

Wells Fargo was not quiescent over these compulsory changes of ownership of gold dust. It hired detectives, it enlisted the aid of sheriffs and police officers of all kinds, and it offered rewards. The time was still about fifteen years before the coming of J. B. Hume, but Wells Fargo fought back. It hired special messengers with rifles and shotguns to ride the stages, and it left no stone unturned to find the stolen treasure and catch the highwaymen. It is said that the shotgun guards were able to stop only about half of the attempted robberies—but that certainly was worthwhile.

And Wells Fargo lived up to its reputation for safety. It made good on every ounce of dust that was taken while in the company's hands.[2]

Probably the most effective publicity for the central route and for overland routes in general came in 1859 when Horace Greeley, the editor of the New York *Tribune,* made a vividly publicized transcontinental trip via the Overland. Greeley was a considerable character in his own right—a leader, a fighter, a man whose movements always made news. He wore boots, and usually one trouser leg was caught on a boot top. He had silken whiskers that overflowed his collar; he wore glasses and a string tie, a tall white hat and a white duster; he carried a whalebone umbrella and a carpetbag. But he wrote, and people read, and nothing all the overland-mail proponents could possibly have done would have focused so much attention on the Overland and on the West. He seems not to have mentioned Wells Fargo, as did most travelers, and Alexander Majors says somewhat sourly that Horace

Horace Greeley, the one and only, editor of the New York "Tribune," was a much better newspaperman than he was a business manager, and presently lost control. He backed Frémont in 1856, and lost. He was nominated for President in 1872 by the Liberal Republicans and by the Democrats, but lost decisively in a bitter campaign with General Ulysses S. Grant; he was relentlessly opposed by "Harper's Weekly," and never recovered from the vilification of the campaign.

Greeley was deadheaded to California—meaning that the overland companies carried him without charge. Majors' lack of enthusiasm is hardly justified on that count, however, for it was customary to give all editors free passage on public transportation in those days, and the practice did not really go out of style until after 1918.

Perhaps it was enough that Greeley thought well of the West, and particularly boosted for a Pacific railroad.

It was in 1859 that one Pardee (probably William I. Pardee, who had been manager of the San Francisco agency) was the express agent for John Butterfield in Washington, D.C., and it rather seems that he had a hand in a test of speed between Butterfield and Hockaday of the central route. Hockaday had long been trying to promote such a test to prove that the central route was the quickest way to California, and so in December, 1859, it was arranged that each line should carry the President's message. Hockaday made early application for copies of the President's address, and spent some $8,000 preparing for the run, but—alas and alack!—the Butterfield agent in St. Louis got his copy and left for Fort Smith without delay, while Hockaday's agent cooled his heels in St. Louis, and it was said that the President had refused to deliver a copy of the address to Hockaday.

Butterfield's line delivered the message in San Francisco on December 26; the mail steamer delivered it on December 28; and Hockaday delivered it in Placerville on January 1. There are many ways to skin a cat, and John Butterfield had no intention of being beaten by a competitor. The arrangements were credited to one A. R. Corbin, a "lobby agent" in Washington. Somehow, it was overlooked that the Hockaday line actually made the run from St. Louis to Placerville in seventeen days.

Gold had been discovered at Denver in the summer of 1858, and the big movement of men came the following spring, and gave rise to the transportation companies that eventually were swallowed up by Ben Holladay and then by Wells Fargo.

Hockaday's route was up the North Platte River once a week in wagons or stagecoaches (his contract was to run until 1860) and the post office nearest Denver was Fort Laramie, some 200 miles away. In November, 1858, one Jim Saunders "with his squaw" drove a small wagon from Denver to Fort Laramie and returned with mail, charging fifty cents for letters, twenty-five cents for newspapers. Apparently Saunders made several trips, but was replaced in the early spring of 1859 by the Leavenworth & Pike's Peak Express of William H. Russell and John Jones. This was an outgrowth of the great freighting firm of Russell, Majors & Waddell that had been formed in 1855 with a contract to carry all army material and supplies to the army posts west of Leavenworth. In the Utah War of 1857–1858[3] the firm had great success by carrying 16,000,000 pounds of government freight,[4] but, once that affair was over, the firm's business was only a fraction of its former business, and Russell wanted to get in on the ground floor at Denver. Majors was cautious, so Russell went into partnership with John S. Jones, and they gave ninety-day notes to the freighting firm (Russell, Majors & Waddell) to finance their operations.

The first coaches of the Leavenworth & Pike's Peak reached Denver in May, 1859, substantially following the Republican River from Leavenworth.

In that same month, Hockaday, having had his mail service cut from weekly to semimonthly (with an accompanying decrease in pay), found himself in trouble, and Russell and Jones bought his mail contract, and, since they would be carrying mail to Utah, changed their route to the Platte River, running semiweekly. Their main business was in passengers, for by their line a man could get to Denver in about a week. The L. & P. P., however, did not have a mail contract, and could carry mail only as express, and even the combination of the L. & P. P. and the Hockaday line did not make expenses. As in California, the government was slow to act, and so it cost the people of Jefferson Territory (the proposed name of Colorado) twenty-five cents to get a letter, ten cents to get a newspaper. Express was generally twenty to forty cents a pound.

It was in 1859 that Russell, Majors & Waddell began to make plans for the Pony Express, which eventually was to break them and throw them into the hands of Wells Fargo.

The directors of Wells Fargo held further talks with the Adams Express Company about Freeman & Company's California Express. The Adams company was opposed, and Wells Fargo's directors passed a resolution to censor the Adams company "for its attitude," and a copy was sent to the Adams company. A committee was appointed to negotiate further, and on October 4 an agreement was signed between Wells Fargo and the Freeman company, by which the Freeman company sold its express business for 1,000 shares of the capital stock of Wells Fargo. Wells Fargo's capital stock was to be increased for that purpose, and if it should be increased more than 1,000 shares, Freeman & Company was to get one seventh of the increase.

On November 17, 1859, the capital stock of the company was increased from $600,000 to

$1,000,000, so it appears that Freeman & Company should have received one seventh of 3,000 shares, or a total of 1,428 and a fraction shares.

Another important item of business was handled: the amendment and extension of the Articles of Association of Wells, Fargo & Company, to take effect January 1, 1862, was authorized, and a committee was appointed to obtain the signatures of all shareholders; the association was to be extended for twenty years.

The usual cash dividends were paid: 5 percent on February 1, 5 percent on August 1.

At the November 17 meeting, James McKay resigned as director, and Ashbel H. Barney was elected to succeed him. The board of directors was then composed of Danford N. Barney, president; N. H. Stockwell, secretary; Charles F. Latham, treasurer; Edwin B. Morgan, Henry Wells, Ashbel H. Barney, E. P. Williams, Benjamin P. Cheney, Johnston Livingston, and William G. Fargo.

Twenty-eight new agencies were opened in 1859 by Wells Fargo: Amador in Amador County, Bear Valley in Mariposa County, Big Oak Flat in Tuolumne County, Clarksville in Eldorado County, Dutch Flat in Placer County, Eureka in Humboldt County, Fort Tejon in Kern County, Fort Yuma in San Diego County (on the route of the Butterfield Overland), Fraser River in Fresno County,[5] Fresno, Gilroy in Santa Clara County, Healdsburg in Sonoma County, Jenny Lind in Calaveras County, Lancha Plana in Amador County, Live Oak in Sutter County, Redwood City in San Mateo County, Salmon Falls in Eldorado County, San Luis Obispo, San Rafael, San Quentin, Seattle in Washington Territory, Springfield in Tuolumne County, Steilacoom in Washington Territory, Tehama in Tehama County, Trinity Center in Trinity County, Ukiah in Mendocino County, Vacaville in Solana County, and Windsor in Sonoma County.

Total agencies operating December 31, 1859: 126.

There is no list by which deletions or changes can be checked, and it will be observed that Gold Hill, listed in Thompson & West's *History of Nevada* as established in 1859, is not included. It is in the 1860 list, however, and it seems likely that the *History of Nevada* is mistaken; it was not quite characteristic of Wells Fargo to go into a new territory so abruptly.

1860 was coming, and Virginia City would be roaring; Wells Fargo would haul (as express) everything from crushing mills to fresh oysters to cut flowers to ladies of the night, for millions were made in Virginia City, and millions were spent. The Wells Fargo agency there would become the richest in all its great empire.

It also would be the year of the Pony Express, the most spectacular of all transportation efforts. The Pony Express did not make any money—in fact, it broke Russell, Majors & Waddell—but it carried the mail with great vigor and complete reliability. Its real problem was that it could not compete with the telegraph.

1860
The Pony Express

The 1860's meant prosperity for California. In fact, the *Alta California* said on October 10, 1860:

> Perhaps at no previous period of our history has there been so widely diffused financial ease among the people of our state as at present. No complaint is heard of "hard times" among the industrial classes, of whatever denomination, and cases of industrial misfortune have, for some time past, been exceedingly rare. This, in a great measure, results from the foreign demand this year for our agricultural products; the employment this demand, in one manner or another, has given to thousands, and the consequent diffusion of ready cash among the people, . . . Altogether the present promises to be a notable year in our progress.

Indeed it was a good year, and so were the rest of the years in the decade.

By 1860, too, public sentiment over the United States began to favor the overland routes over the sea routes, partly because of the efficient conduct of the Butterfield line, and partly from the flamboyant trip of Horace Greeley.

However, it was not unconditional prosperity for the various firms providing transportation on the overland routes. In February, 1860, the new Leavenworth & Pike's Peak Express found itself in financial trouble, and had to turn for help to the freighting firm (Russell, Majors & Waddell), and presently was absorbed by a new company, the Central Overland California & Pike's Peak Express Company, among whose directors were Alexander Majors and William B. Waddell of the old freighting firm, and Jones and Russell. Very soon, then, the Chorpenning contract from Placerville to Salt Lake City was cancelled for "failures" of service, and the contract went to the C. O. C. & P. P. At that point, the C. O. C. & P. P. (later known as "Clean Out of Cash & Poor Pay") controlled the mail service from the Missouri River to California; its total subsidy from the government was $162,000 ($130,000 on the Hockaday contract, and $32,000 on the contract formerly held by Chorpenning).

The transcontinental service was semimonthly, and the C. O. C. & P. P. continued to operate into Denver, three times a week, during the summer of 1860, but soon had to compete with the Western Stage Company, which in August obtained the first government mail contract for service to Denver. It was to run from Fort Kearney, and, since Western also had a contract from Omaha to Fort Kearney, it made strong competition for the C. O. C. & P. P., which cut rates on letters to ten cents, newspapers to five cents. Its stages ran three times a week against Western's one, and so it was able to hold its own on passenger business, but fares were reduced. It had been receiving $100 for passage from St. Joseph, Missouri, to Denver, and that had to be reduced to $75.

The C. O. C. & P. P. obviously was gambling when

A symbolic drawing in R. Guy McClellan's book, "The Golden State," showing emigrants (and one busted emigrant), stagecoach, Pony Express, and telegraph.

it went ahead with the Pony Express in 1860—but the stakes were big: a daily-mail contract between the Missouri River and California. That was the big contract that everybody had been trying to obtain, and that Russell, Majors & Waddell were trying to secure by demonstrating their ability to maintain daily service over the long and hazardous route.

It seems that not even the Butterfield line in the Southwest was doing too well in 1860, for by early spring, says *Old Waybills,*[1] it was apparent that Wells Fargo was the dominant factor in the Butterfield Overland Mail, even though Dinsmore, who was president of Adams Express, succeeded Butterfield as president of the mail company in April.

Facts are hard to come by in the disputed question as to whether or not Wells Fargo got control of Butterfield, but there are numerous secondary indications. For instance, the San Francisco *Bulletin* on February 9, 1863, and again on June 7, 1864, says that Wells Fargo was a heavy investor in the Butterfield Overland Company. (See also Samuel Bowles, *Across the Continent* [Springfield, Massachusetts: Hurd & Houghton, 1866], p. 51.)

> From [Salt Lake City] to Nevada and California, about seven hundred and fifty miles farther, the stage line is owned by an eastern company [Butterfield], and is under the management of Wells, Fargo & Co., the express agents. All this is a daily line, . . . From Salt Lake, Mr. Holliday runs a tri-weekly coach line north and west nine hundred and fifty miles through Idaho to the Dalles on the Columbia River in northern Oregon.

It does not appear that Wells Fargo was *managing* the Butterfield line, but certainly it was acting as agent for it, and had express rights over it. Among

Alexander Majors, early freighter on the Plains, partner in the Pony Express, and partner in the Central Overland California and Pike's Peak Express.

the dispatches carried by the first Pony Express was one that said, "The New York *Herald's* Washington correspondent says the Butterfield Overland Mail is now under the control of Wells, Fargo & Company." No authority is cited in this item, but apparently it was generally believed or known that Wells Fargo controlled the Overland.

There was still a place for the Pony Express. The Overland Telegraph was being constructed, and that, when completed, would provide fast transmission of news. News was not, however, a substitute for mail, and so the cry was louder than ever for a daily mail service, especially inasmuch as it was obvious that the North and the South were drawing further apart. It seemed only a matter of time until the mail service should become daily, and Senator Gwin of California assured William H. Russell that it was necessary, if he hoped to get a daily contract, to demonstrate the feasibility of daily service, and promised that he would support any such attempt. Russell, Majors, and Waddell, therefore, began the Pony Express as a private enterprise, without a mail contract and with no guarantee of one. Alexander Majors says that neither he nor Waddell wanted to take a chance on the Pony Express because they did not believe it could make money, but Russell had been boasting in Washington, and now he said that his pride was involved—so they went along.

They bought about four hundred light ponies (the best they could find for speed and endurance), hired 125 riders, and set to work in the early spring of 1860 to build relay stations over the entire route from St. Joseph to Sacramento, from ten to twenty miles apart; four hundred station attendants had to be hired, and, as with the overland mail, supplies had to be provided.

The schedule was nine days from New York to San Francisco for telegraphic dispatches (since the telegraph lines were already at Carson City on the west and at St. Joseph on the east, the time of nine days would be largely used by the ponies between those two points); it would take thirteen days for letters from New York to San Francisco. The company would charge $5 per half ounce for letters.

The schedule would call for hard riding through dangerous country, and each pony would carry no more than twenty pounds of mail. The riders were selected for small size and weight as well as skill and endurance; William F. Cody was one. The mail was carried in the pockets of a *mochila* (a leather jacket that could be lifted from one saddle and dropped over another to save time during the changing of horses at each station). Each letter, of course, had to bear ten cents in government postage.

Samuel Colt had made in 1848 a .31-caliber belt revolver that was frequently carried by Wells Fargo messengers, but Pony Express riders started with bigger weapons—generally with .44-caliber arms; many shifted to .36-caliber Navy Colts.

The Post Office Department never did subsidize the Pony Express. Although bills were introduced into Congress for that purpose, the Pony Express had to depend on the money received from its customers. That was not enough to meet expenses, since the number of letters first carried was about forty, and increased but slowly to fewer than one hundred until near the end of the Pony's existence, when it reached 350.

However, it seems that the 350 letters per mail were from west to east only; the more conservative East objected to the high rate of postage, and its use of the Pony Express responded to the rate.

A rider's scheduled time was eight miles an hour, day and night—two hundred miles a day; each rider was expected to cover a route of something like 125 miles per trip.

The first Pony Express left St. Joseph, April 3, 1860, and there was great excitement—perhaps more than over the first running of the Butterfield Overland.

Almost immediately the Pony Express ran headlong into the Washoe County Indian War, and had a number of stations burned and service interrupted; but when it commenced running again, the schedule was semiweekly instead of weekly.

In June, soon after the Pony Express got started, the Paiutes went on the warpath in what is now Nevada, and looted and burned several stations, stole horses, and killed tenders. Regular soldiers and volunteers drove the Indians north, and restored service on the Pony Express line. This outbreak cost Russell, Majors and Waddell $75,000, and, during it, the Paiutes got the mailbags once—the only time in the Pony Express' nineteen months that a letter was lost.

Wells Fargo sent letters by Pony Express, and not only used its own franked envelopes but also had special envelopes printed, saying, "Paid from St. Joseph to Placerville per Pony Express."

Service during the bad winter of 1860-61 was slow and irregular; sometimes letters were thirty to forty days getting through. But in the spring, when the weather improved, the service also improved.

During the winter, the Pony Express was not able to maintain its schedule, even though that schedule was extended by the owners to give it a better chance. On one occasion, the Butterfield mail beat the Pony Express by three days—but that was not common.

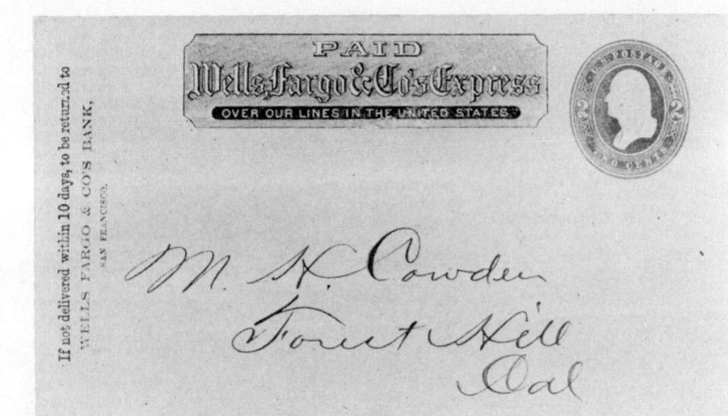

A Wells Fargo frank on a government-stamped envelope, never canceled. From the California Historical Society.

The Pony Express created a new breed of hero—the rider. The thought of those intrepid young riders (many of them were under twenty years old), spurring their ponies across the vast plains, through Indian country, and over mountains, stirred the imagination of the public, and in no time at all the riders became heroes. Sometimes, of course, a rider was not courageous or brave but was afflicted with a spell of practicality, but mostly, it seems, the riders lived up to expectations: Jim Moore rode 140 miles west to Julesburg, for instance, but found the eastbound rider killed in a fight, and immediately made the trip back, covering 280 miles in less than fifteen hours (an average of eighteen miles an hour). Jack Keetly rode for two other men and covered 340 miles in thirty-one hours. Bill Cody is supposed to have ridden 322 miles without stopping.[2]

It was during the Paiute outbreak (the Washoe County War) that Pony Bob Haslam, one of the most famous of all Pony Express riders, made the most spectacular ride. His route was from Friday's Station to Fort Churchill, but one day, when he reached Reed's Station, he found the horses had been taken by the volunteers, so he fed his own horse and rode on to Fort Churchill, fifteen miles away, the end of his route. But the next westbound rider refused to go back through the Indian uprising, and the superintendent offered Haslam $50 to do the job. Haslam took the mail back west. After this 185-

The Wells Fargo assay office built at Folsom, in the Gold Country, in 1860. From the California Historical Society.

mile trip, he slept for nine hours and then had to return—but when he reached Cold Springs he found the station torn to pieces and the station-keeper's body mutilated, the horses gone. He gave his pony a drink and went on to Sand Springs, where he urged the station keeper to go with him to the Sink of the Carson; there he found fifteen men who had had a skirmish with the Indians a few hours before. They advised Haslam to stay at the station until the Indians were under control, but Haslam went on to Fort Churchill (it was Buckland's then). The bonus was doubled, and Haslam, after 1½ hours of rest, went back on his own course over the Sierra Nevada Mountains. He rode 380 miles on that occasion.

Later, Haslam rode Wells Fargo's Pony Express from the Central Pacific at Reno to Virginia City—twenty-three miles—and is said to have covered it in an hour. Again for Wells Fargo he rode in Idaho.[3]

In December, 1860, the Pony Express carried the presidential message to Sacramento in eight days and some hours, but nevertheless it operated at a heavy loss, and as early as August, Russell announced that the line would be discontinued if help should not be forthcoming from Washington. Then some curious circumstances developed. Secretary of War John B. Floyd was an ardent southerner, and during Christmas week, 1860, the story was given to the newspapers, supposedly through Floyd's son-in-law, that Russell was guilty of using Indian trust bonds to borrow—"hypothecating bonds," it was called. Russell was arrested, and the entire business went into the courts.

While these tumultuous events were taking place on the Great Plains and across the Rockies and over the broad face of the western deserts and in the marble halls of the Capitol, Wells Fargo was pursuing its customary course in California and the Southwest. On February 13, 1860, Judge J. R. Robinson wrote a letter to Hiram Rumfield that seems to explain itself:

Office of the Overland Mail Co., 61 Hudson St., N. Y., Feb. 13, 1860. Friend Rumfield: . . . I have been raising a company to work a silver mine in Mexico. . . . Batopilas for $50,000. Fargo, the Barneys and myself are the purchasers, so you see I have the strength of the Overland. This enterprise will be the commencement or introduction of Wells Fargo & Company into Mexico in their express and banking business. J. R. Robinson.

This letter, written on an Overland Mail letterhead, can not be taken lightly, nor can it be explained away as careless talk. A man who writes on company stationery is generally careful in his choice of words.[4]

In 1860, Wells Fargo established agencies at Anaheim in Orange County, Arcata in Humboldt County, Cacheville in Yolo County; Carson City, Nevada; Cloverdale in Sonora County, Comanche in Calaveras County, Coulterville in Mariposa County, Don Pedras in Tuolumne County; Genoa, Nevada; Geyserville in Sonoma County; Gold Hill in Utah Territory[5]; Guaymas, Mexico; Illinoistown in Placer County, Knight's Landing in Yolo County; Mesilla, New Mexico; Mount Ophir in Mariposa County, Nicolaus in Sutter County, Pachecoville in Contra Costa County, San Mateo; Silver City, Nevada; Tucson, Arizona Territory; and Virginia in Santa Cruz County.[6]

This list is noteworthy for several features: the establishment of agencies at Guaymas, at Mesilla and Tucson (both on the Butterfield route), and at Genoa (Nevada's first town) and at Carson City, Gold Hill, and Silver City in the Comstock area.

The Head Minutes show that in November "the matter of Freeman & Company was finally closed by issuing to Freeman & Company 500 shares of Wells, Fargo & Company stock, and giving the Freeman company $50,000 in notes, dated November 15 and payable in 3, 6, 9, and 12 months, with interest." (But it seems that, when they faced it, the directors of Wells Fargo did not want to part with so much stock.)

The company bought the property at 84 Broadway, New York, for $65,000; $15,000 was to be paid in October, while $50,000 was payable in 1865, with semiannual interest at an unspecified percentage.

Rather than issue a large block of stock to Freeman & Company, the director declared a stock dividend of 8 percent on the outstanding shares (5,533), to be paid out of the 467 shares of unissued stock, par value $100.

The company also paid its usual dividend of 5 percent on February 15, and a second dividend of 3 percent on May 1. It was the first time since 1853 that the stock had paid less than 10 percent cash.

The directors were the same as in 1859: Morgan, Danford Barney, Wells, Ashbel Barney, Williams, Cheney, Livingston, Fargo, and Stockwell.

A profit and loss statement of the express department for 1860 shows emphasis on robberies:

June 3, 1860. Recovered of Iowa Hill robbery	$3,068.23
Earnings, foreign express	4,864.62
Profit on transp. of govt. troops to Washoe	7,500.00
Earnings for quarter, Havana & Europ. express	3,585.00
Bal. dust recovered from Iowa Hill Robbery	1,386.87
Recovered from G. Parker, alias Smith, supposed to have been concerned in Shasta roby.	1,515.00
Earnings on foreign express	2,785.00
Express earnings year ending Dec. 31, 1860	$151,128.47
Total	$175,833.19

CHARGES

Jan. 31. Paid Officers Gay and O'Neil for defending treasure in attempted robbery on Angeles Road	$1,330.00
Apr. 30. Louis McLane, traveling exp.	2,141.69
June 30. Iowa Hill robbery	11,811.25
Shasta robbery	22,239.12
July 31. Judgment on O'Neil suit	1,505.06
Robbery at Trinity Center	2,839.30
Exp. paid officers—Shasta robbery	649.00
Exp. paid officers—Iowa Hill robbery	161.00
Aug. 31. Settlement with A. B. Brown, agt. at Marysville—cash short	1,716.00
Iowa Hill robbery—paid officers	540.50
Trinity Center robbery—paid officers	91.00
Sept. 30. Paid office exp., witness and cost	239.00
Oct. 31. Paid officers reward for arrest and conviction of "Cassell" engaged in the Shasta robbery	1,040.00
Officers' expenses—Iowa Hill robbery	52.00
Nov. 30. Reward for recovery of portion of money stolen—Iowa Hill robbery	778.00
Due to M. E. Mills—lawyer	500.00
Sundry exp. officers and witnesses	271.25
Reward officers—recovery of $1515 of the Shasta robbery	475.00
Error Stable Acct. quarter ending Dec. 31	36.00
Total Charges	$48,415.17
Balance, Profit & Loss Acct. Dec. 31	$127,418.02

Nineteen of the items (nearly all the charges) relate to the three robberies at Iowa Hill, Shasta, and Trinity Center, and one relates to a robbery on the Angeles Road (to Los Angeles?). The loss from the three robberies totaled about $37,000, and this item made up most of the "charges" total. These various items indicate the extent to which Wells Fargo went to make robbery of their express shipments unprofitable for the robbers: rewards and expenses for officers, expenses for witnesses, fee for a lawyer, sundry expenses—and possibly the traveling expenses of Louis McLane were chargeable to the robberies.

There had been several developments in the mail situation during 1860: Besides the establishment of weekly service between Denver and Fort Kearney, there had been a change in the Southwest when the Yuma to San Diego leg of the San Antonio & San Diego had been discontinued. There had been a development in the mail service by sea when Vanderbilt had been awarded a contract for trimonthly service via Panama in July.

In 1856, Wells Fargo's gross income from transportation was $251,400 and its net income from express was $44,349.63; in 1860, its gross from transportation was $430,293.41, and its net from express $151,128.47. And with all major competitors eliminated in California, there was no way to go but forward.

This statement, of course, does not give any details on the income or expense from express shipments, but only the total of earnings.

As for the government's mail routes: The Central Overland route became well established during the year, even though the figures on expenses and receipts hardly seemed to justify it. The three central routes cost the post office $908,241 in 1864, and receipts were $125,050.90, while the Panama route cost $350,00, with receipts of $170,825.40. Only the anxiety of men who wanted to hear from home would have justified such an imbalance.

Now 1861 was coming, and with it the outbreak of the Civil War, the removal of the Butterfield Overland Mail Company to the central route, and the completion of the overland telegraph line.

1861

Butterfield Moves North

During the time William H. Russell was under fire in Washington, of course, the Pony Express could not expect any help or any chance to improve its service.

Floyd's testimony in regard to Russell's use of the bonds seems to have disappeared, but most writers believe that it was a conspiracy to embarrass the Pony Express. If so, by whom? Perhaps by Floyd, who might have been trying to forestall communication between the North and California; also, it seems that possibly the Butterfield Overland Mail Company might have had a hand in the affair—since it profited from it. By logical extension, then, since Wells Fargo is presumed to have been in control of Butterfield by that time, the onus at such high levels would fall upon Wells Fargo. However, with the impetus coming primarily from Floyd, it may be that Floyd himself was involved in more items than the mere storing of army supplies in southern towns in preparation for the outbreak of war. Russell was indicted by a grand jury and arrested, then bailed out. He begged to get his testimony on record, but apparently never was allowed to.[1]

Now some unforeseeable factors entered the situation. Congress, under constant pressure, had finally passed the law of March 2, 1861, providing daily mail service on the central route and a semiweekly Pony Express, effective July 1, 1861, for a combined subsidy of $1,000,000 a year, and it seems likely that Russell, Majors, and Waddell were feeling pretty good about that. But the sectionalism of North and South had been growing, and in late March, a number of attacks were made on Butterfield stations in the South; therefore, the Postmaster General ordered the Butterfield route closed, and John Butterfield was ordered to move to the central route and establish his service there (he was allowed two months' pay for damages to be incurred in moving). So, in the final analysis, Butterfield got the daily contract and the Pony Express service too (since the semiweekly Pony Express was to be maintained), notwithstanding the fact that Russell's Pony Express had carried Lincoln's inaugural address from Atchison to California in seven days and seventeen hours.

It must have been a severe blow to Russell, Majors, and Waddell, for they had already spent far more than they had made—and now they were forced to borrow from Ben Holladay. (It appears they had borowed from him at least two years before.) They gave Holladay a mortgage on all their property, and made a deal with Butterfield whereby they were to maintain the Pony Express and were to operate daily coach service from the Missouri River to Salt Lake City, while Butterfield would operate the Pony Express and a daily coach from Salt Lake City to Placerville.

Butterfield apparently lost some of his stock and equipment to the Confederates, but he had almost enough left to stock the line from Salt Lake City to Virginia City, and it seems that the traffic from

Abraham Lincoln, sixteenth President of the United States, 1861–1865. From "The White House Gallery of Official Portraits of the Presidents."

Virginia City to Sacramento was sublet to the Pioneer Stage Line, owned by Louis and Charles McLane.

Since Denver was involved, and naturally wanted to be on the main line of the transcontinental mail, there were strenuous efforts made to route the line through Denver; the distance from the Missouri River to Salt Lake City was substantially shorter through Denver, but the difficulty was in getting over the Rocky Mountains. A party from Denver discovered or explored Berthoud Pass and found it could be used, but it was too late to influence the route. Service had to start July 1, and it started via the old route along the Platte River and through South Pass in Wyoming, which was some 3,000 feet lower than Berthoud Pass.

The Post Office Department made arrangements with Butterfield to start daily coach service over the central route on July 1, and the Butterfield company subcontracted to the Central Overland California & Pike's Peak Express the service east from Salt Lake City; the Butterfield was to operate from Salt Lake City to Carson; the Pioneer Stage Line was to operate from Carson to Placerville.

Now Louis McLane sold the Pioneer Stage Line to Wells Fargo, and the paneling over the doors of the coaches was changed from "Pioneer Stage Line" to "Wells, Fargo & Company." In 1861, for the first time, Wells Fargo actually owned its own stagecoaches.

Now, according to some writers, Wells Fargo acquired control of the Pony Express. Beebe and Clegg say flatly that Wells Fargo took over the Pony Express, April 15, 1861, and I. W. Hellman III, who in 1944 became president of Wells Fargo Bank & Union Trust Company (and whose grandfather had been the first president of the Wells Fargo-Nevada National Bank in 1905), said in an address in 1952 that "The Pony Express that ultimately became a Wells Fargo enterprise . . . the promoters were ruined. Wells Fargo took over the line."

There could have been some confusion in Mr. Hellman's memories, although it is a fact that some of Wells Fargo's envelopes said, "From St. Joseph to Placerville," and also that Wells Fargo issued its own Pony Express stamps in April—a $2 red and a $4 green; a few weeks later it issued a $1 stamp to conform with the new rate set by law, to take effect July 1. These references apparently are to Wells Fargo's function as an agency, however.

If Wells Fargo did indeed control the Pony Express, Ben Holladay's position becomes confusing, for he had already loaned Russell, Majors, and Waddell money for their operations. Shortly after July 1, he would advance more money and take a chattel mortgage on all personal property of the C. O. C. & P. P., and a deed of trust on all its real estate. *Old Waybills* says that Wells Fargo (through the Butterfield company) handled both the overland mail and the Pony Express west of Salt Lake City, but it seems more accurate to say that the Butterfield company handled the facilities. This question is apart from the question as to Wells Fargo's control of the Butterfield company.

An item in the *Alta* for April 30, 1861, indicates that Wells, Fargo & Company was appointed general agent for the Pony Express, and Wells Fargo in turn employed others to act for it in the East—specifically, United States Express in St. Louis, for one. It hardly seems that Wells Fargo, which was not in St. Louis itself, would have acted as agent in St. Louis unless it had been acting as agent generally east of the Missouri River.

The first daily coaches were to run from St. Joseph on the east to Placerville on the west, but the eastern terminal was moved in November to Atchison, across the river, fourteen miles west of St. Joseph. There would be 153 stations on the route (at an average of twelve-and-one-half miles apart), and the fare would be $225 for through passengers, twelve cents a mile for way passengers. Coaches would run seven times a week; express would be carried on Monday when there would be no mail.

The stations erected by the stage company were largely the same, especially along the Platte River: square, one story, of hewn cedar logs, containing one to three rooms. Sometimes they were of one room, with partitions of muslin to separate kitchen, dining room, and bedroom. The roof was laid on a gable log, and was of poles laid as close together as possible. On top of those were put willows, then a layer of hay, and finally a layer of earth or sod and a sprinkle of coarse gravel. Most of the logs were obtained from canyons south of the Platte near Cottonwood Springs in southwestern Nebraska.

Drivers were to receive from $40 to $75 a month, stock tenders from $40 to $50, carpenters $75, harness-makers and blacksmiths from $100 to $125, and division agents $100 to $125 (sometimes advanced to as much as $200 when Indian troubles were bad); express messengers received $62.50 a month.

While William H. Russell was being harassed in Washington, the unofficial territory of Jefferson officially became Colorado Territory, and sometime during that year the capital stock of Wells Fargo was increased to $1,000,000, according to the Head Minutes; it would continue to be a New York corporation until 1866.

The Pony Express, of course, was still running when the Civil War broke out in April, 1861, and played its part in carrying the long-expected news to California.

The New York Times for April 13 said:

> The War Commenced. The first gun fired by Fort Moultrie Against Fort Sumter. The Bombardment

An 1861 advertisement for the Pony Express by Wells, Fargo & Company, Agents. This was printed at the time of the change of rates on July 1, 1861, and apparently was circulated in New York. Postage was 10 cents plus $1 for a half ounce. Note: "Pony Express Envelopes For Sale at our Office."

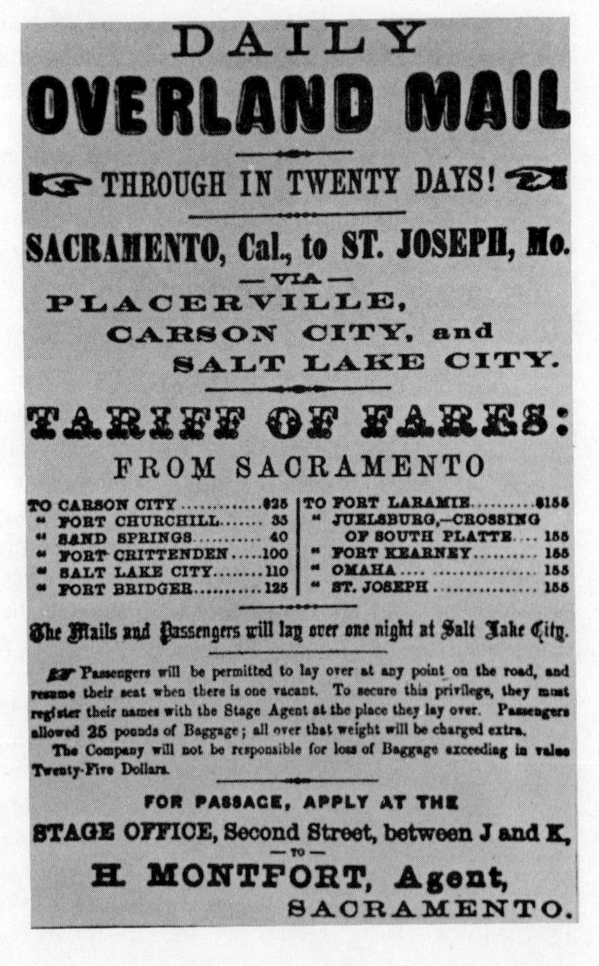

Probably one of the first advertisements for the Overland Mail after Butterfield moved it north from the southern route. Note that it was twenty days from Sacramento, California, to St. Joseph, Missouri.

Continued All Day. Hostilities to Commence Again at Daylight. How the news is received in Washington. Our Charleston Dispatches.—Charleston, Friday, April 12. The ball has opened. War is inaugurated. The batteries of Sullivan's Island, Morris Island, and other points, were opened on Fort Sumter at 4 o'clock this morning.

No reporter today would start a war dispatch with "The ball has opened."

Farther west, the Chicago Daily *Tribune* said:

By Telegraph. The Attack on Sumter. THE SURRENDER! Effect of the News in Washington. Absurd and Contradictory Rumors. President Lincoln's Proclamation. Calls for the State Militia. Action of the States. The prevailing excitement. THRILLING WAR NEWS. The very latest. From the seat of War.

Lincoln's proclamation was printed, calling for 75,000 militia "to facilitate and aid in this effort to maintain the laws and the integrity of the national Union, and the perpetuity of the popular Government, and redress wrongs long enough endured." A correspondent in Washington says, "You cannot imagine the indescribable fury consequent upon the news of the surrender of Fort Sumter, which was manifested here last night." A Chicago reporter says: "Yesterday was a day long to be remembered in Chicago. Whatever the future has in store to continue or increase the present excited state of feeling, the earliest effect of the war news of Saturday evening, was of too marked a nature readily to be paralled in a city usually so quiet on Lord's Day." And the reporter, trying to describe the city rather than show it, adds: "The city was given up to an intense and all-pervading excitement, the like of which has never been known in this country." Chicago was full of public meetings that strange Sunday, and one minister preached a sermon from Matthew 24:6: "And ye shall hear of wars, and rumors of wars: see that ye be not troubled; for all these things must come to pass, but the end is not yet."

In another column on the same page is a classified ad that says:

HEADQUARTERS U. S. Z. C. Company Orders No. 1. You are hereby ordered to appear at your Armory on Tuesday and Friday evening for Company Drill. Awkward Squad drill Monday, Wednesday, and

A cartoon in "Harper's Weekly" for November 23, 1861, celebrating "The first telegraphic message from California. May the union be perpetual." The Civil War had been under way since April.

Many ships stopped at Mazatlán in Gold Rush days, but it is somewhat more quiet there today. This is a photograph of a calm sea on an overcast morning taken by the author.

Friday evenings, until further orders. Per order, J. R. Haydon, Capt. R. W. Wetherell, Orderly.

The United States Zouave Corps was losing no time getting in shape.

One Julian S. Rumsey, campaigning for the mayoralty of Chicago, profited from the news, for the *Tribune* got strongly behind his candidacy in a news item: "Tonight. Sustain the government! Let Chicago speak. Rebuking Treason. The true Union ticket headed by Julian S. Rumsey!"

At Marysville, in California, the *Daily Appeal* would consider the mechanics of the news' arrival more important than the news itself, because its top line and its first paragraph of its story on the Battle of Bull Run said nothing about anything but the Pony Express:

Arrival of the Pony Express. Dates to July 26. Terrible Battle in Virginia. The Pony Express arrived at Edwards Creek Station [100 miles east of Fort Churchill, to which the wires had just been extended] at 8 o'clock night before last. The following dispatch was telegraphed across the mountains to the *Union* [Sacramento *Union*]: Washington, July 21.—Midnight. —The fighting at Bull's Run commenced at 3 a.m. and continued most desperately till 2 p.m. The rebels were driven back inch by inch, leaving their dead on the field. The loss of life on both sides was frightful. The battle has been one of the most severe ever fought on this continent.

How Wells Fargo managed to keep its skirts clean in the turmoil in California is a miracle, for California had been populated by both northerners and southerners, and feeling in the mines was intense. There were fights and pitched battles, and the Copperheads organized to divert to the South the silver shipments from the Comstock.

Generally speaking, 1861 started a period of depression over the country, but that did not extend to the express companies; they were, by that time, carrying more mail than the government, and all their other sources of income responded accordingly. John Butterfield in 1864 organized a coalition of express companies to deliver bundles of ballots to every New York unit in the South, and the various express companies performed a multitude of services all during the war.

Wells Fargo started a pony express from Placerville to San Francisco, July 1, 1861, to "connect with the Overland Mail Company's Pony Express at Placerville," according to the *Bulletin* of June 26, 1861.

One Edward Creighton got a contract from the

government to build a telegraph line west from Omaha toward California; he was to receive $40,000 a year for ten years. The California State Telegraph was to build east to meet Creighton at Salt Lake City, but California State Telegraph stopped at Ruby Valley, in Utah Territory, and Creighton reached that point on October 24. The last Pony Express mail reached San Francisco in November, and the spectacular experiment was over.

There were sixteen new Wells Fargo agencies opened during 1861: Aurora, Nevada; Callahan's in Siskiyou County, California; Chicago in Shasta County; Copperopolis in Calaveras County; Dayton; Lincoln in Placer County; Mazatlán, Mexico; Michigan Bluff in Placer County; Millerton in Marin County; Napa; Nolen's Gap; North Almadon; Port Oxford, Oregon; St. Joseph, Oregon; Snelling in Merced County; and Union, Oregon.

Another list shows twenty-five agencies that ceased operation in 1860 and 1861: Carrollton in San Joaquin County; Cherokee in San Joaquin County; Colusa; Crescent City; Don Pedras, Forest City in Sierra County; Fort Tejon; Fort Yuma; Fraser River in Fresno County; French Bar in Siskiyou County; Fresno; Indian Diggin's in Eldorado County; Live Oak in Sutter County; Mesilla, New Mexico; Michigan City, Napa Springs; Port Oxford, Oregon; Port Townsend, Washington; Portland, Oregon; Prairie City in Sacramento County; Salmon Falls in Eldorado County; Shaw's Flat in Tuolumne County; Tucson, Arizona Territory; Uniontown in Eldorado County; Whatcom, Washington Territory.

From this list, it may be noted that, as soon as the Butterfield route was closed in the Southwest, the offices at Mesilla, Tucson, and Yuma were closed. The early-established office at Oroville, Arizona Territory, seems to have disappeared; from still another list, it may be seen that at the end of 1861 there were 120 offices still in operation. This total included Gold Hill, California, and Gold Hill, Utah Territory;[2] Guaymas and Mazatlán, Honolulu, Los Angeles, Monterey, San Bernardino, San Diego, Santa Barbara, and Seattle.

In 1861, Wells Fargo received, among other things, 230 firkins of butter, shipped by Panama, and, on November 16, 713 firkins; also that year, Wells Fargo shipped a steam fire engine from Baltimore to Sacramento. Wells Fargo was living up to its reputation.

In February, 1861, the board of directors of Wells Fargo learned that all shareholders had signed the amendment to the association agreement of 1859 except two—one of whom was dead; the stock of the other was in litigation.

In June, the directors considered the question of war-risk insurance, since "ocean shipping and land shipping [were] extremely hazardous," and the directors apparently felt secure enough to authorize the president of the firm to use his own discretion on shipments from San Francisco to New York, which obviously included the all-important items of gold and silver.

Directors were Morgan, Danford Barney, Wells, Ashbel Barney, Williams, Cheney, Livingston, Fargo, and Stockwell.

In 1861, the earnings of the express company were quite satisfactory, for the company paid 3 percent dividends on February 1, May 1, August 1, and November 1.

It was in 1861 that Benjamin P. Judah, an eastern engineer who wanted to build a transcontinental railroad, went to Washington to work for a bill under which the government would subsidize the building. He had been there before but had found the congressmen from the North and those from the South so opposed to each other that he could not get any kind of favorable action; now, in 1861, he found the southern senators had gone home to the Confederacy, and Judah put up tremendous arguments to the effect that a transcontinental railroad would be an important factor in holding California in the Union.

1862-1865
The Civil War Years

It is said that Wells, Fargo & Company, along with many other express companies and many businesses that were not common carriers, did not want the transcontinental railroad. Wells Fargo had executive control of the western half of the Overland (from Salt Lake City to Placerville), and thus had guaranteed space for its own shipping as well as the power to exclude that of others; smaller express companies whose business was not overland at all saw a general lowering of rates that would cut their own charges eventually; and private companies foresaw that a railroad would bring in goods that could be sold more cheaply in competition with their own products. An ice company that brought in ice from Alaska was opposed to the railroad.

The Pacific Railroad Bill was passed, however, in midsummer, and was signed by Lincoln on July 1, 1862. It designated two companies to build and operate a railroad from the Missouri River to Sacramento. It would loan the two companies capital at the rate of $16,000 per mile over the prairie, up to $48,000 per mile in the mountains, and it would issue bonds to the companies to provide working capital. Further, it would grant each company ten sections of public land per mile (the sections to be alternate—noncontiguous), and adjoining the right of way or as close to it as possible. (And for generations afterward, the two companies and others made a big business of selling land and of promoting immigration to the land and then selling it.)

The Casement brothers, building for the Union Pacific under General Dodge, started west with Irish workers; the Central Pacific, made up of four Sacramento merchants (Leland Stanford, Collis P. Huntington, Mark Hopkins, and Charles Crocker), built east from Sacramento. It was obvious that the company that laid the most miles of track would make the most money, for, in those days, the price offered for railroad-building on the prairie was generous. Nevertheless, neither line got off to a resounding start. The construction required massive quantities of materials and thousands of laborers. Iron and steel for the Central Pacific had to be shipped around the Horn and were subject to confiscation by the Union for war use, capture by the Confederacy, and the uncertainties of shipping by water. Labor was extremely scarce, and by the end of 1862, the Central Pacific had built only eighteen miles. This is significant, because it would not be long before the Big Four would be in trouble financially because of the unforeseen high cost of getting over the Sierras, and it would seem that an astute investor might have bought a substantial portion of the company at a reasonable price.

For Wells Fargo, it would have meant guaranteed space for its express from Pacific to Atlantic. Wells Fargo was, in 1862, forced to ship via the Central

An attack of Indians on a bull train (wagons pulled by oxen) near Sheridan, Kansas. The action seems remarkably scattered, and the various parties seem remarkably oblivious to one another. From "Harper's Weekly," October 10, 1868.

Overland California & Pike's Peak Express, but by the latter part of 1862 it would find itself at the mercy of Ben Holladay—and he was not easy to get along with. Therefore, it might seem that Wells Fargo would have tried to get control of the Central Pacific rather than hinder it. Perhaps it did, and, if so, perhaps the Big Four were too astute to give up control. At any rate, Wells Fargo seemed to focus its attention on stages and ignore the railroad, so that a shrewd financier, Lloyd Tevis, would eventually seize control of Wells Fargo by obtaining the express-carrying privilege on the two transcontinental railroads.

By 1862, important steps had been taken to facilitate travel between the Gold Country of California and the Silver Country of Nevada. Three toll roads had been built: through Sonora Pass, through Hennesse Pass, and from Placerville. The Placerville road was 101 miles long from Placerville to Virginia City, was wide enough to allow wagons to pass each other, and had turning points where an eight-mule team could turn in a circle. It had been macadamized all the length of its 101 miles at a cost of $500,000, and considerable money was spent every year to maintain it. The fee was $15 for a four-horse team, and $1.50 more for each pair of animals. It must have been one of the best businesses in the West, for the gross revenue for several years was $639,000 a year.

The freight wagon generally used then was the Washoe wagon, made in Stockton or Placerville by John M. Studebaker, whose line of wagons eventually would rule western transportation. The Washoe wagon was stronger, heavier, and deeper than eastern wagons.[1]

In 1862, Wells Fargo was doing $40,000 worth of business a month in letters, express, and freight, on the Overland stages. From San Francisco to Carson City or Virginia City, the express rate was seven to ten cents a pound; to Salt Lake City it was fifty to sixty cents a pound—higher in the winter.

In May and June, 1861, the C. O. C. & P. P. got in trouble and borrowed heavily from Ben Holladay. By the end of 1861, the company owed Holladay

$208,000, and a public auction was held in March, 1862, at which Holladay bid in the entire system. Wells Fargo appears to have had little interest in acquiring control. Holladay said he paid off over $500,000 for the Central California Overland, and he went to work to make something of it.

Holladay was a financier and a capable man on his own account—a rough frontiersman who liked to put on a big show, and frequently did. In 1849, he had gotten a good start in the freighting business by supplying Colonel Kearny's Army of the West in its conquest of New Mexico and California—in which Holladay made big money. In 1849, he had taken $70,000 worth of goods to the Mormons and sold them at a big profit; in 1850, he had taken $150,000 worth of goods to them, sold it, and gone on to California, and in the 1850's had run a freighting business from the Missouri River to California. In 1853, he went in with Chorpenning to carry mail in covered wagons between Sacramento and Salt Lake City, and, when Chorpenning's contract was suspended in 1858, Holladay became surety for W. L. Blanchard.

In 1855, he had observed Russell and Majors start their big freighting business that was to run to 3,500 wagons, out of Leavenworth, and it must have stirred some envy in him. In 1858, he bought $200,000 worth of surplus materials (from the Utah War), and now he was bigger than them all.

He spared no expense to build up the system, and he overlooked no opportunity to advertise it. He made flying trips from coast to coast in his own stages, and saw that those trips were properly publicized. He got numerous smaller contracts, including one to Montana when gold was discovered there, and it seems the mantle of "king of the world's greatest staging empire" must have passed to him in the 1860's.[2]

In May and June, 1862, nine mail sacks and seven Wells Fargo express sacks were burned by Indians at Sweetwater; twenty-one mail sacks were cut open at Ice Springs.[3]

In August, 1862, the Sioux War broke out in Minnesota, and the overland mail was suspended for three weeks. When it was resumed, Holladay had changed the route to go along the South Platte instead of the North Platte; in the Greeley area it turned north and west up the Cache la Poudre, and then crossed the Laramie Plains of Wyoming to the North Platte—all this to avoid the marauding Indians in western Nebraska and eastern Wyoming.

Wells Fargo seems to have started its own pony express between Sacramento and Carson City-Virginia City, and charged ten cents an ounce for letters (which, of course, had to have also the government stamp).[4]

In April, 1862, Wells Fargo's capital stock was increased to $2,000,000 (20,000 shares at $100 each), but, the Minutes say, final approval was not given by the stockholders until November, 1863. An interesting item slips into the Minutes: "Nothing in the line of extending the service, etc., was undertaken during the year on account of the bad aspect of affairs between the United States and Great Britain." Presumably this refers to the unpleasantness between the two countries that arose from England's protest over the Union's stopping a British ship and removing James M. Mason and John Slidell, who were Confederate commissioners on the way to England.

Directors for 1862 were the same as those for 1861.

A stock dividend of 42 percent was paid out of the surplus on May 15 to the amount of 2,940 shares of 3,000 unissued shares, fractional shares to be paid in full; the amount of the dividend was $300,000. In addition, four cash dividends of 3 percent each were paid on February 1, May 1, August 1, and November 1. Whatever else was happening, Wells Fargo continued to make money.

The list of agencies opened during the year shows only four: Strawberry Valley in Yuba County, Washoe City in Nevada, Woodbridge in San Joaquin County, and Woodland in Yolo County.

In 1862, the first United States paper money was issued to relieve an acute shortage of specie. These notes were in denominations of from $5 to $1,000 and were called "demand notes" because they were payable in specie by the treasury.

California particularly disliked the paper money (and in fact the California state constitution prohibited its issuance[5]), and Californians promptly discounted the federal greenbacks 10 percent. The hard-money preference would stay in California for a long time.

Over the nation, too, the people did not have much faith in them, and before long they were depreciated from 50 percent to 100 percent, and prices were often quoted in this fashion: "$25 in gold or $37.50 in Lincoln skins."

Business in the North was good, but prices rose almost three times as much as wages. The South was suffering for money, war equipment, manufactured goods, and quinine.

In this year, also, precut houses were shipped around Cape Horn to Nevada, and probably Wells Fargo had a hand in delivering them.[6]

In 1862, Wells Fargo bought 2,000,000 three-cent envelopes, 15,000 six-cent, 3,000 ten-cent and eighteen-cent envelopes; it bought also 70,000 three-cent stamps and 12,500 six-cent stamps. In that year, too, in San Francisco, Wells Fargo put green mail boxes on the street for the convenience of mailers; the Post Office Department put up red mailboxes.

In 1862, Hiram S. Rumfield, Overland Mail agent at Salt Lake City, spoke of the difference between the feeling of the Mormons toward the Holladay line as contrasted with their feeling toward the Butterfield Overland. "The Mormons have always been hostile in feeling towards the Eastern Division [the Central Overland, or Holladay line] and its management," said Rumfield on June 8, 1862.[7] This animosity apparently had its origin in the fact that the Central Overland had the contract that Heber Kimball, a Mormon, had had canceled.

An employee of Wells Fargo, hunting a stray horse or mule, found gold in the Reese River area in Nevada, and another gold rush was on. Gold was discovered in Alder Gulch, Montana, and the big rush to the second Virginia City was soon under way. It is said that the opening of gold fields in that period saved Ben Holladay from going broke, for the overland mail, express, and passenger revenue alone was not enough to sustain his huge organization. He did, however, get other mail contracts—one from Salt Lake City to Montana.[8]

In 1863, service between the Missouri River and

J. Ross Browne drew this picture to show the sad and cruel end of an Apache—probably killed by Americans, since he was crucified. From "A Tour Through Arizona," in "Harper's Monthly."

Indians chasing a stagecoach marked "Overland Express" (whatever that meant). From J. P. Dunn, Jr., "Massacres of the Mountains."

California was generally good until winter. The government charge on postage dropped from ten cents to three cents per half ounce in March.

Hiram S. Rumfield also contrasted the treatment of the Indians by the Butterfield Overland and by the Central Overland, and said that the treatment had much to do with the fact that the Butterfield Overland did not start having trouble until long after the Central Overland had it. The Butterfield Overland fed the Indians, and Rumfield said it had spent $1,792 for beeves in January, February, and March, 1862, and $20,000 in November (400 head of beeves). Rumfield said in July, "The Eastern Line is not yet free from Indian annoyances and interruptions, and, I think will not be soon, until some of the men now in charge are removed. . . . We have 10 Indians on our line to one on their's and yet we have no trouble with the savages. We give them plenty to eat and that is all they want." About the same time, he wrote: "As game of all kinds has left the valley since the Overland Mail Company established its route along here, the poor savages had had no means of subsistence, except that furnished by the Company. We had fed them liberally acting upon the principle that it is cheaper to feed them than to fight them."

Prices were high in Salt Lake City in January—undoubtedly because of the Indians and the weather; calico was sixty cents a yard and coffee or sugar was sixty cents a pound—some three times normal.

In February, 1863, one of Ben Holladay's brothers, Joseph, killed a man named Greenleaf, and Ben brought all his resources to bear against his brother's conviction; naturally, an outsider throwing his weight around in Salt Lake City did not endear the Central Overland to the Mormons, either.

But in March, 1863, Rumfield told his wife that the Indian troubles had finally come to the Butterfield Overland (in spite of the $20,000 it had spent in November).

"Last Sunday noon," he said, "the unexpected announcement came to us by telegraph from Deep Creek—171 miles west—that a party of hostile Indians, from the north, had suddenly appeared in the valley and that there was reason to fear that they intended to attack the station."

That was one of the big problems in dealing with the Indians: You would get one tribe or band taken care of, and another would appear. Rumfield said at various times that most of the trouble in Utah was caused by Shoshones or Bannacks from the north.

An hour later . . . another message informed us that the indians had made an attack upon the stage, (going east), in the canyon 10 miles west of Deep Creek, killing the driver and mortally wounding a passenger. When the attack was made, it appears that another passenger, Judge Mott of Carson, Delegate to Congress for Nevada, was seated outside with the driver. The driver being shot dead at the first fire of the concealed foe, the venerable Judge with great presence of mind seized hold

No. [illegible]

COMMISSION,

To be attended to by

Forest Hill Office.

WELLS, FARGO & CO.'S

EXPRESS.

From Francisco Gonsalvo
Folsom

To W. F. & Co.
Forest Hill

Folsom 12 Nov 1862

REMARKS.

$1 — [illegible] at the Drugstore at or near your office or P.O. 2 bottles Thompson's Eye Water — cost .50¢ each. — Make charges on return $1. —

Palmer Agt.

Filled Nov 12/62 [illegible]

Returned

Please explain to the Collector that this is for 2 Ranches instead of one and inform him that he must allow it at regular rates as it was his mistake.

Yours
H. Palmer
Agt.

Return fees.

Collector says taxes are paid on all property assessed in name of B. N. Bugby and that he has receipted for same.

W. F. & Co.
P.ville Nov. 17/63. [illegible] White

A commission from Folsom for Wells Fargo at Placerville to pay a man's taxes. Apparently these were paid three days later; then C. T. H. Palmer, Folsom agent, sent a note from the payer insisting the payment was for two ranches instead of one, but the collector said that taxes were paid on all property in the payer's name. The taxes were $5.75, and Wells Fargo's charge was $1—apparently a standard charge for errands of this nature. The original is in the History Room, Wells Fargo Bank.

of the lines and kept the frightened horses in the road. The murderous savages with hideous yells and frantic gestures broke from their hiding places behind the jagged rocks and ran after the stage at their utmost speed; but being outdistanced in the chase, they soon gave up pursuit as unavailing. . . . Judge Mott reached Deep Creek in safety. The dead driver was lying in the forward boot, where the body lodged when it fell from the seat above. Inside the stage was Mr. Liverton, the other passenger, insensible but alive. A bullet had pierced his skull and his brains were oozing from the wound. The wounded man was accompanied by his two little sons, who were unharmed. A party of soldiers . . . arrived at 8 Mile Station early yesterday, (Monday) morning, and found the station buildings in ashes, the horses gone, and the two unfortunate men lying dead, naked and scalped upon the ground. . . . They are doubtless Snake or Sho-sho-ne Indians, and belong to Poco-tel-la's band. . . . This is the first Indian difficulty we have had upon our road since the line was started.

In May, Rumfield advised his wife that he had sent a scalp [Indian] to Doctor B., and Rumfield said: "He can rely upon its genuineness." He made a promise that must have thrilled his wife:

The first nice one I get I will send to you. [As a postscript he added:] Since writing the above I have concluded to send you the scalp I spoke of a month or more ago. The Tanner, as I said, caused some of the hair to come out—which is the reason I hesitated about sending it. [Naturally, he would not want her to have any but a perfect scalp!] The letter herewith I received with the scalp. The injun was killed by Gilbert at Spring Valley Station.

Gilbert's letter of authenticity was apologetic: "Am sorry indeed that I cannot send you as many dozens, I send the scalp complete except a very small piece. You should get some one to tan the skin as it is yet green. I have nothing here to do it with or I would have fixed it all right for you."

Before we censor them too vigorously, let us remember that it was a rugged country, that it was simply a question as to whose scalp would be tanned. It does appear that a man can go primitive pretty fast when his survival is at stake.

Wells Fargo never for a moment forgot its obligation to be of service to its customers, as an old "Commission Envelope" of 1862 well shows:

No. 814. Commission, to be attended to by Forest Hill Office. WELLS, FARGO & CO.'S EXPRESS. From Francisco Gonsalvo, Folsom, to W. F. & Co., Forest Hill. Folsom, 12 Nov. 1862. Remarks. $1 herewith. Buy at the Drugstore at or near your office or P. O. 2 bottles Thompson's Eye Water, cost 50¢ each. Make charges on return $1. Palmer, Agt.

The eye water was bought and delivered, for the endorsement is: "Filled Nov. 12, 62 [the same day]. Chgs. 1. coll. Louis G. G'W. Per K. B. L."[9]

Nothing was too small or too personal for Wells Fargo to undertake at a price.

National banks were authorized in 1863, but California would have none of them, primarily because they could issue banknotes, and banknotes were paper money.

On April 15, 1863, Danford Barney, Benjamin P. Cheney, and William G. Fargo were authorized to go to California "in the best interests of the company," and they went by stage, for on May 25 Rumfield told his wife that "Mr. Barney" would be there for a week or so. Barney, Cheney, and Fargo spent most of July, all of August, and most of September in California. Late that year, the company bought the property at 82 Broadway, New York City, where it had had its headquarters since 1853, for $101,000.

A commission dated November 12, 1863, again demonstrates Wells Fargo's attention to personal tasks:

No. 41. Adv. $5.75, our 1, $6.75. Commission, to be attended to by Placerville Office. WELLS, FARGO & CO.'S EXPRESS. From B. N. Bugby, Folsom, to W. F. & Co., Placerville, to pay taxes on all property in his name and return as adv. chgs. Nov. 12, 1863. Remarks. P. O. R. [?] Filled. Theo. F. Tracy, gt. [agt]. p[er] Roff. Nov. 15/63. over Returned. Please explain to the collector, that this is for 2 Ranches instead of one, and inform him that he must allow it at regular rate, as it was his mistake. Yours, W. A. Palmer, for agt. Return face. Collector says taxes are paid on all property assessed in name of B. N. Bugby—and that he has receipted for same. W. F. & Co. W. D. White. P'ville, Nov. 17, 1863.

Other commissions of those years were equally interesting. One dated at Columbia, March 26, 1862, and directed to the office at San Francisco, said:

"Obtain from pawnbroker T. Salomon a watch & specimen." The pawn ticket and $22 coin were enclosed; Wells Fargo charged him $1.50.

Another from Columbia directed the agent to "procure a copy of Hardy's Military Tactics." Somebody was more than casually interested in the war. The money enclosed was $4, of which $2 was returned.

In 1860, a commission was to "purchase a rifle as per enclosed description. Price not to exceed $75." A check for $60 was enclosed but was returned; the commission was not filled.

Another from Columbia directed the San Francisco agent to "Buy ten shares Hale & Norcross at the lowest market price but not to pay more than $44." There was some correspondence about the price, but the stock was bought and delivered.

A man named Humphreys sent Wells Fargo to collect a bill from a man named Knapp, but the agent reported: "Knapp says Humphreys owes him a bill and when he pays that, he will pay this."

In May, 1861, the Yankee Hill Union Club employed the Wells Fargo agent to "procure a regular (bunting) American Flag 34 stars of good material for the amt $33 sent herewith. As large as possible."

In 1861, Wells Fargo was commissioned to collect $150.40 from Thomas Sprague in Carson City, but the agent there reported: "Cannot collect this has promised to pay time after time always fails. Would pay no doubt if he had money."

A collection from 1868 shows the feeling about paper money: "McKee says—Coin no greenbacks accepted."

Another collection item from 1866 directed: "Accept greenbacks, take part payments if you cannot get the whole amount, and do the best you can." Still another, in the same year, said: "Sell greenbacks and make return in coin."

Nearly all the collection items—and occasionally a commission—were marked "P. O. R.," which might mean, "Protest or Return."

However, one of the most plaintive, perhaps, was dated in November, 1860: "Procure 2 boxes of Dr. Cheesemans Pills." The customer enclosed $2, and Wells Fargo charged him $1 for getting the pills. Exactly what Cheeseman's pills were, is not known to this generation, but it is a good bet that they were either a purgative or a mercury compound.[10]

Again in 1863, a special stock dividend was paid, this time of 100 percent, or 10,000 shares at $100 par value. Also, during the year, there were five cash dividends: 3 percent on February 1, 10 percent on March 16, and 3 percent on May 1, August 1, and November 2. Altogether, Wells Fargo paid 122 percent in dividends for 1863. It seems hard to do much better.

In this year, Wells Fargo carried over $20,000,000 in silver bullion from Virginia City alone, and 4 or 5 percent on that amount is a sizable sum.

In November, 1863, the stockholders finally ratified the increase in capital stock from $1,000,000 to $2,000,000.

Directors at the beginning of 1863 were the same as those in 1862. On October 14, 1863, E. P. Williams resigned as director, and Charles F. Latham, who had been treasurer for several years, was elected in his place.

The list of agencies opened in 1863 shows: Austin, Nevada; Chico in Butte County, California; Clifton, Oregon; Jacksonville in Tuolumne County; La Paz in Yuma County, Arizona Territory;[11] Latrobe in El Dorado County; Markleville in Alpine County; Mayfield in Santa Clara County; "Mexican Coast"; Newcastle in Placer County; Star City in Humboldt County; Telegraph City in Calaveras County; and Unionville in Humboldt County, Nevada. This makes twelve new agencies for the year 1863.

Thirty-two Concord coaches were ordered in 1863 by Louis McLane as president of the Pioneer Stage Company from the Abbot-Downing Company at Concord, New Hampshire; they were shipped around the Horn and reached San Francisco in 1864.

In 1864, began the series of events that were to lead to Wells Fargo's becoming sole owner of all the overland lines in the United States. That was a year of war prosperity in the North and in the West, and it was the year that camels were tried in freight service among Walker Lake, Virginia City, and Austin (they didn't last long). Water was rising in the mines of Virginia City and choking off work, and a Frenchman named Adolph Sutro was trying to interest bankers in a fantastic project to dig a tunnel that would drain the entire Comstock Lode.

Ben Holladay's contract for the overland mail would be up in 1864, and he was trying to get a

Hordes of Indians with bows, lances, and shields attacking a mule-drawn stagecoach of the Butterfield Overland Dispatch (Atchison to Denver). It appears that reinforcements are waiting around the bend. From "Harper's Weekly" for April 21, 1866.

renewal. He was a personal friend of Abraham Lincoln and Postmaster General Blair, but the renewal was blocked for a time by Senator John Conness of California, who was a bitter enemy of Louis McLane and presumably thought to embarrass Wells Fargo. After a good deal of backing and filling, the post office advertised for bids in early 1864, and on the fifth advertisement Holladay responded. By that time there were others bidding, and after a tangle of offers and withdrawals, Holladay got the contract; his contract for the eastern half was at $365,000 a year, and he subcontracted or had the western half made out to the Overland Mail at $385,000 a year. The contracts would expire in September, 1868.

Holladay suffered losses during both 1864 and 1865 from the Indians, with resultant breaks in service, and there were those who groaned when they heard his contract had been renewed. Among these might have been the officers of Wells Fargo, who were unhappy because Holladay had steadily refused to give them a contract to carry their express. United States Express, American Express, and Wells Fargo had tried to make a deal with Holladay, but with no success. Holladay carried his own express, and had his eye on a through expressway to the Atlantic coast. United States managed to place some express on his lines before 1866, but the others were unsuccessful. In 1865, Holladay would arrange with United States and American to carry his express to New York, but he would have no contract with Wells Fargo. He himself carried coin, specie, and gold from Central City, Colorado, to Atchison, Kansas, at 1½ percent, and he brought gold in from Oregon, from Idaho, and from Montana to Salt Lake City and to the East for 4 percent to 5 percent of its value.

In the spring of 1864, the Indians rampaged when a body of Cheyennes took a hundred horses from settlers along the South Platte. The governor appealed for troops but none were available. A Mr. Hungate and his wife and two children were murdered and scalped, and their bodies were exhibited in

Denver. The town went into panic; business houses were closed at 6:30, and all able citizens drilled every night.

By 1864, the Indians had plenty of rifles and ammunition, said the governor of Colorado, and they were encouraged by the absence of soldiers. Two emigrants were killed near Bijou Ranch, and seventeen horses stampeded; then all the horses of the stage company's stock at one station were stampeded, and sixty at another. Five Indians were killed and the stock recovered. A raid was made near Valley Station, and dead cattle, full of arrows, were left everywhere. A general Indian war was anticipated. The stage found two men scalped at Beaver Creek. That was in July, and the next day Indians attacked a train near Larned and killed ten men, leaving two scalped but not dead.

On August 8, several trains were attacked east of Kearny, and fourteen men were killed, some women and children captured. Three men were killed near Gilman's Ranch, and another near Cottonwood. Trains were raided on the Little Blue River, and Mrs. Eubanks and her two children and Miss Roper were captured. The westbound coach came into Fort Kearny and said that not a living soul was on the road within fifty miles. The coach had passed several burned wagon trains and eleven dead persons. Six more whites had been killed at Thirty-two Mile Creek. On August 15, the country was deserted to within forty miles of Atchison. The governor of

Colorado appealed to the citizens to kill all hostile Indians; the overland mail was stopped.

Near Boone's, on the Arkansas River, three men were killed and a woman captured, and a general attack was planned on the frontier towns in Colorado —but this was learned by the whites, and the attack was not made. The postmaster at Denver was ordered to send all mail for the East to San Francisco to be forwarded by water. The Rocky Mountain *News* criticized Holladay, saying he had been purposefully negligent because he had not received a renewal of the contract.

At Latham, west of Denver, 75 passengers and 109 sacks of mail accumulated, and the sacks were piled along the walls to serve as protection from bullets. A large quantity of mail accumulated at Atchison, but was finally sent back to New York to be forwarded to California by sea.

Winter was coming, and the Indians began to think about peace, because they depended largely on governmental charity during the winter. In November, however, troops under Chivington made the notorious attack upon Black Kettle's Cheyennes at Sand Creek and killed several hundred in one of the most debated actions in the history of war. Chivington called it a "battle," but others said it was a massacre.

The Cheyennes from Sand Creek, reinforced by Sioux and Arapahoes, attacked Julesburg and killed fourteen soldiers. The governor of Colorado telegraphed Washington: "The Indians are again murdering travelers and burning trains. . . . We must have 5,000 troops to clean out these savages. . . . The general government must help us or give up the Territory to the Indians."

In 1864, Holladay suffered heavily from Indian raids and from suspension of service because of a general state of war on the plains—as he had suffered in 1862. In a pamphlet apparently published by Holladay later, were fifty-nine pages of affidavits relating to Indian raids. One was by Richard Murray, a driver in Utah:

Mounted messengers pursued by Indians on the Plains. One messenger is falling from his horse; the other, saber dangling, has just shot a redskin in the chest. They should not have ridden so close to the woods. From "Harper's Weekly," January 13, 1866.

Advertisement for a line of five steam-powered river boats. The Stella Whipple *and the* Chippewa Falls *were to run from Fort Benton, Montana (it may have been Dakota Territory or Idaho Territory then), to the Great Falls, while the* Favorite, *the* Hudson, *and the* Frank Steel *would run between LaCrosse, Wisconsin, and Fort Benton. Note that runs would be made up the Yellowstone River also. The whole business avoided the Indians where they were worst: on the Great Plains. This original is in the possession of the Hobart House, Pine Valley, California.*

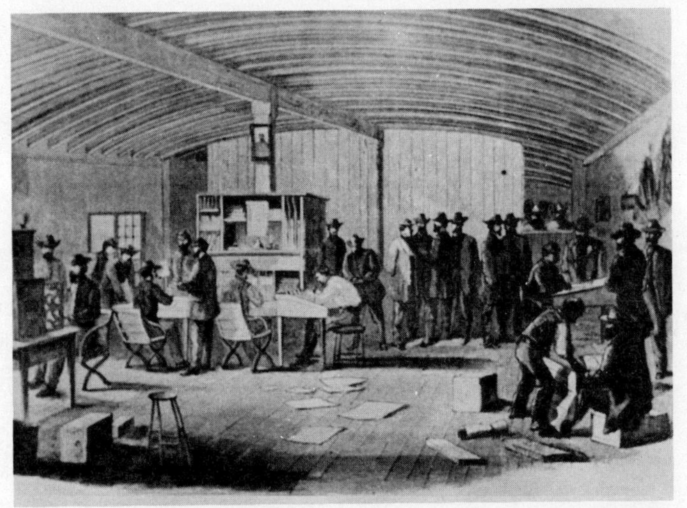

The express companies were active and prominent during the Civil War. This picture shows Adams Express handling the army payroll at City Point, Virginia, during Grant's siege of Richmond in 1864. From "Harper's Weekly."

Affiant states that he was passing from Split Rock Station west to Three Crossing of Sweet Water with the United States mails on the said 17th day of April, A. D. 1862, in company with eight other men, all of the mail party; that they were attacked by a band of Indians numbering thirty or more, who commenced a furious fire upon them with rifles and bows and arrows; that resistance was made by said mail party for hours, when the Indians retreated. Affiant further states that six men out of the nine who composed said party were wounded, one with arrows and five with guns.

Lemuel Flowers, a district agent, said of the same day:

The Indians attacked a party of nine men running two coaches, and commenced a furious fire upon them, wounding six men, including this affiant, whose body was penetrated by two rifle-balls; that after a resistance of four hours the Indians captured nine head of mules, nine sets of harness, and partially destroyed two coaches.

George H. Carlyle made affidavit that:

On the 9th of August, 1864, I left Alkali Station for Fort Kearney. On reaching Cottonwood Springs I learned by telegraph that the Indians had attacked a

> train of eleven wagons at Plum Creek, killed eleven men, captured one woman, and run off with the stock. Upon hearing this I started down the road, and when a few hundred yards off Gillman's Station I saw the bodies of three men lying on the ground, fearfully mutilated and full of arrows. At Plum Creek I saw the bodies of the eleven other men whom the Indians had murdered, and I helped to bury them. I also saw the fragments of the wagons still burning, and the dead body of another man, who was killed by the Indians at Smith's Ranch, and the ruins of the ranch, which had been burned.

Indeed, the Indian war was a real war. And it was not over.

In January, 1865, the American Ranch was burned by Indians and seven persons killed. Other ranches were burned. In late January, the Indians ravaged seventy-five miles of the road along the South Platte, burning wagons and ranches and tearing down the telegraph line. They drove off five hundred cattle and burned one hundred tons of hay, and continued to raid the South Platte for six days. Then they captured two large wagon trains west of Julesburg, and raided Julesburg again, taking food and clothing. Then they moved north to the Powder River country.

Finally, accumulated mail of six tons was sent east from Denver, escorted by forty soldiers, and accompanied by passengers and twenty additional teams of eastbound travelers. The telegraph line required eight miles of poles and twelve miles of wire. Then it was learned that two thousand soldiers were coming.[12]

There would be other encounters with the Indians, but service gradually got back on schedule.

In 1864, there was some trouble in California with Confederacy-inclined bandits; it apparently was not widespread but certainly was symptomatic of the deep feeling in the Gold Country between Confederate sympathizers and Unionists; it is said that the Confederates were trying to capture enough of the silver output of the Comstock to embarrass the Union. At any rate, on the evening of June 30, 1864, the San Francisco-bound stage of the Pioneer Stage Company was robbed by several armed men thirteen miles from Placerville. The leader of the band took the gold bullion that belonged to Wells Fargo, and gave a receipt that read:

> This is to certify that I have received from Wells, Fargo & Co., the sum of $........ cash, for the purpose of outfitting recruits enlisted in California for the confederate states' army. R. Henry Ingram, captain commanding company, C. S. A.

Some or all of the bandits were captured later, and one confessed, and it does seem that they were recruiting and equipping Confederate soldiers. They were called—and probably were—Copperhead guerrillas, but their activities were never on a big enough scale to cause more than annoyance except to those who suffered directly.[13]

The Bank of California, with William Ralston, cashier, opened at San Francisco, July 4, 1864, as a descendant of Garrison, Morgan, Fretz & Ralston; Darius Ogden Mills and Louis McLane were on the board. It opened a branch at Gold Hill on September 4, 1864, and William C. Ralston was launched on the course that was to lead to his death.

On July 14, 1864, the directors of Wells Fargo considered buying the Pioneer Stage Line from Louis McLane, and on December 15, it had been bought for $175,000 in gold payable at San Francisco.

In 1864, the first postal money order was issued, to inaugurate a revolution in the transmission of small sums of money.

Three cash dividends were paid that year: 3 percent on each of three dates: February 1, May 2, and August 1.

The profit and loss statement for 1864 again shows considerable attention to robberies. Apparently the bookkeepers could find no account in which they could enter the cost of robberies.

OTHER CREDITS

Overland Mail Co., rent and commission . . $	900.00
Special contract, Virginia City	1,777.77
Revenue taxes	12,000.00
Washoe robbery, bullion recovered	3,430.79
Claim against insurance company for genl. avge. St. Oregon remitted to Treasurer for credit of California	4,042.82
Express earnings for year	188,255.10
Total Credits	$210,406.48

CHARGES

Robbery, express box, A. Austin ....$	1,522.34
Genl. Avge. Str. Oregon [?]	4,042.82
Reward for arrest and conviction of Fiddletown robbers	1,000.00

Coulterville robbery:		
Willowman Bros. Company	$ 306.00	
Sullivan & Cashman	1,100.00	
D. N. Field	248.00	
Expenses, July	44.00	
Reward to sheriff	500.00	
Expenses—August	565.00	
Expenses—September	175.00	2,938.00
Washoe Road robbery:		
Donahoe & Ralston Co.	$ 534.85	
Levy & Company	700.00	
J. C. Dagley	50.00	
No. Kee & Company	236.00	
H. Kohn & Company	500.00	
F. Garasche	2,240.00	
Reward for post[age?] recovered	2,179.30	
D. B. Sullivan	70.00	
Owens M. Co.	140.00	
Rewards, July	1,790.73	
Expenses—August	702.50	
Reward for robbers killed at San Jose	1,500.00	
Sheriff, expenses	263.08	
I. C. Goods—Lawyer	645.00	
Attorneys in cash Washoe	1,175.00	$ 12,726.46
Old packages sold for charges		783.35
Silver Bar lost, Washoe stage		1,944.08
Robbery, Aurora express		645.00
Hanford arrest—escaped convict		105.00
Total Charges		$ 25,707.05
Balance Profit and Loss Account		$184,699.43

One thing seems obvious from this statement: Wells, Fargo & Company did not hesitate to spend money to track down robbers or to recover stolen treasure. Also, it is interesting to note that, with silver at roughly $1 an ounce, that particular bar of silver weighed about 125 pounds. One wonders what happened. It should be hard to *lose* a 125-pound bar of silver.

It is interesting to observe that $900 was paid to the Overland Mail Company for "rent and commission." Apparently this refers to the Butterfield company, which was now supposedly controlled by Wells Fargo.

The board of directors in 1864 remained unchanged from the close of 1863. Dividends in February, May, and August were 3 percent each.

Only six new agencies were established in this year: Clipper Gap in Placer County, Colfax in Nevada County, Gold Run in Placer County, N. San Juan in Nevada County, Princeton in Colusa County, and Silver Mountain in Alpine County.

In its fourteen years of existence, Wells Fargo had become the most familiar byword of the West. Although the Bank of California was bigger, Samuel Bowles said:

> But there is no institution of the Coast that has interested me more than the Wells & Fargo Express. It is the omnipresent, universal business agent of all the region from the Rocky Mountains to the Pacific Ocean. Its offices are in every town, far and near; a billiard saloon, a restaurant, and a Wells & Fargo office are the first three elements of a Pacific or Coast mining-town; its messengers are on every steamboat, and rail-car and stage, in all these States. It is the Ready Companion of civilization, the Universal Friend and Agent of the miner, his errand man, his banker, his post-office. It is much more than an ordinary express company; it does a general and universal banking business, and a great one in amount; it brings to market all the bullion and gold from the mining regions,—its statistics are the only reliable knowledge of the production; and it divides with the government the carrying of letters to and fro.
>
> . . . It has grown very much into the heart and habit of the people, and even conveys many of the letters upon routes that the government mail now goes as quickly and as safely, though the cost by the latter is much the greatest. . . . Wells & Fargo bought of the government in 1863 over *two millions* of three-cent envelopes, and seventy thousand three-cent stamps; in 1864, the three-cent envelopes were nearly two and a quarter millions, and the extra stamps about one hundred and twenty-five thousand. . . . One long side of the great San Francisco office is devoted to this letter business; clerks wait courteously, and at all hours, on all callers; letters with known or discoverable local addresses are delivered; and for the others, lists of those received each day are regularly posted, so that any one can tell at once, without inquiry, if there be anything for him. . . .
>
> This part of the business of Wells & Fargo is very profitable, and its success, popularity and wide extension, reaching through one hundred and seventy-five different towns and villages, . . . present very effective practical arguments for the government's giving up wholly its post-office department.[14] . . . Private enterprise here does better than the government, and is preferred to it.
>
> The Wells & Fargo Express is mostly owned in New York, but it is managed out here by men of large

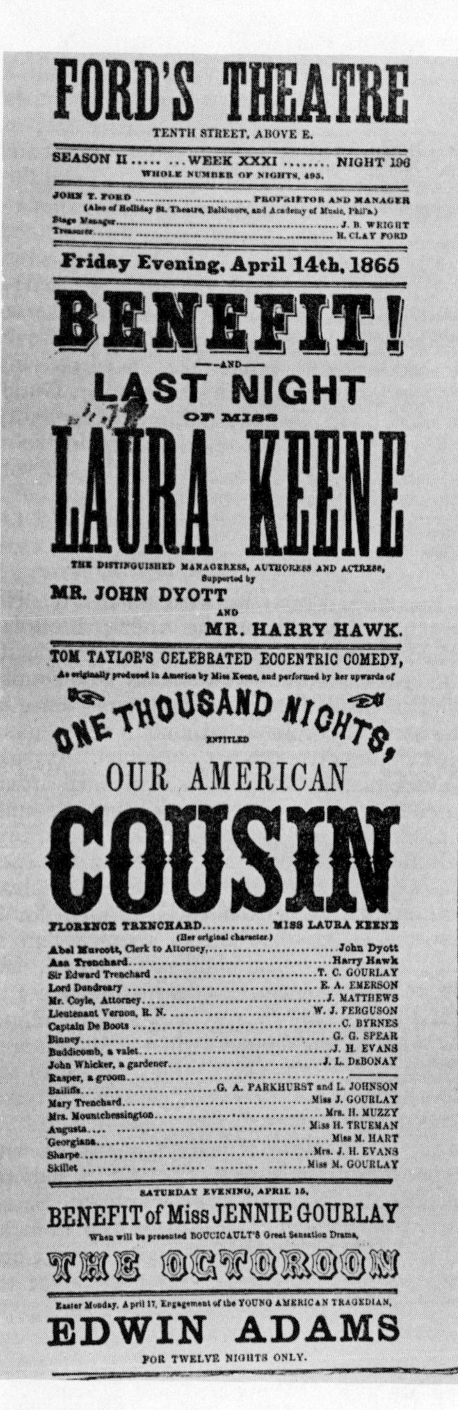

FORD'S THEATRE

TENTH STREET, ABOVE E.

SEASON II ....WEEK XXXI .... NIGHT 196

WHOLE NUMBER OF NIGHTS, 495.

JOHN T. FORD .... PROPRIETOR AND MANAGER

(Also of Holliday St. Theatre, Baltimore, and Academy of Music, Phil'a.)

Stage Manager.. J. B. WRIGHT

Treasurer.. H. CLAY FORD

Friday Evening, April 14th, 1865

BENEFIT!

—AND—

LAST NIGHT

OF MISS

LAURA KEENE

THE DISTINGUISHED MANAGERESS, AUTHORESS AND ACTRESS,

Supported by

MR. JOHN DYOTT

AND

MR. HARRY HAWK.

TOM TAYLOR'S CELEBRATED ECCENTRIC COMEDY,

As originally produced in America by Miss Keene, and performed by her upwards of

ONE THOUSAND NIGHTS,

ENTITLED

OUR AMERICAN

COUSIN

FLORENCE TRENCHARD.............. MISS LAURA KEENE

(Her original character.)

Abel Murcott, Clerk to Attorney,.......................... John Dyott
Asa Trenchard.. Harry Hawk
Sir Edward Trenchard .... T. C. GOURLAY
Lord Dundreary .... E. A. EMERSON
Mr. Coyle, Attorney.................................... J. MATTHEWS
Lieutenant Vernon, R. N. .... W. J. FERGUSON
Captain De Boots .... C. BYRNES
Binney.. G. G. SPEAR
Buddicomb, a valet...................................... J. H. EVANS
John Whicker, a gardener............................... J. L. DeBONAY
Rasper, a groom...——
Bailiffs... .... G. A. PARKHURST and L. JOHNSON
Mary Trenchard...................................... Miss J. GOURLAY
Mrs. Mountchessington................................ Mrs. H. MUZZY
Augusta.... .... Miss H. TRUEMAN
Georgiana... Miss M. HART
Sharpe.. Mrs. J. H. EVANS
Skillet .... Miss M. GOURLAY

SATURDAY EVENING, APRIL 15,

BENEFIT of Miss JENNIE GOURLAY

When will be presented BOUCICAULT'S Great Sensation Drama,

THE OCTOROON

Easter Monday, April 17, Engagement of the YOUNG AMERICAN TRAGEDIAN,

EDWIN ADAMS

FOR TWELVE NIGHTS ONLY.

Handbill for Laura Keene in one of her favorite plays, "Our American Cousin." This one seems to have run nearly three years at the time it was presented in Washington, D. C., the night of Lincoln's assassination—April 14, 1865. From "Century Magazine," January, 1890.

Army men attacking an Indian village at dawn; painting by Charles Schreyvogel. Indians were not ordinarily on their horses so early. Note the troopers mounted with right legs over carbines. From the collections of the Library of Congress.

The main street of Denver City, Colorado, and—among other things—a stagecoach loading for Butterfield's Overland "Despatch." C. A. Cook & Company's banking house was in with Butterfield. A great many ox-drawn covered wagons are in the street. From "Harper's Weekly," January 27, 1866.

Overland mail-coach crossing the Rocky Mountains: scene in Guy's Gulch. From "Harper's Weekly," February 8, 1868.

business experience and great sagacity, and in its enterprise and popular facilities not only strikingly illustrates but greatly advances the civilization of these States. Often it runs special treasure wagons with escort, and frequently its messengers are exposed to great peril from robbers and Indians. Those from Idaho now have to ride wide awake, day and night, with guns and pistols ready loaded and cocked. The stages on which their messengers and treasure were passing were stopped and robbed on the road eight times during 1864; and several serious robberies have also occurred this year, and in one case a messenger was murdered. The managers of the express are influential leaders and movers in the opening of new routes and in establishing lines of stages; even also are high powers in the construction of railroads.[15]

San Francisco saw some of its wildest times in the spring of 1865. A Frenchman named Etienne Derbec had established a newspaper, *L'Echo du Pacifique,* that had prospered; Derbec was a man of decided leanings and had an irrepressible tendency to say what he thought; he was thoroughly pro-French, and sometimes that was misinterpreted as anti-American. Therefore, when, on April 15, 1865, the news of Lincoln's assassination reached San Francisco, the whole town exploded in violence against southerners and against foreigners. Several foreign-newspaper buildings were destroyed; then the mob appeared before the building of the *Alta California,* in which were the *Echo*'s offices, and demanded that the *Echo*'s composing room be destroyed. The mob was stopped by the police, but they eventually demanded Derbec's life. With the help of the police, Derbec managed to stall them off, but his troubles were not over. The English-language newspapers were voluble and even furious, for Derbec had more than once taken an unpopular side. One newspaper said that all French editors were a pestilence; another offered $1,000 for Derbec's head.

Derbec got out that day with a whole skin, but by the next day his plant had been taken over by United States soldiers, who kept it some three weeks and literally wrecked it. They pied type on the floor, twisted his files out of shape, smashed his cuts with hammers, left excrement on the floor and urine in the water buckets. Derbec's business was ruined. He had made as much as $80,000 a year, but was reduced, finally, to poverty. For many years, he tried to recover damages from the government, but was not successful.[16] San Franciscans had little sympathy for anybody whose loyalty was even questioned.

By June, 1865, with the Civil War at an end, soldiers began to be available for service on the plains, and the Indian problem began to be less burdensome. By the latter part of the year, however, more trouble was developing for Holladay: a man named David O. Butterfield (no relation to John Butterfield), seeing that Denver's mail service was actually a spur line from the Overland, started a competition line to run along Smoky Hill River in Kansas, south of the Platte and south of the Republican River. It was something like 150 miles shorter by the Smoky Hill route, and in September, 1865, with the Civil War over, the Butterfield Overland Dispatch made its first trip. A great deal of material had accumulated, and David Butterfield's freight wagons had already carried 150,000 pounds of freight, including seventeen large boilers, nineteen carloads of assorted freight, and (in August) 600,000 pounds to Salt Lake City, and (in July) 150,000 pounds to Virginia City, Montana (at 22½ cents a pound).

The company bought stock and equipment and built stations along the Smoky Hill route, and announced plans for spur roads, and especially for a line from Denver to Salt Lake City via Berthoud Pass, which would be two hundred miles shorter than the route through South Pass. The company extended its line to Central City, past Denver, and the Denver-Central City section apparently was the most profitable section of the line.

The time from Atchison to Denver was from five to six days, but one trip was made on the Holladay line in three days and eleven hours. Holladay reduced the Central City to Denver fare from $6 to $1, but the B. O. D. (Butterfield Overland Dispatch) continued to operate. It had some Indian trouble, and its service was irregular that winter.

In the meantime, the eastern express companies and Wells Fargo began to investigate the possibility of building their own line through Berthoud Pass. They were shipping express east on the B. O. D., and a connection with Salt Lake City would remove completely their dependence on Ben Holladay. Already, according to some, they had contracts with the B. O. D.

In October, 1865, Louis McLane did some flashy

traveling of his own, going from San Francisco to Salt Lake City in three days and seventeen hours.

On February 8, 1865, D. N. Barney was asked to visit London "in reference to a financial agency of the California Railroad Company," so it would seem that Wells Fargo was more than ordinarily interested in the railroad company. And the directors noted that the business of the Pioneer Stage Line, bought from Louis McLane, was discouraging, to say the least, judging from reports received up to September 8.

However, the company went back to its 12 percent dividend in 1865: 3 percent paid on February 1, May 1, August 1, and November 1. Directors for 1865 were the same as those for 1864.

The Oregon Interior Express earned $113,089 up to September 30, and the silver bar apparently was recovered and added $1,316.45 to profit. The company paid $500 reward for its recovery.

It lost $1,130 in coin and $1,250 in gold dust by an explosion; a robbery at Placerville cost $1,145 (and other coin lost and stolen, belonging to A. Bouchard and Clung Wong, was $420). Wells Fargo paid H. T. Langdon for his good will on the North San Juan and Timbuctoo express route, $1,500. A safe lost in an explosion at Yosemite is listed as recovered at a cost of $1,059.62, and a package of bonds delivered to the wrong consignee cost the company $708.60.

However, the express earnings for the year were $144,042.24, and that amount, added to the earnings of the Oregon Interior Express, and reduced by the charges, made a net profit of $221,704.36 for the year.

Ten new agencies were opened in 1865: Albany in Linn County, Oregon; Alta in Placer County; Astoria, Oregon; Baker City in Baker County, Oregon; Boise City in Ada County, Idaho Territory; French Corral in Nevada County, California; Salt Lake City; Shingle Springs in El Dorado County; Sweetland in Nevada County; and Wilmington in Los Angeles County.

The big showdown with Ben Holladay was approaching.

1866

The Great Consolidation

THE EXPRESS COMPANIES HAD MADE enormous profits during the war, and in 1866, Adams paid a 500 percent dividend—$300 in stock and $200 in cash. Its capital was up to $12,000,000, and it was paying 12 percent on that. The Great Northern Express Company paid half its gross income to its parent railroad as rental, and 8 percent on top of that to its shareholders. None of the leading express companies ever issued stock for cash; it was used to buy express-carrying privileges and also to keep down the dividend rate.[1]

Ben Holladay was going ahead. The Concord people had built for him three special four-mule wagons to haul express, each to have a driver and a messenger; the messenger's run to be six hundred miles, to be covered in six days and nights.

Holladay was a big operator; he had steamship lines to Oregon, Panama, Japan, and China. But in February he heard that Wells Fargo, American Express, and United States Express were trying to get out of his clutches, and promptly sent two of his men to ride the B. O. D. as passengers and find out how much business it was doing. The B. O. D. was financed in New York, and, as it happened, he received the report from his agents one day and an ultimatum from Wells, Fargo & Company, American Express, and the United States Express, the next. The big companies demanded, first, a through rate, and, second, a division of business or territory. If he did not come through, they said, they would stock the line from Denver to Salt Lake City and would go around him.

Holladay sent for Edward Bray, president of the Park Bank, who was also president of the B. O. D., and told him exactly what he knew about the business, how much he figured the B. O. D. had lost. He told the president he knew the line had lost over a million dollars and was in shape to lose a lot more, and that he, Ben Holladay, was the only one who could pull him out—but the price would have to be a bargain. The banker, thoroughly cowed by big Ben's dominating manner, called his board together, and they agreed to sell to Holladay by 3 P.M.

Why Park did not contact the express companies may be explained, perhaps, by the fact that the line had indeed lost heavily, that the directors wanted to get rid of it, and that Holladay's personal bluster had built a fire under the bank president.

Holladay got the contract signed and then said, "Now, tell those expressmen to stock their line and be damned!"

Holladay bought the B. O. D. in March, 1865, and with it received 150 large Santa Fé six-ox wagons and fifty large six-mule wagons, and controlled almost five thousand miles of stage lines. He was at the height of his prosperity, and owned a brownstone mansion on Fifth Avenue, another in Washington, and a mansion near White Plains.

Holladay then had seven hundred men in his employ, and owned fifteen hundred horses, seven

The Butterfield's Overland Dispatch stagecoach starting out from Atchison (here horse drawn) for the run to Denver City. From the looks of the baggage on top, there must be a full load of passengers. (The artist seems a little confused between Butterfield's Overland Dispatch and the Holladay Overland Mail and Express Company; practically every stage line was called the Overland.) From "Harper's Weekly," January 27, 1866.

Ben Holladay, the mighty king of transportation who moved a little too far too fast. He was a very competent operator while things were booming, but he extended his capital all over the world, and it caught up with him. He got a splendid cash settlement out of Wells Fargo, but that did not save him.

hundred mules, and eighty coaches and express wagons, besides oxen and freight wagons.

But Holladay, too, had extended himself, and the next few months were frantic ones for him.

The railroads were building from east and west, and by the middle of July, Holladay moved the terminal of his lines to Columbus, Nebraska, one hundred miles west of Omaha, which was then the railhead of the Union Pacific. In September, he moved his headquarters to Fort Kearny. The handwriting was on the wall.

On February 5, 1866, Holladay incorporated as the Holladay Overland Mail and Express Company. The president was Bela M. Hughes, who had been the last president of the C. O. C. & P. P.; secretary and treasurer was John E. Russell; other directors were David Street, Samuel L. M. Barlow, and Ben Holladay. On March 12, 1866, this company bought from Holladay all his mail and express lines west of the Missouri River, a total mileage of 2,670, more or less, and all property constituting the Overland Dispatch Company; Holladay was to receive $3,000,000 in cash. It bought Holladay's mail contracts, wagon-road, stock and good will for $1,500,000, of which $100,000 was to be paid in cash, the rest on notes maturing every three months until October 1, 1867.

On March 19, a contract was made with Henry Carlyle & Company to do the company's freighting from Fort Kearny to the North Fork of the Platte

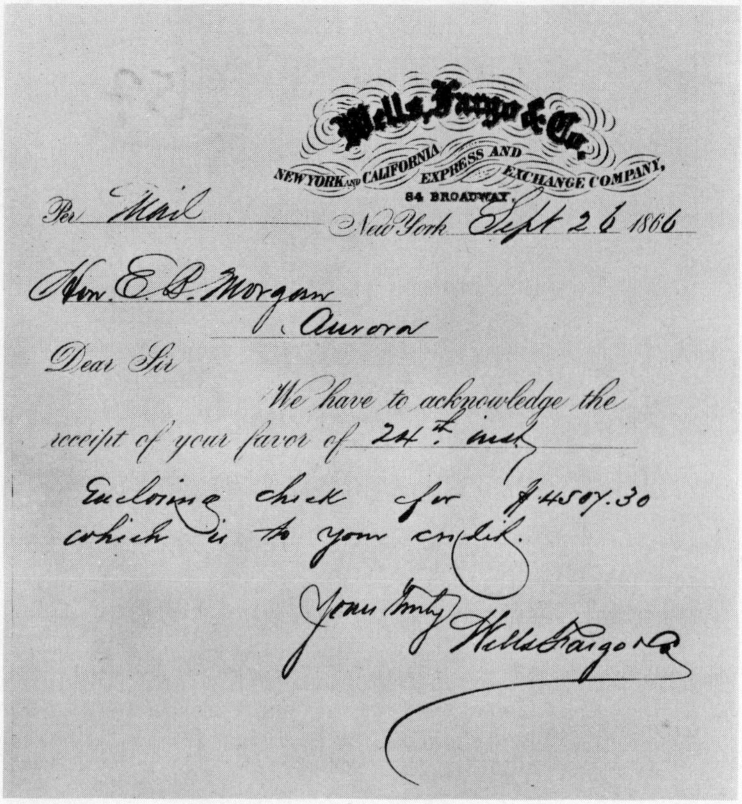
Wells, Fargo & Co.
NEW YORK AND CALIFORNIA EXPRESS AND EXCHANGE COMPANY,
84 BROADWAY

Per Mail New York Sept 26 1866

Hon. E. B. Morgan
Aurora

Dear Sir

We have to acknowledge the receipt of your favor of 24th inst

Enclosing check for $4507.30 which is to your credit.

Yours truly
Wells Fargo & Co

A letter from Wells, Fargo & Co., New York and California Express and Exchange Company, advising E. B. Morgan, the first president, that it was sending him a check for $4,507.30. They were still signing, "Wells, Fargo & Co.," without a personal signature. The original is in the History Room, Wells Fargo Bank.

River, and on March 20, the new company's capital was increased to $10,000,000. On April 23, the president was authorized to establish three assay offices: in Utah, Montana, and Idaho. On June 4, a fare reduction of 25 percent was allowed ministers.

In July, Louis McLane of Wells Fargo reported that he had subscribed to $150,000 worth of stock in a San Francisco assaying and refining business, in the name of Wells Fargo.

On September 16, the Holladay company borrowed $100,000. On October 31, it gave one hundred shares of stock each to William H. Fogg and Samuel L. M. Barlow as their commissions for acting as trustees for Ben Holladay.

In October, the Wells Fargo directors discussed a consolidation with the Holladay company, and it was agreed first to sell the business and good will to the Holladay company for forty thousand shares of the capital stock of $10,000,000 of the Holladay company (which, as will be seen later, gave Wells Fargo control), plus payment for personal property and supplies. No real estate in New York or Chicago was included. The name of Wells, Fargo & Company was to be retained.

On October 31, the directors of Wells Fargo were Morgan, Danford Barney, Wells, Ashbel Barney, Cheney, Fargo, Stockwell, Latham, and Livingston. On that date, however, Fargo resigned, and Louis McLane was elected in his place. The officers then were Danford N. Barney, president; N. H. Stockwell, secretary; and Charles F. Latham, treasurer.

On November 1, the Holladay Overland Mail and Express Company's bylaws were adopted, and the president was authorized to buy the property, good will, and other interests west of the Missouri River of Wells Fargo & Company, the United States Express Company, the American Express Company, the Overland Mail Company, and the Pioneer Stage Company.

The United States Express Company agreed to discontinue its activities west of the Missouri; United States was to receive $447,500 cash or that much interest in 7,975 shares of stock. The Holladay company also made an agreement with the American Express Company for a similar quitting of the territory, for which American was to receive $400,000 cash or that much credit on 7,400 shares of stock.

On November 1, the directors authorized the change of the name to Wells, Fargo and Company, "in accordance with section 11 of the charter." (This refers to the Colorado territorial charter, under which Wells Fargo would operate henceforth.) It is obvious that Wells Fargo had never lost control. Apparently the owners of Wells Fargo had their own reasons for going through this complicated procedure, but it ended up with their ownership of the business, the name, and the good will, while both United States and American were to quit the territory.

On November 12, the name change was ratified by the directors, and at that meeting the following stockholders were represented in person: Wells, Fargo & Company, 39,998 shares; Overland Mail Company, 10,000 shares; U. S. Express, 7,975; American Express, 7,400; Benjamin Hicks, 667; James Cruikshank, 134; A. S. Underhill, 54; R. H. Haydock, 134; H. A. Miller, 200; H. A. Richardson, 54; T. L. Randlett, 27; George Richardson, 67; W. B. Kendall, 67; George E. Cook, 754; A. Bancroft, 12; John Slode, 134; J. H. Puleston, 100. The total number of shares was 67,777, of which Wells Fargo controlled almost 50,000.

On March 19, Eugene Kelly was elected to the board of directors in place of James Enniott; on November 1, Louis McLane was elected to the new Wells, Fargo and Company board in place of William H. Fogg, Ashbel H. Barney in place of Samuel L. M. Barlow, and Danford Barney in place of Walter I. Gurnee. Ben Holladay, who had become president March 13, resigned as president, and Louis McLane became president. Two days later, Calvin Goddard became treasurer.

It is at this point that some persons think the corporate name was changed to Wells, Fargo and Company, but the Colorado incorporation papers show it as Wells, Fargo & Company, and on December 10, Louis McLane sent a notice to Wells Fargo customers in the following words:

Notice. The public, and especially all persons who have heretofore transacted business with WELLS, FARGO & CO., are notified that a consolidation of interests and business between Wells, Fargo & Co., The Pioneer Stage Co., The Holladay Overland Mail and Express Co., The Overland Mail Co., The United States Express Co., and the American Express Co., has taken place, and been effected under a Charter granted by the Territorial Legislature of Colorado, and that all the business heretofore done by either of these Companies west of the Missouri River, or between New York, San Francisco and the China Seas, will hereafter be carried on by Wells, Fargo & Co., under the Act of Incorporation referred to. Louis McLane, President of Wells, Fargo & Co. New York, Dec. 10, 1866. Please acknowledge.[2]

There is some evidence that the stockholders of the first company were paid off in 1867, and the original New York corporation liquidated at that time, but in practice, at least, it seems doubtful that "Wells, Fargo and Company" was ever considered the corporate name.

At any rate, the great deed had been done. Wells, Fargo & Company had become the owner of the greatest staging empire in history.

There are those Holladay admirers who laugh up their sleeves at the easy way in which Wells Fargo was sucked into this deal, pointing out that Holladay knew the days of the stage were numbered, that the Wells Fargo directors closed their eyes to the reality of the railroad, and expected the staging business to last much longer than it eventually did. However, it is a little hard to understand how these nine men could have been fooled so patently. It is suggested that Wells Fargo expected to use its huge quantity of stock and equipment on smaller lines to feed the railroad, and that, in effect, is exactly what it did do.

It really does not seem that Wells Fargo was blind to the implication of the railroad, for in the same year (1866) it was issuing tickets with blanks for insertion of rail to stage changes and stage to rail changes to allow for the constant westward progress of the Union Pacific. It is hard to know the directors' motivations, but it does not seem that they were blind to the results of the railroad construction.

On the whole, it appears to be an academic argument. There were still two and a half years to go.

It did not take the "Harper's" artist long to get rid of most of the baggage on top of the stagecoach. Here the four men (driver and passengers) are shown holding a "council of war" on the Plains. From "Harper's Weekly," January 27, 1866.

It appears that Holladay received $1,500,000 cash and $300,000 in Wells Fargo stock. There was a great deal of maneuvering, but Wells Fargo was in control all the way. It now owned and controlled nearly all the stage lines from the Missouri River to California.

Holladay had owned steamship lines to Oregon, to Japan and China; he had owned railroads, but he had failed to get one of the things he had wanted most: the name, "Overland Mail Company." (David Street, his right-hand man, said Ben had always wanted that name.) Now Ben was on the downhill slope, and, sadly enough, he would not again be on top. He had been a giant in his own right—but even the day of a giant must pass.

There are those who point to Wells Fargo's subsequent earnings, which immediately were somewhat less than they had been. It is a fact that the net express income in 1866 (for the first ten months) was $123,084.84, while in 1867, at ten times the capitalization, it was $199,362.86; thereafter, it dropped to a low point of $133,526.52 in 1870, the year after the railroad was completed, but in 1871 was back up to $227,902.90, and continued to grow from that time on.

During 1866, Wells Fargo paid a little more than its usual handsome dividends, however: 3 percent on February 1, 10 percent on February 15, 3 percent on May 1, 3 percent on August 1, and 3 percent on October 31—a total of 22 percent for the year.

An income and expense statement from October 31, 1866, shows that Wells Fargo paid $569,000 in charges for transportation, $305,000 in "express privilege debit" (paid to other carriers for moving Wells Fargo express), and had net revenue from transportation of $264,000; received $93,000 for carrying letters, and therefore had a gross operating revenue of $357,000. Operating expenses were $231,000, which left a net operating revenue of $126,000; it paid $2,600 in taxes.

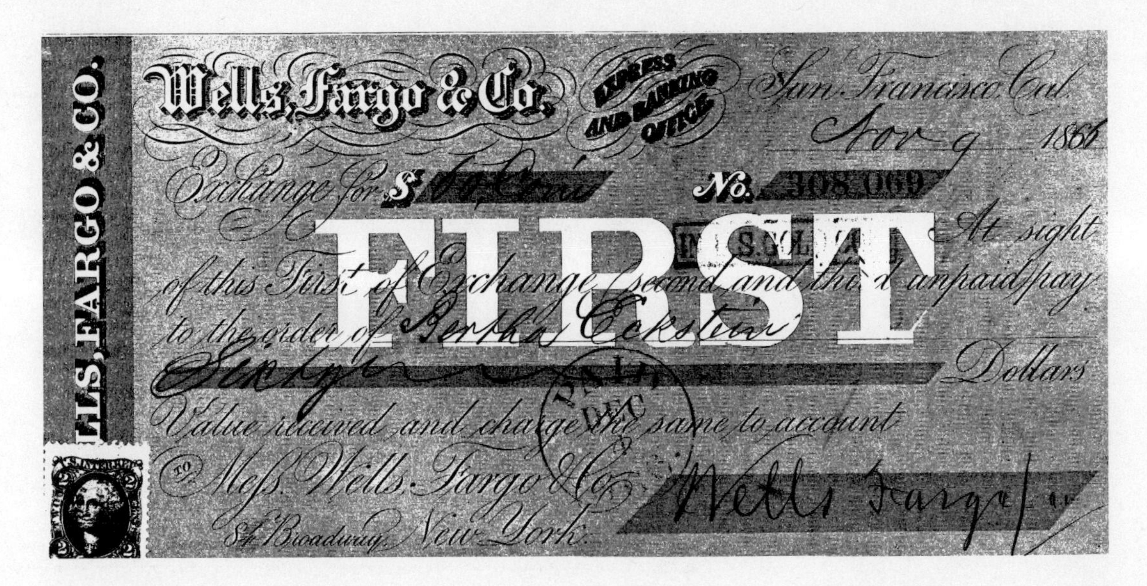

LLS, FARGO & CO.

Wells, Fargo & Co. EXPRESS AND BANKING OFFICE.

San Francisco Cal. Nov 9 1866

Exchange for $ No. 308.069

FIRST

At sight of this First of Exchange (second and third unpaid) pay to the order of Bertha Eckstein

Sixty Dollars

Value received and charge the same to account

To Mess. Wells Fargo & Co.

84 Broadway New York.

Wells Fargo & Co.

A First of Exchange for $60 in gold coin, paid December 4, 1866, by Wells Fargo. Duly legalized with a two-cent Internal Revenue bank check stamp. The original is in the History Room, Wells Fargo Bank.

WELLS,

Wells, Fargo & Co. EXPRESS AND BANKING OFFICE.

Sacramento Cal. Apl 25th 1866

Exchange for $30 Gold No. 297.126

SECOND

At sight of this Second of Exchange (first and third unpaid) pay to the order of A. M. Snyder in U S Gold Coin

Thirty Dollars

Value received and charge the same to account

To Mess. Wells Fargo & Co.

84 Broadway New York.

Wells Fargo & Co.

A Second of Exchange for $30 in gold coin, also apparently stamped paid. This one, dated April 25, 1866, bears also a California stamp for eight cents, applicable to Seconds of Exchange. The original is in the History Room, Wells Fargo Bank.

WELLS, FARGO & CO'S EXPRESS.

WELLS, FARGO & CO.

Value, $ ... Received of ... Valued at ... Dollars

Addressed, ...

which we agree to forward to ... by usual conveyance, subject to the following conditions:

In no event to be liable beyond our Route as herein receipted; not to be responsible except as and in the capacity of forwarders, we not owning or being interested in the means or vehicles of transportation. Nor liable for any loss or damage arising from the dangers of railroad, ocean or river navigation, explosion, fire, etc., unless specially insured by us, and so specified herein. Nor for the negligence or misconduct of the owners of said means or vehicles of transportation, or of their agents or others in charge thereof. And not to be liable in any respect except under this contract.

Charges, $ ... For the Proprietors, ...

Towne & Bacon, Printers, San Francisco.

Receipt at Virginia (City) for ten bars of (silver) bullion valued at $20,766.95 to be forwarded to the Savage Company in San Francisco. The original is in the History Room, Wells Fargo Bank.

WELLS, FARGO & CO'S EXPRESS.

WELLS, FARGO & CO.

Value, $ ... SAN FRANCISCO, ... 1866

Received of ... Addressed ...

which we agree to forward to ... by usual conveyance, subject to the following conditions:

In no event to be liable beyond our Route as herein receipted; not to be responsible except as and in the capacity of forwarders, we not owning or being interested in the means or vehicles of transportation. Nor liable for any loss or damage arising from the dangers of railroad, ocean or river navigation, explosion, fire, etc., unless specially insured by us, and so specified herein. Nor for the negligence or misconduct of the owners of said means or vehicles of transportation, or of their agents or others in charge thereof. And not to be liable in any respect except under this contract.

Charges, $ ... For the Proprietors, ...

Towne & Bacon, Printers, San Francisco.

A receipt given by Wells Fargo to the United States mint for one sealed box valued at $872, to be delivered to the director of the mint at Philadelphia. Wells Fargo's charges were $24.25. The original is at the California Historical Society.

On February 20, Hiram Rumfield wrote to his wife from San Francisco, advising her that he was enclosing "Second of the Coin Draft for $3,000." The first had been sent from Virginia City, and he carefully warned her that if the First had been paid, then this Second was of no value. He spoke of many Indian troubles at that time, and said that he had bought eight yards of silk at $8 a yard in gold, for her to make a dress. They had told him that seven yards would be enough, but he wanted to be sure. He said nothing more about sending her a scalp.[3]

The Second of Exchange was a symptom of the times and the uncertainty of the mails. The company would issue an order for exchange in First, Second, and Third of Exchange, and the buyer would send them by different routes—perhaps one overland, one by Nicaragua, and one by Panama. The payee could cash any one of them.

A First of Exchange issued in San Francisco reads:

> Wells, Fargo & Co. Express and Banking Office, San Francisco, Cal., Nov. 9, 1886. Exchange for $60 coin. No. 308 069. At sight of this First of Exchange (second and third unpaid) pay to the order of Bertha Eckstein Sixty Dollars. Value received and charge the same to account. to Mess. Wells, Fargo & Co., 84 Broadway, New York. [Signed] Wells Fargo & Co.

The draft bears a U.S. Internal Revenue bank check stamp for two cents, and is stamped, "In

The Wells Fargo office at Virginia City in 1866; picture used in "Old Waybills." The sign (probably next door to Wells Fargo), says, "Fast Freight Line."

E HOLLADAY OVERLAND MAIL & EXPRESS CO.

ARRYING THE REAT UGH MAILS

FROM THE ATLANTIC TO THE PACIFIC STATES.

Salt Lake City, Sept 19 1866

Received from Wells Fargo & Co

One Pk

said to contain

Sarah Coken

Virginia City

AGREED, and is a part of the consideration of this contract, that the HOLLADAY OVERLAND MAIL AND EXPRESS CO. are not to be held responsible for any loss or damage except as forwarders only; nor for any loss or damage by the dangers of railroad, ocean or river navigation, leakage, breakage, fire, or from whatever, unless the same be proved to have occurred from the fraud or gross neglect of ourselves, our agents or servants, or unless insured by us (in no case against leakage or breakage,) and in no event is this Company to be liable beyond their route as herein receipted. Valued under Fifty Dollars, unless otherwise stated.

For the Holladay Overland Mail and Express Co.

Roberson

Agent.

Slote & Janes, Stationers, 93 Fulton St., N. Y.

A receipt given by the Holladay Overland Mail & Express Company at Salt Lake City in September, 1866, to Wells Fargo for a box valued at \$20. The original is in the History Room, Wells Fargo Bank.

Wells, Fargo & Co.

San Francisco Nov 16 1860

Exch. for £20

On demand Pay this Second of Exchange (first & third unpaid) to the order of Martha Harrison

Twenty Pounds Sterling

Value received and charge same as advised.

To The Union Bank of London

London.

Wells Fargo & Co

A Second of Exchange for £20 sterling on a London bank. The original is at the California Historical Society.

U. S. Gold Coin" and "Paid, Dec. 4, 1866."

A Second of Exchange, made out in Sacramento, April 25, is for thirty dollars "in U. S. Gold Coin." It is No. 297.126, and bears the two-cent bank check stamp and a California tax stamp that says: "California State Tax. Exchange. Second. Above $20 to $50, 8 cts."[4]

Wells Fargo continued to be of service to the people, as is evidenced in a letter dated April 8, 1866, from G. A. Benzen, district attorney of San Diego County, when he said in the margin: "If you see Doctor Wooster tell him that I paid my note to the agent of Wells Fargo & Co.—$40 coin [gold]—some 6 weeks ago. Thank you kindly for waiting so long."[5]

Obviously the Holladay office in Salt Lake City had been accustomed to accepting packages from Wells Fargo for shipment to the East, and it is equally obvious that, if so, Wells Fargo itself had had no space on Holladay stagecoaches. A receipt given by the Holladay lines in September, 1866, is worded as follows:

> The Holladay Overland Mail & Express Co. for carrying the Great Through Mails from the Atlantic to the Pacific States. Salt Lake City, Sept. 19, 1866. Received from Wells, Fargo & Co. in apparent good order, one pkg. said to contain ———, val. $20. Marked Sarah Cohen, Virginia City. Marked "Paid Through" on San F. W. B. [waybill?] #255. It is agreed, and is a part of the consideration of this contract, that the Holladay Overland Mail and Express Co. are not to be held responsible for any loss or damage except as forwarders only; nor for any loss or damage by the dangers of railroad, ocean or river navigation, leakage, breakage, fire, or from any cause whatever, unless the same be proved to have occurred from the fraud or gross neglect of ourselves, our agents or servants, or unless insured by us (in no case do we insure against leakage or breakage,) and in no event is this Company to be liable beyond their route as herein receipted. Valued under fifty dollars, unless otherwise herein stated. All kinds of fragile ware at shipper's risk. For the Holladay Overland Mail and Express Co. Jos. Roberson, Agent. All kinds of fragile ware at shipper's risk. Chgs. $1.50 paid.

It is rubber stamped or otherwise stamped: "Dangers of War and Fire excepted," but it is hard to know to what this exception is taken.

A receipt given by Wells Fargo about the same time is for bullion (probably silver):

> Wells, Fargo & Co.'s Express. Nos. 521 & 530. Value, $20,766.95. Virginia, Nov. 20th, 1866. Received by Chas. Bormer, Supt., ten 10 bars Bullion valued at twenty thousand seven hundred and seventy-six 95/100 Dollars. Addressed Savage Co. which we agree to forward to San Francisco by usual conveyance, subject to the following conditions:
>
> In no event to be liable beyond our Route as herein receipted; not to be responsible except as and in the capacity of forwarders, we not owning or being interested in the means or vehicles of transportation. Nor liable for any loss or damage arising from the dangers of railroad, ocean or river navigation, explosion, fire, etc., unless specially insured by us, and so specified herein. Nor for the negligence or misconduct of the owners of said means or vehicles of transportation, or of their agents or others in charge thereof. And not to be liable in any respect except under this contract.
>
> Charges, $............... For the Proprietors, Henry L. Roff Wells, Fargo & Co.

This disclaimer of ownership of the vehicles undoubtedly was the usual disclaimer, although it seems that Wells Fargo did own the Pioneer Stage Line over which these ten bars of bullion would have traveled.[6]

A Second of Exchange dated at San Francisco, November 16, is on the Union Bank of London and is for twenty pounds.

A receipt on exactly the same form as that issued at Virginia City was issued by the San Francisco office to the U. S. Br. Mint (United States Branch Mint) for a "Seald Box Val Eight Hundred and Seventy two Dollars," addressed to the Director of Mint, Philadelphia"; the charges were $24.25—a little under 3 percent.[7]

There was one event in 1866 that had nothing to do with the overland mail but did have much to do with Wells Fargo. In 1866, one Julius Bandmann was making the first dynamite ever manufactured, and the site of his manufacturing was San Francisco. Nitroglycerine, a principal component of dynamite, at that time was but newly invented and little known, and it is probable that the several cans of nitroglycerine shipped in care of Wells Fargo were destined for Bandmann. At any rate, the nitroglycerine

The nitroglycerine explosion at Aspinwall in 1866. From "Harper's Weekly," May 5, 1866.

was shipped from New York in tin cans put up in a wooden case like coal oil. The cans leaked a little and stained the wood with an oily fluid, which looked like that from coal oil. The cans had traveled as freight on a Pacific Mail Company steamer, and were set on the dock. Nobody was quite clear as to the contents, and Wells Fargo moved the case to its office at Montgomery and California—the Parrott Building. Somebody tried to investigate the cause of the leakage, and at the first impact of a hammer on a cold chisel, the nitro exploded with a tremendous roar. The entire city felt the shock, and San Franciscans ran for the street, thinking it was an earthquake. The rear of the building was shattered. Samuel Knight, the superintendent of the company, and several other employees were killed.

Some six months before, a Greenwich Street hotel in New York had been destroyed in a mysterious blast, and eventually it turned out that among the guests of the hotel were the promoters of a company formed to import "blasting oil" from Sweden to send to the California mines. And two weeks before the catastrophe in San Francisco, a whole steamship, the *European,* had blown up at Aspinwall, with about fifty persons killed.

Wells Fargo had handled just about everything up to that time, but it finally drew the line on Swedish blasting oil, and wrote a new regulation for the instruction manual:

> Camphene, nitroglycerine, naphtha, benzine, petroleum or other explosive burning fluids; gunpowder, giant powder, oil of vitriol, nitric or other chemical acids; turpentine, matches, phosphorus or loaded firearms, must not be received for transportation.

Nitroglycerine continued to be shipped, but presumably by freight rather than by express, because Charles Crocker, driving his tunnels through the solid granite peaks of the Sierras, saw a great use for this ultra-powerful explosive. Giant powder had not been very effective against the granite, and thus was

The seventy cases of nitroglycerine exploding on the European *took about fifty lives; a second and third explosion sank the ship, which had been towed out to a distance; a fourth explosion wrecked the Panama Railroad Company's freight house, as shown here from "Harper's Weekly."*

too slow; nitroglycerine was treacherous but it was much faster, and Crocker put in his order, and nitro was used to carve out the big tunnel above Donner Lake.

Soon after Wells Fargo absorbed or consolidated with Holladay, Charles E. McLane, Louis' brother, was appointed general agent for the Pacific Coast, and he appointed John J. Valentine superintendent of express.[8]

During 1866, the company continued its policy of expansion, establishing twenty-five new agencies, including several in Portland and Oregon (perhaps feasible for the first time because of Ben Holladay's absence): Browns Valley in Yuba County, Cisco in Placer County, Corvallis in Oregon, The Dalles in Oregon, Eugene City in Oregon, Forbestown in Butte County, Fort Jones in Siskiyou County, Foster Bar in Yuba County, Gibsonville in Plumas County, Howland's Flat in Plumas County, Idaho City in Idaho Territory, La Porte in Plumas County, Lewiston in Washington Territory; Trinity, California, Meadow Lake in Nevada County, Oakland, Roseburg in Douglas County, Rugby City, St. Louis in Plumas County, Salem in Oregon, Smartsville in Yuba County, Susanville in Lassen County, Umatilla in Oregon, Vancouver in Washington Territory, and Walla Walla in Washington Territory.

The company's profit and loss statement for 1866 shows some interesting items. The Oregon Inter Express Company had earned $123,084.84 up to October 31; however, the Oregon Stage Company had lost $250 worth of opium. Wells Fargo had lost another silver bar in the "Ada Hancock" explosion, worth $120.24; Blake's Express had failed to pay $300. A reward of $3,000 had been paid for recovery of treasure and the arrest and conviction of robbers of the San Juan & Nevada Express on May 15. Wells Fargo bought the Downieville Express for $2,075.50 and the LaPorte Express for $3,200, and paid Hop Cik $500 for opium lost, and again

$255.75 for opium lost. It lost $5,000 in coin in a holdup on the Geiger Grade on October 10, and it has a final item of $925 lost on "Old Horse" Collection Department—probably an attempt to collect accounts that had been written off (which apparently was not very successful).

Directors for 1866 were Morgan, Danford Barney, Ashbel Barney, Wells, Cheney, N. H. Stockwell, Charles F. Latham, Johnston Livingston, and Louis McLane.

The number of offices in operation January 1, 1866, had been 172; on October 31, it was 196.

Wells Fargo had the world's greatest staging empire but no express-carrying privilege on the transcontinental railroad—thereby making it possible for a man named Lloyd Tevis to get control of the entire company a few years later.

Whatever the merits of either side of the argument as to who got the best of whom in the great consolidation (perhaps a good answer is that Holladay got his price and got out, while Wells Fargo paid what it had to pay for something it wanted), it is clear that Ben Holladay had already reached his greatest height. He lost most of his far-flung properties after 1866, and some ten years later tried to get the government to pay him for his losses on the plains in the early 1860's, but when he was offered $100,000, he scorned it, and left Washington, to remain away forever. He lost vast farm holdings, mines, Mexican railroads, a salt works—almost everything. His brother Joseph, who had killed a man in Salt Lake City, turned against him and got control. Ben died in 1887; his second wife, Esther, died in 1889, supposedly from poison, while Ben's supposed friends and cronies and his brother managed to get their hands on as much property as possible. Ben's two children finally became the beneficiaries of a $125,000 estate.

1867-1869
Tevis Gets Control

THERE WERE NO STARTLING DEVELOPMENTS in 1867. It was a period of postwar depression for business as a whole, but undoubtedly one of consolidation for Wells, Fargo & Company. A map captioned, "Wells, Fargo and Company's Stage and Express Routes, 1867,"[1] shows the network extending from the "British Possessions" on the north to the latitude of Santa Fé on the south; apparently Wells Fargo was not very active farther south, although at least three lines seem to go farther.

From about Atchison, Kansas, a line goes down to Tahlequah in Indian Territory, and a branch to Fort Smith on the southeast, and another toward the Red River Crossing on the southwest. Solid lines seem to indicate Wells Fargo stage lines while dotted lines probably indicate connecting lines on which Wells Fargo had space for express. From Des Moines a line went up toward Minneapolis, and another to Sioux City and beyond Yankton, South Dakota. From the railhead a little west of Fort Riley, Kansas, a line went up the Smoky Hill Fork to Denver; another turned a little south and went up the Arkansas River to Denver. From Denver there were several connecting lines—one south to Santa Fé and beyond.

The Union Pacific had reached Julesburg in northeast Colorado, and a stage line went from Julesburg up Lodgepole Creek to cross southern Wyoming and reach Salt Lake City, from where it went on across the middle of Nevada to Carson City and Sacramento, and then by boat to San Francisco. One line went north from Salt Lake City to Virginia City, Montana, and on to Fort Benton; another line went northwest from Salt Lake City to Boise City, Idaho, and one to the Columbia River and Portland, Oregon. Another line from Virginia City went north to get around the Bitter Root Mountains, but came back to the Snake River and eventually the Columbia. Another line went north and east from Virginia City, Nevada, to Boise City, Idaho. A principal line (the California & Oregon Stage Line) went north from Sacramento through Oregon and into Washington; the Gold Country was covered with a network of lines; there was a line from Sacramento south up the San Joaquin Valley, and another south from San Francisco along the coast toward San Diego. Principal connecting lines were from the North Platte, near Fort Casper, to Virginia City and Fort Benton (Fort Benton was an important point on the Missouri River in those years); from Boise City west into Oregon; and lines through the southern part of Nevada and Utah; also, Wells Fargo apparently had express rights south from Salt Lake City along the Colorado River—possibly connecting with San Bernardino and Los Angeles over the traditional Mormon Trail.

Thus, it seems that Wells Fargo, through its own lines and many smaller lines, pretty well blanketed the inhabited portions of the West.

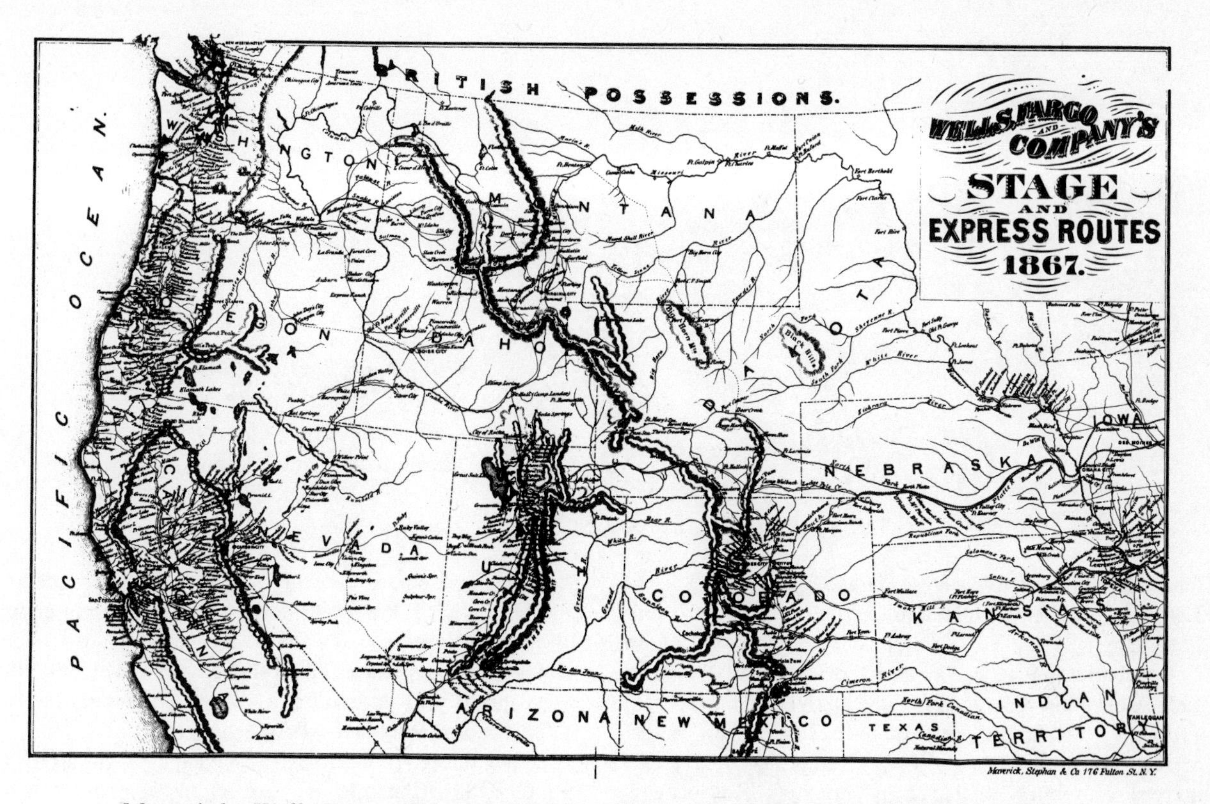

Map of the Wells Fargo "Stage and Express Routes" in 1867. Presumably the solid lines represent Wells Fargo routes, while the dotted lines represent connecting carriers. Map by Maverick, Stephan & Company, New York; the original is in the History Room, Wells Fargo Bank.

Perhaps this map, prepared for Wells Fargo, does not show the southern part of the Southwest because Wells Fargo was not interested in that area. Service had been established from Mesilla, New Mexico, to Tucson, Arizona, and in 1867, it was extended to Los Angeles and made triweekly; before that time, a resident of Tucson, to send a letter to California, had to send it back east to St. Joseph, and then west via the Overland. The extension of the line from West Texas to Los Angeles was on the old Butterfield route. By that time, too, there was a semiweekly line from Los Angeles via San Bernardino to La Paz and Prescott, Arizona.

By the end of 1867, the Central Pacific Railroad had reached Cisco, ninety-four miles east of Sacramento, and the Union Pacific had reached Cheyenne, Wyoming, west of Julesburg, Colorado, while the Kansas Pacific (the Eastern Division of the Union Pacific) was at Hays City, past the middle of Kansas.

Obviously mail-carrying was still an important part of the express or stage-line business, because in 1867, according to *Old Waybills,* there were some charges that Wells Fargo gave government mail careless treatment to build up their own mail-carrying.

Apparently not many early Wells Fargo waybills are still in existence, but a waybill from the California and Oregon United States Mail Line is interesting. It was printed on a sheet about 8½ by 11 inches, and designed to be folded twice across the short dimension, like a letter to be inserted in a No. 10 envelope. On the outside, printed crosswise so it would be readable after the fold, is the following:

WAY-BILL. ——— California and Oregon United States Mail Line. ——— Portland and Yreka. [handwritten:] Monday July 8th 1867. Cal Scovill [printed:] Driver. Agents must insert Time of Departures and Arrivals. ——— [printed and handwritten:] Left Port-

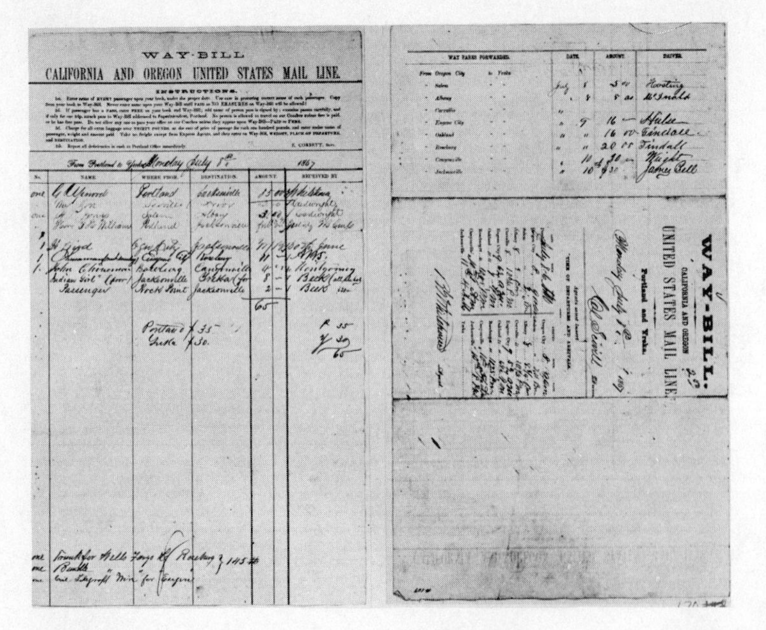

One of the few surviving waybills of the 1860's in the West. The California and Oregon United States Mail Line. The original is in the History Room, Wells Fargo Bank.

land July 8, 6 a.m.; arrived Oregon City, 8, 9 a. m. Left Oregon City 8, 9:10 a.m.; arrived Salem 2:10 p.m. Left Salem 8, 2½ p. m.; arrived Albany 8, 8¾ p. m. Left Albany 8, 9 p. m.; arrived Corvallis 8, 10½ p. m. Left Corvallis 8, 10¾ p. m.; arrived Eugene City [July] 9, 5¾ a. m. Left Eugene City 9, 6¼ a. m.; arrived Oakland 9, 6½ p. m. Left Oakland 9, 7 p. m.; arrived Roseburg 9, 11:25 p. m. Left Roseburg 9, 10:45 p. m.; arrived Canyonville [July] 10th, 5½ a. m. Left Canyonville 10th, 6 a. m.; arrived Jacksonville 10th, 8 p. m. Left Jacksonville 11th, 4 a. m.; arrived Yreka [blank]. B. G. Whitehouse, Agent.[2]

This waybill covers over four days of traveling time, and the longest recorded stops are at Eugene City, one half hour (probably for breakfast), and Canyonville, one half hour (also early in the morning). Apparently the stage did not travel at night in the rough mountain country between Jacksonville and Yreka; it is now about sixty miles by road, so it took probably six hours or more to make the trip.

On the inside, printed at the top, are instructions for the agents:

Way-Bill. CALIFORNIA AND OREGON UNITED STATES MAIL LINE. Instructions. 1st. Enter name of EVERY passenger upon your book, under the proper date. Use care in procuring correct name of each passenger. Copy from your book to Way-Bill. Never enter name upon your Way-Bill until PAID as NO ERASURES on Way-Bill will be allowed!

2d. If passenger has a PASS, enter FREE on your book and Way-Bill; add name of person pass is signed by; examine passes carefully, and if only for one trip, attach pass to Way-Bill addressed to Superintendent, Portland. No person is allowed to travel on our Coaches unless fare is paid or he has free pass. Do not allow any one to pass your office on our Coaches unless they appear upon Way-Bill—PAID or FREE.

3d. Charge for all extra baggage over THIRTY POUNDS, at the rate of price of passage for each one hundred pounds, and enter under name of passenger, weight and amount paid. Take no freight except from Express Agents, and then enter on Way-Bill, WEIGHT, PLACE OF DEPARTURE, and DESTINATION.

4th. Report all deficiencies in cash to Portland Office immediately. E. CORBETT, Supt.

Most of the page is taken up with blanks for the names of passengers:

From Portland to Yreka, Monday, July 8th, 1867

No., Name, Where From, Destination, Amount, Received by.

one G. Alpwood [?] Portland [to] Jacksonville $35.00 [Received by] G. Whitehouse. one Mr. Lyon Scoville [to] driver 2.00 Cartwright. one H. P. Jones Salem [to] Albany 3.00 Cartwright. one Hon. G. H. Williams Portland [to] Jacksonville fnt on?? strdg BGW [apparently initials of the agent] WB [Received by] C. M. C. 1 H. Bird Ogn City [to] Jacksonville W/B 30th June [apparently a layover]. 1 Chinaman (???? Sunday) Eugene City [to] Roseburg 11.00 A. W. S. 1 John Chinaman [most Chinese were so called] Roseburg [to] Canyonville 4.00 Montgomery. Indian girl (poor) Jacksonville [to] Yreka (for) 8.00 Beek (all she had). Passenger Rock Point [to] Jacksonville 2.00 Beek.

Portland $35
Yreka $30
one Trunk for Wells Fargo & Co., Roseburg, [and] one Bundle for Wells Fargo & Co., Roseburg, 145 pounds.
one coil telegraph wire for Eugene.

From this waybill, it may be observed that the agent apparently had some leeway in the matter of fares, since the agent at Jacksonville accepted $8, apparently less than standard fare, and allowed the Indian girl to ride anyway. This makes it seem obvious, too, that there was no discrimination on the California and Oregon. On the back is printed and written:

Way fares forwarded from Oregon City to Yreka.
From Salem to Yreka, July 8, $5.00. Driver, Hasting.
From Albany to Yreka, July 8, $5.00. Driver, McDuald.
From Corvallis to Yreka, July. [Not filled in.]
From Eugene City to Yreka, July 9, $16.00. Driver, Hulse.
From Oakland to Yreka, July 9, $16.00. Driver, Tindall.
From Roseburg to Yreka, July 9, $20.00. Driver, Tindall.
From Canyonville to Yreka, July 10, $20.00. Driver, Wright.
From Jacksonville to Yreka, July 10th, $30.00. Driver, James Bell.[3]

From about the same time, there is evidence of Wells Fargo's wide extension of interests, in the form of an advertisement in a San Francisco newspaper, dated January 1, 1867:

WELLS, FARGO & CO.,
EXPRESS AND EXCHANGE COMPANY, Head Offices, No. 84 Broadway, New York, and N. W. corner California and Montgomery Streets, San Francisco.

Express—Daily to all parts of California, Nevada and Utah. Weekly to Oregon, the Northern Territories and British Columbia. Tri-monthly to New York, Atlantic States and Europe *via* Panama. Monthly to Mexican Pacific Ports. Monthly to Honolulu, Japan and the China Coast.

Bills of Exchange and Telegraphic Transfers on New York, Boston and Philadelphia, payable in the principal cities of the United States and Canada.

Bills on London, Dublin and Paris, at Current Rates.

Letters of Credit negotiated throughout United States' Territory on this Coast.

Credits issued on the New York House exchangeable for Circular Letters, payable in all parts of Europe.

Collections and Commissions of all kinds executed. We undertake to make this a specialty. A General Express Business promptly attended to throughout the United States, Canada, Europe and the China coast.

Bullion, Coin and Articles of special value shipped on the most favorable terms; issued, if desired, under our Open Policies, with the best home and foreign companies.

Orders for Passage from Queenstown, London, Liverpool, Hamburg and Havre, and New York; also from New York to San Francisco.

CHARLES McLANE, General Agent for California.
PHILIP K. DUMARESQ, General Agent for China.

That last item is one we hardly anticipated: general agent for China. Dumaresq's address is not given, but we may assume that he was resident on the China coast, and that Wells Fargo must have been doing important business in that part of the world.

In 1867, Thomas J. Bidwell, a half-brother or nephew of General John Bidwell, was appointed Wells Fargo agent at Chico. It is sometimes said that John Bidwell was the agent at Chico, but the evidence strongly favors Thomas J.

One of the most interesting developments of 1867 was Wells Fargo's order placed with the Abbot-Downing Company of Concord, New Hampshire, for stagecoaches. These orders are now in the form of notes entered in the Order Books of the Abbot-Downing Company. The first occurs on page 120:

Wells Fargo & Co New York April 20/67
Ten. Nine Passenger Coaches inside 3 Seats
Middle Seat 3 fold. Bag foot board Lea[ther] sides
Back Boot. Lea sides & flap. Top Seats usual
End Panel Side Light Projections. Bunters &
Prongs to sill irons Both Ends—Perches Stout under axle
Axle 2⅛ Tire 1⅞x¾ Braces 3¼ wide & 1⅜ thick stout stitched. Track 5 ft 2 in c to c [center to center]
Wheels usual higth [c. q.]
Brakes as usual Strong handles. Evener chains &
Pole clip straps. Stout Sand boxes. cut out under side
Bodies made roomy inside & 3 inch more room between
Back & middle Seats. Corner Pillars ironed strong

at Sills [small sketch] Jacks Stout 2 in wide & jack braces strong
Lead bars and whiffletrees with loose ring. Pole hook stout
All irons, hooks & staples well steeled where wear comes
Steps on Body Single Pad—Candle Lamps Ex large size

Paint Bodies Red Carriages Straw
Letter Wells Fargo & Company (Rail)
U. S. Mail (Top door rail)

Russet Leather Lined. Damask head & fringe
Lea Curtains put on very loose & Damask lined

Weight 2100 lbs. Just

No Canvases on Front Boots

Done at once Sure No delay
Future orders iron clad corners of bodies. Jack Braces stout & [illegible] on Center Jacks Stouter & Clip around the fork [small sketch]

In the margin are ten numbers that probably are the serial numbers of the coaches: 169, 171, 172, 176, 178, 179, 193, 194, 196, 197.

A further notation says: "Chgd May 29, 1867."

The next order was entered on October 8, 1867:

Wells Fargo & Co New York Oct 8th 1867
["Ten" is written in and lined out]
Thirty Nine Passenger Coaches inside 3 Seats
Middle Seat—3 fold. Bag foot board Leather sides
Back Boot. Lea Sides & flap. Top seats Both ends as usual
End Panel Side Light. Projections. Bunters &
Prongs to sill irons Both Ends—Perches stout under axle
Axle 2⅛. Tire 1⅞x¾ Braces 3¼ wide & 1⅜ thick Stout Stitched.
Track 5 ft 2 in c to c. Wheels usual height.
Brakes as usual. Strong handles. Evener chains &
Pole clip straps stout with large shackles. Sand boxes—cut out under side.
Bodies made roomy inside & 3 in more room between back & middle seats. corner Pillars ironed strong at Sills. Iron clad corners of bodies
Jacks stout 2 in wide & Jack Braces 1¼ tapered to 1 in at ea end stout and swelled
in centre Jacks stouter & clips around the fork of the Jack
Lead bars & Whiffletrees with loose rings Pole hook stout
All irons hooks & staples well steeled where wear comes
Steps on body. single Pad—Candle Lamps extra large size
Axle go through nut with hole for Pin. Albany bed plates.
Brake bar carved out fuller at end & handle stouter of best timber
Point Bodies Red Carriages Straw
Letter Wells Fargo & Company (Rail)
U. S. Mail (Top door rail)
Box brace made larger inside layer of jack little stouter at the weld.
Russet Lea lined Damask head & fringe
Leather Curtains put on *very loose* & Damask Lined
No. under drivers seat from 400 up. Numbers to be sent.
Top Canvass. Drivers Apron Leather.
No Canvases or Front Boots
Stout chains & short links. Flap 3 or 4 in wider on a side & 4 straps
Done at once on edges & bottom & old fashioned larger buckle
February 1

In margin: "Weight 2100 lbs." In different handwriting: "Weight 2225 lbs."

In the margin apparently are the serial numbers: 223 [lined out], 227, 229 [lined out], 230, 231, 232 [lined out], 233, 234, [lined out], 235, 236 [lined out], 244, 245, 246, 247, 250, 269, 267, 268, 248, 249, 251, 252, 253, 254, 255, 256, 257, 258, 259, 260, 261, 262, 263, 264, 265.

Also in the margin:

Coaches 227, 230, 231, 233, 235, chgd Jany 10, 1868
Coaches chgd 244, 245, 246, 247, 250 chgd Feby 25 1868
Coaches chgd 248, 249, 251, 252, 253, 254, 255, 267, 268, & 269 chgd Mch 25 1868
Coaches chgd 256, 257, 258, 259, 260, 261, 262, 263, 264 & 265 chgd Apl 13th 1868[4]

It appears that forty Concord coaches were ordered by Wells Fargo and were shipped between April 20, 1867, and April 13, 1868. It is noticeable that some additional specifications were added to the second order, but the same painting and the same lettering were to be used. It appears that Abbot-Downing was to put the Wells Fargo number under the driver's seat from four hundred up, but this order lists only the numbers.

Whatever else might be said, Wells Fargo was not pulling in its horns.

At some point in this period, Wells Fargo also ordered sixty sets of four-horse harness from James R. Hill, and it made the largest lot of harness ever shipped at one time.

By 1867, William C. Ralston very nearly owned the Comstock. He had come far since 1863, when he had organized the Bank of California with D. O. Mills as president and himself as cashier. Ralston was a very big operator: He spent big and he made big. He was the kind who was always in the pink physically and always magnificently groomed; he was suave, urbane, sophisticated—and yet he always had time to greet ordinary workmen by name and to help them generously when they were stricken by misfortune. He was vain, flamboyant, enormously extravagant, impractical, and a born gambler. He wanted what he wanted and would spend any amount of money to get it. He had a princely estate where Belmont is now, south of San Francisco,[5] at which he entertained presidents and foreign nabobs, actors and actresses, anybody of note, anybody who took his fancy. His dining room could seat 110 guests; his mansion was lighted by his private gas plant, and it was said that for years no ship entered the Golden Gate without carrying some priceless china, tapestry, furniture, rug, or work of art for Ralston. He was such a fabulous and popular figure that people gathered at the bank every afternoon to watch him leave. He had great stables at his estate, and always drove his own blooded horses to his own fine carriage, and always raced the train—and always beat it by about a hundred yards, ending his race by dashing across the track that far ahead of it. When he was taking guests home for entertainment, he always arrived just at dusk, when the mansion would be blazing with light. And his wife, like James Birch's and Ben Holladay's, lived apart from him a good deal of the time; Mrs. Ralston lived in Europe—preferably France.

Ralston was also a man who knew how to use

A photograph of thirty stagecoaches and four railroad cars of harness shipped to Wells Fargo in 1868. This picture, by "Edwin G. Burgum, 1934," is on display in the History Room, Wells Fargo Bank. A similar picture on the 1965 "Annual Report" of the Wells Fargo Bank is of a painting owned by the New Hampshire Historical Society.

PHOTOGRAPHIC VIEW OF
Coaches shipped by Abbot, Downing & Co., Concord, N. H.
APRIL 15, 1868.

William C. Ralston, the great spender. He was a flamboyant man who made many friends, but those friends lost no time turning on him when they discovered that he had misused their money. From Ira Cross, "Financing an Empire."

his financial power to get more, and was utterly ruthless in doing it. And whatever he did, his excuse apparently was that he was doing it for San Francisco. More than likely, however, he was just a big operator with still bigger ideas. It is said that he spent as much as $350,000 a year on his living expenses. He owned or controlled a woolen mill, a watch factory, a carriage factory, a silk company, a foundry, a theatre, the Grand Hotel, a tobacco works, a rolling-stock factory, a drydock, and countless other enterprises. He paid the stockholders of the Bank of California 1 percent a month dividend every month, rain or shine. He speculated in mines and real estate, in vineyards and ranches. On any business day, $3,000,000 in gold would pass over his counters. Billy Ralston, in the minds of the people, was San Francisco's greatest citizen.

As a matter of fact, starting in 1865, Ralston got control of the entire Comstock, and was to depend on it three times during his life to save his financial empire. He started taking over the Comstock in 1865 through the work of William Sharon, with whom he had a partnership agreement. Sharon was manager of the Virginia City branch of the Bank of California, and shrewdly and heartlessly used his power and the bank's power to get control. The mines were slowing down; water was rising, and the great deposits had either been mined out or had been flooded with water. An engineer, Adolph Sutro, had a plan to drive a tunnel under Mount Davidson to drain the mines, but Ralston fought it because he knew that it would make Sutro too big, and Ralston could not endure that.

Before long, Ralston, through Sharon, controlled many of the mines of the Comstock, and owned the gasworks, the water system, a lumber industry, and

William Sharon, ruthless partner of Ralston, who finally got himself elected United States Senator and who survived the debacle of the Bank of California and his partnership with Ralston. Some people thought Ralston should have left a huge estate and that Sharon played fast and loose with it, but the truth is that Ralston spent money much faster than he earned it, and it is hard to see how there could be anything left after his reckless building of the Palace Hotel and his enormous personal expenditures. From Ira Cross, "Financing an Empire."

the newspapers. Then he and Sharon used the mines to suit themselves. They started rumors and manipulated stocks, and over and over made huge sums of money out of the gambling spirit of Californians. His banking policy was not to limit loans to men with collateral, but to gamble—to loan money for a share of the enterprise. It wasn't banking; it was pure speculation with the power of a great bank behind him.

For—make no mistake—the Bank of California was the biggest bank of all.

On February 5, 1867, Wells, Fargo and Company bought from the Overland Mail Company "all property of every kind belonging to that company" for a consideration of 10,000 shares of stock. On May 14, the business of the Western Transportation Line was bought from "Mr. Creighton"[6] for $50,000 in cash and $15,000 in stock (150 shares at $100 each).

Early in the year, the president of Wells Fargo was authorized to buy from the trustee of Wells, Fargo & Company the property located at 84 Broadway for $100,000.

At the beginning of 1867, the board of directors of Wells Fargo & Company was made up of Louis McLane, president; Ashbel H. Barney, vice president; James C. Fargo, Danforth N. Barney, Johnston Livingston, Ben Holladay, Benjamin P. Cheney, William H. Fogg, and Eugene Kelly. George K. Otis was secretary and Calvin Goddard was treasurer.

On June 11, William G. Fargo and John Butterfield were elected to the board.

At the end of the year, the company had 207 offices.

In 1867, the company received for transportation $893,552.42, and paid out $452,970.72 for express privileges (it was over half of the revenue); it had other operating revenue of almost $100,000, and operating expenses of $332,099.09; its net operating income was $199,362.86.

There is no record of dividends for 1867.

Nothing very spectacular occurred in 1868. The depression lasted until the middle of the year, and then business improved.

Adolph Sutro, turned down cold by Ralston, and, in fact, stopped cold by Ralston no matter which way he turned, got mad and rolled up his sleeves and

Joshua A. Norton, usually known as Emperor Norton, one of San Francisco's many characters, was born in London, lived in Algoa Bay, Cape of Good Hope, South Africa, and came to San Francisco in 1849 with $40,000. He did well in real estate and mortgages, but in 1853, he tried to corner the rice market but lost everything—$250,000—after which he lost his mind. Thereafter, Norton was a typical hometown jester. He proclaimed himself emperor in 1859, and went around town in a blue military coat with gold epaulettes. He was treated tolerantly by merchants, allowed to eat at free-lunch counters, admitted to public functions without paying, and especially respected at meetings of the state legislature at Sacramento. At times he issued scrip, usually for no more than fifty cents, payable ten years in advance and bearing interest at 4 percent. He proclaimed himself Emperor of United States, Sovereign Lord and sole owner of Guano Islands, and Protector of Mexico (though later he abandoned the protectorate). He was pleasant and congenial on every subject save that of his empire. From Albert Dressler, "Emperor Norton."

set out to whip the California tycoon. People laughed at first at the idea of a nobody like Sutro trying to do something the giant did not want done, but Sutro carried the fight to New York, to London, to Washington.

The silver production of the Comstock was on the way down; it had fallen from $16,000,000 in 1867 to $7,500,000 in 1869. The bonanzas apparently were either played out or flooded out.

However, the production of the Comstock was not a crucial point with Wells Fargo. It rather seems that one of the biggest problems of Wells Fargo—for a change—was with Norton, Emperor the First, one of San Francisco's best known and most beloved characters. Norton was in the habit of dressing up in some sort of military finery and asserting jurisdiction over his subjects; he even issued scrip when in need of money (but never over fifty cents), and got it cashed by forbearing San Franciscans. In the year 1868, one C. Averill left Wells Fargo, and apparently there was more in his resignation than meets the eye, for McLane issued a warning to Wells Fargo agents. But Averill must have been a friend of Emperor Norton, and obviously Norton had a printer friend, for the following imperial document was issued:

PROCLAMATION.

Whereas, Certain parties having assumed prerogatives, pertaining only to my Royal self; And Whereas, in the furtherance of such assumption, they have printed and circulated treasonable and rebellious documents, circulars, sermons and proclamations, calculated to distract and divide the allegiance of my subjects; And Whereas, it has come to my knowledge that a certain seditious proclamation and command has been distributed amongst the most faithful of my agents and supjects [c. q.], of which the following is a copy, to-wit:

"OFFICE WELLS, FARGO & CO.

"San Francisco, July 4th, 1868.

"TO OUR AGENTS:

"C. Averill, formerly Forwarding Clerk, and late Messenger to our Mexican Coast Offices, has left our employ and gone with the Pacific Union Express Company.

"You will treat him as any other employee of an opposition Express Co.

"CHARLES E. McLANE,
"Gen'l Agent."

NOW, THEREFORE, I, EMPEROR NORTON the First, do hereby command that no notice shall be paid to proclamations issued by Pretenders to my authority, ability, and Regal position.

And it is further Commanded, that any violation of this command shall be reported to me, in order that I may banish the offender from my Kingdom.

NORTON, Emperor the First.

San Franciscans had to have their fun. It was the biggest little town in the world.

Wells Fargo's reaction to this cautiously worded edict is not recorded, but one may assume it was not unduly concerned. However, the incident brings into the spotlight another factor that was to be an important one to Wells Fargo: the Pacific Union Express.

Some say that Wells Fargo did not pay any attention to the Pacific railroad because Wells Fargo thought it would not be completed until 1875. But it hardly seems reasonable, especially since the Union Pacific advertised in the New York *Tribune* on August 20, 1868, that it had already finished 750 miles (on June 13, it had announced six hundred miles), that it was employing twenty thousand men, and that "It is now probable that the WHOLE LINE TO THE PACIFIC WILL BE COMPLETED IN 1869 .... THE EARNINGS ... from its Way or Local Business only, during the year ending June 30, 1868, amounted to over FOUR MILLION DOLLARS." This advertisement offered thirty-year 6 percent bonds, and it is highly unlikely that Wells Fargo's directors would remain in the dark as to the projected date of completion.

Edward Hungerford is perhaps close to the truth of the matter when he says that Louis McLane and his brother, Charles McLane, were horsemen, and could not see that stagecoaches might go out of style. At any rate, while Charles Crocker, Leland Stanford, Mark Hopkins, and Collis P. Huntington,[7] the Big Four of the nineteenth century, were struggling to build their Central Pacific east to meet the Union Pacific, it seems that Wells Fargo did not buy a hand in the business, although there must have been many opportunities. In fact, Neill C. Wilson says that Wells Fargo, the Pacific Mail Steam Ship Company, and the California Stage Company fought the railroad at every turn.

Whatever the reason, Wells Fargo did nothing until a man named Lloyd Tevis realized that presently there would be a transcontinental railroad, that it would greatly shorten the time from New York to San Francisco, that Wells Fargo or any other express company would have to have express privileges on it, and that Wells Fargo had none and apparently had made no move to get them.

Tevis was a sound operator. At one time he owned thirteen hundred miles of stagecoach lines in California, streetcar lines in San Francisco, thousands of acres of ranchland, and great herds of sheep and cattle. He reclaimed swamplands in central California; he owned gold and silver mines in California, Nevada, Utah, Idaho, and South Dakota.[8] He was an expressman of experience and a successful businessman, and he got the Big Four to go in with him to organize the Pacific Union Express, which immediately got express privileges from the Central Pacific. Lloyd Tevis indicated at a Pacific Railway Commission hearing in 1888 that D. O. Mills,[9] H. D. Bacon, Leland Stanford, Mark Hopkins, and Charles Crocker went into the organization of the Pacific Union Express (which Tevis in 1888 called the Pacific Express[10]) with him, and that they never did any express business except to have some stationery printed.

Leland Stanford was a Sacramento merchant when he went into partnership with the Big Four. He was slow-thinking, gregarious, ambitious to be a leader but not a match for Huntington's dominating presence. He was full of pious maxims, and an easy man to attack, but also a highly controversial one. He built a palace on two acres of land on Nob Hill. He was Governor of California for one term, and later a United States Senator. He and Mrs. Stanford built Stanford University as a memorial to their son, who died at fifteen, and Mrs. Stanford, after their large estate was tied up in litigation at his death, economized personally for many years to keep the school going. From the California Historical Society.

PROCLAMATION.

WHEREAS, Certain parties having assumed prerogatives, pertaining only to my Royal self; AND WHEREAS, in the furtherance of such assumption, they have printed and circulated treasonable and rebellious documents, circulars, sermons and proclamations, calculated to distract and divide the allegiance of my subjects; AND WHEREAS, it has come to my knowledge that a certain seditious proclamation and command has been distributed amongst the most faithful of my agents and supjects, of which the following is a copy, to-wit:

"OFFICE WELLS, FARGO & CO.

"SAN FRANCISCO, JULY 4TH, 1868.

"TO OUR AGENTS:

"C. Averill, formerly Forwarding Clerk, and late Messenger to our Mexican Coast Offices, has left our employ and gone with the Pacific Union Express Company.

"You will treat him as any other employee of an opposition Express Co.

"CHARLES E. MCLANE,
"Gen'l Agent."

NOW, THEREFORE, I, EMPEROR NORTON the First, do hereby command that no notice shall be paid to proclamations issued by Pretenders to my authority, ability, and Regal position.

AND IT IS FURTHER COMMANDED, that any violation of this command shall be reported to me, in order that I may banish the offender from my Kingdom.

NORTON, EMPEROR THE FIRST.

Emperor Norton apparently considered C. Averill his friend (probably because Averill had treated him to lunch and beer occasionally), and asserted his royal prerogatives against Charles E. McLane. From the History Room, Wells Fargo Bank.

It seems that Tevis' memory was bad on that point. This company, variously called Pacific Express, Pacific Union Express, and Union Pacific Express, was organized, says Stimson, in May, 1868, and seems to have been operating between Reno and Virginia City in 1868, and was carrying express on others' stagecoaches or was operating its own, and was also operating a pony express between Reno (terminus of the Central Pacific) and Virginia City. As a matter of fact, there was considerable rivalry between the pony express riders of the two companies, and the McLanes imported Pony Bob Haslam, the Pony Express rider of six years before, to make the run. Haslam usually beat the Pacific Union Express rider, and the Sacramento *Union* reported the race of July 3, wherein Haslam beat Frank Henderson for the Pacific Union Express by six minutes. Both received their packages before the cars had stopped, and the Pacific Express rider got a headstart of ten rods. Haslam held back to get his bag firmly fastened on his back and passed the other man within one mile. Each man had five changes of horse about four miles apart. Bennett, the driver of the Wells Fargo lightning express wagon, a light buckboard, came near beating both ponies, but, having worn-out horses, could not keep up.

Later, Haslam covered the (now) twenty-one miles in fifty-eight minutes, but Wells Fargo later took their ponies off the route and went to the buckboard. It was a shame, too, because the race had become the daily sporting event of the Comstock area. From time to time a real match race would be worked up, and bets would be made from a two-bit cigar to $1,000 in gold. On such occasions, the sports from Gold Hill, Silver City, and all points round about would gather in Virginia City to watch the race; sidewalks were jammed; balconies, awnings, and housetops were crowded; men and boys climbed telegraph poles to watch the finish.

The buckboard driver made six changes of team—each in only a few seconds. If a bridge was taken up by a freight wagon and a twenty-mule team, the driver charged through the creek. If the narrow road was obstructed, he bounced through the sagebrush.

But all this grandstanding was getting Wells Fargo nowhere with the Central Pacific, and it may be that the Pacific Express was not too much concerned over its regular defeats in the race from Reno.

Early in 1868, the Wells Fargo directors saw the handwriting on the wall, and on May 16, they authorized the president to sell all stage lines, with the provision that the privilege of transporting express on them be retained by Wells Fargo. It seems not impossible that Wells Fargo's general policy of monopolizing express privileges in the West might have had something to do with Wells Fargo's purchase from Ben Holladay. If so, it throws still more confusion on Wells Fargo's failure to get in on the ground floor with the Central Pacific. Had Wells Fargo tried but been stopped because of its own previous reluctance to help with the railroad-building? It seems likely. All the Big Four were small men to start with, and they had plenty of trouble raising money to build the railroad. If it had not been for William C. Ralston, the story might have been different on the Central Pacific. And naturally, if the men of the Big Four had asked for help from Wells Fargo and been refused, they would not have been eager to grant express privileges when the tables were turned.

This is the more interesting because Tevis testified in 1888 that the railroad builders in 1865 were borrowing money from everybody who would lend, and that they often applied to him, and he occasionally accommodated them, although he was afraid they would go down in ruin. Stanford urged Tevis to invest, but Tevis did not want to risk liability for the corporation's indebtedness. At that time, the railroad men were paying 3 percent a month for money. Tevis said that capitalists (and himself) considered the company on the verge of bankruptcy even at the completion of the road.

In October, 1868, San Francisco had an earthquake, and the Bank of California building rocked like a boat in the waves. The wall of Ralston's private office was cracked, and part of the stone cornice came crashing down. Several blocks of reclaimed land slid into the sea and reduced the town's area.

Ralston's clerks were frightened when Ralston reached the bank, for the building was rocking every few minutes. Ralston sent word that everybody in the bank must stand up to business with strictness and cheerfulness, or could not return to work in his bank. Some $650,000 was due the bank that day, but not one cent was demanded from any man in genuine business or production. On the same day, Ralston bought a lot on Market Street for $150,000, a piece of land he had wanted for a long time.

On June 2, Wells Fargo made a bid for the "Salt Lake mail contract" (not otherwise identified) for $91,600. This may refer to the line from Salt Lake City to The Dalles, some eight hundred miles; if so, apparently, Wells Fargo did not get the contract, because in October it was let for $149,000.

On June 19, Wells Fargo accepted a contract to carry mail from Cheyenne, Dakota Territory (then), to Virginia City, Nevada, at $1,314,000 a year. However, there were difficulties and there was delay, and the contract was let to Carlton Spaids of Chicago. Spaids, however, was unable to carry it out, and probably the government requested Wells Fargo to submit a new bid. That was done on October 20, and Wells Fargo presented two choices to the government:

1. It would carry the overland mail six times a week for one year or until the two Pacific railroads should connect, for $1,050,000 a year, and no deduction for the shortening of the distance as the railroads advanced.

2. It would carry the mail for a year or until the two railroads should connect, for $1,750,000 a year, subject to a deduction for every fifty miles of railroad completed and put into service.

The Post Office Department accepted the second proposition, and Wells Fargo went to work under the new contract.

During the year, John Butterfield was dropped from the board of directors and E. B. Morgan was added. John J. Valentine was appointed general superintendent. The headquarters, which had been in New York, was moved to San Francisco. The number of offices at the end of 1868 was 232. There is no record of dividends for this year.

Gross income from expenses was $944,423 in 1868; operating expenses increased to $370,377.73; and the net operating income dropped to $176,516.61—this in spite of the fact that Wells Fargo collected over $50,000 more for transportation than in 1867; a substantial part of the difference came in an increased debit of over $32,000 for express privileges.

Now Wells Fargo was going into 1869, the year of its biggest crisis since its organization. The two railroads were racing to a junction, and the usefulness of the overland stage line was lessening every

A busy room in the post office at Washington: the dead-letter room. The heavy coats and the hat indicate that there probably was no heat in the room—or very little. Service was the watchword in those days, and these men are trying to find an address for every piece of mail, no matter how badly directed. From "Harper's Weekly," February 22, 1868.

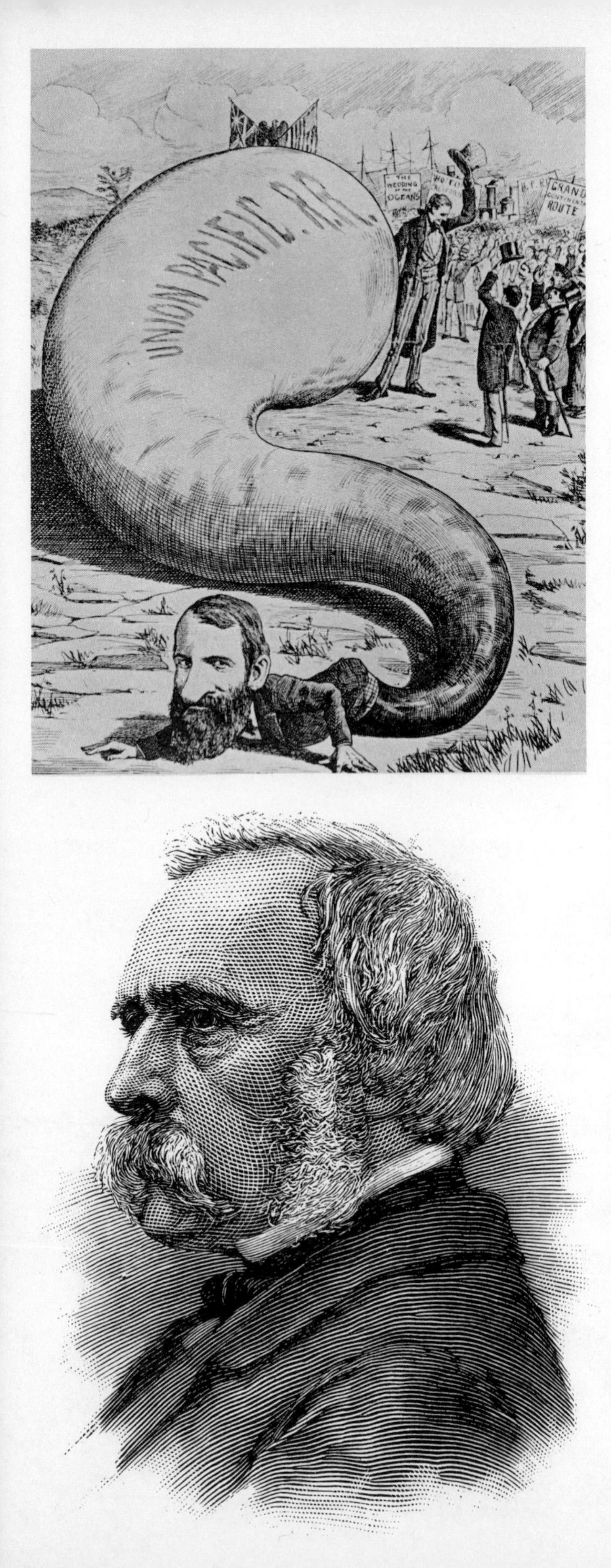

While the country was celebrating the completion of the Union Pacific and the Central Pacific and their joining at Promontory Point near Ogden, Utah, it was learned that Jay Gould, who did not build railroads but bought them (and, some say, wrecked them), had acquired control of the Union Pacific. This cartoon was printed in "Harper's Weekly."

day. General Dodge's Irish terriers were laying track across the broad flatlands of Wyoming at an incredible rate, and Charles Crocker's Chinese coolies were throwing steel across the desert of Nevada and Utah. The Pacific Mail Steamship Company, whose president was Allan McLane (another brother of Louis), had lost much business already, and with the meeting of the rails in June, would lose all mail, express, and passenger traffic. There were rumors that the United States Express Company would take over the Pacific Express franchise and fight Wells Fargo in the West. It did not help that United States was, like Wells Fargo, an offspring of American Express; the danger was real. Wells Fargo had already reduced charges to compete with Pacific, and had been losing money; its stock naturally had declined, dropping at one time to $13 a share. Tevis, Crocker, Mills, and Bacon bought up large numbers of Wells Fargo shares, knowing that the older company was beaten.

Nor did it help that the United States Express Company was also the baby of the Union Pacific Railroad, and held the express franchise from Ogden, Utah, to Omaha.

The railroad company, at the height of its building, had employed 11,000 Chinese and 2,500 white men at $35 a month, and 600 mechanics at from $3 to $5 a day—all payments in gold. The difficulties of buying rail, or bringing ties around the Horn by ship, and of fighting the terrible winters of 1865 and 1866 (the worst winters ever in the Sierras), and the consequent forty-foot snows and avalanches that

Ashbel H. Barney was president of Wells, Fargo & Company, 1869–1870. From "Harper's Weekly," 1887.

Mark Hopkins, one of the Big Four of the Central Pacific Railroad. He was tall, thin, ascetic, and anything but given to extravagance. He was close-mouthed and cautious, and regarded himself as the balance wheel of the Big Four. He died at sixty-five and left an enormous fortune, some of which his widow squandered on buildings of various kinds, she later married a man who was twenty-two years younger and left everything to him when she died. Her adopted son sued the widower and got a settlement of some $8,000,000. From the California Historical Society.

This notice of 1868 (and others like it) are evidence enough that the directors of Wells Fargo knew what the Union Pacific was doing. This was printed in the New York "Tribune," August 20, 1868. Similar notices were published in "Harper's Weekly" and other periodicals.

Special Notices.

750 Miles
of the
UNION PACIFIC RAILROAD

Are now finished, and in operation. Although this road is built with great rapidity, the work is thoroughly done, and is pronounced by the United States Commissioners to be first-class in every respect, before it is accepted, and before any bonds can be issued upon it.

Rapidity and excellence of construction have been secured by a complete division of labor, and by distributing the 20,000 men employed along the line for long distances at once. It is now probable that the WHOLE LINE TO THE PACIFIC WILL BE COMPLETED IN 1869.

The Company have ample means of which the Government grants the right of way, and all necessary timber, and other materials, found along the line of its operations; also 12,800 acres of land to the mile, taken in alternate sections on each side of its road; also United States 30-year bonds, amounting to from $16,000 to $48,000 per mile, according to the difficulties to be surmounted on the various sections to be built, for which it takes a second mortgage as security, and it is expected that not only the interest, but the principal amount may be paid in services rendered by the Company in transporting troops, mails, &c.

THE EARNINGS OF THE UNION PACIFIC RAILROAD, from its Way or Local Business only, during the year ending June 30, 1868, amounted to over

FOUR MILLION DOLLARS,

which, after paying all expenses, was much more than sufficient to pay the interest upon its Bonds. These earnings are no indication of the vast through traffic that must follow the opening of the line to the Pacific, but they certainly prove that

FIRST MORTGAGE BONDS

upon such a property, costing nearly three times their amount,

ARE ENTIRELY SECURE.

The Union Pacific Bonds run thirty years, are for $1,000 each, and have coupons attached. They bear annual interest, payable on the first days of January and July at the Company's office in the City of New York, at the rate of six per cent in gold. The principal is payable in gold at maturity. The price is **102**, and at the present rate of gold they pay a liberal income on their cost.

A very important consideration in determining the value of these bonds is *the length of time they have to run.*

It is well known that a long bond always commands a much higher price than a short one. It is safe to assume that during the next thirty years the rate of interest in the United States will decline as it has done in Europe, and we have a right to expect that such six per cent securities as these will be held at as high a premium as those of this Government, which, in 1857, were bought in at from 20 to 23 per cent above par. The export demand alone may produce this result, and as the issue of a private corporation they are beyond the reach of political action.

The Company believe that their Bonds, at the present rate, are the cheapest security in the market, and the right to advance the price at any time is reserved. Subscriptions will be received in New-York

AT THE COMPANY'S OFFICE, NO. 20 NASSAU-ST.,
and by
JOHN J. CISCO & SON, BANKERS, NO. 59 WALL-ST.,

and by the Company's advertised Agents throughout the United States.

Remittances should be made in drafts or other funds par in New York, and the Bonds will be sent free of charge by return express. Parties subscribing through local agents, will look to them for their safe delivery.

A PAMPHLET and MAP for 1868 has just been published by the Company, giving fuller information than is possible in an advertisement, respecting the Progress of the Work, the Resources of the country traversed by the Road, the Means for Construction, and the value of the Bonds, which will be sent free on application at the Company's offices, or to any of the advertised Agents.

JOHN J. CISCO, Treasurer, New-York.

August 12, 1868.

Charles Crocker, a big man with great force and drive, was actual construction superintendent for the Central Pacific and frequently said, "I built the railroad." In his later years a retired millionaire, Crocker said: "One man works hard all his life and ends up a pauper. Another man, no smarter, makes $20,000,000. Luck has a hell of a lot to do with it." He also said that he did not know much about art. From the California Historical Society.

Collis P. Huntington was in partnership in Sacramento with Mark Hopkins; they bought and sold much heavy goods. Huntington believed in frugality and money-making, in that order. He was big and square and rarely ill. When he went to California in March, 1849, with a capital of $1,200 he was caught (along with thousands of others) on the isthmus awaiting transportation. He did not get away for three months, but, by the time he did get passage for California, his capital was $5,000. He was called hard, cheery, ruthless, dishonest, and without weakness. He had few vanities, and crusading newspapermen of San Francisco, which was a notorious crusading newspaper town, had little luck with him; one of his few vanities was over his hair: He grew bald in later years, and was sensitive about it. He was no reformer and neither a snob nor a devotee of democracy. Huntington was claimed to be the brains of the Big Four. His fortune was the basis of the Henry E. Huntington Library at San Marino, California. From the California Historical Society.

Lloyd Tevis, who said, according to Eric Francis, that he could think five times as fast as any other man in San Francisco, and who became principal owner and president of Wells Fargo in 1872, to remain there for twenty years.

sometimes buried the Chinese until the following spring, made the building unusually expensive for the time.

Ashbel H. Barney succeeded McLane as president, and performed his duties "with sagacity, energy and success."

On February 18, 1869, Wells Fargo directors voted to reduce the capital stock from $10,000,000 to $5,000,000. On March 11, one John Hughes (related to Bela Hughes?) offered to buy the Wells Fargo stage lines centering on Denver, but his offer was declined. In May, a proposition was submitted to consolidate stage lines between Elko and White Pine, Nevada, but no action was taken. Only three days before, the golden spike had been driven at Promontory Point, Utah, to signal the joining of the railroads.

The Chinese set a world's record by laying ten miles of track in twenty-four hours across the salt flats of Utah; they placed one thousand tons of rails that day.

On May 16, Wells Fargo sold the building at 84 Broadway, New York City, to D. N. Barney for $130,000.

It was in 1869 that the financial circles of San Francisco moved over just a little to admit another group of four men who were to become known as the Lords of the Comstock, and were to succeed Ralston and Sharon as the financial giants of San Francisco: John W. Mackay, superintendent of the Kentuck mine; James G. Fair, superintendent of the Ophir mine (both these men were in Virginia City); and James C. Flood and William S. O'Brien, who owned the Auction Lunch Saloon on Washington Street in San Francisco.

Mackay and Fair had discovered that there was a bonanza in the Hale & Norcross mine, and the four Irishmen, with a total of $225,000, went into the market to get control from Ralston. Since the rumor had already been set afoot of the bonanza, shares opened at $2,925, and the Irishmen began to bid, but they were stopped when a bigger San Francisco businessman, Charles L. Low, got into the fight against Ralston. They did, however, make some nice money, for Ralston finally had to pay them $7,100 apiece for the shares they had bought. But something went wrong: No dividends were declared from the Hale and Norcross. Ralston controlled it

John W. Mackay, principal owner of the Kentuck mine, who worked with Fair. Mackay was quiet, unostentatious. He was the youngest, and was always in fine physical shape; he backed James Corbett as heavyweight boxing champion. He had no or little formal education, but read literary journals and studied elementary English grammar. With natural dignity and innate adaptability, he was well liked but far from prominent; he was usually the one who paid the bill. Sometimes he stayed in France with his wife but refused to speak a word of French; he was generous, and during a slack period on the Comstock authorized a grocer to extend credit to miners, and secretly paid some $3,000 a month. He died in 1902, also very wealthy. Sadly enough, he was another rich man who was in effect a widower, since his wife established homes in Paris and London and lived there until she died in 1928, visiting California only twice while Mackay was alive. From the California Historical Society.

James G. Fair, supposedly the brains of the four Silver Kings, a man who believed himself smarter than anybody else and often proved it. He was a very capable mechanic and a shrewd financier, and never felt any compunction at taking advantage of a dull-witted opponent. He was an assistant superintendent in the early years of the Hale & Norcross mine; it was that mine that William Sharon controlled the stock of in 1869, and then lost to the four Irishmen: Fair, Mackay, Flood, and O'Brien. Fair and Mackay, both miners, started the Hale & Norcross coup, and handled it through Flood and O'Brien, who had owned a saloon but became brokers. All four became partners in the enterprise, with Fair owning one fourth. In 1874, they brought in the Consolidated Virginia, which had a profound effect on finances on the West Coast and in New York, Boston, London, and Paris. Fair was an inveterate showman, and sometimes piloted visitors through the mine while posing as a miner. He was elected to the United States Senate at a reputed cost of $350,000; while he was Senator, his wife divorced him on grounds of "habitual adultery" and won one third of the Fair estate—some $5,000,000. He at one time owned sixty acres in San Francisco, but refused to keep his buildings in repair. He suffered from bad health, and his circle of friends was very small—if it existed at all. With $40,000,000, he would spend fifty cents for a hotel room, and was generally unloved. Fair died in 1894, and his death brought forth an unbelievable crop of women who claimed to be lovers, common-law wives, illegitimate children, and secret spouses. His will disappeared and has never been found, but the $40,000,000 estate went to his children. The lawsuits did not end until after 1902. From the California Historical Society.

William S. O'Brien, one of the broker partners of the Silver Kings. In 1857, he opened a saloon in San Francisco in partnership with James Flood. They both were models of sartorial elegance even though their drinks were always a bit (two for a quarter). O'Brien began to play the mining-stock market, and did well. By 1868, they had considerable fortunes, and sold the Auction Lunch and opened a brokerage, where they met Mackay and Fair and joined them in the Hale and Norcross coup over William Sharon, and later brought in the Consolidated Virginia. In 1872, O'Brien and Fair's income was half a million dollars a month. O'Brien was plebeian, unpretentious, and well aware that his wealth $12,000,000 at his death) was largely luck. He was the oldest and least forceful of the Silver Kings, but easily the best liked. He never forgot his friends from pre-Consolidated Virginia days, but on the few occasions he appeared in society, he seemed to belong there. He did not marry, and died in 1878, worth $15,000,000. From the California Historical Society.

but nothing happened, and that summer the stock dropped to $11.50 a share.

Then the four Irishmen moved; they bought up four hundred of the eight hundred shares, and Ralston and Sharon had to buy all the other four hundred that they did not own. One hundred shares were outstanding. Sharon discovered the widow who had them, and wired Ralston in code. But John Mackay had a friend in the telegraph office at Virginia City, one who, like many Comstockers, detested Sharon. He deciphered the message and handed it to Mackay, who called Flood and got the stock that night. The Lords of the Comstock were on their way; at the annual meeting, Ralston and his men were put out, and Fair was made superintendent of the mine. A scheduled assessment against the stockholders was canceled, $728,000 was paid out in dividends; the mine's production tripled that year and quadrupled the next year (1870). At the same time, the Irishmen began to buy mills in the Comstock and jeopardized Ralston's monopoly on that business.

A lot of things had happened that year, but it was only April when a terrible fire broke out in the Yellow Jacket mine, one of Ralston's most dependable sources of silver, and almost destroyed the mine. The shaft was a violent inferno of smoke, flame, poison gas, falling timbers, clouds of dust—and death.

It was not generally known, but Ralston's men had been following a thin streak of ore, and Ralston had been counting on it to widen into a bonanza to cover his extravagances—but the fire destroyed that. Forty-five men died down there, and the fire burned for months at the nine-hundred-foot level. Whenever they tried to open it, flames burst out and drove them back, and eventually the gallery collapsed and had to be abandoned.

Ralston actually was in bad shape, though he kept paying 1 percent dividend on the bank stock every month. The transcontinental railroad had brought in cheap goods and had hurt many in California, especially the numerous factories in which Ralston was deeply involved.

In such an atmosphere, Ralston conceived the Virginia & Truckee Railroad. It was partly a scheme to block off Sutro's tunnel, for one of the selling points of the tunnel was the possibility of using it as a right of way to ship ore out of the mines; it would save lifting the ore to the surface, and it would save the long, hard haul down the mountains in wagons. So, with typical Ralston flamboyance, the Virginia & Truckee Railroad got under way. Ralston bought equipment all over the world, moved in Chinese laborers, and finished the road that year. It was said to be the crookedest road in the world; it descended 1,600 feet in 13½ miles, and the track made seventeen full circles to maintain the grade through the mountains.

In July, Ralston almost went under in spite of his diversionary tactics. It was a financial emergency that would have broken many banks and many businesses if it had not been met with typical Ralston boldness and firmness.

In that month, Jay Gould and his associates cornered the gold market and forced up the price of gold, which caused the metal to be shipped to eastern financial centers. The banks of California, after losing so much coin, were in precarious shape: They had plenty of gold bars in their vaults, but those

James C. Flood, the fourth member of the Silver Kings. While Mackay was an easy mark for long lines of panhandlers, Flood was unapproachable. He built an estate in Menlo Park, the very fashionable suburb of San Francisco; he built an office in the Nevada Block that was almost invulnerable. In 1875, the four partners, by that time involved in many important projects in California, opened the Nevada Bank to compete with William C. Ralston's Bank of California. Ralston said he would send Flood back to selling rum at the Auction Lunch Saloon, and Flood answered that if he should ever sell drinks again, it would be over the counter of the Bank of California. A few months later, when Ralston's bank suspended, Flood left a large sum of money on deposit, although he knew what was happening. Flood was unfailingly loyal, but his latter years were hectic. A man named Squire P. Dewey caused him organized trouble for years, and five of San Francisco's seven newspapers were against the Silver Kings—perhaps for their very bigness. Everybody, crying for more profits and bemoaning their losses on the erratic stock, seemed to forget that they had gotten into it in the first place to make a killing, and might have expected more than ordinary risk—but nevertheless, they screamed. Flood was the ablest financier of the group and was responsible for its stock-market operations. He is the one who held the four men together. Flood became president of the Nevada Bank in 1881 on the retirement of Louis McLane. In 1885, Flood and Mackay got rid of Fair, and Flood hired Brander, who went into wheat speculation and almost closed the bank. To keep it going, Flood and Mackay had to bring Fair back in as president. Flood and Mackay lost $12,000,000, and Flood died two years later. I. W. Hellman took over the Nevada Bank in 1891. From the California Historical Society.

could not be used in over the counter transactions with the public; Ralston sometimes opened his bank in the morning with only $50,000 in the vault. At the same time, the United States mint was not operating, so that a bank could not take gold bars there for minting; there was $14,000,000 in gold coin locked up in the Sub-Treasury in San Francisco, but President Grant had not seen fit to allow San Francisco bankers to exchange gold bars for gold coin. At the same time, Ralston's Bank of California had loaned the Big Four of the Central Pacific Railroad $3,000,000 so it could gain another hundred miles in its race with the Union Pacific (to entitle it to more governmental subsidies), and another $2,000,000 had been invested by San Franciscans in South America. With all these drains on gold coin, San Francisco began to be uneasy, and rumors of a crash were going through the town like a flash fire. Asbury Harpending tells how Ralston met the problem:

While the tension was at its height I called at the Bank of California one afternoon and was ushered into the private office of Mr. Ralston. To tell the truth, I was feeling the pinch myself, and wanted to know something of the outlook.

The banker said I was just the man he wanted to see. "If things go on as they are," he said, "every bank will be closed by tomorrow afternoon. Not one of us can stand a half day's run, and all will go down in a heap. Then look out for hell in general to break loose. This will happen if I don't get a million dollars in coin in the vaults tonight. But I intend to get it, and want you and Maurice Dore to help me. Be at the bank at 1 o'clock tonight, and put on an old suit of clothes, for you will have plenty of hard work to do."

Dore and myself met by appointment shortly after midnight. We were utterly mystified. Together we tramped through the deserted, dimly lighted streets. We found Ralston at the bank with one of its trusty officials. The financier [Ralston] was in high spirits, but counseled caution. We walked noiselessly to the United States Sub-Treasury, then located on Montgomery, between Sacramento and California Streets. A dim light was burning within. Mr. Ralston asked us to halt a few paces from the entrance; then to our great surprise he opened the door of the Sub-Treasury, without challenge of any kind, and closed it after him as he stepped inside. Presently he emerged with several sacks of coin. "Take that to the bank," he said. "The gentleman there will give you something to bring back."

The party at the bank received the cash, tallied it and handed us gold bars for the same value. These we took to the Sub-Treasury, where we found Mr. Ralston smilingly awaiting us with a new cargo of sacks on the sidewalk. We turned over the bars and made another journey to the bank.

Thus, at dead of night, passing to and fro, we transferred in actual weight nearly five tons of gold. We did not get quite as much as Ralston wanted before the light began to break. It was a heart-breaking job from a physical standpoint. I was young and athletic and stood my end of it in good shape. But Maurice Dore was of sedentary habit, soft as mush, and he was on the verge of collapse. He was nearly chest foundered and had a swayback appearance for a month. During all this time, not a person passed to interrupt us. This was doubtless due to a prearrangement with the policeman on the beat.

When the Bank of California opened the next morning a rather ominous looking crowd was in waiting. Lines began to form behind the paying tellers' windows. It wasn't a "run" but a "near-run." Ralston appeared on the scene and looked annoyed, as he said, "Why are you making so many of our customers wait on a busy day? Put more tellers on the windows and have your coin on hand." More tellers went to the windows. Porters brought tray after tray from the vaults. It was amazing how the crowd changed their minds about wanting their money and melted away. And all over the troubled city the report spread that the Bank of California had coin to burn, and the news caused a general relief.

Nevertheless, a serious run started on one of the leading banks [he does not say which one]. Ralston hurried to the spot, mounted a dry goods box and addressed the crowd. He told them they were doing the bank and the city a great injustice. He declared that the bank was absolutely sound—which was the truth. He further told the crowd that they need not wait for a lineup. Just bring their books to the Bank of California and they would be accommodated with the cash there. Again, the crowd slunk away abashed.

Thus, a tremendous panic, the consequences of which might have been world-wide, was averted by a bold front, a nervy bluff backed by a million in cash. Three days later, President Grant reversed himself and allowed gold to be exchanged at the Sub-Treasury for cash, which settled all anxiety. This was brought about through the agency of Jesse Seligman, the New York banker, who gave the President a banquet and then showed him his mistake.

But neither Mills nor Sharon, who were leading officers of the bank [of California], ever knew how Ralston gathered in nearly a million dollars after banking hours that day. All the satisfaction they ever got was that a kind friend had come to the bank's assistance.[11]

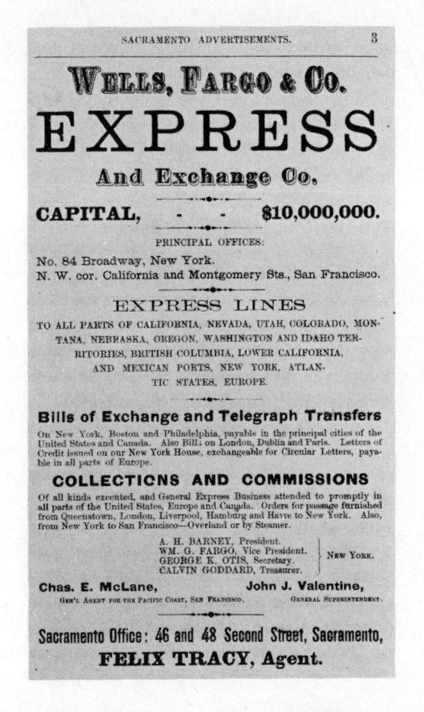

An advertisement from McKenney's "Sacramento Directory for the Year 1870," showing the capital at $10,-000,000, and A. H. Barney, president. From the Bancroft Library, Berkeley, University of California.

It is no wonder that early Californians considered William C. Ralston the greatest hero of San Francisco.

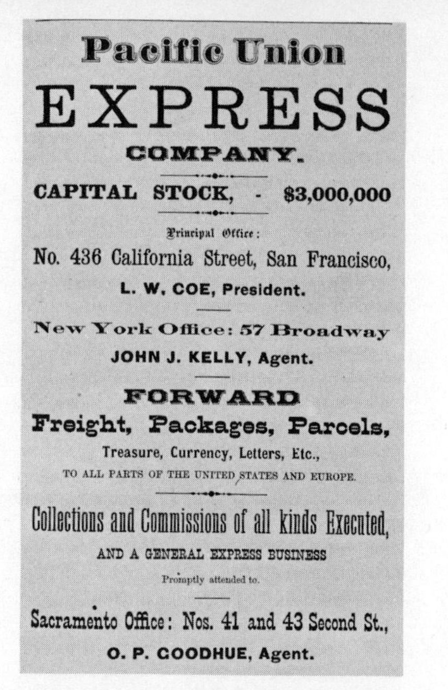

The Pacific Union Express Company, which Lloyd Tevis said later was nothing but a name, apparently was advertising for business in McKenney's "Sacramento Directory for the Year 1870." From the Bancroft Library, Berkeley, University of California.

In June, in a possible desperation attempt to stall off the inevitable, the directors of Wells Fargo voted a subscription for $10,000 in bonds to extend the Kansas branch of the Union Pacific.

But the wheels of fate turned steadily toward a showdown, and on October 4, William G. Fargo and his brother Charles, and A. H. Barney, president of Wells Fargo, met Tevis, Bacon, and Mills at Omaha in what has become known as the Omaha Conference. It was held behind locked doors, but it may be assumed that Tevis showed Fargo and Barney that he already owned a controlling interest in Wells Fargo, and his exclusive ten-year express contract with Central Pacific was something Wells Fargo had to have to maintain its existence.

The Union Pacific had its own express company from Omaha to Salt Lake City, and swap arrangements only were available on through shipments, nothing on local or way business. The man in the saddle, the only man who could negotiate a deal with the Union Pacific was Charles Crocker, and there was not much Wells Fargo could do but accept his terms.

At any rate, an agreement was reached that came to be known as the Omaha Treaty.

There is considerable room for interpretation in the various terms of the Omaha Treaty, but the Head Minutes show that, first of all, the Pacific Express was to turn its business over to Wells Fargo and disband. The Pacific Express Company was to receive $5,000,000 in stock of Wells, Fargo & Company and was to pay to Wells, Fargo & Company 3⅓ percent of $5,000,000 in cash. "All assets previously owned by Wells, Fargo & Company in excess of 3½ percent on its $10,000,000 capital stock were to be distributed to the holders of these shares, thus making the working capital of the reorganized company $5,000,000."

Wells, Fargo & Company gave its own official explanation in a letter to its stockholders dated November 10, 1869:

Sir—

You will have received a notice from the Secretary, informing you of a meeting of the Stockholders, to be held on the 25th day of November to pass upon the question of increasing the capital stock of this Company.

This communication to Stockholders, is to inform them of the purpose and occasion for that increase. You are doubtless aware that a rival company, called the Pacific Express [!], has been organized in California, composed of persons having intimate relations with the Central Pacific Railroad; that it has succeeded in negotiating an exclusive contract with that road for ten years; and that we were lately notified that our business over that road would be stopped, on and after the 1st day of October last. We tried to get from the Railroad equal facilities with the other Express Company, and used every effort and influence in our power, but were refused.

We took legal advice, and the result of that advice was, that although we should in the end, doubtless, be able to compel the granting of equal treatment with other Companies, yet this would only be at the end of a litigation, during which our business would be seriously impaired, and perhaps destroyed, by the interruption and hostility of the Railroad. While preparing to defend ourselves, we received an intimation that the opposition Company was as averse as we to such a litigation as was likely to ensue, and desired a conference. We were already of opinion that the interests of our Stockholders required every effort towards an amicable arrangement, and a Committee, composed of Messrs.

A. H. Barney, William G. Fargo and Charles Fargo, met a Committee of the other Company, at Omaha. The result of the conference has been an agreement (subject to the action of our Stockholders, on the increase of capital stock,) substantially as follows:

Wells, Fargo & Co. is first to withdraw, for distribution among its present Stockholders, all its cash assets, retaining only enough to furnish, with its working property, two-thirds in value of what is requisite to carry on business. The Pacific Express Company is to assign all its contracts and privileges, and pay, in cash, enough to make its contribution equal to one third of what is requisite; and the business is to be carried on upon this united capital by Wells, Fargo & Co. There being no way provided for calling in one-third of our stock, to be re-issued to the Pacific Express Company, to represent its interest in the united property, there is no other course but to make a nominal increase of one-third, that is, to fifteen millions. The increase is made for this purpose only, and nothing is called for from our Stockholders. The assets withdrawn by us will be converted into cash and distributed among the old Stockholders as soon as possible after the increase of stock enables us to carry out the contract.

This arrangement by the Committee will give us practically an exclusive use of the Central Pacific and all roads now or hereafter controlled by it, for the period of ten years; and it has, after full discussion and consideration of the situation in which our property and interests were placed, been approved by the Board of Directors by a nearly unanimous vote, and by all the Stockholders to whom the circumstances have been explained. The carrying out of the contract is dependent upon the increase of stock; and the Stockholders, in passing upon this question, have their interests in their own hands. Should they choose not to make the increase, we have the alternative of abandoning our business upon the railroad, or resorting to litigation for its protection. The delays, interruption to business, and eventual risk of this course is such that the Board of Directors is of opinion that the arrangement above stated is preferable, even as compared with the result of a successful legal contest.

Should your judgment approve this arrangement, and you be unable to attend the meeting, you are requested to execute the enclosed proxy to Danford N. Barney and Wm. G. Fargo, and return to this office.

A. H. Barney, President.[12]

One thing seems reasonably certain: Wells Fargo gave one third of its capital for the Pacific Express franchise, and turned control over to Lloyd Tevis.

Tevis would control Wells Fargo for more than twenty years, and few would regret it. He was capable, shrewd, and daring at the right time, and Wells Fargo would benefit from his interest.

Montgomery Street, looking north from California Street. The picture is labeled "instantaneous"—which means a snapshot. Wells Fargo is on the left. Observe water wagon in right foreground, horse-drawn streetcars at right center. This picture, taken in 1868, was made at the same intersection as that of the Soulé picture of 1854, and looking in the same direction. It appears in Ira Cross, "Financing an Empire," without the name of the photographer.

There was, however, another angle to the Central Pacific franchise: Inasmuch as Tevis and his associates had made a fortune from the use of their railroad interest, other railroads would see the opportunity and would be even harder in their dealings with express companies. Tevis himself became president of the Southern Pacific when the Big Four acquired control of that struggling company in 1869, and he would carry the knowledge of his harsh bargain with Wells Fargo. It was to be a period of wars with many railroads, and Wells Fargo would find itself forced more than once to make a bargain that it did not like.

Under the terms of the settlement in Omaha, Wells Fargo still would not be able to accept or deliver express between Omaha and Ogden; its express had to travel in sealed cars between those points. It was not the best situation, but it gave Wells Fargo access to the East.

On October 14, 1869, Wells Fargo sold a number of its stage lines: Salt Lake to Uintah to Gilmer & Company (as of July 9) for $22,500; Corinne to Fort Benton to Gilmer & Salisbury (as of August 1) for $87,000; Argenta to Austin to J. P. Cope & Company (as of August 1) for $15,000; the Colorado lines (the Smoky Hill lines, which probably included Cheyenne to Georgetown) to Jack Hughes & Company (as of October 2) for $106,000.

By the end of 1869, the board of directors showed many new names, although most of the old ones were still present: Ashbel H. Barney, president; James C. Fargo, vice-president; William G. Fargo, Louis McLane, John Bloodgood (new), William H. Fogg, Danford N. Barney,[13] Henry Kip (new), Charles W. Ford (new), Johnston Livingston, Eugene Kelly, E. B. Morgan, D. L. Einstein (new), Benjamin P. Cheney, Charles Fargo (new), George E. Cook (new), and Prince S. Crowell (new). George K. Otis was secretary, and Calvin Goddard was treasurer; Theodore F. Wood had been appointed assistant secretary on January 27.

In 1869, Wells Fargo had 293 offices; in spite of the losing battle with Tevis, the company had added sixty-one offices that year.

The statement of income and expenses for 1869 has some interesting features: charges for transportation collected by the company were $1,647,446.19, an increase of more than $700,000; expenses for express privilege were $889,018.63—almost double; operating expenses were $630,655.83—up about 70 percent; and net operating income was $170,778.12—$6,000 less than the year before. No dividends are listed for 1869.

The 1870's were coming: the time of William C. Ralston's downfall and the beginning of the Nevada National Bank by the Lords of the Comstock.

OFFICE WELLS, FARGO & CO.,
84 BROADWAY,
NEW-YORK, NOVEMBER 10TH, 1869.

SIR—

You will have received a notice from the Secretary, informing you of a meeting of the Stockholders, to be held on the 25th day of November to pass upon the question of increasing the capital stock of this Company.

This communication to Stockholders, is to inform them of the purpose and occasion for that increase. You are doubtless aware that a rival company, called the Pacific Express, has been organized in California, composed of persons having intimate relations with the Central Pacific Railroad; that it has succeeded in negotiating an exclusive contract with that road for ten years; and that we were lately notified that our business over that road would be stopped, on and after the 1st day of October last. We tried to get from the Railroad equal facilities with the other Express Company, and used every effort and influence in our power, but were refused.

We took legal advice, and the result of that advice was, that although we should in the end, doubtless, be able to compel the granting of equal treatment with other Companies, yet this would only be at the end of a litigation, during which our business would be seriously impaired, and perhaps destroyed, by the interruption and hostility of the Railroad. While preparing to defend ourselves, we received an intimation that the opposition Company were as averse as we to such a litigation as was likely to ensue, and desired a conference. We were already of opinion that the interests of our Stockholders required every effort towards an amicable arrangement, and a Committee, composed of Messrs. A. H. Barney, William G. Fargo and Charles Fargo, met a Committee of the other Company, at Omaha. The result of the conference has been an agreement (subject to the action of our Stockholders, on the increase of capital stock,) substantially as follows:

Wells, Fargo & Co. is first to withdraw, for distribution among its present Stockholders, all its cash assets, retaining only enough to furnish, with its working property, two-thirds in value of what is requisite to carry on business. The Pacific Express Company is to assign all its contracts and privileges, and pay, in cash, enough to make its contribution equal to one third of what is requisite; and the business is to be carried on upon this united capital by Wells, Fargo & Co. There being no way provided for calling in one-third of our stock, to be re-issued to the Pacific Express Company, to represent its interest in the united property, there is no other course but to make a nominal increase of one-third, that is, to fifteen millions. The increase is made for this purpose only, and nothing is called for from our Stockholders. The assets withdrawn by us will be converted into cash and distributed among the old Stockholders as soon as possible after the increase of stock enables us to carry out the contract.

This arrangement by the Committee will give us practically an exclusive use of the Central Pacific and all roads now or hereafter controlled by it, for the period of ten years; and it has, after full discussion and consideration of the situation in which our property and interests were placed, been approved by the Board of Directors by a nearly unanimous vote, and by all the Stockholders to whom the circumstances have been explained. The carrying out of the contract is dependent upon the increase of stock; and the Stockholders, in passing upon this question, have their interests in their own hands. Should they choose not to make the increase, we have the alternative of abandoning our business upon the railroad, or resorting to litigation for its protection. The delays, interruption to business, and eventual risk of this course is such that the Board of Directors is of opinion that the arrangement above stated is preferable, even as compared with the result of a successful legal contest.

Should your judgment approve this arrangement, and you be unable to attend the meeting, you are requested to execute the enclosed proxy to Danford N. Barney and Wm. G. Fargo, and return to this office.

A. H. BARNEY, President.

A stockholders' notice of the action by which Lloyd Tevis came into control of Wells Fargo. This letter is from a negative owned by Basil C. Pearce, a vice-president of the Wells Fargo Bank.

1870-1875
The Great Splurger

PEOPLE IN THE SAN FRANCISCO AREA had been able to see what was coming across the continent on steel rails, even if the directors of Wells Fargo had not: prosperity. In a grand fury of speculation, land was bought and subdivided; town sites were planned; new industries were established; and it appeared that a new era of prosperity was ahead for San Francisco. The tide of immigration had already begun to surge in 1868, and it was said that the newcomers far outnumbered those of Gold Rush days. California was the lend of golden plenty, of unbounded opportunity. Some fifty thousand emigrants reached California in 1868–1869; emigration companies were booming, real-estate speculators were in their glory, and laborers were coming in such numbers as to lower wages and perhaps lengthen the eight-hour day.

However, the completion of the railroad brought unexpected problems. There were no more placer mines for the unemployed. Land prices were too high for those who wanted to buy farms. Worst of all, thousands of unskilled laborers swarmed into San Francisco from the Central Pacific Railroad. Wages went down and the eight-hour day, established during the Civil War, went up. Dock workers, commission merchants, and all those who had been connected with San Francisco's extensive shipping industry, found themselves out of work or out of business.

And it seems that San Francisco and her people also were asleep at the switch, for agents of Chicago business houses were following the railhead of the Union Pacific to obtain trade and customers. The *Chronicle* said that when the "golden spike was driven at Promontory Point, Chicago was reading accounts of the event." And the *Evening Bulletin* enlarged on it:

> The merchants of Chicago and other Atlantic cities . . . acted as though new gold mines of fabulous wealth had been opened up to them on this coast by the laying of the iron tracks across the continent and as if the people were actually starving for supplies. Hence, drummers were sent on by scores and hundreds, soliciting everything from a pair of shoe strings to a well stocked variety store. They canvassed the coast thoroughly, not forgetting the smallest retail establishment, even accosting private individuals at the mines, on the farms, in the work shops and on the street; and as a reward for their perseverance, for the unusual inducements offered, and also for the sake of the novelty of the transaction, they secured a number of orders and subsequently forwarded a large quantity of goods in response to such orders and for speculative account. As a result of these operations, our markets, which were already well stocked, were overburdened with goods, and stagnation was the inevitable consequence.[1]

California had been isolated from the world, and had built up a little province of high prices, great profits, a general recklessness of life, but now the railroad opened the floodgates from the East and poured in emigrants to lower the standard of living. It did not rain during the winter, either in 1869 or 1870, and the drought hurt agriculture and farm laborers, especially in southern California. Real estate dropped, wages and prices dropped, and bankers and financiers were in trouble.

One fifth of the population was unemployed; there were seven thousand unemployed in San Francisco, and a group of businessmen met in the interest of establishing a soup house for the poor. The people naturally blamed the Chinese, and there were many riots, and finally a new state constitution.

There were only four business failures in California in 1869, but there were 270 failures in 1870 and 89 in 1871.[2]

In 1870, after an incredibly difficult fight against unbelievable odds and all the power that Ralston could throw against him, fair and foul, Sutro won the endorsement of Congress for his tunnel, 124 to 42, and Ralston and Sharon were more than ever determined to stop him. What if the man should uncover a new bonanza of his own while digging through twenty thousand feet of rock?

In the same year, Alvinza Hayward, who had rescued Ralston in the Hale and Norcross affair, saw a chance to whip Ralston and make a fortune. He and John P. Jones, who had been the hero of the Yellow Jacket fire, got control of the Crown Point mine and made $30,000,000, largely at Ralston's expense. Business, after all, was business, though certainly Ralston would not have seen it that way.

However, Ralston and Sharon bought the Belcher mine and opened another bonanza that brought them $35,000,000 worth of silver. For a while they were saved.

Mackay had bought up the Bullion mine but found nothing; Fair became superintendent of the Savage mine, but found nothing. Most of the million they had made in Hale and Norcross was gone, and they finally began to buy up Virginia Consolidated from Ralston, sometimes at fifteen cents a share.

One of the first things Wells Fargo did in 1870 was change its head office to San Francisco, since Lloyd Tevis lived there, and the board of directors on February 5 ordered all offices west of the Missouri River to send their remittances to San Francisco instead of to New York.

Notice of intention to reduce the capital stock from $15,000,000 to $5,000,000 was published in *The New York Times* for six weeks commencing July 18, and in the Rocky Mountain *News* at Denver; and on September 1, the capital stock was so reduced. The terms of the contract with the Pacific Express (or Pacific Union Express) Company, dated October 4, 1869, "relative to the distribution of assets to stockholders," were carried out in 1869, "making the net working capital $500,000," say the Head Minutes.

In 1870, the Virginia & Truckee Railroad began operating into Virginia City over the world's most tortuous iron path of twistbacks, hairpins, and crossovers—and Wells Fargo's express was on board.

In September, 1870, one Thomas Mooney, organizer of the California Building, Loan & Savings Society and the Builders' Insurance Company, made a trip to the Orient for his health; suspicion arose, and the savings society was investigated, and it turned out that the bank was in bad shape, that Mooney had operated it for Mooney's benefit. It seemed obvious that Mooney would find the Orient a permanent necessity for his health, and the savings society was forced to suspend, and finally paid off very little to the depositors. Runs were made on all banks, and one on the Hibernia Savings & Loan Society almost closed it; the company had sixteen thousand depositors and $11,000,000 in deposits. The City Bank of Savings, Loan & Discount of San Francisco went bankrupt, but no city-wide calamity resulted, even though the effects of Mooney's trip to the Orient were felt for months.

Wells Fargo was not embarrassed.

In November, 1870, Wells Fargo suffered its first big train robbery. The Central Pacific's No. 1, from Oakland to Ogden, carried a big shipment of gold and silver bullion and greenbacks to meet the payroll of Ralston's Yellow Jacket mine at Virginia City. The train was stopped at Verdi, seven miles east of Truckee, by seven masked men who got $42,000 in gold and gold coin (missing a few bars of gold hid in the firewood), unhitched the engine and went ahead five miles, then put the gold and the money in their boots and disappeared. Twenty hours later and 385 miles east of Verdi, the same train was held up again, and the robbers got $4,000 in bullion and coin.

John J. Valentine, Wells Fargo's general superintendent, offered a $10,000 reward; the United States Post Office offered $500, and the State of Nevada, the county, and the Central Pacific Railroad offered $20,000—and the law forces of the Pacific Coast went to work. Meanwhile, near Verdi, the wife of a tavern keeper, sitting in one side of an outhouse, through a knothole saw a man examining a bootful of $20 gold pieces, after which he lowered the boot carefully into the vault of the outhouse. The man was arrested shortly afterward, and presumably revealed the hiding place of the money. Another member of the gang was found in California but was given a gun-muzzle extradition. The man who had tipped the robbers as to the shipment was arrested. Two men turned state's evidence and got off free; four were given twenty-one years each; the leader got ten years, which was reduced to three; he tried in 1877 to hold up a stage, and was shot by a Wells Fargo messenger. The other robbers were army deserters and were soon rounded up; the Central Pacific's No. 1 would not be robbed again until 1882.

William G. Fargo about the time he became president of Wells, Fargo & Company in 1870. From Alvin F. Harlow, "Old Waybills."

The board of directors was reduced in 1870. William G. Fargo became president; Lloyd Tevis, vice-president[3]; Leland Stanford, Milton S. Latham, C. P. Huntington, Ashbel H. Barney, Darius Ogden Mills, James C. Fargo, and Benjamin B. Cheney were directors. Stanford, Huntington, and Mills were Tevis' associates in the Pacific Express. Theodore F. Wood was secretary, and Calvin Goddard was treasurer.

The number of Wells Fargo offices had jumped to 396.

Wells Fargo's income from transportation charges dropped to $1,559,801.38, and its payment for express privileges likewise dropped, to $686,783.32. Its operating expenses went up to $781,983.89, and its operating income dropped to $133,526.52. That year for the first time, however, it had an income from investment of $73,350 (but no suggestion as to the nature of the investment). Over $140,000 was transferred to the reserve fund that year, and $65,989.77 was paid in dividends; on a capitalization of $5,000,000, that is approximately 1⅓ percent.

In 1871, the mines produced their lowest yield, and this fact, plus the eighty-nine business failures in California, was complicated by an unusual event: the Chicago fire. It seems that after the railroad went through, San Francisco businessmen went to Chicago with activities that required only the use of money and not the hard work of selling; a number of San Francisco insurance companies accepted coverage of buildings in Chicago—only to run into the great Chicago fire of 1871. An enormous amount of money was lost in flames, and San Francisco fire-insurance companies paid off at least $1,500,000, which they withdrew from San Francisco banks, causing bank credit to tighten and the stock market to drop.

Apparently Wells Fargo was continuing its policy of good deeds, for H. L. Stimson says of the company about that time:

> Although inaugurated, like all mundane institutions, for the purpose of making money, this company, by its uniform respect for the rights of individuals, has secured and maintains a hold on the good will of the people exceptional in the history of monopolies.
>
> Probably no other Express Company has received the same unremitting attention from highwaymen and lawless desperadoes; but the promptness and fairness with which losses caused by their depredations are adjusted, has inspired the public with a confidence in its responsibility and integrity that could not easily be shaken.
>
> The company has further augmented its reputation

One drawing of the great fire at Chicago, October 8–10, 1871. From Leonard Louis Levinson's excellent book, "Wall Street."

with the people by the ready interest it has shown in cases of public calamity; and, notably, under its present management [that is, the presidency of Tevis], it has identified itself with the several great relief movements of recent years, which will constitute a luminous page in the nation's history. Thus, it employed, under the personal supervision of its officers, its extended facilities for collecting and forwarding money and supplies, free of charge, to the communities affected by the following calamities: Great Fire of Chicago; Overflow of the Mississippi River; Yellow Fever at Memphis, 1873; Grasshopper Plague of Kansas and Nebraska; Inundation at Marysville, California; Forest Fires in Wisconsin; Great Fire at Virginia, Nevada; and the Terrible Yellow Fever Scourge of 1878.[4]

Wells Fargo had not changed since the days of the 1850's, nor did it limit its helpfulness to California or even to the area west of the Missouri River.

The only bright spot in the 1871 economic picture was the fact that emigration declined substantially, and construction work in Chicago, plus construction in Virginia City after its fire of that year, offered employment to a large number of men. Then, too, in the winter of 1871–1872 there was good rainfall, and even mining stocks recovered.

During that year, Adolph Sutro began to make some headway in his fight to build a tunnel to drain the Comstock, for, with an endorsement by the Nevada legislature and a subscription of $50,000 by the miners of the Comstock following the Yellow Jacket fire, he was offered and accepted $650,000 from Calmont's in London, and went to work with renewed energy.

In 1871, Wells Fargo's income from charges went up to $2,027,150.10; its charges for express privileges vaulted to $1,053,485.78; its operating expenses were $800,678.29, and its net operating income was $227,902.90. It had income from investments of $146,699.39.

The board of directors was not changed.

The company paid $150,000 in dividends that year, approximately 2⅓ percent.

There was transferred to surplus $224,602.29.

The number of offices at the end of the year went up again—to 436.

In the early part of 1872 there was wild speculation in mining stocks. Ralston's Crown Point and Belcher mines had produced a great deal of metal, and the old fever hit the market again. From January to May, the value of silver stocks on the San Francisco exchanges rose from $17,000,000 to $81,000,000, and many mining companies increased their capitalization in accord—eleven companies, in one case, going from $19,598,000 to $74,000,000. The trouble was that only four of the 150 companies listed were paying dividends, and the market broke on May 8; in three weeks the total valuation dropped $61,000,000. Business was paralyzed, and again thousands were unemployed. The effects of that orgy lasted into 1874.

1872 was the year of the Great Diamond Hoax, in which William C. Ralston was involved, and through whose influence others were involved. It is worth recording because it caused considerable uneasiness in financial circles in San Francisco, and also because it caused some to lose faith in Ralston even though he handled it in his characteristically bold fashion, and is said to have protected everybody who was taken in by it.[5]

Two prospectors, Philip Arnold and John Slack, deposited some rough diamonds in the Bank of California, and naturally the news got around, and presently they met Ralston, and appeared to be two simple-minded men who nevertheless were shrewd enough to keep a secret of the location of the place where they had found the diamonds. They were willing to sell Ralston a half interest in their mines, but imposed certain conditions; for one thing, they would take only two men to the field, and the two must be blindfolded. Two men were sent by Ralston, and more diamonds were brought back. Then the men offered to bring back a couple of million dollars' worth of stones as a guarantee of good faith; on delivery, they said they had had the stones in two bags but had lost one of the bags while crossing a river on a raft, but had saved a million dollars' worth. In San Francisco, they poured these out on a billiard table in Harpending's home, and revealed a magnificent pile of diamonds, rubies, and sapphires. It was agreed to send a large sample of the stones to Tiffany's in New York, and, if their value should

A certificate for four shares of stock in Wells, Fargo and Company, dated August 26, 1872, and signed by William G. Fargo. The original is in the History Room, Wells Fargo Bank.

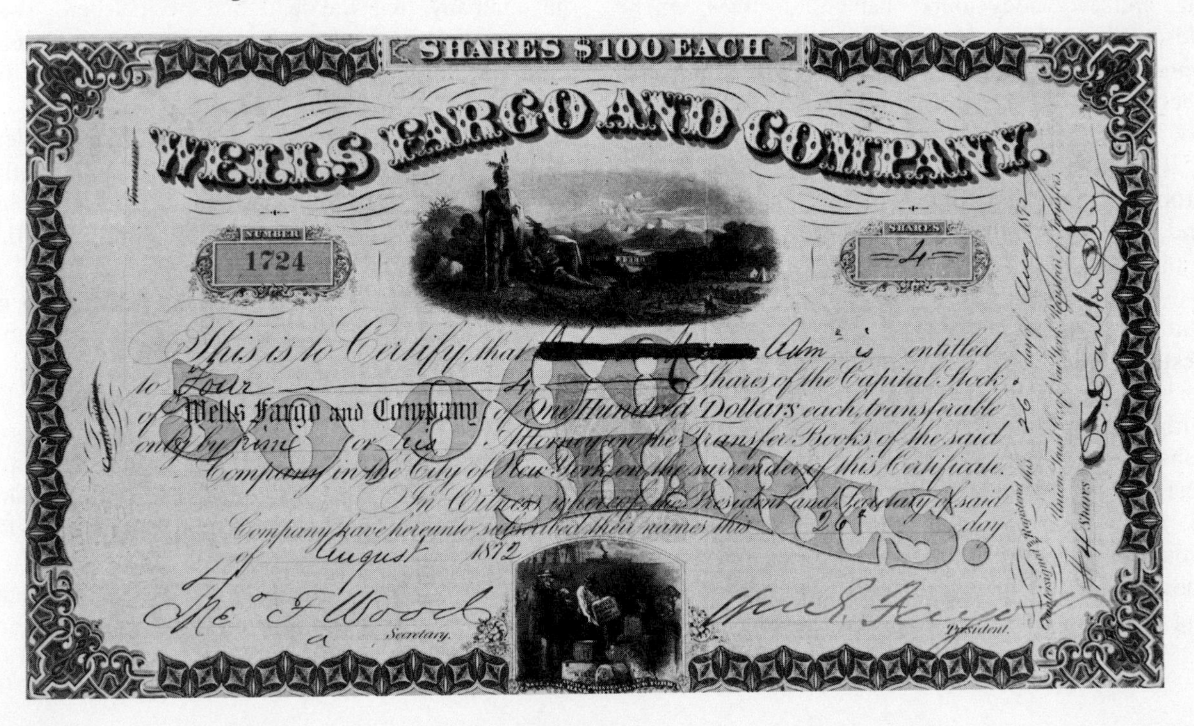

SHARES $100 EACH

WELLS FARGO AND COMPANY.

NUMBER 1724

SHARES —4—

This is to Certify that [illegible] Adm^r is entitled to Four Shares of the Capital Stock of Wells Fargo and Company of One Hundred Dollars each, transferable only by him or his Attorney on the Transfer Books of the said Company in the City of New York on the surrender of this Certificate.

In Witness whereof the President and Secretary of said Company have hereunto subscribed their names this 26th day of August 1872

Secretary.

President.

Countersigned & Registered this 26 day of Aug 1872, Union Trust Co of New York, Registrar of Transfers be verified, then to send a mining expert to the field.

Ralston, Harpending, General Grenville Dodge (who had been chief engineer and builder of the Union Pacific, and later built railroads all over the United States), William M. Lent, and George D. Roberts were the principal financiers, and they contemplated a corporation with a capital stock of $10,000,000 immediately upon approval of the field by a mining expert. Several of them went to New York, and showed the stones to Mr. Tiffany, General George B. McClellan of Civil War fame (not always flattering), Horace Greeley, Mr. Duncan of Duncan, Sherman & Company, and General Benjamin F. Butler. By that time, it seems, there were also emeralds in the bag, but nobody wondered about the geological background of such a mixture. Mr. Tiffany said they were beyond question precious stones of enormous value. He submitted them to his lapidary, and the valuation was set at $150,000. At that rate, they had about $1,500,000 worth of precious stones to begin with.

They hired a nationally known expert, Henry Janin, to examine the field (he later cleared $42,500 from his part in the business), and Philip Arnold demanded $100,000 in cash as a guarantee, but agreed to let it remain in escrow. Then the party left the railroad near Rawlings Spring in Wyoming, spent four days of difficult travel, and camped on a seven-thousand-foot mesa. Everybody began to dig, and everybody found diamonds, rubies, emeralds, and sapphires. For two days they kept finding gems, then staked out a large acreage. They went back to New York, and Baron Rothschild in London got interested.

Ralston and Harpending owned a majority of the property, and they organized the San Francisco and New York Mining and Commercial Company, with a capital stock of $10,000,000, and the thought in several minds was to move the great lapidary cutters of Amsterdam to the Pacific Coast. The businessmen of San Francisco considered it a privilege to be in on the ground floor, and twenty-five men with unblemished reputations were permitted to subscribe $80,000 each—which was paid immediately to the Bank of California. William M. Lent, A. Gansl, Thomas Selby, Milton S. Latham (who would have a long history with Wells Fargo), Louis Sloss, Maurice Dore (who had winded himself carrying gold from the Sub-Treasury one night in July, 1869, to save Ralston's bank), W. F. Babcock, William C. Ralston, William Willis, George B. McClellan, and Samuel P. Barlow were elected directors. Ralston was treasurer. A. Gansl represented the House of Rothschild. Slack and Arnold were paid off with cash to the extent of $300,000, which was received by Arnold.

The stampede began. Articles were printed in the papers; there was something about a ruby as big as a pigeon's egg, worth $500,000, and a tidal wave of prospectors headed for Arizona. The promoters sent a large consignment of diamonds to Rothschild in London, and a party of fifteen miners and surveyors to the field. There were reports that Latham represented prominent British capitalists.

The party in the field found still more gems, including 286 small diamonds. Another package went to Tiffany's and was appraised at $8,000. It was predicted that the company would mine $1,000,000 worth of gems a month, and that the world market would be upset. As yet, however, no stock was placed on the market.

Finally the company posted a map showing the three thousand acres that they had claimed. Then one Clarence King, a government geologist and engineer who had been over the area, could not recall anything that looked like diamond country, so he went to look. He and his associate found diamonds, all right—one with lapidary marks on it. King wired the company that the field had been salted. That was on November 10. Then another party went back to look again, and found the evidence of salting.

About that time, the report came from London that the diamonds were niggerheads, almost worthless diamonds from South Africa. The dealer who had sold them a year before was found, and the scheme was clear. The two men had been lucky at mining and had made some money; they had spent $35,000 for coarse gems, had salted the area, and had made over $600,000.

Arnold went back home to Kentucky, where he retired with, presumably, most of the money, and where no attempt to sue him was successful at all. Slack disappeared, and his end is unknown. Arnold, who apparently got all or most of the money, finally gave up $150,000 for a complete release.

Ralston paid back the twenty-five men who had subscribed $2,000,000. Ralston, Roberts, and Harpending were the losers. Ralston got receipts from the twenty-five men, framed them, and put them on the wall of his office.

The hoax had repercussions for many years, and probably the reactions toward Ralston himself were mixed. In spite of the fact that he, according to Harpending, made good the losses of the twenty-five investors, there were many rumors, and even histories, to the effect that Ralston had made millions selling stock—but it appears not to be so.

Ralston had his hand in other things, including railroad-building, and it may be that he was interested in a map of 1872[6] that shows a railroad that never existed: the Texas & Pacific, south from Gilroy to a point near Los Angeles, and southeast along the route of the Butterfield Mail to Yuma, with a spur from about Vallecito (the Colorado Desert station) to San Diego. The road was never built, but the map certainly indicates the things people were wishing in those days; apparently the railroad builders were wishing too, for the map was prepared by the National Railway Publication Company.

In May, 1872, William Sharon decided that he wanted to be United States Senator from Nevada, and set out to buy the office at any price. It is said that he spent over $800,000 on the campaign, and that his attacks on his opponent, John P. Jones, were vicious and unrestrained—so much so that they backfired and he lost the election. It is thought, too, that Ralston had urged him to run so as to be able to oppose Adolph Sutro in Congress.

In 1872, Valentine called attention to the importance of Wells Fargo's Letter Department in a bulletin to agents:

"Never put our Old Letters in the Post Office for delivery, but keep these instructions before you, and observe them."

WELLS, FARGO & CO.'S OFFICE,

To Agents:

THE LETTER DEPARTMENT is an important feature of our General Express business, and deserves careful and prompt attention at the hands of every Agent, Clerk or Messenger. You will therefore carefully inspect, *at least once a month,* every letter remaining in your offices, to correct any omissions of the Letter or Express Clerk. In addition to the above, upon receipt of this, carefully inspect all letters in your office, and if there are any that can be delivered, deliver them; all those remaining, received prior to January 1st, 1872, return to this office way-billed to Aaron Stein. Please do likewise at the expiration of each quarter; *i. e.,* June 30th, Sept. 30th and Dec. 31st, from this time forward, until otherwise ordered; *returning, at the expiration of each quarter, all letters remaining undelivered, received prior to the expiration of the preceding quarter.*

Yours truly,

Jno. J. Valentine,

Gen'l Sup't.[7]

Directors of Wells Fargo at the beginning of the year 1872 were Leland Stanford, D. O. Mills, Oliver Eldridge,[8] Milton S. Latham, Lloyd Tevis, C. P. Huntington, William G. Fargo, Ashbel H. Barney, and Benjamin P. Cheney. Huntington resigned in April, and Mark Hopkins was elected in his place; Milton S. Latham resigned in April, and the fabulous James Ben Ali Haggin was elected in his place. Lloyd Tevis was elected president in place of Fargo, and Fargo became vice-president. Calvin Goddard resigned as treasurer in June, and apparently that office was not filled until March, 1873.

John J. Valentine was appointed general superintendent of the express department on February 8, 1872.

Two cash dividends were paid that year: 3 percent in January ($150,000), and 3½ percent in July ($175,000).

The number of offices increased to 463.

In the same year (1872), receipts from transportation went up to $2,151,736.13, charges for express privileges rose a little, and gross operating revenue rose $75,000; operating income was up accordingly, to a net income figure of $285,886.17, and there was a net income from investment of $188,664.50, for a total income of almost half a million dollars. There was transferred to the reserve fund $149,550.17, which made that fund total $515,039.71.

Over the country, 1872 ended as a very prosperous year, and that went into 1873 but was stopped dead and turned into a depression by the act that omitted the silver dollar from the coinage and established gold as the monetary standard. Undoubtedly, the drop in the price of silver had an effect on the Comstock, but apparently not a substantial one. Cross says that California was so far from the East that it was hardly affected by the panic along

The cover of Wells Fargo's "Directory of Chinese Merchants, 1873." From the Bancroft Library, Berkeley, University of California.

the Atlantic Coast. At the same time, the trade dollar was created, a bigger dollar with more silver in it, for use primarily in the Orient, and perhaps that coinage offset the demonetization.

In early 1873, James G. Fair discovered a new bonanza in the Consolidated Virginia mine. He took out twenty-five tons a day at $60 a ton, but said nothing. He and his partners had just about gone through $200,000, and they kept still.

While the Bank of California was in serious trouble, Consolidated Virginia stock fell lower, and Flood and O'Brien bought it up. Then Fair struck still another deposit that refined $93 to $632 a ton, but still said nothing. They had just located the greatest body of ore the world has ever known, but they continued to mine quietly. (How it was possible to keep it a secret remains a mystery, but apparently the secret was well kept.)

In October of that year, Mills retired from the Bank of California, and Ralston was elected president; he kept Mills's name on the board of directors, apparently for the prestige of Mills's reputation. Ralston himself was busy building the Palace Hotel, to be the most magnificent piece of architecture conceivable. It was to cost a million dollars a floor, and would strain Ralston's credit more than once—primarily because he apparently knew no bounds when it came to expense. Marble statues, colonnades, a fountain big enough to float boats, silks, damask, furniture of exotic woods, clocks, hardware, and blankets from his own factories, flooring from a ranch that he bought just to get the oak trees—there was never any end to the expense, and now Ralston's unbridled extravagances began to hurt him. His bank had a capital of $5,000,000, but it had loaned $3,518,177.02 to William Sharon & Company, the partnership of Ralston and Sharon, and in February, those various companies were not paying interest, and the loans were uncollectible. Ralston still paid 1 percent a month dividend, and the directors could hardly complain, but they were uneasy, for two thirds of the bank's assets were frozen. Ralston finally quieted the directors by "taking personal responsibility," and securing an agreement signed by

The great and magnificent, superlavish Palace Hotel, as it is shown in William M. Thayer, "Marvels of the New West." It was opened in December, 1875, and its first big function was a dinner in honor of Lieutenant-General Philip H. Sheridan, the famous Indian-fighting general. The building of the hotel helped to break William C. Ralston, who bought a ranch to get oak trees to make furniture for it, and it would last until the fire of 1906, when Enrico Caruso would run down the great stairway clutching an autographed photograph of Theodore Roosevelt.

Mills and by Colonel J. D. Fry, Ralston's father-in-law.

Ralston had his back to the wall. He was called generous (and was), a patron (and was, for those he liked), a banker (which seems doubtful), a tycoon (obviously), a philanthropist (perhaps), a very democratic man (which he was), and a demagog (which he was). He was a grand actor, a grandiloquent leading man, but perhaps the wrinkles were beginning to show around his eyes.

The Palace Hotel was draining him, and everywhere he went he must have felt the pressure for money.

Now Fair and Mackay, knowing they had found a bonanza, began to oppose Sutro to avoid paying the $2 a ton charge that would be levied for drainage if the tunnel should ever be completed. Sutro kept hammering away at the rock, making up to thirty feet a day, while the four Irishmen explored their huge body of ore in the Consolidated Virginia in every direction. They ran drifts and crosscuts, sank winzes, made upraises. There was a mountain of ore; they started at the eleven hundred-foot level and dropped to the fifteen hundred-foot level, and there was still ore. Wealth, unlimited wealth. It meant power for the four men, and it would mean disaster for Ralston's banks, his hotels, his factories, his mills, his railroads, his wheat fields, his vineyards, his ranches, and his steamship lines. His empire was so precariously balanced that any other great fortune would destroy it. But still nobody in San Francisco knew about the colossal bonanza in the Consolidated Virginia. The four men organized or reorganized the California Mining Company; Consolidated Virginia sold at $45 a share. The four men were miners —not speculators—and they continued to take out silver while William Sharon constantly belittled them; they were working themselves out on nothing but a small deposit, he said. Every time he said it, the stock dropped, and the four men began to buy it up. The original 10,700 shares of each mine had been divided into 180,000, each share representing less than 1/14 of an inch.

While Ralston and Sharon were fighting the four

silver kings in 1873, Wells Fargo was tired of being plagued with holdups, and John J. Valentine hired a man who could stop them: James B. Hume, a New York man who had become marshal of Placerville after he reached California. He was intelligent and shrewd, cool and courageous, and soon became sheriff of El Dorado County; soon afterward he went to Carson City as warden of the state prison. Not long afterward, Tevis and Valentine hired him, and he was to build a splendid reputation—no small part of which was due to the cooperation of sheriffs and local officials. Hume's policy was to let the local officials collect the rewards, and Wells Fargo reaped the benefit of that policy.

Hume was perhaps as admirable personally as he was officially. He had little formal education but a highly analytical mind. He was soft-spoken and looked benign; he disliked lies or deceptions; he was tolerant and got along with everybody, and often helped settle quarrels in the neighborhood where he lived in Oakland.

He was 6 feet, 1 inch tall, weighed two hundred pounds, and was very powerful; he had light brown hair, beautiful blue eyes, and a mustache; his hair turned white at sixty. He did not marry until he was fifty-nine. He was never ill, and it was a good thing, because he did not trust doctors. He kept a can of quinine in the pantry, and when he thought he might be sick, he stuck a knife blade in the can, brought it up with as much quinine as it would hold, stuck the knife in his mouth and turned it over, and chased the quinine down with bourbon. He liked a Doctor Clark in Stockton, who once stopped a nosebleed for him, and sent for Clark when he was dying.

In Oakland, he had a garden and was especially interested in roses. He bought many gourmet foods and much Roquefort cheese, and drank California claret wine with his dinner every night. His son Sam would visit him in San Francisco, where he would be sitting with his feet on the desk; he wore beautiful handmade boots. He would take Sam to a bar with him, and people would criticize him for it, but Hume would say, "Too many boys get into trouble because they are curious about what is inside a saloon. But Sam knows, and he won't ever be a drunkard, because he won't be curious. He knows."

Toward criminals he was a humanitarian, and gave many of the young ones a second chance; his son Sam said in later years that none ever betrayed him. Frequently he went to the governor and got a man pardoned or his sentence commuted. Released criminals would go to visit him, and he would give them a Southern Pacific pass back home and $10 of his own money.

James B. Hume, who often could tell who had committed a crime by looking at the scene. He helped sustain the motto: "Wells Fargo is good." From the History Room, Wells Fargo Bank.

Between them and him, catching them was a business and did not extend to his personal feelings—nor did they, as a rule, have any animosity toward him.

This is the man who fought transgressors against Wells Fargo for thirty-two years. Here was the man who could often finger the criminal by looking at the scene of the crime. He is also the man who thought his chief assistant, John N. Thacker, was a good man though he sometimes brought home the wrong criminal.[9]

In 1873, the Wells Fargo board was: Lloyd Tevis,

Five of James Hume's stalwarts. The significance of the hatchet and the broken-open box is not obvious. Left to right, they are Tom Cunningham, Captain A. W. Stone, B. K. Thorn, J. N. Thacker, and H. N. Morse. From the History Room, Wells Fargo Bank.

A portrait of J. N. Thacker, who became James Hume's right-hand man, although Hume said that sometimes he brought in the wrong man. From the History Room, Wells Fargo Bank.

A map of Wells Fargo routes in July, 1874. The original is in the History Room, Wells Fargo Bank.

president; William G. Fargo, vice-president; Ashbel H. Barney, Benjamin P. Cheney, D. O. Mills, Leland Stanford, James Ben Ali Haggin, Oliver Eldridge, and Mark Hopkins. Only Fargo, Barney, and Cheney were left of the old crowd. James Heron was secretary, and Theodore F. Wood was assistant secretary; Homer S. King, who would be prominent in the company for a long time, was elected treasurer on March 18.

A 4 percent dividend ($200,000) was paid in January, and 4 percent more in July.

The total number of offices was 592.

Income from transportation charges rose to $2,418,149.12, and express-privilege debits to $1,298,703.12. Operating expenses rose a little, and operating income went up to $346,608.06. Income from investment was $234,439.18. Amount transferred to reserve fund was $180,000, making the total almost $700,000.

The fight between Ralston and Sharon and the four silver kings was still going on. Sharon scorned the four Irishmen, but they continued to buy their own stock. Then, tired of Sharon's abuse, as soon as they had control, they invited Dan DeQuille to visit their mine. DeQuille (a pseudonym) was a newspaperman but also a mining expert and a careful one. Therefore, when he came back to the surface and said the two mines would produce $3,000,000 a month for ten years—a total of $360,000,000—the financial world was staggered. The director of the United States mint verified DeQuille's report, and Philip Diedesheimer, the man who invented the method of timbering that made the Comstock possible, estimated the probable yield at $1,500,000,000.

Ralston must have been shocked, but he didn't show it. He and Sharon had sold their shares in those mines; Sharon had been mistaken in belittling the bonanza. It is said that Sharon himself was safe, but Ralston didn't know that. He supposed that, with the partnership agreement that made either him or Sharon responsible for the other's debts, he was

... that Ralston, like most plungers,

... created unprecedented excitement in ..., in Paris, in Berlin. Sutro got another million ...lars from his Scottish bankers, and drove ahead with his tunnel.

Ralston was desperate, but Sharon convinced him that the real body of the bonanza was in the Ophir mine, and Ralston got ready to plunge. He would get control of the Ophir at any cost. Then he heard that Sutro was about to get a $2,000,000 loan from the government, and the Bank of California put William Sharon up as candidate for the United States Senate again.

Wells Fargo was minding its own business. A "Map of the Western States Showing the Express Route of Wells Fargo & Co., July, 1874," indicates principal routes from San Francisco to Salt Lake City, with a line from Salt Lake City to Virginia City, Montana, and another from Virginia City to Portland; one from about Winnemucca, Nevada, northeast to Boise City, Idaho, and still another southeast through central Nevada; another from San Francisco through Shasta, California, and north to Portland and beyond; one south through the San Joaquin Valley to Los Angeles, with a branch going up the east side of the Sierra Nevadas; still another from San Francisco along the coast to Los Angeles and then east to (probably) La Paz on the Colorado River in Arizona; and a line south from Los Angeles to San Diego and then east to Yuma.[10]

Directors of Wells Fargo at the beginning of 1874 were Lloyd Tevis, president; William G. Fargo, vice-president; Ashbel Barney, Cheney, Stanford, Haggin, Eldridge, Hopkins, and C. R. Greathouse. Greathouse resigned in December and was replaced by Mills. King was treasurer, Heron secretary, and Wood assistant secretary.

A 4 percent dividend was paid in January, and another 4 percent in July, as usual.

The number of offices was 609.

Income from express dropped a little, and charges for express-carrying dropped in proportion. Operating expenses dropped, and operating income rose to $392,000. Income from investments was $192,000, and total combined income was $584,000—slightly over that of 1873. The transfer to reserve was $184,000, which made the total in that fund $880,000.

While Wells Fargo continued to follow its logical course, events elsewhere were heading for a showdown. The tremendous wealth pouring forth from the Consolidated Virginia and the California inflamed the financial world, and speculation in Comstock mines spiraled upward at a dizzy rate, impelled, naturally, by Ralston's no-limit effort to get control of the Ophir mine. The stock had started at $60 in December, 1874, and reached $350 a share in January. At that price, the Ophir was worth about $31,000,000, while the entire available capital on the Pacific Coast for mining was about $20,000,000! Of course, Consolidated Virginia went up too—from $230 in December to $790 in January. San Francisco was mad with excitement and the frantic fever of gambling. Lucky Baldwin sold a large block of stock to Ralston and made a profit of $2,000,000. James R. Keene, Ralston's broker, bought big blocks of stock and resold them to Ralston. William Sharon bought up large blocks of Ophir stock, and then, as soon as he was elected Senator (he won it this time), he began to unload; he sold all his stock and then sold short; the price dropped precipitously, and he filled his short sales at far less than he had contracted for. (Altogether, it was said, Sharon made over a million dollars, enough to pay for his wildly extravagant senatorial campaign and leave a considerable profit.) It appears that Ralston did not know why the market had broken. The stock continued to sink lower and finally reached $50 a share; Ralston could not stop it.

San Francisco reeled under the impact of the stock-market crash. Ralston must have staggered too, for it had cost him $3,000,000 to get control of the Ophir mine—and that $3,000,000 had been squandered, for there was nothing in the mine to justify it.

Sometime in 1875, Louis McLane returned from New York, where he had gone to exercise the presidency of Wells Fargo, and was invited to come into the Bank of California, which he had helped to incorporate—but McLane declined. He might not have been able to judge between horses and steam locomotives, but he knew a losing bank when he saw one.

At the same time, the high price of gold in the East again had drawn heavily on the gold supply in

San Francisco—some $30,000,000 being shipped in the first eight months (twice that of 1874). The price of wheat was high, and some $5,000,000 was needed to move the California crop to market. This means that some $20,000,000 in gold (gold coin, of course) was lacking from San Francisco's usual supply needed to conduct business, and that fact was known to businessmen and financiers, and caused business to slow down.

Then too, the panic of 1873 was still having an effect, and, as a matter of fact, commercial failures in the United States were 50 percent more than those of 1873.

California had largely escaped the impact of the events of 1873, but the winter of 1874–1875 produced little rainfall or snow, with consequent bad effect on agriculture and mining.

Ralston kept up his personal expenditures as usual. He built a magnificent new stable and bought new blooded horses; he entertained at Belmont ever more magnificently, and spent money ever more freely. His friends could throw expensive parties in restaurants or theatres, and Ralston would pay the bill. The San Francisco *Call* and the San Francisco *Bulletin,* seeing—as any sensible man must have seen—that Ralston was on a collision course, attacked him furiously. The fury was all the more pronounced because Ralston, when he lost heavily on the Ophir stock, turned in desperation to another of his favorite projects, the Spring Valley Water Company, which he proposed to sell to the City of San Francisco for $15,500,000—a neat profit, since it could have been bought in 1874 for $6,000,000. (Ralston had cornered the stock on Spring Valley, but had had to borrow from $3,000,000 to $4,000,000 at 6 percent to do so.)

In May, 1875, the Consolidated Virginia and the California mines were producing about $1,500,000 worth of silver a month, and in May they began to distribute $300,000 a month in dividends.

The four Irishmen (Fair, Flood, Mackay, and O'Brien), having become the fourth ruling hierarchy of the Comstock, had decided to have their own bank, and in July it was almost finished. They did not seem particularly disturbed by the stock market. In fact, they were accused at times of selling their own stock to drive the price lower so they could buy up more. They also were accused (by Ralston's friends) of locking up the $5,000,000 of their cap in gold to drive down the market, and it seems th had also $1,500,000 in gold coin in the bank oı Donohoe & Kelly.

About that time, Adolph Sutro's tunnel broke through into the Savage mine, and the great project was completed. Within a short time, Sutro brought the Big Four to terms, although he relented a little and agreed to take $2 a ton for ores assaying over $40, $1 a ton for lesser ore. In no time at all, he was receiving $200,000 a month from the tunnel.

But Ralston, who had swung his weight for so long, was in trouble. Even William Sharon unloaded most of his bank stock, and the shrinkage in value of mining stocks hurt the bank immeasurably, since much of its collateral was in the form of mining stocks.

The day for the public election on the purchase of the Spring Valley Water Company was drawing near and the *Call* and the *Bulletin* attacked Ralston viciously.

Louis McLane looks mellow in his later years. From the History Room, Wells Fargo Bank.

...s entrenched behind bank-counters ... comfortable chairs. . . . His ring is pow- ...ason of wealth. It is above the law. The ...es which it yields are not of the bar-room, ...-gathering or sailors' boarding-houses. Its methods resemble Washington rather than New York. Its head is depraved. It hatches the worst designs against its own body. Its dangers smack of the villa, bank and palace rather than the back-alley and slum. For all that, its bite is more vicious than that of New York's Tweed Ring.

They accused Ralston of wanting the huge profit from the Spring Valley Water Company to buy more villas, more palaces, more Lucullan luxuries, more fast horses; they said the wheels of his chariots hurled dust into the faces of the people to blind them. They said that Spring Valley water would be more expensive than Ralston's Belmont champagne.

Ralston had only two nervous symptoms: His face turned red, and he tore up paper into long strips and dropped them on the floor. And these days he was tearing up a lot of paper. Then the Associated Press sent a dispatch to New York:

> We are afraid that a good many of the Pacific Coast dollars will be found stuffed with straw before their $5,000,000 hotel, $20,000,000 water works, $100,000,-000 railroads, and big bonanzas generally are all settled up. Some of their banks are "kites," with very long tails, and it would be well for these rich men to pause in the mad career of their fancied prosperity before adding electricity to their movements.[11]

The Oriental Bank of London seemed to lose confidence in Ralston. Then Ralston wired Washington to get a million dollars from the Sub-Treasury, but failed. The Nevada Bank was not to open until October, when their new building at Montgomery and Pine would be ready, but on August 25, James C. Flood asked Ralston for his money (that was on deposit in the Bank of California) in gold coin. It is not known how much money he had in the Bank of California, but it apparently was several hundred

A contemporary drawing of the crush around William C. Ralston's Bank of California at the time of the run. From Beebe and Clegg, "U. S. West, the Saga of Wells Fargo."

thousand dollars, and Ralston sent word that he would send Flood back to sell rum over the counter of the Auction Lunch Saloon. Flood replied that he would soon be able to sell rum over the counter of the Bank of California. Ralston saw him immediately, and said he had not enough coin to pay the withdrawal check. Flood then gave him three checks —one dated August 26, one August 27, and one August 28. The first was paid when presented; the second and third were never presented, perhaps to avoid the stigma of Flood's having closed the Bank of California. Now stocks began to drop again; Consolidated Virginia went down fifty-five points. Ophir eighteen. And the lower the stocks went, the weaker was the bank. Ralston's friends came in to trade their stocks in the bank, and he took them for real estate and other properties; other stockholders in the bank threw great blocks of stock on the market, and again, that last week in August, mining values plummeted, losing as much as $42,000,000. At that moment, word reached Ralston that the mayor would veto the Spring Valley Water Company deal. Ralston then got $750,000 from Mills, giving him his stock—a one-third interest—in the Virginia & Truckee Railroad. But that still was not enough, and on August 25, Ralston took $2,000,000 worth of bullion in a refinery that he controlled, to the United States mint to be turned into $20 gold pieces.

The next morning (August 26, 1875) a huge block of Ophir stock was thrown on the market—offered by Sharon or by the Bonanza Kings (Fair, Flood, Mackay, and O'Brien). Consolidated Virginia and Ophir began to drop, and apparently Flood and O'Brien were out to break Ralston to secure their preeminence in San Francisco's financial world.

Then at 11 o'clock, William Sharon's broker appeared with an unlimited order to sell the three stocks as long as there was a bid. The three stocks kept dropping. By noon, Consolidated Virginia was down fifty points, Ophir was down eighteen points to thirty-six. Was it a scheme to break Flood and O'Brien and establish Ralston again as the big man in the financial world? Many thought it was, that it was a fight to the death between Ralston and the Comstock Kings.

Presently it became apparent that Flood and O'Brien were taking a licking but were staying on their feet, and only then it became obvious to som[e] of them that Flood and O'Brien had not been hurt, that Ralston had been ruined, and that Sharon had lost very little.

At 2:30 that afternoon, the Bank of California was jammed, and the customers were crowded up on the street. There was a run on Ralston's bank.

The news spread through the financial district like a bombshell, and then through San Francisco, and the whole city moved toward the great gray stone building at California and Sansome. The bank was jammed with frenzied depositors trying to get their money, and nobody else could get inside, but through the windows they could see stacks of gold coins on the counters, and more trays being brought up as the tellers paid it out. People fought to get inside, they tried to climb in through the windows, they waved passbooks and slips of paper. The police arrived to keep order. Then the great bronze doors swung to, but a small iron-wicket door in the center of the bronze ones remained open; people who continued to try to fight their way in to get their money, continued to leave with gold instead of paper. The street was filled with thousands, and the great hero of San Francisco was damned and cursed. Flood and O'Brien were blamed by some, while the bank paid out the silver from Ralston's Crown Point and Belcher mines, and the $2,000,000 in coins from the refinery's bullion. A long-time depositor tried to deposit $40,000 in the bank, but could not get through the crowd—to his good fortune.

The run had started at 10 o'clock, when a large number of big checks were presented. Lucky Baldwin tried to draw his entire balance—$1,000,000—but was persuaded to accept $250,000. More big checks came in, for as much as $200,000. They were paid without a murmur, but the run did not stop; the crowd in the street increased; the bank was crowded with depositors, and by 2 o'clock, a person could hardly move. Three of his friends tried to get in to deposit, all told, $130,000, and it was then that Ralston closed the bronze doors, for he would not accept the deposits of his friends.

Closing hour was 3 o'clock, but by 2:30, the crowd outside in the street was a mob, shouting, screaming, demanding their money. At 2:35, a clerk told Ralston there was only $40,000 left in the vault. Ralston telegraphed New York, Boston, and Chi-

cago to stop payment; he ordered the doors closed; the depositors were ushered out by the police.

The directors gathered in the back room, and Ralston told them that over $1,400,000 in cash had been paid out. Then he assured everybody that Flood and O'Brien had nothing to do with it; he said there simply was not enough money in the state.

At 5 o'clock the next morning, Ralston sent his wife to her foster father, and said that they would rise again even if they had to live on a hundred dollars a month. Ralston went by the Palace Hotel, although he had long since turned over his share of it to Sharon. At the Bank of California, the street was a sea of excited faces. Windows and balconies were filled with spectators; men were on roofs, straddling gables, hanging to chimneys. The bank, of course, did not open.

Ralston executed a deed of trust, turning over everything he owned to William Sharon, and the deed was notarized. At noon, there was a meeting of the board, while newsboys called extras. The Bank of California, the bank that meant everything to California, the bank that *was* California, had failed. Ralston told the directors exactly what had happened to the bank's money. Mills and Sharon were there, and others whose wealth was well known. He owed the bank, said Ralston, some $4,000,000, Sharon $2,000,000, others $3,500,000. He had used that enormous sum of money, he reminded them, to make San Francisco the greatest city of the West. He admitted that he owed $9,000,000 but had assets of only half that much—and he presented a plan for reorganization of the bank with himself as president.

The directors were shocked, and said some harsh things. Where was the $2,000,000 worth of Comstock bullion that had been in the refinery? Where was the collateral for $1,000,000 in loan to irresponsible men? Why had the bank stock been overissued? Why was Mills's name still carried on the books? Not even Sharon, Ralston's bosom friend, tried to defend him. How could he? It mattered not that he had made them all millionaires. What really mattered was that he had used their millions and their names to put himself in a position to misuse the money of others, and he had squandered for himself and spent unwisely. No directors under the sun could have decided otherwise. The directors whispered together and then asked Ralston to leave the room.

William C. Ralston at the time of his death in 1875. From "Harper's Weekly," September 25, 1875.

Sharon offered a resolution that Ralston be asked to resign. It could not have been otherwise. Mills was appointed to deliver the request, and a few moments later Ralston, greatly shaken, signed his resignation. Ralston had lost much more than a personal fortune; he had lost the idolization of the multitudes, and that had always been dear to him; perhaps it was the only thing that had been his assurance that he was a man. And now, with the multitudes turned against him, he had nothing left. He departed from the bank; there was no horse and groom there, because they were all in Sharon's hands now. Ralston walked to the North Beach to get away from the growl of the mob. He went to the Neptune Bath House whence he was accustomed to swimming in the ocean on many afternoons, and swam out as far as he could, and did not come back.

There are those who grow indignant over the suggestion that Ralston may have committed suicide, but it is hard to understand why suicide is more reprehensible than spending other persons' money. The coroner's report[12] shows that Ralston had no water in his lungs, and this is taken to be proof that

he did not drown intentionally. However, this fact does not prove anything as to suicide, but merely that he did not die of drowning. The postmortem report says: "Immediate cause of death: asphyxia with cerebral congestion." Perhaps a compromise speculation can be offered here. It was said that Ralston was unusually flushed during the day, and it was said also that he swam out much farther than usual; therefore, it seems possible that he did go into the bay with the idea of committing suicide, but the extra exertion on top of high blood pressure killed him before he even reached a decision. The point that the insurance company paid off promptly after the postmortem examination is of doubtful validity, because most suicide clauses are effective only for a year after a policy is taken out.

San Francisco was stunned over Ralston's death. William Sharon took the partnership contract that made him equally liable with Ralston for all their activities and disposed of it. Sharon was one of the richest men in California, but the other men closest to Ralston, now blaming Sharon, avoided him. The California Theatre closed its doors for that night. Crowds surged around newspaper bulletin boards and watched the constant stream of dispatches. There were mobs in Virginia City and Gold Hill, and a National Guard detachment stayed on duty all night in Virginia City; C Street was jammed with people, and utterly impassable. The London gold exchange was in an uproar. Wall Street went into a panic. There were fears that the *Call* and the *Bulletin* would be sacked. Some were still asking: How is it possible?

They might better have asked: What has taken it so long?

The great crash of Friday, August 27, would be remembered for a long time. There were runs on other banks, but none was forced to suspend. The National Gold Bank & Trust Company paid out $1,000,000, as did the London & San Francisco Bank, Limited. There were 237 business failures that year in San Francisco, with total liabilities of $5,281,111.

It seems likely that Ralston's wife and four children did not suffer for want of money, for his wife's foster father, Colonel Fry, was wealthy.

The Bank of California was in such bad shape that the directors could not close it, for it would have ruined some of them and would have caused great difficulty in the financial world of the Pacific Coast. William Sharon started a reorganization, and subscribed $1,000,000 to replace the dissipated capital. Ralston had overissued the stock by 13,180 shares to replace Mills's stock, but had left Mills's stock in Mills's name; therefore, Mills subscribed $1,000,000; James R. Keene, Ralston's broker, $1,000,000; E. J. Baldwin, $1,000,000; and others, to a total of $7,000,000. (Only 20 percent of the total was called in.)

Sharon finally got back the 13,180 shares—some at par value—to avoid a suit that would have brought out the irregularities of the bank. Sharon settled Ralston's indebtedness to local savings banks ($4,655,000) for $1,500,000. Harpending thought Ralston was worth at least $15,000,000, and wondered where the rest had gone. It does not really seem hard to answer. Mrs. Ralston later sued Sharon for an accounting, and Sharon said there never had been anything, but offered $250,000 in full settlement, which Mrs. Ralston accepted.

With Mills as president, and with $2,000,000 in coin on hand, the Bank of California opened again on October 2 without incident. It was too important to the finances of the West to remain closed.

A few days after the Bank of California reopened, the Nevada Bank, with Louis McLane president, opened, and the stock exchanges reopened.

There was good rainfall afterward, that boded well for agriculture and mining. San Francisco recovered from the most catastrophic event in California history, and perhaps the really miraculous thing about it was the reopening of the Bank of California.

Frederick L. Lipman, who was later to be president of the Wells Fargo Nevada National Bank, in 1931, spoke of his memory of the closing of the Bank of California:

> I remember it very well; I remember the day in school the teacher told us the Bank of California failed. You can't have any idea what the Bank of California was in those days. The Bank of California was an important bank; so was ours and many of the others, but none of the banks today [1931] are of the importance of the Bank of California in those times.[13]

Wells Fargo kept a level head during that time, and its primary concession to the possibility of trou-

D. O. Mills in, perhaps, the 1850's, and later, perhaps when he became president of the reorganized Bank of California, which was too important to be allowed to go broke. From Ira Cross, "Financing an Empire."

ble was the generous display of stacks of $20 gold pieces on its counters.

In 1931, Frederick L. Lipman was asked if Wells Fargo had any financial part in developing the Comstock, since the Bank of California had major mining interests there. He was asked if perhaps Comstock mining securities represented a portion of Wells Fargo's investment, and he replied no, the bank would never put its money into such stuff as that. "Even a badly run bank wouldn't do that." However, it seems that before Lipman's time it was different (Lipman entered the bank in 1883), for the Head Minutes show that on April 9, 1875, Wells, Fargo & Company made a quitclaim deed to John C. Packard for mining property on Fintic Mining District known as the Young Lion Lode, the Desert Lode, the Montant Lode, the Left Bower, the Eureka Lode, and the Eureka Twin Lode (that is, the Eureka Mine). The quitclaim was later revoked and the mine sold to William W. Chisholm for $29,588.83.

Perhaps Wells Fargo did not indulge too much in mining investments, or perhaps it learned its lesson in time. Nevertheless, the substantial amounts entered in the annual statements under "Net Income From Investment," though conservative, may indicate some mining properties.

In January, 1875, a new federal law authorized the post office to handle merchandise at ½ cent an ounce, with lower rates for newspapers. The express companies protested, but without success. Then the railroads of the country began organizing their own express services. With the government starting to carry parcels, it might have looked like the beginning of the end, but it was not as bad as it looked, because it would be thirty-eight years before the parcel-post service would be offered.

The year 1875 was the first year of operations by the infamous bandit, Black Bart, the PO8, who was plague to Wells Fargo for eight years. In August, 1875, a stagecoach without a passenger and without a shotgun messenger was following the Russian River when a man stepped into the road and said in a deep and hollow voice: "Throw down the box!"[14]

The man was wearing a long linen duster and a floursack over his head, and had a double-barreled

A reward poster for Black Bart, signed by James B. Hume, Special Officer of Wells, Fargo & Company. From the History Room, Wells Fargo Bank.

ARREST. STAGE ROBBER.

These Circulars are for the use of Officers and Discreet Persons only.

About one o'clock P. M. on the 3d of August, 1877, the down stage between Fort Ross and Russian River, was stopped by a man in disguise, who took from Wells, Fargo & Co.'s express box about $300 in coin and a check for $205 32, on Granger's Bank, San Francisco, in favor of Fisk Bros. On one of the way-bills left with the box, the robber wrote as follows:

I've labored long and hard for bread—
For honor and for riches—
But on my corns too long you've trod,
You fine haired sons of bitches.
BLACK BART, the Poet.

Driver, give my respects to our friend, the other driver; but I really had a notion to hang my old disguise hat on his weather eye.

Respectfully
B. B.

It is believed that he went into the Town of Guernieville about daylight next morning.

About three o'clock P. M., July 25th, 1878, the down stage from Quincy, Plumas Co., to Oroville, Butte Co., was stopped by one masked man, and from Wells, Fargo & Co.'s box taken $379 coin, one diamond ring said to be worth $200, and one silver watch valued at $25. In the box, when found next day, was the following: [Fac simile.]

here I lay me down to sleep
to wait the coming morrow
perhaps success perhaps defeat
And everlasting sorrow
I've labored long and hard for bread
for honor and for riches
But on my corns too long youve trod
You fine haired sons of bitches
let come what will I'll try it on
My condition cant be worse
and if theres money in that Box
Tis munny in my purse
Black Bart
the Po8

About eight o'clock A. M. of July 30th, 1878, the down stage from La Porte to Oroville was robbed by one man, who took from express box a package of gold specimens valued at $50, silver watch No. 716,996, P. S. Bartlett, maker.

It is certain the first two of these crimes were done by the same man, and there are good reasons to believe that he did the three.

There is a liberal reward offered by the State, and Wells, Fargo & Co. for the arrest and conviction of such offenders. For particulars, see Wells, Fargo & Co.'s "Standing Reward" Posters of July 1st, 1876.

It will be seen from the above that this fellow is a character that would be remembered as a scribbler and something of a wit or wag, and would be likely to leave specimens of his handwriting on hotel registers and other public places.

If arrested, telegraph the undersigned at Sacramento. Any information thankfully received.

J. B. HUME, Special Officer Wells, Fargo & Co.

T. T. 1.

PACIFIC DIVISION
OF THE
Atlantic and Pacific Telegraph Company.

The rules of this Company require that all messages received for transmission shall be written on the message blanks of the Company, under and subject to the conditions printed thereon, which conditions have been agreed to by the sender of the following message.

LELAND STANFORD, President.
R. P. HAMMOND, General Manager.
F. L. VANDENBURGH, Gen'l Supt.
San Francisco.

114

Marysville 7 1875
Received at S F Oct 7 1875 9 A. M.
To L F Rowell
Asst Supt
Meyers is entitled to reward in both whenever payable
J B Hume

Please Answer by this Line.

A telegram from James B. Hume to settle the question of rewards payable. Hume invariably let somebody else collect the reward, and thereby received excellent cooperation from other law officials. (Leland Stanford was president of the Pacific Division of the Atlantic and Pacific Telegraph Company at that time.) The original of this telegram is in the History Room, Wells Fargo Bank.

James B. Hume considered all angles, as here when he suggested that Valentine hire a lawyer named Farley to keep him from being retained by the men arrested. This message was sent by the Western Union Telegraph Company. The original is in the History Room, Wells Fargo Bank.

estern Union Telegraph Company.

JAS. GAMBLE, General Supt., San Francisco.
WILLIAM ORTON, President, G. H. MUMFORD, Secretary, New York.

156

Plymouth Cala 16 1875
Received at San Francisco, July 16 1875 5 P M
To J J Valentine Genl Supt W F & Co
Have arrested Humphrey and Randolph workmen at mill I think it important to Employ Farley to assist prosecution & keep him from defending accused
J B Hume
24 pd P

REWARD!

WELLS, FARGO & CO'S

Express was Robbed this Morning, between Ione Valley and Galt, by two men, described as follows:

One elderly, heavy set, and sandy complexion. The other tall, slim, and dark complexion.

$200 Each and one-fourth of the Treasure recovered, will be paid for the ***arrest*** and ***conviction*** of the robbers.

JNO. J. VALENTINE, Gen. Supt.

San Francisco, May 3d, 1875.

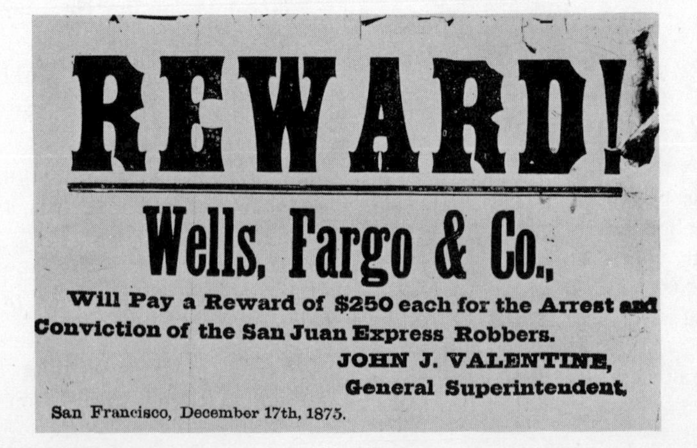

REWARD!
Wells, Fargo & Co.,
Will Pay a Reward of $250 each for the Arrest and
Conviction of the San Juan Express Robbers.
JOHN J. VALENTINE,
General Superintendent.
San Francisco, December 17th, 1875.

Reward posters distributed by Wells Fargo in 1875 usually offered about $200 and often one-fourth of the treasure recovered. An interesting point is that many of these posters are dated the day of the robbery; it rather seems that local agents may have gotten on the telegraph wires and have been authorized to offer rewards and to have posters printed. The many different type faces and styles of typography indicate that most of these posters were printed near the place of the robbery. All originals are in the History Room, Wells Fargo Bank.

shotgun pointed in the general direction of the driver. The holdup man got $300 in coin and a check on a San Francisco bank.

A search of the grounds later turned up the West's most famous bit of doggerel:

> I've labored long and hard for bread,
> For honor and for riches,
> But on my corns too long you've tred
> You fine-haired sons of bitches.[15]
> [Signed] THE PO8.

Black Bart was to rob twenty-eight stagecoaches before James Hume could finally catch up with him.

Two telegrams show the way James B. Hume worked for Wells Fargo. One is dated July 16, 1875, and was sent by the Western Union Telegraph Company to J. J. Valentine from Plymouth, Colorado: "Have arrested Humphrey and Randolph workmen at mill I think it important to employ Farley to assist prosecution to keep him from defending Answer J. B. Hume." The second was sent by the Atlantic and Pacific Telegraph Company from Marysville on October 7 to L. F. Rowell, Assistant Superintendent: "Meyers is entitled to reward on both whenever payable. J. B. Hume."[16]

There were plenty of other holdups to keep Hume busy in 1875. A reward poster dated May 3, 1875, says:

> Wells, Fargo & Co.'s Express was Robbed this Morning, between Ione Valley and Galt, by two men, described as follows: One elderly, heavy set, and sandy complexion. The other tall, slim, and dark complexion. $200 EACH and one-fourth of the Treasure recovered, will be paid for the *arrest* and *conviction* of the robbers.
> JNO. J. VALENTINE, Gen. Supt.
> San Francisco, May 3d, 1875.

In July, the price for information went up:

> $2750 REWARD. Wells, Fargo & Co.'s express box on Latrobe & Fiddletown Stage Route, was Robbed to-day, by two men, one mile from Plymouth, of $7000 in Gold. We will pay $500 EACH for Arrest and Conviction of the Robbers, and one-fourth of any portion of Treasure recovered.
> JNO. J. VALENTINE, Gen. Supt.
> San Francisco, July 5, 1875.

Ten days later the express box on "Coast Line Stage Co's Route, from Soledad, was Robbed this morning, by two men, about ten miles north of San Miguel," and $250 each was offered for arrest and conviction. Nothing was said about one fourth of the treasure; perhaps the amount was negligible.

Eleven days after that, the box on the Sonora and Milton Stage Route "was Robbed this morning, near Reynolds' Ferry, by one man, masked and armed with sixteen shooter[17] and double-barreled shotgun. We will pay $250 for Arrest and Conviction of the Robber."

On July 27, the box was robbed of $160 in gold notes by one man on the route from Sonora to Milton, "near top of the Hill, between the river and Copperopolis," and $250 and one fourth of the money recovered was offered as a reward. On August 17, a robber "stopped the Quincy Stage and demanded the Treasury Box" near the old Live Yankee Ranch about seventeen miles above Oroville. Apparently he got nothing, but Rideout, Smith & Co., Wells Fargo agents at Oroville, offered $500 reward.

In October, three men tackled the stage on the Milton and Copperopolis route, but apparently got nothing; however, Wells Fargo offered $200 each for arrest and conviction. On November 10, three men robbed the Silver City bound stage near Boise City, Idaho Territory, and $250 each, plus one fourth of the treasure recovered, was offered by William B. Morris, agent at Boise City.

On December 1, Copperopolis got back into the news when the Chinese and Copperopolis Stage was robbed by one man about two miles from Burns Ferry (Ruplee's Bridge), on the Tuolumne county side, of $600 in coin and gold dust. A reward of $300 was offered, plus one fourth of the treasure recovered. This time the robber was described: "A Mexican, lightish complexion, rather short and thick set; weight about 150 lbs.; had a moustache and short growth of beard." This poster is about 7 by 10 inches, printed the long way, and, although signed by Valentine and dated at San Francisco, it was printed by the Tuolumne Independent Press. The great variety of type faces used on these posters indicates that all were printed locally rather than in San Francisco, and also explains how it is possible for most of them to say "today" or "this morning." Probably the local agents got in touch with Hume

by telegraph to get authority for the rewards.

On December 16, an early Christmas shopper stopped the San Juan Stage near Smartsville, and the Marysville agent offered $250 reward and one quarter of the treasure recovered, in Valentine's name. On the following day, in a poster distinguished by the presence of at least seven wrong-font letters in the dateline, Wells Fargo offered $250 each for the arrest and conviction of the "San Juan Express Robbers."[18]

From the quick reaction of Wells Fargo, it appears that James B. Hume was waging a relentless war on the robbers of Wells Fargo boxes.

On March 11, 1875, F. M. Trym of New York was appointed "customhouse broker" with power of attorney to act for Wells Fargo. On October 14, Frank W. F. School was appointed customhouse broker in San Francisco with power of attorney. On the same day, Dudley Evans was appointed attorney for the state of Oregon.

Directors at the beginning of 1875 were: Lloyd Tevis, president; James Ben Ali Haggin, vice-president; William G. Fargo, Ashbel H. Barney, Benjamin P. Cheney, Leland Stanford, Mark Hopkins, Oliver Eldridge, and C. R. Greathouse; the Minutes say that Greathouse resigned in February and that Darius Ogden Mills was elected in his place. King, Heron, and Wood were secretary, treasurer, and assistant secretary, respectively.

The company paid its usual cash dividends of 4 percent in January and 4 percent in July.

The number of offices was 407, a reduction of 202 from the figure of 1874. Exactly the reason for this economy wave is not apparent.

Income from transportation charges for 1875 was $2,390,000; payment for express-carrying privileges was $1,206,000; operating expenses were $830,000, and net income was $409,000. Income from investment, $227,000; total income, $636,000. Almost $236,000 was transferred to the reserve fund, which became $1,116,000. No reduction in operating expenses is apparent; in fact, an increase is recorded in spite of the great reduction of offices; however, 1876 would show a decrease, and that would continue through 1880, which would show $1,737,000 in operating expenses.

It rather seems that 1875 was potentially the most dangerous period in Wells Fargo's history, but it seems also that Wells Fargo got through it without trouble. It may be, of course, that Wells Fargo suffered losses during that time, and that those losses suggested the closing of 202 offices.

Wells, Fargo & Company's bank at the northeast corner of California and Sansome streets after the separation of express and banking. This must have been soon after the separation (which occurred in 1876), because a horse-drawn car is seen on Sansome Street in the picture (one would not think two horses could pull a car up steep California Street), and it was in 1876 that the cable-car company, financed largely by Leland Stanford, began operations. The bank of Wells, Fargo & Company was at this location for fifteen years, 1876–1891. From the History Room, Wells Fargo Bank.

1876-1879
Bad Years for San Francisco

THE YEAR 1876 WAS NOTABLE FOR the separation of the banking and express departments. Up to that time, and for a long time after, there was actually no cashier in the banking department. Since it was not a bank but merely a department of Wells Fargo, its decisions were handled by officers of the company rather than officers of the bank. One of its important functions, aside from expedition of the express business and accommodation of customers who came to it as customers of Wells Fargo, was to hold the money made and accumulated by the express department. Up to 1876, both departments carried on in the same building at the northeast corner of California and Montgomery streets, but in 1876, the two departments were separated. It was something of an odd situation, but Wells Fargo people did not mind, because Wells Fargo was always good.

The reminiscences of Frederick L. Lipman show the position of the banking department when he says that in 1883 Henry Wadsworth was treasurer of Wells Fargo and cashier of the bank, and signed whichever title was applicable; Lipman says that there was no valid signature of anybody as cashier, but Wadsworth was a general officer of the company and had the right to sign "Wells Fargo & Co."—a right given only to the president, sometimes a vice-president, and the treasurer. When that signature was written, it was not signed "by" anybody.

The title of president, says Lipman, means the managing officer of a corporation, but the bank was not a corporation, and therefore when Homer King became "president" of the bank in 1892 it was merely a title; his authority was as treasurer of Wells Fargo.

The bank had the entire capital and surplus of Wells Fargo to deal with. In 1900, according to Lipman, the express profits amounted to over $100,000 a month, and every month the bank would get a check from the express company that it would add to its undivided profits, and by 1905, the banking offices in New York, Salt Lake City, and San Francisco had a capital of something over $16,000,000, while customers' deposits amounted to only $11,000,000. But this $16,000,000 was the capital of Wells, Fargo & Company, although it was allocated to the bank—a book entry only. At that time, the express company had only about $2,000,000 in buildings and equipment, and the rest of it was available for banking purposes.

Naturally, Wells, Fargo & Company did all its banking business with the Wells, Fargo & Company bank.

The president of the company was always a banker, says Lipman, until Valentine became president in 1892. Valentine was one of the most capable expressmen in the United States, but was not a banker.

The bank held the capital structure of Wells, Fargo & Company, and the express department

SHARES $100 EACH

No. 72

100 Shares

Arizona & New Mexico Express Company

This is to Certify that Charles H. Wells Esq. Trustee is entitled to One Hundred Shares of the Capital Stock of the ARIZONA & NEW MEXICO EXPRESS COMPANY, Transferable only in person or by Attorney on the Books of said Company at their office in the City of Cleveland, on surrender of this Certificate.

5000 SHARES.

CLEVELAND, Ohio. Jany 12th 1876

F. M. Prentiss Secy.

Henry Wells Prest.

Wm. Vick Treas.

This Certificate not valid unless Countersigned by the Treasurer.

A certificate for the Arizona & New Mexico Express Company, signed in 1876 by Henry Wells, whose picture is on the certificate. The original is in the History Room, Wells Fargo Bank.

VIRGINIA DIST. STOREY CO. NEV.

CAPITAL 10,800,000 DOLLARS.

108,000 SHARES $100 EACH

NUMBER 3069

75 SHARES

SAN FRANCISCO

This Certifies, that F. G. Berry Trustee is entitled to Seventy Five Shares of the Capital Stock of the WELLS FARGO MINING CO.

Transferable on the Books of the Company by endorsement hereon and surrender of this Certificate.

INCORPORATED JAN. 28 1875.

SECRETARY.

PRESIDENT.

The name of the company and the use of the stagecoach in the picture indicate that Wells Fargo did indeed get into the mining business in Virginia City in 1875, although the names of the directors are not familiar ones in Wells Fargo history. The original is in the History Room, Wells Fargo Bank.

Jas. B. Hume,

Special Officer W., F. & Co.

OFFICE, ROOM 28, WELLS, FARGO & CO'S BUILDING,
(Sansome and Halleck Streets,)
RESIDENCE, NO. 1466 8TH STREET,
West Oakland, near "Center Station."

The business card of James B. Hume, sometime after 1876, when the express office moved to Sansome and Halleck streets. The original is in the History Room, Wells Fargo Bank.

$800 REWARD!

IN ADDITION to the $300 offered by the Sheriff of this County,

We will pay a reward of $250 for the capture and delivery of George Little, alias Dick Fellows, alias Richard Perkins into the custody of the Sheriff of Kern county. Said Perkins, together with a Chinaman, broke jail on the night of the 9th inst., is about 5 feet 9 inches high, heavy built, short, thick neck, blue eyes auburn hair and full beard same color, has pleasing, genial face and manner, right leg was broken near ankle and was in bandages when he escaped; is under sentence of eight years for stage robbery.

A further reward of $250 will be paid for the arrest and conviction of person or persons who aided him in his escape. By order, JNO. J. VALLENTINE, Gen'l Sup't.

Office Wells, Fargo & Co., Bakersfield, Kern Co., Cal., January 11, 1876.

They really wanted Dick Fellows. (Valentine's name is misspelled.) The original is in the History Room, Wells Fargo Bank.

kept an account with the bank in which it deposited its receipts and from which it paid its expenses; then every month it sent the bank a check from that account, and the check represented undivided profits.

Gradually, as the banking business had to be carried on in conformity with stricter and stricter rules and authority, the banking business became more specialized, but Lipman believed the close connection with the express business helped keep the bank on an even keel.

In commenting on the Bank of California's involvement with mining stocks, Lipman said that Wells Fargo might have owned hotels and restaurants, but that the company did not contribute directly to the Comstock development; perhaps he should have said, "on a large scale." In this connection, an interesting document is in the possession of the History Room of the Wells Fargo Bank in San Francisco: a stock certificate of the Wells Fargo Mining Company of California, dated at San Francisco, February 3, 1876. It has in the margin: "Virginia Dist. Storey Co. Nev." and shows a four-horse stagecoach labeled W. F. Mining Co., with a lady in the front seat, another lady in the back seat, and six men on top besides the driver. The certificate indicates that the company was capitalized at $10,800,000, in shares of $100 each, and had been incorporated January 28, 1875. The incorporation papers[1] show that the company was formed to develop and sell mines located in Virginia District, to transact a general mining and selling business, and to buy and sell mining stocks for the benefits of its stockholders. The time of its existence was to be fifty years, and its incorporators were D. L. McDonald, O. R. Johnson, A. C. Taylor, H. Z. Wheeler (all of San Francisco), and George W. Hammer of Virginia City.[2]

There is no direct tie-up here except for the name, but that seems to be enough. The charter was forfeited December 13, 1905, for failure to pay license tax for the year ending June 30, 1906.

The History Room has also a certificate for 100 shares of stock in the Arizona & New Mexico Express Company, dated at Cleveland, Ohio, January 12, 1876, and signed by Henry Wells; the capital was five thousand shares at $100 each.

In Wells Fargo's separation of departments in 1876, the banking department was moved to California and Sansome, and the express department to Sansome Street near Halleck, but the bank continued to operate as a department, exactly as before.

The reorganized Bank of California continued to maintain its place as the leading bank of San Francisco. The San Francisco clearing house was organized that year to eliminate the necessity of each bank's dealing with each other bank, and at that time the leading banks of San Francisco were, in order of importance: the Bank of California, the Nevada Bank (opened in 1875), the Anglo-American Bank, Ltd., Lazard Frères, and Wells Fargo.[3] Steamer days by that time had been changed to the thirteenth and the twenty-eighth of each month. The Southern Pacific railroad was completed from San Francisco to Los Angeles, but the Texas & Pacific decided not to build between San Diego and El Paso, although it had already laid ten miles of track out of San Diego. Business slowed down, with real-estate values declining.

A great centennial exposition was held in Philadelphia, and tourist travel to California dropped off.

Although it was a period of general depression, and commodity prices were low, express rates were

the highest in history. Harlow gives some rates charged by Adams in 1876: Cincinnati to Augusta, Georgia, $4.75 per 100 pounds; to Raleigh, North Carolina, $6; to Wilmington, North Carolina, $7.

Wells Fargo was after stage robbers with all its power, for on January 11 it advertised an $800 reward for the capture of an escaped prisoner:

> In addition to the $300 offered by the Sheriff of this County, We will pay a reward of $250 for the capture and delivery of George Little, alias Dick Fellows, alias Richard Perkins, into the custody of the Sheriff of Kern county. Said Perkins, together with a Chinaman, broke jail on the night of the 9th inst., is about 5 feet 9 inches high, heavy built, short, thick neck, blue eyes, auburn hair and full beard same color, has pleasing, genial face and manner, right leg was broken near ankle and was in bandages when he escaped; is under sentence of eight years for stage robbery. A further reward of $250 will be paid for the arrest and conviction of person or persons who aided him in his escape.

It is dated at Bakersfield.

In December, 1876, the company bought some stables on Webb Street between California and Sacramento.

At the beginning of 1876, the Wells Fargo board of directors was: Tevis, president; Haggin, vice-president; William G. Fargo, A. H. Barney, Cheney, Stanford, Mills, Eldridge, and Hopkins. Heron was secretary; Wood, assistant secretary; and King, treasurer.

Wood resigned in February, and H. B. Parsons was elected in his place; King resigned in May, and Henry Wadsworth from Salt Lake City was elected in his place. King had managed Wells Fargo for several months in 1873 during Tevis' absence in Europe, but now he went into the stock-brokerage business under the name of Latham & King.

Wells Fargo paid the usual cash dividends: 4 percent in January and 4 percent in July.

The number of offices went up to 438.

In 1876, the gross earnings from transportation were $2,322,000; express-carrying debit, $1,117,000; "other operating revenue" was $54,000. Operating expenses were $793,000; net income was $460,000; income from investment, $217,000; total income, $678,000. Transferred to reserve, $278,000, for a total in that fund of $1,394,000.

Rainfall during the winter of 1876–1877 was about half as much as usual, and therefore the year got off to a bad start. Cross points out that California in 1877 had 146 banks, and believes it is amazing that more of them did not fail, because a bank could be established with as little as 10 percent of the capital stock paid in—and that not always in cash (promissory notes without security were sometimes accepted). There was no state inspection of banks, no requirements as to reserves, capitalization, or banking practices, and nothing to prevent any person who wanted to, from setting himself up as a banker.[4]

Since sometime in 1875 the Consolidated Virginia mine had been paying $1,000,000 a month in dividends, but in January, 1877, it was announced that the Consolidated Virginia would not pay its $1,000,000 dividend, and a panic took place in mining stocks. Prices crashed to the lowest recorded levels, and within three months the two leading mines had lost $140,000,000 in value. Most of those stocks were held in San Francisco, and it set off the most serious and prolonged business depression in California. During that year, there were 451 failures with liabilities of $11,736,276. Agriculture did nothing. Thousands of unemployed men hunted work, and the newspapers commented upon the appearance of tramps, a "specimen of humanity . . . new to the Pacific Coast." A great many persons were destitute; crime increased; uncontrolled crowds gathered on street corners to hear an ignorant drayman, Dennis Kearney, preach, "The Chinese must go." He organized the Workingmen's Party of California and forced the drafting of a new state constitution.

In a lighter but no less serious vein, expressmen came in for the abuse that traveling men have always received the world over, when a correspondent who signed only "M." wrote the *Expressman's Monthly* to voice a traditional complaint:

> . . . For the express benefit of farmers and residents living along the line of the various Railroads, who have grownup daughters, who fortunately or unfortunately for all concerned, have a particular hankering after train men, that a rule be adopted . . . compelling messengers to remain inside their car with closed doors during transit between stations. . . . In the last eighteen months I have purchased nine pairs of hinges for my front gate, and repainted the top board of the fence for several yards each side of it, a number of times, where it has been rubbed off by the girls waiting the

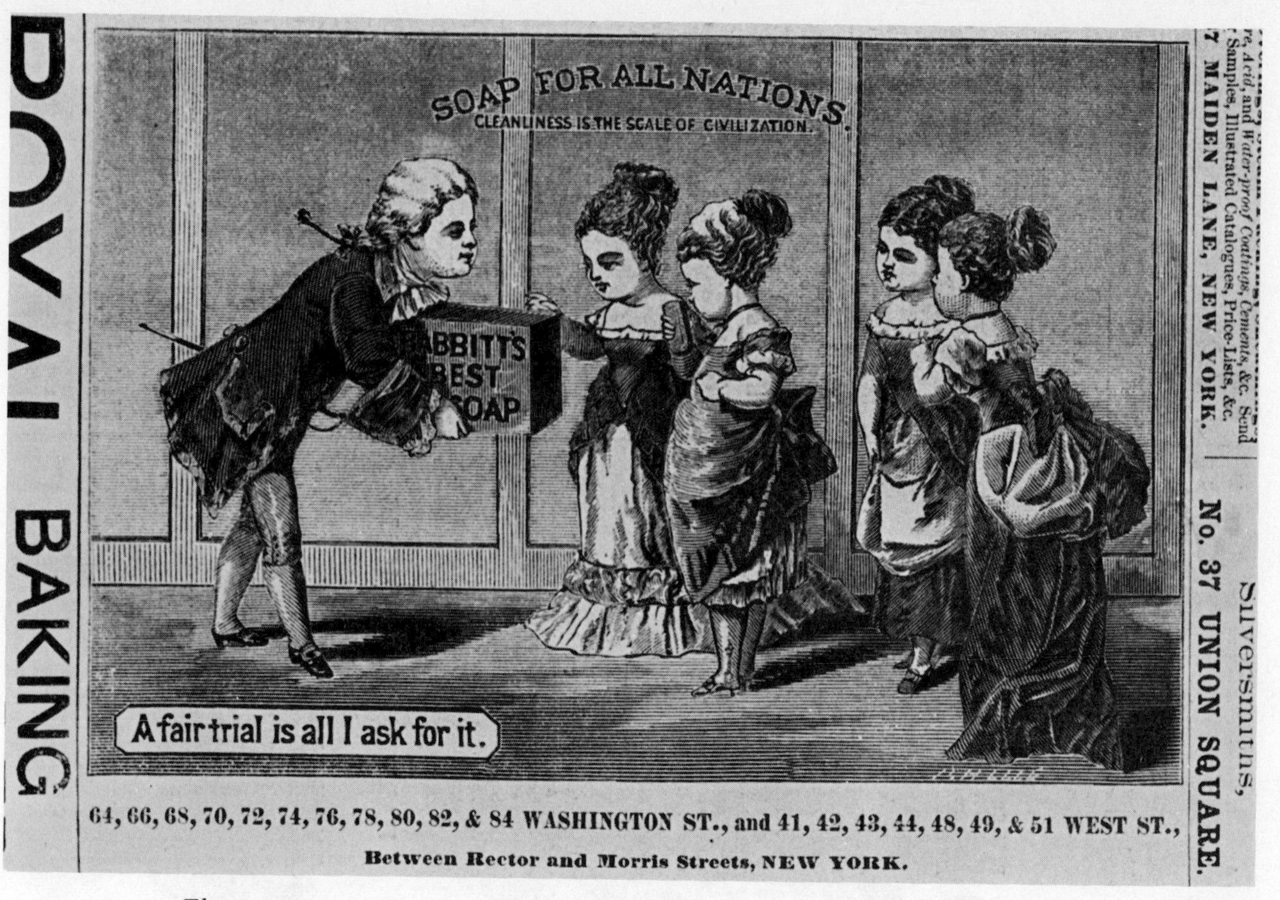

There was money in other things besides gold-mining, and in these years of panic B. T. Babbitt figured out a way to get it when he went into the soap business and became one of the biggest merchandisers of the century. His advertisement says: "Soap for all nations. Cleanliness is the scale of civilization." From "Harper's Weekly," 1878.

passage of trains; and what is worse still, I have at this time a professor engaged in teaching my seven daughters the use of the left hand, their right arms having become paralyzed from excessive use in throwing kisses to messengers.

My goodness! The writer goes on to suggest that the express companies hire females "so as to give the girls a rest from the roost, and the boys a chance to sit on the fence a while. I am not quite seventy yet, and will take my turn with the rest."[5]

Alvin Adams died in 1877, but Adams Express continued without pause.

On Wells Fargo board for 1877, Tevis continued as president, and his long-time partner, Haggin, continued as vice-president; Cheney was replaced by Charles Crocker, but otherwise the personnel of the board was the same as that of 1876.

The usual cash dividends of 4 percent were paid in January and July.

The number of offices increased to 459.

Income from transportation charges was up to $2,150,000, while payments for express-carrying privileges were down to $918,000; operating expenses were $780,000; operating income was $490,000; income from investment, $183,000. Transferred to reserve, $273,000; total in that fund, $1,666,000.

1878 was not a recovery year, partly because of the Kearney agitation and the uncertainty of a possible new state constitution. During this year, there were 532 business failures, with liabilities of $11,600,130. Banking was still catch-as-catch-can, and 1878 was one of the most discouraging periods in California banking. An old firm, Hickox & Spear, suspended in January with assets and liabilities

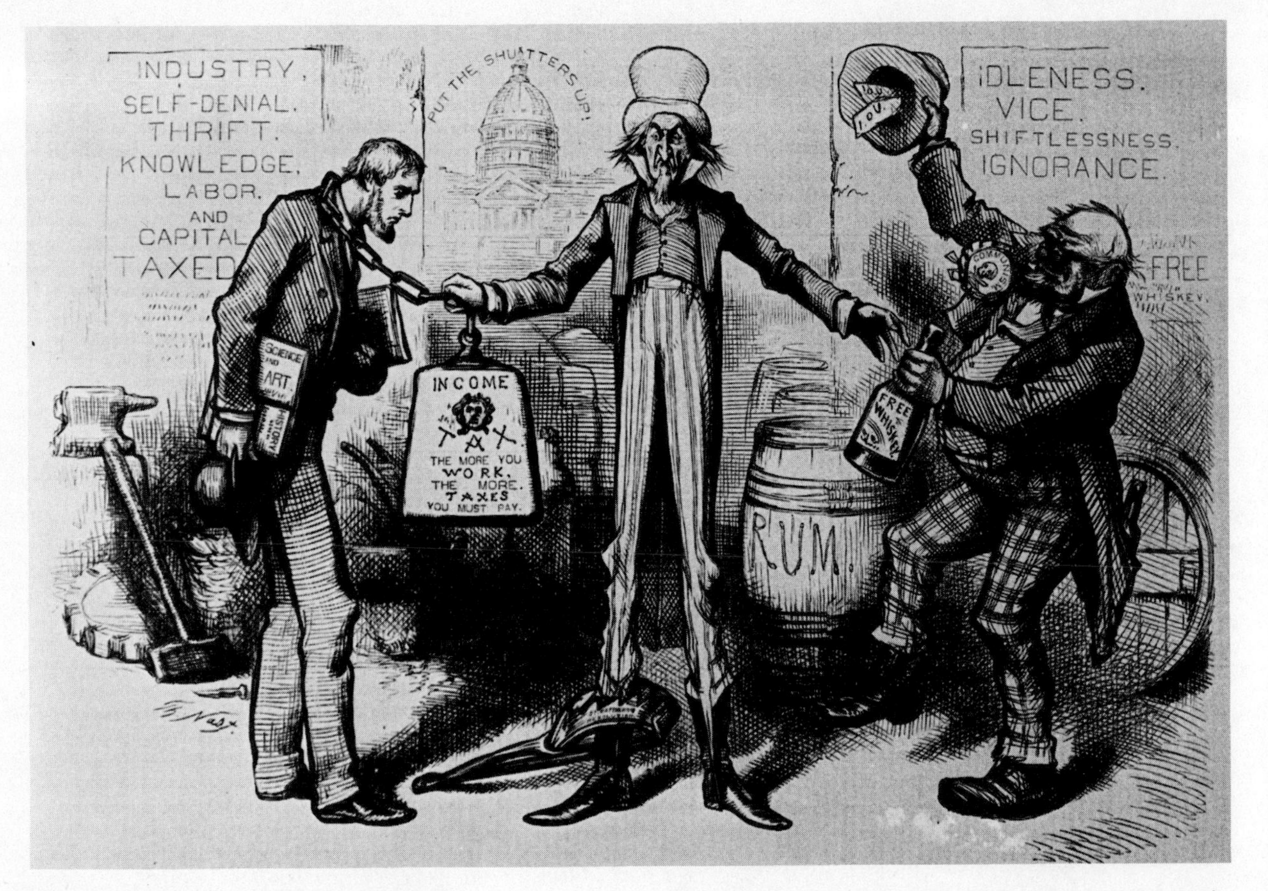

Even in 1878, they were concerned about income-taxing the worker and giving to the idle. This cartoon by Thomas Nast appeared in "Harper's Weekly," March 2, 1878. Uncle Sam has just given the man wearing a button labeled "Communism" a bottle of free whiskey, and is about to hang a millstone on the neck of science, art, and industry. The words over the national Capitol are, "Put the shutters up!" and it may be noted that Uncle Sam has his foot in a bear trap.

equal, but with inability to meet a large payment in New York without endangering its creditors. The need for banking laws was emphasized by that failure, even though the *Alta California* in 1872 had said: "[The legislature] has no more right to control or examine the affairs of a private banker than those of a private shoemaker."

The state constitutional convention started in 1878 and ran into 1879, creating uncertainty; savings banks attacked the new constitution and lost public confidence. During 1877, 1878, and 1879, eighteen San Francisco banks and four banks outside San Francisco closed, with a loss of some $3,000,000 to depositors, while at the same time the public was withdrawing its money from all savings banks and from many commercial banks. Some $8,000,000 was invested in United States bonds, much was sent to Europe for safety, some was spent on real estate and on mining stocks, and some was buried in the ground. Altogether deposits decreased nearly $15,000,000 during these two and a half years to June, 1879.

Several big banks reduced their capital stock—the Bank of California by $2,000,000, the Nevada Bank by $7,000,000. Real estate fell 20 percent in value, 50 percent in sales. Hotels suffered from lack of business, and suicides became almost epidemic, two hundred suicides occurring in San Francisco alone during those three years.

In 1878, a boy named H. G. Hanley was hired by Tevis as a messenger boy at $25 a month, and he said it took him an hour to reach the bank from his home by horse and buggy. Later, he said, they had a streetcar drawn by mules along California Street; it had to have an extra mule to go up Nob Hill, and it took twenty minutes to get up the hill. Since there were no telephones, no electric lights, no streetcars over most of his territory, a messenger boy covered a good deal of ground on foot every day.[7]

An important event of 1878 was the passage of the Bland-Allison Act to counteract the "Crime of '73"—the demonetization of silver. Western people campaigned for a return to bimetallism, and found support from inflationary elements who wanted more money to circulate to raise farm prices and industrial wages. The bill, passed over the veto of President Hayes, required the Secretary of the Treasury to buy not less than $2,000,000 and not more than $4,000,000 worth of silver a month, and to convert it into coins. The Nevada mines immediately went into full production, and soon were digging out more silver than ever before.

In 1878, the express-carrying contract with the Central Pacific Railroad expired, and Wells Fargo made a new contract with the Central Pacific and the Southern Pacific, which were substantially one and the same. The new contract had some interesting provisions:

1. Carloads only to be carried at the convenience and option of the railroad company. Presumably this meant that whenever the express company should ship in full carloads, such cars would be subject to the railroad company's facilities.
2. Free transportation privilege. That is, that personnel of the express company would not have to pay fares.
3. The railroad company agreed to use Wells Fargo's mail service.
4. Settlements were to be made on or before the tenth day of each month.
5. Wells Fargo would pay four times first-class freight rate for every ton of freight it shipped over the railroads, but if it should ship over one hundred tons, the rate would be three times first class, and if it should exceed 150 tons, the rate would be two times first class. And since Wells Fargo had the exclusive right over both roads, it could keep whatever it could charge above those costs.
6. The railroad was to allow a 10 percent reduction for carrying letters.
7. The consideration for the contract was $1,250,000 in Wells Fargo stock—$825,000 to the Central Pacific, $425,000 to the Southern Pacific.
8. The contract would last for fifteen years.

It was a highly important contract, because it put Wells Fargo on board the Southern Pacific, which was already in Los Angeles and was turning east; and it kept all other express carriers off the Central Pacific.

To pay the two railroad companies, Wells Fargo increased its capital stock to $6,250,000.

Directors for 1878 were the same as those for 1877, but Mark Hopkins died during the year and was succeeded by Charles B. Brigham.

It paid its usual 4 percent dividends in January and July, on its $5,000,000 capitalization.

The number of offices this year was 489.

In 1878, the gross income from transportation was about the same as that for 1877 ($2,113,000); express-carrying charges were $937,000; operating expenses were down a little ($751,000). Income from investment rose to $229,000; transferred to reserve, $287,000. For the first time there appeared a profit and loss adjustment debit, which is a deduction from the reserve fund, leaving the balance in that fund, $1,290,000. For some reason, the balance in the reserve fund was as of February 8, 1879, rather than as of December 31, 1878.

In 1879, the depression was still dominant in San Francisco, but perhaps was getting ready to ease up, for in that year there were more failures (772), but the liabilities were less than for 1878 ($7,967,854).

Black Bart was still robbing stagecoaches, but by this time there was $800 on his head. He had left another bit of verse—his last, and he remained faithful to his flour-sack disguise. James B. Hume finally found that Bart was a brown-haired man turning gray, with soft, slender hands, two missing front teeth, heavy eyebrows, and brilliant blue eyes; he looked, said Hume's informant, like a preacher.

Hume spread the word, and went back to his rose bushes. He knew by that time that Black Bart used no horses, that he traveled the mountain country on foot.

In November, 1879, the board of directors of Wells Fargo ratified a contract dated June 1, 1879, between the United States and three express companies (Wells Fargo, American, and United States) for the transportation of coin and bullion between San Francisco and New York; intermediate points were covered, as well as the routes between Carson City and Reno, Denver and Cheyenne, Helena and Ogden, and Boise City and Ogden. (There were United States mints at Denver and San Francisco, and there had been one at Carson City since November, 1869.)

The rates from San Francisco to New York were to be \$2.50 per \$1,000 in gold, \$10 per \$1,000 in silver; from intermediate points and for other routes, the charges would be proportional, based on distance. Between San Francisco and Boise City (presumably by stage), the charge would be \$14.50 per \$1,000 for gold bullion (1.4 percent).

In December, the amount of capital to be used in the banking department was fixed at \$5,000,000, and at about the same time, the office of the company was designated as the southerly corner of F and Holladay streets, in Denver. This does not necessarily signify a change in the general offices from San Francisco, but perhaps was done because Wells Fargo's charter was a Colorado charter.

At the beginning of the year 1879, the board of directors was made up of Tevis, president; Haggin, vice-president; Fargo, Barney, Crocker, Stanford, Mills, Eldridge, and George E. Gray. In September, Haggin resigned, and Charles F. Crocker, son of Charles Crocker, was elected in his place.

The number of offices in 1879 was 524.

The usual cash dividends of 4 percent were paid in January and July; the January dividend was \$200,000, and the July dividend, on a capital of \$6,250,000, was \$250,000.

In 1879, the gross income from transportation dropped to \$1,737,000, and express-carrying payments dropped to \$771,000; operating expenses also dropped (to \$699,000), and the operating income was \$395,000. Income from investment, \$244,000; transferred to reserve, \$89,000 (a drop of almost \$200,000), bringing the reserve to \$1,380,000.

The turbulent years of the 1870's were finally at an end, and the 1880's would be more quiet and more prosperous.

The Early 1880's

THE 1880'S WERE BETTER TIMES IN California. The great postwar depression was over, and when it was realized that the United States Treasury had accumulated a surplus of $200,000,000 in gold, public confidence was restored, and greenbacks were accepted at par value for the first time since their issuance in 1862. In California, the people still preferred gold and silver, and it was customary for a person buying a newspaper to leave pennies of change lying on the counter.

In 1880, Emperor Norton I, who had once taken issue with Wells Fargo, died, and was accorded a fitting funeral. (It was said that he once had been wealthy, but had lost his money in bank failures and had lost his reason along with it.)

During that year, President Hayes and General Sherman made a stage trip to Yreka in northern California, and it is hardly worth noting that Yreka would never be the same. One wonders how much Wells Fargo had to do with the safety of the presidential party.

In that year, Wells Fargo began to operate over the Mexican National Railway between Veracruz and Mexico City, and went into western Mexico over the Sud Pacífico de México, down the west coast through Sonora, Sinaloa, Nayarit, and Jalisco to Guadalajara. Wells Fargo initiated with Mexico a rapport that still exists.[1]

Also—and in some ways more important, because it opened up another crosscontinental route—Wells Fargo went into El Paso that year over the Santa Fé Railroad. It came in from the east via Santa Fé and Albuquerque, and for a while it went no farther west because the Santa Fé was blocked west of El Paso by the Southern Pacific. The two roads (the Santa Fé and the Southern Pacific) met at Deming, New Mexico, from which point the Santa Fé went southeast to El Paso. The Southern Pacific was sensitive about other tracks' crossing its own—especially those of a rival.

About that time, the Southern Pacific built from Nogales, Arizona, to Tepic and Guadalajara, and presumably Wells Fargo operated over that line.

In 1880, the president of Wells Fargo was authorized to start negotiations with the Santa Fé for express-carrying from Atchison, Kansas, to Kansas City, Missouri, and throughout Kansas, Colorado, and New Mexico. Wells Fargo was reaching for the big one—a run into Chicago and then to the East, bypassing the Union Pacific.

The Wells Fargo bank had many important accounts in the 1880's—not that of Haggin & Tevis (both of whom were on the board; their account was carried at the Nevada Bank). It carried the account of Scofield & Tevis (this Tevis was not Lloyd Tevis, but a relative of his in the oil business; Scofield became president of the Standard Oil Company); Wells Fargo had the Pacific Coast Oil Company, of which Scofield was president. It had a number of bankers' accounts: the First National

of Denver, the State National of El Paso, the Utah National Bank of Salt Lake City, the Washoe County Bank of Reno, the First National of Dillon, Montana, and the First National of Deadwood, South Dakota; it had the Bank of Hawaii when it was started in the 1890's.

Wells Fargo had the Henry Cowell Lime & Cement Company and other accounts of the Cowell family. The Nevada Bank had the Fuller family accounts and the Southern Pacific; the Wells Fargo Bank always handled the Wells Fargo account.

The Wells Fargo bank lost the Standard Oil account after Tevis' day (after 1892), when the Sub-Treasury notified the bank that it could no longer receive silver subject to counting. The Wells Fargo Bank also said it could not count the silver because it had many customers who deposited large amounts of silver—Wells Fargo Express was one, and Standard Oil was another. Standard Oil did not like that decision, and changed its account to the Anglo-American Bank.

In the latter 1880's, the bank loaned much to the Pacific Improvement Company (the Central Pacific Railroad)—usually $100,000 in a note—and it loaned a great deal to the wine and wheat-growing industries; it loaned to Haggin & Tevis' subsidiaries but always on good collateral.

In the 1880's, said Frederick L. Lipman, bank accounts were handled substantially as they were in the 1930's, except that loans were made in the form of overdrafts. If a company was granted a credit of $100,000, it was privileged to overdraw its account $100,000, and the charge was made each day for the amount of that day's overdraft.[2]

Notes in the 1880's read, "———% a month" instead of per annum. Around 1883, rates on individual loans of, say, $1,000 were about 1 percent a month, but not many loans were made at that rate. Most business loans were made at ¾ percent a month, sometimes less. Most borrowing was on the overdraft system.

Interest was never allowed on credit balance, and there were no savings accounts.[3]

Paper money was still not considered money in the 1880's. Greenbacks were treated like checks, and were received at face value, but all payments were made in gold coin. The paying tellers had $20 trays, and each teller had a gold shovel (?), and they all were expert at handling the $20 gold pieces. The $20 pieces were never counted; they were stacked; the teller stacked twenty of them ($400) and measured the others against that stack. If a customer came in to cash a check for $20,000, he expected to take away gold coin.

Paper money had ceased to be discounted in 1879, when the government resumed specie payment. More easterners came into California, and greenbacks were better tolerated. (Los Angeles resisted paper money longer than did San Francisco.)

Elijah Mason Cooper came out from Chicago about that time to be manager of the express department, said Eric Francis. Cooper had a long, venerable gray beard and a closely shaved upper lip and looked like a prophet from the Bible, but he was a wonderful pool and poker player, and liked wine, according to Francis, though it never affected his brain even when it made him stagger. One night Cooper got off the boat in Oakland somewhat inebriated, and a Wells Fargo porter escorted him to the train. A few days later, Cooper fired the man for interfering with his personal business. Francis said "Elijah the Tishbite" was one of the sharpest men in the business, drunk or sober, and Francis said, "He was the brains of Wells Fargo, in my opinion."

Lipman came into the bank in 1883 as a note clerk, at the age of seventeen. The note clerk attended to the bank's loans and to the collateral for them, and also handled collections and bullion. Collections were handled in a big book, where the clerk registered every item and all pertinent information; for fifty or sixty items a day, he had to spend about two hours in the book. By 1930, they were handling fifteen to twenty thousand items a day, and no item under $100 was recorded. The note clerk also took care of mining stocks that belonged to customers; the clerk registered the stock certificates and put them in a big wallet and kept them in the vault, and it was four or five years before anybody but Lipman touched that wallet. It was never checked and never audited except by Lipman.[4]

It was Lipman who introduced the Boston ledger system to the bank in the late 1880's, and since this system was important in the bank for fifty years, it merits description.

The old-fashioned system of bookkeeping involved one page for each customer, and a description of every check entered on his account. But it was discovered that the descriptions were not worth the

trouble, and those were dropped and made way for the Boston ledger. This involved a ledger arranged like a modern teacher's classbook, except that the Boston ledger is about thirty-six inches square—as far as a bookkeeper can conveniently reach. When the ledger was open, down the left side would be perhaps thirty-six names of customers. To the right would be columns, each one headed by the day of the month, and since the space for one day opposite one name was about an inch square, the bookkeeper could make a number of entries in it: debits and credits, footings (a footing is the total of the previous entries), and balance. In this way, some thirty-six customers' accounts for a period of about three months were summarized in one book. (And, as in a classbook, each name was written only once.) Likewise, the bank could prove its own books by adding and subtracting the entries down the column for a given day.

The Boston ledger's weakness appeared when the bank's business began to grow, and it took a huge force of bookkeepers to keep up with it; sometimes on Monday morning one third of a force of eighty bookkeepers would fail to appear. There was also a problem caused by the bank's increasing complexity: that of sorting checks by their destination—as, for instance, to collection, transit, clearing house, home bank, and so on. Since the boys who sorted the checks did not always know where they ought to go, there were troubles caused when the bank tried to prove its own books at the end of the day. So, before World War I, bookkeeping machines were beginning to come in that could hold totals and subtotals and transfer them to control sheets.

Wells Fargo did not make the change abruptly because of the problem of putting bookkeepers out of work, but gradually, as the bookkeepers retired, it went over to bookkeeping and posting machines, and by the late 1930's that changeover was complete. The new machines, of course, required accurate sorting, and banks then developed the batch system, which enabled the bank to prove up its own books at the end of the day against the totals of the various batches. This system, refined, is essentially still the system used by the high-speed computers of modern banking.[5]

Wyatt Earp was a shotgun messenger for Wells Fargo in Tombstone from 1879 to 1882, as was the equally great law officer Jeff Milton. A Texas ranger, Arizona ranger, chief of police in El Paso, deputy sheriff, customs inspector, and deputy United States marshal were messengers for Wells Fargo in Arizona in the 1880's.

Some of San Francisco's local color of the 1880's is related by Eric Francis, who came from Australia and worked for Wells Fargo from 1882 to 1902. He tells of delivering the summons to each director to attend a meeting of the board of directors, written in Mr. Heron's fine copperplate handwriting.[6] First he would go up on Nob Hill to the home of Governor Stanford. The butler would ask, "Who shall I say?" and Francis would answer, "A messenger from the secretary's office." Stanford would read the notice and say, "Present my compliments to Mr. Heron and tell him it will give me pleasure to attend the meeting next Wednesday afternoon at 2 p.m." He would then offer the boy a glass of wine, which was always declined.

On the day of the meeting, the boy would go into the vault and get some $10 gold pieces and give each director $10 as his attendance fee; then he would go out on the street and walk around until the meeting was over. Often Crocker, Stanford, and Huntington would pat him on the head and give him a dollar. The boy did not like being tipped because, he said, he did not want to feel like a porter at the Palace Hotel, but he was advised to take the dollar and forget it.

In the express building was Wells Fargo's famous letter department, where thirty-five ponies were kept saddled. This service was used a great deal by merchants who wanted to send a message to some other part of town; the delivery fee was twenty-five cents. According to Francis, the letter riders galloped their horses through the streets.

Wells Fargo had the finest horses in the city to pull the big express wagons; the horses were bought by the stable superintendent, Zachariah Birdsall, a hook-nosed Quaker who knew horses well.

Nor did Wells Fargo forget its Chinese friends, for it had Dane Son, who wrote letters for the Chinese and handled their correspondence, since Wells Fargo's Chinese business was heavy all over California.

Francis recalls also C. A. Klinkner, the Red Rubber Stamp Man, who anchored his donkeys and carts in front of the Wells Fargo office. His delivery boys drove the donkeys to pull small, gaudy, red-

colored two-wheeled carts, and Klinkner dyed the donkeys red, yellow, blue, green, and other colors. Whenever one of the donkeys would return after a trip, the other donkeys would greet him with penetrating brays that could be heard for blocks, and Francis thought that Klinkner encouraged that performance as a form of advertising.

The board of directors of Wells Fargo in 1880 was the same as that in 1879 except that Charles F. Crocker was vice-president in place of Haggin, who had resigned.

In 1880, John J. Valentine was general superintendent,[7] according to H. L. Stimson, and under him were S. D. Brastow and L. F. Rowell, assistant superintendents. H. B. Parsons was assistant secretary and agent in New York; H. M. Francis was cashier of the banking department in New York; and D. B. Horton was cashier of the express department in New York.

An interesting letter appears about this time in relation to the mail:

WELLS, FARGO & COMPANY.
Exchange, Banking and Express
General Superintendent's Office.
San Francisco, Sept. 1st, 1880

To Agents:

In several instances recently W. F. & Co.'s Gov't Franked Envelopes addressed to points west of Ogden, have been received by messengers from the offices sending, with the stamps not properly cancelled. Messengers are expected to correct such omissions, but that does not excuse an agent's or clerk's negligence, and we urge upon all employes the importance of carefully cancelling the Gov't stamps in all cases except on letters destined for points east of Ogden, which are to be placed in U. S. Mail.

JNO. J. VALENTINE,
Gen'l Supt.[8]

Since Wells Fargo had no express rights between Ogden and Omaha, and could ship only in sealed cars between those points, obviously letters destined for points between those two cities could not be delivered by Wells Fargo.

Cash dividends of 4 percent were paid as usual in January and in July, on the new capitalization of $6,250,000.

The number of offices at the end of the year was 561.

The income from transportation in 1880 was up a little to $1,754,000; express-carrying charges were $691,000; operating expenses were almost the same at $700,000; net income from express was $388,000, and income from investment was $262,000. Transferred to reserve, $149,000, making the total in that fund $1,529,000.

In 1881, Wells Fargo rode into Kansas City, Missouri, on the Santa Fé, and now had an eastern outlet not dependent on the Union Pacific.

The number of offices in 1881 was 714, a jump of 153.

At that time, says Bancroft, Wells Fargo had 800 offices[9] and 1,300 men, and traveled over 17,000 miles by stagecoach, 8,000 miles by rail, and 12,500 miles by sea. The goods it handled yearly amounted to $25,000,000.

In February, 1881, a contract between Wells Fargo and the Santa Fé Railroad was ratified by Wells Fargo's board, but the Minutes do not give any details at all.

During 1881, Wells Fargo obtained an express-carrying franchise from another new railroad, the Denver & Rio Grande.

In July, the mine known as El Sauce, on the ranch of the same name, in the municipality of Commander, in Baja California, was sold to the San Bruno Copper Company—another item that indicates Wells Fargo's interest in mines.

The board of directors of Wells Fargo was the same in 1881 as that in 1880 except that William G. Fargo died that year and was succeeded on the board by his younger brother, James C. Fargo.

In 1881, the company received $2,420,000 from transportation (a big jump—almost $700,000); its express-carrying charges likewise jumped (to $1,043,000—an increase of almost $350,000); presumably these two big increases were the result of the contract with the Santa Fé. Operating expenses likewise went up (to $884,000), and the total net income from express was over half a million. Income from investment was $284,000. A brand new account appears this year: surplus, to which $250,000 was allocated; this fund would receive no further allocations until 1892, the year after Lloyd Tevis' presidency. Transferred to the reserve fund, $51,000 (a drop of $99,000); total in reserve fund, $1,580,000.

The usual cash dividends of 4 percent were paid in January and July.

In 1882, came the first express money order. That form of transmitting money had been inaugurated in 1864 by the United States Post Office, and had been so successful that by 1880 more than $100,000,000 a year was being sent that way. James C. Fargo, president of American Express, told one of his employees, Marcellus F. Berry, that he wanted a money-order form that would be foolproof and not subject to being raised. A few weeks later Berry came up with the form that provided for the agent to tear off figures on the side, down to the amount for which the order was issued. It was as near proof against being raised as a man could devise, and American sold twelve hundred of them in the first six weeks, and presently they were on sale in railroad stations and drug stores. They cost five cents up to $5, and eight cents up to $10.

Black Bart got back into the news in 1882 when he held up the stagecoach from LaPorte to Oroville. Bart was standing so he was protected by the lead horses and at the same time keeping his shotgun pointed at the driver, but the Wells Fargo messenger, George Hackett, swung his shotgun to his shoulder and fired. The horses reared and plunged; Bart was thrown to one side but not hurt. Hackett fired at Bart as the coach lunged by, but Bart, unhurt, sprang up and ran into the woods.

There was, too, another train robbery of Central Pacific train No. 1 in eastern Nevada. The messenger with the Wells Fargo shipment was Aaron Y. Ross, who had been a shotgun messenger for Wells Fargo in Montana, in Nevada, and in Utah. Ross was another 6 feet, 4 inch giant, and weighed 250 pounds.

On this run, some outlaws had chased the Chinese out of the bunkhouse at Montello, a signal stop. It was early morning and most of the passengers and crew of the train were asleep, including Ross. He was awakened by a sudden stop, and a man's voice shouted: "Hop out!" while he poked a rifle muzzle through a crack in the door.

Ross was paid for defending the treasure, and he defended it. There was only $600 in gold in the box, but the principle was the same as if it had been a million. Ross refused to get out or to open the doors. The outlaws began to fire, and Ross fired back. For three hours and twenty minutes they tried to overcome Ross with hot lead; forty bullets entered the car; countless more hit around the doors. Ross was hit several times but not seriously. His left arm was wounded and he was covered with blood, but he continued to load and fire his Winchester.

Finally the outlaws forced the engineer to ram the express car with the mail car. They tried it three times but it didn't work, perhaps because the engineer did not try very hard. The west bound train, No. 2, came onto the siding, stopped, was motioned on by the engineer (with a revolver in his back). No. 2 went back onto the main line and continued west, but the conductor of No. 2 gave an alarm at the next station, and a posse came to the rescue. Hold-the-Fort Ross had held it. Ross's hand was torn by a bullet and his groin discolored by a spent ball; he wanted a day off.

In the mail car, which the outlaws had used as a battering ram, was half a million dollars in silver bullion.

At seventy-five, Ross was still a messenger for Wells Fargo, and in that year Ross escorted 342 bars of silver (about the same amount as had been in the mail car) from Oakland to New York. For honesty and for ability, the company knew a good man when it had one.

A statement made out November 30, 1882, by Steere & Colby, East Oakland, to D. B. Hinkley, gives a little information on express charges (Steere & Colby was agent for Wells Fargo): "Tr [unk]. & Valise 1.00 Pkg. 25, Trunks 1.50, Ex. Tk. from San Mateo 1.00, Ex Tk. S. F. 1.50 Valise 25." Perhaps "Ex" means extra large; at any rate, it cost $1.50 to get that trunk from San Francisco to East Oakland; a valise (suitcase) was twenty-five cents and a package was twenty-five cents.[10]

In 1882, the Wells Fargo board of directors made a contract with the Chicago, Burlington & Quincy Railroad Company under which Wells Fargo was to pay the Burlington $7,500 a month—twenty-two cents per mile per day for 1,250 miles, less two cents a mile for franked packages.[11] The Burlington during the 1870's had built a network of lines from Chicago west to Kearney, Nebraska, and a line from Denver to Cheyenne; during the 1880's it would go up to Minneapolis and St. Paul, northwest to Billings, Montana, and west to Denver. This would seem to be an important step for Wells Fargo—especially

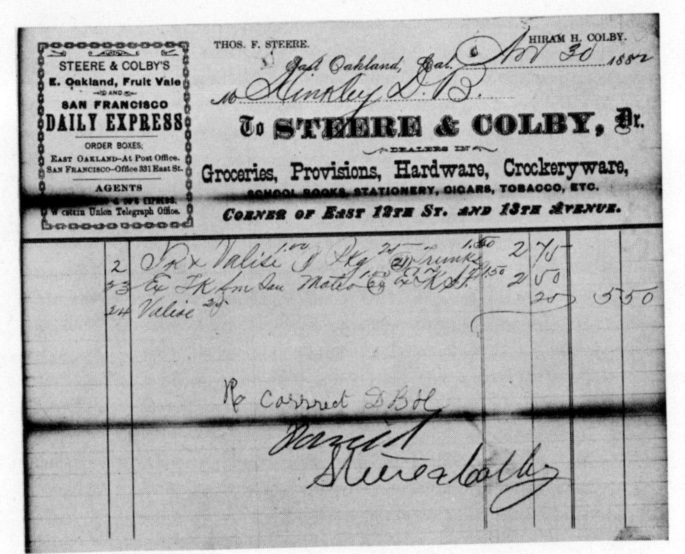
STEERE & COLBY'S
E. Oakland, Fruit Vale
AND
SAN FRANCISCO
DAILY EXPRESS
ORDER BOXES,
East Oakland—At Post Office.
San Francisco—Office 331 East St.
AGENTS
Western Union Telegraph Office.

THOS. F. STEERE. HIRAM H. COLBY.
East Oakland, Cal. Nov 30 1882
Mr Hinkley D.B.
To STEERE & COLBY, Dr.
DEALERS IN
Groceries, Provisions, Hardware, Crockeryware,
SCHOOL BOOKS, STATIONERY, CIGARS, TOBACCO, ETC.
CORNER OF EAST 12TH ST. AND 13TH AVENUE.

Steere & Colby

Steere & Colby's bill for express. This company operated the San Francisco Daily Express and acted as agents for Western Union Telegraph and Wells, Fargo & Company's Express. The original is in the History Room, Wells Fargo Bank.

since it involved no stock transfer and no percentage of earnings.

On the same day, the company ratified an agreement under which the Adams Express Company retired from the Santa Fé and from the Denver & Rio Grande Railroad. Sadly enough, the terms are not given.

In 1882, Mills left the board of directors, and the membership was: Lloyd Tevis, president; Charles F. Crocker, vice-president; Ashbel H. Barney, Leland Stanford, James C. Fargo, Benjamin P. Cheney (back again), Oliver Eldridge, Charles Crocker, and George E. Gray.

Charles F. Crocker resigned in August, and was replaced by John J. Valentine, the well-liked general superintendent. Wadsworth, Heron, and Parsons were treasurer, secretary, and assistant secretary, respectively.

The usual cash dividend of 4 percent was paid in January and July.

The number of offices was up to 927, an increase of over 200, due, no doubt, to the additional territory added along the Santa Fé and the Burlington.

In 1882, following Wells Fargo's expanding network, income from transportation charges again went up (to $3,045,000), and express charges to $1,314,000; operating expenses also went up (to $1,143,000); income from investment was $340,000. There were two transfers to the reserve fund—one in

"Alert and Faithful." "Wells, Fargo & Company's Express." "List of Offices, Agents, Correspondents, etc." for 1883. The original is in the History Room, Wells Fargo Bank.

WELLS, FARGO & COMPANY'S
EXPRESS.

LIST OF
OFFICES, AGENTS,
CORRESPONDENTS,
ETC.
PRESENTED
WITH COMPLIMENTS OF
THE COMPANY.
#2154
July 1st 1883

June of $168,000, one in December of $283,000; apparently the reserve fund was increased by a profit and loss adjustment of $297,565.60, and the total of the reserve fund at the end of the year was $2,328,000.

In 1883, according to Lipman, there were two officers in the Wells Fargo Bank, and four tellers—not a very imposing staff for a bank that conducted a rather imposing business.

In the same year, Wells Fargo rode into New Orleans with the Santa Fé Railroad, and added to its mileage.

In November, 1883, Black Bart made his last appearance on the winding road from Milton to Sonora in Calaveras County; it was the scene of his first effort and the scene of many holdups in 1875. The stage, coming from Sonora now, had $4,100 in amalgam and $500 in cash, and Bart stepped out just as he had done eight years before.

The driver was Reason McConnell, who was something of a hero in his own right. The box was fastened to the floor of the stage, and Bart, with his shotgun swinging, sent McConnell to unhitch the team and take them over the hill while he attacked the Wells Fargo box with a hatchet. Bart got the treasure, and McConnell or a young fellow with him began firing. Bart apparently was hit, and he left a handkerchief, his hat, a magnifying glass, and a case for field glasses. On the handkerchief was what came to be the West's most famous laundry mark: F.X.O.7.

Hume began to trace the laundry mark in a dozen towns, and finally located it in San Francisco on the ninety-first try in that town. They found Bart and arrested him, and to the chagrin of city detectives, they found that for years Black Bart had eaten at the same bakery with them, and had often talked to them.

Black Bart had been the plague of Wells Fargo, for he never robbed any other express company's shipment. His method of operation was so simple it was unbelievable: of course he knew when a stage carried treasure, because he talked to the drivers.

Black Bart hardly measured up to the super-criminal myth that had grown up around him. He was a rather stupid man who figured out an elementary scheme of robbing, and followed it. Perhaps he traveled on foot because he did not like horses. He probably read about the flour-sack device in a

Poor old Black Bart was finally caught. He had gotten by for years because he didn't know enough to be clever, but was finally trapped by a laundry mark. From the History Room, Wells Fargo Bank.

book. (One cannot help wondering what he did with his derby hat when he wore the flour sack.) He tried his simple routine, and got by with it. The newspapers analyzed his methods, and he studied the analyses, and continued to follow the pattern. It was so simple that it fooled Hume for eight years, for, literally, the only way to catch him was to be on hand at one of his holdups—until he left the handkerchief. As long as the pattern went smoothly, he was invincible, but when the pattern went wrong, he was in trouble. There is not even any assurance that he was prepared to shoot, for his shotgun was empty on that last holdup.

He was sent up for six years (he was then fifty-five), but was released in 1888, and disappeared. Where he went, nobody knows, although reports came in to Wells Fargo for years that Black Bart was here and there.

One of the finest descriptions of Wells Fargo services in the nineteenth century appears to be contained in a list of offices printed in 1883, that survived in the agency at Columbia in the Gold Country. The cover shows a dog sitting on a Wells Fargo express box in front of a big iron safe, surrounded by baggage and packages, and characterized by the words "Alert and Faithful."[12]

The pamphlet, of some forty-eight pages all told, is entitled "Wells, Fargo & Company's Express. List of Offices, Agents, and Correspondents, etc. To which is appended other data of public interest, including the Tariff-Graduating Table of the company." Jno. J. Valentine was general superintendent of the Express Division. Division superintendents were S. D. Brastow, San Francisco, Western Division; L. F. Rowell, San Francisco, Southwestern Division; Dudley Evans, Portland, Northern Division; E. L. Patch, Kansas City, Eastern (A. T. & S. F. and A. & P. Lines); W. J. Hancock, Council Bluffs, Eastern (C. B. & Q. and D. & R. G. Lines); C. T. Campbell, Houston, Southern Division.

Assistant superintendents were Felix Tracy, Sacramento; William Pridham, Los Angeles; F. L. Clark, Council Bluffs; Jas. H. Langtry, City of Mexico.

Route Agents: L. A. Hall, San Francisco; H. L. Tickner, San Francisco; H. R. Smith, Deming, New Mexico; M. L. Crowell, San Francisco; Eugene Shelby, Portland; L. A. Garner, Kansas City; E. B. Allen, Pueblo; J. W. Nichols, Albuquerque; C. S. Potter, Lincoln; Jno. MacCulloch, Houston.

Assistant route agents: Wm. H. Taylor, Los Angeles; J. K. Duncan, Albuquerque; Amador Andrews, Portland.

T. P. Carroll was auditor; J. S. Bunnell was assistant auditor;[13] C. W. Banks was cashier of express; and Aaron Stein was purchasing and supply agent.

Officers of the bank were shown separately: Lloyd Tevis, president (and president of Wells Fargo); H. Wadsworth, cashier (and treasurer of Wells Fargo); H. B. Parsons, agent in New York (and assistant secretary of Wells Fargo); J. E. Dooly, agent in Salt Lake City; C. C. Pendergast, agent in Virginia, Nevada; E. F. Pierce, agent in Carson City.

Principal agencies of the company were listed at Atchison, Kansas; Chihuahua, Council Bluffs, Denver, El Paso, Galveston, Guaymas, Honolulu, Houston, Kansas City, Lincoln, Los Angeles, City of Mexico, New Orleans, New York, Oakland, Ogden, Omaha, Portland, Pueblo, Sacramento, St. Joseph, Salt Lake City, San Antonio, San Francisco, San Jose, California; Seattle, Washington Territory; Sioux City, Iowa; Stockton, California; Topeka, Kansas; Tucson, Arizona Territory; and Virginia, Nevada.

Special correspondents were listed at Boston, Chicago, Cincinnati, St. Louis, Panama (probably at Chagres or Panama City); Bremen and Hamburg, Germany; Le Havre, France; Liverpool, London, Paris, Rome, and Florence.

On page 8 the advertisement says:

> Scope of country over which the service of Wells, Fargo & Co's Express extends. The company's lines, covering more than 33,000 miles, extend over railroad, steamboat, and stage routes through the United States and territories west of the Missouri & Mississippi Rivers, also, in British Columbia and Mexico, and by steamers from San Francisco, to all Pacific coast ports, Alaska and the Sandwich Islands, and, from New York, to Liverpool, London, Havre, Paris, Hamburg, and all the principal points in Europe, connections are made at eastern termini with the American, Adams, Southern, and United States Express Companies, thus reaching nearly every Hamlet, Town, and City in the United States and Canadas.

Page 10 shows the "Character of Business Transacted":

> It carries and delivers money, valuable parcels, packages, merchandise, letters, etc. Collects invoices, drafts,

notes, bills, coupons, dividends, and other paper. Fills commissions, records deeds, pays taxes for non-residents, serves legal papers, etc., etc. Reclaims baggage and other property at depots, hotels or warehouses, and redeems goods in pawn. Transfers money by telegraph, within specified points. Attends to orders for goods and household supplies, to be returned by express, etc., etc. Foreign and domestic exchange. In addition to the operations of the regularly-organized banks of the company, at New York, San Francisco, Salt Lake, Virginia, Nev., and Carson, orders for exchange are taken at all offices where there is call for it.

Page 12 lists:

Points to Consider. Quick Despatch . . . by the swiftest trains, steamers, and stages. . . . Losses or damages . . . will be promptly made good. Free Cartage and Delivery. At principal offices, and wherever the business justifies the keeping of a horse and wagon, goods are called for and delivered without cost to shipper or consignee.

Page 14 considers the advantages of sending money by express rather than by mail:

The Express vs. the Mail. Money will be saved . . . by Wells, Fargo & Co's Express instead of by mail. . . . Losses or damages will be adjusted. Low Rates. Only 25 cents is charged on any sum of money not exceeding $25—or small package [of merchandise] not over 1 lb. weight and $25 value, between any of its offices west of the Mississippi, except those in Mexico and on ocean routes. Between all points reached by the Northern Pacific Express west of Helena, Montana.

The following special rates are given on all sums [of money?] not over $300: $20 or less,—15 cents. [Various rates for different weights up to 100 pounds.] Over 100 to 125—50 cts. . . . Over $250 to $300—1.25. Special and favorable rates are made for farm products: —Fruit, vegetables, butter, eggs, etc. and for game, fish and oysters. Printed Matter.—Books, Sheet Music, Chromos, Engravings, lithograph, posters, and other matter wholly in print, sent by manufacturers, publishers or dealers . . . packages of 4 pounds or less, at 8 cents per pound.[14]

Page 16 notes that Mexico's revenue laws are of more than ordinary stringency, and that, therefore, "too much care cannot be taken to secure an accurate manifest and custom-house clearance."

Page 18 considers the "Pacific Ocean Routes" to:

Alaska, offices having been opened at Sitka, Wrangel and Harrisburg, and with the Hawaiian or Sandwich Islands, west and south, an office having been established at Honolulu, which will be followed by others at the principal towns and plantations of that flourishing group. Shipments are taken, also, at owner's risk and charges prepaid, for Auckland, Sydney, Melbourne, Yokohama, Nagasaki, Hiogo, Hongkong and Shanghai.

Page 20 deals with shipments to England and Continental Europe. However, following the explosion of 1866, "Gunpowder, acids, and other articles of a combustible or an explosive character cannot be sent." Shipments to Spain, Portugal, Africa, Japan, China, the Mediterranean coast, and South America, would be wholly at the owner's risk, and charges must be prepaid.

Page 22 gives a tariff table to foreign points; the rates are from New York, and are in gold coin. Under two pounds could go to England for seventy-five cents, to France or Germany for $1, to Rome for $2.50, to St. Petersburg or Moscow for $2.50, to Spain or India for $3.50, to Panama for $1, or to South America for $5. Up to one hundred pounds could be sent to England for $7, to France for $12 or Germany for $7.50, to Spain or India for $28, to Panama for $6, or to South America for $15. These were rates for merchandise, not for money or jewels.

On page 24 the company advertised "the transfer of money by telegraph." It said the practice was "rapidly extending, and growing in favor. In cases of sudden emergency, it offers every possible advantage for applying the pecuniary remedy at once and efficaciously. The company pays money by telegraph, between all its principal agencies, at reduced rates and with unequaled promptness." The charge was twenty-five cents for sums under $50, fifty cents up to $100, and ½ percent over $100.

On page 26 are listed some 130 offices authorized to make and pay money transfers by telegraph. These include Chihuahua, Guaymas, Hermosillo, Maricopa in Arizona Territory (probably Maricopa Wells), "Phenix," [!] Prescott, Silver City (New Mexico), Tombstone, Tucson, Tuscarora in Nevada (a booming mining town then), and Willcox in Arizona Territory.

On page 28 Wells Fargo devotes a page to its letter department, and gives a list of its San Francisco drop boxes, with their locations and hours of

service. The first pickup was at Kearny and Bush at 5:15 A. M., and by 7:20 pickups had been made at about 100 boxes out of the 113 listed. Certainly no time was wasted, for a pickup was made at Grand Central Market at 5:33, one at Battery and Washington at 5:34, one at Battery and Clay at 5:35, one at Battery and Sacramento at 5:36, one at Battery and California at 5:37, one at California and Front at 5:38, and the next at Clay and Front streets at 5:41. It is obvious that more than one man made the pickups, since there are other pickups scheduled at the same time. Another round was made between 1 and 2 o'clock, another at about 3, and four at about 7 P.M. All letters had to be enclosed in government franked envelopes, with W. F. & Co.'s frank, to be carried by express.

On page 30 the company advertises its purchasing and commission department: "Trading, etc., by express" to satisfy the public's "most peculiar wants" and avoid "the old-fashioned and inconsiderate practice of imposing upon friends and acquaintances." The company emphasized that it contemplated "no invasion of local mercantile interests," but was designed to purchase items that could not possibly be had in the home market. The charge was twenty-five cents upward for purchases under $10, 5 percent plus express charges on purchases over $10, but "quick and liberal" reductions on much larger sums.

Pages 38 and 39 give the names of offices arranged by states. It shows 433 offices in California, 16 in Colorado, 4 in Iowa, 90 in Kansas, 34 in Louisiana, 4 in Missouri, 146 in Nebraska, 48 in Nevada, 75 in Oregon, 44 in Texas, 8 in Utah, 3 in Alaska, 37 in Arizona Territory, 11 in Idaho Territory, 3 in Montana, 36 in New Mexico, 31 in Washington Territory, 1 in British Columbia, 1 in the Hawaiian Islands, 1 in Lower California, and 41 in Mexico. The total, 1,167, is in very close agreement with the figure in the Head Minutes—1,163.

On page 40 is an interesting table showing the product of precious metals in the West, as taken from the annual published estimate of the general superintendent of Wells Fargo. In 1882, California produced $14,700,000 worth of gold (most of it shipped by express), $509,000 in silver, $300,000 in ores and base bullion, for a total of $16,300,000. Nevada produced $750,000 in gold, about $10,000,000 in silver. Colorado produced $26,000,000—nearly all in silver; Arizona $9,000,000, mostly silver; Utah and Montana, each about $8,000,000, predominantly silver in both states. Idaho produced a little over $3,000,000 and New Mexico $3,667,000. The total for 1882 is $92,400,000, of which gold represents 33 percent and silver represents 54 percent.

There is also shown the production by years from 1870 to 1882. In 1870, the total was $52,000,000, and it rose steadily to $96,000,000 in 1877, then dropped but rose again to $89,000,000 in 1882. In 1870, the production of gold was valued at $34,000,000, silver $17,000,000, and lead $1,000,000. In the peak year (1877), gold was worth $45,000,000, silver $46,000,000, and lead $5,000,000. In the last year shown (1882), gold was worth $29,000,000, silver $48,000,000, lead $8,000,000, and copper, first valued in 1880, was listed at $4,000,000.

A table of distances shows that from San Francisco it was 871 miles to Salt Lake City, 1,606 miles to Denver, 2,366 miles to Chicago, and 3,278 miles to New York. It was 482 miles to Los Angeles, 650 to San Diego, and 978 to Tucson.

The Head Minutes for 1883 say: "The head office was also now located at San Francisco, California," which makes it seem that perhaps the head office was indeed at Denver for a time.

In 1875, the Northern Pacific Railroad had thrown out the United States Express Company from its line across the northern tier of states, and organized its own express company. This is the background for the notation in the Minutes that on December 11, 1882, Wells Fargo had started a suit against the Northern Pacific Railway Company. It appears that Wells Fargo won that suit and did carry express on the Northern Pacific for two years or more, but in 1886 the Supreme Court of the United States reversed the previous decision, and Wells Fargo had to leave the Northern Pacific.

In 1883, Wells Fargo's fifteen-year contract with the Southern Pacific expired, and was renewed, with the Southern Pacific to get 40 percent of the gross receipts from Wells Fargo's express operations on its lines.

The board of directors for 1883 was the same as that for 1882 except that Charles F. Crocker replaced Ashbel H. Barney. The officers were the same.

The usual 4 percent dividend was paid in January and in July.

The number of Wells Fargo offices that year increased to 1,163, as noted.

In that year, the charges for transportation brought in $3,507,000, and the express-carrying expenses were $1,518,000; operating expenses were $1,397,000; income from investment was $315,000. Transferred to reserve fund, $430,000; debited to profit and loss adjustment, $128,000, which reduced the increase in the reserve fund, leaving it, in total, $2,630,000.

A new depression began in 1884 and extended through 1885. There had been five years of farm prosperity, but overproduction in the United States and heavy competition from wheat-growing countries abroad caused prices to drop (they would not recover until 1896).

In 1884, Wells Fargo had a grand accounting over its experiences with holdup men, and it found that in the fourteen years starting in 1871 there had been 313 robberies against Wells Fargo, 34 attempted robberies, and 23 burglaries; 4 train robberies and 4 attempted train robberies. There had been 2 Wells Fargo guards killed and 6 wounded; 4 stage drivers killed and 4 wounded. There had been 16 stage robbers killed, 7 hanged by citizens. There had been 7 horses killed, and 14 stolen from teams. There had been 240 convictions—a remarkable record in those early days.

The value of treasure stolen and immediately made good to customers was $415,312.55; rewards paid totaled $73,451; prosecutions and incidental expenses cost $90,079; salaries of guards and special officers cost $326,417. Therefore, it had cost Wells Fargo for robbers attacking 8 shipments by train and 347 shipments by stage (and 23 burglaries), over the 14 years, $905,259.55—close to a million dollars. Thanks to men like Valentine, Hume and Thacker, it was a splendid record.

On January 10, 1884, the company was operating over twelve railroads: the St. Paul & Omaha; the Sioux City & Pacific; the Southern Pacific System; the Atchison, Topeka & Santa Fé; the Denver & Rio Grande; the Mexican Central; the Sonora Railroad Company; the Southern Pacific Company; the Morgan, Louisiana, Texas & New Orleans; the Galveston, Harrisburg & San Antonio; the Silver City & Deming Pacific; and the Atlantic & Pacific Company.

The huge territory covered by these roads called for a reorganization, and Wells Fargo was divided into an eastern department and a western department, with general headquarters at San Francisco. The eastern department had headquarters at Omaha, and W. J. Hancock was made general superintendent; the western department had headquarters at San Francisco, and E. N. Cooper was general superintendent. Sometime later, Valentine was made general manager of Wells, Fargo & Company, over Hancock and Cooper.

The board of directors at the beginning of 1884 was: Tevis, president; Valentine, vice-president and general manager; James Heron, secretary; George E. Gray, Bela M. Hughes (from C. O. C. & P. P. days), Charles J. Hughes, S. A. Walker, E. B. Allen, and Charles F. Crocker. It seems that considerable infighting was going on, for in February Charles J. Hughes, S. A. Walker, and E. G.[15] Allen resigned, and were replaced by Charles Crocker, Eldridge, and Stanford. Heron resigned from the board in March, and Charles Fargo of Chicago (another younger brother of William; the Fargos had seven brothers in the express business) replaced him. In July, James S. Bunnell was appointed assistant secretary in the absence of H. B. Parsons.

The usual cash dividends of 4 percent were paid in January and again in July.

The number of offices this year was 1,369.

Income from transportation was $3,684,000, while the expense of express-carrying privileges dropped to $1,511,000; operating expenses were $1,513,000; income from investment, $330,000. In 1884, $506,000 was transferred to the reserve fund, which reached $3,126,000.

The reserve fund was reaching sizable proportions.

The Late 1880's

1885 WAS A QUIET YEAR. THE DEpression did not let up. The Comstock was dead, and the mint at Carson City was closed by the government.

On November 16, after a dog-eat-dog fight between the Southern Pacific and the Santa Fé, the first Santa Fé train left San Diego, and presumably Wells Fargo was aboard. Santa Fé was really in southern California, which the Southern Pacific had tried to preserve as its private territory.

Directors of Wells Fargo were: Tevis, president; Valentine, vice-president, Stanford, Charles Crocker, James C. Fargo, Gray, Charles Fargo, Charles F. Crocker, and Oliver Eldridge.

Wadsworth, Heron, and Parsons continued to hold their jobs.

There is no figure on the number of offices.

The usual 4 percent cash dividend was paid in January and in July.

Gross income from express in 1885 was $4,007,-000, and payment for express-carrying was $1,600,-000; operating expenses were $1,711,000; net income from express was exactly $700,000; net income from investment was $284,000. Transferred to reserve fund, $484,000; debited to profit and loss adjustments, $369,000; total in the reserve fund, $3,-242,000.

Business turned up in 1886, but for some reason, Wells Fargo's income did not reflect it; it increased, but not much.

There were fifteen holdups that year, and the total lost was $2,600, most of which was recovered.

Bela M. Hughes was appointed general counsel for the company.

The directors for 1886 were the same as those for 1885, but in August, William Norris was elected to replace Charles Fargo. The officers remained the same.

The usual cash dividend of 4 percent was paid in January and in July.

Income from express-carrying in 1886 was $4,025,000; express-carrying expenses were $1,604,-000; operating expenses were $1,830,000. Net income from express dropped to $637,000, and income from investment dropped to $254,000. Transferred to reserve, $391,000; debited to profit and loss adjustment, $44,000; the reserve fund now totaled $3,589,000.

The year 1887 dawned with considerably more promise of excitement. Prices of farm products would not go up much, but the year would start a long drought that would hurt farmers and ranchers all over the West.

It was that year that somebody tried to get a world corner on wheat, and almost wrecked the Nevada Bank. The four Lords of the Comstock had not gotten along since 1881, when Louis McLane had retired and Flood had succeeded him. O'Brien had died in 1879. By 1885, the quarrels had come into the open. Fair, a strange, irascible man at best,

said that if they should not give him a larger voice, he would withdraw and organize his own bank. So in April that year, Fair and Flood sold out to Mackay, who promptly sold a quarter interest back to Flood, who became president. Flood's health was not the best, and he hired George L. Brander as cashier, while he himself went into semiretirement, and both the partners paid little attention to the bank.

In 1887, the financiers of San Francisco observed that somebody was making heavy purchases of California wheat (a bumper crop), and moving the wheat into clipper ships. It seemed obvious that someone was trying to corner the market—a gamble that might break the gambler or make him a huge fortune. There was talk that the Bank of Nevada was behind it, that the Lords of the Comstock were trying the same tactics they had used in their stock speculations. It seems also that the bank had made heavy loans in the wheat business, and owned some wheat warehouses. The purchases continued, all handled by John Rosenfeld, a broker, who would not reveal the name of his client. It was estimated later that some $21,000,000 was spent on wheat, and by early summer the price was up to $2.19 a hundred pounds (about twice its usual value).

Flood, in town one day, ran into William Alvord, the president of the Bank of California, and Alvord said the heavy borrowing of the Nevada Bank was making financiers nervous. Mackay, back in New York from Europe on the same day, learned that New York banks were overloaded with Nevada Bank paper. Mackay in New York and Flood in San Francisco were flabbergasted; the bank had a paid-up capital of $7,000,000 and was doing a profitable and safe business. Both men had large sums on deposit. They exchanged telegrams, and Flood then confronted Brander, the bank's cashier, with the facts and asked for an explanation. Brander finally admitted the truth: that he had been convinced that he could buy up 1887 wheat at low rates, hold it until prices went up, then sell at an enormous profit.

But some unforeseen factors entered in: in spite of the drought, the wheat crop had been good in California, and also in Australia, Argentina, and Europe.

It is said that Brander actually was trying to make money for the bank, but at one point he seemed on the verge of losing and taking a $400,000 loss,

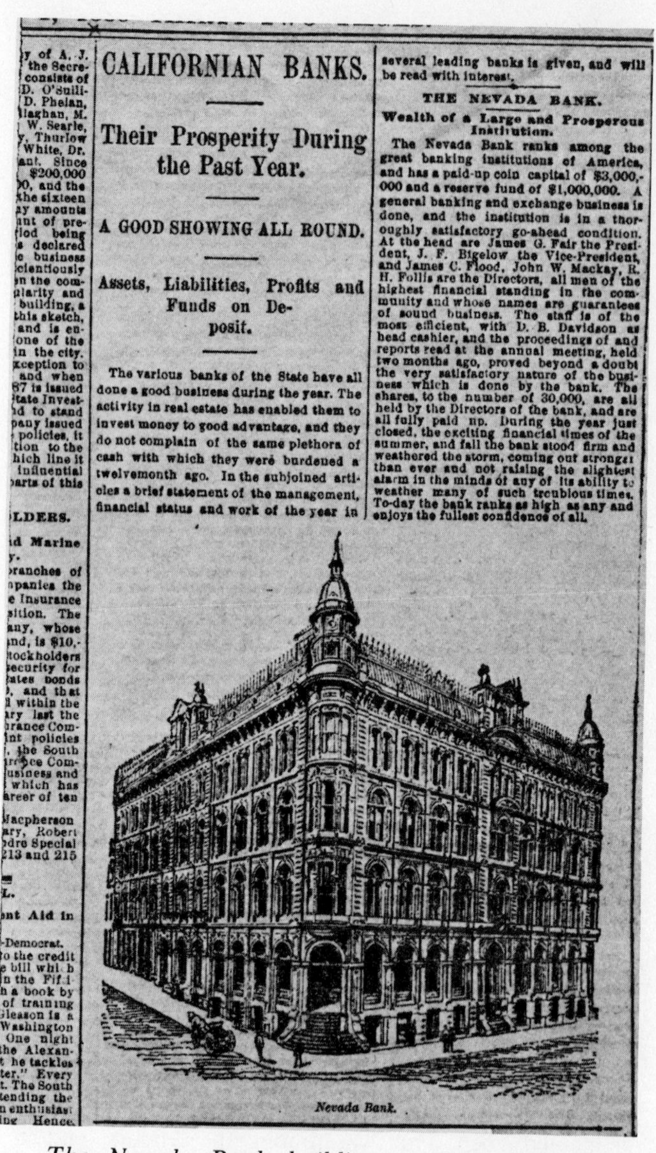

CALIFORNIAN BANKS.

Their Prosperity During the Past Year.

A GOOD SHOWING ALL ROUND.

Assets, Liabilities, Profits and Funds on Deposit.

The various banks of the State have all done a good business during the year. The activity in real estate has enabled them to invest money to good advantage, and they do not complain of the same plethora of cash with which they were burdened a twelvemonth ago. In the subjoined articles a brief statement of the management, financial status and work of the year in several leading banks is given, and will be read with interest.

THE NEVADA BANK.

Wealth of a Large and Prosperous Institution.

The Nevada Bank ranks among the great banking institutions of America, and has a paid-up coin capital of $3,000,000 and a reserve fund of $1,000,000. A general banking and exchange business is done, and the institution is in a thoroughly satisfactory go-ahead condition. At the head are James G. Fair the President, J. F. Bigelow the Vice-President, and James C. Flood, John W. Mackay, R. H. Follis are the Directors, all men of the highest financial standing in the community and whose names are guarantees of sound business. The staff is of the most efficient, with D. B. Davidson as head cashier, and the proceedings of and reports read at the annual meeting, held two months ago, proved beyond a doubt the very satisfactory nature of the business which is done by the bank. The shares, to the number of 30,000, are all held by the Directors of the bank, and are all fully paid up. During the year just closed, the exciting financial times of the summer, and fall the bank stood firm and weathered the storm, coming out stronger than ever and not raising the slightest alarm in the minds of any of its ability to weather many of such troublous times. To-day the bank ranks as high as any and enjoys the fullest confidence of all.

Nevada Bank.

The Nevada Bank building at Pine and Montgomery streets in 1888. James G. Fair was president; J. F. Bigelow, vice-president; James C. Flood, John W. Mackay, and R. H. Follis were directors. It had a paid-up coin capital of $3,000,000 and a reserve of $1,000,000. This picture, a drawing rather than a photograph, was printed in the San Francisco "Chronicle," January 1, 1888. From the History Room, Wells Fargo Bank.

Charlie Banks, a good man with a streak of larceny and a rebellion against his marriage. From Beebe and Clegg, "U. S. West, the Saga of Wells Fargo."

so he had continued to buy wheat. He exhausted the bank's funds and borrowed heavily. Mackay had a million dollars in negotiable securities in the vault for his wife, and Flood had $600,000 in government bonds for his sister. Brander used them all, and by the time Mackay reached San Francisco, the bank's assets were $368, and they could see nothing but failure. However, the Bank of California feared to see the Nevada Bank go down because of the effect of such a failure on other banks, and loaned the two men $1,000,000 on their personal notes. Other wealthy men put up more money, and the bank remained open. Fair was among the lenders, and in August he became president.

By that time, the price of wheat was down to $1.35, and the Nevada Bank liquidated as best it could, with a loss of as much as $12,000,000. Flood died two years later. Fair was succeeded by Mackay as president, since Mackay and Flood still owned most of the stock, and in 1891, the Nevada Bank was sold to Isaias W. Hellman of Los Angeles, who ten years later combined it with the Wells Fargo Bank. Mackay was a director of the Wells Fargo Nevada National Bank until he died; James L. Flood, son of James C. Flood, was a director until his death, and his son was a director.

Brander got off free, and started an insurance firm, but made false reports and fled back to Edinburgh.[1]

The second interesting event of 1887, and one that caused a great deal of embarrassment if not pain to Wells Fargo, was the defalcation of Charlie Banks.

Charles W. Banks was his full name, and he acted as cashier of the Wells Fargo Bank. In those days, as always, San Francisco was a gay and lively city, and everybody who could afford it, took part in its activities—including the officers of Wells Fargo. Among these was Charlie Banks, who had the distinction of being known as an intellectual. He was handsome, and, like many men of those days, wore a full beard; he knew the best people. He had been an aide-de-camp to General Banks during the Civil War, and was a strict disciplinarian in the bank, a good fellow outside. He belonged to the Union Club, the Bohemian Club, the San Francisco Art Association, and several scientific clubs. He had a copy of the first edition of Burton's unexpurgated *Arabian Nights* that his fellow members from the Union Club would come in to borrow. He had the only oil-immersed microscope west of the Mississippi River, which he loaned to scientific societies up and down the coast. Eric Francis said he had never met a man who had Banks's all-around ability; he could add several columns of figures faster than anybody else, and he could write in five different styles of penmanship. He was lively and quick-thinking and kept everybody around him on their toes.

He was generous with those who worked for him; Eric, at sixteen, had passes on the railroads, franks for his express matter, and Banks's ticket to the Mercantile Library. Banks collected penpoints and was fond of French gumdrops, and would send Eric down to Marron's Candy Factory on Merchant Street to buy two pounds for fifty cents. It rather seems that Eric sampled them on the way back, for he said they were the greatest he had ever tasted.

One day in early 1887, Banks told Tevis he would like to have an extra day off over the weekend to do some fishing in the Russian River, and Tevis said yes, he had been working hard; why not take three or four days?

(Eric Francis said he told him he was going to his ranch on Howell Mountain near St. Helena; that he often went up on the 4 o'clock train on Saturday afternoon, and came back Sunday evening.)

Charlie thanked him and left. At the end of the three or four days, Charlie did not appear. At the end of the week he was still gone, and Tevis put the accountants to work on his books and found that he was short as much as eighty or one hundred thousand dollars.

Tevis turned it over to Valentine, and Valentine sent for Hume and told him to find Banks fast; he thought Banks would have shaved off his beard, but Hume said that Banks was not in San Francisco, that three ships had sailed for the South Seas the day after he was to go fishing. Hume thought he had gone on the *Star of India* and would turn up in the Cook Islands or some place from which he could not be extradited. Valentine told him to keep looking in San Francisco. Three weeks went by, and Valentine threatened to send for Pinkerton. Hume told him to write two letters, without dates. One would be a letter of apology from Valentine to Hume; the other would be Hume's resignation—and Hume proposed that one of the letters be mailed within three months.

Hume turned Banks up, all right, in Rarotonga—a long way off. He had sailed on the *City of Papeete,* and the skipper identified Banks, though without the beard. A wonderful fellow, said the skipper; he gave every man $5 when they crossed the equator.

Wells Fargo was stuck, because Banks could not be extradited from Rarotonga. Unofficially, Wells Fargo offered a reward to any ship captain who would shanghai Banks and bring him back, but none did.

There were a thousand stories about Banks when the news got out, and the Sunday papers were still printing stories in the 1920's. One was that he had gone blind and had learned to read Braille. Another was that he had married 250-pound Queen Matea; another, that he was secretary to Queen Matea and had married one of her princesses. But Hungerford had the most likely answer: he found from a young man who came from Rarotonga that Banks was living there under his own name, was representative of a British trading company, and was the British consul for Rarotonga; he had regrown his beard, and he was still an inveterate reader. He wrote to some of the Wells Fargo old-timers.

The story about his marriage to the queen probably was true; also the story about his marriage to one of the princesses—marriage sometimes being a rather elastic term and supposedly more loosely constructed in the South Seas than in New England.

He was said to have speculated in stocks before his embezzlement, but there is no evidence of that. Eric Francis said his wife was "anything but congenial"—and that has led many men to make a break. It was said that he had a harem in the old Nevada Bank building at Pine and Montgomery; it was said also that he had three mistresses in different parts of town, so it is not at all likely that he isolated himself from females in Rarotonga. It rather seems that he did not get along with his wife, and that he decided to go some place where he could enjoy life without the harassing restrictions of Anglo-Saxon civilization.

How did he get away with the money? Wells Fargo did not tell, but Eric Francis said he was always asking him to save big bills—$50 and $100—and that he would give Eric change for them out of a tin box marked "Suspense."

In any event, it was a case that Wells Fargo solved but about which the company could do nothing. And the embarrassment at having one of its important men default was far more important than the loss of the money.

In September, 1887, Wells Fargo leased the first and second floors of a building at New Montgomery, Jessie, and Mission streets for ten years at $2,050 a month for five years, $2,300 a month for the next five years.

Directors were the same as for 1886, with Norris in place of Fargo; officers were the same.

The usual cash dividend of 4 percent was paid in January and in July.

Income from express in 1887 was $4,107,000; express-carrying charges were $1,613,000; operating expenses were $1,869,000. Net income increased, and income from investment was up to $296,000. Transferred to reserve, $466,000; credited to profit and loss adjustment, $141,000 (was this to cover Charlie Banks's retirement to Rarotonga?); the reserve fund now had $4,195,000.

For a number of years, railroads and shippers had been experimenting with the shipment of perishable foods. Perhaps Henry Wells had started it with his fresh oysters, and by the late 1860's apparently there were some refrigerator cars. By 1877, Swift & Company built ten special "reefers" to haul fresh meat, and a few years later Armour & Company began to ship meat under the refrigeration (ice). The South-

west, opened up to railroads in the early 1880's, needed all kinds of fresh fruits and vegetables, and Wells Fargo saw the need and reacted to it. The company persuaded the Santa Fé to fit a baggage car with refrigerators and to place such cars in service on passenger trains to assure prompt delivery. The new car went into service between Kansas City and Phoenix and Tucson sometime before April, 1888, when the Santa Fé went into Chicago. It hauled express in the form of meat, poultry, eggs, fresh refrigerator cars in red-ball freight trains, but ahead of the season and after the season fruits and vegetables were sent by fast express: strawberries from Sacramento, asparagus from New Jersey, lettuce from the San Joaquin Valley; grapefruits, dates, and figs from Southern California; carrots and a dozen other items from the Imperial Valley of California; apples, grapes, peaches, pears, and other fruits from western New York and northern Ohio, and fruits from the Northwest. The kosher markets of the East

Wells, Fargo & Company's bank on the northeast corner of California and Sansome in 1888; note the telephone wires. From the History Room, Wells Fargo Bank.

vegetables, and fresh fruit, and soon was bringing in $1,000 a trip.

The Santa Fé rigged up more refrigerator cars, and so did the Southern Pacific. The idea took like wildfire, and refrigeration was used to move oranges and lemons from California, cantaloupes from Rocky Ford, Colorado, peaches and strawberries from Arkansas. Refrigerator cars were used in freight service for many foods, but express was faster for perishable items. The railroads in general (or many of them) were not able to build refrigerator cars, but Wells Fargo was, and by 1918 it would have 175 refrigerator cars of its own—the finest ever built.

In-season shipping came to be done largely in demanded live fish from the Great Lakes, and Wells Fargo, working with the Baltimore & Ohio, got cars containing freshwater tanks and machinery for aerating the water; the fish were in perfect condition when they reached New York or Boston. Wells Fargo men iced refrigerator cars and met fishing ships in Seattle and Tacoma, advised by wireless of the ships' arrival, and then shipped the catch east to Boston and Baltimore.

Chicago, of course, was the great railroad center of the United States, and Wells Fargo wanted to be there. So did the Santa Fé Railroad. Eastern roads were building west, paralleling the Union Pacific, but the Union Pacific, now out of money, was not

able to move east from Council Bluffs and Omaha. But the Santa Fé bought a small line, built five bridges between Kansas City and Chicago, and rolled into Chicago in April, 1888, with Wells Fargo on board. Wells Fargo, at long last, had a straight chute from San Francisco to Chicago—well, not straight exactly, but certainly not subject to the whims of the Union Pacific. Wells Fargo had been a long time reaching that terminus, and it wasted no time moving on east and completing the line. It absorbed the Erie Express and entered New York City over the Erie Railroad, becoming the first transcontinental express line in the United States—all the way on its own rails, with the right to do business every mile of the way, a right it had not had over Ben Holladay's stagecoach lines or over the Union Pacific.

Wells Fargo paid the Lake Erie & Western Railroad a $500,000 cash bonus, and agreed to pay it 40 percent of the gross earnings, with a guarantee of $500,000 a year. The plant of the Erie Express Company was taken by Wells Fargo at its appraised value, and contracts and leases were assumed by Wells Fargo. The contract was over the Erie and all leased lines except the Northern Railroad of New Jersey. The Erie Express Company assigned to Wells Fargo its contract with the Chicago & Atlantic Railroad and with the Erie Railroad to give Wells Fargo the right to operate over the Cleveland, Columbus, Cincinnati & Indianapolis Railroad.

Neither Adams nor American had direct access to California, and Wells Fargo was in the driver's seat.

Wells Fargo and the Santa Fé Railroad had agreed on a new contract on November 1, 1887, and that contract was approved in May, 1888. As might be expected, the Santa Fé people were aware of the value of that exclusive franchise and were not giving it away. Gross earnings were to be divided fifty-fifty, and Wells Fargo guaranteed $160 a mile per year on the main line, $60 a mile per year on branch lines; the contract applied to all subsidiary Santa Fé lines, of which there were many, especially the Gulf, Colorado & Santa Fé lines in Texas, and the Atlantic & Pacific Railroad, Western Division (the Frisco), as long as the Santa Fé should operate it.

Other lines included were the Chicago, Kansas & Western; the California Central; the California Southern; the Chicago, Santa Fé and California; the Manhattan, Alma & Burlington; the St. Louis, Kansas City & Colorado; the Southern Kansas; and the Leavenworth, Topeka & Southwestern. Quite an imposing array of mileage, and it left Wells Fargo preeminent in the West. Within a few years, American Express would ride into Los Angeles across the deserts of Nevada in a Union Pacific baggage car—but that was another story.

On May 3, 1888, Wells Fargo was authorized to apply to the Secretary of the Treasury of the United States for designation as a common carrier under the act of 1880, and to deliver a bond to the United States for the port of New York ($500,000) and another for the port of San Francisco ($250,000).

Grover B. Simpson was appointed attorney for the company in September.

Officers and directors for 1888 were the same as those for 1887.

The usual cash dividend of 4 percent was paid in January and in July.

Sadly enough, there are no figures on the number of offices.

Gross earnings from express were $5,982,000; express-carrying expenses were $2,461,000. Income had increased $1,874,000, express-carrying charges $850,000. Operating expenses likewise went up (to $3,185,000); and the net result is that net revenue went down to $403,000 (a drop of $282,000). Net income from investment was $367,000. Transferred to reserve fund, $250,000; debited to profit and loss account, $516,000; the total of the reserve fund dropped a little (to $3,928,000).

In 1889, the railroad prosperity was in full boom, and the Carson City mint was reopened.

Lots for a new stable were bought on Folsom Street in San Francisco for $50,000.

The express company retired from Montana this year, but the Minutes give no other information. The fact is that Wells Fargo had sold its passenger and mail business to the Gilmer & Salisbury Overland Stage Company in 1869, and therefore had retained only its express and banking business, but by 1889 gold shipments had fallen off, and in that year the railroads across Montana were completed. Also, the population in Montana was still very small, and there probably was not enough business to enable Wells Fargo to operate profitably.

On November 1, the company made a new contract with the Erie Railroad and changed the guarantee of $500,000 a year to $450,000 a year until March 16, 1893.

EXPRESS WELLS, FARGO Y CIA.
Precio, 15 ctvo.
FRANCO EN LA REPUBLICA MEXICANA
Y POR TODAS LAS LINEAS DE LA COMPAÑIA
Para cartas ½ oz. á los Estados Unidos exclusivamente
Señor Manuel Ray
Forest Hill Placer county
California

An envelope bearing Wells Fargo's frank printed in Spanish: Wells, Fargo & Company, Express. Price, 15 centavos [9 of them went to Wells Fargo]. Stamped in the Mexican Republic, and [good over] all the lines of the company. Rubber stamped: For letters of ½ ounce to the United States exclusively. The cancellation is a blot, but the letter was stamped at Mazatlán and sent to Forest Hill, California. The original is at the California Historical Society.

A money order for $10 issued in March, 1889, and good through June (about three months); apparently it was not cashed. The original is in the History Room, Wells Fargo Bank.

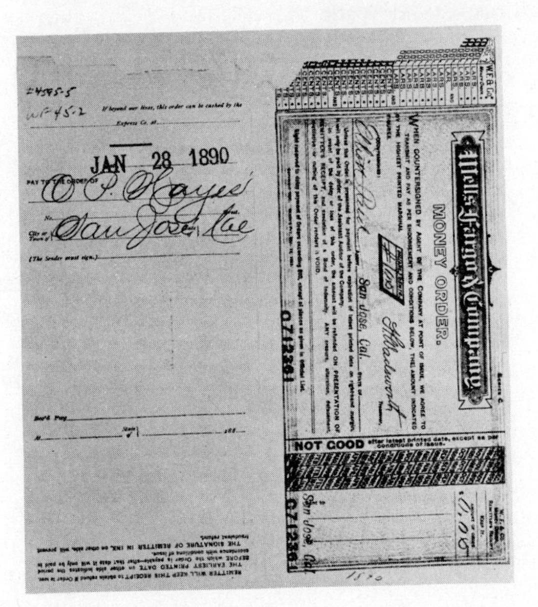
JAN 28 1890
O. P. Hayes
San Jose Cal
Wells Fargo & Company
MONEY ORDER.
NOT GOOD

Whether this was a joke is not certain—but this money order for five cents was made out in 1890, and apparently was never cashed. The original is in the History Room, Wells Fargo Bank.

If you want to send money to any point, get a WELLS, FARGO & CO'S EXPRESS Money Order. It is cheap, safe and handy, and can be bought at any office of the Company, and is payable everywhere.

If you want to forward packages, goods or valuables to the West, to Mexico or Europe, WELLS, FARGO & CO'S EXPRESS will serve you well, and at low rates.

In 1891, Wells Fargo was running this small advertisement in the "Century Magazine," showing lines from San Francisco to New York, Los Angeles to Mexico City, El Paso to Chicago, New York to New Orleans, and New Orleans to El Paso.

Wells Fargo made a contract with the Pittsburgh & Western Railway, under which Wells Fargo was to pay the P. & W. 40 percent of the gross earnings, and to advance a loan of $50,000, to be repaid without interest by March 15, 1892; the contract to start March 15, 1890. The 40 percent due the railway might be applied against the note—but not over $2,100 in any month—until the principal should be paid.

In 1889, Wells Fargo was running a small advertisement in the *Century Magazine,* in which it said:

> If you want to send money to any point, get a WELLS, FARGO & CO'S EXPRESS Money Order. It is cheap, safe and handy, and can be bought at any office of the Company, and is payable everywhere. If you want to forward packages, goods or valuables to the West, to Mexico or Europe, WELLS, FARGO & CO'S EXPRESS will serve you well, and at low rates.

A tiny map shows the North American continent in skeleton form, and lines connecting the following cities: Victoria, Portland, San Francisco, Los Angeles, El Paso, Chihuahua, Mexico City, Kansas City, Omaha, Chicago, New York, Cincinnati, St. Louis, and New Orleans.

A money order dated March 24, 1889, sent by R. Taylor at Oakwood, California, to George Dudley, shows a form substantially the same as that used by American Express: the heading is "Wells, Fargo & Company";[2] on the left margin is an arrangement for the agent to tear off the paper down to the proper amount; it can be made for any sum from one cent to $49.99.[3] It had also an arrangement of dates on the right, and had to be cashed before the latest date not torn off; in this case, it was June, 1889. If the order should be lost, the amount would be refunded on presentation of remitter's receipt and execution of a bond of indemnity. A small line at the bottom says: "Berry's Pat. Dec. 12, 1882," and four lines at the bottom give some information on the extent of Wells Fargo's operations:

> ☛ This Money Order CAN BE DEPOSITED IN BANK, and remitted by bankers, merchants or others, who may cash it, as "Exchange," payable at New York, Boston, Buffalo, Cleveland, Detroit, Cincinnati, Louisville, St. Louis, New Orleans, Chicago, Milwaukee, St. Paul, Kansas City, Omaha, Denver, Salt Lake, San Francisco and over 7000 other places.

There were some changes in the membership of the board of directors in 1889: Tevis remained president; Valentine remained vice-president and general manager; Charles Crocker had died in 1888, and W. F. Goad[4] was elected in his place; the officers were the same.

The usual cash dividend of 4 percent was paid in January and in July.

Gross earnings from express were up to $6,525,000, and expenses up to $2,851,000; operating expenses were $3,220,000; income from investment, $353,000. Transferred to reserve, $366,000; debited to profit and loss, $12,800; total in the reserve fund reached $4,281,000.

This year, for the first time, we have an official statement of the number of miles over which Wells Fargo operated. It reached the astounding total of 45,780.

The home of the bank at Sansome and Market streets from 1891 to 1905. From the History Room, Wells Fargo Bank.

The Turbulent 1890's

BANKS IN THOSE DAYS DID NOT USE present-day high powered advertising methods; in fact, they were not aggressive at all, for the theory of those days was that there was always new business to be had, and that, if one bank did not get it, another would. People opened bank accounts, said Frederick Lipman, because they had money to put away, and they would open them whether or not the bank advertised. Banking was not a matter of merchandising. Frederick Lipman said that he invented the officer's call on prospective customers, that he had to make the officers understand that when they called on a man, they did not have to ask him for business.

In those days, Wells Fargo did not make many loans on real estate; that was considered business of the savings bank, and Wells Fargo generally sent real-estate loans to them, according to Lipman.

The savings account was not characteristic of American commercial banks, but it was very popular in Europe. Some banks, like the Bank of Amsterdam, had savings accounts only, and did not pay out over the counter but only transferred money on the books. (Personal checks came after the savings account.)

Lipman said there were two types of savings accounts: one, such as is common now, was called a "Term Deposit Account," and the depositor could not draw out his money for six months, or had to give notice; the other, the "Ordinary Savings Account," did not require notice. Actually, the second type is more typical of today's savings account, which technically requires notice but in practice seldom does. Commercial banks did not start savings accounts until about 1918 or 1920.

Nor did depositors follow the officer of a bank when he went to another bank. Depositors seemed to want to do business with a certain bank, said Lipman, not necessarily with a person in that bank.

Most banks did not attempt to specialize (although, of course, banks did invariably tend to loan more heavily in certain fields). Lipman said that specialization was contrary to good banking, that a bank, then as now, needed both depositors and borrowers. Specialization, he said, was worse for a bank than for any other business.

Directors on the board, said Lipman, never represented their own institutions, but rather acted as directors of Wells Fargo. When Edward Harriman of the Southern Pacific was on the board, he did not represent the Southern Pacific Company. Mr. Bell of the American Can Company was on the board, but he did not represent the American Can Company.[1] Only when there was a very large amount of stock represented would any company have an understanding that it should be on the board. For instance, Wells Fargo Express had an agreement that it be represented on the board of the Wells Fargo Nevada National Bank, and perhaps the Southern Pacific had a contract that entitled it to representation on the board of Wells, Fargo & Company—not on the bank's board.

Perhaps the most important event of 1890 was the

President
THE NEVADA BANK, 1890-1905
WELLS FARGO NEVADA NATIONAL BANK, 1905-19
FOUNDER, UNION TRUST COMPANY, 1893

Isaias W. Hellman of Los Angeles, who took over control and management of the Nevada Bank in 1891 and the Wells Fargo Bank in 1905; he founded the Union Trust Company in 1893, and all these came together in 1923. He was president of the Wells Fargo Nevada National Bank 1905–1920, and his grandson, also named I. W. Hellman, is still on the board of directors of the Wells Fargo Bank. From the History Room, Wells Fargo Bank.

saving of the Nevada Bank by Isaias Hellman of Los Angeles. Obviously the Nevada Bank had not recovered from the devastating raid of its former cashier, and by 1890 it was in bad shape, since it lacked men who were bankers.

Isaias had been born in Bavaria, had come to Los Angeles at seventeen and gone to work in a clothing store. By the time he was forty, he was known internationally as a banker.[2] He helped organize and finance the Los Angeles City Water Company, the Main Street car line, the Pacific Electric Railway. In 1890, either the businessmen of San Francisco sought him out or he was looking for room to expand—or both. At any rate, he went to San Francisco and "undertook the rehabilitation" of the Nevada Bank. (Cross says he "saved the bank," which does not seem farfetched.) It was Hellman who would organize the Union Trust Company, who would engineer the consolidation of the Nevada National Bank with the Wells Fargo Bank. His son, Isaias W. Hellman, Jr., would be a vice-president of the Union Trust Company, would be elected president of the Wells Fargo Nevada National Bank at the death of his father, only to die one month later. I. W. Hellman III would become a vice-president of the Wells Fargo Bank & Union Trust Company.

Isaias Hellman, Sr., went into San Francisco and interested many wealthy businessmen, and set to work with his customary energy to make a bank out of the remains of the Nevada Bank. At that time, according to Frederick Lipman, there was only one real banker in the Nevada Bank (John L. Bigelow), and the reorganization would take some doing.

Wells Fargo made an agreement in 1890 for the building of stables in Jersey City, New Jersey, for $89,400.

Officers and directors were the same as those in 1889.

Total mileage over which Wells Fargo operated dropped to 39,600—for what cause is not apparent.

The usual cash dividend of 4 percent was paid in January and in July.

Gross receipts dropped slightly to $6,516,000, while express-carrying expenses dropped to $2,701,000; perhaps the retreat from Montana accounted for this and also for the fewer miles of operation. Operating expenses dropped to $3,064,000, and the result was that net operating revenue went up sharply to $837,000. Net income

from investment was $371,000. Transferred to reserve fund, $680,000; debited to profit and loss account, $59,000, and credited to the same account, $58,000; total in the reserve fund, $4,961,000.

Many banks, says Cross, incorporated in 1891—but not Wells Fargo and not the Nevada Bank.

The year 1891 was notable for the first American Express travelers' check, which had gotten its start in 1890 when James C. Fargo, who was president of American Express as well as director of Wells Fargo, made a trip to Europe and encountered difficulty in getting money on his letters of credit. When he returned, he told M. F. Berry (the same man who had designed the money-order form in 1880) to work up a foolproof check that would be negotiable. The result was the familiar express-company check of today, which the purchaser signs on purchasing and again in cashing, as identification. American Express promised to make good on any check stolen and forged, and so the travelers' check was born. About the only difference in a travelers' check then and now is that then the value was stated only in dollars, pounds sterling, francs, and lira. Currencies then were stable.

It is said that before long an American Express check was better in some countries than gold.

In that year the two most important branches of the Wells Fargo Bank turned up short, and the resulting embarrassment cost Tevis his job as president of Wells Fargo. Carson City was first. In June, E. F. Pierce, the bank's agent at Carson City, came in to confess that he was in bad shape. Lipman was sent to examine the bank and found it $150,000 short—quite a sum for a small bank. Tevis went to Carson City, and between them they got the bank in shape and sold it to the Bullion & Exchange Bank there for the amount of the deposits plus a fair sum for the bank building.

Then Tevis sent Lipman to Virginia City to look over the books there, and warned him not to take anything for granted. Prendegast, the manager, was an old and trusted employee, but Lipman was to make a careful audit. He got there on July 5, and Mr. Prendegast detained him with talk; he had known Lipman's father, who had died eighteen years before. But finally Lipman examined the balance sheet and saw that it did not balance.

It was customary for the Virginia City manager and other managers in mining country to receive mining stocks as collateral. They would enter them on a big register and send a copy to San Francisco, but it was easy to enter fictitious names of owners and fictitious stock certificates. Lipman asked Prendegast for the certificates of deposit, and, when he examined them, found that, although they were carried on the books at $15,000, they came closer to $200,000. Lipman said, "Mr. Prendegast, this thing is not right." He telegraphed Wadsworth, who was shocked, and went to work to straighten it out. Wadsworth came up to help, and they tried to sell the bank. Lipman was to be married July 25 but could not get away, so his prospective bride came to Virginia City with her sister-in-law and Lipman's brother, and they were married there. Wadsworth sold the bank to the Nevada Bank, and Isaias Hellman sent Bigelow to take charge. In taking over the deposits, said Lipman, Bigelow received nothing but $20 gold pieces.

Wells Fargo had a branch bank in New York City at that time, but it was decided not to send Lipman there to audit.[3] He was sent, however, to Salt Lake City, where the branch bank was almost as big as the home bank in San Francisco. John E. Dooly was the manager—a wealthy man, shrewd and likeable. Lipman got into Salt Lake City early in the morning, and hurried to the bank to get there before it opened, but the teller's cash had already been distributed, so he had to count that first and count the vault cash later. He found the cash $9,000 short, and the assistant cashier went out to the T. R. Jones Bank and got $9,000 in $20 bills, and wrote out a check form for it. He came in with the $9,000 under his coat while Lipman was counting the tellers' cash again, and on the final count it was all there. There was no question of defaulting, said Lipman; it was just an error. But Wells Fargo several years later sold the bank to the Walker Brothers—four Mormons who were successful at everything they touched.

There was considerable criticism and not a little apprehension among the directors over these affairs. Tevis had trusted other banking men to take care of certain things, but they had not delivered the goods. He had sent J. L. Browne, assistant cashier, to check on the branches, but Browne, says Lipman, "could not have audited a nickel-in-the-slot machine. He was a well-meaning man but not up to a mediocre clerk in ability."[4] There was no excuse for the failure of a bank president to perform, and feeling began to build up against Tevis.

In 1891, Wells Fargo bought property for stables on State Street in Chicago. W. J. Hancock, division superintendent of the eastern division, died in November.

Officers and directors for 1891 were the same as those for 1890.

In 1891, Wells Fargo's mileage was 40,437.

The usual 4 percent cash dividend was paid in January and in July.

Income from express was $6,855,000; express-carrying charges were $2,798,000; operating expenses were $3,224,000; income from investment jumped to $531,000. Transferred to reserve fund, $920,000; debited to profit and loss, $392,000 (probably to cover the defalcations); total in reserve, $5,488,000.

Wells Fargo began on August 1, 1892, to operate over the St. Louis and San Francisco Railway, but it discontinued service on the Burlington & Missouri Railroad Line in Nebraska, and it discontinued service on the Pittsburgh & Western Railroad.

E. A. Stedman was appointed general agent in February.

At a directors' meeting August 11, 1892, Tevis was voted out. Some say that Valentine forced him out—for Valentine was rigidly honest and did not like anything that smacked of irregularity. There was no reflection on Tevis' honesty, only on his carefulness. In banking, carelessness can be as bad as dishonesty.[5]

At any rate, there was a shakeup, and Tevis was out. Valentine became president of Wells Fargo in August.

Wadsworth remained treasurer, and became a director of Wells Fargo; Heron continued as secretary; Parsons, who was managing the New York bank, continued as assistant secretary.

Board members after August 11 were Valentine, Stanford, W. F. Goad (vice-president), James C. Fargo, George E. Gray, Dudley Evans[6] (in place of William Norris; Evans was elected second vice-president), Eldridge, Charles F. Crocker, and Lloyd Tevis.

The Head Minutes say the bylaws were amended in August and the capital increased from $5,000,000 to $6,250,000. However, that had been done on February 5, 1879, and there is no record of a reduction. The steady 4 percent dividends since that time had been on a capital stock of $6,250,000.

In spite of all the turmoil, the usual cash dividend of 4 percent was paid in January and in July.

Mileage operated in 1892 was 37,766.

At the end of 1892, Wells Fargo had 2,829 offices.

Gross income from express in 1892 was $7,059,000; express-carrying expenses were $2,918,000; operating expenses were $3,430,000; investment income was $424,000; and $241,141.51 was added to the surplus account. Transferred to reserve, $463,000; debited to profit and loss, $406,000; credited to profit and loss, $4,000; the reserve fund totaled $5,750,000 exactly. The surplus fund rose from $250,000, where it had been since 1881, to $491,000.

This marks the end of the statement showing the disposition of amounts transferred to the reserve fund. Exactly what was done with that fund does not appear, for no corresponding entry appears in connection with the surplus fund or any other.

The year 1893 was notable for a number of events, but perhaps the most important one was the panic that struck about the middle of the year. The big firm of Baring Brothers in London had failed in 1890, and the feeling of panic had spread over Europe and the United States.

The panic caused British investors to sell American securities and drain gold from the United States. At the same time, United States revenue dropped because of the McKinley Tariff Act, and expenditures increased because of the pension grants of the Harrison administration. The gold reserve dropped to $100,000,000 in April. Investors and speculators began to liquidate. Depositors doubted the solvency of the national government and of the banks, and began to demand their funds in gold. On May 5, the selling fever hit the New York Stock Exchange, and the stock market started down, crashing on June 27. Banks were closing; big stores, factories, and mines closed down. Unemployment was widespread when the bottom dropped out of the market on June 27.

President Cleveland called a special session of Congress to repeal the Sherman Silver Purchase Act and halt the depletion of the gold reserve (which dropped to $80,000,000 by the end of the year). The effect of the repeal was disastrous in western mining areas, and undoubtedly had a strong impact on Wells Fargo.

However, Wells Fargo men had seen the whole thing coming and had protected themselves. One big

borrower in the East, said Lipman, owed Wells Fargo $700,000, and sent word that it hoped Wells Fargo would not call in that loan. The bank said it would accept $150,000 and not bother the borrower. The $150,000 was paid, and Wells Fargo kept its word.

The panic ceased in August, but it would be several years before the country would fully recover. A total of 15,242 business firms failed, with losses of almost $350,000,000, and 642 banks closed their doors, with liabilities of $211,000,000; 81 of those banks were on the Pacific Coast.

Lipman said the Wells Fargo Bank had no particular trouble in 1893, but he recalled that he went to a bank in Tacoma that owed Wells Fargo, and asked for more security. He put some money on the train by express, and took the same train to see if the bank could offer some security.

I stood outside in the lobby, looking across the street, and I saw a bank die—actually saw it. [It was not the one he had come to visit.] There was a queue in front of it there, and at a certain time of day they pulled down their shades, stopped the people that were there from coming in. The bank never opened again. Well, they [the other bank] had to give me the securities I insisted upon or I wouldn't give them the money. I gave them the money, but you can imagine the situation this bank was in when I loaned them any money. They owed us already.

On that trip, I had a bank in Seattle that also owed us money. It wasn't asking us for any more money, but I was asking for better security. I got the security, and the loan was entirely collected sometime later.

I went over to Spokane, got there on Saturday. I went to the bank, and they suggested that I come after 12 o'clock; they were too busy. So I did. They owed some money. I got some more security then—and we never collected except on the new security I got. After talking to them on Saturday afternoon, I took the train back. The bank never opened its doors again. That was another case—I was there on Saturday morning before the bank closed; I was there Saturday afternoon after they closed; and when Monday morning came, they did not re-open.

We had a bank in Fresno, and the president said to me, "If you will send the money down to us, we will just keep it, and if we can't stay open, we will ship that money back to you before we close." We lent them the money, and they didn't close.

Isaias Hellman had complained about the overdraft system of loaning money since he had come to San Francisco. It was a way of making loans, as explained by Frederick Lipman. The customer would apply for permission to overdraw up to a certain amount, and his overdraft was figured each day and he was charged for it at the rate agreed upon beforehand. Adolph Sutro, early in 1893, was borrowing on the overdraft system and paying 6 percent a year —a very low rate, said Lipman. The overdraft system was bad in many ways: It got the customer into bad habits; it fostered the idea that if the customer wanted to overdraw, the bank was honor bound to pay his checks.

During the panic of 1893, Hellman proposed to Thomas Brown, head of the Bank of California, that they drop the custom, and all San Francisco bankers got together and made a clearing-house agreement to stop it, and all lived up to the agreement.

Victor Rossetti in 1893 went to the Wells Fargo Bank to ask Homer King for a job. He was well recommended and was hired, then discovered that the pay was only $20 a month. "I was very disappointed," he said, "but the prospects looked good, and I stayed. The previous office boy had been fired because he could not copy letters without blurring them. In those days, we used a wet cloth in making copies, and unless it was done carefully, the copies would smear. There was no carbon paper, of course. I stayed, working in every department and on every ledger they had. And in 1905 I was elected to the first official position—assistant cashier."[7]

James J. Corbett ("Gentleman Jim," the prizefighter) worked as a teller at the Nevada Bank from 1893 to 1897—not at the Wells Fargo bank as sometimes reported.

In the fall of 1893, Wells Fargo made a new contract with the Southern Pacific for all lines of the S. P. system and the San Antonio & Aransas Pass (which was not at that moment a part of the system, but would be later). It was an expensive contract for Wells Fargo, for the company agreed to pay the Southern Pacific $1,750,000 in stock, and 40 percent of the gross earnings. (Earlier that year the company had renewed its fifty-fifty contract with the Santa Fé. Those were hefty percentages, and they reduced Wells Fargo's net profit for a few years.)

In this year, the Commercial National Bank of

Portland suggested that Wells Fargo buy it and make it a branch bank. The Commercial National had been hurt by the panic, but, of course, Wells Fargo had not, so Homer King sent Lipman to Portland to look it over. Lipman was a banker, but he had not learned that good faith could be ruined by bad judgment, so he recommended the purchase. Homer King went up to look it over, and he too thought it was a good buy. Wells Fargo bought it, but it turned out badly, and Valentine was so annoyed about it that he put an inferior manager in it and ran the bank his own way, and, says Lipman, thus ran into a heavy loss on the bank. The man he sent to act as assistant cashier was Harry Hanley, and Valentine said there was nothing wrong with Hanley except that he was not big enough for the job. The entire project eventually cost Wells Fargo $300,000.

In that year Mike Tovey, one of Wells Fargo's legendary express messengers, who never had lost a treasure box, was killed from behind by a highwayman who got away with nothing.

Isaias Hellman had been interested in the trust end of banking, and in 1893, two months after he took over the Nevada Bank, he established the Union Trust Company of San Francisco, the first real trust company in that town. It opened for business April 3, 1893, and by January 1, 1895, had $1,520,604 worth of trust accounts. Isaias W. Hellman, Sr., was president of the Union Trust Company at its organization, C. de Guigne was vice-president, and S. P. Young was cashier. Its directors were Hellman, Louis Gerstle, Henry F. Allen, C. de Guigne, Robert Watt, Henry L. Dodge, A. Borel, John D. Spreckels, Homer S. King, George T. Marye, and James L. Flood—many familiar names. Isaias W. Hellman, Jr., became cashier in 1895, vice-president in 1903, and succeeded his father as president in 1916; he served until his death in 1920, and was succeeded by Charles J. Deering. These antecedents are important in the history of Wells Fargo because in 1924 the two companies were consolidated. (By that time, of course, Wells Fargo would be the Wells Fargo Nevada National Bank, and so the Hellmans would come into strong control of the Wells Fargo name.)

The contract with the Southern Pacific was made on October 9, according to the Head Minutes, and in addition to 40 percent of the gross earnings, Wells Fargo paid $725,000 in cash and $1,750,000 in stock, divided as follows: Southern Pacific, 16,625 shares and $688,750 cash; San Antonio & Aransas Pass Railway, 875 shares and $36,250 cash. Operations under this contract did not begin until December 10.

Wells Fargo also began operations on the Colorado Midland Railway in 1893, replacing the Denver & Rio Grande Express Company.

The Santa Fé contract, according to the Minutes, was not a simple renewal, for Wells Fargo raised the percentage of gross earnings to fifty-five, and guaranteed $1,450,000 (the Minutes do not say whether the guarantee was a cash payment as it had been previously).

Wells Fargo vacated the Missouri Valley Lines—which included the Sioux City & Pacific, the Fremont, Elkhorn & Missouri Valley, the Chicago, St. Paul, Minneapolis & Omaha, and the Black Hills & Fort Pierre—on June 1, and relinquished them to the American Express Company.

The Minutes for 1895 say that the bylaws were revised on August 8, 1893, but apparently the revision was not approved by the stockholders until sometime between January 15 and July 16, 1894, for the dividend rate changed between those dates. The new dividend rates indicate that the capitalization was increased from $6,250,000 to $8,000,000 to take care of the stock paid to the Southern Pacific. However, the two dividends in 1893 were paid as usual in January and July, 4 percent each, for a total of $500,000.

In 1893, there was a considerable shakeup in the board of directors. The starting members were Tevis, Valentine, Stanford, Goad, Fargo, Gray, Evans, Eldridge, and Charles F. Crocker. Stanford died in June, and the old expressman and railroad man, Benjamin P. Cheney, was elected in his place.[8] On August 10, Tevis resigned under pressure (primarily from Valentine), and Henry Huntington was elected; Goad resigned, and Homer S. King was elected; James C. Fargo resigned, and John J. McCook was elected.

At the shakeup in August, Gray was elected vice-president in place of Goad, whose election to that office had not been noted; Homer S. King was elected treasurer in place of Wadsworth; Valentine continued as president (he had held that office for a year), and Evans continued as second vice-president.

Homer S. King was called in to be treasurer of the company and manager of the bank. He spoke of himself as president of the bank, says Lipman, who

Homer S. King, who managed the bank for a number of years and who finally was nominal president 1902–1905 while he was treasurer of Wells, Fargo & Company. In January, 1905, he went to the Bank of California and set off rumors of the sale of the Wells Fargo bank to Isaias W. Hellman. He was succeeded by Frederick L. Lipman (acting for Wells Fargo), until the opening of the Wells Fargo Nevada National, April 22, 1905. From the History Room, Wells Fargo Bank.

Lloyd Tevis in later years, with a fuller beard. The only complaint against him was that he relaxed banking practices too much.

points out again that there was no president of the bank, since the bank itself was only a department of the company.

Wells Fargo was operating over 36,171 miles at the end of 1893, a considerable reduction from the high point of 45,780 in 1889.

Gross receipts for 1893 were $6,984,000, a slight decline; but express-carrying privileges were up to $3,221,000, an increase of over $300,000; "other operating revenue" was $92,000; operating expenses were up a little to $3,487,000; net income from investment was $416,000. The surplus account increased to $660,000. No more figures are available on the reserve fund.

In 1894, the panic continued, but there is little personal record of Wells Fargo for that year.

The directors were Valentine, president; Gray, vice-president; Evans, second vice-president; Cheney, Huntington, McCook, Eldridge, and Charles F. Crocker. Evans resigned as director in September, and Aaron Stein was elected; Crocker resigned, and

John J. Valentine, long-time general agent for Wells Fargo, who, some said, worked to get Lloyd Tevis out of the presidency in 1892. Valentine became president of Wells Fargo, and was an excellent expressman but not a good banker, said Lipman. Valentine would be president until the advent of Dudley Evans in 1902. From the History Room, Wells Fargo Bank.

Evans was reelected. James Heron died, and Stein was elected secretary in his place. Evans was reelected second vice-president; King was treasurer and H. B. Parsons was assistant secretary.

Wells Fargo paid a 4 percent cash dividend of $250,000 on January 15, and a 3 percent cash dividend of $240,000 (presumably after the new capitalization had taken effect).

The company operated over 36,308 miles in 1894.

The gross transportation receipts were $6,356,000, the express-carrying charges $3,152,000; thus the gross receipts were down over $600,000. Expenses were $3,101,000, a drop of nearly $400,000, so apparently Wells Fargo, hit by the panic, was retrenching; net income from investment, $368,000; the surplus account declined to $564,000. It was the first time since 1872 that the annual dividend was less than 8 percent.

A recovery from the panic began in 1895, and in that year Wells Fargo finally came to terms with the Post Office, and quit carrying mail. For forty-three years it had thumbed its nose at the Post Office and gone ahead to carry mail anyway, long after it agreed to collect Uncle Sam's stipend and remit to him, but now, perhaps, the United States mail service was improving, and apparently Wells Fargo's mail-carrying activity no longer was as profitable as it had been, so the green Wells Fargo collection boxes came down in San Francisco, in Sacramento, and in Portland. A great era had passed, and Wells Fargo carried no more mail except in Mexico.

In 1895, Stein resigned as director, and Charles F. Crocker was elected; Benjamin P. Cheney died in July, at the age of eighty, and his son, Benjamin P. Cheney, Jr., was elected. The officers were unchanged.

In 1895, the mileage was 36,551—about the same.

Cash dividends of 3 percent were paid in January and in July.

In 1895, the gross receipts from transportation were up to $6,721,000—a sizable increase; express-carrying charges were $3,319,000—a substantial increase; operating expenses were $3,233,000; income from investment, $374,000 (for three years the income from investment had exceeded net income from express); the surplus account went up to $677,000.

In 1896, William Jennings Bryan's intensive silver

campaign keynoted another depression, but in that year the Santa Fé Railroad reached San Francisco at long last in spite of a vigorous and no-holds-barred fight by the Southern Pacific. The two railroads brought prosperity to San Francisco, and Wells Fargo rode the crest. It had contracts with both roads, but the roads were bitter competitors, and Wells Fargo had a problem maintaining peace.

In 1896, there is evidence that holdup men were still busy in some parts of the country (on trains, of course), as shown by a letter from C. H. Young, assistant superintendent of the Colorado-New Mexico Division, to William Pridham, assistant superintendent at Los Angeles:

> Herewith I hand you for your information, copies of statements from Messengers Kohler and T. G. Hutchison, regarding attempted holdup, train No. 802 at Rio Puerco last night, of which I wired you today. We were certainly very lucky in this case. Deputy United States Marshal Loomis was on the train and he killed a man who is said to be Cole Young [Younger?], who, I believe, is charged with numerous robberies in Arizona. Original of these reports sent to Supt. Rowell. I do not anticipate any further trouble soon, but think it well to caution messengers to be on the lookout. I will post a bulletin here [in Albuquerque] for west-bound men.[9]

A small map of this letterhead of "Wells, Fargo & Co's Express" bears the legend: "Ocean to Ocean," and shows lines to, among others, Portland, Los Angeles, Honolulu, Salt Lake City (via Los Angeles only), Denver, Deadwood, Helena, Omaha, Kansas City, St. Louis, Chicago, Boston, New York, New Orleans, Houston, El Paso, Guaymas, Zacatecas, Guanajuato, City of Mexico, and Vera Cruz.

The Head Minutes show evidence of activity in several directions. The bylaws were amended in June, but the Minutes do not give the import of this revision. Apparently, the capitalization was not changed, for the Minutes continue to show a 3 percent dividend, amounting to $240,000, for several years.

The Minutes say that in 1895 a new contract was made with the Santa Fé in 1895 because some of the lines had gone into receivership, and that in February, 1896, the contract was terminated because of the receiverships and the disintegration of the Santa Fé lines. In May, the system was reorganized, and the roads remaining under the Santa Fé system were the Southern Kansas Railway of Texas; the Gulf, Colorado & Santa Fé; the New Mexico & Arizona; and the Sonora Railway.

The Frisco became an independent road and included the Atlantic & Pacific, "Central Division" (Seneca and Sapulpa); the Wichita & Western Railway became an independent road, as did also the St. Louis, Kansas City & Colorado; the Manhattan, Alma & Burlingame; and the Atlantic & Pacific (this one in a receivership). All those but the Manhattan, Alma & Burlingame were parts of the Santa Fé system in 1893.

A contract was approved with the Chicago, Great Western Railroad, which would guarantee the road $80,000 a year.

An interesting item appears in the Minutes for 1896: "On August 1, 1896, began operation of the New Jersey & New York Railroad as an independent road." Without further information, it sounds as if Wells Fargo went into the railroad business in 1896.

Elijah Mason Cooper, manager of the Pacific Department of Wells Fargo, died in July.

The officers and directors remained the same as those for 1895.

In January and in July, 3 percent cash dividends were paid, and the amount of each was $240,000.

Wells Fargo's lines covered 35,924 miles, a small reduction from 1895.

Charges for transportation were $6,937,000—about $200,000 increase; express-carrying charges were $3,714,000—almost $400,000 increase; operating expenses were lower, $3,079,000; net income from investment, $378,000; the surplus fund increased to $779,000.

In 1897, Wells Fargo entered St. Louis through a contract with the Frisco, which was originally the Saint Louis & San Francisco but lost out in the fight between the Southern Pacific and the Santa Fé, and did not reach San Francisco; it nevertheless had a going business west of St. Louis. The contract with the Frisco was for ten years.

This is the year that the Wells Fargo Bank and the Nevada Bank were the last two San Francsico banks to succumb to the custom of paying interest on bank balances, according to Lipman; interest was paid on "some" balances, he said.

On January 12, 1897, a new contract for ten years was made with the Chicago, Great Western Railroad, with a guarantee of $84,000 a year. (The

old contract was less than a year old, and had guaranteed $80,000 a year.)

In July, the Santa Fé assumed control of the "Atlantic & Pacific" (the quotes are in the Minutes) Railroad Company and the Albuquerque & Mojave under the name of Santa Fé & Pacific Railroad; and at the same time the New Mexico & Arizona and the Sonora Railway passed from Santa Fé control to that of the Southern Pacific.

In August, 1897, it was decided to liquidate the Commercial National Bank of Portland, and it was sold to the United States National Bank; Wells Fargo lost $300,000 on the Commercial National.

On August 12, the first remarks were made about "rate troubles in Texas," but no explanation is given.

On December 2, attention was called to the competition in carrying money by the government mail service; apparently, Wells Fargo was feeling a loss of business.

A new office building was begun in San Francisco, to be completed in 1899, and on July 13, the Christian Endeavor Convention was held at San Francisco, and some forty thousand persons attended. It is not explained how this item got into the minutes of the board of directors.

Officers and directors for 1897 were the same as those for 1896 except that Charles F. Crocker died, and John Bermingham was elected in his place.

Cash dividends of 3 percent were paid in January and in July.

Miles operated over: 36,147.

Gross receipts from express, $7,064,000; express-carrying charges, $3,237,000—down almost half a million dollars (apparently the reorganization of the Santa Fé system was good for Wells Fargo); operating expenses, $3,335,000; income from investment, $386,000. The surplus fund grew to $992,000.

In 1898, according to I. W. Hellman III, speaking in 1952, the Wells Fargo Bank had thirty employees, including three girls but no armed guards. Twice a day, said Hellman, Reade's Express (not Wells Fargo!) came around to the bank with a wagon, and took gold and silver to the clearing house. Money always meant gold coin. They stacked $20 gold pieces in piles of $400 (twenty coins), $10 pieces in stacks of $200, $5 pieces in stacks of $100; the tray held $20,000 of any denomination. There were no pennies then, said Hellman. Everybody paid to the nearest nickel, though a seven-course dinner was only fifty cents. Silver was not legal tender over $5.

Steamer Day was on the thirteenth and the twenty-eighth, said Hellman, and was used largely by merchants.

In 1898, the Nevada Bank became the Nevada National Bank, while Wells Fargo continued to operate under state laws—as it does today. On that subject, Frederick Lipman said:

> We rather think we're better off as a state bank. We became a state bank because of the real-estate loans, as I said, but since that time, and since the government in Washington has become what it is, we think we are better off being under an authority right in this state than being governed by authorities in Washington. Naturally we don't want to do things that aren't good banking, but it's better to be here. The national bank authorities, for instance, probably would have had us issue preferred stock. But this way, they have nothing to say about this bank, and we never ask them for a favor. We expect to be carefully examined, and we expect fault to be found if there is any fault to be found. But we don't owe them anything and we expect no concessions. That means something to us.

Probably late in 1898, the Wells Fargo express office left the Sharon Estate on New Montgomery Street and moved to its new express building at Second and Mission streets.

The mint at Carson City was finally abandoned for good, and only an assay office was retained there.

The Spanish-American War broke out in April, and the company offered its services to the Secretary of the Treasury to float a popular loan. It was not a big war, and in many parts of the country, business continued about as usual.

A man named Harry Helen went into the bank in January, 1898, and later left his reminiscences to tell of conditions at that time, and he especially recalled many names of those who worked in the bank. It was at Sansome and Market streets, and was called "Wells, Fargo & Company's Bank." Valentine's offices were with the express company at Second and Market. Homer S. King was manager of the bank, Henry Wadsworth was cashier, and Frederick Lipman, assistant cashier. Henry A. Brown was the only paying teller, and his assistant was named Hess. There were two receiving tellers, John B.

Maynard and Frank Cullen (the latter was killed on a vacation trip in the mountains).

"There was nothing but gold and silver in those days," said Helen, "No currency and no pennies."

The departments were: the clearinghouse department, the note department, exchange department, and a bookkeeping department. In those days, they balanced the passbooks with just a debit and a credit, and there were no statements at the end of the month. At the end of the month, all canceled checks from outside San Francisco were mailed (or deadheaded by Wells Fargo express).

The collection department was the working department; all the work was distributed by it, and so was the incoming mail. There was no transit department. A Miss Ellsworth handled the cash collections and cash remittances.

There were three bookkeepers in the bookkeeping department: Henry King, who handled general books; Mr. Wade, who handled correspondents' books; and Walter Moore, who handled banks and bankers' books. Bert Wadsworth, son of Henry Wadsworth, handled the clearinghouse. Harry A. Miller, John Miles, and Stuart Smith were, more or less, chief clerks. Smith later became president of the Bank of California. Victor Rossetti, who was assistant note teller under Nathan Stein, became president of the Farmers & Merchants Bank at Los Angeles. George McKean was in charge of the exchange department.

Helen's job was varied: He went to the post office at the Ferry Building for the mail, helped the porter bring out the books in the morning, and changed the dates on the desks. He followed the mail to the collection department, where the receiving teller would prove up and sort the checks: collection items, country items, and so on; the teller would distribute the checks to the various departments. Helen looked over the checks for endorsements, helped with the clearinghouse department, took care of customers who came in to find out their balances, get canceled checks, and other things. He ran errands, filed and recorded correspondents' letters, and in the evening helped each department complete the day's work. The last task, of course, was to get out the day's mail. It was nothing unusual, he said, to work from 7 A. M. to 7 P. M., and he got $14 a month for it; then he was raised to $20, which was paid in a $20 gold piece in an envelope. He said that in those days it was not unusual to make a loan (presumably small and for a short time) by giving the paying teller an I. O. U.

Lunch in those days often was taken free with a five-cent glass of beer, and a man could get bologna, cheese and crackers, and other similar items. However, if he felt like splurging, for fifteen cents he could go to the Fly Trap in the flatiron building on Sutter and Sansome, across from the bank, or for twenty cents he could get a full-course lunch with soup, wine, and dessert.

Market Street had cable cars, but horse-drawn cars ran along Sutter Street.

Three young men worked in the mailing department: Al Rosetti (Victor's brother), Bill Bachelor, and Helen.

In June, Wells Fargo made three new contracts: with the Colorado & Midland Railroad for five years at 50 percent with a guarantee of $30,000 a year; with the Texas Central for three years at 50 percent with a guarantee of $7,200 a year; and with the Rio Grande & Western at 50 percent with a guarantee of $100,000 a year.

Officers and directors remained the same as for 1897, with Bermingham in place of Crocker.

The usual 3 percent dividend was paid in January and in July.

Mileage operated in 1898—37,849, an increase of fifteen hundred miles.

Gross receipts from express: $7,880,000—an increase of over $800,000; express-carrying charges, $3,729,000—an increase of almost half a million dollars; operating expenses, $3,686,000; income from investment, $452,000; the surplus fund went over a million: $1,110,000.

From 1899 to 1903, the country would be blessed with the prosperity of giant mergers, that would lead into a period of corporate prosperity and a subsequent period of trustbusting.

In 1899, ornate cages were installed on the counters at the Wells Fargo Bank. From about this year, too, a set of specifications for Wells Fargo harness has been found that clearly sets out the way the harness is to be built in such language that a good harness maker today could reproduce it.[10]

In 1898, some highwaymen tried to rob the Wells Fargo express car of a Santa Fé train near Daggett Station but were foiled by the engineer, and in 1899, Valentine had a gold watch and chain en-

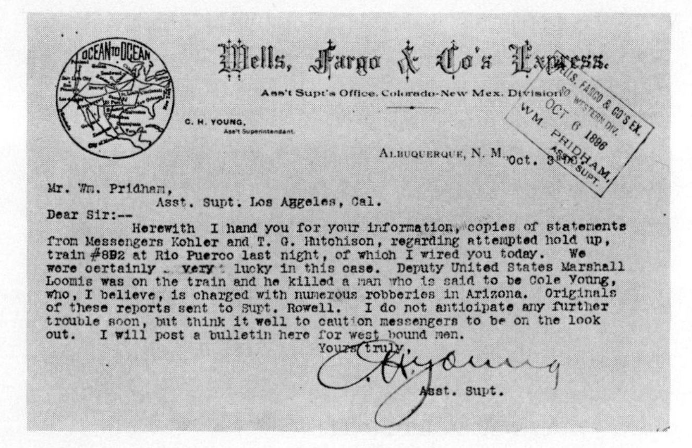

Wells, Fargo & Co's Express.
Ass't Supt's Office, Colorado-New Mex. Division
C. H. YOUNG,
Ass't Superintendant.
WELLS, FARGO & CO'S EX. SO. WESTERN DIV. OCT 6 1896 WM. PRIDHAM, ASST. SUPT.
ALBUQUERQUE, N. M. Oct. 3'96.

Mr. Wm. Pridham,
Asst. Supt. Los Aggeles, Cal.
Dear Sir:--
Herewith I hand you for your information, copies of statements from Messengers Kohler and T. G. Hutchison, regarding attempted hold up, train #8B2 at Rio Puerco last night, of which I wired you today. We were certainly very lucky in this case. Deputy United States Marshall Loomis was on the train and he killed a man who is said to be Cole Young, who, I believe, is charged with numerous robberies in Arizona. Originals of these reports sent to Supt. Rowell. I do not anticipate any further trouble soon, but think it well to caution messengers to be on the look out. I will post a bulletin here for west bound men.
Yours truly,
C. H. Young
Asst. Supt.

A letter of 1896 headed "Wells, Fargo & Co.'s Express," relating to an attempted holdup. (The man killed was not Cole Younger.) The original letter is in the History Room, Wells Fargo Bank.

graved for him (the traditional thank you from Wells Fargo to employees who had defended the express), along with the following letter:

WELLS FARGO & COMPANY,
EXPRESS AND BANKING.
San Francisco, August 8, 1899.

Mr. Daniel B. Bunnell,
Engineer Santa Fe Pacific Train,
Los Angeles, Cal.

Dear Sir:

In taking official action to manifest our appreciation of the commendable conduct of our own employes—Blakeley and Hutchison—in the attempted hold-up and robbery of the train near Daggett Station, Saturday morning, November 19th, 1898, which has been unavoidably delayed until now by a steady pressure of other important duties, while consulting the correspondence had on the subject at the time, I find your name appearing so very creditably therein as their coadjutor—however handicapped for a while by the excessive attentions and partiality the robbers showed you—that I cannot forbear thanking you also for the service thus rendered the Company, and sending you a small token as evidence of the fact. Please find herewith a gold watch, chain and charm,—the former engraved as follows:

To
Daniel B. Bunnell
For intrepid action
November 19th, 1898
Wells Fargo & Company.

which accept with our best wishes for your health and welfare.

JNO. J. VALENTINE
President.[11]

On May 4, 1899, the bylaws were amended, and again on August 3 they were amended, but there is no hint as to the reason or reasons.

On May 1, Wells Fargo began carrying express on the Colorado Southern Railway and the Fort Worth & Denver City Railway, a total distance of 810 miles. In the same year, the Santa Fé bought the San Joaquin Valley Railroad.

On August 10, 1899, according to the Head Minutes, the "parcel post agitation was first mentioned." There are no other details, but the fact is that the express companies were known to be highly profitable, and public opinion was beginning to turn; newspapers and some politicians demanded that the government get into the parcel-carrying business and reduce the cost of carrying packages.

Lloyd Tevis died in October.

Directors and officers were the same as those for 1898, but in August, Andrew Christeson was elected director in place of Benjamin P. Cheney; it is not said that Cheney resigned, nor is any other information given.

In January and in July, the usual cash dividend of 3 percent was paid—a total of $480,000, which indicates that the capital stock had not changed.

Number of miles operated over in 1899: 38,001.

Total gross receipts continued to rise, and reached $8,650,000; express privileges cost $4,213,000; operating expenses were $3,796,000; net income

from investment, $483,000. The surplus fund went up almost $700,000 to $1,785,000, but the reason is not apparent; combined income was up only $187,000, and the usual dividends were paid; it rather seems there were two reserve funds: the surplus fund and the "dividends and profit and loss adjustment" account, for in 1898, $854,000 was charged to this latter account, but in 1899, only $482,000 was charged to it (and nearly all that was dividends).

Wells Fargo had been in business almost half a century, and had gone through some hectic times, but more were to come: the merger with the Nevada National Bank, dominance of the company by the great railroad tycoon, Edward P. Harrington, and the beginning of governmental control. This period would also see the separation of the bank from the express company, and the distribution of nearly $27,000,000 in dividends in one year—315 percent on the capital stock.

OFFICE OF THE PRESIDENT.

Wells Fargo & Company,
Express and Banking.
San Francisco, August 5, 1899.

Mr. Daniel B. Bunnell,
Engineer Santa Fe Pacific Train,
LOS ANGELES, CAL.

Dear Sir:

In taking official action to manifest our appreciation of the commendable conduct of our own employes - Blakeley and Hutchison - in the attempted hold-up and robbery of the train near Daggett Station, Saturday morning, November 19th, 1898, which has been unavoidably delayed until now by a steady pressure of other important duties, while consulting the correspondence had on the subject at the time, I find your name appearing so very creditably therein as their conductor - however handicapped for a while by the excessive attentions and partiality the robbers showed you - that I cannot forbear thanking you also for the service thus rendered the Company, and sending you a small token as evidence of the fact. Please find herewith a gold watch, chain and charm,- the former engraved as follows:

To
Daniel B. Bunnell
For intrepid action
November 19th, 1898
Wells Fargo & Company.

which accept with our best wishes for your health and welfare.

Very truly yours,

Jno. J. Valentine
President.

John J. Valentine's letter of presentation of a gold watch to Daniel B. Bunnell "For intrepid action." The original is in the History Room, Wells Fargo Bank.

1900-1905

Separation of Express and Banking

IN 1900, THERE WAS STILL A BOOM because of the merger prosperity, but it would turn to a small depression in the latter part of the year. Gold was discovered at Tonopah, Nevada, inaugurating the last great bonanza, and in that year the production of gold and silver in Nevada reached an all-time low after their first discovery and production.

The Santa Fé Railway ran its first passenger trains (that carried express) over the San Joaquin Valley Road from Bakersfield to San Francisco on July 1, and naturally Wells Fargo was on board.

The directors for 1900 were the same as those for 1899, and the officers were the same, but Aaron Stein died in March, and was succeeded by Charles H. Gardiner on the board. Gardiner served temporarily as secretary, but was succeeded by Nathan Stein, brother of Aaron.

Aaron Stein had run the stationery department, according to Eric Francis; he was handsome, with white hair, mustache, and goatee, and had a very slow but distinct enunciation. He was a clever man, and the "Colonel House" (ghost writer) to Valentine, and was supposed to be the real author of a piece entitled *Gold,* that received great credit during the McKinley presidential campaign in 1900.

The usual dividends of 3 percent were paid in January and in July, for a total of $480,000.

Total mileage operated over: 40,798.

Gross income from express jumped to $10,151,000; express-carrying charges were $4,832,000; operating expenses increased to $4,282,000; net income from investment, $473,000. The surplus fund went up almost a million dollars to $2,634,000.

In 1901, the depression soon ended, and the merger prosperity took hold again under President Theodore Roosevelt.

In that year, Collis P. Huntington died, and left to his heirs 475,000 shares of Southern Pacific stock —47.5 percent of the outstanding capital stock. And Huntington's death opened the way for the last big conquistador of the Wells Fargo company: Edward H. Harriman.

Harriman, born in 1852 as the son of an Episcopalian minister, married into a wealthy family in New York and presently got control of a small New York State railroad line and sold it to the Pennsylvania Railroad at a handsome profit by showing the Pennsylvania president the advantage of a feeder line that could carry Pennsylvania coal to a port on Lake Ontario, from whence it could be shipped downriver to Canada, a big market for coal.

In 1887, he used clever parliamentary tactics at a stockholders' meeting of the Iowa Central (a line leased by the Illinois Central) to upset the great house of Drexel, Morgan & Company, and in 1890, he made a financial forecast that enabled the Illinois Central to pull in its horns in time to escape the panic of 1893.

Harriman was soon able to buy a seat on the New York Stock Exchange and began to buy and sell railroad stock. In 1883, he became vice-president of the Illinois Central, and in 1903, he would be president. He worked with Stuyvesant Fish and

Kuhn, Loeb & Company, and formed a syndicate to buy the Union Pacific, which had been in receivership since 1893; Jay Gould had had control, but Gould was not a railroad man but a financier, and had the reputation of wrecking any road that he bought. It appears that the Union Pacific (General Dodge's creation in those hectic days of the late 1860's and the titanic race with Charlie Crocker's coolies) was now pretty well stripped, and Harriman organized a syndicate to take it over, because he was dreaming of a transcontinental railroad that he would control.

The Union Pacific owed the government $53,000,000, and Harriman figured an even hundred million would do a job on it. Kuhn, Loeb & Company thought they could get it from Germany, but Harriman opened their eyes by borrowing it from the Illinois Central. In the meantime, Harriman personally was buying Union Pacific stock at a low price wherever he could find it. If Harriman could control an Atlantic to Pacific line, he could challenge the railroad giants of the East.

He had a train rigged up with a special platform, and had himself pushed backward over every mile of the Union Pacific while he watched the track, the land, the stations, the water towers, the roundhouses, and everything else that had a bearing on his investment. That made a hit, and he got $25,000,000 in Wall Street to reduce curves and grades and buy new rolling stock—especially bigger locomotives. In 1900, he paid a dividend on Union Pacific stock.

He had tried to buy the Central Pacific from Collis P. Huntington, whom he had known for some time, but Huntington would not sell. Then Huntington died in the fall of 1900, and left his widow and his nephew, Henry E. Huntington, 475,000 shares of Southern Pacific stock—which of course controlled the Central Pacific. Harriman had boasted that he could control any railroad with 35 percent of its capital stock, and within seven months he had 37.5 percent; by the summer of 1901, he controlled 45.49 percent—1,000,000 shares, and by September, 1901, he was president of the Southern Pacific. He got $18,000,000 to modernize the Southern Pacific, and started on a huge program. It is said that he told the general manager to spend it in a week, but it was not spent that fast or carelessly. They dug tunnels, straightened track, and built a cutoff across the Great Salt Lake.

Portrait of Edward H. Harriman. From the New York Public Library.

Dudley Evans, the southern colonel who became president of Wells Fargo in 1902 and remained so until he died in 1910. From the History Room, Wells Fargo Bank.

Meantime, in the same year (1901), Harriman got into a titanic struggle with James P. Hill and J. P. Morgan for control of the Burlington and the Northern Pacific—but lost. And in the process, he brought down the wrath of the Roosevelt administration and its trustbusting era.

Harriman was the biggest railroad operator in the West, and he was getting ready to move in on Wells Fargo. The Southern Pacific owned $1,530,000 of Wells Fargo's capitalization of $8,000,000, and Harriman owned the Southern Pacific.

The Santa Fé Railway took control of the Mexican Central Railway in 1901, and Wells Fargo was on that road. A new contract was made with the Santa Fé, to run for fifteen years and thereafter until six months' notice should be given to either party; the Santa Fé was to get 55 percent of the gross earnings.

Wells Fargo entered into a number of fifteen-year-and-six-month notice contracts, but at a smaller percentage of the gross. It made contracts with the Erie Railroad, the Chicago & Erie, the Northern Railroad of New York, the New Jersey & New York, and the New York, Susquehanna & Western. Also, the Santa Fé, Prescott & Phoenix was absorbed by the Santa Fé and became a part of the system.

The Harriman syndicate, as noted in the Head Minutes, acquired a controlling interest in the Southern Pacific on February 1, 1901, and President Hayes resigned from the Southern Pacific board in September, and Harriman was elected president.

A suit for taxes of the Southern Express Company was compromised in October, and Wells Fargo paid $35,000 to have the suit dismissed.

The directors at the beginning of 1901 were the same as those for 1900, but John J. Valentine died in the latter part of December, at sixty-three. Eldridge resigned in November, and Nathan Stein was elected. The officers were the same as those of 1900 (noting that Nathan Stein had succeeded Aaron Stein as secretary).

Total mileage operated over in 1901: 42,670.

Wells Fargo had been making, it appears, as much as 30 percent earnings on the capital, but had held the dividend rate down; this year was the same: a 3 percent dividend in January, and another in July.

Gross receipts from express, $11,829,000; carrying charges, $5,767,000; operating expenses, $4,725,000; income from investment, $503,000. The surplus fund took another healthy jump to $4,137,000.

In January, 1902, Colonel Dudley Evans became president of Wells Fargo. Evans was a southern gentleman, an ex-officer of the Confederate army, and a friend of Valentine, who also had been a southerner. Evans had been with Wells Fargo since soon after the Civil War, and was agent or manager at Portland until he was transferred to Omaha in the late 1880's as manager of the Central Department. He moved to Kansas City, then to New York. He was completely honest, and accumulated several hundred thousand dollars, of which, obviously, a substantial part was in Wells Fargo stock. The colonel was a very capable man, but he was not

accustomed to doing business with the shrewd operators of Wall Street. As soon as he heard of Harriman's coup on the Southern Pacific, he sat back to wait for Harriman to send for him, and perhaps he was a little smug, because Wells Fargo had long wanted a contract on the Union Pacific, and now, Evans felt, it was about to forge the final link in a transcontinental express empire. So Evans waited for Harriman, and while he waited, ordered Wells Fargo signs to be painted for all the Union Pacific stations from Ogden to Omaha, Denver, and Kansas City.

But Harriman did not send word, and finally Evans went to Harriman. It wasn't exactly etiquette for the president of the proud old express firm, but he went anyway—only to be told by Harriman that the Union Pacific had given the contract to the American Express Company, and that within months American would be in Ogden, Portland, and Los Angeles—all Wells Fargo citadels.

Harriman was not concerned with Wells Fargo's heritage of pride and position—or was he? Is it possible that he resented that position, and that he gave the contract to American as a reprimand?

Years later, Frederick Lipman said that he found the Salt Lake City branch short in 1902, as short as the Carson City and Virginia City branches put together, eleven years before. The assistant cashier and a paying teller had taken the money and "cooked up" the books. Apparently, however, Wells Fargo took no action, and it may be presumed that Dooly, the manager, made up the shortage.

Wells Fargo had given the Alaska Packers' Association a credit line of $1,500,000, but about 1902, some New York men formed the Pacific Packing & Navigation Company and ran it speculatively, according to Frederick Lipman, and made things difficult for Alaska Packers. The banks had to carry Alaska Packers for a while, and Lipman went on the board for Wells Fargo, Frank Anderson for the Bank of California. They got Alaska Packers "out of the woods," but Alaska Packers still had a big debt that the Wells Fargo bank had to write off.

That loss was a factor in the merger of Wells Fargo with the Nevada National Bank in 1905.

Frank Todd in 1952 told about going to work for Wells Fargo in 1902. He dressed in a black derby hat, a three-inch stiff collar, pointed-toe shoes, and a fancy silk vest, and was interviewed by "a most courteous and kindly gentleman," Homer S. King,

Receipt for one Gila monster, dated at Gila Bend, Arizona, in 1902. The original is in the History Room, Wells Fargo Bank.

and told to report for work the following Monday.

> And there a boy's dream was fulfilled. . . . Since I could not have been a pony rider or a shotgun messenger, at least now I was a part of that fabulous institution, Wells Fargo & Company. Office boy, one-man mail department—and I would not have traded jobs with the king of all Britain. Then, a bank clerk was a somebody—a man of distinction; ye Gods, how the mighty have fallen. Today even the CIO sheds bitter tears over our miserable plight.

At that time, the bank staff consisted of some thirty persons: Homer King, president; Lipman, assistant cashier; Frank B. King, (later) assistant cashier; Victor Rosetti, assistant chief clerk; and Harry Helen, clearinghouse clerk. There were two stenographers, the telephone girl, one woman clerk, four bookkeepers using the old Boston ledger system, and one adding machine that was then the ninth wonder of the world.

The tellers and those in responsible positions, said Todd, were middle-aged men—some past middle age, with years of experience behind them.

Wells Fargo shipped many strange things in its time, but none stranger, perhaps, than the Gila monster it shipped from (appropriately) Gila Bend, Arizona, in 1902. The Gila monster is a peculiarly repellent beast that inhabits the Sonora desert; he is slow and relatively harmless, but he will bite if tempted too far, and when he bites, he hangs on and grinds, and injects a most unpleasant poison into the wound. There has never been a very heavy traffic in

Gila monsters, but on May 31, 1902, H. D. Morey, the Wells Fargo agent at Gila Bend, gave a receipt to P. Slater for "1 Box screened said to contain 1 Gila monster valued at Fifty dollars." It was addressed to C. B. DeVry, Lincoln Park, Chicago, and probably was delivered in good condition—though it would have been admitted by all concerned that not too much was known about a Gila monster's health.

The Gila monster, of course, was by no means whatsoever an unusual piece of express for Wells Fargo. Tropical fish were often carried, their water being kept constantly warm. Wells Fargo had carried the first ice commercially shipped to Los Angeles in the 1850's. It cost 12½ cents a pound in San Francisco, was packed there in blankets, and must have gone by sea. The loss by melting made it cost twenty-four cents a pound, but the grocer-saloonkeeper who ordered it, got the best patronage in town.

Live game had been shipped in early days, but dead game was also carried, one shipment from Dubuque to New York (fifty cases) in 1858 costing $3,000 in express charges. In the early 1880's, ducks, rabbits, snipe, quail, prairie chickens, wild turkeys, grouse, squirrels, and so forth, were hung together on a heavy wire or a small rope and shipped without icing or crating from Kansas and the Indian territory to Kansas City and St. Louis.[1]

In 1883, the Pacific Express moved sixteen hundred rabbits from Jerseyville, Illinois, and in 1896, the company shipped fifteen hundred pounds of live bullfrogs east from Paragould, Arkansas. A famous frog and turtle farm at North Judson, Indiana, kept Pacific Express going in that area around 1900.[2]

Live chickens, ducks, geese, and guinea fowls were shipped by express, as well as calves without crates, and sometimes, says *Old Waybills,* the stench of animals, dung, boxes of imported cheese, barrels of fish, baskets of crabs and lobsters, and, perhaps, cages of Gila monsters made the express car considerably stronger than a sun-drenched garbage dump, so that the messenger had to have an impervious nose and a strong stomach.

Crated dogs were shipped in the 1890's, as well as crated cats, and just after the Civil War the express companies did a good business shipping the trained horses on which Adah Isaacs Menken, Kate Fisher, and other famous Mazeppas made their thrilling and titillating exits at the end of the play. Wells Fargo shipped at least one horse for Miss Menken to Virginia City.

In the late 1890's, the Belgian hare craze swept the country; in 1900, there were six hundred rabbit breeders in and around Los Angeles, and the express companies did a tremendous business delivering rabbits. A few years later, it was pigeons (to raise squabs), and again the express companies benefited—to the point where some wondered if the express companies were behind those businesses!

Homing pigeons were for many years shipped in coops to express agents with a request that they be liberated at a certain point. Fingerling fish were sent everywhere by express, and baby chicks, of course, have been a standard express item for over half a century.

In 1916, a sitting hen was sent from California to New York by Wells Fargo and American, the box being labeled, "Sitting hen—eggs expected to hatch. Handle with care." It was a publicity stunt, but expressmen took good care of the expectant mother; the eggs hatched en route, and only one chick died.

One hundred packages of silkworm eggs were carried by Wells Fargo in 1876, en route from Japan to Italy. And in the 1870's, sparrows were shipped from England to America to eat the caterpillars. A camel was shipped by express in 1899 from Sells-Forepaugh's circus at Columbus, Ohio, to New York to appear in the stage play, *Ben Hur*. Between 1870 and 1890, lions, tigers, leopards, bears, elephants, alligators, and hippopotamuses were shipped by express. Live animals, of course, could not be shipped by freight, but had to go by express so they could be watered and fed. Bears, prize bulls, and five hundred-pound boars have been shipped by express. Even whales were shipped in the late 1870's, but did not arrive in good condition. Monkeys, kangaroos, hyenas, echidnas, mandrills, pythons, and a herd of Philippine water buffaloes were shipped by express, and many were the harassing experiences of express messengers who found themselves prisoners in the baggage car with a maddened lion or bear loose in the car. In the late 1890's, reindeer were brought from Lapland and sent to Alaska and the Northwest Territory, and the great herds of reindeer in the North Country today have a trace of Wells Fargo blood in their ancestry.

Many insects were shipped by express, and in

1926, a man in the state of Washington captured and shipped ladybugs in boxes with wire screen on two sides; expressmen were required to sprinkle the boxes with water once a day.

Racing and breeding horses were sent by express, and Wells Fargo had horse cars built with removable stalls; in 1912, Wells Fargo sent a special train of five such cars from New York to North Dakota with fine Percheron horses from France and Belgium for breeding purposes.

Wives and children had been shipped by express from the early days of the Gold Rush, and Negro slaves were shipped freely. A Kansas man went broke in Texas and had himself shipped home to his wife, express collect. (It cost her the regular passenger fare plus an additional fee—and one wonders if she paid it with a smile.)

In Washington in 1881, there were no hospital ambulances (as we know them now), and the fatally wounded President Garfield was carried from the White House to the railroad station in a steel-tired Adams delivery wagon.

Bodies of human beings have been shipped by express since very early days. But in the 1850's, there was no embalming, and, when the weather was warm, a body could be offensive, and sometimes the express messenger set the body on the front platform of the car.

It was Wells Fargo that brought the world's biggest pump from Pennsylvania to Tombstone in a special car to pump water out of the mines. (It didn't work; the flooded mines gradually went out of business.)

It was Wells Fargo that transported five huge turbine deep-well pumps, in three baggage cars, from Los Angeles to the American Zinc Company mines at Mascot, Tennessee, in four days, where freight would have taken ten or twelve days. The company made money by using express and saving time, for the lack of the pumps was costing the zinc company $5,000 a day.

Wells Fargo carried seven ostriches in September, 1913, and in the same year, it sent 1,821 pounds of ginseng to China—value, $7,873.50. Skunks were refused—perhaps under the head of volatile substances.

Wells Fargo carried the world's biggest gold brick. The limit by mail was 4 pounds, but this brick weighed 218 pounds and was worth $51,750; it was shipped from Dawson, Yukon Territory, to Selby, California. Wells Fargo, of course, was the great gold carrier of the West, but, even after the Cali-

Six men removing President Garfield from an express wagon (name of the express company is not given) to the railway train to take him to the seashore. From "Harper's Weekly," 1881.

fornia Gold Rush was over, the company still was called on to carry gold. It carried a shipment from Dawson to Seattle of $1,250,000, another of $1,500,000. In 1891, the company carried $6,665,000 worth of negotiable bonds from New York to Monterrey, Mexico, on one waybill; the carrying charges were $30,500. It carried a shipment of $3,500,000 in gold from Ottawa, Canada, to Mexico City—and President Elmer Jones went with it.

The United States Express, by the way, handled the biggest gold shipment up to 1913—$43,000,000 in gold coin from Baltimore and Philadelphia for $50,000. But in 1915, a British battleship brought $53,000,000 to Halifax, consigned to J. P. Morgan & Company, to pay for munitions. American Express representatives joined the Dominion Express at Halifax, and escorted it to New York in five steel baggage cars (there were seven hundred sacks), guarded by forty men with rifles and pistols. A decoy train, empty, preceded it. There was no insurance on the gold, and American's capital stock then was about $18,000,000.

Wells Fargo's bylaws were amended on October 7, 1902.

The Mexican Central Railway acquired the Monterrey & Mexican Gulf Railroad, and Wells Fargo began to operate over the latter line.

The directors at the beginning of 1902 were the same as those for 1901: Valentine (whose name was not removed until January 2), Christeson, Henry E. Huntington, Gray, King, McCook, Evans, Nathan Stein, and Bermingham. On January 2, E. H. Harriman was elected in place of John J. Valentine, and Evans became acting president. F. D. Underwood was elected in place of A. Christeson; W. O. S. Thorne was elected in place of Nathan Stein; and W. T. Van Brunt was elected in place of John Bermingham. The control had passed to the East. Officers at the beginning of 1902 were Valentine, president; Gray, vice-president; Evans, second vice-president; King, treasurer; Stein, secretary; and Parsons, assistant secretary. Evans was elected acting president in January, and president in September. Parsons was elected secretary, and Stein was elected assistant secretary in September; King was elected president of the bank in September.

Total number of miles: 43,052.

In January and in July the usual 3 percent cash dividends were paid, and in January, an extra 2 percent was paid—making $640,000 in dividends in 1902.

Gross receipts from express were $13,394,000; carrying charges, $6,275,000; operating expenses, $5,212,000; income from investment, $657,000; the surplus fund took a healthy jump to $6,490,000.

In 1903, Harriman surveyed the situation, and found many things he did not like.

The bank, which had in its possession the surplus of Wells, Fargo & Company, was operating on capital stock of $8,000,000 and surplus of $8,000,000—which made a capital of $16,000,000, while it had deposits of only $11,000,000 or $12,000,000, and it was obvious that no bank could make any money on that basis. Money had to be used to make money. Another factor that Harriman disliked was the emphasis on certain phases of business when it came to making loans. At that time, for instance, Wells Fargo had made heavy loans to wheat growers in the San Joaquin Valley, and at various times it loaned heavily in the wine business, lumber business, and others. Harriman considered these loans too risky when they represented a large part of the bank's business; a bad year in wheat, for example, could wipe out the bank. Harriman was especially concerned because he knew the splendid condition of Wells, Fargo & Company, and he had bought heavily of Wells Fargo stock.

Harriman had known Isaias Hellman, president of the Nevada National Bank, because he and Hellman had worked together in financing the Los Angeles Street Railroad Company. In 1901, Harriman had wanted Hellman to take the Wells Fargo Bank, but Hellman was already president of Nevada National, and had gone about as far as he could go because he had no adequate help with the Nevada bank; it had grown up to be a one-man bank.

Harriman now wanted to close the Wells Fargo Bank, but there was strong opposition. Wells Fargo was an institution, and the bank was the strongest bank in the West; *nobody* could close down Wells Fargo. So Harriman gave up the idea of closing the bank, but began to look around for somebody to sell it to. That somebody, of course, was Isaias Hellman.

In 1903, gold was found at Goldfield, Nevada, and started another boom in that direction. The railroad was built into Goldfield, and Wells Fargo's express car rode behind the engine.

Directors for 1903 were Evans, president; Homer

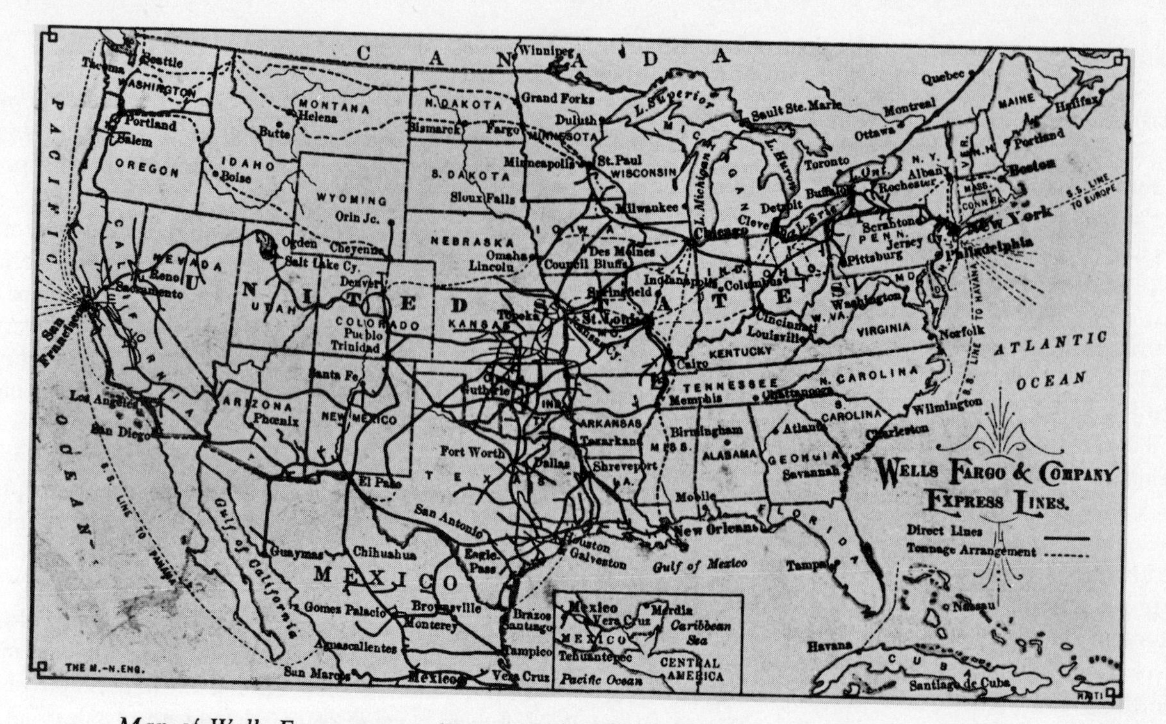

Map of Wells Fargo express lines in 1904, when Wells Fargo was very solid in the central part of the United States and in the West and Southwest. The original is in the History Room, Wells Fargo Bank.

S. King, treasurer and nominal president of the bank; F. D. Underwood, Huntington, McCook, Gray, Harriman, Van Brunt, and Thorne. H. B. Parsons was secretary; Nathan Stein was assistant secretary.

Number of miles operated over: 45,758.

A 3 percent cash dividend was paid in January, and another in July; a 1 percent cash dividend was paid in January, and again in July. Total for the year: 8 percent.

In 1903, the gross express receipts were $14,906,000; express-carrying charges were $6,961,000; operating expenses were $5,880,000; income from investment, $706,000; the surplus fund increased more than $2,000,000 to a total of $8,655,000.

In 1904, Harriman started negotiations to sell the bank to Isaias Hellman; Homer King did not approve, and accepted an offer to become president of the Bank of California. Business in general was not good in 1904 because of the so-called rich man's panic, but Harriman was involving himself in various transportation projects on the West Coast, especially in Oregon.

A statement of Wells Fargo & Company, Express and Banking, similar to the statements that banks still issue quarterly, is dated August 1, 1904, and shows the directors: Evans, president (office in New York); King, treasurer, San Francisco; Harriman, W. D. Cornish, McCook, Thorne, F. D. Underwood, William F. Herrin, Huntington, Gray, Van Brunt, and J. Kruttschnitt (who had been general superintendent of the Southern Pacific and had started rebuilding that road under Harriman's direction). H. B. Parsons, New York, was vice-president and secretary; and Nathan Stein, San Francisco, was assistant secretary. Harriman was not a man to accept an office in the corporations he controlled.

By law, the New York bank had to be a state bank, and was not a branch bank but an independent bank, with Evans president, Parsons cashier.

In the express division, Evans was president, J. S. Bunnell of San Francisco was auditor; E. A. Stedman was manager at New York, R. A. Wells at Kansas City, and A. Christeson at San Francisco (probably the same Christeson who had been on the board until September, 1902).

In the bank, King was listed as president, Lipman as cashier, and Frank B. King and John E. Miles as assistant cashiers. H. B. Parsons was cashier at New York, H. L. Miller at Salt Lake, and R. Lea Barnes at Portland.

Paid-up capital was shown as $500,000, surplus as $5,750,000, and undivided profits as $9,666,000. Deposits by banks and bankers were $2,188,000, and by individuals $7,808,000. Assets were loans, $16,085,000; bonds, stocks, and warrants, $2,732,000; real estate, $2,140,000; due from banks and bankers, $1,701,000; cash, $3,250,000.

The folder shows total mileage as 48,439, and numbers of offices as 4,210.

A small map on one page of the folder shows that Wells Fargo was operating over the Union Pacific by arrangement from Omaha to Denver, directly from Denver to San Francisco; from Minneapolis through Montana to Seattle over the Great Northern, and also from Minneapolis through Montana over the Northern Pacific; and over the Union Pacific by arrangement from Cheyenne to Portland. The strongest network of short lines seems to be in Kansas and Oklahoma (Oklahoma Territory then), with another heavy concentration on the Gulf Coast of Texas, and lines north and south from San Francisco.

In August, H. B. Parsons was elected a director—the thirteenth on the board.

In January and again in July, the company paid a 4 percent cash dividend—a total of 8 percent, apparently to the discontent of the stockholders. By the end of the year, Wells Fargo stock was selling at $215 a share.

Gross receipts from express, $16,180,000; express-carrying charges, $7,572,000; operating expenses, $6,303,000; income from investment, $811,000. The surplus went up to $11,156,000.

Then came the eventful year of 1905.

In the last part of January, King went to the Bank of California, and that move precipitated the merger between Wells Fargo and the Nevada National.

When it had become evident in 1904 that there would be a merger, Homer King did not like the idea of Hellman's coming in, because he wanted to be president of the bank officially as well as actually, so he went to New York to talk to Harriman. Harriman told him to see Hellman, and Hellman said that he was not a young man, that he had a place at the lake where he liked to spend his time, that he went East occasionally and would be away much of the time; it added up to the fact that he had no objection whatever to King's being manager of the bank, but that, of course, there could be only one president: Mr. Hellman.

About two years before, the Bank of California had brought Frank Anderson from the American Exchange National Bank in New York to be its executive vice-president. It seemed that Anderson was competent but a little too young, so they offered the presidency to King, who accepted it. King's move started rumors of the impending merger.

The board of directors of Wells Fargo, in the meantime, at a meeting in New York made Lipman president of the bank, and Lipman chose Frank B. King for cashier "because there wasn't anybody else."

Lipman's primary job at that time was to hold the business of Wells Fargo in the face of the many rumors. Lipman had had a poor impression of the Hellmans because of the closing up of affairs of the Virginia City branch of the Wells Fargo bank; Bigelow had represented the Nevada National and was one of its trusted officers, but he could not say that the Nevada National would assume its half of a $550 expense until he should talk to Mr. Hellman, who was at the lake. Then, when Bigelow later came into the merged bank as vice-president, his salary had to be raised $3,000 to equal that of Lipman, who was cashier. Lipman said he never did have a conversation with Isaias Hellman, Sr.

Lipman was manager of the Wells Fargo bank and the one to make the deal on Wells Fargo's side. In the meantime, Isaias Hellman, Jr., asked Lipman to see him, and wanted to know where Lipman stood. Lipman answered: "Mr. Hellman, I have been accustomed to participating in bank management and to contribute my judgment, and there will be no place for me in a combination where all the talent will be furnished by others."

"I want you to go on and be cashier of the new bank," said Hellman. "What is your salary?"

"It is $10,000."

"We expected to pay you $10,000 to start with."

Lipman said, "I am ready to do so as long as I find that the objectives of the new bank do not conflict with my own ideals." And that, Lipman said later, was the last word they ever had on the subject.

Isaias W. Hellman in 1905, at the time of the formation of the Wells Fargo Nevada National Bank, when he became president. From Ira Cross, "Financing an Empire."

Hellman, Sr., was in Europe, and the merger could not be completed as readily as it might have been. Nevertheless, the Wells Fargo Nevada National Bank opened for business April 22, 1905, with Hellman president and Lipman cashier. The Nevada's capital was $3,000,000 and its surplus was $1,500,000; it paid its stockholders a dividend to reduce the combined amount to $1,500,000—10,000 shares at $150 each. The wells Fargo bank had assets of $2,000,000 capital and $1,000,000 surplus by putting in a mass of assets exceeding the deposit liabilities by $3,000,000. There was a new issue of stock, sold to the public at $200 a share—$2,000,000 all told—which contributed $1,000,000 to the capital fund and $1,000,000 surplus. It made a total capital of $9,000,000 and a surplus of $3,500,000, and $158.33 on each share due to the two banks.

It seems that Hellman paid Wells, Fargo & Company in stock of the new bank.

Directors of the Wells Fargo Nevada National were: Isaias W. Hellman, Sr., president; Isaias W. Hellman, Jr., and F. A. Bigelow (from the Nevada bank), vice-presidents; Frederick L. Lipman, cashier; Frank B. King, George Grant, William McGavin, and John E. Miles, assistant cashiers. Harriman became a director of the bank; he was also on the board of the National City Bank of New York, but no others. Also on the Wells Fargo-Nevada board were W. F. Herrin, prominent in the South Pacific hierarchy, and Dudley Evans.

So, after fifty-three years of existence as a department of Wells, Fargo & Company, Express, the Wells Fargo Bank was separated from the express business and went its own way. The express business would henceforth be centered in New York. The Wells Fargo Nevada National Bank would continue to do business with the Wells Fargo Bank in New York,

Frederick L. Lipman, who was nominal president of the Wells Fargo bank from January to April 22, 1905, president of the Wells Fargo Nevada National Bank, 1920–1923, and president of the Wells Fargo Bank & Union Trust Company from 1924 to 1935. From the History Room, Wells Fargo Bank.

The same Nevada Bank building at Pine and Montgomery streets in 1905—probably in the very early morning. From the History Room, Wells Fargo Bank.

but that bank in turn was sold to another New York bank. At this late hour, there could be an actual bank president of Wells Fargo, for it was now an independent bank on its own (combined, that is, with the Nevada National).

Lipman, who was to be a power in San Francisco banking circles for a long time, had been born and educated in San Francisco, and spent his entire life with Wells Fargo; for many years, he was considered the dean of bankers in San Francisco, and was considered the epitome of integrity.

The huge surplus of Wells, Fargo & Company, of course, did not go with the bank. Wells, Fargo & Company received 200,000 shares of stock in the new bank, and the huge surplus was used by Harriman to finance reconstruction of the Union Pacific, and, after Harriman's death, it was distributed as dividends.

Isaias Hellman did not care for branch banks, and had closed out all the Nevada National branches before the merger. Wells Fargo still had two, and he proceeded to sell them out.

The Portland branch of the Wells Fargo Bank had started out as the Commercial National, but Valen-

tine had closed it out and made it a branch of the Wells Fargo Bank. The company continued to operate it, but the management was poor, and the bank was sold in 1905 to the United States National.

In that same year, the Salt Lake City branch was sold to the Walker brothers of Salt Lake City, and the Wells Fargo Nevada National Bank was out of the branch banking business.

The Head Minutes say: "The Auditing, Cashier and Money Order Departments were removed from San Francisco to 51 Broadway and 100 Warren Street, New York City, January 1, 1905."

At the beginning of 1905, the board of directors of Wells, Fargo & Company was made up of Evans, president; Parsons, vice-president and secretary; King, treasurer and president of the bank; Underwood, Huntington, Van Brunt, Kruttschnitt, McCook, Gray, Harriman, Thorne, William F. Herrin, and Cornish. Nathan Stein was assistant secretary. R. S. Lovett was elected to the board on August 10 in place of King; Parsons was elected vice-president, treasurer, and secretary at the same time; and A. Christeson was elected assistant secretary. Lipman's name does not appear, of course, because he was not an officer of Wells, Fargo & Company, but an employee of the Wells Fargo Nevada National Bank.

Gross receipts from express for 1905, $17,070,000; charges for carrying express, $8,072,000; operating expenses, $6,768,000; income from investment, $542,000 (a decrease of $269,000—apparently the result of losing the bank as an investment). The surplus fund increased $400,000 to $11,560,000. It is obvious that the express business continued to roll.

Total mileage: 51,566.

In January and in July, Wells, Fargo & Company paid its usual 4 percent dividends, a total of $640,000.

The most catastrophic event in the history of the West was about to come: the great earthquake and fire of 1906. It would not be a particular hazard to Wells, Fargo & Company, Express, but it would try the new bank—as in fact it would try all banks and the very banking system itself. It would be a time of great peril, and both the great names of Wells Fargo would have a chance to show the stuff they were made of.

On the second day, looking eastward toward the fire. From "Collier's," May 5, 1906.

1906
Earthquake and Fire

THE WELLS FARGO BANK HAD BEEN through many crises, but never one as totally unforeseeable in its occurrence and as completely unpredictable in its results as was the earthquake of 1906 and the resulting holocaust of fire. The earthquake struck in the early morning of April 18, 1906. Power lines were broken, gas mains fractured, water pipes severed in countless places, chimneys cracked. Fire broke out in a thousand spots at once, and the only effective tool to fight it was dynamite. By the night of the third day, a great pall of smoke hung over the peninsula, and three fourths of the city had been burned.

For a while, the city was in utter chaos. Most persons were without homes, without money. Soldiers shot looters on sight, and a man dared not try to open his own safe. Drayage firms gave their services free of charge; the army pitched hundreds of tents and established hospitals; railroads and ferries carried passengers without charge until the crisis was over; newspapers were published in the plant of the Oakland *Tribune;* firms set up temporary offices in unburned buildings and advertised the addresses to their employees. Banks were generally in good shape and stood firm; the United States mint acted as a sort of central bank until the bank vaults cooled and the various banks could get to their books and their gold and silver assets. It was a time of trial for San Francisco, and the city, the state, the nation, and the world responded wholeheartedly.

San Francisco had already outgrown the early wild days of the Gold Country and the Comstock, of speculation and the get-rich-quick fever. It would, perhaps, never quite outgrow that policy of "devil take the hindmost," but it was making progress. It was a city of solid fortunes, of great pride, of culture.

On the night of April 17, 1906, the Metropolitan Opera Company of New York was in town, and Enrico Caruso sang in *Carmen;* he was to appear in *Pagliacci* on the eighteenth. Ralston's Palace Hotel was still one of the wonders of the West with its eight-foot-thick walls, and Caruso, of course, stayed there. The daughters of James Fair were building the Fairmont Hotel to their father's memory. Smart shops like the City of Paris and the White House (both still in existence) made San Francisco women the best dressed in the world and contributed to San Francisco's reputation as a city of gracious living. Before and after the great performances at the Tivoli Theatre, wealthy homes would ring with gay parties of bejeweled and beautiful women, of swallowtail-coated and white-tied men. Governors, ambassadors, commercial tycoons, great artists, and rajahs were entertained in a constant round of dinners and parties, and the Palace Hotel, like no other in the world, blazed with light from evening to morning.

In the midst of all this gaiety, the earthquake occurred in the early morning. The *Chronicle* had issued its April 18 edition, closing at about 2 A. M.;

it was a sixteen-page edition, and its principal story was one of Charles Evans Hughes, who had been retained by the Department of Justice to investigate the operations of coal companies engaged in interstate commerce. (Hughes had the same beard in 1906 that he would have running for President against Woodrow Wilson in 1916.)

Not many descriptions of the earthquake itself seem to exist, but one very good one is a letter written by Antoine Borel to his parents:

> Dear Papa & Mamma & Sisters: A terrible thing has hapened. San Francisco is no more. There was a frightful shock on Wednesday morning at 5:13—buildings fell right and left. Our house on Washington suffered a good deal. The fence on Franklin Street was thrown on the street. Every chimney fell down, crushing the building in several places. Many persons killed downtown. Many boarding house totally destroyed. Market Street near the ferries sank many feet. Van Ness near Vallejo sank down over 4 feet. Portions of the City Hall were destroyed, but worst of all was the fire. The whole city is destroyed— . . . Every street went up in flames. The big mains of the Water Co. were broken by the shock, so there was no water down town. . . . Alfred and the children and myself—when we saw the fire eating all before it began to pack a few necessary things. . . . We engaged a gasoline to cross the bay to Alameda. . . . The Nevada Bank was blown up by the soldiers, who came from all parts of the state. There was "martial law" in town and when we went to the bank they denied us entrance. The only buildings so far not known destroyed are the Mint, Post Office, and some in the Park district. The heat is intense. The smoke is awful. [Later:] The house was saved from fire though the demon crept to Van Ness and acrossed over to the Claus Spreckels house—destroyed it—also swept out California Street—ruined Zeile house block. . . . All Van Ness Avenue is totally destroyed on the East Side, in fact from the ferry building to parts of Franklin and from Telegraph Hill to the Potrero—all gone!! . . . Reports say our vaults at the bank are safe. . . . We saw Mr. I. W. Hellman who has great hopes for the new city. . . . Ogden Mills and his father [D. O. Mills] said the Mills building in S. F. would be rebuilt. Ant.[1]

Since plants were damaged and power service was disrupted, apparently no San Francisco paper issued an edition immediately after the earthquake. Not until the nineteenth did the *Call,* the *Chronicle,* and the *Examiner* issue a combined edition from the plant of the Oakland *Tribune,* but the very first announcement was made in the Oakland *Tribune* on Wednesday, April 18, the day of the earthquake. An extra said:

> SAN FRANCISCO DOOMED! GREAT EARTHQUAKE! Death and Destruction Sweep the Bay Cities! Hundreds Die in Ruins! This morning at 5:14:48 o'clock an earthquake shock was experienced in Oakland and a number of other California cities. The temblor lasted for 28 seconds. Many chimneys in private houses, mercantile establishments and manufacturing institutions were knocked down. In some cases, holes were torn in the walls of business places, but no structures were entirely demolished [in Oakland]. Water for a time was cut off from consumers, and telegraph and telephone service was interrupted. The loss will aggregate several hundred thousand dollars. Five lives were lost. Three victims were crushed to death in a rooming house [in Oakland]. In San Jose and San Francisco the loss of property and life was excessive, especially in the latter place where the eastern part of the city, including the Palace Hotel, the Call Building, the Chronicle Building and the City Hall and a number of other structures were reduced to ashes by fire that broke out in the dismantled structures. The loss there will run into many millions.

This report, of course, is told primarily from the Oakland viewpoint. Since the lead paragraph says the Palace Hotel was reduced to ashes, this edition must have come out sometime after 5 P. M. The Call Building, one of the first to burn, was a roaring furnace by 11 A. M. the first day. The Post Building was also burned, and apparently all San Francisco newspaper buildings were destroyed.

The Oakland *Tribune* said: "To the people: Keep cool. Keep your heads. Keep your courage. Don't exaggerate. Don't get panic-stricken."

General Funston, of the United States Army at the Presidio, sent word to the mayor of San Francisco, Eugene E. Schmitz, asking if he needed help. The mayor said he did, and by 9 o'clock in the morning of April 18 there were two thousand regular-army soldiers patrolling the streets; by that night there were five thousand.

Warnings were issued against looting, against building fires in houses, and against congregating in crowds. In San Jose a placard was posted: "WARNING! Notice is given that any person found Pilfering, Stealing, Robbing, or committing any act of Lawless Violence will be summarily HANGED. Vigilance Committee."

The Call-Chronicle-Examiner

SAN FRANCISCO, THURSDAY, APRIL 19, 1906.

ARTHQUAKE AND FIRE: AN FRANCISCO IN RUINS

DEATH AND DESTRUCTION HAVE BEEN THE FATE OF SAN FRANCISCO. SHAKEN BY A TEMBLOR AT 5:13 O'CLOCK YESTERDAY MORNING, THE SHOCK LASTING 48 SECONDS, SCOURGED BY FLAMES THAT RAGED DIAMETRICALLY IN ALL DIRECTIONS, THE CITY IS A MASS OF SMOULDERING RUINS. AT SIX O'CLOCK LAST EVENING THE FLAMES SEEM- PLAYING WITH INCREASED VIGOR, THREATENED TO DESTROY SUCH SECTIONS AS THEIR FURY HAD SPARED DURING THE EARLIER PORTION OF THE DAY. BUILDING THEIR IN A TRIANGULAR CIRCUIT FROM THE START IN THE EARLY MORNING, THEY JOCKEYED AS THE DAY WANED, LEFT THE BUSINESS SECTION, WHICH THEY HAD ENTIRELY DE- ATED, AND SKIPPED IN A DOZEN DIRECTIONS TO THE RESIDENCE PORTIONS. AS NIGHT FELL THEY HAD MADE THEIR WAY OVER INTO THE NORTH BEACH SECTION AND ING ANEW TO THE SOUTH THEY REACHED OUT ALONG THE SHIPPING SECTION DOWN THE BAY SHORE, OVER THE HILLS AND ACROSS TOWARD THIRD AND TOWNSEND TS. WAREHOUSES, WHOLESALE HOUSES AND MANUFACTURING CONCERNS FELL IN THEIR PATH. THIS COMPLETED THE DESTRUCTION OF THE ENTIRE DISTRICT KNOWN E "SOUTH OF MARKET STREET." HOW FAR THEY ARE REACHING TO THE SOUTH ACROSS THE CHANNEL CANNOT BE TOLD AS THIS PART OF THE CITY IS SHUT OFF FROM ANCISCO PAPERS.

AFTER DARKNESS, THOUSANDS OF THE HOMELESS WERE MAKING THEIR WAY WITH THEIR BLANKETS AND SCANT PROVISIONS TO GOLDEN GATE PARK AND THE BEACH TO SHELTER. THOSE IN THE HOMES ON THE HILLS JUST NORTH OF THE HAYES VALLEY WRECKED SECTION PILED THEIR BELONGINGS IN THE STREETS AND EXPRESS WAG- ND AUTOMOBILES WERE HAULING THE THINGS AWAY TO THE SPARSELY SETTLED REGIONS. EVERYBODY IN SAN FRANCISCO IS PREPARED TO LEAVE THE CITY, FOR THE IS FIRM THAT SAN FRANCISCO WILL BE TOTALLY DESTROYED.

TOWN EVERYTHING IS RUIN. NOT A BUSINESS HOUSE STANDS. THEATRES ARE CRUMBLED INTO HEAPS. FACTORIES AND COMMISSION HOUSES LIE FORMER SITES. ALL OF THE NEWSPAPER PLANTS HAVE BEEN RENDERED USELESS. THE "CALL" AND THE "EXAMINER" BUILDINGS, EXCLUDING ON STEVENSON ST

The first page of the "Call-Chronicle-Examiner" of April 19, 1906. The three papers went together and printed this edition in an Oakland plant.

Effects of the shock on two f... uses on Howard Street near 18th in San Fr...

WARNING!

NOTICE IS GIVEN that any person found Pilfering, Stealing, Robbing, or committing any act of Lawless Violence will be summarily

HANGED

Vigilance Committee.

SAN FRANCISCO DOOMED

EXTRA **Oakland Tribune.** EXTRA

GREAT EARTHQUAKE!

DEATH AND DESTRUCTION SWEEP THE BAY CITIES!

HUNDREDS DIE IN RUINS!

Possibly the very first extra on the great San Francisco fire (San Franciscans don't like to refer to it as the earthquake, since most of the damage was caused by fire). This newspaper was issued on Wednesday evening, April 18, 1906, by the Oakland "Tribune." The quake had hit at a little after 5 o'clock that morning.

The Vigilance Committee must already have been organized, or else it was put together in a hurry. There is no evidence that it hanged anybody. Printed in the fiftieth anniversary edition of the Oakland "Tribune."

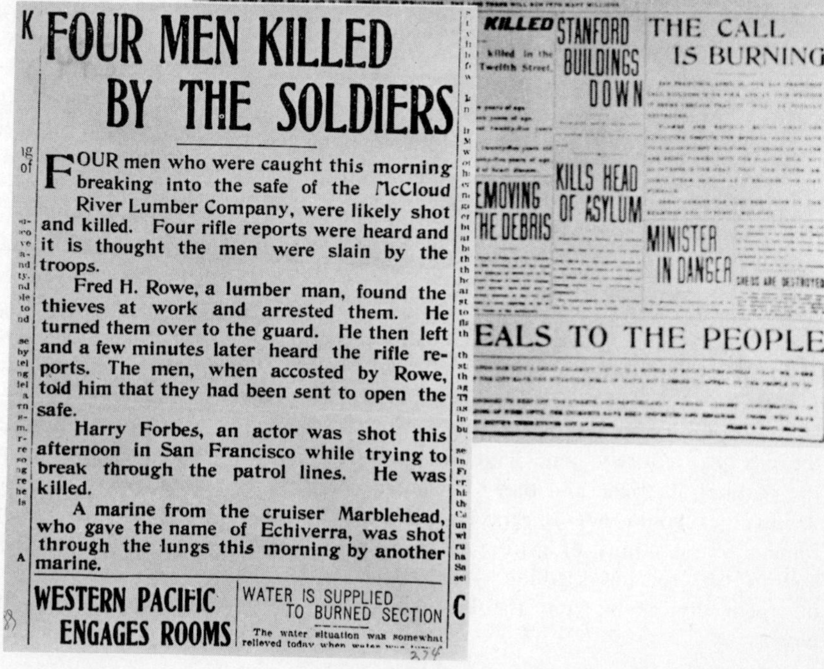

FOUR MEN KILLED BY THE SOLDIERS

FOUR men who were caught this morning breaking into the safe of the McCloud River Lumber Company, were likely shot and killed. Four rifle reports were heard and it is thought the men were slain by the troops.

Fred H. Rowe, a lumber man, found the thieves at work and arrested them. He turned them over to the guard. He then left and a few minutes later heard the rifle reports. The men, when accosted by Rowe, told him that they had been sent to open the safe.

Harry Forbes, an actor was shot this afternoon in San Francisco while trying to break through the patrol lines. He was killed.

A marine from the cruiser Marblehead, who gave the name of Echiverra, was shot through the lungs this morning by another marine.

WESTERN PACIFIC ENGAGES ROOMS

WATER IS SUPPLIED TO BURNED SECTION

The water situation was somewhat relieved today when water ...

KILLED — STANFORD BUILDINGS DOWN — THE CALL IS BURNING — EMOVING THE DEBRIS — KILLS HEAD OF ASYLUM — MINISTER IN DANGER — EALS TO THE PEOPLE

In spite of the general good order, there was some trouble, and probably this report of six men shot (five killed) is accurate. It was printed in the "Bulletin," April 21, 1906.

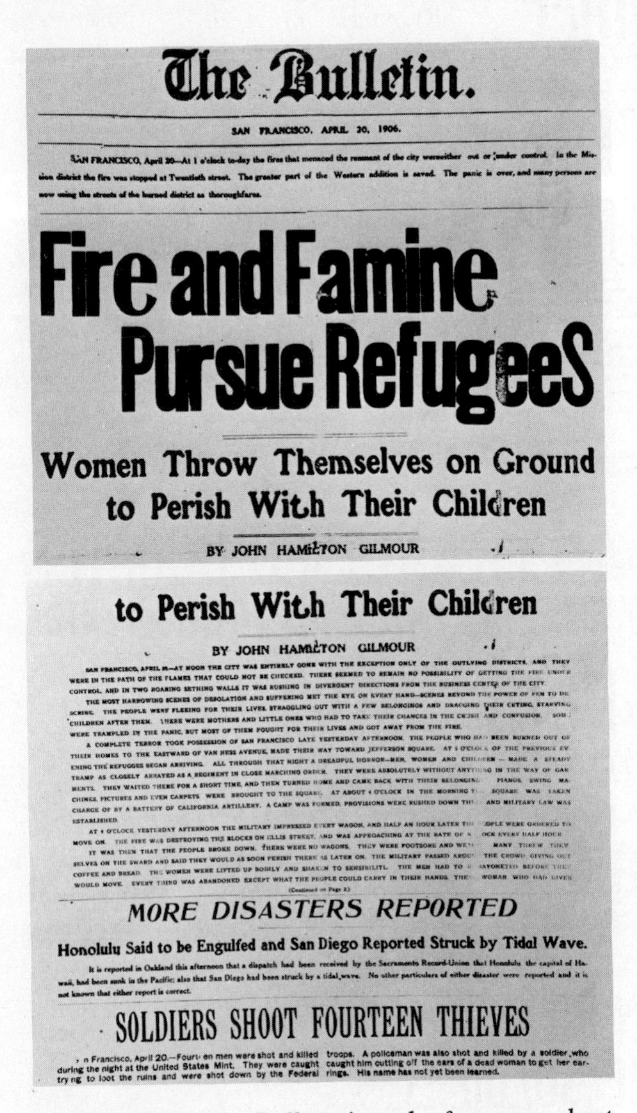

The Bulletin.

SAN FRANCISCO, APRIL 20, 1906.

SAN FRANCISCO, April 20—At 1 o'clock to-day the fires that menaced the remnant of the city were either out or under control. In the Mission district the fire was stopped at Twentieth street. The greater part of the Western addition is saved. The panic is over, and many persons are now using the streets of the burned district as thoroughfares.

Fire and Famine Pursue RefugeeS

Women Throw Themselves on Ground to Perish With Their Children

BY JOHN HAMILTON GILMOUR

to Perish With Their Children

BY JOHN HAMILTON GILMOUR

SAN FRANCISCO, APRIL 20—AT NOON THE CITY WAS ENTIRELY GONE WITH THE EXCEPTION ONLY OF THE OUTLYING DISTRICTS, AND THEY WERE IN THE PATH OF THE FLAMES THAT COULD NOT BE CHECKED. THERE SEEMED TO REMAIN NO POSSIBILITY OF GETTING THE FIRE UNDER CONTROL, AND IN TWO ROARING SETHING WALLS IT WAS RUSHING IN DIVERGENT DIRECTIONS FROM THE BUSINESS CENTER OF THE CITY.

THE MOST HARROWING SCENES OF DESOLATION AND SUFFERING MET THE EYE ON EVERY HAND—SCENES BEYOND THE POWER OF PEN TO DESCRIBE. THE PEOPLE WERE FLEEING FOR THEIR LIVES, STRAGGLING OUT WITH A FEW BELONGINGS AND DRAGGING THEIR CRYING, STARVING CHILDREN AFTER THEM. THERE WERE MOTHERS AND LITTLE ONES WHO HAD TO TAKE THEIR CHANCES IN THE CRUSH AND CONFUSION. SOME WERE TRAMPLED IN THE PANIC, BUT MOST OF THEM FOUGHT FOR THEIR LIVES AND GOT AWAY FROM THE FIRE.

A COMPLETE TERROR TOOK POSSESSION OF SAN FRANCISCO LATE YESTERDAY AFTERNOON. THE PEOPLE WHO HAD BEEN BURNED OUT OF THEIR HOMES TO THE EASTWARD OF VAN NESS AVENUE, MADE THEIR WAY TOWARD JEFFERSON SQUARE. AT 5 O'CLOCK OF THE PREVIOUS EVENING THE REFUGGES BEGAN ARRIVING. ALL THROUGH THAT NIGHT A DREADFUL HORROR—MEN, WOMEN AND CHILDREN — MADE A STEADY TRAMP AS CLOSELY ARRAYED AS A REGIMENT IN CLOSE MARCHING ORDER. THEY WERE ABSOLUTELY WITHOUT ANYTHING IN THE WAY OF GARMENTS. THEY WAITED THERE FOR A SHORT TIME, AND THEN TURNED HOME AND CAME BACK WITH THEIR BELONGINGS. PIANOS, SWING MACHINES, PICTURES AND EVEN CARPETS WERE BROUGHT TO THE SQUARE. AT ABOUT 4 O'CLOCK IN THE MORNING THE SQUARE WAS TAKEN CHARGE OF BY A BATTERY OF CALIFORNIA ARTILLERY. A CAMP WAS FORMED, PROVISIONS WERE RUSHED DOWN THERE AND MILITARY LAW WAS ESTABLISHED.

AT 4 O'CLOCK YESTERDAY AFTERNOON THE MILITARY IMPRESSED EVERY WAGON, AND HALF AN HOUR LATER THE PEOPLE WERE ORDERED TO MOVE ON. THE FIRE WAS DESTROYING THE BLOCKS ON ELLIS STREET, AND WAS APPROACHING AT THE RATE OF A BLOCK EVERY HALF HOUR.

IT WAS THEN THAT THE PEOPLE BROKE DOWN. THERE WERE NO WAGONS. THEY WERE FOOTSORE AND WEARY. MANY THREW THEMSELVES ON THE SWARD AND SAID THEY WOULD AS SOON PERISH THERE AS LATER ON. THE MILITARY PASSED AROUND THE CROWD GIVING OUT COFFEE AND BREAD. THE WOMEN WERE LIFTED UP BODILY AND SHAKEN TO SENSIBILITY. THE MEN HAD TO BE BAYONETED BEFORE THEY WOULD MOVE. EVERY THING WAS ABANDONED EXCEPT WHAT THE PEOPLE COULD CARRY IN THEIR HANDS. THE [illegible] WOMAN WHO HAD GIVEN

(Continued on Page 2.)

MORE DISASTERS REPORTED

Honolulu Said to be Engulfed and San Diego Reported Struck by Tidal Wave.

It is reported in Oakland this afternoon that a dispatch had been received by the Sacramento Record-Union that Honolulu the capital of Hawaii, had been sunk in the Pacific; also that San Diego had been struck by a tidal wave. No other particulars of either disaster were reported and it is not known that either report is correct.

SOLDIERS SHOOT FOURTEEN THIEVES

San Francisco, April 20.—Fourteen men were shot and killed during the night at the United States Mint. They were caught trying to loot the ruins and were shot down by the Federal troops. A policeman was also shot and killed by a soldier, who caught him cutting off the ears of a dead woman to get her earrings. His name has not yet been learned.

The "Bulletin" came out April 20, published in Oakland, with a headline replete with wrong-font letters. The "Bulletin" sensationalized it to such an extent that one wonders if John Hamilton Gilmour was actually on the scene.

The bottom half of the same page, carrying out the sensationalism of the top half; the reports of Honolulu and San Diego were somewhat exaggerated, as was the report that soldiers had shot fourteen men trying to loot the United States Mint. It was all in the tradition of James King of William, who had established the "Bulletin."

On April 20, the *Bulletin* issued a four-page sheet, probably printed in some commercial shop in Oakland. The *Bulletin* showed strong evidences of its heritage of extravagance from the times of James King of William:

FIRE AND FAMINE PURSUE REFUGEES. WOMEN THROW THEMSELVES ON GROUND TO PERISH WITH THEIR CHILDREN. By John Hamilton Gilmour. San Francisco, April 20.—At noon the city was entirely gone with the exception only of the outlying districts, and they were in the path of the flames that could not be checked. There seemed to remain no possibility of getting the fire under control, and in two roaring seething walls it was rushing in divergent directions from the business center of the city.

The most harrowing scenes of desolation and suffering met the eye on every hand— scenes beyond the power of pen to describe. The people were fleeing for their lives, straggling out with a few belongings and dragging their crying, starving children after them. There were mothers and little ones who had to take their chances in the crush and confusion. Some were trampled in the panic, but most of them fought for their lives and got away from the fire.

A complete terror took possession of San Francisco late yesterday afternoon. The people who had been burned out of their homes to the eastward of Van Ness Avenue, made their way toward Jefferson Square. At 5 o'clock of the previous evening the refugees began arriving. All through that night a dreadful horror— men, women and children—made a steady tramp as closely arrayed as a regiment in close marching order. They were absolutely without anything in the way of garments. They waited there for a short time, and then turned home and came back with their belongings. Pianos, swing [sewing?] machines, pictures and even carpets were brought to the square. At about 4 o'clock in the morning the square was taken charge of by a battery of California artillery. . . .

At 4 o'clock yesterday afternoon the military impressed every wagon, and half an hour later the people were ordered to move on. The fire was destroying the blocks on Ellis Street, and was approaching at the rate of a block every half hour.

ENTIRE CITY OF SAN FRANCISCO IN DANGER OF BEING ANNIHILATED

Big Business Buildings Already Consumed by Fire and Dynamite---30,000 Smaller Structures Swept Out and Remainder Are Doomed

PANIC-STRICKEN PEOPLE FLEE

SAN FRANCISCO, April 18.—This city lies in smouldering ruins and total annihilation seems to be its fate. The magnificent business district lying between the water's edge and Tenth street and even still farther west is destroyed, and there is scarcely any hope of saving but a few of the magnificent skyscrapers that have been erected during the last ten years.

... of the fire and all the intervening streets are practically under martial law.

Mayor Schmitz to prevent disorder ordered all of the saloons closed. There were but few cases of theft reported.

The Call building is already destroyed utterly and it is probable that the Examiner building and the Chronicle building will also be destroyed.

The Emporium is reduced to ashes as is the Flood building. The mag- ... broken by the earthquake during the early progress of the fire nothing could be done to stay the hungry blaze.

BUILDINGS DYNAMITED.

More than 150 buildings were dynamited with hope that the fire could be kept within a certain district.

In the business district, at Sansome and Bush streets, the flames are supposed to be under control. Twenty buildings were dynamited in this district.

BIG FIRE IN MISSION

SAN FRANCISCO, April 18. —A great fire is raging in the

EMPORIUM IN RUINS

SAN FRANCISCO, April 18. —The Emporium is a mass of

FATEFUL BUILDING

SAN FRANCISCO, April 18.—The [illegible]

THEATERS RUINED

All of San Francisco's best

The "Bulletin" for April 20 carried out its tale of gloom and destruction: "Panic-Stricken People Flee."

It was then that the people broke down. There were no wagons. They were footsore and weary. Many threw themselves on the sward and said they would as soon perish there as later on. The military passed around the crowd, giving out coffee and bread. The women were lifted up bodily and shaken to sensibility. The men had to be bayoneted before they would move. . . . Then a woman, who had given birth to a child during the early hours of the morning was put in a government wagon and sent to Golden Gate Park. . . .

A similar reign of terror raged in the district from California Street to the waterfront. . . . The fire had leaped Van Ness Avenue and was eating its way westward. Its explosions were heard every few minutes. . . . The detonations continued all through the night as the buildings were being blown up. . . .

There is absolutely nothing left of Van Ness Avenue. Never in the history of dynamite has that explosive done such terrible work. . . . Grant Avenue towards Sutter was a hill of brick, and smoke was issuing from either side of the street. . . . The smoke was dense and the heat terrific. . . . Market Street never presented such a spectacle. People in all conditions alike from the poorest Chinaman to the well-to-do merchant were hurrying to the ferry carrying extra suits of clothes on their arms or tied up in towels. At the Ferry Building the employees of the Southern Pacific Company are giving milk to the women and children and invalids. As the ferryboat *Oakland* pulled out of the slip, the *Slocum* and another government vessel, the latter packed with refugees, also started for Oakland.

It can be understood that there must have been individual scenes of terror and tragedy, but the many reports of the event do not seem to support Mr. Gilmour's excited prose. There are several mentions of the good humor of the people, and many pictures that support it; apparently there are few—if any—pictures that indicate panic.

Jack London, reporting from San Francisco for *Collier's* as an eyewitness, gave quite a different picture:

Remarkable as it may seem, Wednesday night [April 18], while the whole city crashed and roared into ruin, was a quiet night. There were no crowds. There was no shouting and yelling. There was no hysteria, no disorder. I passed Wednesday night in the path of the advancing flames, and in all those terrible hours I saw not one woman who wept, not one man who was excited, not one person who was in the slightest degree panic-stricken.

Before the flames, throughout the night, fled tens of thousands of homeless ones. Some were wrapped in blankets. Others carried bundles of bedding and dear household treasures. Sometimes a whole family was harnessed to a carriage or delivery wagon that was

weighted down with their possessions. Baby buggies, toy wagons, and go-carts were used as trucks, while every other person was dragging a trunk. Yet everybody was gracious. The most perfect courtesy obtained. Never, in all San Francisco's history, were her people so kind and courteous as on this night of terror.

All night these tens of thousands fled before the flames. Many of them, the poor people from the labor ghetto, had fled all day as well. They had left their homes burdened with possessions. Now and again they lightened up, flinging out upon the street clothing and treasures they had dragged for miles.

They held on longest to their trunks, and over these trunks many a strong man broke his heart that night. The hills of San Francisco are steep, and up these hills, mile after mile, were the trunks dragged. Everywhere were trunks, with across them lying their exhausted owners, men and women. Before the march of the flames were flung picket lines of soldiers. And a block at a time, as the flames advanced, these pickets retreated. One of their tasks was to keep the trunk-pullers moving. The exhausted creatures, stirred on by the menace of bayonets, would arise and struggle up the steep pavements, pausing from weakness every five or ten feet. . . . In the end, after toiling for a dozen hours like giants, thousands of them were compelled to abandon their trunks.

[At 1 o'clock Wednesday morning] at the corner of Kearny and Market Street, . . . surrender was complete. There was no water. There was no dynamite. Now from three sides conflagrations were sweeping down. The fourth side had been burned earlier in the day. In that direction stood the tottering walls of the Examiner building, the burned-out Call building, the smoldering ruins of the Grand Hotel, and the gutted, devastated, dynamited Palace Hotel. . . . At Union Square a man offered a thousand dollars for a team of horses. . . .

All day Thursday and all Thursday night, all day Friday and Friday night, the flames still raged. Friday night saw the flames finally conquered, though not until Russian Hill and Telegraph Hill had been swept and three quarters of a mile of wharves and docks had been licked up.

There is quite a difference between "bayoneted" and "stirred on by the menace of bayonets." Perhaps Mr. Gilmour was the panic-stricken one.

On that first day, the mayor issued a proclamation that helped to maintain order:

PROCLAMATION by the Mayor: The Federal Troops, the members of the Regular Police Force, and all Special Police Officers have been authorized to KILL any and all persons found engaged in looting or in the commission of any other crime. I have directed all the Gas and Electric Lighting Companies not to turn on Gas or Electricity until I order them to do so; you may therefor expect the city to remain in darkness for an indefinite time. I request all citizens to remain at home from darkness until daylight of every night until order is restored.

I Warn all citizens of the danger of fire from damaged or destroyed chimneys, broken or leaking gas pipes or fixtures, or any like cause.

E. E. SCHMITZ, Mayor.

Dated, April 18, 1906.

The Southern Pacific Company carried people away from San Francisco free on its ferryboats.

The *Bulletin* for April 20 was published from 1058 Broadway in Oakland, but on the twenty-first it was published from the plant of the Oakland *Herald* at Fortieth Street and San Pablo Avenue—at which plant, said the *Bulletin,* two morning papers of San Francisco were published.

PROCLAMATION

BY THE MAYOR

The Federal Troops, the members of the Regular Police Force, and all Special Police Officers have been authorized to KILL any and all persons found engaged in looting or in the commission of any other crime.

I have directed all the Gas and Electric Lighting Companies not to turn on Gas or Electricity until I order them to do so; you may therefor expect the city to remain in darkness for an indefinite time.

I request all citizens to remain at home from darkness until daylight of every night until order is restored.

I Warn all citizens of the danger of fire from damaged or destroyed chimneys, broken or leaking gas pipes or fixtures, or any like cause.

E. E. SCHMITZ, Mayor.
Dated, April 18, 1906.

The burning city from Portsmouth Square to the Ferry Building. From "San Francisco in Ruins," published by Leon C. Osteyee.

Proclamation by the mayor of San Francisco, advising that any person caught in commission of a crime may be killed. Printed in "Collier's," May 5, 1906.

Governor George C. Pardee, using the office of the mayor of Oakland, worked from 8 A. M. to 3 A. M., directing the dispatching of troops, granting of passes, receipt of hundreds of carloads of meat, groceries, and supplies arriving every hour from all points on the Pacific Coast.

All persons were prohibited from crossing the fire lines without a pass, and many persons lined up before the office where ex-Governor Budd issued passes, because they had left members of their family behind and wanted to look for them. Twenty thousand persons were camped in Presidio Park. The army at the Presidio in San Francisco issued three thousand wall tents, one thousand buckets, and one thousand blankets.

The weather was fine, and there was no suffering from cold or rain.

On April 20, according to the *Bulletin,* the cashier of a Market Street bank was killed by a soldier while he was opening a vault. This seems somewhat doubtful, because the vaults must have been still very hot on the twentieth.

Pass for Paul Calman, signed by the adjutant general of California. Owned by his son, Eugene Calman of San Diego.

PERMANENT PASS

GOVERNOR'S OFFICE
Oakland

April 25 1906

PASS MR. Paul Calman

through the lines in SAN FRANCISCO.

By order of GEO. C. PARDEE

GOVERNOR OF CALIFORNIA

Attest: J B Lauck

Adjt. Gen. of Cal.

The Vigilance Committee, which apparently had been a functioning organization, had headquarters on Union Street, and sent volunteers to patrol districts along the waterfront where refugees were camped. One man wore a badge, carried a ten-gauge shotgun, and had a handful of fourteen-gauge shells, but had no power to arrest anybody.

On the twentieth, E. H. Harriman passed through Chicago on a special train for San Francisco. He said that all his lines and all the steamship interests that he controlled would be placed at the service of San Francisco.

"All the motive power of the Harriman lines," he said, "have been instructed to do everything possible, and with the utmost energy. . . . I have ordered the collection and immediate despatch of supplies from Los Angeles, Sacramento, Oakland, and other points. All such shipments . . . will of course be handled without charge of any kind to the shippers." He was going to aid in his orders by being on the ground himself.

The records of the appellate court and the records of the county clerk were all destroyed.

The United States Sub-Treasury was burned, and on Friday neither the assistant treasurer nor the deputy could be found, and it was feared they had lost their lives. J. H. McClure, an assistant bookkeeper, wired Secretary of the Treasury Shaw from Oakland:

> San Francisco completely destroyed by fire following earthquake. Subtreasury burned yesterday afternoon. Under difficulty reached wreck of building this morning [Thursday]. Vaults appear intact. Found no guards. Finally communicated with General Funston and secured detail of one company of soldiers. Unable to locate assistant treasurer and therefore acted on own responsibility. Chaotic conditions. Mint buildings and vaults safe. Please arrange with Secretary of War for military protection to Treasury vault.

The bank vaults and safety deposit vaults of the city were pronounced safe by experts. The *Bulletin* said that fourteen men had been shot and killed during the night at the mint, caught trying to loot the ruins. This seems doubtful, because the mint, with its own water system, was one of the few buildings not burned. The *Bulletin* also said that Honolulu had been sunk in the Pacific and that San Diego had been stricken by a tidal wave. The *Bulletin* likewise, in a story extravagant with phrases like "robbers of the dead, pillagers of the defenseless living" (to take up space in the absence of facts), spoke of the "soulless, sordid shopkeepers" who "pounced upon the terror-stricken refugees . . . like vultures" and charged fantastically prohibitive prices. One firm the next day announced that it had advanced prices a little to keep a few persons from buying out the stock; another report says that a shopkeeper who raised his prices was surrounded by an officer and troops and ordered to give away his goods.

Men walking and running, buildings falling in flames, a shell still standing, street-car cables dropping—all these were caught in this picture as the building on the left leaned perilously outward. From the anniversary edition of the Oakland "Tribune."

The United States Mint was saved, but not without a battle—a seven-hour battle, as a matter of fact.

The mint was built in 1874 of granite and sandstone blocks, massive enough to resist fire. Iron shutters protected the lower windows, but those on the top floor were exposed, and a tarred roof on top was vulnerable to heat. Wooden tanks and other inflammable materials on the roof were a menace.

As the fire drew closer, soldiers and mint employees threw great timbers and tank staves into the courtyard below, where there were some thirty tanks of copper sulphate. The mint had its own well, and the engineer pumped water to the eighty or so men on the roof. The fire swept up Fifth Street and the heat increased to a dangerous degree. The Metropolitan Hall, the Lincoln School, and the Emporium went up in flames. By that time, a roaring north wind raced the fire through the Windsor Hotel and the Emma Spreckels Building, and sheets of flame shot up two hundred feet high, until the fire burst out on the northwest corner of the mint "like the breath of a second Pelee."

The twin chimneys from the refinery (which was covered with a tarred roof) were dropping bricks

Market Street burning on both sides, the Ferry Building in the distance. Photograph by W. E. Worden, from the History Room, Wells Fargo Bank.

The San Francisco branch of the United States Mint. From Frank Soulé, et al., "Annals of San Francisco."

and stones from time to time, but a few firefighters under Firechief Kennedy of Oakland continued to throw buckets of water on the tarred roof.

On the upper windows, men played a slender stream of water from a one-inch hose on the windowsills and frames, while the floor inside was awash with diluted sulphuric acid, but soldiers and employees fought from this floor as long as possible (presumably in rubber boots). Finally, however, the glass windows melted, and the fire poured into the building. The hose was abandoned, and the fighters withdrew to the floor below. "The roar of falling walls, the thunder of bursting blocks of stone, the din of crashing glass swelled to an unearthly diapason," said Harold French, an employee. It sounded like an attack by heavy artillery. Deep in the basement and sub-basement, artillerymen with blanket rolls and rifles stayed on guard in the strangling smoke.

Then the full fury of the fire across the street was burned out, and the firefighters went back upstairs to extinguish the blazing inner woodwork. The roof was swept by a hose and the copper-sheathed surface was cooled so that men could walk on it. An army officer with an ax tore up sections of tar and directed water beneath them. At 4 o'clock the mint was pronounced safe, and employees went out upon the hot cobblestones to learn about their own homes.

"There were sensational rumors," said the *Chroncle,* "of an attack of thieves upon the mint in which fourteen were killed in the attempt, but it is needless to advertise the fact that the garrison of the mint is equal to any emergency that may arise."

In the *Bulletin* for April 21, notices like these appeared on the front page:

"Will Mrs. J. M. Daly please communicate with son in care of The Bulletin."

"Miss Mae Scott will come at once to her brother at 598 Jean Street, Oakland."

"William Eager, foreman of Bulletin press rooms, report at Oakland Herald office Monday morning."

"Eustace Cullinan of The Bulletin staff is requested to report at the Oakland Herald Office Monday morning."

2 SAN FRANCISCO, THURSDAY, APRIL 19, 1906

AT LEAST 500 ARE DEAD

NO HOPE LEFT FOR SAFETY OF ANY BUILDINGS

(Continued From Page 1.)

the fire away from the swept section toward Mission street, they made their way to the point of the hotel until the old place began to crumble away in the blaze.

The City Hall is a complete wreck. The entire part of the building from Larkin street down City Hall avenue to Leavenworth, down from top of dome tothe steps is ruined. The colossal pillars supporting the arches at the entrance fell into the avenue far out across the car tracks and the thousands of tons of bricks and debris that followed them piled into a mountainous heap. The west wing sagged and crumbled, caving into a shapeless mass. At the last every vestige of stone was swept away by the shock and the building laid bare nearly to its McAllister street side. Only a shell remained to the north, and the huge steel frame stood gaping until the fire that swept from the Hayes Valley set the debris ablaze and hid the structure in a cloud of smoke. Every document of the City government is destroyed. Nothing remains but a ghastly past of the once beautiful structure. It will be necessary to entirely rebuild the Hall.

Mechanics' Pavilion, covering an entire block, went before the flames in a quarter of an hour. The big wooden structure burned like tinder and in less time than it takes to write it was flat

the streets, looking for missing relatives and rescue parties parties were formed to go into the burning blocks to save life. Here and there the grim-faced men dug out the unfortunates who had gone down into the shapeless piles of debris when the big shock came. Man fought to save man and many times did the sickened crowds turn away as they saw the rescuers driven back by the flames that reacheddown through the ruins to claim their victims.

Steadily the fire found its way into the uptown retail districts. From the sout hand east the south side of Market was attacked. One by one the familiar buildings went down. Levi Strauss and Company, Zellerbach and Company, Holbrook, Merrill and Stetson, Hicks-Judd Company, D. N. and E. Walters, W. W. Montague, the Donohoe estate building, Uhl Brothers, the Bancroft Building,—all the places that have made the San Francisco business district. Everyone of them went. They can't be enumerated. The work of the fire demon was too complete to make that necessary. From Mission to Market and east to Ninth the many-storied structures were gutted. True, many of these places had crumbled when the earth shook, but evidence of this was removed in the path of the flames.

From Second to Third streets Market street held its own until late in the afternoon. The Call Building was ablaze, but the Examiner Building the Palace Hotel, the Grand, and the other structures toward Second street stood. Two attempts were made to dynamite the new Monadnock Building when it was seen that the Hearst structure was doomed. And slowly

EFFECTS HEROIC RESCUE

The disaster brought forth hundreds of heroic deeds. About the only persons in the awoke when the trembler occurred were the mechanical workers of the newspapers, policemen and saloonmen. Among the heroes were Emile Dengel, foreman of "The Examiner" stereotyping department, and several of his men. After the first crash, and upon their escape from the building they were passing Krumm's cafe when they heard cries for help coming from beneath the debris of the place. Dengel rushed out to a passing hose cart, seized an axe, and with his great strength began chopping a hole through the structure to release its captive inmates.

A woman's voice kept saying

MAYOR CONFERS WITH MILITARY

(Continued From Page 1.)

responded. Among those promptly on hand were Hartley and Herbert Law, capitalists, the brothers Magee of Thomas Magee & Sons, real estate men; J. Downey Harvey, of the Ocean Shore Railway Company, ex-Mayor James D. Phelan, Garrett McEnerney, the prominent attorney; ex-Judge C. W. Slack, W. H. Leary, manager of the Tivoli Opera House; J. T. Howell, of Baldwin & Howell, real estate men; former City Attorney Franklin K

4 SAN FRANCISCO, THURSDAY, APRIL 19, 1906

LOSS IS $200,000,000

HEARTBREAKING SCENES AT THE PAVILION

FIVE KILLED IN OAKLAND THEATRE

MARTIAL LAW IS DECLARED

SAN JOSE IS RUINED

REFUGEES GO TO OAKLAND

SANTA ROSA IS A TOTAL WRECK

OFFICER KILLED IN DYNAMITE EXPLOSION

The "Call-Chronicle-Examiner" estimated the dead at five hundred, and printed a summary of the progress of the fire.

The "Call-Chronicle-Examiner" for April 19 (the day after the earthquake) estimated the money loss at $200,000,000. Later estimates made it $500,000,000.

On Sunday, April 22, the "Chronicle" announced that the fire was being brought under control, that the banks had plenty of money in the vaults, but, since the vaults could not be opened for thirty days, the governor had declared a financial holiday for possibly as long as thirty days.

San Francisco Chronicle.

VOL. LXXXVIII. SAN FRANCISCO CHRONICLE, SUNDAY, APRIL 22, 1906. NO. 97

FORCE OF THE FIRE IS AT LAST SPENT BANKS ABLE TO MEET THE EMERGENCY

PLENTY OF MONEY IN THE VAULTS

Financiers Want Thirty Days in Which to Put Affairs in Shape for Business

THIRTY DAYS OF HOLIDAY.

Governor Pardee yesterday, after a conference with financiers, agreed to declare a legal holiday from day to day as long as the emergency demanded. The Governor will confer with the Bankers' Committee from time to time. This will give the banks opportunity to reorganize their forces.

Issuing Meat Rations From a Commissary Department.

WINE USED TO FIGHT FLAMES

Long Hard Battle on Russian Hill Near Water Front---Docks Are Saved.

NO DANGER OF NEW EARTHQUAKE

URGENT CALL FOR NURSES

Persons without homes or whose relatives were missing were urged to register at the Ferry telephone booth, at Golden Gate Park, at Twenty-fifth and Bryant, at Park Lodge in the Presidio, at Sixth and Mission, and the Seventeenth Street station, and at the Black Point Ferry, or in Oakland, Alameda, or Berkeley. Registration lists from all these places were sent to the general office at Franklin Hall, Fillmore and Bush, to be kept on record.

The relief committee designated nine substations for distribution of food throughout the city.

Mrs. William Kreft's baby was killed in bed by a flying brick, but she carried the body through the streets of San Francisco, over to Oakland, and finally to Alameda, where she had relatives.

Insurance adjusters were at work, but there was little they could do but find offices to work out of.

The State Board of Bank Commissioners issued a statement saying that there was plenty of money and that all depositors would be paid in full. Eastern banks that owed money to the banks in California, were instructed to pay through the United States Mint.

Twenty men were said to have been shot Friday night for refusing to help fight the flames. Two men were shot down for insulting women. The grocery firm of West, Elliot & Gordon turned over its entire stock of $60,000 worth of food to the committee for the relief of the hungry. Mayor Schmitz asked the postmaster to carry letters without stamps on them. Four men who tried to break into a safe were shot and killed.

On Sunday, April 22, the *Chronicle* said the fire was over, that the banks had plenty of money but that it might be thirty days before the vaults could be opened and business could be resumed. Baltimore had recently had a disastrous fire, and word from Baltimore bankers was that some of them had opened their vaults within two weeks, before they had cooled off, and the books and papers had burst into flame upon the opening; therefore, the bankers of San Francisco wanted enough time for the vaults to cool.

The governor declared a legal holiday, to be maintained as long as the emergency lasted. Homer S. King, president of the Bank of California and president of the clearinghouse, had to borrow money for his personal expenses. King said there was more than $200,000,000 in gold coin in the mint. Isaias Hellman sent east for $5,000,000 to build a new building or buildings. There was not expected to be any trouble among the insurance companies.

Able-bodied men were impressed into service by soldiers to help clear the streets.

By Sunday evening, twisted tracks had been repaired and streets had been cleared so that many lines of trolley cars were able to resume full operation as soon as power should be available. Unused streetcars were placed so they could be used as shelter by women and children. Transportation on every line was absolutely free to individuals and for supplies of all kinds, and an army soldier was stationed on every car to prevent abuse of the free privilege.

By that time, every railroad that had a terminus in or near San Francisco had offered to take every refugee to any point in California without charge.

Chimneys had to be inspected throughout the city to avoid further fires, and it was proposed, first, that every house owner strip the plastering or partitions away from his chimney to be sure there were no cracks in it. It was also proposed to burn sulphur in the stove or chimney and stop up the top, to see if fumes could be detected in the house, and the Board of Works was contemplating requisition of all available supplies of sulphur.

Experts of the Spring Valley Water Company (Ralston's company that he had wanted to sell the city in 1875) spent two and a half days examining the mains and reservoirs, and said the company had enough water for almost two years. The problem, of course, was with broken mains, but the company had already repaired pipes and was, by Friday, sending six million gallons a day into the city. The normal consumption for San Francisco was thirty-five million gallons a day.

The Chinese section was destroyed, and the Chinese Six Companies bought cars of provisions from along the coast, the Los Angeles Chamber of Commerce sent carloads of provisions, and a Chinese ship arrived with a huge cargo of rice. Portland sent $130,000 and a trainload of supplies; Spokane sent four cars of provisions and twenty-five cars of flour.

Church committees distributed wagonloads of sandwiches and coffee to crowds that waited many hours for trains. Fourteen cars of provisions from Sacramento, Modesto, Bakersfield, and Fresno were received—including one carload of hard-boiled eggs.

That food was sent to the Presidio for distribution by the army.

John D. Rockefeller donated $100,000 and directed Standard Oil to give another $100,000, while Rockefeller's chief of staff, H. H. Rogers, gave another $100,000.

Chicago sent $500,000, Boston sent $1,000,000, and New York sent $1,750,000. Arizona sent two trainloads of supplies and $75,000 in cash. Kansas City sent $500,000.

Every big theatre in New York held a benefit; George M. Cohan, Sarah Bernhardt, Mrs. Leslie Carter, Julia Marlowe, E. H. Sothern, James K. Hackett, and many other famous men and women of the theatre held benefits.

In Los Angeles, the famous Jim Jeffries, the prizefighter, took a wagonload of oranges and, with the help of Battling Nelson, sold them on Spring Street at $1 apiece for San Francisco. Blanche Bates in New York was playing in David Belasco's hit, *The Girl From the Golden West,* and when she came to the final line, "Farewell, San Francisco!" she collapsed and was not able to finish.

On April 23, the Clearing House Association called a meeting to discuss proposed measures to relieve distress. Over $76,000,000 in cash and securities lay in the overheated vaults. It was proposed to establish a "Clearing House Bank" at the mint. The Clearing House Bank was opened on May 1, with a teller from each bank in attendance. Each bank took care of its own depositors, and paid up to $500. Savings-bank depositors were not allowed to withdraw funds until the bank officials were satisfied, but before any man was given a check on the Clearing House Bank, he was required to sign a promissory note for the amount.

The clearinghouse itself was located in the ruins of the directors' room of the Mercantile Trust Company of San Francisco at 464 California Street (where the Wells Fargo Bank is today).

The commercial banks introduced a system of "special accounts" (in reality, new accounts) in which customers could deposit funds and against which they could draw checks. By May 9, all checks dated prior to April 18 had been cleared, and on May 23, all restrictions were removed, and the bank cashed checks as usual.

There was no run, no excitement. If a depositor had lost his check stubs in the fire, he called at the bank and got a statement of his balance.

More than $42,000,000 in gold was imported from New York and from Europe, but none of it was ever needed.

One unexpected result was that tramps (hoboes) flocked to San Francisco to get the free handouts. Some said they had not lived so well for years, and authorities took all possible precautions to avoid giving foods and supplies to such persons.

Streets were being cleared, and the *Call-Chronicle-Examiner,* April 19, carried an important notice:

KEEP OUT OF THE WAY OF THE AUTOMOBILES. The people must give right of way, every consideration and all assistance possible to their machines and their drivers now engaged in most heroic messenger service. Expedition is the chief need in the gigantic task of caring for the sick, the hungry and the homeless, and in forwarding the plans for the restoration of the city destroyed and the salvation of the city remaining. There is no speed limit in a time like this, and had it not been for the swiftness of the automobiles the great work now under way would have been dragging for days. KEEP OUT OF THE WAY OF THE AUTOS!

On Wednesday and Friday of the second week, the coroner organized a crew of men to remove the bodies that had been buried in Portsmouth Square the first day of the fire. Thirty bodies were disinterred, and either moved to Laurel Hill or delivered to undertakers at the request of relatives. Then the crew went to Washington Square and disinterred the bodies there. Most of them had been buried in a long trench; of the thirty buried there, seventeen were unknown, and a heart-rending scene took place when a father and a son identified bodies of their respective families. Three bodies were of Chinese, one of a Japanese.

The *Chronicle* for Thursday, April 26, said several banks put cotton banners on residences overlooking the tented camps of the refugees in the square, and they also proposed to pay depositors as much as $500 on their accounts, but checks and blanks had yet to be printed, and it might be three weeks more before the banks could make any of those preliminary payments. The Crocker-Woolworth bank would open with $13,000,000 in coin. Hellman said: "The banks are all right. We must be patient and

This picture, printed in the "Chronicle," shows the rebuilding of the Anglo-Californian Bank, to open about June 1.

The Price of the "Chronicle" is 5 cents. No dealer, carrier or news agent is authorized to charge more.

San Francisco Chronicle.

Chronicle Business Office, 1804 Fillmore Street, San Francisco. Branch office, 1236 Broadway, Oakland.

VOL. LXXXVIII. SAN FRANCISCO, CAL., THURSDAY, APRIL 26, 1906. NO. 101

City Banks Will Soon Resume Business

MINT WILL CASH CHECKS OF BANKS

Measures Are Taken to Permit the Early Resumption of Business

MILITIA CENTER OF HOT CONFLICT

Appeal for Recall of State Troops and a Petition for Their Retention

CLEARING AWAY DEBRIS AT THE CHRONICLE BUILDING. M.H. DE YOUNG STANDING IN FRONT OF DOORWAY. CHAS. DE YOUNG AT HIS LEFT.

BEST NEWS IN BRIEF PARAGRAPHS.

Milk will be supplied free by the Dairymen's Association until May 1st.

Electric street lighting will be resumed in three districts to-night.

Street cars will probably be running this morning on a number of lines.

Work of dynamiting walls in ruined district proceeding rapidly.

Labor Council resolves that wage scale shall not be increased.

Fifteen of the thirty-nine planing mills in the city escaped the fire and some are now in operation.

Forty telephones in operation yesterday.

The "Chronicle" for April 26 indicates that banks are about to get back into business. It would not be exactly routine, for the checks would have to be cashed through the Clearing-House (and for not more than $500). A depositor had to have his check approved by an officer of the bank. Note the "Best News in Brief Paragraphs" and the story that shows conflict among the army, the national guard, the police, citizens' police, vigilantes, and other voluntary organizations, some of which had "interfered most energetically."

This notice by Wells Fargo appeared in the "Chronicle," April 26. Wells Fargo was trying to get back to the job of forwarding express.

Wells Fargo & Co. Express

NOTICE TO CONSIGNEES.—We have a large quantity of freight and merchandise express shipments, consigned to people formerly doing business in San Francisco, now on hand at Oakland, and detained at Sacramento and Los Angeles, awaiting forwarding as soon as the present congestion can be relieved. It is therefore imperative that consignees send their instructions for disposition of goods at once to my office, room 68, Bacon block, Oakland, Cal. A. CHRISTESON, Manager.

the strong help the weak. I will do all I can to help build up the city again, and it will be done. The outlook is most encouraging considering the extent of the calamity that has just befallen us."

W. A. Simonsen, vice-president of the National City Bank of New York, took the first train out of New York for San Francisco. (Harriman was on the National City Bank's board of directors.)

"We stood up for Galveston [the flood of 1900]," said Simonsen. "We stood up for Baltimore, and now we are going to stand up for San Francisco."

The savings banks of Oakland were paying up to $30 without notice. Streetcars would start to run in San Francisco that day (Thursday, April 26). President Roosevelt gave the Secretary of War authority to disburse $2,500,000 in congressional appropriations through the Mint and the Sub-Treasury. Milk would be supplied free by the Dairymen's Association until May 1. Electric lighting would be resumed in three districts that night. The work of dynamiting walls in the ruined district was proceeding rapidly. The Labor Council resolved that the wage scale should not be increased. Forty telephones were back in operation on April 25.

The Wells Fargo Nevada National Bank had opened its headquarters at 2020 Jackson Street, which was the home of E. S. Heller; at his home also was located the office of Heller, Powers & Ehrman, lawyers, and that of the Union Trust Company. The paper was filled with advertisements of temporary quarters, in which all employees were requested to report at once. An announcement of Levi Strauss & Company said that all salaries of employees would be continued until further notice, and asked employees to register their names in Oakland. (Levi Strauss was on the board of the Wells Fargo Nevada National Bank.)

Wells Fargo & Co. Express ran a notice in the *Chronicle,* April 26:

NOTICE TO CONSIGNEES.—We have a large quantity of freight and merchandise express shipments, consigned to people formerly doing business in San Francisco, now on hand at Oakland, and detained at Sacramento and Los Angeles, awaiting forwarding as soon as the present congestion can be relieved. It is therefore imperative that consignees send their instructions for disposition of goods at once to my office, room 68, Bacon block, Oakland, Cal. A. CHRISTESON, Manager.

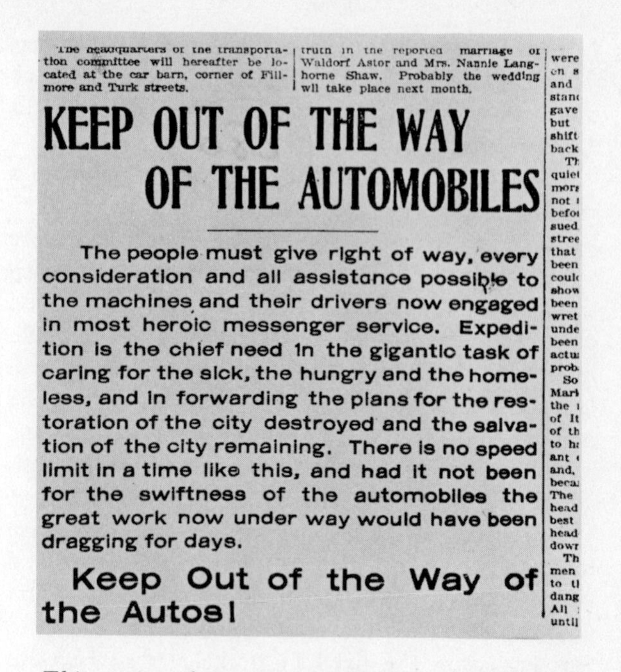

tion committee will hereafter be located at the car barn, corner of Fillmore and Turk streets.

Waldorf Astor and Mrs. Nannie Langhorne Shaw. Probably the wedding wll take place next month.

KEEP OUT OF THE WAY OF THE AUTOMOBILES

The people must give right of way, every consideration and all assistance possible to the machines and their drivers now engaged in most heroic messenger service. Expedition is the chief need in the gigantic task of caring for the sick, the hungry and the homeless, and in forwarding the plans for the restoration of the city destroyed and the salvation of the city remaining. There is no speed limit in a time like this, and had it not been for the swiftness of the automobiles the great work now under way would have been dragging for days.

Keep Out of the Way of the Autos!

This notice about the automobiles appeared in the "Call-Chronicle-Examiner" for April 19.

On the classified-ad pages there were some eight pages of "Business Personals," consisting largely of addresses at which various persons could be found.

Some $2,300,000 in relief funds was contributed by individuals, by organizations, and by governmental agencies aside from Congress. San Diego sent $25,000; Los Angeles sent $100,000 in cash and a large quantity of supplies.

The deposits of the Wells Fargo Nevada National Bank had been $16,000,000 at the time of the merger in April, 1905, and had risen to $24,000,000 by the time of the earthquake in April, 1906—a heavy responsibility to be hit by fire. But the bank, as Lipman said many times, was always good, and it was only a question of working out the details.

Lipman and his family were awakened in their home in Oakland on the morning of April 18 by the earthquake, which seemed to last an unusually long time. His chimney broke down, so they all got dressed, and went out in the street. It was a nice morning, but chimneys were falling all around. It did not interfere with cooking, for they were cooking with gas, but it did make it impractical to use the

heating facilities: the fireplace and the coal furnace. They had breakfast, and he started for San Francisco at his usual time, taking with him his dress suit for *Pagliacci* that night.

From the boat, he could see smoke rising from a number of places in San Francisco, and it seemed to be spreading. He went up California Street, and there were fires not far from him, but he could get through all right; he went to the Western Union office and sent the last telegrams that got through, instructing their New York correspondents to call loans that were out and send them $3,000,000. (The money was sent, and lay in the mint through the entire period; it cost the bank $9,000 in interest, although it was never touched.)

As the fire got nearer the bank, those inside were told by firemen to leave; they locked the vaults and left; the fire came on, and the bank was burned that day. On Thursday, they would not let him return to San Francisco (he lived in Berkeley), so he went to Oakland and telegraphed correspondents in New York, London, and Paris: "Building destroyed vaults intact credit unaffected."

On Friday, he got into the city and found the fire was just being stopped at Van Ness; everything east of Van Ness was burned.

On Monday, they opened offices at the home of E. S. Heller. They got around the dining-room table and dumped the accumulated mail; their last business day had been the preceding Tuesday. They went to small stationery stores to buy children's composition books to write in; all the big stores were burned. They met around the table, opened the mail, and discussed the situation. The United States Mint agreed to give space to the banks (desk or teller space, probably), but each bank was located in some private home, and the checks that each bank was to honor had to be drawn by that bank or permitted by that bank. Wells Fargo had a paying teller in the mint, but he did not pass on the checks. One had to go to the bank headquarters to have his check certified, and then it would be cashed at the mint.

Of course, they could not get into the vault, and so they had no books. If a person claimed to have an account in the Wells Fargo Nevada National, somebody tried to remember it. They paid everybody, and Lipman said their losses were probably no more than $200.

One of the convenient things about the Heller home was that it had a fair-sized safe for the family silver.

They waited for the vaults to cool off, and one day Bigelow, the vice-president, came in with a pale face and said the books were destroyed. Lipman said the next half hour was the worst he ever lived in his life; he pictured his future being devoted to trying to restore the records.

They still used the Boston ledger, a book where the names were in the left-hand column, and every other column meant a day. The names were all footed up at the bottom, and to prove the books, they had the customers' statements kept up to the day. The ledger would be used as transactions came in during the day, and the next morning the bookkeepers would change books, and would post the checks on the statements. Then they would figure the balance, and that would prove with the ledger. So they had, for each section of the output, the ledger of the last statements, and these would check with the Boston ledger.

Lipman went downtown—the longest trip he ever took in his life. He did not say on what day the vault was opened, but he recalled that when they had put the books away in a hurry on the eighteenth, some of them had been just thrown on the floor. This book vault was built on the bank floor, one story above the basement, and on a framework, so the fire in the basement had cooked the vault, and what had been on the floor was a floury ash. But then they found that only one ledger had in fact been destroyed out of fifteen or sixteen. Besides, at the bottom of the vault they found the lower part of the destroyed book—the binding edge, where the paper had been pressed together, was saved, and it gave the footing of every page, so they had something to go by. They found the relative statements for that ledger, and they had the footings, and they proved up to within $100.

The gold and silver in the vault—$3,000,000 worth—was unharmed.

Bigelow, by the way, was so unnerved by the events of the fire that he resigned; Lipman became vice-president, and Frank King became cashier.

The bank moved into the Union Trust Building, which had stood well, being a fireproof building (probably gutted, although Lipman did not say so). Lipman said the Union Trust Company took the Market Street frontage, and the bank took the

Montgomery Street frontage. It was a grand old building, and still was the home of the bank until 1962. In January, 1966, it was still standing, but was about to be demolished to make way for a new building.

The mint had had tons of silver quarters, and they were used for exchange for at least a month. The fire had started on April 18, and the Wells Fargo Nevada moved into its new quarters on May 21.

The Fairmont Hotel had been gutted; the walls of the Palace Hotel stood, but the building was entirely gutted. The Parrott stone building, Wells Fargo's home for so long, still stood.

Wells Fargo Express was also busy during the turmoil. It had three hundred horses and almost as many wagons in the big stables on Folsom Street, and it loaned them to whoever requested them, without security. People used them to move beds, mattresses, tables, chairs, and trunks. They went to the Presidio, to Golden Gate Park, and far beyond, but all that equipment was returned—the dark-blue-and-gold wagons and trucks, the fine horses, the splendid harness. And well it was returned, for Wells Fargo needed the equipment to clear the city and start to rebuild it.

The Red Cross people worked like supermen. The Southern Pacific Railroad brought in 1,300 carloads of supplies without cost, and took out 224,000 refugees without cost.

After the fire, paper currency began to be used freely for the first time.

Wells Fargo Express set up a circus tent at Franklin and Golden Gate Avenue, and put its sign on the tent; soon after, it had a crude one-story building. The express company had built a fine six-story building at Second and Mission for its headquarters on the Pacific Coast; that building stood, but was gutted, and records there were completely destroyed. For a while, a two-story wooden flat at Bush and Franklin was the headquarters of Wells, Fargo & Company on the Pacific Coast; then Wells Fargo put up a two-story wooden building next to it, and finally restored the original building and added two floors.

Wells Fargo men performed heroically during the fire, as was traditional. The big blue-and-gold wagons and trucks carried hundreds of tons of supplies without cost, and, by the end of April, express rates were slashed to help store owners restock their shelves.

Some $500,000,000 was lost in the fire, and the insurance totaled $202,000,000. Insurance payments began to come in, and the Wells Fargo Nevada handled huge sums over its pine counters at Market and Montgomery.

An English company paid its losses with sixty-day bills of exchange on London, and wanted Wells Fargo to receive their sixty-day time drafts the same as cash; Lipman said it put the company in the class of companies that did not pay in full, even though its credit was first class even after the fire.

By September 1, with the unusual amounts of insurance money going through the bank, the total deposits were $30,000,000, but in November, they were back to $16,000,000.

San Francisco banks were tried by fire, and not found wanting. Wells Fargo Express had lived up to its reputation of more than fifty years.

The Head Minutes show no cognizance of the great fire. The bylaws were amended in June and again in July, and the amendments were ratified in August.

The officers and directors for 1906 were the same as those at the end of 1905.

A cash dividend of 4½ percent was paid in January, and another in July—a total of 9 percent, or $720,000,000.

Total mileage: 55,060.

Gross receipts for 1906, $20,301,000; express-carrying charges, $9,792,000; operating expenses, $7,680,000; income from investment, $621,000. Apparently, the separation of the bank affected the income from investment but not much else. The surplus fund mounted to $14,715,000.

The next big event would be the panic of 1907.

1907-1918
End of Express Service

THE PANIC OF 1907 WAS CAUSED BY the inability of many banks to cope with conditions brought about by great expansion of commerce and industry, plus the introduction of many new banking functions. Some of these new functions caused otherwise sound banks to get in trouble, as, for instance, in the case of a bank that had both commercial and savings departments but allowed its commercial deposits to become intermingled with its savings functions and real-estate loans. The panic was set off by a stock market decline that started in March, an enormous number of business failures in mid-year, and finally, in October, the suspension of the Knickerbocker Trust Company in New York. It was one of the country's great depressions, and many suffered from it.

The Wells Fargo Nevada National Bank had no particular trouble, said Frederick Lipman. They had felt for some time that it was coming. The bank had a large customer, the branch of a big eastern concern that owed the bank $700,000; the parent house in the East sent word to the bank, hoping that the bank would not call on them for the money. Lipman said, "We will ask for only $150,000, which would be the proper reserve against this loan. You pay that to us and we will let you alone." The eastern concern was overwhelmed with gratefulness; they paid the $150,000, and the bank carried them through.

In 1907, coin was scarce, and Lipman said he had to "tend to the clearing house to deal with conditions of the bank there." Presumably the bank members of the clearing house pooled their coin, in effect, and depended upon payments by the clearing house, because on January 6, 1908, the bank sent notices "To our depositors and correspondents It will not be necessary for you to continue stamping checks drawn on this bank 'Payable through the Clearing House.' Coin conditions having become practically normal. Frank B. King, Cashier."[1]

Exactly what this instruction means is not quite clear today, but it is known that a severe shortage of coin developed in October, and legal or special holidays were proclaimed from October 31 to November 30; then the legislature passed laws to declare holidays from December 2 to December 21. In the meantime, to relieve the coin shortage, clearinghouse loan certificates were issued for the banks and the public. The banks deposited security with the clearinghouse, and were allowed to issue up to 75 percent of the market value in loan certificates of $1,000 to $10,000 denominations, bearing 8 percent interest. Some $12,000,000 of this material was out on December 24. The banks also issued circulating script, without interest, against the clearinghouse loan certificates, in denominations from $1 to $20. Altogether, approximately $100,000,000 in coin was withdrawn from California by the end of 1907, and this was replaced by some $30,000,000 in certificates. The California Safe Deposit & Trust Company was not able to produce assets acceptable to the

clearing house and was forced to close—for each member of the clearinghouse was responsible for the loan certificates of all.

In this light, it rather seems that the member banks did business among themselves with loan certificates, and conserved what coin they had by depositing it with the clearinghouse, which perhaps had the authority to pay with coin when it was absolutely necessary.

Wells, Fargo & Company Express paid a 5 percent cash dividend in January, and another in July—a total of $800,000 that year. It was this kind of thing—8 to 10 percent dividends while the company was earning 30 to 40 percent—that annoyed the stockholders of Wells, Fargo & Company; likewise, the fact, now common knowledge, that Harriman was borrowing from $10,000,000 to $15,000,000 at a time, at extremely low rates, to use in his railroad deals. *Old Waybills* says that the express company controlled the Wells Fargo Bank, whose deposits exceeded $20,000,000, but it seems that "controlled" is a strong word. Undoubtedly Harriman, through his holdings, influenced the bank, but it would seem that Isaias Hellman and Frederick Lipman would have stopped any untoward loans to Harriman.

The smaller stockholders formed a committee, employed counsel, and tried to get control of the company. Harriman was alarmed, and sent a crew of men through the country to buy up the stock. He raised the dividend rate to 9 percent and then, in 1907, to 10 percent, and the stock rose as high as $300 a share. The stockholders' committee sold out at those prices, and Harriman had eliminated the opposition.

Dudley Evans had said in answer to the complaints of the stockholders that the directors' aim had always been "to conserve the investment upon a sound and stable basis, rather than the speculative policy of larger and fluctuating dividends. . . . Dividends should not be put upon a scale that may not be maintained, and that would restrict the growth and resources of the company."

During the panic, the price of newspapers dropped to one or two cents, and pennies finally began to be used in San Francisco. This was the year that Colonel Epes Randolph of Virginia, on orders from the Southern Pacific Railroad, dumped thousands of tons of rock (and the cars in which the rock was hauled) into the breach in the Colorado River and saved the entire inland sea (now known as the Imperial Valley) from flooding.

The officers and directors for 1907 were the same as those for 1906, but Van Brunt resigned in November, and Stuart R. Knott was elected. R. S. Lovett resigned in December. Parsons died that year, and A. W. Zimmerman was elected secretary pro tem in November.

Total mileage in 1907: 56,544.

Gross receipts, $23,495,000; express-carrying expenses, $11,085,000; operating expenses, $9,437,000; income from investment, $994,000 (the highest point yet). The surplus fund increased more than $3,000,000 to $18,084,000.

In 1908, the country was in the full grip of the panic, but neither the bank nor the express company suffered.

That year, according to *The American West,* there was perpetrated the last holdup of a Wells Fargo box from a Concord stage; it was on the Rawhide-Manhattan run, and a posse chased the holdup men in open touring cars and roadsters.

In 1908, the Aldrich-Vreeland Act was passed by Congress, allowing national banks in emergencies to issue circulating notes. It also established the National Monetary Commission, which investigated banking and currency systems in the United States and Europe, and made recommendations that eventually led to the Federal Reserve Act of 1913.

The years 1908 and 1909, then, inaugurated an era of reform in banking.

There are no entries in the Head Minutes in relation to the directors or officers for 1908. On August 13, the bylaws were amended, and in January and in July, dividends of 5 percent were paid.

Total mileage: 58,209.

Gross receipts, $23,947,000; express-carrying charges, $10,796,000; operating expenses, $10,181,000; income from investment, $1,721,000 (a big increase). The surplus fund went on up to $21,794,000.

In 1909, Guy Giffen rode shotgun on the last horse-drawn stage that carried Wells Fargo treasure between Tonopah and Manhattan, Nevada. There were no regular gold shipments from Manhattan, but, when there was one, the Wells Fargo agent hired Giffen to ride with the driver. He made a number of trips, and then, on the last trip, a man

came out from behind a rock with his shovel reversed. Both Giffen and the driver thought it was a holdup, but Giffen paused in pulling the trigger, and the man explained himself. Giffen quit the job, somewhat shaken by his near killing of an innocent man.[2]

In this year, the Southern Pacific Railroad was the largest stockholder in Wells Fargo; Harriman was seventh with 1,524 shares, and five other stockholders were clerks in the offices of Kuhn, Loeb & Company, who, with Harriman, controlled the Southern Pacific![3]

The panic ended early in 1909, and a period of good times set in. The California legislature passed a new set of banking laws, following recommendations of a committee of bankers.

In many respects, one of the important developments of 1909 was Harriman's unexpected death at the age of sixty-one. This threw control into the hands of Kuhn, Loeb & Company, and the great surplus fund of Wells, Fargo & Company would soon be distributed.

The officers and directors of Wells, Fargo & Company at the beginning of 1909 were: Dudley Evans, president; F. D. Underwood, H. E. Huntington, Stuart R. Knott, Julius Kruttschnitt, H. W. DeForest, John J. McCook, George E. Gray, E. H. Harriman, W. O. S. Thorne, W. D. Cornish, William F. Herrin, and A. K. VanDeventer. Officers but not directors were E. A. Stedman, vice-president; R. A. Wells, vice-president; A. Christeson, vice-president and assistant secretary; A. W. Zimmerman, treasurer and secretary. In September, B. H. River was appointed assistant treasurer.

In May, Knott and Cornish resigned, and were replaced by William Mahl and Frederic V. S. Crosby.

Harriman died on September 9. He had been president of the Southern Pacific for eight years, and had spent $240,000,000 on the line. And that was only one of his many interests.

Total mileage of Wells Fargo: 59,900.

The Head Minutes do not give the dividends, but other sources indicate a total of $800,000, or 10 percent, as in 1908.

Gross receipts for 1909, $26,682,000; express-carrying expenses, $12,844,000; operating expenses, $10,857,000; income from investment, $1,653,000. The surplus fund rose to an all-time high of $27,211,488.73.

In 1910, the huge melon was cut. The fat cat of Montgomery Street was made to give up its surplus. After Harriman's death, his executors proceeded to declare dividends: 5 percent on January 15, 300 percent on February 15, 5 percent on June 15, 5 percent on December 15—for a total of 315 percent. The huge surplus was distributed to the extent of $26,796,740. Never had American business seen anything like that. The gold bars had to come out of the vaults of the Wells Fargo Nevada National Bank and from many other places. The dividends were not all in cash; 200 percent was in stock—$16,000,000 worth, but at the price of Wells Fargo stock it was better than cash, and it was still the greatest melon-cutting in financial history.

It was in 1910 that Elmer Jones, who was later to be president of Wells Fargo, was building up Wells Fargo business in Mexico when the Díaz regime collapsed, and Jones went all over Mexico to watch out for Wells Fargo's interests. Jones with some companions on horseback was traveling in the northern part of the state of Sonora (Pancho Villa's stomping ground) one day when he was met by a number of guerrillas who pointed rifles at them and demanded: "Viva Villa? Viva los Estados Unidos?"

Elmer Jones smiled and answered: "Viva Wells Fargo."

The guerrillas smiled and came to shake hands.

Early in 1910, American Express Company bought up substantial amounts of Wells Fargo stock and acquired a large interest in the company. By June 30, Wells Fargo was capitalized at $24,000,000, of which $3,000,000 was a bonus to the Southern Pacific. Wells Fargo's investment in real property and equipment was then $6,000,000; it was taking in $66,000 a day, and turning over its investment every three months. Naturally, the public was aware of this mint in express-company form, and resentment had built up long before, so that in 1910 it was no surprise when the Mann-Elkins Act was passed to declare express companies to be common carriers.

In April, Dudley Evans died, and ended another era.

The board of directors at the beginning of 1910 was Evans, president; Underwood, Huntington, Kruttschnitt, DeForest, William Mahl, McCook, Gray, Thorne, Herrin, VanDeventer, Crosby. E. A. Stedman was vice-president; R. A. Wells, vice-president; A. Christeson, vice-president and assistant sec-

retary; A. W. Zimmerman, secretary and treasurer; and S. H. River, assistant treasurer.

E. A. Stedman was elected to the board in place of Evans; Kruttschnitt was replaced by Richard Delafield, and VanDeventer was replaced by William Sproule.

Charles A. Peabody was elected to the board to fill Harriman's place in February; George Gray resigned, and Paul M. Warburg was elected; Underwood was appointed managing director in May, and resigned in November. Crosby resigned, and L. F. Loree was elected in October. William Sproule was elected president of the company.

Total miles of operation in 1910: 67,964.

Gross receipts, $25,171,000; express-carrying privileges, $12,022,000; operating expenses, $10,920,000; net income from investment, $1,369,000. In spite of the enormous dividends that year, the surplus fund remained at $4,437,000.

In 1911, Wells Fargo made twenty-year contracts with the Missouri Pacific-Iron Mountain System, the Wabash Railroad, and the Texas & Pacific, and a contract with the St. Louis & Southwestern System; these contracts meant replacement of the Pacific Express Company on almost the entire Gould system. Contracts for from one to twenty years were made with the Wheeling & Lake Erie Railroad, the Ann Arbor Railroad, the Missouri, Oklahoma & Gulf, some electric lines in Ohio, and some minor roads.

Service was extended throughout Alaska and the Yukon Territory under contracts with the White Pass-Yukon Route, Copper River & Northwestern Railroad, and various steamship lines operating from San Francisco and Seattle. The Head Minutes say, "While this is practically a summer service only, the progress of development in this section gives promise of future business for the express company."

The operating divisions of the company were reorganized to handle the expanded territory "with close supervision of the operating details combined with economical management."

A new system of accounting that had been under preparation for some time was put into effect on October 1, to relieve the operating staff and leave it free to superintend, solicit, and build up business. The Auditing Department was moved to Chicago.

E. E. Honn was appointed general auditor, and J. V. VanLoan was appointed assistant treasurer.

A final note shows which way the wind was blowing: "The company, together with the other express companies, was confronted with numerous inquiries and investigations by state commissions and the Interstate Commerce Commission as to the reasonableness of its rates, regulations, and practices."

Directors at the beginning of the year were Sproule, president; Underwood, Huntington, DeForest, Mahl, McCook, Richard Delafield, Thorne, Herrin, Peabody, Paul Worburg, Loree, and Stedman. Officers were the same as those for 1910, but Wells resigned in August and his position was abolished; Zimmerman resigned in July, and Charles Gardner was elected secretary and B. H. River was elected treasurer; Sproule resigned as president in October, and Burns D. Caldwell was elected in his place. Richard Burr was appointed comptroller in August.

Caldwell was a handsome man with a shock of snow-white hair, a million-dollar smile, and always a fresh white carnation; he telephoned his wife twice a day. It was his aim to give the express company a good traffic organization like that of a railroad; he obtained great men and produced magnificent results. He paid careful attention to public relations and advertising.

Caldwell hired Fred S. Holbrook as vice-president in charge of traffic (he was from the Vermont Central, while Caldwell was from the Delaware, Lackawanna & Western); he got John W. Newlean from the Union Pacific as comptroller; Charles W. Stockton was general counsel; Davis G. Meller, a Wells Fargo man, was made foreign traffic manager; Dudley T. Mervine, another Wells Fargo man, became general superintendent of transportation; Edward Hungerford was made advertising manager. Stedman was a general manager at Chicago, Andrew Christeson at San Francisco—and these two had, as general superintendents, F. J. Hickey at New York, Grover B. Simpson and H. B. Calkins at Chicago, Gerrit A. Taft at Houston, Elmer R. Jones at Los Angeles, and Clifford R. Graham at San Francisco.

At about that time, ready-made clothing was becoming popular all over the country, and Wells Fargo and other express companies made it possible for small merchants to stock ready-mades without investing a prohibitive amount of capital. Ready-mades could be brought in quickly by express, so that the merchant had only to carry a few sizes, colors, and styles. The merchant could send a telegram to New

York, and within a few hours the desired item of clothing would be delivered.

Wells Fargo had been shipping fish, meat, and fresh fruits and vegetables by refrigerated cars since Mervine had first used a baggage car. In 1896, Wells Fargo was hauling oranges, lemons, and bananas from Seattle to Dawson in ten days, to Fairbanks in sixteen days.

Wells Fargo brought back gold, and sometimes used dog teams—a typical run being from Iditarod to Seward, 479 miles. The first dog-team run was made by two teams of eight dogs each, and carried $559,000 in gold. It took fifty-four days in the dead of winter, reached Seward on February 6, 1912, and five days later was in a bank in Seattle. On one 376-mile run, Wells Fargo used horses to pull sleds holding $600,000 in gold in eleven days. Wells Fargo also shipped small fortunes in walrus ivory and northern furs.

By 1911, Wells Fargo had offices in Shanghai and Manila, and was getting ready to invade Europe. Wells Fargo also began to make refrigerator cars and lease them to the railroads.

Total number of offices, 5,204.

Total mileage: 60,850. (The Minutes show a figure as of October 1 of 63,461.)

A 5 percent dividend was paid in June, and again in December. Apparently the capital stock was not quite $24,000,000, because the Head Minutes show the amount of each dividend as $1,198,370.

Gross receipts, $27,973,000; express-carrying charges, $13,331,000; operating expenses, $12,518,000; income from investment, $1,298,000. The surplus fund moved up to $5,513,000.

In 1912, Caldwell made his moves in Europe, where the American Express Company had become very powerful. Wells Fargo had a system of money orders and travelers' checks, and now it went after the tourist business. It had a commercial office in Threadneedle Street in London, but now it established a tourist office near American Express on Charles Street, and in Paris it established another office on the Rue Scribe near the American Express.

On the night of March 12, 1912, what is said to be the last Wells Fargo holdup on a train took place near Dryden, Texas, when a gang of robbers stopped the Texas Sunset Flyer and required David A. Trousdale, the Wells Fargo messenger, to open the safe. Trousdale opened the safe but persuaded the robber to take a package that was supposed to contain something valuable, and, when the robber reached for the package, Trousdale crushed his skull with an oyster mallet. Then they took the dead man's revolvers and set a trap for the other robber, who fell for it and got shot through the brain. Seven guns, several sticks of dynamite, a bomb, and a pint of nitroglycerine were found on the robbers' bodies.

By 1912, Wells Fargo's interest in Cuba was extensive, along with its interest in Mexico. It was operating over eighty thousand[4] miles, it had a $3,000,000 interest in the Wells Fargo Nevada National Bank, it had a paid-in capital of $24,000,000, and a surplus of $7,000,000. But William Randolph Hearst was after the four big express companies—Wells Fargo, Adams, American, and United States—and feeling was growing against the fantastic earnings of the companies, a feeling that Hearst could fan better than anybody on earth.

The Head Minutes say that the increase in gross earnings in 1912 was largely due to the new railroads taken over in 1911— a total of some seventeen thousand miles, embracing a large number of trunk-line railroads. The company was concerned first of all with establishing a standard of service similar to that on other Wells Fargo lines. Therefore, say the Minutes, net earnings were small, and this, added to the fact that adjustments in accounts were made to conform with the new accounting system, resulted in a net figure not much larger than that of 1911, while the gross figure was up almost $7,000,000.

The new accounting system involved large expenses for printing, expert accountants, new employees because of the removal of the department to Chicago, many more employees for the new lines, and an extra force for the "extensive work of compilation of statistics in the rate investigation of the Interstate Commerce Commission." Also, the Minutes say, "owing to the extremely high price of provender for horses that prevailed during most of the year," there was an increase in that item alone of some 50 percent. However, in the larger cities, the company began to use auto trucks in place of horses and wagons.

The company was the largest carrier of perishable foods in the nation, and orders were placed for new refrigerator cars and rebuilding jobs on the old ones.

In this year, too, Edward Hungerford, the new

advertising manager for Burns Caldwell, began publication of *The Wells Fargo Messenger,* a house organ that "met with great favor and appreciation by Wells Fargo and was most helpful in promoting the company's efficiency and usefulness."

The directors for 1912 were the same as those for the end of 1911 except that McCook was dropped and Caldwell was added.

Officers were: Caldwell, president; Stedman, vice-president; Christeson, vice-president and assistant secretary; B. H. River, treasurer; Charles Gardner, secretary; Richard Burr, comptroller; E. E. Honn, general auditor; and J. A. VanLoan, assistant treasurer.

J. W. Newlean was appointed comptroller in April, and Richard Burr was appointed assistant secretary in October.

Mileage according to the Head Minutes: 89,703.

Cash dividends of $2,396,740 were paid in 1912, indicating two 5 percent dividends.

Gross receipts in 1912, $34,723,000; express-carrying charges, $16,917,000; operating expenses, $15,706,000; income from investment, $1,311,000. The surplus fund rose to $6,959,000.

In 1913, the long-delayed parcel post service began; the government started handling parcels as a part of the mail service, and this was to be the death knell of most express companies in the United States; Pacific and United States would soon go under, and the character of Wells Fargo's business and the business of all express companies would undergo drastic changes.

Business was good in 1913, but changes caused by new federal laws, by trustbusting, and by regulations of bodies like the Interstate Commerce Commission caused many individual problems.

It was in 1912 or 1913 that Elmer Jones had trouble securing the money the company was making in Mexico. The company's headquarters was in the ancient palace of the Duke of Albuquerque, and in the inner patio Jones decided to bury the earnings. Under the paving stones he dug a big hole and buried the safes, with gold and silver bullion, bank notes, and valuable papers, and then replaced the stones. During the Huerta regime he put $756,000 of company funds in the ground, and a few days later he was summoned to the office of the president, who smiled and said that the government was going to issue $13,000,000 worth of bonds, and that he would

EVEN A YOUNG GIRL
MAY TRAVEL ALONE
if she carries Wells Fargo Travelers Checks. Because they protect the hoider against loss by theft or accident.
Your pocketbook is insured—when you carry Wells Fargo Travelers Checks. You insure your house and your life—why not your ready money when traveling?
WELLS FARGO & COMPANY

A girl dressed in the sloppy clothes of 1914 may travel alone if she carries Wells Fargo traveler's checks even though, in 1914, girls seldom traveled alone. This was an advertisement of Wells Fargo.

be pleased if Wells Fargo would take $756,000 worth. Jones took them—and they were good.

During those days, two baggage cars carrying a million dollars' worth of silver bars were wrecked on the way to Vera Cruz in a wild section of the country. When the cars were found, they were empty. But Jones appealed to General Emiliano Zapata, and they found all the missing bars but two, which were found later under a dead burro. There was also a single bar of pure gold worth $45,000, and they eventually found that in a shed near San Luis Potosí.

It was in 1913 that the Federal Reserve System became a part of the United States' financial system. That financial system had been established during the Civil War, according to Cross, and had now lasted much too long—during a period of great industrial expansion, of exploitation of natural resources, the growth and control of trusts, and the expansion of foreign trade in a search for world markets.

The United States had about 28,000 banks, one third of which were under federal law, and over all this vast complex of financial affairs there was no unifying agency. Federal law required too much in reserves, and did not distinguish between demand deposits and savings deposits. The seasonal movement of crops created heavy seasonal demands for money, and monetary stringencies were habitual. The amount of money in circulation was so clumsily administered that it could not expand with the requirements of the market. The import and export of gold were not regulated, and the treasury system, established in 1846 to make the United States government its own banker, had proved clumsy and wasteful.

The Aldrich-Vreeland Act of 1908 had authorized national banks to issue currency, and established a commission to study banking and currency systems; it was largely approved by the American Bankers' Association. In the presidential campaign of 1912, however, both parties condemned the Aldrich Plan of reform, but Woodrow Wilson, after his election, took a personal interest in it, and a set of laws, later to be known as the Federal Reserve Act, was passed in December, 1913. It created the Federal Reserve Board, twelve Federal Reserve banks, and member banks; none of the Federal Reserve banks were to be owned by the government, but by member banks. Savings and demand deposits were separated, and reserves were reduced against both. Federal Reserve notes were created, with elasticity in the reserve requirements for them. Reserves could not be pyramided. The Federal Reserve banks were to act as the fiscal agents of the government, and the independent treasury system was abolished as of 1920.

Because of the European war, which started in August, 1914, the twelve Federal Reserve banks began simultaneous operation, November 16, 1914. No bank was compelled to buy stock in the twelve banks, but all the stock was held by national and state banks. This new system brought considerable stability at a time when stability was greatly needed, for World War I was under way.

Wells Fargo directors for 1913 were the same as those for 1912, but in October, A. Christeson was elected in place of William Sproule. Officers were the same except that J. W. Newlean was elected vice-president, W. B. Clark was elected assistant secretary, Richard Burr was made assistant comptroller, and J. A. VanLoan became assistant secretary.

Total mileage: 96,847.

Dividends paid in 1913 were $2,157,066, which indicates a dividend (or dividends) of 9 percent.

Gross receipts, $32,310,000; express-carrying charges, $16,123,000; operating expenses, $15,305,-000; income from investment, $1,290,000. The surplus fund rose to $7,079,000.

In 1914, the war broke out in Europe, and thousands of United States tourists found themselves stranded, and struggled to return to the United States—many of them abandoning luggage in the rush. F. S. Holbrook, the traffic vice-president of Wells Fargo, was in Germany, and as soon as the excitement began to simmer down, he began to gather the abandoned luggage, and shipped four hundred trunks to New York at Wells Fargo's expense.

Wells Fargo's offices in London and Paris stayed open during the war and served the men and women of the American armed forces, but the offices projected for Berlin, Hamburg, Brussels, and Rome never were opened, and the war ended Wells Fargo's activities in Europe.

It was in 1914 that banking and government officials had to devise a way to wean San Franciscans from gold, since a free market in gold obviously was an invitation to the enemy to drain American gold

reserves; and this was done, as told before, by taking away all gold except the $20 pieces.

The war depression hit in the middle of 1914, and Wells Fargo, which was making contracts for service in Argentina, stopped its activities there and brought a sudden end to its plans to expand into South America.

The express companies had to contend with parcel-post competition for the entire year (compared to only six months of 1913), and parcel-post rates were reduced and weights extended in certain zones, to make the competition more difficult.

New rates ordered by the Interstate Commerce Commission applicable to all interstate express business went into effect February 1. Rates were reduced from 12 to 15 percent in all but six of the thirty-nine states in which the company operated. This became known as the zone system of charges that was worked out by Franklin K. Lane, who would later be Secretary of the Interior under Woodrow Wilson. In the first five months of reduced rates—February to June—gross revenue decreased some $926,000, while operating expenses decreased $493,000, and payments to railroads decreased $313,000. Only $211,000 was earned during the five months.

The United States Express Company folded on June 30, and Wells Fargo grasped the opportunity to make contracts with thirty-seven more steam and electric lines, totaling 12,904 miles, and including the Baltimore & Ohio System; the Cincinnati, Hamilton & Dayton Railroad; the Chicago & Eastern Illinois; the St. Louis & San Francisco System; the Central Railroad of New Jersey; and the Philadelphia & Reading Railway; all these were short contracts.

Eighteen refrigerator cars were rebuilt in 1914, and 158 refrigerator and ventilator cars were in service during the year.

Directors for 1914 were the same as those at the end of 1913, but Worburg resigned in September, and Jacob H. Schiff was elected in his place; W. A. Harriman was elected in place of William Mahl in October.

Officers were the same as for 1913 except that J. W. Newlean was made vice-president and comptroller, and F. S. Holbrook was elected vice-president in October.

Until the earning potential of the company could be better gauged, the directors reduced the dividend rate; in June it was 4 percent, and in December it was 3 percent for a total of $1,677,718.

Total mileage in 1914: 99,017.

Gross receipts for 1914, $34,009,000; express-carrying charges, $17,393,000; operating expenses, $16,200,000; income from investment, $1,128,000. The surplus fund rose to $7,306,000.

About the middle of 1915, business began to improve because of the war in Europe, and Wells Fargo, doing a fast-growing business, went after better earnings. Application was made to the Interstate Commerce Commission in March for relief from the reduced rates that had been in effect since February 1, 1914; the express companies (apparently they all were in it) estimated that if their requests should be granted, they would earn from 3 to 4 percent on their gross revenue. The request for advance was confined to packages below one hundred pounds to avoid forcing a change in the commission's rate-structure system, and it was granted, to be effective September 1, 1915. By the end of the year, a similar increase was granted for intrastate business in about one half of the states in which Wells Fargo operated, and commissions for reductions had been filed before the commissions of the other states.

The Head Minutes reported pleasure over the new attitude toward the express companies.

> In the hearing before the commissions . . . as well in in its [the commission's] decision granting the application, marked encouragement was to be found in the attitude of appreciation and good will shown, both by the public and the commission, toward the express companies. The shipping public did not oppose the advance, while the commission strongly commended the express companies for the good faith and earnest effort with which they had met the situation.

It was whistling in the dark, however. The seeds of discontent had been planted over long years of earnings and perhaps sometimes a very unpleasant independence on the part of employees of some express companies, and it was not to be wiped out in a few months of penance.

The mileage operated over increased to 114,691, about fifteen thousand miles over 1914, due primarily to extension of Wells Fargo service over the lines of the defunct United States Express Company. The only other important contract during the year, say

the Minutes, was made with the Denver & Rio Grande System, comprising 2,308 miles in Utah and Colorado.

The company completed its rebuilding of its 146 refrigerator and ventilator cars, but because the perishable-goods business was growing, it ordered thirty-five new cars, to be ready January 1, 1916.

The directors for 1915 were the same as those at the end of 1914. Officers were the same except for the addition of F. S. Holbrook, vice-president and traffic manager, and W. B. Clarke, assistant secretary.

A 3 percent dividend was paid in June and another in December—a total of $1,438,044.

Mileage was 114,691.

Gross revenue from express, $41,846,000; express-carrying charges, $21,507,000 (these two increases were the result of increased mileage). Operating expenses, $18,479,000; income from investment, $1,033,000 (the Minutes say that this drop resulted from the discontinuance of payment of dividends upon the stock of the Mexican Express Company and of interest upon Mexican government and railroad securities owned by the company). The surplus fund climbed to $8,997,000.

On June 1, 1916, the company adopted a revised benefit and pension plan for employees "in recognition of the loyalty and devotion of the company's employees and as an encouragement to continuity of employment and increased expertness in the exacting work." Pension allowances were increased, and allowances were made for sickness, accident, and other disability, and to dependents of dead employees by continuing a salary. Directors estimated this revision would cost $200,000 a year.

The board also established allowances for employees who went into military service: for single men without dependents, the allowance, added to the military pay, would be enough to make up one half the company's rate of pay to the employees; for married men, the company would make up all differences between military pay and company pay. This program was expected to cost about $25,000 a year.

Toward the end of the year, minor-salaried employees were granted an increase in pay that was expected to cost the company about $300,000 a year.

The directors for 1916 were the same as those for 1915, and the officers were the same.

Total mileage: 107,529 (there is no explanation for this reduction).

Gross receipts, $50,403,000; this very substantial increase in earnings (almost $9,000,000) resulted largely from two factors not considered normal: the activity in business because of the war boom and the use of express for goods that ordinarily went by freight but that could not well do so because of the unusual demands on freight facilities. Again the Minutes are optimistic, saying:

> An encouraging feature has been a growing appreciation of the express during a time in which its service proved of greatest value to both the public and the railroads. There probably never was a period heretofore in which the benefit to the shipping public of the express as a specialized form of transportation in which expedition and personal service are fundamental, was so fully demonstrated.

However, the directors reckoned without one William G. McAdoo, son-in-law of President Wilson; Mr. McAdoo had ideas of his own on efficiency and costs.

Express-carrying expenses, $25,854,000; operating expenses, $22,213,000; net income from investment, $1,167,000. In either 1915 or 1916, the directors made an adjustment to the profit and loss fund to depreciate the Mexican securities, since Wells Fargo was no longer receiving dividends from them.

In June, the company paid a 3 percent dividend; in December, it paid another 3 percent; and on December 28, it paid a 33⅓ percent dividend—for a total of almost 40 percent, or $9,427,000. American and Adams were paying some fantastic dividends, too, and it was axiomatic that those things would not go sight unseen. Wells Fargo's surplus fund went down to $4,020,000, but it was still a sizable reserve.

Wells Fargo's general balance sheet of December, 1916, shows that Wells Fargo owned some $11,000,000 in real estate and equipment, and $10,000 in the Knickerbocker Express Company; other investments (stocks, bonds, notes, and other) totaled $22,173,000. Current assets were $16,000,000, deferred assets, $1,166,000. Total assets were nearly $51,000,000.

Liabilities: capital stock authorized, $24,000,000

(but not issued, $32,600, which means outstanding stock was $23,967,400). Wages unpaid were $3,851,000; unpaid money orders, checks, and drafts were $3,735,000; express-carrying charges payable were $3,205,000; unmatured interest, dividends, and rents payable were $8,708,000; accrued depreciation on equipment was $2,103,000. The profit and loss account in June was $10,195,883.63, and there was a "miscellaneous profit and loss item" of $93,000. Net income for July, $420,000; in September, it went up to $542,000, and in December, it dropped to $292,000. Total profit was $12,728,000; dividends were $8,708,155.33.

In equipment, the company owned in cars (railroad cars), $750,000; horses, $1,323,000; automobiles $353,000; wagons and sleighs, $1,018,000; harness, $205,000; office furniture and equipment, $813,000; safes, $261,000; trucks, $345,000; line equipment, $280,000.

The list of miscellaneous investments is not particularly significant but it is interesting: a farm in Cook County, Illinois, $47,000; a stable in Sacramento, $4,000; unimproved lots in San Francisco, $37,000; a ranch in Sonoma County, California, $38,000; unimproved land in Wheeler County, Texas, $1,600. It is impossible to know how the company came into possession of these assorted assets, but it is worth observing that most of them are land.

We have no figures for 1917, but probably the express companies continued to make money. In 1918, however, it was a different story. McAdoo was spreading the idea of unionism, and wages were going up. Also, the government seized rail equipment and caused many delays to express shipments, which resulted in suits, and, as an industry, the express business lost $17,000,000 in the first half of the year. Thus, the big companies were ready to be plucked when McAdoo, Secretary of the Treasury, "suggested" that the big companies unite into one big express organization—which would be, naturally, under McAdoo's authority. Wells Fargo, American, and Adams (which included the Southern Railway) were to merge into a single agency to be known as the American Railway Express.

The Southern Railway declined, and organized an independent Southeastern Express; its president, Fairfax Harrison, had withdrawn from President Wilson already, and chose to go its own way, which it did until Harrison died and the consolidation was finally made with the American Railway Express.

The American Railway Express Company was capitalized at $30,000,000, and the express companies were to subscribe for the stock at par; they were to transfer to the new corporation everything but their cash, treasury assets, and the office buildings of American in New York and Chicago and of Wells Fargo in Portland. It was technically a partnership with the government, and the profits were to be divided with the government—the company getting the first 5 percent, the government coming in for one half of the profits above 5 percent, and getting up to as much as three fourths of everything over 13 percent. The changeover was made on June 30, 1918.

The president of the new agency was George C. Taylor, who had succeeded James C. Fargo as president of the American Express Company; chairman of the board was Burns D. Caldwell. American retained its great travel agency abroad. Wells Fargo received $10,075,400 in stock of the American Railway Express, and still had twenty thousand shares in the Wells Fargo Nevada National Bank, and interests in Mexico and Cuba. It sold its own unsold shares to its stockholders at $1 per share, although not for a long time had Wells Fargo stock been below $100. Elmer Jones bought the Mexican and Cuban interests in 1919 for $640,000; and in 1924, he bought from the Harriman estate all the Wells Fargo stock it held of the United States company, Jones making arrangements with Charles A. Peabody and Robert W. DeForest, the executors of the Harriman estate. The shares of Wells Fargo were taken by the American Express Company (51 percent) and by another group headed by Jones and including officials of American and Wells Fargo. Headquarters of Wells Fargo remained at 65 Broadway, New York, where it continued to do business under the 1866 Colorado charter. In behalf of himself and American Express, Jones controlled 80 percent of Wells Fargo in the United States.

Adams Express Company stayed in business as an investment company, but Wells Fargo sold its twenty thousand shares of bank stock and all but went out of the operating business.

All the 25,000 employees of Wells Fargo were not happy over the change, and some were particularly bitter when the famous old Wells Fargo signs

Elmer Ray Jones had been with Wells Fargo since 1893, and finally became president. In 1910, William Sproule succeeded Dudley Evans; in 1911, Burns D. Caldwell succeeded Sproule; in 1918, David G. Meller became president of Wells Fargo although it no longer was in the express business in the United States. In 1919, Elmer Ray Jones bought Wells, Fargo & Company Express in Mexico and Wells Fargo in Cuba, and in 1924 headed a group of men to buy Wells, Fargo & Company in the United States from the Harriman estate, and became president. He was succeeded in 1956 by Ralph T. Reed; in 1960, Howard L. Clark became president; in 1963, R. D. Beals became president; and in 1964, James A. Henderson became president. Wells Fargo at present is a holding company, with subsidiaries in the armored-car and coin-auditing and coin-rolling business in twelve southern and eastern states.

were torn down all over the country, and the name was stricken from telephone books. Probably the last sign to go, according to Hungerford, was that atop the Wells Fargo building at Second and Mission in San Francisco, which was still standing in 1922; it was soon torn down, however, and only the lintel stone remained to proclaim, "Wells, Fargo & Co., Express Building."

Wells Fargo retained its corporate identity, but American was the only one that continued to be an operating company. At the close of the war, none of the express companies wanted to start over, and the Railway Express was continued. In 1929, however, the railroads created the Railway Express Agency, with stock spread among eighty-six principal railroads.

By 1933, the Chase National Bank owned the American Express Company, while the American owned 51 percent of Wells Fargo.

In 1929, the Chase Securities Corporation (for the Chase National Bank) bought control of American; in 1934, it was reorganized as Amerex Holding Corporation, and by 1950 held 99 percent of American Express Company stock.

American Express, as heir to all the express tradition, came into prominence again in the great panic of 1933 when it became apparent that the banks of the country were in bad shape. American called in as much money as it could from its larger branches, got some of its own money from the Chase National Bank, got all it could from the Railway Express Agency (which handled American Express money orders and travelers' checks), and got $1,000,000 from the New York clearinghouse. At the moment of crisis, therefore (a Saturday morning), American had $10,000,000 in silver, gold, silver and gold certificates, and every legal form of American currency. As people all over the country began to present their travelers' checks for payment in cash, the branches telephoned New York and told American what they would need; the Miami, Florida, office had a line of people a mile long waiting to cash their checks. American shipped out from $1,000,000 to $2,-000,000 a day, by train, plane, and automobile. American Express offices abroad paid their travelers' checks according to a schedule (since dollars had no value at that time), and guaranteed to pay the difference, if any, when trading should be resumed.

American held out for ten days, and then the demand was substantially over except for normal business.

Wells Fargo still carries express, and in 1947 shipped thirteen tons of gold from Montreal to Mexico City—this time by plane under the personal care of Elmer Jones. Wells Fargo in Mexico then owned the largest tourist agency in Mexico (along with American), ten big stores handling farm equipment, automobiles, and trucks, and in 1949 had a fleet of fifty armored cars in New York City. It also operated extensively on the nation's railroads through the Wells Fargo Carloading Corporation, that handled fast freight.

Back in San Francisco, the Wells Fargo Nevada National Bank continued to grow. Isaias W. Hellman died in 1920, and I. W. Hellman, Jr., became president, only to die within a few weeks and leave the presidency to Frederick L. Lipman. Lipman said later that the panic of the 1920's was second only to the great panic of 1933—but the bank came through, thanks to Lipman's two cardinal policies: (1) the bank must be prepared under any conditions to meet the utmost demands of depositors; and (2) funds arising from the deposits may in part be put to productive use to create earnings. In the 1920's, there were high earnings and great speculation, but Wells Fargo had been through those things before: the gold boom of the 1850's, the silver boom of the Comstock in the 1870's, World War I, and so the bank, under Lipman in the 1920's, got through in fine shape.

At the close of business February 28, 1920, the Wells Fargo Nevada National Bank had total assets of $86,430,000, of which nearly $17,000,000 was in cash, $44,000,000 in loans and discounts. Its capital was $6,000,000, its surplus and undivided profits, $5,685,000; its deposits were $55,488,000.

On June 30, 1923, the Union Trust Company, a Hellman organization, had total resources of $41,000,000, including $7,000,000 in cash, $20,000,000 in loans and discounts; it had $1,200,000 in capital stock, and surplus of $2,688,000; "due depositors," $36,000,000.

Six months later, the Wells Fargo Nevada National Bank showed total assets of $94,000,000—of which $20,000,000 was cash, $54,000,000 loans and discounts, $13,500,000 United States bonds and securities. Its capital was $6,000,000, surplus $5,253,000, deposits, $64,000,000. Frank B. King was vice-president and cashier; Lipman was president.

On January 1, 1924, these two—the bank and the trust company—were merged, and a new corporation was formed, the Wells Fargo Bank & Union Trust Company; the Wells Fargo Bank began to handle savings accounts that year for the first time.

In 1927, the bank started the Wells Fargo Investment Company to loan money to new banks, because, as a bank, they were more restricted than the national banks. They got fooled once, Lipman said, by a man in San Diego.

There is some information on banking from the trust angle, in the reminiscences of W. D. Kelley, who joined the Union Trust Company as a legal officer. The administrative staff when Kelley joined was made up of Mr. Greene, Percy Wood, John Shields, Grover, Frank Brickwedel, and Kelley.

In 1948, W. D. Kelley said:

In the old days, a person would come to the counter with new business, and the one least occupied at the

I. W. Hellman, Jr., who was president of the Wells Fargo Nevada National Bank in April and May, 1920, when he died and was succeeded by Frederick L. Lipman. From Ira Cross, "Financing an Empire."

moment in our administrative staff would wait on him, whether it was an escrow, a guardianship, a depositary, a living trust, a court trust, or the executorship of an estate—and from that time the same staff member usually handled that matter.

The real estate division was staffed by one man, and that meant that the principal management of the real estate in the several estates we handled, devolved upon the administrative staff. I administered several ranches, and one I especially remember had a payroll of over $35,000, and was a continuous nightmare of weather conditions and crop uncertainties. This ranch was later sold for about $160,000, cash over the counter, and it was a great relief.

I was involved in another case in what apparently was a bankrupt estate, and we eventually greatly benefited the beneficiaries by refusing to sell an interest in the land at the appraised value of $800. We demanded the reservation of minerals, and shortly afterward leased the land to oil-prospectors for a cash bonus of $50,000; the land soon produced plenty of oil, and made royalties of more than $60,000 a year. Naturally, the estate did not go bankrupt after all.

When I joined Wells Fargo in 1920 we had resources of about $38,000,000; in 1924, when we consolidated with Union Trust, we had resources of about $135,000,000. Then on December 31, 1947, we had resources of over $500,000,000. We had grown enormously.

In 1925, incidentally, the old stone building of John Parrott that had first been jinxed and later exorcised by the Chinese of San Francisco was finally torn down. It had stood through earthquake, fire, and an explosion of nitroglycerine, and they had to tear it down to get it out of the way.

Following the panic of 1933, banking laws were reorganized, and Frederick Lipman said later: "There was only one good thing about that legislation: it forbade the payment of interest on commercial deposits."

Lipman retired as president in 1935, and R. B. Motherwell became president. I. W. Hellman III became president in 1943. In 1954, the bank resumed the title that all old Wells Fargo men had always hoped it would resume: Wells Fargo Bank. It also merged with the First National Bank of Antioch, and a year later with the First National Bank of San Mateo County.

But the biggest merger of all was to come in 1960: that with the American Trust Company.

Since the American Trust Company has a long and honorable lineage, it is well to recapitulate its history briefly. Its earliest antecedent, the San Francisco Accumulating Fund Association, was founded April 27, 1854, with an office at 174 Clay Street (one half block below Kearny). The incorporators were E. W. Burr, to be the reform mayor of San Francisco following the Vigilance Committee activity of 1856; Albert Miller, founder of the American Trust Company tradition, whose descendants would still be on the board in the 1960's; Christian Otto Gerberding, who was to be publisher of the *Evening Bulletin;* and William F. Herrick, a merchant with whom many persons had left personal papers in tin boxes (it was called a "Tin Box Custody"). On the board of directors were Frank Soulé, editor and publisher of the *Chronicle;* E. Crowell, an importing druggist; Joseph F. Atwill, a music dealer; Joseph Britton, a lithographer and printer; J. H. Atkinson; J. R. West; A. D. Hatch; P. Coggins; Calvin Lathrop; George H. Goddard, surveyor; and T. D. Rodgers, an attorney. The association kept its funds with Lucas, Turner & Company.

In 1857, Burr, Miller, Herrick, John Archbold, James de Fremery, and Charles Pace incorporated a new bank—in fact, the first bank incorporated in California: the Savings and Loan Society, an outgrowth of the San Francisco Accumulating Fund Association that had its office at 171½ Washington Street. The society was successful, and for the first half year paid dividends at the rate of 9 percent, the second half year at 19½ percent. It was reincorporated in 1865, and all through the years including 1872 it paid dividends of from 10 to 12 percent.

The San Francisco Accumulating Fund Association was formally ended February 25, 1862, with a payment of $217.39.

The Savings and Loan Society in 1860 moved to 169 Clay Street, and in 1891 to Sutter and Montgomery.

Along another line of descent, in 1862, the San Francisco Savings Union was formed—the first bank to be incorporated under California's first banking act (that of 1862). The incorporators were James de Fremery, Albert Miller, and John Archbold. The union's office was at 513 California Street, then was moved to 529 California; by 1867, it was at 530 California, and in 1906, it moved into the famous old Parrott Building. This firm was the first to introduce

on the Pacific Coast a successful plan for accumulation of savings, and a systematic plan to use those savings for loans on real property for a term of years on an amortizing basis.

De Fremery was president until 1883, and Miller was then president to 1898.

In 1910, the Savings and Loan Society and the San Francisco Savings Union went together to form the Savings Union Bank of San Francisco, which in 1911 was changed to the Savings Union Bank & Trust Company.

Along still another line, the Mercantile Trust Company of San Francisco was organized in 1899 to specialize in trust business. The first president was Frederick W. Zeile, whose custom it was to ride shotgun with the stagecoach driver when gold was being shipped; N. D. Scott and Henry T. Scott were vice-presidents; and John D. McKee was cashier. Directors were William Babcock, Wakefield Baker, H. S. Breeden, Warren D. Clark, W. F. Detert, F. G. Drum, C. E. Green, M. H. Hecht, William G. Irwin, Darius Ogden Mills of Bank of California fame, E. S. Pillsbury, and Claus Spreckels.

In 1899, the office was at 236 Bush Street, in 1904, at 464 California Street (present address of the Wells Fargo Bank); and in 1910, the Mercantile National Bank was formed, and the commercial business of the Mercantile Trust Company of San Francisco was transferred to it.

In 1920, the Savings Union Bank & Trust Company was merged with the Mercantile National Bank of San Francisco; John D. McKee of the Mercantile National became chairman of the board, and John S. Drum of the Savings Union became president; the name was changed in 1922 to the Mercantile Trust Company of San Francisco.

San Francisco is still heavily oriented toward its Chinese population. This is a poster in a department-store window. Photograph by the author.

The word "American" got into the long line through an entirely different channel—from the other side of the house, so to speak. In 1871, the Security Savings Bank was formed, with John Parrott, the longtime San Francisco banker, president, and Henry Babcock, vice-president. This bank did not change its name until 1920, when it became the Security Bank and Trust Company.

Along still another line, the American Bank and Trust Company was formed in December, 1887, with P. E. Bowles, president; Francis Cutting, vice-president; W. B. Wightman, vice-president; and James J. Fagan, cashier. It first had offices in the Mills Building, then moved to the Merchants' Exchange Building, then to California and Montgomery, where the Wells Fargo Bank is now.

In 1906, the Mercantile Building was not burned, and the bank's offices opened on April 25, five days after the fire, although the safe deposit vaults were not opened until May 7.

In 1902, the name was changed to the American National Bank, and in 1923 this bank and the Security Bank and Trust Company merged to become The American Bank of San Francisco.

Along a different line, the Alameda County Savings & Loan Society was formed in 1874, and went

R. B. Motherwell, president of the Wells Fargo Bank & Union Trust Company, 1935–1943. From the History Room, Wells Fargo Bank.

into the First National Gold Bank of Oakland in 1875, and into the First National Bank of Oakland in 1880. On still another line, the First Trust and Savings Bank of Oakland was organized in 1908, and became The First Savings Bank of Oakland in 1914, and The American Bank, Oakland, in 1922.

The two Oakland banks and the American Bank of San Francisco went together in 1924 to form The American Bank.

In 1927, finally, the American Bank side of the family and the Mercantile Trust side of the family came together, having already acquired some thirty-one other banks, to form the American Trust Company. The two sides of the big family had already opened forty-five branch offices, and up to 1954 the American Trust Company acquired eight more banks and became a giant institution.

Then in 1960, the American Trust Company merged with the Wells Fargo Bank; the American Trust hierarchy went into control of the banking business while the Wells Fargo hierarchy controlled the trust business. The cycle finally was complete: the Wells Fargo Bank had merged with the San Francisco Accumulating Fund Association, started in 1854 as a savings bank. Ransom M. Cook became president.

One family retained its identity all the way through the hundred and twelve years from 1854 to 1966: the Millers. Albert Miller started with the accumulating fund association in 1854, and was succeeded by C. O. G. Miller, Robert Watt Miller, and in 1966,

I. W. Hellman III, president of the Wells Fargo Bank & Union Trust Company from 1943 to the merger with the American Trust Company in 1960. He was still on the board of directors in 1966.

Robert W. Miller of the Pacific Lighting Corporation.

In 1962, the big new bank moved from the old Wells Fargo Nevada National Bank site to new quarters at 464 California Street.

For 1964, the annual report of the Wells Fargo Bank (and American Trust Company), still a state bank, shows deposits of $3,312,000,000 and loans of $2,224,000,000. It was a colossus of banking—the eighteenth largest bank in the United States.

Ransom M. Cook (American Trust Company) was chairman of the board in 1964; H. Stephen Chase (American Trust Company) was president; I. W. Hellman (formerly I. W. Hellman III, and president of the Wells Fargo Bank from 1943 to 1960) was chairman of the board from 1960 to 1964, when he retired from the chairmanship but retained his directorship; F. J. Hellman (the fourth member of the family in direct descent) was vice-chairman of the board of the new bank, but died in September, 1965.

Cash on hand December 31, 1964, was $506,908,000; total assets were $3,784,333,731. Capital stock was $88,715,670 at $10 par per share; surplus was $91,000,000; undivided profits were $57,486,000; there were capital notes, due in 1989, of $75,000,000.

This huge structure had grown from an original capital of some $300,000—only $75,000 of which was paid in.

Wells Fargo has not changed in some respects, though. In 1964, the bank increased the capital stock

Opposite:
A third view north on Montgomery Street (ninety-eight years after the one in "Financing an Empire") from the intersection of Montgomery and California. Entirely typical today. Montgomery is a one-way street, and here are pedestrians, buses, automobiles, and a cable car with passengers riding the steps. Photograph taken in 1966 by the author. In the 1854 picture, California Street does not seem to go straight across Montgomery as it does here.

The new, modern Wells Fargo Bank building at California and Montgomery streets; this is the California Street entrance. The tall Wells Fargo building south on Montgomery Street has no connection with the bank.

The banking structure in 1954 had gone back to its original name (Wells Fargo Bank), and after 1960 and the merger with the American Trust Company, this was the insigne adopted.

from 6,000,000 to 12,000,000 shares, and declared a 75 percent stock dividend; the new annual dividend rate was set at $1 per share, which is 10 percent on the par value. Dividends paid in 1964 totaled $8,872,000.

In one respect, certainly, the bank has taken a turn that neither Isaias W. Hellman I nor Frederick Lipman would have foreseen back in 1920: it had in January, 1966, some two hundred branch banks throughout northern and central California.

On November 10, 1966, there were further changes of office: Ransom M. Cook left the chairmanship of the board of directors and became chairman of the executive committee; Cook was sixty-seven. H. Stephen Chase, sixty-three, retired as president and became chairman of the board. Richard P. Cooley, forty-two, who had joined the bank in 1949, was elected president and chief executive officer. The bank then had 216 offices and its assets were $4,100,000,000.

The Wells Fargo Bank has come a long way since those early days when the surplus exceeded the deposits, but one thing has not changed. Frederick Lipman said it in 1946: "Wells Fargo is always good."

"We were always rich," said Lipman. "It was just a cinch. It did me good personally. I never had any feeling of inferiority. Our bank was good. We never even felt like boasting about it. We took it for granted. Wells Fargo was always good."

This building, designed by Clinton Day, was built in 1910 by the Union Trust Company at Market and Grant avenues. In 1963, the elaborate carved granite surface was cleaned, the ornamental ironwork was repaired, new paneling and draperies were added, and a 25-foot crystal-and-brass chandelier was hung. It is the present Union Trust Office of the Wells Fargo Bank. Picture taken in 1966 by the author.

Ransom M. Cook was president of the American Trust Company in 1960, and became president and chief executive officer of the Wells Fargo Bank and American Trust Company. He was succeeded in 1964 by H. Stephen Chase, and became chairman of the board of directors; on November 10, 1966, he became chairman of the executive committee and remained a director of the bank. From the Wells Fargo Bank.

Known to three generations of Westerners, the Nevada Bank Building at Market and Montgomery streets, built in 1893 as the Union Trust Company Building, occupied in 1906 by the Wells Fargo National Bank, renamed the Nevada Bank Building. From the History Room, Wells Fargo Bank.

H. Stephen Chase, who became executive vice-president of the Wells Fargo Bank and American Trust Company in 1960, and president in 1964, succeeding Ransom M. Cook. He served as president until November 10, 1966. From the Wells Fargo Bank.

Richard P. Cooley, formerly executive vice-president of the Wells Fargo Bank and American Trust Company, was elected president November 10, 1966, at age forty-two. Wells Fargo Bank was then the United States' eleventh biggest bank, with 216 offices and assets of $4,100,000,000. From the Wells Fargo Bank.

Notes

1852: The Beginning

1. As an indication of the confusion in bank notes, Ira B. Cross, *Financing an Empire* (Chicago: S. J. Clarke, 1927), p. 117, quotes from a journal of 1840: "Started from Virginia with Virginia money; reached the Ohio River; exchanged $20 Virginia note for shinplasters as a $3 note of the Bank of West Union; paid away the $3 note for breakfast; reached Tennessee; received a $100 Tennessee note; went back to Kentucky; forced there to exchange the Tennessee note for $88 of Kentucky money. In Virginia and Maryland compelled to deposit five times the amount due, and several times detained to be shaved [discounted] at an enormous per cent. At Maysing exchanged $5 note, Kentucky money, for notes of the Northwestern Bank of Virginia; reached Fredericktown; there neither Virginia nor Kentucky money current; paid a $5 Wheeling note for breakfast and dinner; received in change two $1 notes of some Pennsylvania bank, $1 Baltimore & Ohio Railroad, and balance in Good Intent shinplasters; 100 yards from the tavern door all notes refused except the Baltimore & Ohio Railroad; reached Harpers Ferry; notes of Northwestern Bank in worse repute there than in Maryland; deposited $10 in hands of agent; in this way reached Winchester; detained there two days in getting shaved. Kentucky money at 12%, Northwestern Bank at 10."

2. There does not seem to be any information on the exact way in which he shipped them except that he shucked them first, but perhaps the shipping was not much different from that into the Texas Panhandle about 1910, when oysters were shucked and put in five-gallon milk cans pretty well filled with ice.

3. The government had supported one Enoch J. Humphrey as an expressman, and he was allowed to advertise the government as his partner—but Wells fought back, and Buffalo businessmen, also individualists, gave their business to Wells. Alden Hatch, *American Express* (Garden City: Doubleday, 1950), p. 24.

4. In 1850, there was an important realignment of express moguls in the East, from which emerged two companies (Wells, Butterfield & Company and Livingston, Fargo & Company) that formed and owned the American Express Company.

5. "We saw a few days ago a beautiful specimen of gold from the mine newly discovered on the American Fork. From all accounts the mine is immensely rich; and already, we learn, the gold from it, collected at random and without any trouble, has become an article of trade at the upper settlements." (California *Star,* April 1, 1848.)

6. On December 9, 1848, an advertisement by Dewitt & Davenport in the New York Daily *Tribune* announced a guidebook, *The Gold Mines of California,* "from the notes of a returned volunteer" (that is, from a man who had been in Stevenson's Regiment in the Mexican War), edited by G. G. Foster, which would be published next Wednesday (December 13) at twenty-five cents—and apparently it was so published. Also on December 9, Berford & Company announced Emory's *Notes of a Military Reconnoissance* (from Fort Leavenworth to San Diego with Kearny) at $2. J. J. Disturnell advertised maps of California and Mexico, with special attention to the gold regions, from $1.50 down. On December 11, D. Appleton & Company announced a second edition of Edwin Bryant's *What I Saw in California* at $1.25, and Colonel Frémont's *Narrative* at twenty-five cents. On December 15, H. Long & Brother advertised the government edition of Emory's report at $2, and the firm of Stringer & Townsend advertised *California in 1849,* by Fayette Robinson, "shortly." The description of all books was intended to catch the eye of the gold-hungry emigrant.

7. It is said that Gail Borden, who first canned evaporated milk, invented the meat biscuit, in which he mixed meat broth with flour and cooked it for some friends who made the trip to California in 1850; he sold the biscuits for a time. Hundreds of interesting advertisements appeared for gadgets, one of the most interesting being in a Boston paper in 1850: "Fessenden's Patent Pocket Filter, an article adapted to the wants of the traveller, especially to those of the California Emigrants and Miners. Manufactured and for sale, Wholesale and Retail, corner of Beach and South Streets, Boston." A hazardous guess is that this referred to a water filter.

8. Could this be the W. C. Gray who had bought out Silas Tyler in 1836?

9. There is an interesting speculation as to the reason for this lack of attention—especially in Missouri, which was always receptive to any startling tale. Since over four months elapsed from the date of the edition and its receipt in St. Joseph, could it be that the overland express had not panned out, and that the *Star* had finally sent the special edition to the East by steamer?

10. Thomas G. Wells, apparently no relation to Henry Wells, had been a printer and publisher in New England, and his brother-in-law, Hamilton Willis, was a banker in Boston. Wells built a "fireproof" brick building and chose to remain inside it in San Francisco's sixth great fire in May, 1851. He was severely burned, and never recovered, and his bank suspended October 3, 1851.

11. In fairness, one should say that the *Alta California* on September 22, 1850, named five companies—Adams; Gregory; Haven & Livingston; West & Co.; and Berford & Co.—and said: "We believe all these expresses dispatch special messengers by each steamer. They have also agents on the Isthmus and at New York to attend to the dispatch of goods." How many of these actually had messengers, and how many had "arrangements" with ship's pursers or even with one of the regular messengers such as those of Adams, is hard to say.

12. *The Expressman's Monthly,* II, No. 10 (October, 1877), 298.

13. This writer does not know how to check the use of "and" and "&" in these many firm names short of an expenditure of time that is not available. Harlow tends to use "and" most of the time, but we have, on the whole,

used "&" because there is much evidence (primarily in newspaper advertisements, which are not reliable in matters like this) for the ampersand. Moreover, and this factor does not encourage us to try to run these down, corporate names were constantly changing, and it is safe to say that many were changed from "and" to "&" or vice versa at various times.

14. According to *U. S. West* by Lucius Beebe and Charles Clegg (New York: Dutton, 1949), three firms (Wells & Company; Livingston & Fargo; and Butterfield, Wasson) merged to form Wells, Butterfield & Company and Livingston, Fargo & Company, and these two became the co-owners of the American Express Company. Livingston & Fargo was to receive all the profits from west of Buffalo, while Wells, Butterfield & Company was to receive the profits from east of Buffalo.

15. In 1848, says *U. S. West,* California produced $250,000 worth of gold; in 1849, $10,000,000 worth; in 1850, $41,000,000; and in 1851, $60,000,000. Inasmuch as express rates varied from 3 percent to about 5 percent of the value for transportation to the East, it is obvious that a lot of money was to be made from that item alone.

16. In fact, Adams was so far dominant in the early days that it is said that when the end-man in a minstrel show asked his partner, "For what purpose was Eve created?" that the audience responded as if drilled: "For Adam's Express!"

17. Nor should it be overlooked that Adams was doing tremendous freight business around Cape Horn.

18. This seems a little strange on the part of Butterfield, because he had already pioneered with stage lines and canal boats, and had already organized a transportation service across the Isthmus of Panama. Interestingly enough, it would be John Butterfield who would negate American Express' entry into the travel business.

19. Henry Wells, William G. Fargo, Johnston Livingston, and James McKay were also on the board of the American Express Company.

20. There is some conflict here with later "facts," but the rate of Wells Fargo's expansion in California suggests that $75,000 was the starting capital.

21. The advertisement is dated July 1, but does not seem to be in the *Alta* of that date or that of the second.

22. This was 114 Montgomery Street, the address of Sam Brannan's new red-brick building. Some pictures of Wells Fargo's first office show a stone building, while most references to it say the building was of red brick. The picture on page 29 of Lucius Beebe and Charles Clegg's *U. S. West,* showing a narrow, two-story brick building, is more likely to be the original. Brannan's own office was three buildings away, and the *Herald* was in that building in the early days.

Brannan was California's indefatigable promoter, who had arrived in San Francisco as a Mormon elder, and was so successful in California that Brigham Young wrote him a letter requesting him to remit his tithing, which President Young thought would be about $10,000, plus $20,000 to help Brother Young in his labors, plus $20,000 to be divided between Brothers Kimball and Richards, who were also in straitened circumstances. Brannan replied that the Lord had entrusted that property to him, and he would release it only on a written order from the Lord.

Today, 114 Montgomery Street is numbered 440 Montgomery Street, and the Wells Fargo Bank's History Room is only a few feet from it.

23. According to Edward Hungerford in *Wells Fargo,* the company was first incorporated as Wells, Fargo & Company—which changed in 1866 to Wells, Fargo and Company. Today's letterheads show, "Wells, Fargo & Company," while the bank letterheads (now entirely separate, of course) show simply "Wells Fargo Bank."

24. The Parrott Building stood through the earthquake of 1906 and was not demolished until the late 1920's.

25. A banker's bill of exchange is an order drawn by one bank upon another to pay a sum of money to the order of a specified person or to the bearer, on demand or at a fixed or determinable future time; in today's usage a "bill of exchange" means an order payable in a foreign country or in foreign currency. A draft is an order drawn by one party upon another calling for payment of money to a third party on demand or at some specified time; a bank draft is drawn by one bank upon another, and today it usually means an order payable in dollars within the United States. A check is an order drawn upon a bank, payable on demand. Information furnished by E. E. Munger of the Wells Fargo Bank.

26. A question arises as to how much money-lending there was in the early affairs of Wells Fargo and Adams. It is worth noting that Adams in 1852 was advertising, "No loans made," but one suspects, from various indirect references, that perhaps both houses were loaning money, even though that was not a prominent part of either business.

27. Professor Jerry Thomas, head bartender at the El Dorado Saloon, invented the Tom and Jerry and the Blue Blazer. The Pisco Punch was invented in the Bank Exchange Saloon (John Bruce, *Gaudy Century*). The martini was invented on the steamboat *Chrysopolis* in the Sacramento River near the town of Martinez in 1859. (See Robert E. Pearson, "Martini," in the *Butterfield Express,* I, No. 1, October, 1962.)

28. And also that one might make a general deposit, subject to his own withdrawal and also, perhaps, subject to loss if Wells Fargo should go bankrupt; or he might make a special deposit, not subject to loss in case of insolvency. This apparently was common practice in the Gold Country, for Andrew Todd has already spoken of both kinds.

29. Opposite page 103 of the *San Francisco Directory for the Year 1852-53, Embracing a General Directory of Citizens: A Street Directory: A New and Complete Map of the City, and an Appendix of General Information, an Almanac, etc.* "First Publication . . . 1852."

30. F. Argenti was to finance Raousset-Boulbon's abortive filibuster in Sonora in 1854.

31. In 1856, he would make a vicious attack on James P. Casey and, refusing even to let Casey present his side of the story, he would be shot by Casey, who in turn would be hanged by the Vigilantes.

32. While Edward Bosqui says the house was destroyed by James King (who was capable of it), it is only fair to say that Palmer, Cook & Company was also financially involved in William Walker's king-size filibuster in Nicaragua, Charles A. Frémont's presidential campaign of 1856, and

state funds. Politics and money are an explosive combination.

33. One should not forget the close tie-up between Wells, Fargo & Company and the American Express Company.

34. If California in the 1850's was freewheeling, we are at an utter loss for a word to describe the volcanic situation in Nicaragua and the piratical actions indulged in by all parties. One of the most curious trios of modern times was involved in this complicated affair: William Walker, "the gray-eyed man of destiny"; Cornelius Vanderbilt (the commodore himself); and the kingdom of Great Britain. Vanderbilt was the winner.

35. For a condensed narrative of the filibusterers, see Dorothy Loomis' series, "The Men Who Would Be Kings," starting August 8, 1965, in the San Diego Sunday *Union*.

36. Until the Gadsden Purchase in late 1853 (ratified in June, 1854), all of present Arizona south of the Gila River was a part of Sonora.

37. The same notices were carried of Adams, Gregory, Todd, and many others, principally because the newspaper of the 1850's was largely dependent on other newspapers for any news from outside its own community.

38. Reuben W. Washburn, the first banking manager of Wells Fargo who sometimes is said to have been not very competent, was spoken of by Eric Francis in his reminiscences: "W. Washburn, a quiet little old gentleman, who at one time was the only man who could sign Wells Fargo & Co.... When I knew him he was in the stationery department, a pensioner; he became feeble-minded toward the last, and used to go around picking up scraps of paper." This was in 1882 or later. (Manuscript in the History Room, Wells Fargo Bank.)

Gold—The "Ruin" of California

1. The California *Star,* March 18, 1848.

2. In February, 1847, the name had been changed from Yerba Buena to a more American-sounding name.

3. Those who love San Francisco are the first to deny any claim of normality for her.

4. In 1849 alone, nine thousand Gold Rushers followed the Gila Trail through Arizona—then a part of Sonora, Mexico. See Ralph Bieber, *Southern Trails to California in 1849* (V of the *Southwest Historical Series;* Glendale: Clark, 1937), 62.

5. In fact, the Sonorans were the first to rush to the gold fields, starting in 1848.

6. In 1849, seven hundred ships arrived in San Francisco harbor, bringing forty thousand passengers; it is estimated that four thousand sailors deserted to go to the mines.

7. "Brigham" probably was Dexter Brigham, Jr., who had been a partner of Harnden since 1840. It now appears that it was Brigham who had gone to California in 1849 for the Harnden company, but that by 1852 the company had dropped the enterprise, and Brigham had remained to act as Vanderbilt's agent in San Francisco.

8. By "nearly $3000," presumably he meant Wells Fargo's charge for transporting gold and packages; the *Alta California* of February 16 shows $73,448 in treasure shipped by Wells Fargo, and that implies that up to 4 percent (depending on how much of the gold belonged to Wells Fargo) was the charge for shipment to New York. The usual charge, according to Ira B. Cross, *Financing an Empire,* was from 3 to 5 percent.

9. From the History Room, Wells Fargo Bank, San Francisco.

10. Frequently referred to, but Irene Simpson, director of the History Room at the Wells Fargo Bank, says she has never seen one.

11. Bankers and express companies had been assaying in the Gold Country from the beginning, so this was no new duty. The assaying was done for ¼ percent of the value—four to five cents an ounce—and the assayer would melt the dust, cast it into an ingot, chip off tiny pieces to test for its fineness, then usually stamp the bar to show its weight and fineness. It was, of course, highly important to the miner to be able to trust the assayer, for a dishonest assayer could cheat the miner in many ways.

12. Waybill: A list of goods or passengers carried by any common carrier.

13. *Harper's Weekly, Frank Leslie's Illustrated Weekly,* and others of like persuasion; the *Illustrated News* had lasted but one year, and *Gleason's, or Ballou's,* had expired in 1859. (All were modeled after the *London Illustrated News.*) The pictorial papers of that time were from eight to sixteen tabloid pages. *Harper's* in 1863, for instance—filled with Civil War news—was usually sixteen pages and weighed about two ounces.

14. The "Mr. Knight" who canceled the Boise route probably was Samuel Knight, superintendent of Wells, Fargo & Company, who was killed in the great nitroglycerine explosion of 1866.

15. It was not long before somebody realized that Wells Fargo had made a mistake, and sent an agent out again in August to buy out Tracy & King, who had gone into Boise after Blake left.

1853: A Year of Races and Records

1. Here we come face to face with the problem that has beset Wells Fargo historians for many years: Some records of the company in San Francisco were burned in the fire of 1906, following the earthquake, and sometimes data are missing, or one set of facts seems to contradict another. In an article by Ruth Teiser and Catherine Harroun, "Origin of Wells, Fargo & Company" (in *The Bulletin of the Business Historical Society* for June, 1948), it is said: "On April 23 [1852], these payments [the balance] were called for." However, in a manuscript in possession of the History Room of the Wells Fargo Bank in San Francisco, it is said the securities for the subscriptions were surrendered on May 3, 1853—which makes it seem that the original payments were not called in until 1853.

It is well to describe that manuscript, since most of our data on management will be taken from it. There are three volumes, entitled, "History of Wells Fargo & Company: a Joint Stock Association Express Company, 1852-1866"; "History of Wells Fargo & Company, a Corporation: Successors to Holladay Overland Mail and Express Co., 1866-1916"; and "Wells Fargo and Company... Statements of Income and Expenses, 1866-1917." These appear to be extracted from the original minutes of Wells, Fargo & Company, perhaps by L. O. Head, an employee of Wells Fargo from 1900 to 1918, and vice-presidential assistant of

American Railway Express until 1927, since they are marked, "Property of L. O. Head," etc. This manuscript will hereafter be referred to as "Minutes."

2. John Parrott was born in Virginia in 1810, and made a fortune in Mazatlán; he went to San Francisco in 1849 with $300,000 in Mexican currency and was always considered a man of experience, prudence, and sound judgment. His bank, Parrott & Company, was one of the strongest on the West Coast. (Ira B. Cross, *Financing an Empire,* I, 211.)

3. Since the mail contracts were held in the Atlantic by George Law's United States Mail Steam Ship Company, and in the Pacific by William H. Aspinwall's Pacific Mail Steam Ship Company, Vanderbilt could not carry "mail," or, rather, could not get paid for it unless it should be carried as express.

4. Steamer Day is usually considered to be the first and fifteenth of each month. See E. A. Wiltsee, *Gold Rush Steamers* (San Francisco: Grabhorn Press, 1938), p. 32; see also Frank Soulé, *et al., Annals of San Francisco* (New York: D. Appleton & Co., 1854). However, there are references to other days; for instance, Frederick L. Lipman, in an interview (a copy is in the History Room, Wells Fargo Bank), says that in the 1880's, Steamer Day was the 13th and the 28th, and that it lasted until 1906 or later. However, by Lipman's time it was no longer a banking date but a merchants' date. In the beginning, it was customary for everybody to pay his bills by Steamer Day, and to regulate all his business by that day, but in the 1880's, says Lipman, bills were due sixty days after Steamer Day.

5. John Bruce, *Gaudy Century* (New York: Random House, 1948).

6. It is interesting to note that the *Alta California,* which was heavily biased in favor of the Pacific Mail, was not much favored by Wells Fargo, perhaps because Adams was already in rather solidly with the *Alta;* at least, it seems so from the regular reports in the *Alta* from Sacramento, San Joaquin, and other places, that carried a byline: "Per Adams & Co.'s Express." However, Adams did not have an exclusive claim on the *Alta*'s affections, for occasionally, under Adams' byline, the *Alta* says: "We are also indebted to Wells Fargo for news from this community."

7. Since "all the baggage" was saved, and most express traveled in trunks.

8. Cornelius K. Garrison apparently got started as a gambler in Panama City, became a banker and commission merchant and an early mayor of San Francisco. In Nicaragua he was in partnership with R. S. Fretz, and in the *Alta California* in January, 1856, there is an advertisement for Garrison, Morgan, Fretz & Ralston, bankers. (William C. Ralston had joined the firm in September, 1851, and in the 1870's would emerge as the most important banker in California.) In Panama in 1849, Garrison fought a duel with Vicissimus Turner, in which each one was to hold the other's coat lapel and fire. They were both inebriated, and Garrison had to loan Turner a percussion cap from his own revolver. This anomaly titillated each man's sense of humor, and the only problem that remained was for each man to find his way home.

9. To be specific, Henry Wells, William G. Fargo, Johnston Livingston, and James McKay.

1854: The Last Great Year of Gold

1. In 1857, Birch would start the first transcontinental mail, the San Antonio & San Diego Mail Line, and in 1857, on the way back to see his wife, who did not want to live in California, he would be drowned in the sinking of George Law's *Central America.*

2. See "Edward, Letter to a Loved One," in the *Butterfield Express,* III, No. 8 (June, 1965).

3. H. H. Bancroft, *History of California* (VII; XXIV of the *Works*), 709.

4. Zeke Daniels, *The Life and Death of Julia C. Boulette* (Virginia City: Lamp Post, 1958).

5. The low character of most Frenchwomen in California at that time was so commonly accepted in California that the following item from the *Alta California* of February 10, 1853, is worth thinking twice about: *"Arrival of Female Emigrants.*—The French ship *Sansonette,* from Havre, having on board upward of two hundred and fifty female emigrants arrived yesterday morning. The great portion of these people, it is said, come to join their husbands, and to reside permanently in the country. They are all from the farming or working classes of France, industrious and respectable." While this type of characterization was not uncommon in a frontier area, one cannot but feel an undercurrent of relief in the editor's announcement.

6. Theodore T. Johnson, *Sights in the Gold Region and Scenes by the Way* (New York: Baker & Scribner, 1849). Although Johnson describes the scene in 1849, it had changed very little in 1854. In fact, it does not seem there was any permanent change until after the Civil War.

7. Most foreign coins were legal tender until the Act of February 21, 1857, and some newspapers regularly reported the equivalent values in dollars. As late as 1892, at least, the New York *Tribune*'s *Almanac* had a page of such values, and since the values were given in gold and silver "coins," we may assume there were still foreign coins in circulation at that time. Because of the shortage of gold and silver coins in the Southwest, Mexican coins were always well accepted, and in Missouri in the 1830's practically no other coin was in circulation.

San Francisco always liked hard money; in fact, soon after the beginning of World War I (1914), it was the only city in the world where gold was freely used as an item of exchange, and bankers so dreaded the howls of protest that would come from any attempt to stop the interchange of gold (and therefore its falling into the hands of enemies), that they had to use a subterfuge: They allowed gold to circulate only in $20 denominations.

8. The standard marine telegraph signals, used by this semaphore, were similar to the arm signals of a Boy Scout and the Morse code. Both arms out straight meant a sidewheel steamer (and that meant a mail steamer, since that was the fastest kind of ship, and mail steamers were the only ones—for a while, at least—that had that equipment); one arm straight out to the right (from the viewer's point of view) and the other up and to the right (the international semaphore signal for *W*) meant a brig; the opposite —straight out to the left and up to the left—was a brigantine; one arm up on the right (at a 45° angle, that is), a schooner; one arm up on the left, a sloop. The uninhibited

character of San Francisco theatre audiences and their quick response to a familiar situation is demonstrated by the story of an early-day actor who came out upon the stage—perhaps having caught his wife or sweetheart in the arms of another—and threw his arms wide and cried in anguish: "What does this mean?" (A stupid question, perhaps, but it is not the ideal time to invent a clever saying.) The audience responded with a roar, as one man: "Sidewheel steamer!"

9. Scrip: A certificate to the effect that the holder is entitled to payment.

10. This account is taken largely from the *Memoirs* of Sherman, who, having resigned his commission in the army, was a partner in the banking firm.

11. An acknowledgment that a bill is just and due, and an agreement to pay it.

12. Bancroft says that rich and poor suffered alike; that some hid their losses to avoid embarrassment, while some of Meiggs's confederates on the city council repudiated just debts to hide their complicity. Meiggs became a railway contractor in Chile and Peru, and acquired wealth and fame. In later years, he bought up most of his notes at a big discount. The California legislature passed an act of pardon—unconstitutionally, says Bancroft—but the governor vetoed it.

13. The "bigger building" site is now (1966) occupied by the Wells Fargo Bank.

14. Interestingly enough, Adams & Company (at a rental of $3,000 a month) and Page, Bacon & Company, both of whom moved into the Parrott Building, went broke within a few years, while Wells, Fargo & Company prospered. Whether it has resulted from the stubbornness of the contractors or from the prayers and incense of the Chinese, Wells Fargo always has enjoyed and still does predominantly enjoy the patronage of the Chinese people in San Francisco. It rather seems that the powers that be of Wells Fargo recognized the fact that the Chinese handled money too; at any rate, Wells Fargo received most of the Chinese patronage throughout the Gold Country.

15. Alexander McLeod, *Pigtails and Gold Dust* (Caldwell, Idaho: Caxton, 1948).

16. Where the United Bank of California is now.

17. Original in the History Room, Wells Fargo Bank.

18. Copy from the History Room, Wells Fargo Bank.

19. In May, 1854, Senator John B. Weller, Democrat from California, presented the petition to the Senate of the Thirty-fourth Congress.

20. Bancroft, VI, 589.

1855: The Great Banking Panic

1. Protest: A formal declaration that payment has been demanded but not made. An item from the St. Louis *Democrat* for August 25, 1847, throws some light: "We understand that the Ohio and Mississippi Railroad Company have ordered a locomotive to be constructed which shall be propelled by *hot air*, on an entirely new principle . . . coal sufficient to take the machine to Cincinnati can be carried in a single barrel." Perhaps the bank was overcome by the hot air.

2. Anna McAllister, *Ellen Ewing* [Sherman's wife] (New York: Benziger, 1936), pp. 117–118.

3. One can hardly avoid asking an obvious question: What did James King of William have to offer that was worth $1,000 a month? Ira B. Cross says that King had lost his own bank because a former employee had misused funds, implying that King was a good banker in other respects.

4. Original in the files of the California Historical Society, San Francisco.

5. Alexander McLeod, *Pigtails and Gold Dust* (Caldwell, Idaho: Caxton, 1948), p. 89.

6. The *Uncle Sam* did sail on Monday but was not able to take any pleasant news back East. She carried no gold from Page, Bacon; Adams; or Wells Fargo.

7. Copy from the History Room, Wells Fargo Bank, and printed by permission of Irene Simpson, Director.

8. The agent must not have observed the date very carefully.

9. If so, apparently the money did not last long, for one J. C. Wood in 1857 became superintendent for James E. Birch, of the San Antonio & San Diego Mail Line, and made a lengthy report to the Postmaster General. It turns out that "J. C. Wood" was Isaiah Churchill Woods, the same man who is said to have gone to Australia in 1855. He was an experienced expressman, and so his selection was not entirely unlikely, but San Franciscans didn't like it at all. Apparently their opinions did not change, either, for on October 11, 1858, the *Bulletin* said: ". . . the extreme southern route, running from Los Angeles to San Antonio, Texas, of which the notorious I. C. Woods is the ruling spirit." Perhaps this reaction to Woods had much to do with San Francisco's holding her nose at the San Antonio & San Diego, and dubbing it the Jackass Mail. During the Civil War, Woods was personal secretary and adjutant to General Frémont. (Heitman's *Register* lists Isaac W. Woods as captain of volunteers, September–November, 1861.) Daniel C. Haskell died in an almshouse.

10. He first published the *Bulletin* October 8, 1855, and he attacked Palmer, Cook & Company on October 11, and again on November 6 and 7.

11. We must concur with Bosqui: It is a vicious attack. The damnable part of the whole thing, however, is that the officers of Palmer, Cook & Company *were* politicians before they were bankers, and it does seem that somehow Palmer, Cook & Company wound up with $560,000 of Adams money. (See Ira B. Cross, *Financing an Empire*, I, 184–195.)

12. Taken from Alvin F. Harlow, *Old Waybills*, p. 169.

13. According to an item in the *Alta California* for March 2, a receivership was chosen to protect the depositors, because, under such arrangement, the creditors would not get anything until after the depositors were paid off in full. An insolvency, on the other hand, would prorate the assets among both depositors and creditors. In any case, says the *Alta*, the banker could not legally withhold his personal property from the settlement—even his homestead.

14. Noyes had been the Adams agent at Placerville.

15. A bit equals one eighth of a dollar. Its usage started back in Missouri when the people, lacking small change,

would cut a Mexican peso into eighths with tin snips, each eighth being one bit.

16. But Bancroft says (VII, 149) the agents paid twenty-five cents per letter so they would *not* have to stand in line, which from some standpoints is even worse. However, one of the things that accompanied the general crackdown of the post office in 1855 was the fact that the Nevada agents *decided* to stand in line, says Bancroft.

17. From the reminiscences of Eric Francis in the History Room, Wells Fargo Bank.

18. It sounds as if the *Goliah* was regularly late.

19. Reprinted by permission of Elizabeth Wayrynens, Alpine, California; full text published in the *Butterfield Express,* I, No. 8 (June, 1963).

20. This letter, written at Grass Valley, Nevada County, is owned by J. Mark Rhoads, a San Diego attorney, and was published in the *Butterfield Express,* III, No. 12 (November, 1965).

21. Louis' father had been president of the Baltimore & Ohio Railroad, and his brother Charles, with Louis' help, would organize the Pioneer Stage Line from Virginia City to Placerville, which Wells Fargo would buy in 1864. Louis had commanded an artillery battalion under Frémont in the California Battalion in 1847, and had gone into the express business in 1850. He would one day be president of Wells Fargo, and would be an incorporator of the Bank of California and first president of the Nevada Bank of San Francisco.

22. *Arraster:* A mill to crush the quartz ore, usually crudely made of heavy stones; from the Spanish *arrastra,* since it was the Sonorans, among the first in the Gold Country, who showed the miners how to crush the quartz. The very first mining was placer-mining, in which the gold occurs loose in gravel and requires only washing for separation; the second is quartz-mining, where the gold occurs in streaks of quartz in rock, and must be crushed before it can be washed.

23. Which substantiates the story that Vanderbilt was getting $40,000 a month from the transit company.

24. And the expenses must have been enormous, for various computations put the total of his forces at as much as 6,000. Another source gives it as 2,288. Either way, the expense of maintaining a large body of men in the field is formidable.

25. The *Alta California* shows that Palmer, Cook shipped $40,722 in "treasure" on the *Uncle Sam,* but nothing on the *John L. Stephens,* which sailed on the same date, and on which Wells Fargo shipped $288,728.

26. This must be the same Hornsby who was a first lieutenant of cavalry of Company B, Texan-Santa Fé Pioneers, in 1841. See Noel M. Loomis, *The Texan-Santa Fé Pioneers* (Norman: University of Oklahoma Press, 1958).

27. Was this also a three-way blackmail? Walker had recently "examined" the books of the transit company and had found it owed the Nicaraguan government $450,000; Walker sent French to New York to collect the money from Vanderbilt, plus 10 percent of the profits. In the course of things, Parker H. French proposed that the transit company carry recruits to Walker for a $20 fare; Vanderbilt agreed to that, and one thousand recruits were sent to Nicaragua under that agreement. It seems undoubtable that the transit company was in on the deal, and Wiltsee says that Garrison was trying to work out from under his agreement with Vanderbilt.

28. The Costa Ricans fought Walker at Rivas, and defeated him, but at heavy cost. Before it was over, however, cholera broke out among the Costa Ricans, and out of an army of seven thousand men, only five hundred returned to Costa Rica.

29. A. Delano is the author of *Chips from the Old Block* and other books. This description of his diligence as a Wells Fargo agent comes from Thompson & West's *History of Nevada County.*

30. Oroville is a problem. John O. Theobald, Phoenix, Arizona, has no record of a Wells Fargo office at Oroville, a gold-mining town in Arizona at this period; however, the Head Minutes for 1855 show "Oroville, Yuma County, A. T."—which is pretty definite. The Minutes continue to show "Oroville" through 1862. There was, of course, an Oroville in the Gold Country also.

31. This is not the Vallecito in the desert east of San Diego, but, most likely, is the one in Calaveras County at that time.

32. The History Room at the Wells Fargo Bank has a receipt signed by Baldwin & Company, reading as follows: "Wells, Fargo & Co.'s Express. Value, $100.00 Rattlesnake Mch 2 1855 Received from John Pellet Check from Forest City Office #281. One Hundred Dolrs. Addressed Wells Fargo & Co. which we agree to forward to San Francisco for collection and deliver proceeds to order of John Pellet. W. F. & Co. will not be responsible for the contents of any valuable package unless that value is expressed in the receipt, nor will they be responsible for any loss or damage from Fire, or the dangers and accidents of Navigation and Transportation, from goods being improperly packed, or from any cause whatever, unless the same be proved to have occurred from the fraud or gross negligence of ourselves, our agents or servants. For the Proprietors, Baldwin & Co., agts."

On the left end, within a small border, is the following:

WELLS, FARGO & CO.'S
EXPRESS & EXCHANGE COMPANY,
Capital, $500,000.
Principal Offices, 16 Wall-Street, New-York,
114 Montgomery-St., San Francisco.

1856: Year of the Vigilantes

1. These facts, taken from the minutes, are at variance with those relating to Janes and McLane as given in Chapter 5.

2. From the advertisement in the *Alta California* in early 1856: "☞ For the better security of ourselves and the public, Agents in California and Oregon are furnished with 'appointments' or commissions, specifying their powers as our Agents. Such appointments they are required to keep exposed in their places of business."

3. Original in the History Room, Wells Fargo Bank.

4. There may be a record as to the final outcome of this mountain of castile soap, but we have not found it.

5. This refers to the fall of Sebastopol in the Russian Crimea in the Turko-Russian War, in which England,

France, and Turkey were allied against Russia and Austria. Sebastopol was an important Russian fort that finally gave way under siege.

6. In 1855, says Bancroft (*History of California* VII, 149), the amounts were $24,900 to express companies, $2,067 to the post office.

7. Quoted from Alvin F. Harlow, *Old Waybills,* pp. 155-156.

8. This figure, taken from Stimson, *History of the Express Companies,* p. 261, probably includes three-cent, six-cent, and ten-cent envelopes, and possibly some stamps, but it indicates about 150,000 letters carried a month. Interestingly enough, the *Alta California,* October 7, 1853, reports the total cash receipts for stamps and envelopes at the San Francisco post office from October 1, 1854 to October 1, 1857 was $318,668.71; therefore, it appears that Wells Fargo's purchases were close to 60 percent of the total sales at San Francisco. Bancroft (VII, 151) says the figure was $140,000 a month—but it seems that a zero must have slipped in.

9. In 1856, Broderick manipulated the Know-Nothing legislature to prevent its filling the expired term of William M. Gwin, the Southern or Chivalry leader (the senatorship had been vacant since March, 1855); in 1857, Broderick and Gwin compromised, Gwin getting the rest of his own term that would expire in 1860, and Broderick getting the term that would expire in 1863. But Broderick split with President Buchanan and lost much of his patronage to Gwin, even though Buchanan was Democratic. Broderick also lost prestige because of his senatorial record, but in 1859 he campaigned in California and made statements that caused him to be challenged to a duel by Judge David S. Terry of the state supreme court. Broderick was killed, and, says Carl Wheat, his death had a profound influence throughout the nation. See Wheat, "California's Bantam Cock," in *California Historical Society Quarterly,* IX, No. 3 (September, 1930), 285.

10. It was said that the immediate cause of the dispute between Cora and Richardson was the demeanor of a notorious prostitute, Belle Cora, mistress of Cora, toward Richardson's wife. Under the conditions of those days, it is not unreasonable.

11. It seems that Casey had given his mistress in New York a number of valuable gifts, and that he had repossessed those gifts when they parted company; and for that act of repossession—which might have been pretty stormy—she charged him with grand larceny, and he was convicted and sentenced. Casey wanted all those facts published in the *Bulletin,* but King was not willing.

12. William T. Coleman was a commission man and merchant, and his exemplary conduct as president of the Vigilantes was one of the bright spots of a murky era. He not only conducted the Vigilantes' actions honorably and cautiously, but he also used excellent judgment in a touchy situation.

13. As a matter of fact, Sherman was not in sympathy with King at all, for he said in his report: "King deserved to be cowhided, but he carried arms always, and repeatedly announced that . . . he would fire. Finally he goaded Casey to madness, and Casey shot him. . . . The ringleaders of the Know Nothing mob have influenced the populace . . . they make a martyr of King, forgetting that he always carried loaded-weapons, and that by this and his abuse of people proved himself as much a murderer as Casey." From a letter by Mrs. Sherman to her parents, quoting Sherman; see Anna McAllister, *Ellen Ewing* (New York: Benziger, 1936), p. 149.

14. Isaac Jones Wistar, who was in a law firm in San Francisco at the time, and definitely opposed to any such extra-legal activity as the Committee of Vigilance "where a full and fair judicial organization of the public's own choosing already prevails," says that Casey had distinctly said, "Draw and defend yourself." But it is interesting to note that Wistar, having deplored "mob violence" in no uncertain terms, then turns about face and excuses Casey's attack on King because "there was none but a violent remedy to be had." *Autobiography of Isaac Jones Wistar* (New York: Harper's, 1937), pp. 315, 320.

15. Is is also interesting to observe that Wistar says, in connection with the Vigilantes' trial of Cora, that he had an "alleged but secret midnight trial without counsel or witnesses for the prisoner, or the safeguard of lawful oaths and general rules administered by a qualified and impartial judge." Bancroft says the trial was fair and impartial, and that Cora was allowed to select a man from the tribunal to act as counsel, and that such counsel, M. F. Truett, selected an assistant; that the trial lasted from 12 o'clock noon until 6 o'clock, May 20. All evidence is to the effect that trials before the Committee were conducted strictly on legal principles. Perhaps Wistar, a lawyer, was influenced by the fact that he had been Cora's counsel in the regular courts, that an application by a lawyer to appear in Cora's behalf before the Committee was rejected, that such actions as the Committee's tended to cut down the income of counsel, and that the Committee said that lawyers were responsible for half of the maladministration of justice.

16. King had the biggest funeral—two miles long—but Casey had a good one, for his coffin was followed by eighty-four carriages, eighty horsemen, and four hundred persons on foot. Cora, however, had the best coffin, provided by Belle (who was married to him just before the hanging): It was of solid mahogany, with silver nails, a silver scroll, and sides of gilt scrollwork; the lining was of white satin.

17. Still another well-educated observer, Edward Bosqui, seemed to be of two minds about one's taking the law into his own hands. In his *Memoirs* (San Francisco: privately printed, 1904), he does not like the Vigilantes at all, and he says (p. 127): "Soon the community had in its midst a power organization of armed men in open rebellion against the law." But a few pages later (p. 138), he tells of a squatter on Frémont's land, and says: "I was a disgusted witness of legalized outrages. Consequently, I adopted a very different course in my dealings with squatters than was in accord with the strict interpretation of the law. In fact, I frequently took matters into my own hands, constituting myself both judge and jury. . . . Without process of law, I forcibly evicted them. . . . Care was taken that equity and justice were on our side." As with Wistar, it seems to depend largely on whose ox is gored.

18. The Second Committee of Vigilance was active from May 15, 1856, to November, 1859; then it disbanded, after handling prudently and successfully one of the most dan-

gerous experiments in human history: that of the people's taking the law into its own hands.

19. The Know-Nothing party, or Native American party, arose in the early 1850's to oppose immigration and Catholicism. It was run like a secret society, and its members always claimed to know nothing about it when they were put on the spot. They voted slavishly as they were told to vote, and in 1854 the party won many public offices. In 1856, however, it backed Millard Fillmore against Buchanan, Democrat, and Frémont, Republican (called Black Republican because the party opposed slavery), and lost heavily.

20. It seems that many men must have shared this kindly feeling toward French. He was a genius for doing the wrong thing at the wrong time; he became minister from Nicaragua under the ambitious filibusterer, William Walker, only to be fired soon for "rapacity" and other qualities. French was involved in many questionable affairs (among them a ginseng con game), and was accused of being a spy in the Civil War, and was arrested. He tried to get damages from the government, and was last known in Washington, drinking whiskey and chloroform. The time and place of his death are unknown. See Edward McGowan, *The Strange Eventful History of Parker H. French* (Los Angeles: Glen Dawson, 1958).

21. Pretty fast work—getting kerosene in San Francisco in mid-1856, for it was first manufactured on Long Island in 1855. It may have been whale oil or camphene.

22. The public had subscribed $36,000 for Mrs. James King. See Theodore H. Hittell, *History of California* (San Francisco: N. J. Stone & Co., 1898) III, 622.

23. The *Herald* was a victim of the rampaging turmoil. After King's shooting, the *Alta California,* the *Journal,* and the *News* called for support of the Vigilantes, while the *Chronicle* was at first undecided, and the *Herald* issued a naïve call for order, definitely siding against the Vigilantes. Later it reversed itself, but it was too late. The merchants of Front Street, indignant over the *Herald's* stand, withdrew their advertising and notified the auctioneers, who promptly did the same. (In San Francisco of that period, unconsigned merchandise arriving by ship was unloaded on the beach and sold at auction, and the auctioneers' announcements were enough to support a newspaper; the *Herald* had been so favored for some time.) Advertisers swarmed into the office to cancel their advertising, and lines of people formed in the street to cancel their subscriptions. The *Herald* survived for a time, but lost most of its income immediately.

24. This account is taken from Bancroft, VII, 616 ff.

25. Bancroft then says, "This company [Wells Fargo] then entered into arrangements to assist Bates in his nefarious transactions, who permitted A. E. Rowe, president of the Pacific Express, and others, to speculate with the state's money deposited with them, by reason of which $124,000 was lost to the treasury." Bancroft offers no evidence as to Wells Fargo's alleged part in this conspiracy, and, since Bancroft is often biased and sometimes reckless in his statements, one may be justified in doubting that this statement represents more than Bancroft's annoyance with express companies. At times he speaks of Wells Fargo as a monopoly, with connotations of evil; again (VII, 151) he calls it an "unobjectionable monopoly." *U. S. West* says, without documentation, that in 1856 Wells Fargo loaned the state $83,000 and loaned the City of Sacramento $65,000.

26. Joseph Palmer and Frémont had been close friends since 1850, Frémont staying at his house for months at a time. Palmer handled affairs connected with Frémont's huge mining-holdings in the Mariposa country, and it is said that Palmer obtained Frémont's nomination as candidate for the Black Republican party. Palmer also broke with Senator Gwin and backed David C. Broderick, which latter action contributed much to his downfall because of his association with men of Broderick's unscrupulousness.

The company had bought large blocks of real estate on credit, and altogether it does not seem that Joseph Palmer, the senior partner of the firm, adhered to banking principles. The immediate cause of the failure, of course, was the firm's refusal to pay its drafts (*refusal* meaning failure). The firm suspended on July 29, 1856, and was legally dissolved on January 21, 1857.

27. He might have spared us that last remark. However, he went on for several columns of six-point type in the Owego, New York, *Gazette* for March 5, 1855.

28. Later, it would be very expensive for Wells Fargo, when certain companies (notably the Southern Pacific and the Santa Fé), knowing that Wells Fargo had to have use of their lines, would demand and get 50 percent or more.

29. Exactly what practice is not stated; perhaps this was a general order relating to too-generous credit—for it is beginning to appear that Wells Fargo officials in California had considerable discretion and were inclined to be quite generous when occasion suggested it.

1857: Year of the Jackass Mail

1. The *Register,* May 20, 1857.

2. Crabb's brother-in-law in Sonoita, Jesús Ainsa, spent thirty-two months in prison, sometimes under sentence of death, but finally was released. John Cosby failed to appear with the thousand men, but became abruptly rich. (It is strange that he died in an accident soon afterward.)

3. An item in the San Francisco *Herald* for August 1, 1858, says: "The Overland Mail Stage which left this city, for St. Louis and Memphis, on Friday morning last, carried off a large letter mail, destined as follows: St. Louis City (letters) 25, for distribution from postoffice 229; Memphis City 4, for distribution from postoffice 102; New York City 90, for distribution from postoffice 111; Little Rock City - - -, for distribution from postoffice 18; for other offices outside California, and made up direct 62. Total, 641. The mail of November 5th, carried 261 letters, and a comparison between the two will show the remarkable increase that has taken place." Nevertheless, at ten cents a letter, the income from letters mailed in San Francisco was only $64.10. It was not untypical, for in the fiscal year ending in 1860 the Panama route had cost over twice as much as it received, while the Salt Lake City to Placerville line had cost $83,241, while receiving $978.50.

4. From this distance, it rather seems that Birch—if he had lived—might have had the ability and the backing to do the same thing—if he had had the same contract. But unfortunately, as the sages have pointed out, *if's* don't count.

5. Most of this data on the early overland mails is taken from LeRoy R. Hafen's excellent book, *The Overland Mail* (Cleveland: Clark, 1926).

6. Pronounced "Kor'-pen-ning," according to Henry H. Clifford, Los Angeles, a collector of postal covers and a student of early mail history.

7. This reference was to the trip across the Colorado Desert on mules. It is hardly necessary to point out that a mule is not a jackass. It seems, from various reports in the San Diego *Herald*, that the first westbound mail crossed in wagons, and subsequent mail in coaches. Apparently the only mule-back mail was in the first month or so.

8. Firing the anvil was a pleasant custom in the 1850's to celebrate anything that needed celebrating. There were several methods of firing the anvil, but one common way was to fill the hole on top of an anvil with black powder, and lay a train of powder in a groove to one side, then set another anvil upside down over the first anvil. Light the powder and run! It made a tremendous boom, and threw the second anvil ten or twelve feet into the air.

9. Twenty-one of these mules were captured on Devil's River by the Indians.

10. From *Report to Hon. A. V. Brown, Postmaster General, on the Opening and Present Condition of the United States Overland Mail Route Between San Antonio, Texas, and San Diego, California*, by J. C. Wood [Isaiah C. Woods], Superintendent. In *Senate Executive Document No. 1*, Part IV, Vol. IV, 35th Congress, 2nd session. Printed in 1968 in *Brand Book No. 1* of San Diego Westerners; annotated by Noel M. Loomis.

1858: The Great Overland Mail

1. During the San Antonio & San Diego's one full year of operation, the cost to the government was $196,000 and the total income was $601. One item of interest might be the reason for the Postmaster General's letting the contract to Birch when he was about ready to let the bigger contract to Butterfield. It could have been friendship for Birch in the first place, or pressure by Butterfield in the second place, or the Postmaster General's personal desire to get service established over the southern route.

2. This was the reason for the monster petition signed by 75,000 Californians in 1854.

3. It is idle speculation, but Frémont was backed by Joseph C. Palmer, the San Francisco banker, and it would have been convenient to Wells Fargo.

4. *Leslie's Weekly* for November 27, 1858, says that about 1818 John Butterfield was connected with the old Red Bird line of mail coaches between Albany and Buffalo; that among his many enterprises, he started an electric telegraph company with Samuel F. B. Morse and Amos Kendall, and was president of it for a long time; on the other hand, he had declined to enter the Atlantic cable company that, backed by Cyrus Field, laid a cable in 1858 but was not able to use it for more than a few weeks (the successful cable was laid in 1865).

5. Butterfield, Fargo, Livingston, and Spencer were on the board of American Express; Fargo, Barney, Livingston, and Williams were on the board of Wells, Fargo & Company; Dinsmore and Livingston were president and director, respectively, of Adams Express Company; Holland was the treasurer of American Express Company; Kinyon, Crocker, and Hawley became division superintendents on the Butterfield line; Moulton was a capitalist.

6. Postal receipts for the first year of operation were $27,229.94; in 1860, they were $119,766.76—more than received from the ocean route, for the first time.

7. Details of the Overland Mail are taken substantially from Roscoe Conkling's excellent book, *The Butterfield Overland Mail* (Glendale: Clark, 1947).

8. Edward Hungerford, *Wells Fargo*, p. 59.

9. Rupert N. Richardson, "Some Details of the Southern Overland Mail," in *Southwestern Historical Quarterly*, XXIX, No. 1 (July, 1925), 7.

10. This was a development of the post horn, used on early coach roads, and even by John L. Swaney, the mail carrier on the Natchez Trace in 1796.

11. See Conkling, II, 134 ff.

12. In the California Historical Society *Quarterly* for December, 1966, W. Turrentine Jackson, in his article, "A New Look at Wells Fargo, Stagecoaches and the Pony Express," gives some figures that support this supposition. Quoting from the minute books of the Overland Mail Company, which he has recently examined, Jackson says that seven of the twenty shares of the Overland Mail Company were owned by directors or large investors in Wells Fargo and that four of Overland's ten directors were also directors of Wells Fargo; that Wells Fargo & Company served as the banker without security for the Overland in the Far West; that by mid-1858, Wells Fargo had loaned the Overland $17,000, and the borrowing continued; that in March, 1959, Butterfield was authorized to borrow $25,000 from Wells Fargo; that Louis McLane became general manager of the Overland in California. Congress in 1859 failed to pass the post office appropriation bill, and that made the Overland's position very difficult. On March 17, 1860, the Overland owed Wells Fargo $162,400, and John Butterfield was ousted as president, and replaced by William B. Dinsmore. In 1866, Wells Fargo would come out of the great consolidation with about three fourths of the total stock.

13. From the San Francisco *Bulletin*, for instance, and from David Broderick, who said: "Give us Butterfield and Tehuantepec, and California will be satisfied."

14. "California's Bantam Cock, the Journals of Charles E. DeLong," in the *California Historical Quarterly*, IX, No. 4 (December, 1930), 390.

1859: The Fabulous Comstock

1. Virginia City is some seven thousand feet high on the east slope of Mount Davidson, and C Street, its main street, runs crookedly north and south, the town being essentially narrow east and west and long north and south. On the south, immediately adjoining, and not far from the old Wells Fargo building, is Gold Hill, and down the canyon from Gold Hill is Silver City. The top of Mount Davidson is west of Virginia City, and therefore the town slants down toward the east.

2. Most of this material on robberies is taken from Alvin F. Harlow, *Old Waybills*. There is much more, including several books on Joaquín Murrieta and on Captain

Harry Love (who got the reward for removing Murrieta's head). For one of the strangest executions on record, conducted by Love, see "The Stage," in the *Butterfield Express,* I, No. 12 (October, 1963), which tells the story of C. E. Bingham, an actor, who on a ship to Panama consorted with a thrice-married-at-nineteen girl named Sue Denin, and was sentenced by his fellow shipmates to be punished. An execution squad of seven was chosen, and blindfolded! Strangely enough, one bullet struck Bingham in the spine and paralyzed him for life. Such was homespun justice in the 1850's.

3. This somewhat abortive affair was brought on, says *Old Waybills,* by the machinations of a disappointed mail contractor (who must be Hockaday) and the southern sympathies of the Secretary of War, John B. Floyd, who wanted to get the army as far west as possible in anticipation of the Civil War.

4. The freighting firms had 3,500 wagons and 40,000 oxen, and after the Utah War they stored the wagons on several acres of vacant ground near the Great Salt Lake (reminiscent of hundreds of acres of ships stored north of San Francisco after World War II, and hundreds of acres of planes stored in Arizona). The Mormons bought the $175 wagons for $10 each and used the iron to make nails. Alexander Majors says, in *Seventy Years on the Frontier* (Chicago: Rand, McNally & Co., 1893), pp. 144–145, that they lost all but 200 of the oxen in severe storms that winter in the Ruby Valley, where they were wintering them. The firm also lost 1,000 oxen to Indians west of Fort Kearny that year.

5. Probably named after the Fraser River strike in British Columbia; apparently it never attained post office status.

1860: The Pony Express

1. Alvin F. Harlow, *Old Waybills,* p. 236.

2. There are many who say that Cody did not ride for the Pony, but Henry B. Sell and Victor Weybright (*Buffalo Bill and the Wild West,* p. 30) say that Cody, at fourteen, talked the terrible-tempered Ben Slade into giving him a job. (Slade was later hanged by Vigilantes at Virginia City, Montana.) There are many unofficial lists of riders, but no company records to uphold them. Alexander Majors says Cody was a rider for the Pony.

3. For a while, Haslam was a deputy United States marshal at Salt Lake City, but that must have been too confining, for he became the first messenger to ride the stagecoach between Denver and Salt Lake City after Wells Fargo bought out Ben Holladay in 1866. He was a long-time employee of Wells Fargo, but finally moved to Chicago to go into business.

4. Copy in the possession of B. C. Pearce, Wells Fargo Bank.

5. Contrary to Thompson and West's date of 1859.

6. According to the Head Minutes.

1861: Butterfield Moves North

1. Alvin F. Harlow, *Old Waybills,* p. 235, says that the Pony Express never had a chance because President Buchanan was the tool of southern Democrats, the Postmaster General was hostile, and the Butterfield company was hostile and was backed by the express companies.

2. This apparently had nothing to do with the Comstock, since it is listed in Utah Territory (and Nevada Territory had been created in 1861); in 1912, Gold Hill, Utah, was a telegraph office in the mountains near the Nevada-Utah state line, a little north of the middle.

1862–1865: The Civil War Years

1. See William S. Greever, *The Bonanza West* (University of Oklahoma Press, 1963), pp. 145–146.

2. One can only speculate as to what drives such a man —but in this case it may be deduced. Holladay was rough and probably uncouth, and then, as many such men do in an effort to build themselves socially, married a society girl. The marriage could not have been very satisfactory, because she spent much of her time in Europe while Ben was traveling or working in the West. They had four children, all of whom came to tragic ends. A later marriage in Oregon produced two children.

3. J. V. Frederick, *Ben Holladay* (Glendale: Clark, 1940).

4. Although Virginia City does not appear in the Minutes, Hungerford says an agency was established there in 1861.

5. Article IV, Sections 34, 35.

6. Those were not the first prefabs to reach California, however, because Thomas Whaley had shipped one to San Diego in the 1830's.

7. Archer Butler Hulbert, "Letters of an Overland Mail Agent in Utah," in American Antiquarian Society *Proceedings* for October, 1928, p. 268. Hulbert says that Rumfield was assistant treasurer of the Butterfield Overland, and Stimson says he was general manager and superintendent, but the letters as printed indicate that he was the agent at Salt Lake City.

8. Interestingly enough, Holladay said that the mail was the most profitable of all his branches of income. *Old Waybills,* p. 265.

9. Copy from the History Room, Wells Fargo Bank.

10. These commissions are in the History Room or in the collection of B. C. Pearce in the Trust Department, Wells Fargo Bank.

11. La Paz, a mining camp, was established ten miles above Ehrenberg on the Colorado River in 1862, and was the first county seat of Yuma County. In 1863, there were five thousand men working the placers in that area, and there was still a Wells Fargo station there in 1870, when the river moved away and left La Paz high and dry.

12. This narrative of the Indian War of 1864–1865 is taken partly from LeRoy R. Hafen, *The Overland Mail,* pp. 255 ff., and partly from *Harper's New Monthly Magazine,* LI, No. 303 (August, 1875).

13. Benjamin Franklin Gilbert, "The Confederate Minority in California," in the *California Historical Quarterly,* XX, No. 2 (June, 1941).

14. And this when the author was traveling with Schuyler Colfax, speaker of the United States House of Representatives. Apparently Wells Fargo was doing well at seven cents a letter. Bowles, *Across the Continent,* p. 295 ff.

15. Would that Mr. Bowles had been a little more explicit in his remark about railroads.

16. From the book by A. P. Nasatir, *A French Journalist in the Gold Rush* (Los Gatos, Calif.: Talisman Press, 1964).

1866: The Great Consolidation

1. See Alvin F. Harlow, *Old Waybills,* pp. 460 ff.
2. Original in the collection of M. C. Nathan.
3. Printed in American Antiquarian Society *Proceedings,* October, 1928. Reprinted by permission.
4. Both this First and this Second of Exchange are in possession of the History Room, Wells Fargo Bank, San Francisco. Miss Irene Simpson, director of the History Room, says that she has never seen a Third of Exchange. This system was abandoned by 1900, because it involved too much bookkeeping to be sure only one of the three would be paid.
5. Zelma Bays Locker, "Rambles Among Books," in the *Butterfield Express,* III, No. 7 (May, 1965).
6. Original in the History Room, Wells Fargo Bank, San Francisco.
7. This receipt and the Second of Exchange on London are in the possession of the California Historical Society, San Francisco, and are printed by permission.
8. Valentine had been Wells Fargo agent at Virginia City in 1864, and had been transferred to San Francisco. He was, said some, the greatest of all the great expressmen, and in 1893, would replace Lloyd Tevis as president of Wells, Fargo & Company.

1867–1869: Tevis Gets Control

1. Original in the History Room, Wells Fargo Bank.
2. Copy from the History Room, Wells Fargo Bank. The discrepancy between the time of arrival and the time of leaving Roseburg is in the original.
3. Original in the History Room, Wells Fargo Bank, San Francisco.
4. Copies furnished from the original Order Books by the New Hampshire Historical Society. Specifications checked by John D. Frizzell, Oklahoma City, builder of old-time stagecoaches.
5. It is now the campus of the College of Notre Dame, and the Sisters of Notre Dame have restored the original Ralston mansion.
6. Not otherwise identified.
7. Crocker was a big man (250 pounds), a driver, and a leader. He had left home at an early age, and had been a placer miner and a merchant in Sacramento; he was the superintendent of construction for the Central Pacific. Stanford had been a placer miner and a successful merchant in San Francisco. Uncle Mark Hopkins, the mentor, had been a merchant at Placerville. Huntington had left home at fourteen and had been a merchant in Sacramento; he became the Central Pacific's agent in New York.
8. He would also own, in partnership with George Hearst, the great Homestake gold mine in the Black Hills of South Dakota, and the huge Anaconda copper properties in Montana.
9. Mills had been a merchant and banker in Stockton and Sacramento, and was president of Ralston's Bank of California.
10. An error. "Pacific Express" was the name of the company formed at the fall of Adams Express in 1855.
11. Asbury Harpending, *The Great Diamond Hoax* (Norman: University of Oklahoma Press, 1958), pp. 92 ff.
12. Negative in possession of B. C. Pearce, Wells Fargo Bank.
13. There is disagreement over Barney's first name; most writers make it "D. N. Barney"; Hungerford makes it "Danforth"; however, the notice to stockholders of December 10, 1869, signed by A. H. Barney, his brother, makes it "Danford." He signed "Danford" in the incorporation papers for the New York Elevated Rail Road Company in 1871.

1870–1875: The Great Splurger

1. The *Chronicle,* June 12, 1870; the *Bulletin,* August 6, 1870.
2. This description of business in California in the 1870's is taken from Ira B. Cross, *Financing an Empire,* I, 363 ff.
3. Eric Francis said that Tevis "barked" at people. "Talk quickly and to the point," he would say. "I can think five times as fast as any man in San Francisco." And so he could, says Francis; he was a mental wonder and one of the smartest men in town.
4. *History of the Express Business* (New York: 1881), pp. 264–265.
5. Most of our information on this affair comes from Asbury Harpending, who seems to be an unusually fair and honest commentator. In one place he says that Ralston was a long-cherished and lamented friend, that he was "gold-bricked" by the Big Four.
6. From R. Guy McClellan, *The Golden State.*
7. Original in the History Room, Wells Fargo Bank.
8. Captain Oliver Eldridge, says Eric Francis, was a tall, grim man with white side whiskers who would come frequently to the secretary's office and clear his throat and say, "By the way, Mr. Heron, I have some letters here I would like to have mailed." Mr. Heron would hand them to the boy with a wink, and the boy would put stamps on them, thus saving Captain Oliver a few cents.
9. From an interview with Samuel J. Hume, the son, at about age seventy-six—the same age at which James Hume traveled to Wisconsin to get a criminal—at Berkeley, California, December 26, 1960. Samuel Hume died soon afterward.
10. Original in the History Room, Wells Fargo Bank.
11. Much of the information on Ralston's course, and especially on the actions of mining stocks in the San Francisco markets, comes from George D. Lyman, *Ralston's Ring* (New York: Scribner's, 1950).
12. Copy furnished by Dr. Frank M. Stanger, San Mateo County Historical Museum.
13. Manuscript in the History Room, Wells Fargo Bank.
14. At least, that is the way it has been handed down. As a matter of fact, there are indications that much of Wells Fargo's treasure was carried in safes fastened inside the coach. See the letters of Charles T. Blake, *supra.*
15. Original reward poster in the History Room, Wells Fargo Bank.
16. Originals in the History Room, Wells Fargo Bank.
17. This is one of the few documentary references to a sixteen-shooter, and, as pointed out in the author's book, *The Texan-Santa Fé Pioneer* (Norman: University of Oklahoma Press, 1958), since there do not seem to be any

records of firearms with sixteen-chamber cylinders, even as experimental weapons, this probably refers to a Remington arm with two eight-shot cylinders designed to be interchanged in the heat of battle. By 1875, of course, metallic cartridges were common, and the extra cylinder, which never had been successful, was not needed as much as in the days when the cylinders had to be loaded by hand. However, it has always been true that firearms are used long after they are obsolete (in fact, most of the rifles used in the Civil War were muzzle loaders), and so the appearance of a "sixteen-shooter" is not phenomenal although unusual enough to cause comment by Wells Fargo.

18. The originals of all the posters are in the History Room, Wells Fargo Bank, San Francisco.

1876–1879: Bad Years for San Francisco

1. Copies furnished by the Secretary of State, Sacramento, California.

2. No more is known about these men, but an 1876 San Francisco directory lists "Devitt L. McDonald, Mining Company, 328 Montgomery, Room 13, dwl. 732 Sutter; Arthur S. Taylor, Stock Broker, office 411½ California, Room 2, dwl. 1704 Pacific; and Horace Z. Wheeler, Assistant Appraiser, Customs House, 1803 Jones."

3. A clearinghouse is organized to save time and money in the settlement of each bank in a city with every other bank. The first clearinghouse in the United States was in New York City in 1853, and the practice was for each bank to send a representative to the clearinghouse at a given time each day, with items to be collected from other banks in the city. In 1908, the forty-eight banks of New York cleared all their items with one another from 10 o'clock to 10:45, and all payments were made by 1:30. By that year, the clearinghouse was used to make the supply of money (gold coin and paper) go further among the banks.

4. Ira B. Cross, *Financing an Empire,* I, 432.

5. From *The Expressman's Monthly,* II, No. 10 (October, 1877), 303.

6. Manuscript in the History Room, Wells Fargo Bank. Mr. Hanley eventually became a teller.

The Early 1880's

1. In his reminiscences, Eric Francis says: "When Wells Fargo was making preparations to establish offices in Mexico, I met many prominent Mexicans, friends of Mr. Heron, who conducted the negotiations in the French language, as that was the diplomatic language in the Mexican government then. When Heron went to Mexico with J. J. Valentine and party, they took a car full of champagne among other things. . . . I remember paying some corking big jewelry bills, for jewels and other gewgaws for the wives of governors, and so forth."

2. The overdraft system lasted until the panic of 1893, when Isaias Hellman persuaded the banks to make a clearinghouse agreement to do away with it.

3. The Wells Fargo Bank and the Nevada Bank were the last two to succumb to the practice of paying interest on credit balances, about 1897, said Lipman. However, he said, country bank balances did draw about 3 percent interest.

4. This material on the inner workings of the bank has been taken from the reminiscences of Frederick L. Lipman in the History Room, Wells Fargo Bank.

5. This information is from John Conlon, retired vice-president of the Wells Fargo Bank, who joined the bank in 1917, and eventually became head bookkeeper. He says emphatically that the development of laborsaving bookkeeping methods for banks did not put anybody out of work, but in fact made more work in the long run. Interview at the Wells Fargo Bank, February 2, 1966.

6. Heron had been an ensign in the United States Navy and had served under Commodore Sloat on the *Savannah* when Sloat captured Monterey in 1846, and therefore must have been a shipmate of Louis McLane. Heron, said Francis, was a gentleman; he had been in the diplomatic service in Paris, and spoke French like a native Frenchman.

7. Valentine, says Stimson, was a man of stern integrity and a man of urbane dignity; he was very generous and was universally loved. (*History of the Express Business,* p. 267.)

Hungerford says that Valentine was a thoroughgoing expressman, bearded, and always wore boots—in which he stood 6 foot, 4 inches tall. His second love (after the company) was his library in his beautiful home in Oakland. He liked writing and writers, and knew many of them; John Greenleaf Whittier dedicated a poem to him.

8. Original in the History Room, Wells Fargo Bank.

9. H. H. Bancroft, *History of California,* VII, 151.

10. Original in the History Room, Wells Fargo Bank.

11. It seems to figure out at about $16,000, but the Minutes say $7,500.

12. This is not the bulldog that later characterized Wells Fargo advertising.

13. Perhaps a relative of Daniel B. Bunnell.

14. It rather seems that Wells Fargo anticipated the educational materials rate by some seventy-five or eighty years.

15. Mr. Allen's initials are given as "E. B." and "E. G." in the Minutes.

The Late 1880's

1. This narrative of the attempted corner in wheat is taken from Oscar Lewis, *The Silver Kings* (New York: Knopf, 1959).

2. In spite of the change from the ampersand to "and" in 1866, most Wells Fargo material still shows the ampersand.

3. The History Room, Wells Fargo Bank, has a money order for five cents.

4. Goad was not a banker or a Wells Fargo man, but a capitalist, says Lipman.

The Turbulent 1890's

1. This may be an error, because Bell's name does not appear on any of the official lists of directors.

2. He was at all times an optimist, says Ira B. Cross, *Financing an Empire* (IV, 222). He had faith, he stood for law and order, for morality and decency. In some respects his broad vision, his sound judgment, and his unquestioned

integrity made him a superman. He was humane and just, and never took advantage of another man's bad fortune. He always conducted his banks on a safe basis, and was always ready for an emergency. But he was not a speculator or a boomer. He believed in investment, but not speculation.

3. Lipman finally did audit the New York bank in 1900.

4. Information on this phase of Wells Fargo's banking activities comes from an interview with Lipman by I. W. Hellman III, a copy of which is in the History Room, Wells Fargo Bank.

5. Valentine was a prime expressman but not a banker, says Lipman. Also, adds Eric Francis, he was a man who did not like an idea unless he thought of it first.

6. Evans, said Eugene Shelby, had been a colonel in the Confederate army, and was good company and well liked socially. He became a very competent expressman, and was a division superintendent at Portland, then succeeded Hancock as superintendent at Omaha; later he went to Kansas City, and finally to New York to succeed Hancock, who died there. Evans would be president of Wells Fargo when Edward Harriman would get control of the Southern Pacific. Evans started poor but accumulated a fortune of several hundred thousand dollars by "dint of thrift and foresight." He was chivalrous and courteous, and respected by all.

7. From an article in the San Francisco *Herald Express*, January 29, 1957.

8. Cheney was originally a New Hampshire stage driver who organized Cheney & Company in 1842, and eventually covered northeastern New England and sold out to American. He organized the United States and Canada Express, and sold it in 1882, but remained a large stockholder in Wells Fargo, American, National, and others. He helped to finance the Santa Fé and the Northern Pacific, and had much to do with getting Wells Fargo on those two roads. He was a director of the Santa Fé from 1873 to 1894.

9. Original in the History Room, Wells Fargo Bank.

10. Printed in full in the *Butterfield Express*, III, No. 7 (May, 1965). Original in the History Room, Wells Fargo Bank.

11. Irene Simpson, director of the History Room of the Wells Fargo Bank, says she has not been able to find any record of the total number of watches awarded in this traditional manner. (It may be noticed that the company name is printed here, in 1899, with an ampersand.)

1900–1905: Separation of Express and Banking

1. Alvin F. Harlow *Old Waybills*, p. 441.

2. This Pacific Express (the third one) had been formed by Jay Gould to conduct the express business of the Union Pacific and the Kansas Pacific railroads.

1906: Earthquake and Fire

1. *San Francisco Is No More*, Ronald G. Fick, ed. (Menlo Park: 1963).

1907–1918: End of Express Service

1. Copy from the History Room, Wells Fargo Bank.

2. Information from Giffen's widow, Helen Giffen, who is director of the Society of California Pioneers library. Giffen died in 1960, and the rifle is in the History Room of the Wells Fargo Bank.

3. Alvin F. Harlow, *Old Waybills*, p. 468.

4. According to Edward Hungerford, *Wells Fargo;* much of this information is taken from Hungerford.

Index

[*Figures in italics refer to illustrations, captions, or wording in illustrations.*]